3rd edition

THE HUMAN PORTRAIT

Introduction to Cultural Anthropology

MICHAEL B. WHITEFORD, *Iowa State University*

JOHN FRIEDL

PRENTICE HALL, Englewood Cliffs, New Jersey 07632

Library of Congress Cataloging-in-Publication Data

Whiteford, Michael B.,
    The human portrait : introduction to cultural anthropology /
  Michael B. Whiteford, John Friedl.
      p.   cm.
    Friedl's name appears first on the earlier edition.
    Includes bibliographical references and index.
    ISBN 0-13-446105-3
    1. Ethnology.   I. Friedl, John.   II. Title.
  GN316.W53   1992
    306--dc20   91-17621
                                                          CIP

Acquisitions editor: Nancy Roberts
Editorial/production supervision and
   interior design: Serena Hoffman
Cover design: Ben Santora
Prepress buyer: Debra Kesar
Manufacturing buyer: Mary Ann Gloriande
Photo researcher: Fran Antmann
Photo editor: Lorinda Morris-Nantz

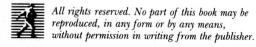

Printed in the United States of America
10 9 8 7 6 5 4 3 2

ISBN 0-13-446105-3

PRENTICE-HALL INTERNATIONAL (UK) LIMITED, *London*
PRENTICE-HALL OF AUSTRALIA PTY. LIMITED, *Sydney*
PRENTICE-HALL CANADA INC., *Toronto*
PRENTICE-HALL HISPANOAMERICANA, S.A., *Mexico*
PRENTICE-HALL OF INDIA PRIVATE LIMITED, *New Delhi*
PRENTICE-HALL OF JAPAN, INC., *Tokyo*
SIMON & SCHUSTER ASIA PTE. LTD., *Singapore*
EDITORA PRENTICE-HALL DO BRASIL, LTDA., *Rio de Janeiro*

To Patty, Scott, Chip, and Cindy from M.B.W.

To Mary, Joe, Sarah, and Ben from J.F.

Brief Contents

Contents

PART FOUR
SOCIAL ORGANIZATION

10 Economic Systems: Gifts, Obligations, and Other Exchanges   278

11 Dispute Resolution and Social Control   295

12 Magic, Witchcraft, and Religion   314

PART FIVE
THE DYNAMICS OF ANTHROPOLOGY

Preface

We human beings all share a common biological heritage that determines much of our behavior, placing at least some limits on our physical and intellectual accomplishments. Yet each society has made its way to the present along a different historical path, and so is in many ways unlike any other. The lesson of cultural anthropology is that we are both similar to and different from all other people around the world. Anthropology teaches us tolerance and understanding by showing us that, just as other ways of life may seem odd to us, so our way of doing things is equally strange to others. To bring some sense of reality to this lesson is the goal of this book.

The subject of cultural anthropology is presented here according to a particular sequence of ideas that follows the authors' thinking about how to organize a college course. We begin with a general overview of the field of anthropology. Having raised the question of what human culture is and what it is not, in Chapter 2 we proceed to discuss how human culture came to be, and what makes human beings similar to and different from other animals. In Chapter 3 we examine the concept of culture. In Chapter 4 we focus on the approaches and methods anthropologists use to study human culture, and in Chapter 5 we consider the topic of language, which has its own special place in the study of culture.

In the next two chapters we look at the major generic types of subsistence strategies and how they relate to specific forms of social and political organization. Hunting and gathering, horticultural, pastoral, and agricultural societies have been the principal areas of anthropological interest and investigation since the beginning of this century.

We then look at some of the basic social institutions, providing some insight into how anthropologists view different cultures. We focus on social structure and social organization in Chapter 8, followed by kinship and marriage in Chapter 9, economic systems in Chapter 10, and dispute resolution and social control in Chapter 11. In Chapter 12 we look at different approaches to dealing with the supernatural.

The final chapters raise important questions about anthropology and its application to contemporary society. Chapter 13 considers social and cultural change, including planned change in the area of applied anthropology. Chapter 14 provides a brief overview of cultural anthropology today, illustrating how the field has changed over the past several decades, and how those changes have led to some current interests in the field.

Each chapter ends with an article designed to serve several purposes: to illustrate important concepts in the text; to provide a break in the style and structure of the book, which the reader may welcome; and because the articles are well written, interesting, and in some cases humorous, to bring to life what anthropology is, or what it can be.

The instructor may wish to reorder the sequence of this book, and this can be done without difficulty. Although ideally the text flows from one chapter to the next, each chapter stands as an independent unit and can be read in a different order from the one proposed by the authors. Recognizing that no single book will suit all ways of teaching cultural anthropology, we have tried to make this one as flexible as possible, and the instructor should not feel bound to follow it to the letter.

Having taught introductory anthropology for many years, we are both very much aware that such courses are often a student's only formal exposure to anthropology. We have tried to address student criticisms concerning the heavy use of jargon in anthropology textbooks. Sometimes technical terms are unavoidable, but we have consciously tried to write in a jargon-free style and to present the subject matter in a clear and direct manner, without "writing down" to the students who will read it. When specialized terms are introduced, they are set in bold type and explained, so that they can be understood rather than simply memorized. Recognizing that examinations are a routine part of college life, we have also included a glossary at the end of each chapter that defines any specialized terms used. Basically, however, what we have tried to do is to write a book about anthropology for nonanthropologists.

Another important feature of this book is the extensive use of examples from American culture as well as from other cultures around the world. As teachers, we have found that while students are interested in the subject matter commonly found in anthropology, they often want it to be brought home for them. We believe that it is important to be able to apply what we know about human culture to our own society as well as to nonindustrialized societies. Thus, when we write about social organization, we refer not only to non-Western societies but to American society as well. When we write about kinship, religion, or political organization, we include examples from American society to compare and contrast with examples from elsewhere in the world. Similarly, the photographs throughout the text contrast what may appear to be bizarre scenes from non-Western societies with familiar scenes from our own daily lives. We firmly believe that this juxtaposition helps make anthropology more relevant for most people.

A few other devices are used to aid in the process of learning. Each chapter contains, besides the glossary, a summary of the chapter contents, questions for discussion that explore issues raised in the chapter and en-

courage relating them to contemporary problems, and an annotated list of suggested readings for those who wish to pursue the subject matter of the chapter further. We hope that both students and instructors will find these teaching aids helpful.

Many people shared their ideas with us and otherwise contributed their efforts to the final product. At Prentice Hall we especially would like to thank Nancy Roberts and Serena Hoffman.

This and the previous edition benefited from the thoughtful and insightful comments and suggestions of a number of colleagues: Cecil H. Brown, Thomas Greaves, Leonard W. Moss, Ailon Shiloh, Joseph R. Walsh, Bob Carola, Richard Scaglion, Meredith Weiss-Belding, Paul Stoller, Helen Schuster, Shumin Huang, and Linda Whiteford. The following reviewers also provided useful commentary: William Leons, University of Toledo; Kaja Finkler, University of North Carolina at Chapel Hill; Simon D. Messing, South Connecticut State University; and John H. Belding, Quinsigamond Community College.

John Friedl would like to thank his family for their support and encouragement—Mary, Joe, Sarah, and Ben. Michael B. Whiteford appreciates the support of his wife, Patty, and offspring, Scott, Chip, and Cindy. He would also like to acknowledge a special debt of gratitude to his family of anthropologists: his father, Bud, who with his mother, Marion, produced anthropologists in the forms of brother Scott and sisters Linda and Laurie (the latter of whom is not an anthropologist, but an urban planner concerned with many of the same issues). Add to this brother-in-law Doug Uzzell (also an anthropologist), and at times family get-togethers resemble the annual meetings of the American Anthropological Association in microcosm. Finally, he would also like to thank his colleagues in anthropology at Iowa State University, who over the years continually shared their insights and perceptions about cultures past and present.

Mainly, we both would like to thank our students. We hope their interests, questions, and concerns about anthropology and the way it is taught are reflected in this book. If there is an abundance of enthusiasm evident in the pages that follow, it is because teaching anthropology has been such a rewarding experience.

Michael B. Whiteford
John Friedl

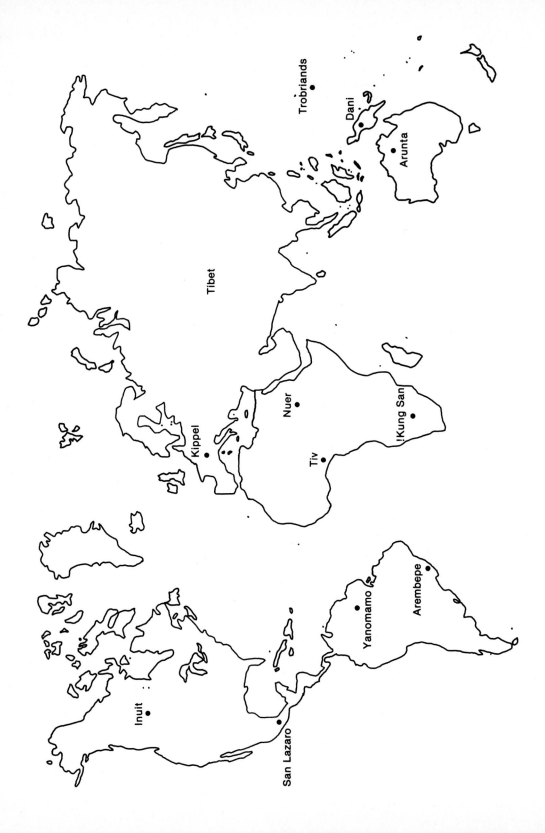

Trobriands

Dani

Arunta

Tibet

Nuer

!Kung San

Kippel

Tiv

Inuit

San Lazaro

Yanomamo

Arembepe

1

What Is Anthropology?

On the first day of class we often ask students in our introductory anthropology courses what the term *anthropologist* means to them. Their responses include images of archeologists stripping jungle foliage from Mayan temples, Jane Goodall observing chimpanzee behavior, or a khaki-clothed individual hunkered next to a campfire, swatting away pesky biting insects while collecting vital bits of information from a slightly bemused, scantily dressed native crouched nearby. Often the term is associated with the origins of human beings or with finding the "missing link." Almost inevitably, a student will bring in a bone found during the summer on the family farm or while camping, or someone will show up with a piece of pottery or chipped stone and ask that we identify the object—frequently wanting to know how much it's worth! All of these situations describe activities of anthropologists, but they do not begin to cover the jobs of anthropologists who work in museums, businesses, clinics or hospitals, government agencies, social change projects, and many other fields.

Information on what anthropology is comes from a variety of sources. Many people got their first exposure to the exciting work done by members of the Leakey family in East Africa through family subscriptions to *National Geographic*. Others have enjoyed reading articles by individuals like Penny Patterson, whose efforts to teach great apes how to communicate using sign language have made the gorilla Koko something of a celebrity. Public television specials on the work of a number of anthropologists have gone a long way in publicizing the diversity of the discipline. In addition, Steven Spielberg's exciting films dealing with the trials and tribulations of Indiana Jones have created a fanciful and romantic, if somewhat unrealistic, image of anthropology.

Rarely is anyone at a loss in defining *anthropology*. If there is a problem, it is that people have too many notions about just what the discipline involves. This confusion goes well beyond the confines of introductory classes. Elsewhere in the academic setting we frequently hear: "But isn't that what sociologists do?" "Isn't anthropology really just the study of 'primitive' societies?" or "Don't you folks just dig up dead Indians?" Curriculum committees struggle over whether the discipline should be categorized as a social or a biological science, or whether it rightly belongs in the humanities. In fact, anthropology has been described as the most scientific of the humanities and the most humanistic of the social sciences. Furthermore, it is the only one of the social sciences (or humanities, as the case may be) that has a strong biological science component. On the one hand, anthropology is all-encompassing because of the seemingly wide range of interests of its practitioners; on the other hand, it is often befuddling exactly because of its breadth and diversity.

This book is an introduction to the subject of anthropology, and in particular, to cultural anthropology. Let us begin by defining the subject of this book. Next we will trace the development of anthropology as a discipline distinct from the other social sciences. We will then look at the four subdisciplines within the field of anthropology to see what different anthropologists are interested in, and how these interests fit together and build on one another to give us an overall perspective for understanding all of human behavior.

The word *anthropology* is derived from two Greek words, *anthropos* (man) and *logos* (study). Anthropologists study the similarities and differences in how people look, how they talk, and how they behave, both in the past and in the present. They are interested in all aspects of the human species and human behavior, in all places and at all times, from the origin and evolution of the species to the way people live today.

Only in the last hundred years has anthropology been recognized as a separate area of formal study. The first academic position in anthropology was held by Edward Tylor in Oxford, England, in 1884. Four years later Franz Boas became the first professor of anthropology in the United States—at Clark University in Massachusetts.

Edward Burnett Tylor (1832–1917)

Edward Burnett Tylor is frequently called the father of modern anthropology. His early interest in foreign peoples and their customs was sparked by archeological research in Mexico, together with studies of the native Mexican-Indian cultures he encountered. Later he became involved in the controversy over the theory of cultural evolution, which he defended against the contemporary views of religious orthodoxy. In 1884 he was appointed to the first academic position in anthropology, at Oxford University.

While the scientific study of anthropology is relatively recent, this cannot be said of interest in anthropological matters. People have always been curious about themselves and have always asked anthropological questions and sought answers to those questions in the spirit in which anthropologists conduct research today. Of course, we have no written records to take us back to the dawn of the human species, but for as far back as we do have records, they indicate that people had an interest in human nature and in the diversity of the world around them.

Herodotus (484?–424? B.C.), the Greek historian who is sometimes called the father of history, might also be called an anthropologist. In writing about the events of his time, he raised a number of questions about the differences between the Greeks and the peoples who lived in surrounding areas. He believed that the peoples encountered by the Greeks in the Persian Wars represented an earlier stage of Greek society. Unfortunately,

Herodotus, like many of his contemporaries, felt that if you weren't Greek, you were "savage" or "barbaric." (The word *barbarian* comes from the Greek word *bar-bar*, a cognate of the English *bow-wow*, describing the sound of a dog, indicating that anyone who spoke a language other than Greek was less than human.) Nevertheless, it is from his writings, based on observations and interviews, that later scholars were able to get a picture of what life was like in Egypt at that time.

A later historian, Thucydides (460?–400? B.C.), in his accounts of the Peloponnesian War, made an even stronger statement of the notion that the "barbarians" represented a stage through which Athenian culture had already passed in its rise to civilization. Thus he was not only comparing different groups, but also analyzing the differences, trying to understand what caused them and explain the current state of his own society.

In Western Europe the age of exploration and discovery that followed the decline of the Middle Ages created greater interest in the variety of peoples and customs in other parts of the world. European explorers, adventurers, missionaries, and travelers came into contact with societies whose people behaved in ways that the Europeans found very strange. In letters and journals they described these societies in the utmost detail. The more contact they had with different cultures, the more information was collected and published, creating even greater interest in the study of other peoples. Although some of the early attempts at scientific analysis of foreign customs and peoples of radically different appearance were quite naive—almost comical from our viewpoint—still, they were the first step toward the development of anthropology as a science. Are these strange peoples in the far corners of the earth related to each other, and to us? How do their customs compare with ours? And how can we explain such a wide range of behavior? These were the kinds of questions asked by the early anthropologists. Never mind that today such questions seem simplistic. If they had not been asked and at least partly answered, we wouldn't be any farther along than our fifteenth-century forerunners were.

The Rise of Anthropology in the Nineteenth Century

It wasn't until the nineteenth century that anthropology began to take shape as a separate field of study. It came together from many different directions, with roots in the natural sciences, the social sciences, and even humanistic disciplines like history and folklore. By the end of the nineteenth century, anthropology had clearly narrowed its focus to four main areas: (1) studies of the physical aspects of the human species, including human biology and evolution; (2) studies of language, mainly the diversity of the world's spoken and written languages; (3) archeological studies of past civilizations; and (4) studies

of the cultural similarities and differences among existing societies, particularly those of the non-Western world.

These four fields are still at the core of anthropology, and today every anthropologist is expected to be acquainted with them. But it is interesting to look at the way these seemingly diverse approaches were brought together as anthropology developed into a formal discipline and defined its boundaries with regard to other social sciences.

In the nineteenth century **physical anthropology** was perhaps most directly concerned with the concept of race, especially in the United States, where the tensions that led to the Civil War fostered scientific investigation of racial differences. The roots of physical anthropology can be found in the natural sciences of that period, including biology, botany, and zoology. These fields had a long tradition of recording all the diverse species of animals and plants discovered in different parts of the world and trying to figure out the relationships among them, as well as how they had grown apart and changed—in other words, their **evolution.**

Of course, these early investigations suffered from the problems that were common to all scientific fields at that time. Their measurements were crude at best, and their knowledge of human anatomy and physiology was limited. But with each new experiment and each new discovery, another piece was added to the puzzle. Anthropologists became more aware of the relationships between human beings and other animals. They began to understand some of the obvious differences among human populations; they learned how physical features like skin color or hair type or even height and general body structure were tied in with the environments in which people had lived for very long periods.

Without evidence of our past, there could be no anthropology. That evidence was provided by **archeology.** Although in the nineteenth century archeology was not considered a branch of anthropology, its subject matter was of crucial importance to physical anthro-

When early European explorers first made contact with individuals in other lands, such as these Maori from New Zealand, they concluded that not only were they strange and bizarre people, but that their ways of life eventually would evolve to resemble what existed in western Europe. But these newly "discovered" people often thought that the first Europeans they encountered were themselves not quite human!

pologists. Archeologists are concerned primarily with **prehistory**—the period of human existence prior to the keeping of written records or historical accounts. Their aim is to reconstruct the origins and spread of culture by examining any remains of past societies that we are fortunate enough to find. Although archeology is best known for its dramatic discoveries of ancient cities and the "great" civilizations of the past, it also provides us with a vast amount of information about ancient people and their customs.

Throughout the nineteenth century, as physical anthropologists were puzzling over the differences among humans, evidence of earlier and somewhat different human forms poured in from around the world. Fossil forms of humanlike animals, some with thicker skulls or larger teeth or slightly different facial shapes, forced scholars to rethink their theories of human evolution or creation. But even more important, in many cases the bones of ancient people were found in association with tools and other material possessions, often indicating not only that they must have looked different from modern human beings but that they lived by different means as well; that is, they had a different *culture.*

As archeologists provided more information about ancient peoples around the world, their work became more valuable to physical anthropology. At the same time, knowledge of past civilizations contributed to other areas of interest and formed the link that tied them to the growing field of anthropology. One such area was *linguistics*, the study of human language and languages.

Much of the work in linguistics in the nineteenth century and even earlier was devoted to detailed descriptions of peculiarities in the speech of various groups of people, or to tracing the history of related languages in an attempt to find some common form from which they had developed. Increased interest in language was a result of the expansion of European economic and political interests throughout the world, but for a long time it remained more of an art form than a science. People who, for one reason or another, had an opportunity to learn another language might do so, but often without any attempt at developing a scientific approach to the study of language as a whole.

As questions about human evolution came to the forefront of anthropological study, it became obvious that our evolutionary past made it difficult to draw the line between humans and nonhumans. One thing that most people felt comfortable in citing as a difference between humans and nonhumans was the use of language. Humans are able to communicate through speech and, in the case of civilized societies, writing; other animals cannot. Out of this interest in studying earlier forms of language, combined with the realization of the uniqueness of spoken language to humans, the field of **anthropological linguistics** developed.

Archeology contributed to the study of language by providing information about the origins and early forms of written language. And physical anthropology contributed its interest in the study of human evolution and human variation in both the past and the present. But the greatest contribution to anthropological linguistics, and the area that tied it most firmly to the field of anthropology, came from the comparative study of contemporary peoples throughout the world. This area of study is called **cultural anthropology.**

The site of Teotihuacan, in central Mexico, can lay claim to being the first true city of the Americas. Built around the time of the birth of Christ, it was considerably more advanced from an architectural and engineering perspective than were European cities at that time.

Cultural anthropology had very different origins from those of other subfields of anthropology, but it was almost a foregone conclusion that they would eventually come together. Cultural anthropology studies the similarities and differences in the behavior of various groups of people. It grew out of people's natural curiosity about the ways of life observed in groups other than their own. The farther away these groups are, the more different they are likely to be.

Early accounts of other cultures came from a limited number of sources—soldiers who conquered the peoples of other continents, traders who brought home the riches of other lands, and missionaries who set out to convert the "heathens" to Christianity. But as Europe gained greater control over other societies, the way was opened for scholars interested in learning about these societies and studying them in a more scientific way.

Increased knowledge about human cultural diversity led to attempts to systematize these differences. The outcome was a theory of cultural evolution that paralleled the theory of biological evolution. Evolutionary theory proved to be the link that tied the four subfields of anthropology together in the early days of the discipline. Cultural anthropologists applied an evolutionary model to contemporary societies in an attempt to set up a scale on which to rank all known cultures. From this scale they reconstructed the evolutionary history of human society, from its earliest and most primitive stages up to the present level of civilization.

Physical anthropologists brought in the biological theory of evolution, based on the work of Darwin and others, and tried to relate it to cultural evolution. Much of the work of physical anthropology in the nineteenth century was designed to prove that there was a correlation between cultural and racial types. People with less advanced cultures were thought to represent earlier stages in biological evolution, and this idea was used to explain cultural differences. Of course, such theories both arose from and contributed to the prevailing racism of the period, but if we are to understand the development of anthropology, we must view it in this context.

Linguistics and archeology were also concerned with evolution, and this helped make anthropology a unified field. Anthropological linguists were interested in the evolution of language and used both contemporary cultural-anthropological studies and those of archeologists to reconstruct earlier languages and trace their change over time. Later, as physical anthropologists became interested in studying the evolution of the capacity for culture, including the human capacity for speech and symbolic communication through language, anthropological linguists turned their interest in that direction as well.

For its part, archeology fit in well with the evolutionary tendencies of anthropology in the nineteenth century. The study of past civilizations was an important contribution to the record of cultural and biological evolution, and to a lesser extent (through the records of literate civilizations) it helped document changes in language over time. Archeologists and cultural anthropologists often worked together in plotting out the world's societies, both past and present, on an evolutionary scale.

The Branches of Anthropology Today

Physical anthropology   Today the four subfields of anthropology remain at the core of the discipline. Physical anthropology considers the human species as a biological entity as well as a social animal. Some physical anthropologists are concerned primarily with prehuman and early human species, or **fossil hominids.** Others concentrate on the similarities and differences among the various **primate** species, which include not only humans but monkeys and apes as well. This area of study is called **primatology.** A third area, known as the study of human variation, or **anthropological genetics,** deals with contem-

Physical anthropologists study primates such as baboons in order to understand human evolution and the capacity for culture.

porary as well as historical variations among human populations. It is concerned with such topics as the adaptation of a group of people to a specific climate, the natural immunity of some peoples to certain diseases, and the all-important question of racial differences.

By studying human nature, the variety of peoples in the world today and in the past, and the relationship of the human species to other species, we are better able to understand why we behave the way we do. The physical anthropologist gives us valuable information about our physical structure. For example, it is important to know the effects of being able to walk erect on two feet rather than having to use our hands to steady ourselves.

By providing answers to the question of what makes human beings unique among animals, physical anthropology gives us the first clues to the meaning of human behavior. It tells us the basis for that behavior and the limitations on it. It tells us why we should expect others to behave within those limita-

tions, and what variations are possible. In other words, physical anthropology spells out the limits of human behavior. Perhaps most important, it teaches us that no matter how much diversity we might find in the world around us, the most remarkable fact is not how different people are but how similar they are, and this is a crucial lesson in getting along in the world today.

A case for physical anthropology: Lactase deficiency   Whether they are studying fossils, primates, or human genetics, physical anthropologists are interested mainly in the interaction between the biological and cultural aspects of humans, as the following example illustrates. In much of the world a physiological condition makes a large proportion of the adult population unable to digest milk properly.

Because many adults cease to produce the enzyme lactase, some peoples of East Africa, like this Nuer woman, along with white Euro-Americans, are among the relatively few population groups that continue to consume raw milk as adults.

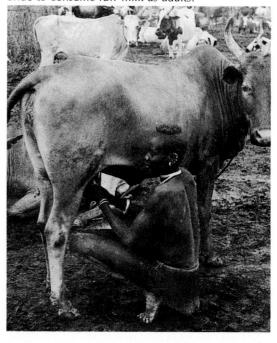

An enzyme called **lactase** is needed to digest milk; without it, milk causes the bowels to become distended and leads to cramps, gas, and diarrhea. Almost every infant has the capacity to produce this enzyme, but in only two population groups is this ability kept through adulthood. If this seems odd to some of us, it is because the United States contains one of these two populations: white Euro-Americans. The other population is the Nilotes of East Africa. Significantly, these are the two main groups who practice dairying in which raw milk is consumed. Of course, other groups also raise cattle. Typically, however, they do not drink milk as such, but consume it in other forms that can be digested more readily.

The Chinese, for example, engage in dairying, but adult Chinese generally do not consume raw milk. Although the inability to produce lactase is not universal among Chinese people, cultural values and taste preferences lead even those who can digest raw milk to avoid it.

The conclusion we can draw from this study is that cultural evolution has paralleled biological evolution. Cultural values, in the form of a taste preference for milk, changed along with genetic changes leading to the ability to drink milk. Before dairy animals were domesticated, early humans would not have consumed milk after two or three years of age, and adults would not have needed to produce lactase. The taste for milk probably did not change until the genetic capacity to digest it was gained. At any rate, this study helps us understand the interplay between genetic and cultural change and between biology and culture. It also teaches us that the American habit of drinking milk throughout our adult lives is not only unnecessary but also undesirable in most cultures. The advertising slogan "You never outgrow your need for milk" would not be effective in most other parts of the world!

Archeology Archeology, the branch of anthropology that is devoted to the study of the human past, often focuses on the period before people began to keep written records. Archeologists study the origin, spread, and evolution of culture by examining the remains of past societies. They share the task of other kinds of anthropologists in that they are trying to understand human behavior. The difference is that their materials are generally the unwritten records of past societies. They can't sit down with living members of those societies and talk about what they have found. They can't even observe living people, but must interpret the material evidence left by people long dead. Many archeologists distinguish between *prehistoric archeology*, which is the study of extinct cultures that left no written records, and *historic archeology*, which is the investigation of those groups for whom there are written materials to accompany the archeological evidence.

Archeology is limited by the nature of the evidence it deals with. For one thing, we cannot examine the activities of prehistoric

FIGURE 1.1 Lactase Deficiency in Selected Population Groups.

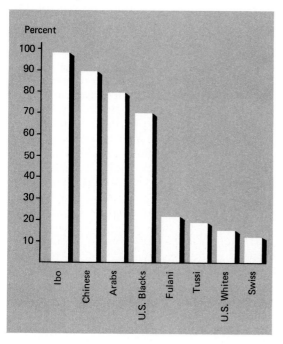

people. We have almost no way of knowing what they believed, what they valued, or even how they organized their society. We can guess a few things—for example, that early human beings believed in a form of magic created by imitating the image of a natural object. One interpretation of the famous prehistoric cave paintings in southern France and Spain is that they were meant to ensure success in a hunting expedition by showing a successful hunting scene.

Another limitation on archeology is that what remains are only the durable materials of a past culture. These are not necessarily what the people might have left if they had wanted to show us what was important to them. Prehistoric peoples did not have the future in mind when they dumped their garbage or buried their dead; they did not provide us with a time capsule containing records of their way of life. Thus, not only must we interpret the materials they left behind within the limited context in which we find them, such as a burial site or a refuse pit; we must also try to paint a picture of an entire way of life without the hope of ever finding physical evidence for much of that picture. We can make an inventory of the kinds of tools or weapons early humans used at a given site, and we can note which ones are found most often, how they are made, and so forth. But we can never know what a tool meant to the person who used it. We can only make guesses based on our involvement with the material of our culture.

What, then, can archeology contribute to our understanding of human culture and social behavior? First, we can learn much about the technology of early peoples through their material remains, as well as through analysis of such aspects of their life style as what they ate. We can tell, for example, whether a particular group lived mainly by hunting or fishing or by farming. A second aspect of the life of early peoples that is revealed to us through archeology is their economic practices. For example, sometimes we find pottery or jewelry made from materials that are known to have been avail-

able only in distant places. This usually means that these items were not made at the site but were obtained through some other means—either by traveling to the place where they were available or by trading with other groups. If we put together a picture of the distribution of such items over time, we can get an idea of the interactions among neighboring groups, and this in turn gives us clues about other aspects of culture that might have been borrowed or traded as well.

Less evident than economics or technology, but still recognizable, is the political and social structure of past cultures. We can assume a great deal about the way a city was organized from the layout of the buildings and the types of housing found there. For example, if we find a large temple in the center of an ancient city and it is surrounded by fairly large dwelling sites, while the buildings on the outskirts of the settlement are smaller, we know that there were probably at least two classes of people and that the temple was at the center of the city not only in a physical sense but socially as well.

Finally, archeological evidence can reveal a great deal about certain aspects of the religious and spiritual life of ancient societies. We can recognize sacred objects by their location in centers of religious activity or in burial sites. When we are fortunate enough to find temples or other religious structures, we can determine their importance and their influence on the society. But in other areas it is very hard to interpret the evidence. Thus we know little about ancient peoples' belief systems, or their values and morals, their feelings about spirits, and so forth. Even when we find material objects that might suggest such beliefs, we cannot ask anyone to explain their meaning but must go on what we know about other aspects of that society and later societies that seem to be similar to it.

In sum, archeology gives us a chance to look into the past of the human species. But it is like doing a jigsaw puzzle with most of the pieces missing, and without a picture of the finished puzzle on the box to work from.

Cave paintings, like this one from Spain, not only give us important clues about what types of animals existed at that time, but archeologists can often make inferences about hunting methods and even about how these people might have interacted with the supernatural.

We have a few things that fit together; we can guess about many others; but we really don't have enough to put it all together with complete confidence. Every new piece we find fits somewhere, though, and we never know when the next piece will give us the key to a whole new section of the puzzle of life in prehistoric times. That is the challenge and the excitement of archeology.

A case for prehistoric archeology: Stonehenge Among all the ancient stone monuments in the world, **Stonehenge** is one of the most magnificent and perhaps the most mysterious. Situated on a grassy plain in southern England, it consists of a ring of huge stones, some of them weighing 50 tons or more, perched on vertical supporting stones of equal size rising almost 13 feet above the ground. These stones were moved to their present site from quarries 20 miles away in an effort that began some 4,000 years ago and may have taken 1,200 years or more to complete.

It is somewhat surprising that a project that involved as many people for as long a period was not described in legends or paint-

Stonehenge, in southwestern England. Although we know little about the way of life of its builders, we do know enough about their technology to explain how they constructed this huge monument.

ings, so that today we still do not know for sure why it was built or how it was used. A strange thing about Stonehenge (and other monuments like it) is that, unlike other large temples, it was not surrounded by dwelling places. Thus if it was the major focus of a settlement of people—as it must have been—then it must have had special significance to be off-limits for residential purposes.

Modern-day archeologists have been able to show how ancient men and women would have been able to build such a monument using the tools and technology available at that time. It would have required great skill to carry out such a project using levers, counterweights, and other advanced tools, but it is clear that with a large work force and enough time it could have been done. What archeologists have not been able to discover is why these ancient people devoted so much backbreaking labor to their task. We know from written records that the pyramids of Egypt were built in honor of the Pharaohs who commissioned them. Lacking written records of Stonehenge, we can only guess about its origin. A number of explanations have been suggested, some more plausible than others. It may have been a shrine or temple where its builders worshipped. It may have been used as a marketplace or a royal palace. It has even been suggested that it was built by aliens as a landing pad for their spaceships!

A recent theory about Stonehenge has generated much debate. In *Stonehenge Decoded* Gerald Hawkins claims that Stonehenge is an ancient observatory and that the positions of the stones were calculated to permit the prediction of the exact moment of sunrise on the summer solstice, as well as eclipses and other astronomical events. Hawkins used computer analysis to support his claim. Although many archeologists have criticized Hawkins's work because he assumed that some fallen boulders were once placed in perfect order to enable the builders of Stonehenge to view astronomical events and because he used some outdated measurements, he has presented strong evidence that Stone-

henge was indeed a prehistoric observatory. But how it is tied in with the religion of the people who built it we will probably never know.

A case for historic archeology: The garbage project About a decade ago a study was conducted in Tucson, Arizona, that involved the analysis of household refuse. The project was very interesting and demonstrated that archeologists' methods can be used to tell us some very important facts about contemporary household food consumption patterns. In the early and mid-1970s archeologists and nutritionists from the University of Arizona analyzed garbage from hundreds of households over a period of several years. Refuse was sorted and identified (for example, "ground chuck" as a variety of "beef"), cost was noted, weight of tossed-out but once-edible food noted, and so forth. The research team allowed for the fact that some households had garbage disposals, which would reduce the amount of their garbage. Other factors such as compost piles and household pets were assumed to reduce the amount of organic materials tossed into the family garbage can. Researchers concluded that their refuse findings represented minimum levels of discard.

What did they find? The research took place during a period of relatively high inflation when food prices rose by an average of 11 percent per year. One might expect that people's strategies would include: (1) reducing the amount of food obtained; (2) looking for cheaper foods; and (3) throwing away less. The results showed that overall there was a reduction in the quantity of food coming into people's houses, although there were some interesting twists to this observation that were related to household income. Perhaps, the authors reasoned, the reduction simply corresponded to national trends that had been going on for a number of years, among them the increasing tendency of American families to eat out. One observation was particularly interesting; food consumption had actually increased in the areas with

Much of the material remains used by archeologists to interpret how people lived during prehistoric times have come from garbage pits. Similarly, today's garbage can tell a lot about contemporary people.

the poorest households, although these families substituted less expensive items for more costly ones, indicated by a decline in meat, fish, poultry, and cheese consumption and an increase in the consumption of grain products.

Patterns related to who threw out what and how much during this period were also tied to income. The amount of discarded food among the poor decreased significantly. In contrast, more affluent people tossed out a larger portion of their estimated food resources than before.[1]

This study, using data collected by archeological methods, is notable because it shows

an important side of socioeconomic behavior that reveals a lot about the economics and efficiency of food use.

Anthropological linguistics   The study of language from an anthropological viewpoint is the third branch of modern anthropology. Of course, linguistics is also a separate field of study, but anthropologists who specialize in linguistics today are concerned with the relationship between language and cultural behavior. They ask questions about a language from the point of view of the human species, rather than trying to describe the language or its structure. The central focus is still on people, and language is viewed as part of the social world.

One area of anthropological linguistics is the study of the origin of language. This

[1] William L. Rathje and Gail G. Harrison, "Monitoring Trends in Food Utilization: Application of an Archaeological Method," *Federation Proceedings*, no. 1(1987): 49–54.

could just as well be a question for physical anthropologists. At present there is an important controversy over which of the fossil hominids was the first with the capacity for speech. Another area of interest is the role of language in social behavior. This is a fairly new field known as *sociolinguistics*, and it is concerned with the way we use the language we speak (or various forms of it, for we all know different variations of the English language, which we use in different contexts).

A third area of interest in anthropological linguistics is the study of *folk categories*, that is, the units of meaning into which a language breaks up the universe. Every language conveys much of the content of a culture in the items that it labels with separate words. For example, in one Inuit (a native word for Eskimo) language there are 12 separate and unrelated words for wind and 22 words for snow. That is, 22 different kinds of snow are recognized and given names that are not just different forms of the same root word but different words altogether. It is not important to English speakers that there are many types of snow, so we use adjectives to describe these variations—*wet snow, powder snow,* and so on. We may occasionally use different words, such as *sleet* or *hail,* but that is about all the variety our language allows. On the other hand, we have a large vocabulary to deal with technological aspects of our culture that are important to us. Look at all the words we have for the automobile: *sedan, convertible, coupe, fastback, wagon, bus, van, truck,* and so on. Obviously, we would not expect a member of a society in which automobiles are not found to make such distinctions; to them a car is a car, period. But then, to us snow is snow, period.

The idea that the structure and content of one's language affects one's thought processes is a fascinating one. If you have ever studied a foreign language, you have found that there are some words that simply cannot be translated into English. This illustrates the importance of language in shaping the way we look at the world. Each language has certain words that describe experiences or feelings that are peculiar to the group of people who share that language and culture. It is often impossible to translate such a word literally into English, for there is no way to capture its essence in a single English word. Instead, we usually end up with several words in a rather awkward phrase that may convey some of the meaning but is never really satisfactory. Thus learning a foreign language is not merely an exercise in memorization but a lesson in cultural anthropology as well, for by learning the language we learn something about the way other people think and about the ways in which they are different from us. Language gives us insight into culture, and as such it is a valuable tool for studying and understanding people.

A case for anthropological linguistics: Color categories One of the most intriguing examples of folk categories is the colors that different languages recognize. We all know that there is a very wide range of colors in nature. If you have ever tried to decide what color to paint your house and have pored over dozens of color charts at the paint store, you know how many variations of the same color there can be. We can look at ten different shades of green, and even though we can see that they are different, we still call them all "green," thus lumping them into the same category. An interesting experiment is to take finely graded color samples (such as those on a custom-mixed paint color chart) ranging from green to blue, including perhaps 20 or 30 shades. If you look at both extremes, you can easily say that one is green and the other blue. The hard part is drawing the line between one shade and another, saying that one belongs to the category "green" and the other to the category "blue." In fact, sometimes we get around this problem by inventing another category, "blue-green."

In our language the category "blue-green" is really not a separate category but merely a convenient label for the transition between two categories. We know this because we do not have a separate word for it. This indicates

To the Inuit, variations in the texture of snow are extremely important, a fact reflected in their language.

to us that, while blue and green are significant, the transition from one to the other is less so. But in another language there could easily be a word that designates "blue-green" as a separate category. Certainly there is no reason why this could not be done—after all, isn't green a transition between blue and yellow?

Here we begin to see how language can affect the way we order the universe. It sets up artificial categories into which we plug our perceptions. The point is that they *are* artificial; our culture, through our language, determines the way we order our perceptions. If one language can set up more categories for color than ours does, certainly another

language can set up fewer such categories. The Navajo term for green includes blue and purple. The Zuni Indians use a single term for both yellow and orange. Some Indian languages have words for only two or three colors, and every colored thing is placed in one of these two or three categories. This does not mean that those people are color-blind, only that the distinctions we make between certain colors are not important in their culture. It doesn't mean that they can't tell the difference between a cardinal and a robin. It simply means that they don't classify them as different in terms of color, even though they can perceive color differences. To most of us red may simply be red, whereas to an interior decorator there are important differences among scarlet, vermilion, crimson, maroon, magenta, and cerise. The study of language in other cultures as well as our own can help us realize the important fact that we must not attempt to judge differences in terms of our own culture but instead must understand them in the context of the cultures in which they occur.

Cultural anthropology   We come now to the main subject of this book, cultural anthropology. In a strict sense, we could include archeology and anthropological linguistics under this heading, for they are both concerned with culture. But since these subfields are generally considered separate from the major focus of cultural anthropology, it is better to treat them separately.

Cultural anthropology, as the term is commonly used today, generally refers to the study of existing peoples. Further, it takes a comparative approach; that is, its aim is to understand and appreciate the diversity in human behavior, and develop a science of human behavior through comparison of different people throughout the world. In the United States we often distinguish between two areas of cultural anthropology: ethnology and ethnography. **Ethnology** is the comparative study of culture and the investigation of theoretical problems using information about different groups. **Ethnography** is simply the description of one culture; it is not a comparative study. In other words, an ethnological study is based on two or more ethnographies; the latter provide the raw material for the former. To avoid confusion we will use the term *cultural anthropology* to cover both of these areas, but you should know what the terms mean since you will come across them in other anthropological readings.

Thus the work of the cultural anthropologist consists of two main tasks: to *describe* the cultures of other peoples and to *compare* them. As we saw in the example of color categories, these tasks are not easy, since putting something from another cultural con-

Cultural anthropologists traditionally studied non-Western people, such as the dancers from Guinea Bissau, West Africa.

text into the concepts and words available in the English language is not always possible. In fact, we might consider an anthropologist's description of a foreign culture to be a cultural translation. The aim of the description is to make clear to the reader just what it is like to live as a member of the other culture lives. Accurate descriptive work, or cultural translation, is the basis for comparative studies, which are crucial to understanding human behavior.

Other social sciences have the same goal as anthropology in that they attempt to understand human behavior. What makes cultural anthropology different? Perhaps the most obvious difference is that the scope of anthropology is much broader than that of any other social science. Economics deals only with economic behavior, and political science focuses on political behavior. Cultural anthropology, on the other hand, is concerned with these and other areas from a comparative perspective, and especially with the interrelationships among all areas of behavior in any particular society. It overlaps every other social science in at least some areas, yet it retains its individuality.

The distinction between history and anthropology was a subject of intense debate for many years. Is anthropology, after all, merely the study of human history in all its various forms? Although this debate has subsided, one cannot truthfully say that it has been completely resolved. No anthropologist can work without an awareness of the past, of the sequence of events that led to the situation being studied. In describing another culture or comparing aspects of two cultures, the anthropologist cannot ignore history.

But there is no doubt that history and anthropology are separate. For one thing, historians focus on past events, and their study of values, motivations, and behavior is directed toward explaining why things occurred the way they did. Anthropology seeks to generalize from such explanations. It is not enough to say that history is more of an art and anthropology more of a science, or that anthropologists use history more than

historians use anthropology. Indeed, it is often hard to tell history from anthropology, although it helps to note that historians focus on past events, in contrast to the cultural anthropologist's emphasis on contemporary events.

A more difficult distinction to make is that between cultural anthropology and sociology. One important difference between these two fields is that sociology is concerned with the study of our own society, while anthropology is a *comparative* discipline that focuses on all societies at all times. Sociology is interested mainly in the present; anthropology deals just as much with the past. However, these contrasts are growing less valid every day as anthropologists adopt sociological methods and sociologists adopt the comparative approach of anthropology.

Another way of looking at the difference between sociology and anthropology is to note that sociology tends to be quantitative, while anthropology tends to be qualitative. What this means is that the sociologist generalizes from broad surveys of large numbers of people and the anthropologist relies on close knowledge of a few members of a group to form impressions. Although these impressions might not be valid for the society as a whole (quantitative), they are valid in greater depth for the small sample studied (qualitative). The anthropologist may spend weeks finding the answer to a particular question, mainly out of intense personal involvement in the study. The sociologist, on the other hand, cannot afford to become deeply involved in surveying a larger sample of the society. This is not to condemn either discipline but, rather, to point out a basic difference between them. Perhaps it is best illustrated by the comment of an anthropologist who, in poking fun at expensive studies of inner-city social problems conducted at a great social distance, described a sociologist as someone who spends $50,000 to find a whorehouse. (One wonders if after all this expense the sociologist might not be led into the parlor only to find an anthropologist playing the piano.)

Thus the major difference between anthropology and sociology probably lies in the methods used. Anthropology uses intensive methods of study; sociology tends to employ broader, more extensive methods.

A case for cultural anthropology: Culture and psychology   A few years ago one of the authors was asked to serve as a consultant to the Child Psychology Division of the medical school at Ohio State University, where he taught. A case had been referred to the division, and the director thought it would be of interest to see whether there were other cultures in which the behavior in question was acceptable. The case concerned a foster mother who had been found to be imposing toilet training on an infant who had been placed in her care. The infant was only a few months old, and training at such an early age is unacceptable in American culture. As the story unfolded, it became apparent that the woman had taken good care of the child, shown warmth and affection toward it, and in all other ways was an ideal foster parent. However, the fact that she had trained the infant to defecate while she held it over newspaper alarmed the officials assigned to the case.

The author was asked, as a consulting anthropologist, to cite references to early toilet training in other cultures. It appeared that the medical personnel in charge of the program thought that if an anthropologist could show that such a pattern was practiced elsewhere, it would be more acceptable to local officials. He was able to cite a few examples of early training, although none as early as the case under study. But the main thrust of his presentation was that to understand the practices of the mother it was necessary to know something about her own culture and background. If this was a common practice within the subculture of American society in which she had been raised, and if it was successful (that is, if people raised this way turned out to be healthy, normal individuals in American society), then we should not be so quick to question its

This Swedish preschool scene suggests that toilet-training practices vary greatly from one culture to another.

validity. He was even able to get the caseworker to admit that the mother herself had been trained this way, as had several other members of her family.

The difference between psychology and anthropology comes through strongly in this example. The approach of the cultural anthropologist was to see whether what was considered deviant in middle-class American culture was acceptable in another cultural setting. However, the main concern of the psychologists and psychiatrists was whether the child was being raised according to the norms of American society, and they took those norms to be the way they, as white, middle-class Americans, had been raised. Deviation from those norms was forbidden, no matter whether it was acceptable and common in another culture or in another American subculture. They spoke of the "harm" that would come to the child as if the absence of a strict middle-class upbringing was by definition harmful. There was a discussion among the Freudians about the possibility of the child's sexual identity becoming confused and about the failure of the mother to relate to anything but an "empty" baby. But no sense of relativity was shown; no mention was made, for example, of other "deviant" practices in other cultures that produced healthy, normal adults.

Holism: The Trademark of Anthropology

In concluding this chapter on the definition and scope of anthropology, it is worth pointing out again that anthropology, as distinct from all other social sciences, is an integrated approach. It includes the study of the physical nature of the human species, our past, our unique capabilities as well as our limitations, and the tremendous variety and startling similarities among different cultures. The anthropological approach is sometimes described as holistic because it integrates so many different areas of concern. It is not just the study of economic behavior or the structural relations between social groups. It tries to understand all human behavior in all contexts, in all places, and at all times. And it does this by drawing from many different disciplines, as well as from the four subfields of anthropology.

The anthropologist brings to his or her study a wide background. Biology and physiology are frequently required for graduate students in physical anthropology; geology, geography, ancient history, and sometimes even architecture are needed by the archeologist; and cultural anthropologists have come from all walks of life. To study peasant society cross-culturally we have to know something about agriculture; to study personality cross-culturally we must have a background in psychology; and so on for every possible area of study within cultural anthropology.

Let us clarify this by an example. Suppose we want to compare the ways in which children learn their culture in two different groups. Because the primary topic of concern is culture, we would logically assume that cultural anthropology would be the place to start. But when we look deeper we find that cultural anthropologists must have information from a number of different fields to conduct such a study. For example, we must know something about psychology to understand the formation of personality and character in infancy. We must understand at least some areas of elementary education to comprehend the process of training in the early years. It would help if we had some knowledge about the physical nature of the infant and its growth and development; this we could obtain by studying physical anthropology. Linguistics would give us a better understanding of how a child learns a language and the patterns that are formed in the infant's brain at that early age. In addition to all of these factors, we must be familiar with the culture of each group in order to understand the attitudes of parents toward children in those societies. (Do they favor males over females? Do they expect males to accept different roles from females at an early age? Do parents treat their children with much care and personal attention, or do they leave them relatively unattended?)

As this example shows, **holism** in anthropology is the attempt to get the whole picture, to put it all together, and to apply knowledge from many different fields to the understanding of any aspect of behavior. It is this holistic approach, more than anything else, that distinguishes anthropology from other social sciences. And it is this approach that makes an anthropological study so difficult to carry out and at the same time so rewarding.

At this point we might address the question of the relevance of anthropology to students in an introductory course. While we will take up this issue in greater detail in the last chapter, it is important as we begin this journey to recognize some of the valuable contributions made to everyday life by anthropology—particularly cultural anthropology, as this is the focus of the text.

Throughout this book we employ a comparative, cross-cultural perspective. As will become apparent, we deal with themes that emphasize global similarities and diversities. Although there are a number of institutions, such as the family, that appear to share many similar features, there are also numerous differences in how people in other cultures behave and live out their daily lives. A cross-cultural, comparative outlook is increasingly important for living in today's world.

In recent years a great deal has been said and written about the "global village." After all, Coca-Cola is consumed in almost 200 countries, and you can now buy a "Big Mac" in Moscow—as well as in McDonald's outlets in numerous other countries. "Guess" designer jeans and Swatch watches are worn by trendy teenagers from Bogotá to Kuala Lumpur, as they wander along, moving in time to the invisible voices of Madonna or the Kinks, who call to them from their Sony Walkmans. A couple of decades ago anthropologists began writing about the revolutionary impact transistor radios were having on isolated regions of the world. In many respects the information being brought into communities by these small battery-powered radios created a level of sophistication previously unknown. Peasant villagers and tribal peoples began to obtain a sense of being part of a much larger and more complex environment than many had ever previously suspected. Today a similar process is occurring with even greater implications. In remote jungles of the Amazon and in isolated regions of the Sahara desert, satellite dishes receive the news of international events, as well as the most recent episodes of "Roseanne," "L.A. Law," and cartoons of "Teenage Mutant Ninja Turtles." Thanks in part to an explosion of information access, a greater global *savoir-faire* exists than did only a few years ago. Although the context in which information is received and processed probably differs quite a bit, today the chances are good that the average New Guinea tribal villager, French peasant, and Wall Street broker all have heard about the recent political events that have transformed Eastern Europe. Conrad Kottak[2] mentions that when he first conducted research in a Brazilian fishing village two decades ago, villagers' knowledge about life outside of the local area was understandably limited—they asked whether elephants lived in the United States. By the 1980s the level of inquiry was much more urbane, thanks in large measure to vastly improved communications with the outside, television being one of the main reasons.

At first glance this apparent veneer of cultural global homogeneity might lead many overly complacent or insensitive North Americans to assume that the whole world is becoming more and more like them. This, of course, is not the case. Over the past couple of decades it has become clear—at times, painfully so—that much of the world simply does not wish to mirror United States culture. There are exceptions, of course. Our music, clothing, and other fashion styles, our television programs and certain of our technologies seem to cross political and cultural boundaries with surprising ease. But to many Americans it often comes as a shock when our political values, ideas about human rights, and other ethical or moral concerns and values are firmly and even violently rejected. Although this rejection is hard to accept, it is essential that we develop some appreciation of the cultural reasons behind it. The interlocking nature of global economies alone demands such understanding.

The oil shortages of the mid and late 1970s pounded home American dependence on the outside world in order to heat our homes, drive our automobiles, run our factories, and do the myriad other things many of us take for granted. Today more than 6,000 United States companies have some operations abroad; overseas investments currently run about $300 billion. Fully one-third of United States corporate banks derive more than half their total earnings from overseas credits,

[2] Conrad P. Kottak, *Prime-Time Society* (Belmont, Cal.: Wadsworth Publishing Co., 1990), pp. 13–14.

and one out of eight domestic manufacturing jobs depends on exports. In spite of efforts to reduce the need to import such products as petroleum, the United States still gets almost two-thirds of its essential raw materials from foreign countries. No sector of the economy or element of society is exempt from this interconnectedness.

One of the authors of this text teaches at a midwestern university, Iowa State University. Many people are not aware of it, but Iowa is the number two state in the country in the export of agricultural products, including everything from machinery to oats. It currently leads the nation in the export of meats and ranks number two in shipping feed grains and dairy products to other parts of the world. Thus, though many Americans imagine that their livelihood is unaffected by what takes place in southern Africa or in Bangladesh, this is no longer true.

We feel that a cross-cultural, comparative perspective is important for understanding your own culture. Anthropologists have long argued that examining other life styles stimulates critical reflection on your own cultural patterns. Just as studying a foreign language can help you to understand better the structure of your own language, the study of another culture can help you appreciate your own way of life. In studying cultural anthropology students will undoubtedly be led to reexamine certain concepts they have held for a long time. Ethnocentrism—the idea that our way of doing things is correct and any other way is weird—is probably a universal human trait. Certainly one of the things anthropologists have learned over many years of cross-cultural investigations is that no single group of people has a monopoly on prejudice and ethnocentrism.

As you study different cultures, we will ask you to challenge your own values and notions. You will be encouraged to place what you are reading or discussing in the appropriate cultural context. As you deal with your ethnocentrism, you will develop a culturally relative perspective. Cultural relativism means refraining from forcing your own cultural judgments on other cultures. Some of the situations and customs you will read about in this book will strike you as somewhat incomprehensible, even bizarre. You will need to ask yourself: How do these things fit into the total cultural pattern of the society I am studying?

Summary

Anthropology began to take shape as a separate field of study in the late nineteenth century, with a focus on four main areas. *Physical anthropology* deals with the evolution of the human species, the relationship between humans and other primate species, and the variations within human groups in the world today. From physical anthropology we learn of the ability for bearing culture that distinguishes humans from other animals. *Archeology* deals with reconstructing the evolution of culture on the basis of the limited information about past societies that remains thousands of years later. Much of what archeology can tell us about the past is based on inference from societies we can observe in the present. *Anthropological linguistics*, the third field within anthropology, treats the relationship between language and culture and how language and communication function in human social behavior. *Cultural anthropology* is the study of human societies, both present and past; it seeks to describe the wide variety of cultural forms and to compare and analyze them, with the goal of understanding human behavior.

Anthropology is related to other social sciences in that all share a common interest in understanding human behavior. It differs, however, in that it is a broader approach: Economics focuses on economic behavior, political science on political behavior, and so on. In contrast, *holism*, a multifaceted approach, is the trademark of anthropology. Holism is the ability to consider a wide variety of viewpoints in understanding human behavior: for example, the physical anthropologist's knowledge of the human capacity for culture, the archeologist's information about past examples of human behavior, the anthropological linguist's assumptions about the role of language and communication in social relations, and the cultural anthropologist's understanding about the variety of culturally accepted behavior in the world today. All of these approaches contribute to the breadth of anthropology as a discipline.

Glossary

anthropological genetics   The area of physical anthropology that studies contemporary and historical variations among human populations, focusing on the way groups are related to environmental pressures (such as climate and altitude) in a specific region.

anthropological linguistics   The subdiscipline of anthropology that is concerned with the relationship between language and cultural behavior.

archeology   The subdiscipline of anthropology that focuses on the reconstruction of the origin, spread, and evolution of culture. This subdiscipline is often seen as having two components: prehistoric archeology, which is concerned primarily with the period of human existence prior to written records; and historic archeology, which studies groups for whom there are written records.

cultural anthropology   The subdiscipline of anthropology that is based on a comparative approach to the study of existing peoples, with the aim of understanding the diversity of human behavior through the comparison of different peoples throughout the world.

ethnography   The branch of cultural anthropology concerned with the description of a single culture.

ethnology   The branch of cultural anthropology concerned with the comparative study of culture and the investigation of theoretical problems using information about different groups.

evolution   The continuous natural process by which the genetic characteristics of populations of plants and animals change in response to forces in the environment. In a more general sense, evolution refers to slow, gradual change of any type.

fossil hominids   Past forms of prehuman and early human species studied in physical anthropology.

holism   The approach used in anthropology that combines a wide variety of disciplines in the study of human behavior, based on the understanding that all parts of a culture are interrelated.

lactase deficiency   The physiological condition, common to most of the world's population groups, in which a person is unable to digest milk properly because of the inability to produce the necessary enzyme (lactase).

physical anthropology   The subdiscipline of anthropology that is concerned with the study of human evolution and human variation.

prehistory   See *archeology.*

primate   The order in the Linnaean taxonomy that includes monkeys, apes, and humans.

primatology   The area of physical anthropology that is concerned with the similarities and differences among the various primate species—monkeys, apes, and humans.

Stonehenge   An archeological site in southern England made up of a ring of huge stones, which may have been used to predict astronomical events.

Questions for Discussion

1. One of the most obvious features of American society is the racial diversity of its people. In many areas of life in the United States members of one racial group predominate over members of others: for example, blacks participate in sports such as professional basketball, football, and boxing in greater proportion than they are represented in the overall population; whites frequently dominate sports such as tennis, golf, and swimming. To what extent are these differences biological and to what extent are they cultural?

2. Suppose your town were suddenly struck by a major catastrophe that wiped out the entire population and left only the physical remains, such as buildings, cars, and so forth. What inferences would future archeologists be likely to draw from these remains a thousand years from now? What aspects of your life would go undiscovered because no lasting records survived? What does this tell us about today's archeological reconstruction of the past?

3. If language is so closely related to culture, can we ever hope to achieve an international language (such as Esperanto) as long as there are cultural differences in the world? What would be the limitations on communicating in such a language? What would be the benefits of such a language?

Suggestions for Additional Reading

Physical Anthropology

JOHN FRIEDL, "Lactase Deficiency: Distribution, Associated Problems, and Implications for Nutritional Policy," *Ecology of Food and Nutrition*, 11 (1981): 37–48.

STEPHEN J. GOULD, *The Mismeasure of Man* (New York: W. W. Norton, 1981). A critique of scientific racism, focusing on the history of ranking human groups by theoretical measures of intelligence.

HARRY NELSON and ROBERT JURMAIN, *Introduction to Physical Anthropology* (St. Paul, Minn.: West Publishing Company, 1979). One of many textbooks on physical anthropology, offering a complete and easy-to-read introduction to the field.

Archeology

JOHN R. F. BOWER, *In Search of the Past: An Introduction to Archaeology* (Chicago: Dorsey Press, 1986). A very readable compendium of the field, with a focus on method.

DON BROTHWELL, *The Bog Man and the Archaeology of People* (Cambridge, Mass.: Harvard University Press, 1986). An exciting chronicle of the research surrounding "bog bodies," centuries-old human corpses unearthed in exceptionally well-preserved condition from peat bogs.

BRIAN M. FAGAN, *People of the Earth: An Introduction to World Prehistory*, 3rd ed. (Boston: Little, Brown, 1980). A thorough textbook surveying the field of prehistory, including a number of theoretical approaches and all geographic areas.

IAN TATTERSALL, ERIC DELSON, and JOHN VAN CONVERING (Eds.), *Encyclopedia of Human Evolution and Prehistory* (New York: Garland, 1988). A one-volume encyclopedia of human evolution, physical anthropology, and prehistoric archeology, referencing recent popular and technical literature on the subjects.

RUTH WHITEHOUSE and JOHN WILKINS, *The Making of Civilization* (New York: Alfred A. Knopf, 1986). A concise, colorfully illustrated history of world civilization as discovered by archeology, including an extensive bibliography.

Anthropological Linguistics

NANCY PARROTT HICKERSON, *Linguistic Anthropology* (New York: Holt, Rinehart and Winston, 1980). A brief introductory survey of language from the anthropological point of view, including the methods anthropologists use in studying language.

BRENT BERLIN and PAUL KAY, *Basic Color Terms: Their Universality and Evolution* (Berkeley, Cal.: University of California Press, 1969). A more detailed and theoretical look at the area of color categories, discussed in the case study on anthropological linguistics in this chapter.

WARD H. GOODENOUGH, *Culture, Language and Society* (Menlo Park, Cal.: Benjamin/Cummings, 1981). A short book clarifying the nature of culture by means of linguistics.

Cultural Anthropology

HERBERT APPLEBAUM (Ed.), *Perspectives in Cultural Anthropology* (Albany, N.Y.: State University of New York Press, 1987). Authoritative articles exposing the major theoretical underpinnings of cultural anthropology.

JAMES F. DOWNS, *Cultures in Crisis*, 2nd ed. (Beverly Hills, Cal.: Glencoe, 1975). A short, entertaining book especially valuable for its illustrations of how the basic principles of cultural anthropology can help in solving some of the major "crisis areas" of our society.

General Anthropology

Natural History (New York: American Museum of Natural History, 1900–present). Every issue has something of interest for students of anthropology.

ERIC R. WOLF, *Anthropology* (New York: Norton, 1974). Now available in a reprinted paperback edition, this is a short but insightful look into the growth of anthropology as a discipline and as a concept.

Culture and the Contemporary World
JAMES SPRADLEY and DAVID MCCURDY

Over the years the works written or compiled by these two authors have been read by thousands of anthropology students. This thoughtful piece cogently introduces and thoroughly explores a number of concepts important to the discipline. But the article goes beyond that, and in the process offers insights about what anthropology and the study of human culture can teach us about others and ourselves, and why, as global citizens, this is useful and important.

Many students associate cultural anthropology with the study of primitive peoples. They picture the anthropologist as that slightly peculiar person who, dressed in khaki shorts and pith helmet, lives among some exotic tribe in order to record the group's bizarre and not altogether pleasant customs. Like most stereotypes, this one is not completely true but it does reflect anthropology's traditional interest in describing the culture of less complex societies. In the last century, when anthropology became a recognized discipline, its members collected and analyzed the growing numbers of reports on non-Western peoples by missionaries, travelers, and colonial administrators. This tradition continued into the twentieth century, although the collection of data was refined by actual fieldwork. Impressed by the variety of human behavior, anthropologists sought to record these cultures that were vanishing before the onslaught of Western civilization. Such studies continue among remote groups, and reports of this research are regularly found in professional journals.

During recent decades, however, anthropologists have developed wider interests. As primitive groups have been obliterated or assimilated, anthropologists have increasingly studied subcultures within more complex societies. Certainly World War II and the Cold War stimulated this trend. The United States government employed anthropologists to describe societies in whose territories we fought. The Cold War years, marked by competition with the Russians

James Spradley and David McCurdy, eds., *Conformity and Conflict: Readings in Cultural Anthropology*, 6th ed., pp. 1–10. Copyright © 1987 by Barbara A. Spradley and David W. McCurdy. Reprinted by permission of HarperCollins Publishers.

for influence in developing nations, led to studies of peasant life styles and culture change.

Today, however, our position in the world has changed. Americans are less welcome in developing nations. Concurrently, problems in our own country have multiplied and taken the center stage of national concern. It is not surprising that anthropologists have extended their attention to subcultures within our own society.

But what can anthropology contribute to an understanding of American life? After all, other social scientists have been doing research in this country for years. Is there anything special about anthropology? In many ways the answer to this question is no. The various social sciences often share the same interests. Yet, as a result of their intensive cross-culture experience, anthropologists have developed a unique perspective on the nature and the significance of *culture*. This view has emerged from over a century of fieldwork among populations whose behavior was dramatically different from the anthropologists' own. Why, for example, did Iroquois women participate with apparent relish in the gruesome torture of prisoners? How could Bhil tribesmen put chili powder in the eyes of witches, blindfold them, and swing them over a smoky fire by their feet? What possessed Kwakiutl chiefs to destroy their wealth publicly at potlatch ceremonies? Why did Rajput widows cast themselves upon their husbands' funeral pyres? Why did Nagas engage in raids to acquire human heads? In every case, anthropologists were impressed by the fact that this "bizarre" behavior was intentional and meaningful to the participants. Bhils wanted to swing witches; to them it was appropriate. Kwakiutl chiefs made careful investments to increase the wealth they destroyed. These acts were planned; people had a notion of what they were going to do before they did it, and others shared their expectations.

Culture

The acquired knowledge that people use to interpret their world and generate social behavior is called *culture*. Culture is not behavior itself, but the knowledge used to construct and understand behavior. It is learned as children grow up in society and discover how their parents, and others around them, interpret the world. In our society we learn to distinguish objects such as cars, windows, houses, children, and food; to recognize attributes like sharp, hot, beautiful, and humid; to classify and perform different kinds of acts; to evaluate what is good and bad and to judge when an unusual action is appropriate or inappropriate. How often have you heard parents explain something about life to a child? Why do you think children are forever asking why? During socialization children learn a culture, and because they learn it from others, they share it with others, a fact that makes human social existence possible.

Culture is thus the system of knowledge by which people design their own actions and interpret the behavior of others. It tells an American that eating with one's mouth closed is proper, while an Indian knows that to be polite one must chew with one's mouth open. There is nothing preordained about culture categories; they are arbitrary. The same act can have different meanings in various cultures. For example, when adolescent Hindu boys walk holding hands, it signifies friendship, while to Americans the same act may suggest homosexuality. This arbitrariness is particularly important to remember if we are to understand our own complex society. We tend to think that the norms we follow represent the "natural" way human beings do things. Those who behave otherwise are judged morally wrong. This viewpoint is *ethnocentric*, which means that people think their own culture represents the best, or at least the most appropriate, way for human beings to live.

Although in our complex society we share many cultural norms with everyone, each of us belongs to a number of groups possessing exclusive cultural knowledge. We share some categories and plans with family members alone. And our occupational group, ethnic group, voluntary society, and age group each has its distinctive culture. Instead of assuming that another's behavior is reasonable to him, that it is motivated by a different set of cultural norms, we frequently assume that he has intentionally violated accepted conventions. In their attempt to build bridges of understanding across cultural barriers, anthropol-

ogists have identified the universality of ethnocentrism many years ago. The study of subcultures in our own society is another attempt to further mutual understanding, as some of the selections in this volume indicate.

How do anthropologists discover and map another culture? Are their methods applicable in the United States? Typically anthropologists live among the people of the society that interests them. They learn the culture by observing, asking questions, and participating in daily activities—a process resembling childhood socialization or enculturation. Obviously, the anthropologist cannot become a child, and must try to learn the norms in a strange group despite his or her foreign appearance and advanced age. Those who study in the United States have followed a similar procedure.

More than anything else, the study of culture separates anthropologists from other social scientists. Other scholars do not ignore culture; they assume their subjects have it, but their main interest is to account for human behavior by plotting correlations among variables. Some social scientists have explained the rise in the American divorce rate as a function of industrialization; this hypothesis can be tested by seeing if higher divorce rates are associated with industrialization and mobility. Anthropologists share a concern for this kind of explanation; for example, many have employed the Human Relations Area Files, a collection of ethnographies describing several hundred societies, as data for testing more general hypotheses. Almost every anthropologist starts with an *ethnography*, the description of a particular culture, and such studies are required to understand the complexity within American society.

As anthropologists have encountered, studied, and compared the world's societies, they have learned more about the concept of culture itself. As we have seen, culture is the knowledge people use to generate behavior, not behavior itself; it is arbitrary, learned, and shared. In addition, culture is adaptive. Human beings cope with their natural and social environment by means of their traditional knowledge. Culture allows for rapid adaptation because it is flexible and permits the invention of new strategies—although change often apepars to be painfully slow to those who are in a hurry for it. By the same token, the adaptive nature of culture accounts for the enormous variety of the world's distinct societies.

Culture is a system of interrelated parts. If Americans were to give up automobiles, then other modes of travel, places for courtship, marks of status, and sources of income would have to be found. Culture meets personal needs; through it, people seek security and a sense of control over experience. Indeed, every tradition includes ways to cure the sick, to prepare for the unexpected, and to support the individual. In a complex society with many ways of life in contact with each other, change is persistent. It may be illusion to think that people can control the course of change, or can modify the resulting culture conflict. But if we can understand human cultures—including our own—the illusion may become reality.

Culture and Values

It is easy for people to feel that their own way of life is natural and God-given. One's culture is not like a suit of clothing that can be discarded easily or exchanged for each new life style that comes along. It is rather like a security blanket, and though to some it may appear worn and tattered, outmoded and ridiculous, it has great meaning to its owner. Although there are many reasons for this fact, one of the most important is the value-laden nature of what we learn as members of society. Whether it is acquired in a tribal band, a peasant village, or an urban neighborhood, each culture is like a giant iceberg. Beneath the surface of rules, norms, and behavior patterns there is a system of values. Some of these premises are easily stated by members of a society, while others are outside their awareness. Because many difficulties in the modern world involve values, we must examine this concept in some detail.

A value is an arbitrary conception of what is *desirable* in human experience. During socialization all children are exposed to a constant barrage of evaluations—the arbitrary "rating system" of their culture. Nearly everything they learn is labeled in terms of its desirability. The value attached to each bit of information may result from the pain of a hot stove, the look of disapproval from a parent, the smile of appreciation from a teacher, or some specific verbal instruction. When parents tell a child, "You should go to college and get a good education," they are expressing a value. Those who do not conform to society's rating system are identified with derogatory labels or are punished in a more severe way. When a Tlingit Indian says to his nephew, "You should marry your father's sister," he is expressing one of the core values of his culture. When a young couple saves income for future emergencies, they are conforming to the American value that the future is more important than the present. When a tramp urinates in an alley, he is violating the value attached to privacy. All these concepts of what is desirable combine cognitive and affective meanings. Individuals internalize their ideas about right and wrong, good and bad, and invest them with strong feelings.

Why do values constitute an inevitable part of all human experience? That human potential is at odds with the requirements of social life is well known. Behavior within the realm of possibility is often outside the realm of necessity. There are numerous ways to resolve the conflict between what people *can do* by themselves, and what they *must do* as members of society. It is a popular notion that prisons and other correctional institutions are the primary means by which our society enforces conformity, but this is not the case. Socialization may be ineffective for a few who require such drastic action, but for the vast majority in any society, conformity results from the internalization of values. As we learn through imitation, identification, and instruction, values are internalized. They provide security and contribute to a sense of personal and social identity. For this reason, individuals in every society cling tenaciously to the values they have acquired and feel threatened when confronted with others who live according to different conceptions of what is desirable.

Cultural Relativism

A misconception about values has been spawned by science and, in particular, by the anthropological doctrine of cultural relativism. Some have maintained that it is possible to separate values from facts, and since science is limited to facts, it is possible to do "value-free" research. By an exercise in mental gymnastics, the very scholars who admit the influence of values in the behavior of others sometimes deny it for themselves. Preferences operate whenever an individual must *select* one action from a multitude of possible courses. Anyone who decides to observe one thing and not another is making that decision on the basis of an implicit or explicit conception of desirability. Science is an activity that makes many value judgments—including which approaches to information gathering are the best. When biologists decide to examine the structure of the DNA molecule using an empirical approach, rather than a mystical, intuitive, or religious one, they are doing so with reference to their sense of what is desirable. Even the decision to study DNA rather than some other substance involves an exercise of values. When doing research on human behavior, the influence of one's values is undeniable. The "objective observer" who is detached from the subject matter, who refrains from allowing values to influence observations, is a myth. This fact does not suggest a retreat from the *quest for objectivity*. It does not mean that social scientists are free to disparage the customs encountered in other societies, or to impose their morals on those being studied. Skilled anthropologists are aware of their own values and then approach other cultures with tolerance and respect. They *identify* rather than *deny* the influence of their own viewpoints. They strive to achieve the ideal of value-free research but realize that it would be naive to assume such a goal possible.

Cultural relativism rests on the premise that it is possible to remain aloof and free from making value judgments. Put simply, this doctrine is based on four interrelated propositions.

1. Each person's value system is a result of his or her experience, i.e., it is learned.
2. The values that individuals learn differ from one society to another because of different learning experiences.
3. Values, therefore, are relative to the society in which they occur.
4. There are no universal values, but we should respect the values of each of the world's cultures.

Cultural relativism has enabled the uninformed to understand what appears to be strange and immoral behavior. Although we may not believe it is good to kill infants, for example, we have found it intelligible in the context of a native Australian band. Although Americans generally believe in the desirability of monogamous marriage (or at least serial monogamy), we have found the practice of polygamy in other societies to be comprehensible when related to their cultures. This view presents numerous difficulties. Does one respect a society that believes it best to murder six million of its members who happen to be Jewish? How do anthropologists respect the values of a head-hunting tribe when their own heads are at stake?

Moreover, all the statements in this doctrine of relativism are either based on implicit values (i.e., empiricism), or they are outright statements of desirability. The belief that it is good to *respect* the ideals of each of the world's cultures is itself a "relative" value. An extreme relativism is based on the philosophy that it is best to "let everyone do his or her own thing." Given unlimited resources and space this might have been possible, but in the modern world this philosophy represents a retreat from the realities facing us. It absolves the believer from the responsibility of finding some way to resolve conflicts among the world's different value systems. What is needed today is not a "live and let live" policy but a commitment to a higher, more inclusive, value system, and this requires changes that are extremely difficult to achieve.

Conformity and Conflict

Every social system is a moral order; shared values act as the mortar binding together the structure of each human community. Rewards and punishments are based on commonly held values; those persons achieving high status do so in terms of cultural rating systems. These values are expressed in symbolic ways—through food, clothing, wealth, language, behavior—all of which carry implicit messages about good and bad. The pervasiveness of values gives each person a sense of belonging, a sense of being a member of a community, the feeling of joining other human beings who share a commitment to the good life. But the moral nature of every culture has two sides—it facilitates adaptation and survival on the one hand, but it often generates conflict and destruction on the other. Let us examine each of these possibilities.

For almost a million years, people have successfully adapted to a variety of terrestrial environments. From the frozen tundra to the steaming jungle, people have built their homes, reared their children, performed their rituals, and buried their dead. In recent years we have escaped the thin layer of atmosphere surrounding the earth to live, if only for a few days, in outer space and beneath the ocean. All these achievements have been possible because of a unique endowment, our capacity for culture. Wherever people wandered, they developed patterns for organizing behavior, using natural resources, relating to others, and creating a meaningful life. A genetic inheritance did not channel behavior into specialized responses but instead provided a reservoir of plasticity that was shaped by values into one of the many ways to be human. Children in every society do not learn the entire range of potential human behavior—they are taught to *conform* to a very limited number of behavior patterns that are appropriate to a particular society. Human survival depends on cultural conformity, which requires that every individual become a specialist, be committed to a few values, and acquire knowledge and skills of a single society.

This very specialization has led to diversity, resulting in a myriad of contrasting cultures. This volume contains only a small sample of the different symbolic worlds created by people in their attempt to cope with the common problems of human existence. We will see how the generosity of the American Christmas spirit stands in contrast to the daily sharing among the Bushmen. Chicago suburbanites and natives of the Brazilian jungle both adorn their bodies with paint, clothing, and rings, but neither can comprehend how the other defines these symbols. All elements of human experience—kinship, marriage, age, race, sexuality, food, warfare—are socially defined and valued. The difficulty of moving from one cultural world to another is immense.

Cultural diversity has fascinated people for centuries. The study of strange and exotic peoples has attracted the curious for many generations. In the isolation of a remote jungle village or South Sea island, anthropologists found a natural laboratory for carrying out research. Their research reports often seemed more like novels than scientific studies and were read by both professionals and laymen; seldom did any reader feel threatened by the strange behavior of far-off "savages."

But isolation rapidly disappeared, sometimes by virtue of the anthropologists' intrusion! Exploration gave way to colonization, trade, and the massive troop movements of modern warfare. Today it is impossible to find groups of people who are isolated from the remainder of the world. Instead we have a conglomeration of cultures within a single nation, and often within a single city. Anthropologists need only walk down the street from the university to encounter those who have learned a culture unlike their own. Individuals with different language styles, sexual practices, religious rituals, and a host of other strange behavior patterns sit in their classrooms or play with their children on the urban playgrounds. Anthropology today is a science concerned with understanding how people can survive in a world where village, hamlet, city, and nation are all *multicultural*. In isolation, each value system was interesting. Crowded into close and intimate contact, these distinct culture patterns often lead to conflict, oppression, and warfare. Barbara Ward has eloquently summed up our situation:

> In the last few decades, mankind has been overcome by the most change in its entire history. Modern science and technology have created so close a network of communication, transport, economic interdependence—and potential nuclear destruction—that planet Earth, on its journey through infinity, has acquired the intimacy, the fellowship, and the vulnerability of a spaceship.[1]

[1] Barbara Ward, *Spaceship Earth* (New York: Columbia University Press, 1966), p. vii.

In a sense, our greatest resource for adapting to different environments—the capacity to create different cultures—has become the source of greatest danger. Diversity is required for survival in the ecological niches of earth, but it can be destructive when all people suddenly find themselves in the same niche. Numerous species have become extinct because of their inability to adapt to a changing *natural* environment. Culture was the survival kit that enabled us to meet fluctuating natural conditions with flexibility, but now we are faced with a radically altered *human* environment. Successful adaptation will require changes that fly in the face of thousands of years of cultural specialization. Our ingenuity has been used to develop unique cultures, but thus far we have failed to develop satisfactory patterns and rules for articulating these differences. Can we survive in a world where our neighbors and even our children have different cultures? Can we adapt to the close, intimate fellowship of a spaceship when each group of passengers lives by different values?

Toward a Multicultural Society

What is required? In the first place, instead of suppressing cultural diversity by stressing assimilation into the mainstream of American life, we must recognize the extent to which our culture is pluralistic. We must accept the fact that groups within our society are committed to disparate and sometimes conflicting values. The second requirement for a truly multicultural society is that we continuously examine the *consequences* of each value system. What is the long-range effect of our commitment to a "gospel of growth"? What are the results of a belief in male superiority? How do our values of privacy affect those without homes? What is the consequence for minority groups when all students are taught to use "standard English"? As we study American culture we must discover the effect of our dominant values on every sector of life. The ideals that have made this country what it is have also been destructive to some citizens. In our efforts to assimilate ethnic groups, we have destroyed their pride and self-identity. In our attempt to offer the advantages of education to American Indians, we have induced them to become failures because our schools are not able to educate for diversity. In order to demonstrate the tolerance built into American values, we have created the "culturally deprived," but the sophistication of labels does not conceal our prejudice. The absence of men in the families of the urban poor is a logical consequence of welfare institutions created from a single value system. The consumer suffers from dangerous products because in our culture productive enterprise is more important than consumer protection. We have only begun to understand some of the consequences of our values, and during the next few decades our survival will demand that the study of values be given top priority.

Finally, the most difficult task for the contemporary world is to induce people to relinquish those values with destructive consequences. This will not be simple, and it probably will not occur without a better understanding of the nature and the function of the world's many value systems. People's capacity to learn has not yet reached its full potential. In every society, children learn to shift from *egocentric* behavior to *ethnocentric* behavior. In deference to de-sirable community standards, individuals give up those things they desire, and life in a particular society becomes secure and meaningful, with conventional values acting as warp and woof of social interaction.

Can we now learn to shift from *ethnocentric* to *homocentric* behavior? Can we relinquish values desirable from the standpoint of a single community but destructive to the wider world? This change will require a system of ideals greater than the conventions of any localized culture. The change will necessitate a morality that can articulate conflicting value systems and create a climate of tolerance, respect, and cooperation. Only then can we begin to create a culture that will be truly adaptive in today's world.

2

The Origin
and Evolution
of Culture

In this chapter we will briefly examine the process of biological evolution that has been going on for millions of years. Our interest in that process will be to see how culture arose as a response to the natural environment—not the only response, but one of many. After laying out the basic processes of evolution as described by Darwin and other natural scientists, we will trace the evolution of the capacity for culture, beginning with mammals and continuing through the primates to the earliest humanlike species. Finally, we will see how the introduction of culture into human societies has influenced biological evolution, and how the combination of biological evolution and cultural change leads to what we call biocultural evolution.

Evolutionary Theory

Have you ever asked yourself why you look the way you do? Think about it for a minute: Why do you stand up instead of walking on all fours? Why do you speak the way you do? Why are your hands and feet shaped the way they are? All of these features are the result of millions of years of gradual change known as *evolution*. In humans this process resulted not only in the physical features that are easily seen but also in other, less obvious features that make us different from other animals and give us greater control over our environment. In other words, human culture is a result of biological evolution.

Although the theory of evolution is commonly linked with Charles Darwin's publication of *The Origin of Species* in 1859, many of the ideas that Darwin put forth in his book had been discussed for at least a century. In fact, Darwin's grandfather, Erasmus Darwin, argued for evolutionary theory before Charles was even born. What *The Origin of Species* contributed to the theory was a clear statement of the process by which evolution occurs, which we call **natural selection.**

In 1831 Darwin set out on a round-the-world voyage on the ship *H.M.S. Beagle*, serving as the ship's naturalist. Over the next five years he made detailed observations of plants and animals, noting their similarities and differences and comparing them with fossils of extinct species. From his study of the similarities among existing species around the world, together with the similarities between living and fossil species, he gradually came to the conclusion that some species were related to one another through common lines of descent, a view that clearly challenged the biblical notion of a single Creation of all the various life forms in the world. It remained for Darwin to pull together the loose ends of various theories of evolution that had been discussed in scientific circles for some time, and to support his own version with evidence gathered during his voyage on the *Beagle*. In 1859 he finally accomplished this task.

Darwin's evolutionary scheme is based on three main points:

1. There are variations among individuals of a given species. Some are obvious, and you can see them if you look around a roomful of people—they differ in height, hair color, facial features, bodily structure, and so forth. Other differences are less obvious and may not even be visible. They include differences in blood type, running speed, and eyesight or hearing. Darwin's point was that variation occurs naturally among all populations.

2. As long as the environment is stable and there is enough food, most variations will not have much meaning for the survival of the individual. But when environmental pressures arise because of population growth, climatic change, the disappearance of a major food source, or a number of other things, some of the variations in the population will become more important for the survival of individuals who have those qualities. For example, if we look at a

Charles Darwin's voyage on the H.M.S. Beagle, *shown here at anchor in the Straits of Magellan at the tip of South America, led to his discovery of the principle of natural selection.*

population of birds of the same species, we will note that some have longer beaks than others. Now, as long as there is enough food for all, the length of the beak is not important. But if food becomes scarce, it is possible that those birds with longer beaks will be able to dig deeper into the ground or into the bark of trees for food, and therefore will have a greater chance of survival. This notion is commonly called **survival of the fittest,** meaning not the strongest but those best suited to a particular environment. The key to natural selection is not just the fact that individuals with certain variations may survive at a greater rate than the rest of the popu-

lation, but that they will produce a larger proportion of the next generation. This leads to the third point in Darwin's scheme.

3. Those individuals whose variations enable them to survive at a higher rate will pass on their traits to a larger proportion of the next generation through the process of *inheritance.* Thus from one generation to the next the population will change in response to changes in the environment. This is the process by which evolution takes place. It operates on the level of the population, not the individual, and it entails the selection of traits and changes in the distribution of those traits in a popula-

tion over time. It has nothing to do with a plant or animal's becoming "better" or "higher." It means becoming better adapted to a particular set of conditions, that is, better able to survive.

You might ask what place Darwin's theory of biological evolution has in the study of cultural anthropology. The importance lies in the answer to the question we raised earlier: Why do we look the way we do? We might just as well have asked why we behave the way we do. The concept that provides the answer to these questions is natural selection. For millions of years there were no humans on earth and there was no such thing as culture. Darwin helps us understand why culture evolved and why our physical appearance and biological makeup are the way they are. We can assume that the early ancestors of human beings were engaged in a struggle to get a living from their environment, just as all forms of life have been since

the beginning of time. In some settings this was fairly easy and there was little pressure to change. In other settings, perhaps as a result of population growth or a change in the environment, there was greater competition for a limited supply of food. Under such conditions certain advantages became more important, so that prehumans with those traits survived and passed on their traits to their offspring. Some of these advantages led to the origin of culture and to the development of the human species. In order to understand how culture came about, we must first see it as resulting from biological evolution.

The Origins of Culture

Modern scientists estimate that the earth is 5 to 6 billion years old. Life is thought to have begun 3 to 4 billion years ago. By comparison,

Charles Darwin (1809–1882)

Charles Darwin is the man most often linked with the discovery of evolution. Actually, his major contribution to evolutionary theory was the concept of natural selection. He saw organisms in competition against the forces of nature, and those best able to cope with the pressures survived at the highest rate and passed on their advantageous characteristics. Although Darwin did not mean for his theory of evolution to be applied to human social and cultural change, it was proposed by many social scientists that cultures evolved in a struggle for survival, just as animals did. Inappropriately called "social Darwinism," this vulgar misunderstanding of Darwin's work caused considerable harm as it was ultimately used to justify white supremacist policies of Western nations in their domination of Third World peoples.

EVOLUTIONARY TIME CHART

Geologic Era	Epoch	Approximate Time (years before present)	Event
PRECAMBRIAN		5–6 billion	Origins of earth
PALEOZOIC		3–4 billion	First life
		450–500 million	First vertebrates (fish)
		400–450 million	First land plants and animals
		350–400 million	First amphibians
		300–350 million	First reptiles and insects
MESOZOIC		225 million	First dinosaurs
		180–200 million	Age of dinosaurs, first mammals
		110–130 million	Extinction of dinosaurs
CENOZOIC	Paleocene	60–70 million	Placental mammals
	Eocene	50–60 million	Early primates
	Oligocene	30 million	Monkeylike mammals
	Miocene	25 million	Early apes
	Pliocene	3–12 million	Terrestrial hunting primates, earliest human ancestral branch (*Ramapithecus*)
	Pleistocene	10,000–3 million	Humanlike ancestors (genus *Homo*)

most of the evolution of humanlike creatures has taken place in a very short time—the first mammals began to evolve from reptiles perhaps 200 million years ago, and the first placental mammals (i.e., mammals that give birth to live young, as opposed to the egg-bearing platypus or marsupials such as the kangaroo) date back about 130 million years. Monkeylike mammals with relatively large brains and tendencies toward social behavior have existed for roughly 30 million years, while terrestrial primates who engage in some hunting as well as gathering have been around only about 15 million years.

The first humanlike animals appeared some 3 million years ago, around the beginning of the epoch known as the Pleistocene. This was the time of the great ice ages, when drastic changes in climate affected life throughout the world. This climatic change may account for the more rapid evolution that produced modern human beings in such a short period; that is, the pace of natural selection may have been quickened because of environmental changes and the resulting pressures on our primate ancestors. In retracing the path of biological evolution, we will look first at the evolution of mammals, then at that of primates as an order within the mammalian class, and finally at that of humans, who are included in the order of primates.

The evolution of mammals   Early mammals evolved from reptiles some 200 million years ago. To understand why mammals evolved, and what advantages they have over reptiles, we can compare some of the important physical features of the two types of animals. For one thing, reptiles are cold-blooded, which means that their body temperature changes with the temperature around them. In many cases this means that during the winter reptiles remain dormant because their body temperature is reduced to a point that precludes much activity. But even in warmer climates most reptiles must feed during the daylight hours, when it is warmer, and are less active during the night, when the temperature drops.

In contrast to reptiles, early mammals had the advantage of being warm-blooded. Because they have a constant body temperature regardless of their environment, mammals can compete with reptiles by remaining active throughout the night and throughout the year. Thus it is probable that the earliest mammals were nocturnal—that is, were most active during the night, when they would not be in danger from reptilian predators and in some cases would be able to obtain food with little if any competition. Of course, being warm-blooded, they could also function during the daytime hours, and this gave them an even greater advantage.

This change toward warm-bloodedness also gave mammals a geographic advantage in that they could exploit a wider range of climates and spread out over a wider territory. If the climate changed, either from one season to another or over a period of years,

The opposable thumb and big toe are important adaptations enabling primates to manipulate tools. The human foot later evolved for walking, while the foot of the orangutan adapted for climbing.

they were in a better position to survive by adapting to the new climate. Thus mammals could adapt to a wider range of environmental conditions and yet compete successfully with reptiles in the same environment. Over many millions of years, mammals spread throughout the world, while many less adaptable reptilian species became extinct.

The evolution of primates The earliest primates began to appear after the time that dinosaurs had become extinct, beginning almost 50 to 60 million years ago. They differed from other mammals in a number of ways, all of which can be traced directly to the biological makeup of modern humans.

They tended to be larger and to have a more **erect posture,** and they had larger brains in proportion to their body size.

Perhaps the most important feature of the early primates is that they were arboreal; that is, while they exploited food sources on the ground as well as those in trees, for the most part they lived in the trees. Because they lived in trees, early primates were subject to selective pressures that brought about a number of other changes. Moving through the trees required improved eyesight and motor coordination. This led not only to the evolution of stereoscopic sight with greater depth perception, which was needed for jumping from one branch to another, but also to color vision, which is useful in telling live branches from dead ones or ripe from unripe fruit.

Other senses changed along with eyesight. The sense of touch became more important, since the precision required for moving in the trees had life-or-death meaning for primates. An animal that is running along on the ground can make a mistake in judgment, fall, get up, and be on its way again, but a slight mistake in the treetops can be fatal. The forelimbs, or hands, of primates therefore became more sensitive, and the fingers became more mobile. Claws were replaced by flat nails, and most important, the thumb and big toe became **opposable,** which means that they could be moved opposite to some or all of the fingers or toes. This means that primates could manipulate objects with their hands, rather than grasping them with their teeth, as other mammals do. Later on, the arms grew distinct from the legs and became able to rotate, flex, and extend. All of these changes are important in terms of the way early primates gathered food and caught small animals, both in treees and on the ground.

Life in the trees also led to changes in patterns of bearing and raising offspring, making the infant more dependent on its mother. Lacking a permanent and protected home for raising children, primates were under selective pressure to have one or at most just a few offspring at a time. And to ensure the survival of the species under such conditions, a large proportion of the off-spring must survive. Whereas a fish may lay thousands of eggs to yield one offspring that survives to reproduce, a primate that bears only one baby must take care of it in order to increase its chances of surviving. Over time this pressure led to greater dependency in primate offspring, both before and after birth.

One way to ensure higher survival rates is to increase the amount of maternal care during pregnancy and after the birth of the child. Once a fish has laid its eggs, its duties are over. Among mammals, the period of care is extended by the fact that the mother must nurse the infant for some time. But in the higher primates the period of dependency becomes even longer.

Yet another change that was brought about by early primate life was greater intelligence. All of the previous changes, such as better eyesight or more nerves in the hands, required an increase in the size of the brain. The reduction in the number of offspring placed a premium on a longer life span, and this provided more chances to learn through experience. Learning, as opposed to instinctual response, is clearly a superior means of adapting to the environment, since it allows the individual to meet changes with new techniques; more important, it allows one to adjust one's behavior on the basis of one's

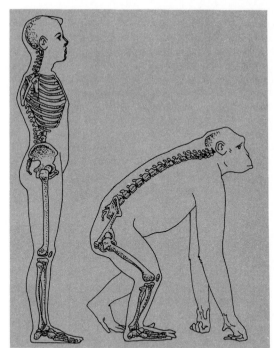

FIGURE 2.1 Erect Posture in Humans Frees the Hands for Making and Using Tools.

experiences (successes or failures). But the greater the role of learning, the more pressure there was for increased brain size to allow for the memory of past experiences.

All of these changes occurred gradually over millions of years. The earlier, smaller, monkeylike primates gave way to larger, apelike ones about 25 million years ago, and by 15 million years ago they had spread throughout Asia and Africa and into parts of Europe as well. These larger species evolved into the modern great apes, including the gorilla, the chimpanzee, the gibbon, and the baboon, as well as through the prehuman ancestral line that eventually led to our own species. They display more social behavior than most other primate species, and they resemble humans in many ways.

Higher primate behavior One of the most obvious and important similarities between apes and humans is that both engage in social behavior. As noted earlier, one reason for this is the extended period of infant dependency among primates, which promotes learning and other kinds of social behavior. Another factor is the diet of primates. Studies have shown that cooperation and movement in groups is required when the food supply is scattered, as is the case with the diet of tree-dwelling primates. This is especially true for hunting, and in fact we find cooperative hunting parties not only among primates but also among other predatory animals such as wolves or lions.

Another interesting aspect of social behavior among some primates is the evolution of a pattern of behavior called **dominance.** Many primate groups are arranged in a hierarchy similar to the "pecking order" of chickens. In such a group there are strong divisions between the dominant males of the group—usually the older, larger, and stronger ones—and other members, including, in descending order, younger and less dominant males, adult females, younger juveniles of both sexes, and infants. This strict hierarchy of dominance serves a double purpose: It aids in the defense of the group by allowing the strongest males to present a united front against attackers, and it keeps the younger members from straying too far from the protection of the dominant members of the group.

Patterns of dominance are maintained through submission behavior, behavior that allows one animal to reaffirm its dominance over another. A subordinate baboon will "present itself" to a dominant one by going up to it and turning its back in a submissive, nonthreatening posture. If it did not behave in this way, the dominant animal might take its approach as a challenge to its authority and try to repel it. Since the dominance hierarchy of a group is constantly changing, such challenges are part of everyday life, especially among the younger members.

Another important aspect of social behavior in primates is the organization of some groups into what might loosely be termed *family structures.* Studies of Hamadryas baboons in Ethiopia have shown that they do not live in promiscuous hordes. Although the troop might contain 60 members or more, it is broken down into smaller family units, each with only one sexually active male and one or more females. There seems to be no cross-mating among these family units. Studies of some other primate species indicate that they have similar familylike units.

Several possible selective advantages might explain this pattern. First, it appears that family structures are found mainly where

Chimpanzees engage in mutual grooming, which not only rids them of pesky insects and is an important aspect of socialization, but also reinforces the dominance hierarchy of the group.

food is scarce, suggesting that a small but stable group such as a family unit has an advantage in obtaining food. Perhaps it reduces competition, which could divide the larger group if all members competed with one another for food. Yet at the same time it would allow the group to remain large enough to offer protection to all of its members when they could not protect themselves alone.

A second advantage of the family life style of some primates is the creation of an "economic" bond whereby males obtain food for females and their young. As the attention of the mother is devoted to her young, she has less time to devote to obtaining food. But when a male has exclusive sexual rights to a female (or group of females), this bond benefits both the female and the offspring because the male provides food when necessary. Along similar lines, among nonhuman primates the males tend to be much larger and more powerful than the females—the differences between the sexes are greater than among humans. Thus the alignment of one or more females with a male creates a situation in which the females and their young are protected from predators and other dangers. If females were to forage for food alone or with infants, they would be less likely to survive than if they stayed together in a larger group.

Finally, family structures become more important among primates as childhood is prolonged and the learning of social behavior becomes more necessary. The role of the male in the family increases the infants' opportunity to learn from individuals of both sexes. To a baby fish, having a male around to teach it how to behave is not of any value since the fish has everything it needs to know programmed into it at birth. But to a baby monkey the experiences of growing up can spell the difference between life and death later on.

Another aspect of primate social behavior—curiosity—is related to learning and prolonged infancy and is an important factor in the evolution of culture. Curiosity seems to be innate in primates, including humans. On an island off the coast of Japan where experimenters were working with a troop of macaques, the researchers set out toys for the monkeys to play with. The monkeys avoided the toys for a full day. The next day the researchers put the toys under an overturned crate, out of the direct sight of the monkeys. When they returned, all but two of the toys were gone; the two that were left were rubber snakes. Interestingly, the juveniles seemed to be the most curious of the monkeys—they were at a time of life when learning is fastest. Moreover, the juveniles were the most expendable members of the troop, since they had not reached reproductive age and were not mature enough to offer protection to the rest of the group.

Early Human Culture

All aspects of the social and biological evolution of primates are important if we are to understand the origins of culture among humans. Estimates of when humanlike creatures began to diverge from apes vary according to the method used to determine the dates. Evidence from the fossil record indicates that our humanlike ancestors and apelike relatives began to follow separate evolutionary paths as much as 15 million years ago. More recently, comparisons of the blood of humans and apes have shown that the divergence of these species may have begun as recently as 7 or 8 million years ago. Regardless of which estimate we accept, it is clear that we are not descended from a creature just like a modern ape. Even though modern apes may be our closest relatives, they have changed over the past several million years, just as we have, and they may be just as different from our common ancestor as we are. Yet by studying modern apes and their behavior, as physical anthropologists do today, we can gain deeper insight into features that probably were already present in our ancestors—not only biological features but social ones as well.

Similarities between humans and other primates   By looking at some of the more obvious similarities between humans and apes, especially chimps, we can make a pretty good guess as to the traits that were present among the earliest humans and formed the basis of the first human culture. Of course, we cannot be sure that something we see in modern chimps was present millions of years ago, but the greater the similarity, the more likely it is that both species inherited a biological or social trait from a common ancestor.

The "yawn" display of this chimpanzee is not a sign of being sleepy, but is a threatening gesture to warn potential challengers. An adult male chimpanzee is the equal of most potential predators, whereas the adult human, lacking the massive teeth and upper body strength of the chimpanzee, must rely on intelligence and cultural conditioning for survival.

For example, biologically we share the same blood groups with chimps, and both species are subject to such diseases as measles, influenza, syphilis, and even the common cold. Among all higher primates, chimps show less sexual dimorphism than any other species except humans. (The term **sexual dimorphism** refers to the structural differences between males and females.) Chimps, more than other primates, are *omnivorous*, meaning that, like humans, they will eat both meat and vegetable matter. In all these cases it is much more likely that our common ancestors had the same characteristics than it is that chimps and humans both evolved along parallel lines.

Several other similarities were mentioned in the last chapter. Chimps in the wild not only use tools but invent and manufacture them as well. When a chimp prepares a stick for getting termites out of their nest, it may do so at some distance from the site where the tool will be used. This indicates that the chimp can conceive of a situation without actually being in that situation. This use and manufacture of tools suggests that chimps and humans shared a common evolutionary line.

As we will discuss shortly, chimps have the ability to communicate in a symbolic language. Although they do not have the equipment for speech and clearly lack the intelligence to use language to the extent that a normal human beng can, there is no denying that chimps can and do learn language and use it to communicate with humans, and in more recent studies even with other chimps. They also have a complex set of gestures and facial expressions like those used in human nonverbal communication. Apparently these abilities were also derived from a common source; at least, the information we have suggests that these characteristics were present in early human populations.

The role of hunting   Perhaps the most important similarity between humans and chimps is that both engage in hunting. This involves cooperation to obtain other animals for food, and group sharing after the kill. Many primates will eat insects but not larger game. In some cases, if a primate happens upon a small animal such as a lizard, it will kill and eat it, but only baboons and chimps regularly eat meat, and only chimps have been seen actually hunting for it.

Hunting has been a major factor in human evolution. It has led to cooperation among hunters, the sharing of food, and even division of labor by sex (that is, men hunt and women gather vegetable foods). Hunting was also important in the evolution of tools and weapons for both killing and preparing the animals. Finally, food sharing and the division of labor in hunting and gathering require a minimal type of "home" or meeting place so that the food may be shared rather than eaten on the spot. And as we will see, this concept of a "home base" is very important in both a biological sense (in that it helps extend the life span of humans) and a social sense (in that it serves as the focus of social life).

In relating hunting to biological evolution, we can see some trends in the changes that occurred in humans and other primates. Primate evolution included the replacement of claws with nails, the development of opposable thumbs, and the movement of the eyes to the front of the face, resulting in better stereoscopic vision or depth perception. These were discussed earlier as adaptations to life in the trees. Yet other animals, such as squirrels, lack these characteristics but do quite well in the trees. It may be that these adaptations are suited to other, more "human" kinds of behavior. The grasping hands and opposable thumbs may be adaptations to the requirements of hunting small animals—something the squirrel cannot do with its forelimbs. Stereoscopic vision helps in the trees, but it also helps on the ground; the predatory cats make good use of it. Thus these characteristics may have been adaptations to hunting, not just to living in the trees.

Social bonds If hunting was an important factor in early human culture, an equally important factor was the social bond created by the relationship between males and females. This bond was enhanced by a major change in human sexuality that did not occur in other primates. Mature human females are sexually receptive throughout the year, whereas other higher primates may mate for only a week or two every year. In most primates and other mammals the female is receptive—that is, she can engage in intercourse—for only a few days before and after ovulation. This receptivity is signaled by odors and by swelling of the genital area. Human females are unique in that they do not have a limited period of receptivity. In humans there are no signals correlated with ovulation and no biological limits on when intercourse may occur.

Anthropologists who have studied this aspect of human biological evolution have suggested that it is related to **bipedalism**—walking on two feet with an upright posture. In bipedal animals it is more difficult to see the visual signal of receptivity, namely, the swelling of the genitals. Similarly, as human evolution led to increased sensitivity and better vision, there was a corresponding decline in the sense of smell, which became less important for survival. In the course of human evolution those females who were receptive more often (regardless of their chances of conceiving) would have had more chances to reproduce. Their genetic differences allowing for greater receptivity would thus have been transmitted to their offspring through natural selection.

Another sign that evolutionary pressure led to this important difference in reproductive behavior is seen in observations of primates in captivity. Rhesus monkeys in cages engage in mating behavior at all stages of the menstrual cycle, not just during ovulation. Likewise, macaques and other monkeys may mate year round in captivity. While these observations do not seem directly related to human behavior, since humans are not captive animals, they do indicate that, given certain environmental changes (i.e., selective pressures), there is enough variability in primates so that abnormal behavior may become normal under different conditions. This may indeed have happened in the course of human evolution.

Learning and infant dependency Another important element in early culture that was based on biological evolution was the role of learning and the resultant mother-infant interaction. Nonhuman primates have a fairly long life span, upwards of 40 years for chimps and as much as 30 years for orangutans. They also have a long immature phase during which the infant is dependent and learning takes place.

As learning became more important, it led to changes in the biology of reproduction among primate females. Although pregnancy is almost as long in apes as it is in humans, the ape infant is far more independent at an earlier age than the human infant. Human infants not only mature more slowly but have much less control over their bodies, and their size at birth is a much smaller proportion of their adult size. As a result of these factors, human dependency lasts much longer and takes up a greater percentage of the life span.

The length of the human dependency period is based on two factors: the size of the brain and the fact that humans are bipedal. The human brain is larger in proportion to body size than the ape brain, making the head larger. This leads to greater difficulty in childbirth. Bipedal locomotion and erect posture limit the size and shape of the pelvis, including the angle of the pelvic opening. Hence the human infant is born at an earlier stage of development so that the larger head can fit through the smaller pelvis. Among apes development can proceed further before the infant is born, resulting in a more mature, less dependent infant requiring less maternal care.

It is easy to see how natural selection has influenced the length of the human gestation period, the amount of time the fetus is carried in the womb. We can assume that there is a genetic factor that affects the length of gestation, so that the offspring will inherit the tendency to carry the fetus for the normal length of time or for a shorter or longer period if the mother has that tendency herself. However, if the mother tends to deliver early, the infant will be less developed than normal and will have a lower survival rate (as premature babies do today). On the other hand, if the mother tends to deliver late, the infant may be too large to fit through the birth canal easily, and the complications of birth are more likely to kill either the infant or the mother, or both. Thus human beings, like other animals, have a fairly consistent gestation period—but in humans this leads to a long period of helplessness outside the womb. It might be interesting to consider the effects of modern medicine on the direction of natural selection in this regard. Caesarean births increase the life chances of babies that might not otherwise fit through the birth canal, and advanced medical techniques can improve the survival rates of premature babies. In both cases genes are allowed to enter the breeding population that might not have otherwise.

The importance of the home base We have touched on some of the elements of early social behavior in humanlike primates that led to the origin of culture. Another factor in the life of early hunting groups, the *home base*, also affected human evolution. The home base is a major factor in the increased life span of humans; and a longer life span means more opportunities for learning. If there is a home base where an individual can remain when he or she is ill, avoiding predators and recovering, then that individual can get very sick and still survive. Further, if an individual can survive an illness, it is not necessary to have built-in immunities in order to migrate from one area to another where new diseases will be encountered. This gives humans a greater range, allowing them to move into new areas more easily. The same is true for injuries—broken or sprained limbs can be nursed back to health without loss of life, provided that there is a home base where one is protected. Compare this to a situation in which if a member cannot keep up, he or she is simply left behind without any protection.

Improved technology and human evolution
Social organization was a major step in human biological and cultural evolution, but equally important was improved technology. Only with adequate technology could humans move out of the tropical climate of Africa and into the cooler climates of Europe and Asia. The oldest manufactured tools have been found in association with prehuman ancestors dating back almost 4 million years. The significance of these finds is that although primates may have used tools much earlier, they did not make them from stone or bone, nor did they use them nearly as much as these later, more humanlike creatures did. The items found include stone tools that could be used to kill larger animals, butcher them, and clean the hides for clothing.

It is important to remember that technology includes not only the physical objects of a culture but also how they are used and the behavior that surrounds their use. Henry Ford revolutionized the automobile industry by inventing the assembly line—a major change in the *organization* of production without any great change in the tools used to make automobiles. Likewise, early hunting societies made important advances not only in the kinds of weapons and tools they used but in the organization of hunting parties as well. One man with one spear cannot always be expected to produce one-tenth the amount of game that ten men with ten spears can produce. Thus we can trace improvements in human technology both by looking at the remains of tools and by reconstructing the ways in which they were used.

The earliest fossil remains from Europe date back to a time when the climate was cool at best and during the ice ages may have been sub-Arctic at worst. People survived by hunting large game, which required a great deal of cooperation and sophisticated tools. Another important technological advance

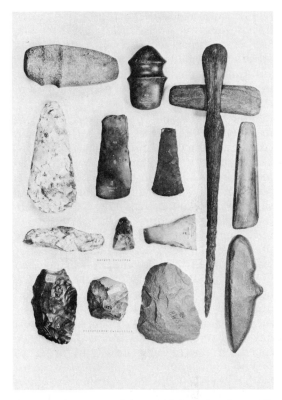

Compared to some of the sophisticated and complicated tools of today, these implements may appear crude. In fact, our early human ancestors were skilled toolmakers.

was the use of fire, which allowed early humans to cook their meat; this killed the more harmful parasites and aided digestion. The use of fire also led to improvements in the manufacture of tools; stone is easier to work with when heated, and finer edges can be made if the core is heat-treated. In the same way, wooden or bone tools are stronger and sharper when they have been tempered by heat.

The first evidence of the use of fire is generally thought to date from about 500,000 years ago. This evidence comes from a cave in Choukoutien, near Beijing, China. But we do not know whether fire was used regularly, and, more important, we do not know whether it was created on purpose or taken from a natural source, such as a fire caused by lightning. We do have clear evidence that the Neanderthals who lived in Europe from 100,000 to 50,000 years ago could start a fire, and that this ability enabled them to remain in the area despite the low temperatures of the most recent glacial period.

The Neanderthal people were, like us, members of the species *Homo sapiens*. Their culture included clothing, stone tools, wood and bone tools, and fairly permanent settlements, as well as the use of fire. Evidence at Shanidar Cave in Iraq and at archeological sites in France indicates that the Neanderthals engaged in ceremonial burial of the dead, including placing flowers and flint tools in the grave. There is also evidence that they cared for the living: One find in Iraq included the skeleton of a crippled person who would have had to be supported from childhood until his death at about 40 years of age. Other sites contained skeletons of people who must have had severe arthritis and also must have relied on the help of others in order to survive. This shows that, at the very least, people were kept alive even if they could not produce food—a very "human" behavior.

Physically, Neanderthals differed from modern humans in several rather minor ways: They had slightly larger brains, aver-aging about 1,540 cc, compared to our average of about 1,350 cc; their skulls were slightly thicker, with heavier brow ridges; and they had larger teeth and stronger jaws. These characteristics are not much different from what might be considered an extreme case in a modern human being. Our image of Neanderthals as short, hairy brutes carrying heavy clubs simply does not fit, and at least one anthropologist has suggested that if we saw a neat, well-dressed Neanderthal man on a crowded subway train, we might not even look twice!

The fact that Neanderthals are classified in the same species as modern humans means that it would be possible for them to interbreed with modern humans. Indeed, this theory is often used to explain why they apparently disappeared about 50,000 years ago. It is possible that at this time the human species was divided into two subspecies and that either the more modern type was better able to compete, and hence drove the Neanderthals into extinction, or the two populations began to interbreed and the Neanderthal traits gradually disappeared. In any case, the Neanderthals have a separate subspecies name, *Homo sapiens neanderthalensis*, whereas our subspecies is called *Homo sapiens sapiens*.

(From left to right): gorilla, Homo erectus pekinensis, and Homo sapiens sapiens. Note the reduced size of the jaw and brow ridge and the increase in brain size in contemporary humans.

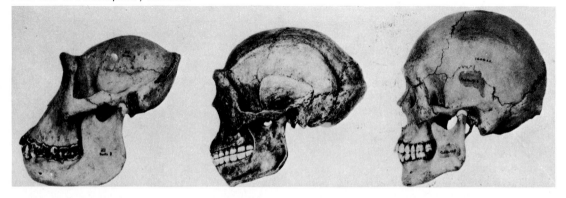

The Concept of Biocultural Evolution

As the title of this chapter indicates, we have been discussing the evolution of culture as part of the ongoing process of biological evolution that led to the human species as it exists today. Human culture would not have been possible without some changes in the physical makeup of our prehuman ancestors, such as the opposable thumb, erect posture and bipedalism, and increased brain size and intelligence, to name but a few. Language adds another element to culture, providing a far more efficient and effective means of communication than exists among other primates. The point of this discussion has been to show how culture became possible as a product of a unique sequence of events, and that all human groups share the same biological basis for culture.

At the same time, we must recognize that human groups are different from one another, not only biologically and physically, but culturally as well. While all humans have the capacity for culture, every human society has created a different kind of culture, with different rules for interacting, for marrying, even for speaking. Human culture has become such a powerful factor that it has changed the course of biological evolution, and it has changed it in different ways for different groups of people. Whereas the evolution of the *capacity* for culture was a result of biological evolution alone, now that we have culture it has become a part of our environment; in fact, it often determines our environment. In evolutionary terms, this means that biological evolution now is a result not just of *natural* selection but also of *cultural* selection.

Natural selection acts on human populations in an environment that is shaped by culture; thus to some extent culture bypasses natural selection. This does not mean that biological evolution ceases; rather, the course of evolution is changed. Since we can define evolution at its most basic level merely as the changes that occur in the gene pool of a population over time, there will always be evolution. Cultural practices may alter the natural environment, either consciously or unconsciously, so that what might have happened "naturally" does not happen. For example, through medical science (a product of culture) we can change the environment in which a person exists by inoculating that person with something that will prevent disease. On a wide scale, such a practice introduces a new element into the process of natural selection. It removes certain environmental pressures (certain diseases) and may replace them with others (population pressure).

We can refer to this new type of change, which combines biological and cultural processes, as **biocultural evolution.** In applying this concept to human populations, anthropologists have been able to look at the uniqueness of human evolution in a way that was not possible before. We have achieved a far better understanding of how we became the way we are by looking at the combination of factors that brought us here.

One of the clearest examples of the interaction between culture and biology in the course of human evolution is the disease known as **sickle-cell anemia.** Medical science had long puzzled over this disease, which affects the red blood cells—a person who suffers from it has little chance of surviving to adulthood. If, as seemed to be the case, it had a genetic basis, it did not make sense that a disease that was so harmful would exist in such a large proportion of certain populations. In other words, we would expect natural selection to weed out individuals with the genetic tendency for sickle-cell anemia, so that the number of people with this disease would be kept down.

In the 1950s it was discovered that despite its harmful effects on some members of the population, the sickle-cell tendency actually benefited others. In order to understand how this is true, we must look at the interaction between sickle-cell anemia and another disease—malaria. That is, sickle-cell anemia occurs mainly in areas where there is a high incidence of malaria, one of the most serious diseases of humans. Briefly, the way these two diseases interact is as follows: Among the tens of thousands of genes that a person inherits, certain ones determine the nature of the blood. Some affect such things as blood type and immunities, while others affect hemoglobin, the part of the blood that carries oxygen to the red blood cells. If an individual inherits "normal" genes from both parents, that person will have "normal" blood and will not suffer from sickle-cell anemia. On the other hand, if an individual inherits "sickle-cell" genes from both parents, the hemoglobin will not be able to carry enough oxygen to the red blood cells. As a result, he or she will suffer from anemia, circulatory problems, and related symptoms, and will almost always die at an early age. The reason the disease is called sickle-cell anemia is that when the red blood cells do not get enough oxygen they become distorted or shaped like a sickle.

Under normal conditions we could expect that, because people who have "sickle-cell" genes would not survive to reproduce, the disease would be kept to a low rate. The key to its existence in large numbers of people is that those who inherit the "sickle-cell" gene from one parent *only* are more resistant to malaria than people with two genes for "normal" blood. The reason is that malaria affects the human bloodstream in the form of a parasite called *Plasmodium*. The *Plasmodium* requires oxygenated red blood cells for its survival, and the sickle-shaped cells do not give it enough oxygen. In those individuals who have both "sickle-cell" and "normal" genes, 70 to 80 percent of the blood cells are normal and the rest are sickle-shaped. But even the normal cells are affected, in that whereas normal red blood cells usually have a life span of about 120 days, these people's cells will only last about 90 days, which is too little time for the *Plasmodium* to mature and take its toll. Thus a person who has inherited the sickle-cell gene from one parent and the normal gene from the other will be resistant to malaria and will have a condition known as **sickle-cell trait.** If we look at the process

Normal blood cells (left) *and sickle-shaped cells* (right).

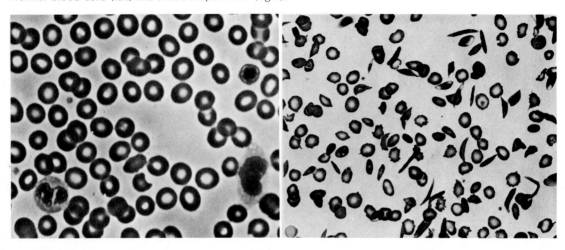

of natural selection as it affects a population in an area where malaria occurs, we can understand why sickle-cell genes exist in such large numbers. Even though they are a disadvantage to some people—those who suffer from anemia—they are an advantage to others—those who are resistant to malaria. When we consider that malaria affects over 350 million people in the world today, it is clear that such an advantage would be an important factor in natural selection.

But what does this have to do with culture, and why is it an example of biocultural evolution? To answer this question we need to know something about malaria and how it is transmitted. The parasite that causes malaria, *Plasmodium*, lives in a certain kind of mosquito, the *Anopheles*. When the mosquito bites a human, it transfers some of these parasites to the human bloodstream, where they settle into the red blood cells. Normally, human populations did not inhabit areas where malaria was present because if they did the disease would wipe them out.

However, within the last few thousand years, as the human species has undergone both population growth and technological progress, there has been more pressure on the land. New agricultural techniques allowed people to clear areas that formerly were tropical rain forest in order to grow food to support a larger population. But the clearing of these lands created conditions that favored mosquitoes as well, since mosquitoes require stagnant water (for breeding) near large groups of humans and animals (for feeding). Thus technological changes led to the spread of people—and malaria—into such areas as central and western Africa. At this point the "sickle-cell" gene became an advantage and began to spread.

The sickle-cell complex illustrates the interaction between biological and cultural factors in the process called biocultural evolution. Before human actions caused changes in the environment, both malaria and sickle-cell anemia were relatively rare in certain regions. People did not move into areas where they were likely to get malaria, and the malaria agent did not spread into areas where conditions were not favorable to it. Thus the genetic tendency for sickle cells was rare because it was disadvantageous. But when cultural factors were introduced, the balance shifted and malaria became a problem. In response, a biological change occurred in the form of a new balance in the gene pool that provided resistance to malaria.

The story does not end here, however. Cultural factors have continued to affect the balance of nature, thereby changing the course of biological evolution. For example, many people have migrated from central and western Africa to the United States, originally as slaves. Some of these people brought with them the genes for sickle cells, but because malaria is no longer a problem in North America, this trait does not provide the advantage it did in Africa. One recent result has been the development of genetic counseling programs—a cultural intervention in the biological process of mating—which try to reduce the number of people who might suffer from sickle-cell anemia.

Other cultural factors have also entered into this process of biocultural change. New agricultural techniques have reduced the number of mosquitoes, for example, by removing the ponds in which they breed. Likewise, culture (in the form of technological change) has created pesticides like DDT that are used to kill mosquitoes, with the result that malaria has been reduced or eliminated in many parts of the world. Again, this means that the genes for sickle cells are no longer advantageous to the populations in these areas.

The example of sickle-cell anemia shows us that through culture human beings can change the environment. As a result of this unique ability, we can no longer look at evolution strictly in biological terms; we must also include those changes that have resulted from cultural activity. It is within this framework that we will look more closely at the evolution of human culture.

Summary

Human beings are a product of evolution, as is every other living form on earth. Both our physical makeup and our capacity for culture are the result of biological evolution. Evolution works through *natural selection,* in which pressures in the environment act on the natural variation in a population, letting some members of the population survive, and thereby pass on their traits to the next generation, at a greater rate than others. It is this difference in rate of reproduction, as well as the resulting change in the frequencies of genes from one generation to the next, that is the basis for evolutionary change over time.

Humanlike creatures are relative latecomers on the earth, having existed for only 4 millions years. Humans share a number of characteristics with other mammals, but they also share many characteristics with other primates that set them apart from the rest of the mammalian class: They have upright posture, stereoscopic vision with greater depth perception, improved sense of touch together with decreased sense of smell, nails rather than claws, opposable thumbs, a reduced number of offspring with greater infant dependency, and above all, increased intelligence.

Humans and other higher primates differ from other animals not only physically but behaviorally as well. For example, they are organized into structured groups with some type of authority pattern, and they learn a lot of their behavior, particularly during infancy. But in the course of evolution humans developed culture, which set them apart from other higher primates. Early humans relied upon a home base that gave them greater protection from predators and at the same time enabled them to overcome the effects of disease and injury. As a result, the human life span could increase, and the role of learning and experience became more important in adapting to the environment. Also, technology improved so that the physically weaker but more intelligent humans could compete successfully with other animals for food. Once humans were able to use fire and to make tools and clothing, they could survive in a wide variety of climates and take advantage of many different sources of food.

In looking at how we came to be the way we are today, we must recognize the importance of both biological and cultural change. But culture is itself a product of biological evolution, and as human culture continues to change the environment in which people live, it causes further biological evolution. The interaction of these two processes of biological and cultural change is called *biocultural evolution.* An example discussed in this chapter is the sickle-cell gene, which spread throughout populations in Africa and the Mediterranean and into the western hemisphere. Individuals who have a combination of sickle cells and normal red blood cells are resistant to malaria. Thus the spread of the sickle-cell gene is in part a response to the pressures of the environment and a part of the process of biological evolution. Yet, at the same time, the spread of malaria in central and western Africa was caused by culturally induced changes in the environment, making the spread of the sickle-cell gene a product of cultural evolution as well. Biocultural evolution is the interaction of these two processes.

Glossary

biocultural evolution The interaction of biological and cultural factors in the continuing process of adaptation to the environment.

bipedal locomotion The ability to walk upright on two feet. Like humans, nonhuman primates can stand on two feet, but they cannot do this for long periods of time, nor can they extend their legs to straighten their knees.

dominance In some primate groups a pattern of social behavior based on a hierarchy usually associated with differences in age, sex, and physical strength.

erect posture The ability to stand upright so that the arms and hands are free for other activities, such as making and using tools.

natural selection The principal process of evolutionary change as described by Darwin. Those best suited to the environment contribute more offspring to future generations, changing the genetic makeup of the population over time.

opposable thumb The ability to cross the thumb over the other fingers, allowing a grip that is useful in the manufacture and use of tools.

sexual dimorphism Differences in individuals based on their gender, as in the different size or different physical appearance of the average male and female. Humans and chimps have less sexual dimorphism than many other animals.

sickle-cell anemia The hereditary disease that affects the red blood cells, and is widespread in areas of the world where there is a high rate of malaria.

sickle-cell trait A hereditary condition in which an individual possesses roughly half normal red blood cells and half sickle-shaped red blood cells. Such an individual is usually resistant to the disease malaria, but suffers no ill effects of sickle-cell anemia.

survival of the fittest The principle in natural selection that those members of a population best adapted to their environment will tend to live and to reproduce at a greater rate than the rest of the population, thereby contributing a greater proportion of genes to the next generation.

Questions for Discussion

1. Which of the five senses is most important to you for survival in the modern world, and why? Which is least important?

2. From what you have learned about the evolution of the human species, how would you evaluate some current practices that seem to go against the "natural" tendencies of the human species, such as vegetarianism and birth control?

3. If through the application of medical science we are able to keep people alive who would not have survived to reproductive age 100 years ago, what does this mean for the continued evolution of the human species? Has evolutionary change ceased now that we can control our environment?

Suggestions for Additional Reading

LOREN EISELEY, *Darwin's Century* (New York: Atheneum, 1958). An entertaining narrative of the rise of evolutionary theory in the nineteenth century and the people who contributed to it.

JOHN G. FLEAGLE, *Primate Adaptation and Evolution* (New York: Academic Press, 1988). An examination of basic anatomical and behavioral similarities and differences among the major groups of living and extinct primates, including the bipedal primates.

JAMES L. FORBES and JAMES E. KING (Eds.), *Primate Behavior* (New York: Academic Press, 1982). A broad overview of primate behavior as analyzed by a varied group of researchers in fields of anthropology, primatology, biology, psychology, and linguistics.

STEPHEN J. GOULD, *The Panda's Thumb* (New York: W. W. Norton, 1980). Entertaining, insightful essays on evolutionary theory, including a biological analysis on the evolution of Mickey Mouse.

FRANK B. LIVINGSTONE, "Anthropological Implications of Sickle-Cell Gene Distribution in West Africa," *American Anthropologist*, 60 (1958): 533–562. An early but still valuable discussion of the evolutionary interaction of biological and cultural forces that led to the spread of the sickle-cell gene.

JOHN E. PFEIFFER, *The Emergence of Man*, 3rd ed. (New York: Harper & Row, 1978). A more detailed analysis of the evolution of *Homo sapiens* and the origins of human culture.

HENRY ROTHSCHILD (Ed.), *Biocultural Aspects of Disease* (New York: Academic Press, 1981). An interdisciplinary exploration of the relationships between ethnicity and health.

G. LEDYARD STEBBINS, *Processes of Organic Evolution*, 2nd ed. (Englewood Cliffs, N.J.: Prentice Hall, 1971). A thorough and readable analysis of the processes of evolution.

SHERWOOD L. WASHBURN and RUTH MOORE, *Ape into Man: A Study of Human Evolution* (Boston: Little, Brown, 1974). A detailed look at the process of human evolution and a consideration of the important characteristics that set humans apart from other primates.

Game: The Prehistoric Origin of Sports

CARL SAGAN

Carl Sagan was sports editor of his high school newspaper and captain of a championship intramural basketball team in college. It is his misfortune to be devoted to the New York Knicks.

We can't help ourselves. On Sunday afternoons and Monday nights in the fall of each year, we abandon everything to watch small moving images of 22 men—running into one another, falling down, picking themselves up and kicking an elongated object made from the skin of an animal. Every now and then, both the players and the sedentary spectators are moved to rapture or despair by the progress of the play. All over America, people (mainly men), transfixed before glass screens, cheer or mutter in unison. Put this way, it sounds stupid. But once you get the hang of it, it's hard to resist, and I speak from experience.

Athletes run, jump, hit, slide, throw, kick, tackle—and there's a thrill in seeing humans do it so well. They wrestle each other to the ground. They're keen on grabbing or clubbing or kicking a fast-moving brown or white thing. In some games, they try to herd the thing toward what's called a "goal"; in other games, the players run away and then return "home." Teamwork is almost everything, and we admire how the parts fit together to make a jubilant whole.

But these are not the skills most of us use to earn our daily bread. Why should we feel compelled to watch people run or hit? Why is this need transcultural? (Ancient Egyptians, Persians, Greeks, Romans, Mayans and Aztecs also played ball. "Polo" is Tibetan.)

There are sports stars who make 10 times the annual salary of the President; who are themselves, after retirement, elected to high office. They are national heroes. Why, exactly? There is something here transcending the diversity of political, social and economic systems. Something ancient is calling.

Most major sports are associated with a nation or a city, and they carry with them elements of patriotism and civic pride. Our team represents *us*—where we live, our people—against those other guys from some different place, populated by unfamiliar, maybe hostile people. (True, most of "our" players are not *really* from here. They're mercenaries and with clear conscience regularly defect from opposing cities for suitable emolument: A Pittsburgh Pirate is reformed into a California Angel; A San Diego Padre is raised to a St. Louis Cardinal; a Golden State Warrior is crowned a Sacramento King. Occasionally, a whole team picks up and migrates to another city.)

Competitive sports are symbolic conflicts, thinly disguised. This is hardly a new insight. The Cherokees called their ancient form of lacrosse "the little brother of war." Or here is Max Rafferty, former California Superintendent of Public Instruction, who, after denouncing critics of college football as "kooks, crumbums, commies, hairy loudmouthed beatniks," goes on to state, "Football is war without killing . . . Football players . . . possess a clear, bright, fighting spirit which is America itself." (That's worth mulling over.) An often-quoted sentiment of the late coach Vince Lombardi is that the only thing that counts is winning. Former Washington Redskins' coach George Allen put it this way: "Losing is like death."

Indeed, we talk of winning and losing a war as naturally as we do of winning and losing a game. In a televised U.S. Army recruitment ad, we see the aftermath of an armored warfare exercise in which one tank destroys another; in the tag line, the victorious tank commander says, "When we win, the whole team wins, the whole tank wins—not one person." The connection between sports and combat is made quite clear. Sports fans (the word is short for "fanatics") have been known to commit assault and battery, and sometimes murder, when taunted about a losing team; or when prevented from cheering on a winning team; or when they feel an injustice has been committed by the referees.

The British prime minister was obliged in 1985 to denounce the rowdy, drunken behavior of British soccer fans who attacked an Italian contingent for having the effrontery to root for their own team. Dozens were killed when the stands collapsed. In 1969, after three hard-fought soccer games, Salvadoran tanks crossed the Honduran border, and Salvadoran bombers attacked Honduran ports and military bases. In this "Soccer War," the casualties numbered in the thousands.

Afghani tribesmen played polo with the severed heads of former adversaries. And 600 years ago, in what is now Mexico City, there was a ball court where gorgeously attired nobles watched uniformed teams compete. The captain of the losing team was beheaded, and the skulls of earlier losing captains were displayed on racks—an inducement possibly even more compelling than winning one for the Gipper.

Suppose you're idly flipping the dial on your television set, and you come upon some competition in which you have no particular emotional investment—say off-season volleyball between Burma and Thailand. How do you decide which team to root for? But wait a minute: Why root for either? Why not just enjoy the game? Most of us have trouble with this detached posture. We want to take part in the contest, to feel ourselves a member of a team. The feeling simply sweeps us away, and there we are rooting, "Go, Burma!" Initially, our loyalties may oscillate, first urging on one team and then the other. Sometimes we root for the underdog. Other times, shamefully, we even switch our allegiance from loser to winner as the outcome becomes clear. (When there is a succession of losing seasons, fan loyalties tend to drift elsewhere.) What we are looking for is victory without effort. We want to be swept into something like a small, safe, successful war.

The earliest known organized athletic events date back 3500 years to preclassical Greece. During the original Olympic Games, an armistice put all wars among Greek city-states on hold. The games were more important than the wars. The men performed nude; no women spectators were allowed. By the eighth century B.C., the Olympic Games consisted of running (*lots* of running), jumping, throwing things (including javelins) and wrestling (sometimes to the death). While none of these events was a team sport, they were clearly central to modern team sports.

They were also central to low-technology hunting. Hunting is traditionally considered a sport, as long as you don't eat what you catch—a proviso much easier for the rich to comply with than the poor. From the earliest pharoahs, hunting has been associated with military aristocracies. Oscar Wilde's aphorism about English fox hunting, "the unspeakable in full pursuit of the uneatable," makes a similar dual point. The forerunners of football, soccer, hockey and kindred sports were so-called "rabble games," recognized as substitutes for hunting—because young men who worked for a living were barred from the hunt.

So, perhaps team sports are not just stylized echoes of ancient wars. Perhaps they also satisfy an almost-forgotten craving for the hunt. Since our passions for sports run so deep and are so broadly distributed, they are likely to be hard-wired into us—not in our brains but in our genes. The 10,000 years since the invention of agriculture is not nearly enough time for such predispositions to have evolved. If we want to understand them, we must go much further back.

The human species is hundreds of thousands of years old. We have led a sedentary existence—based on farming and domestication of animals—for only the last 3 percent of that period, during which is all our history. In the first 97 percent of our tenure on Earth, almost everything that is characteristically human came into being. We can learn something about those times from the few surviving hunter-gatherer communities uncorrupted by civilization.

We wander. With our little ones and all our belongings on our backs, we wander—following the game, seeking the waterholes. We set up camp for a while, then move on. In providing food for the group, the men mainly hunt, the women mainly gather. Meat and potatoes. A typical itinerant band, mainly an extended family of relatives and inlaws, numbers a few dozen; although annually many hundreds of us, with the same language and culture, gather—for religious ceremonies, to trade, to arrange marriages, to tell stories. There are many stories about the hunt.

I'm focusing here on the hunters, who are men. But women have significant social, economic and cultural power. They gather the essential staples—nuts, fruits, tubers, roots—as well as medicinal herbs, hunt small animals and provide strategic intelligence on large animal movements. Men do some gathering as well, and considerable "housework" (even though we have no houses). But hunting—only for food, never for sport—is the lifelong occupation of every able-bodied male.

Preadolescent boys stalk birds and small mammals with bows and arrows. By adulthood they have become experts in weapons-procurement; in stalking, killing and butchering the prey; and in carrying the cuts of meat back to camp. The first successful kill

TEAMS AND TOTEMS

USA Basketball	USA Football	Japanese Baseball	North American Baseball	!Kung Named Groups
Hawks	Cardinals	Hawks	Blue Jays	Ant Bears
Bucks	Eagles	Swallows	Cardinals	Elephants
Bulls	Falcons	Carp	Orioles	Giraffes
Mavericks	Seahawks	Buffaloes	Cubs	Impalas
Bullets	Bears	Lions	Tigers	Jackals
Clippers	Bengals	Tigers	Astros	Rhinos
Nets	Broncos	Whales	Athletics	Steenboks
Pistons	Chargers	Braves	Braves	Wildcats
Rockets	Colts	Ham Fighters	Brewers	Ants
Spurs	Dolphins	Dragons	Dodgers	Lice
Supersonics	Lions	Giants	Expos	Scorpions
Cavaliers	Rams	Orions	Indians	Tortoises
Celtics	Jets		Mariners	Bitter Melons
Jazz	Bills		Mets	Long Roots
Kings	Buccaneers		Phillies	Medicine Roots
Knickerbockers	Chiefs		Pirates	Carrying Yokes
Lakers	Cowboys		Rangers	Cutters
Pacers	49'ers		Royals	Big Talkers
76'ers	Oilers		Twins	Cold Ones
Trail Blazers	Packers		Yankees	Diarrheas
Warriors	Patriots		Red Sox	Dirty Fighters
Nuggets	Raiders		White Sox	Fighters
Suns	Redskins		Angels	Owners
	Steelers		Giants	Penises
	Vikings		Padres	Short Feet
	Giants		Reds	
	Saints			
	Browns			

Teams associated with cities have names, and so do hunter-gatherer groups worldwide. The names are sometimes called totems. At the far right are some from the !Kung San people of Botswana. Of course there are differences. It's hard to imagine an American sports team named the Diarrheas ("Gimme a 'D' . . ."). Or even the Big Talkers. And one in which the players are called the Owners would probably cause some consternation in the front office.

of a large mammal marks a young man's coming of age. In his initiation, ceremonial incisions are made on his chest or arms and an herb is rubbed into the cuts so that, when healed, a patterned tattoo results. It's like campaign ribbons—one look at his chest, and you know something of his combat experience.

From a jumble of hoofprints, we can accurately tell how many animals passed; the species, sexes and ages; whether any are lame; how long since they passed; and how far away they are likely to be. Some young animals can be caught by open-field tackles; others with slingshots or boomerangs, or just by throwing rocks accurately and hard. Animals that have not yet learned to fear man can be approached

boldly and clubbed to death. At greater distances, for warier prey, we hurl spears or shoot poisoned arrows. Sometimes we're lucky and, by a carefully coordinated rush, can drive a herd of animals into an ambush or off a cliff.

Teamwork among the hunters is essential. If we are not to frighten the quarry, we must communicate by sign language. For the same reason, we need to have our emotions under control; both fear and exultation are dangerous. We are ambivalent about the prey. We respect the animals, recognize our kinship, identify with them. But if we reflect too closely on their intelligence or devotion to their young, if we feel pity for them, our dedication to the hunt will slacken; we will bring home less food, and again our band may be endangered. We are obliged to put an emotional distance between us and them.

So contemplate this: For a million years, our male ancestors are scampering about, throwing rocks at pigeons, running after baby antelopes and wrestling them to the ground, forming a single line of shouting, running hunters and trying to terrify a herd of startled wart hogs upwind. Imagine that their lives depend on hunting skills and teamwork. And good hunters were also good warriors. Then, after a long while— a few thousand centuries, say—a natural predisposition for both hunting and teamwork will inhabit many newborn boys. Why? Because incompetent or unenthusiastic hunters leave fewer offspring. I don't think how to chip a spearpoint out of stone or how to feather an arrow is in our genes. That's taught or figured out. But a zest for the chase—I bet that *is* hard-wired. Natural selection helped mold our ancestors into superb hunters.

The clearest evidence of the success of the hunter-gatherer lifestyle is the simple fact that it extended to six continents and lasted a million years. After 40,000 generations in which the killing of animals was our hedge against starvation, those inclinations must still be in us. We hunger to put them to use, even vicariously. Team sports provide a way.

Some part of our being longs to join a small band of brothers on a daring and intrepid quest. The traditional manly virtues—taciturnity, resourcefulness, modesty, consistency, deep knowledge of animals, love of the outdoors—were all adaptive behavior in hunter-gatherer times. We still admire these traits, although we've almost forgotten why.

Besides sports, there are few outlets available. In our adolescent males, we can still recognize the young hunter, the aspirant warrior—leaping across apartment rooftops; riding, helmetless, on a motorcycle; making trouble for the winning team at a postgame celebration. In the absence of a steadying hand, those old instincts may go a little askew (although our murder rate is about the same as among the !Kung San, the present-day hunter-gatherer people of Botswana). We try to ensure that any residual zest for killing does not spill over onto humans. We don't always succeed.

I think of how powerful those hunting instincts are, and I worry. I worry that Monday-night football is insufficient outlet for the modern hunter-gatherer, decked out in his overalls or uniform or three-piece suit. I think of that ancient legacy about not expressing our feelings, about keeping an emotional distance from those we kill, and it takes some of the fun out of the game.

Hunter-gatherers generally posed no danger to themselves: because their economies tended to be healthy (many had more free time than we do); because, as nomads, they had few possessions, almost no theft and little envy; because greed and arrogance were considered to be not only social evils but also pretty close to mental illnesses; because women had real political power and tended to be a stabilizing and mitigating influence before the boys started going for their poisoned arrows; and because, when serious crimes were committed—murder, say—the band collectively rendered judgment and punishment. Hunter-gatherers organized egalitarian democracies. They had no chiefs. There was no political or corporate hierarchy to dream of climbing. There was no one to revolt against.

So, if we're stranded a few hundred centuries from when we long to be—if (through no fault of our own) we find ourselves, in an age of nuclear weapons, with Pleistocene emotions but without Pleistocene social safeguards—perhaps we can be excused for a little Monday-night football.

For Further Reading

A good anecdotal summary of professional sports and its admirers is *Fans!* by Michael Roberts (New Republic Book Co., 1976). A classic study of hunter-gatherer society is *The !Kung San* by Richard Borshay Lee (Cambridge U. Press, 1979). Most of the hunter-gatherer customs mentioned in this article apply to the !Kung and to many other nonmarginal hunter-gatherer cultures worldwide—before they were destroyed by civilization.

3

The Concept of Culture

Since the subject of this book is cultural anthropology, we ought to have a clear idea of what we mean by **culture**. Everyone uses this term quite freely; *Time* and *Newsweek* talk about the culture of this or that, TV broadcasters bandy the word around, but, in fact, most people have only a vague sense of what it means. Even social scientists don't always agree on how to define culture; two anthropologists once collected more than 160 meanings for the term!

Sometimes we think of culture as referring to the life style of the upper class. In order to "have culture" one must attend the opera, art museums, and the like. At other times we might call a person "uncultured," meaning uncouth or rude, although as anthropologists conceive the term, there is no such thing as an uncultured person, since everyone is a member of a cultural tradition. The list of definitions goes on and on. Yet obviously there must be some commonly accepted meaning of culture if cultural anthropologists are to work together and compare their knowledge and understanding of human behavior.

In this and the following chapters we will define culture and then consider how it is maintained, as well as how anthropologists study it.

Defining Culture

Culture is the aspect of our existence that makes us similar to some people, yet different from most of the people in the world. We are all basically the same physically in that we are members of the same species. And we are all different in that each of us has a unique personality. It is culture that binds us together into a group sharing a certain degree of similarity that overcomes individual differences while setting us apart from other groups. Thus when we speak of culture we mean a way of life that is common to a group of people, a collection of beliefs and attitudes, shared understandings, and patterns of behavior that allow those people to live together in relative harmony, but set them apart from other peoples.

Culture is the blueprint for how a group of people should act. Culture is what makes us Americans rather than Germans, Chinese, or Bantu. It is our culture that assists us in figuring out what to do, how to act, how to choose among various alternatives. In other words, cultural understanding becomes a problem-solving device.

A good definition of culture as it is used in anthropology is the one proposed by Edward Tylor more than 100 years go in his book *Primitive Culture*. Tylor was a major figure in anthropology in the nineteenth century, and his lasting contributions to the field are evident in the fact that his definition of the main subject of anthropology has withstood the test of time. Tylor defined culture as *that complex whole which includes knowledge, belief, art, morals, law, customs, and any other capabilities and habits acquired by man as a member of society.*

That complex whole . . . Let us take a closer look at this definition to see what some of its implications are. First of all, culture is not just a series of unrelated things that happen to have been thrown together by a group of people as they wandered around the earth. It is a complex whole, an integrated unit. The parts of any culture fit together—not just the physical aspects, such as tools, houses, and clothing, but the nonmaterial aspects as well, such as knowledge, belief, art, morals, law, customs, and other capabilities and habits. They form a context for each other. Law and morals and customs must be based on knowledge and belief, and must be reflected in the way people act toward one another.

. . . acquired by man . . . Second, Tylor's definition tells us that culture is acquired by human beings. This has several implications, among them that culture is not inherited or instinctive, and also that culture is unique to the human species. Many anthropologists no longer believe that culture is a uniquely human characteristic, and we will discuss this

problem in more detail in a later section of this chapter. But the fact that culture is *acquired* or learned is important in understanding why people behave the way they do. People learn a culture from the members of their group. If you had been born and raised in Japan, you would speak fluent Japanese and feel perfectly comfortable following Japanese customs and traditions. There is no biological basis for one culture as opposed to another, just as there is no relationship between a person's racial characteristics and his or her culture.

Alfred Kroeber provided an interesting example to illustrate this distinction between the inborn character of most nonhuman behavior and the learned culture behavior of human beings. Suppose we hatch some ant eggs on a deserted island. The resulting ant colony will be almost exactly like the parent generation of ants, including their social behavior. Ants have a set of rules they follow in acting together as a group, but these rules are not learned as a result of interaction with other ants of the parent generation. They are instinctive and part of the heredity of ants in each new generation. That is why we can be sure that the newly hatched ants will look and act exactly like their parents, even though they have never seen them.

Suppose we do the same with a group of infants from our own society (pretending for the sake of argument that it is possible). Certainly we would not expect the same results—a generation of people just like their parents. Rather, the result would be a group of people essentially without culture. If they were somehow able to survive (which would also be impossible), they might develop their own culture, different from any other way of life on earth. They would not speak a language that could be understood by anyone else, nor would they dress or eat or do anything else in a way that reflected their parents' culture. Although born of American parents, there is no way that these individuals could acquire American culture without being taught. Only in science fiction can testtube babies be programmed for a specific way of life before they are born.

Social behavior, such as these Chinese people practicing group exercises, is an example of how individuals acquire culture as members of a group.

. . . as a member of society. A third implication of Tylor's definition is that culture is shared and that learning takes place within the confines of a group. Culture is a group phenomenon, not an individual one; it pertains to societies, or people who share a way of life. Of course, ants and bees are organized into what we call societies, as are some higher primates, including baboons and chimpanzees. But we distinguish between the social life of these animals, which is largely instinctive, and the social life of human beings, which is mostly learned or acquired.

Socialization:
Learning the Culture

Social behavior is based on mutual or shared expectations. We are able to operate in our normal daily routine because we have complete confidence that other people will behave in a *predictable* and *orderly* way, responding to the same cues in the same way that we do. If this were not so, we could not have the kind of society that we do. When driving in the United States, for instance, we expect everyone will stay on the right side of the road. Normally, we can anticipate what other drivers will do, how they will behave behind the wheel. That is part of the culture we have learned. Yet there might be variations in the cultural rules. For example, the driving patterns found in small towns differ from those common in large urban areas.

Cultural anthropologists are interested in how people learn the proper behavior in each social setting, and what cues trigger that behavior. We want to know how people learn the values they share as members of the same group. And we try to show how all of what we learn and the way we learn it fits together into a pattern.

Socialization is the process of learning to be a member of a society; it is a process that is slightly different in every society. Groups of people vary in the way they teach their new members to act, and these differences

and similarities in teaching and learning the culture are important to the anthropologist. Socialization includes the teaching and learning of all aspects of culture. It is not limited to physical activities such as table manners or driving a car; it includes values, morals, attitudes, suspicions—literally everything, mental as well as physical. Furthermore, socialization is never really complete, because no individual is an exact replica of his or her parents, either socially or physically.

In studying those aspects of personality shared with all other members of a society, anthropologists assume that there is some pattern or regularity in the way children of a culture are brought up and in the things they learn. Learning the culture begins in infancy and continues throughout life, as a person adapts to changing social and material conditions. In studying culture and personality anthropologists focus on the relationship between the way a culture molds its youths'

Much of human behavior is learned through the process of socialization. By imitating adults, this child learns the behavior appropriate for this situation.

personalities and their psychological makeup in later life. In other words, we look for regularities both in the way children are raised and in the way adults behave, assuming that early childhood experiences have a lot to do with the formation of adult personalities. We study the techniques practiced by parents and other socializing institutions such as schools or peer groups. In each case we try to see how these experiences affect behavior in the adult population, assuming that values learned in infancy have a way of showing up in adults.

For example, the anthropological approach can help us understand personality patterns in our own culture. Adult behavior in American society is reinforced through the way we train our children. Positive values such as individual achievement, competition, and freedom of choice are a strong part of almost every American parent's approach to child rearing. Negative values are transmitted just as strongly to children by parents, teachers, peers, and even impersonal media such as television. We cannot underestimate the role of television in transmitting American

A twentieth-century version of armed warriors dressed for battle. Is violence becoming a pattern of American culture?

culture to the youth of today, particularly its effect of homogenizing the members of the impressionable young age group that is growing up in a "TV culture." In our present-day society, with its increasing wave of crime and violence and the apparent loss of realism concerning war and the death and destruction it brings, we are beginning to look at the relationship between television programming and cultural values more closely. In a study of television programs aired on Saturday morning—prime time for young children—the following results were discovered: 89 percent of the time was devoted to entertaining rather than educational programs, including 70 percent cartoons; 62 percent of all programs were animated; three out of ten dramatic segments were saturated with violence, and 71 percent had at least one instance of human violence. Another interesting conclusion was that although in 52 percent of the programs the violence was directed at humans, in only 4 percent did this result in death or injury. Is it any wonder that our children are growing up with the idea that violence is entertaining and relatively harmless?

Television has also brought war and conflict into our living rooms, a sort of adult version of Saturday television for the kids. The close network coverage of the hostage crisis in Iran, bombings in Lebanon, and worldwide terrorism has created a feeling of artificiality about conflict for Americans. Slightly more than two decades ago TV coverage of the Vietnam War divorced millions of Americans from the outside world by illustrating how far removed from it they were—they could sit down in the evening and watch people killing one another, then go to bed as if it were just another average day. Hundreds of people—not just soldiers, but civilian men, women, and children—could die in a single day's fighting, but life rolled on for us just as it always had, with none of the hardships or insecurities of a

An extremely malnourished mother and child from East Africa. The mass media deluge us with news of global problems, but has this made us insensitive to these issues?

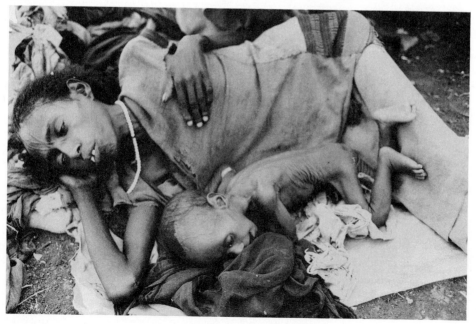

country engaged in a battle for its own survival. More recently, we have experienced the same kind of contradictions regarding the massive starvation among Cambodian and Kurdish refugees and the plight of hungry Ethiopians, yet because we see so much of the suffering of the world through our TV sets, we become almost insensitive to it.

Indeed, television is becoming increasingly important as an institution for socializing the young members of American culture, and its role in molding their minds and teaching them American values and the American way of life is growing at a startling rate. We can no longer speak of the family as the primary institution for child training—it must now share the spotlight with "the tube."

We should qualify the anthropological approach to the study of culture and personality by noting that there is always a wide range of personalities within a given society. When we speak of similarities, we do not mean a uniform personality trait found in all members of the society; rather, we are referring to a personality type that is found most frequently. We may speak of a society as being characterized by aggression, by cooperation, or by a strong feeling of anxiety. This implies that this characteristic will be dominant in most members of that society, but it by no means says that other personality types do not exist at the same time; in every "passive" society there will be aggressive individuals. Moreover, dominant personality types can change rapidly within a culture. For example, during the era when Hitler was in power in Germany, the Jews as a group offered relatively little armed resistance. There were minor uprisings, but the Jewish population of Europe did not band together and stand against Hitler's soldiers in armed conflict. Yet their descendants who make up a large part of the population of Israel today have developed exactly the opposite personality type. Partly as a result of the Jews' experiences in Europe a generation ago, the Israelis of today defend themselves and their country in a way that has enabled them to survive in hostile surroundings.

Do Other Species Have Culture?

Recently anthropologists have begun to ask whether culture is unique to humans or whether some nonhuman behavior might also be considered cultural. We know that culture has a biological basis. (See Chapter 2.) The *opposable thumb*, found in other primates as well as in humans, enables us to make and use tools and hold objects. *Bipedal locomotion*—walking on two feet instead of four—and *erect posture* free the arms and hands for other uses. In the course of human evolution we have become more dependent on our *sense of sight* at the expense of other senses, especially hearing and smell. The human species has fewer offspring and a prolonged childhood, so that the infant is relatively defenseless. (Compare a 5-year-old child to a 5-year-old horse, which is fully mature and can take care of itself.) These factors and many other results of evolution have led to our use of culture to adapt to the environment, making up for our physical weakness. We compensate for our lost strength, claws, long teeth, and other defenses by using tools, language, and cooperation. But these aspects of human life can also be found in nonhuman primate behavior.

We used to think that tool use was the dividing line between human beings and other animals. Lately, however, we have found that this is not so. Chimpanzees are able not only to use tools but also to make them—something much more advanced than simply picking up an object and using it. For example, chimps have been observed stripping the leaves and twigs from a branch and inserting it into a termite nest. When the termites bite at the stick, the chimp removes it and eats them—not unlike the way we use a fork!

For some time we assumed that, whereas human beings learn their culture, other animals could not be taught such behavior; and even if they could learn, they would not teach one another the way people do. This too has been shown to be untrue. A group of Japanese macaques (a type of monkey) being studied at the Kyoto University Monkey Center in Japan were given sweet potatoes by scientists who wanted to attract them to the shore of an island. One day a young female began to wash her sweet potato to get rid of the sand. This practice soon spread throughout the group; that is, it became *learned behavior*, learned not from human beings but from other monkeys. Now almost all members of that monkey group wash their sweet potatoes, but other macaques who have not come into contact with this group do not; thus we have a "cultural" difference on a nonhuman level.

If making and using tools and learning and sharing behavior are not the things that make human behavior different from nonhuman primate behavior, what about language? Even the use of language can no longer be considered the dividing line between human behavior and that of nonhuman primates, as we saw in the previous chapter. Of course, there are limits on the culture of nonhuman primates. As far as we know, no ape society has developed such institutions as religion, law, ethics, or econom-

ics. While some chimps may be able to learn sign language, this form of language is limited in its ability to communicate abstract ideas; with our spoken language, we can communicate our entire culture to anyone who understands that language. Perhaps the most important thing we have learned from studies of nonhuman primates is that the line dividing us from them is not as clear as we used to think it was. As Ralph Linton noted more than 50 years ago in his classic book *The Study of Man*:

> The ability of human beings to learn, to communicate with each other, and to transmit learned behavior from generation to generation . . . and their possession of a social as well as a biological heredity . . . are features which link man to the other mammals instead of distinguishing him from them. The differences between men and animals in all these respects are enormous, but they seem to be differences in quantity rather than in quality. . . . In each of these things, the human condition is such as might logically be expected to result from the orderly working-out of tendencies already present at the subhuman level.[1]

Chimpanzees are now known to be able to make and use simple tools. Here two chimps are using long stems of grass to get termites out of a nest.

Cultural Universals

So far we have been dealing with qualitative differences between human beings and other primates, showing how human social behavior is different. Another way of understanding the fundamental difference between people and apes is in the quantitative separation between them—the sheer amount of cultural behavior practiced by human beings as opposed to the relatively small amount found among other primates. Anthropologist George Peter Murdock has made up a list of what he calls **cultural universals**, basic solutions to the problems of living that are found in one form or another in all cultures. This

[1] Ralph Linton, *The Study of Man* (Englewood Cliffs, N.J.: Prentice-Hall, 1936), pp. 78–79.

list gives us a general feeling for the humanness of our species by pointing out how many different kinds of behavior are shared by all human beings no matter where they come from. We may be able to define some nonhuman behavior as "cultural," but this does not mean that other animals have a culture in the same sense that we do, as this list shows. In reading over some of the universals presented below, think about their form in your own culture, and then try to imagine them in any form among chimps or baboons or other nonhuman species.[2]

age grading	hair styles
athletics	hospitality
bodily adornment	housing
calendar	hygiene
cleanliness training	incest taboos
community	inheritance rules
organization	joking
cooking	kin groups
cooperative labor	kin terminology
cosmology	language
courtship	law
dancing	luck superstitions
decorative art	magic
divination	marriage
division of labor	mealtimes
dream	medicine
interpretation	modesty
education	mourning
eschatology	music
ethics	mythology
ethnobotany	numerals
etiquette	obstetrics
faith healing	penal sanctions
family	personal names
feasting	population policy
fire making	postnatal care
folklore	pregnancy usages
food taboos	property rights
funeral rites	propitiation of
games	supernatural
gestures	beings
gift giving	puberty customs
government	religious ritual
greetings	residence rules

sexual restrictions
soul concepts
status
  differentiation
surgery

tool making
trade
visiting
weaning
weather control

Some of these cultural universals can also be found among nonhuman primates. Baboons, for example, have a form of age grading, community organization, courtship, division of labor, education (if the term is interpreted loosely), games, gestures, sexual restrictions based on differences in status, tool making to a limited degree, and so forth. But the sheer quantity and elaboration of human culture outweighs all of these similarities. It is hard to imagine a baboon troop in a state of mourning over a deceased member. It is even harder to imagine talking to a chimp (in sign language, of course) about its philosophy of death or immortality. Apes, to the best of our knowledge, do not have a mythology or a folklore, they do not recognize a system of law other than the natural "law of the jungle," and it would be impossible to convey to them the meaning of an institution like marriage.

Culture Shock

Although the basic types of cultural behavior are universal, in most cases they differ in form from one culture to another. The potential for cultural variation is enormous; the only limits are that a particular way of doing something must get the job done and that it must fit in with the rest of the culture. Take adornment of the body. In the United States we have many ways of changing the natural appearance of the human body. On a fairly simple level, some people do things such as comb their hair a certain way, pierce their ears, or polish their nails. Others have parts of their body designed with tattoos, permanent mutilations of the body following patterns that are unique to our culture. (Tattoos in other cultures are quite different from

[2] George Peter Murdock, "The Common Denominator of Cultures," in Ralph Linton (Ed.), *The Science of Man in the World of Crisis* (New York: Columbia University Press, 1945), p. 123.

ours.) Still others have cosmetic surgery such as nose jobs, hair transplants, and silicone injections to change their appearance. Young people often try to look older—men grow facial hair; women arrange their hair in certain ways—while older people try to look younger by having their faces lifted, wearing trendy clothes, or dyeing their hair.

In other cultures the ways in which the body is adorned are quite different. Some of the better-known examples, such as the extended lower lip of the Ubangi women, or a bone inserted into a pierced nose, seem bizarre to us. But in every culture we find some form of adornment. Among some South American Indian tribes boards are tied firmly against the head of an infant to change the shape of the skull. Among the Dugum Dani, a highland tribe in New Guinea, women and young girls have a finger amputated as part of the funeral service for a close relative so that they will be reminded of that person for the rest of their lives. Such an alteration of the body is not decorative, but it serves a purpose in religious and family life. It is not likely that a woman will forget the individual for whom she sacrificed a finger! The problem for most of us, however, is that we can't readily cast aside our inner feelings and accept foreign customs that are different from what we have been taught is right or beautiful or the best way of doing something. That is why the study of other cultures is so interesting: It teaches us to look at cultural variation without imposing our own values on a way of life that is different from ours. Anthropologists who go to live in a foreign culture leave their own culture behind and enter a situation in which they do not know all the rules of proper behavior. In time, they learn a new culture and are able to describe and analyze it. This is the way cultural anthropologists do research; it can be exciting, but it can also cause problems.

Living and working in a foreign culture can be lonely and frustrating; we must disregard much of our own cultural background in order to get along in the new situation. In

Though the actual designs may be unique, the practice of bodily adornment is a cultural universal.

the process of shedding our cultural preferences, we often experience what is called **culture shock**. This is not limited to anthropologists; if you have ever spent much time outside your own country, or even in a different subculture within your country, you have probably had a taste of it. Culture shock is the feeling of depression and frustration that overcomes people when they first begin to comprehend the tremendous difference between the way of life they are used to and the way of life in the new setting. It happens to all people, not just anthropologists but immigrants, tourists, and anyone else who must get used to a different way of life.

Why does culture shock occur? In the process of being brought up in a society, every person is trained to accept the values of the group and to follow its unwritten rules of behavior. But it does not stop there, for acceptance of a particular way of life is not based simply on fear of punishment or social isolation. As part of the process of learning a culture, we are taught to believe in that culture, to feel that it is the right way and the best way to live. Its values are not merely seen as the ones that fit that particular way of life; they are thought to be the best ones for all people. Any way of doing things that does not follow the same value system is wrong, if not repugnant.

Thus when a person leaves his or her own culture and enters another one, old values come into conflict with new ones. The solutions to the problems that people face every day are not the same from one culture to another, and patterns of behavior, norms, and morals differ as well. This leads to intense frustration. For one thing, when working in a new language it is frustrating not to be able to express oneself completely, both in doing fieldwork and in revealing feelings and emotions. Not being able to keep up with a conversation or eavesdrop on others can be hard to cope with, especially when we are trying to get across the message that we, too, are human, that we are very much like the people we are working with, and that we have something to contribute to their conversa-

tions and their lives. This lack of communication is something we have all experienced in our own society. There are gaps between generations, between the sexes, between occupational groups—between any two groups—and we all know how upsetting it can be not to be able to bridge them.

While working in a village in the Swiss Alps two decades ago, one of the authors was curious about which aspects of their traditional culture the villagers accepted and which they rejected, and why. To find out the effects of modernization on a farming village, he asked all kinds of questions about personal identity, morality, self-evaluation, attitudes toward family and friends, goals

The strange customs of a foreign culture can lead to culture shock, and leave one looking rather silly as well.

and ambitions, and so forth. At the same time, he wanted the villagers to get to know him better, so he tried to engage them in conversation. But somehow, whenever he started talking to them about his personal experiences, the topic always shifted to the key issues in their picture of America. They could not have cared less about his values, attitudes, goals, and so on. What they wanted to know was why Jackie Kennedy had married Aristotle Onassis. Did she really need the money? And did Lyndon Johnson really have John Kennedy killed, and how did he get away with it? Did they still wear guns in the wild West and ride horses and shoot each other in the streets? Did gangsters in Chicago still carry submachine guns and rub each other out in gang wars? The more he protested against this image of his culture, which they had apparently picked up from TV, movies, and popular magazines, the less they wanted to talk to him about America. He was ruining their fun by telling them things they did not want to hear, so they avoided him. During all the time he was there he was never able to portray himself to them, and despite all his attempts to alter his image he remained a mystery to both the adults and young people of the village.

Anthropologists, as well as others who spend a lot of time going back and forth between cultures, frequently talk about the shock of coming back to their own culture and how difficult the readjustment process is. For those of us who have spent time working in rural areas of the developing world, coming back to the United States and walking into a supermarket or mall is frequently a shock. We are overwhelmed by the variety and amount of consumer items and the comparative affluence of the shoppers. Other things—like concern about punctuality and the lack of social amenities when people meet—often jump out as strikingly different to the returning anthropologist or Peace Corps Volunteer. We don't remember such things from before. What has happened? Although we look forward with eager anticipation to returning to our home country, this excitement frequently is tempered when we get back and find ourselves the "odd ones out," victims of culture shock in our own society.

Ethnocentrism

Culture shock can be an excellent lesson in relative values and in understanding human differences. The reason culture shock occurs is that we are not prepared for these differences. Because of the way we are taught our culture, to some degree we are all *ethnocentric*. This term comes from the Greek root *ethnos*, meaning a people or group. Thus it refers to the fact that our outlook or world view is centered on our own way of life. **Ethnocentrism** is the belief that one's own patterns of behavior are the best: the most natural, beautiful, right or important. Therefore other people, to the extent that they live differently, live by standards that are inhuman, irrational, unnatural, or wrong.

Ethnocentrism is the view that one's own culture is better than all others; it is the way all people feel about themselves as compared to outsiders, no matter how liberal and open-minded they might claim to be. People will always find some aspect of another culture distasteful, be it sexual practices, a way of treating friends or relatives, or simply a food that they cannot manage to get down with a smile. This is not something we should be ashamed of, because it is a natural outcome of growing up in any society. However, as anthropologists who study other cultures, it is something we should constantly be aware of, so that when we are tempted to make value judgments about another way of life we can look at the situation objectively and take our bias into account.

Enthnocentrism can be seen in many aspects of culture—myths, folk tales, proverbs, and even language. For example, in many languages, especially those of non-Western societies, the word used to refer to one's own tribe or ethnic group literally means "man-

What is attractive in one culture may be abhorrent to another. Here an Asmat tribesman from Indonesia displays various forms of adornment.

kind" or "human." This implies that members of other groups are less than human. For example, the term *Eskimo*, used to refer to groups that inhabit the Arctic and sub-Arctic regions, is an Indian word used by neighbors of the Eskimos who observed their strange way of life but did not share it. The term means "eaters of raw flesh," and as such is an ethnocentric observation about cultural practices that were normal to one group and repulsive to another. On the other hand, we find one subgroup among the Alaskan natives calling themselves *Inuit*, which means "real people" (they obviously did not think eating raw flesh was anything out of the ordinary). Here, then, is a contrast between one's own group, which is "real," and the rest of the world, which is not so "real." Both terms, *Eskimo* and *Inuit*, are equally ethnocentric—one as an observation about differences, the other as a self-evaluation. However, *Inuit* is now seen as a more appropriate term because of its origin.

Shifting from language to myths and folk tales, we find a good example of ethnocentrism in the creation myth of the Cherokee. According to this story, the Creator made three clay images of a man and baked them in an oven. In his haste to admire his handiwork, he took the first image out of the oven before it was fully baked, and found that it was too pale. He waited a while and then removed a second image; it was just right, a full reddish-brown hue. He was so pleased with his work that he sat there and admired it, completely forgetting about the third image. Finally he smelled it burning, but by the time he could rescue it from the oven it had already been burnt, and it came out completely black!

Food preferences are perhaps the most familiar aspect of ethnocentrism. Every culture has developed preferences for certain kinds of food and drink, and equally strong negative attitudes toward others. It is interesting to note that much of this ethnocentrism is in our heads and not in our tongues, for something can taste delicious until we are told what it is. We have all heard stories about people being fed a meal of snake or horse meat or something equally repugnant in American culture, and commenting on how tasty it was—until they were told what they had just eaten, upon which they turned green and hurriedly asked to be excused from the table.

Certain food preferences seem natural to us. We usually do not recognize that they are natural only because we have grown up with them; they are quite likely to be unnatural to someone from a different culture. In southeast Asia, for example, the majority of adults do not drink milk, as a result of lactase deficiency in the population. To many Americans it is inconceivable that people in other parts of the world do not drink milk, since to us it is a "natural" food. In China dog meat is a delicacy; but the thought of eating a dog is enough to make most Americans feel sick. Yet we can see how this is part of a cultural pattern. Americans keep dogs as pets and tend to think of them as almost human. Therefore we would not dream of eating dog meat. Horses, too, sometimes become pets, and horse meat is also rejected by most Americans, although not because of its taste. You may have eaten it without even knowing it, and you probably would not recognize it if someone didn't tell you what you were eating. On the other hand, we generally do not feel affection for cows or pigs, and we eat their meat without any feeling of remorse. In India a cow receives even better care than a horse or even a dog receives in our country, and the attitude of Indians toward eating beef is similar to our feeling about eating dog meat. On the other hand, in China dogs are not treated as kindly as they are in the United States. Since they are not pets, the attitude of Chinese people toward dogs is similar to our attitude about cows.

We learn to be ethnocentric as part of growing up in our society. One day, while browsing in a bookstore, one of the authors happened upon a geography textbook that had been used in grammar schools in the United States around 1920. It is entitled *Our Wonder World, Volume 1: The World and Its Peoples*. It begins with a discussion of the heavens, the place of the earth in the heavens, the origin of the earth, and the nature of the earth's surface, and the animals that live and have lived here. It then goes into the story of human evolution and the evolution of culture.

Of particular interest to us as cultural anthropologists are the two chapters on human variation and cultural diversity: "The Queer People of the World" and "Other Peoples of the World." In "The Queer People of the World," subtitled "The Black, Brown, Red, and Yellow Races and Their Ways," the reader is taken on a tour of some of the more bizarre customs of other cultures, which are described in highly ethnocentric terms. The chapter begins with a statement about awareness of cultural differences:

To be queer is to be different from what is ordinary and normal. Each one of us decides from his own experience and surroundings what is natural and reasonable. Then we feel that everybody who departs from these ways of ours is a bit queer.

So "queer peoples" are no more strange and odd to us than we are to them. If you visited some of the places and tribes about which you are going to read, you would find yourself such an odd sight that children and grown persons would turn and follow you in the streets, just as you might turn and follow a circus parade if you met one. In the great human family there are many peoples whose ways and habits are unlike ours, and our interest is in these very differences. Some are uncivilized, and do take us back to a kind of life more like that of our ancestors than anything we are acquainted with; others are highly civilized, but their civilization is on another plane from ours.[3]

Despite this statement, the chapter goes on to make some claims that are totally unscientific and are unacceptable in light of our current knowledge about other cultures. In the subsection "Peoples of the Negro or Black Division" we read the following:

First, let us take some of the black peoples, who live mostly in the Sudan, South Africa, and Australasia, but have migrated to many other parts of the world. Some of the most interesting of these black-skinned peoples live still in Africa. The true black people are the Negroes, whose home is in the middle part of Africa. They are the people with the beautiful white teeth. The home of the Bantu race is the great southern section of Africa. They are not so black as the Negroes. Both peoples are brave, intelligent, and able to adapt themselves to new conditions and take on civilization. Smaller tribes are the Pygmies, the Hottentots, and the Bushmen, all far below the Negroes and Bantu in intelligence.[4]

[3] *Our Wonder World* (Chicago: Geo. L. Shuman, 1918), p. 308.
[4] Ibid.

The scene shifts to "The Wild Bushmen," who are described in some detail. It is interesting to note how white middle-class American standards continually creep into this description. How could a schoolchild who read the following description of a non-Western society avoid feeling superior?

> Almost every people has passed through a hunting stage in its development. The Bushmen stayed at that stage. They represent the typical hunters of the world. Free of all property, never settled in one place, never held by any industries or agricultural ties, they range the hunting grounds of Africa. Their arrows are tipped with wood, bone, or stone. They need no home, for they can make one in a few hours out of brushwood. Their usual garb is a robe of sheepskin thrown over the body and fastened with a sharp thong. The Bushman needs no fireplace or cooking utensils, for his only way of preparing food is to throw the raw flesh on the fire or on hot stones for roasting.[5]

Compare this description of !Kung San[6] society with that written by the anthropologist Richard B. Lee.[7] After a long study of the way San relate to their environment, Lee concluded that they were the original "leisure class." He estimated that because of the way they obtained food from their environment, they could survive quite well, with a balanced diet and high caloric intake, on only a few hours of work each day. The rest of their time they could devote to leisure without fear of starving. Given the harshness of their desert surroundings, it is not likely that the extra labor required to acquire and maintain such trappings of civilization as industry and agriculture would be worth the effort. Yet as we read the old textbook account of San culture we come away with a very different feeling. The reason is clear: It is full of ethnocentric statements; values are injected and comparisons are made on a purely subjective basis. Strange practices are portrayed not as different but as inferior.

But this story does not end here. A few pages later we read about the "Fuzzy-Haired Papuans":

> You have all heard of cannibals, that is, savages who eat human beings. You will be surprised to hear that these Papuans, who can be so polite to one another, were, until within recent years, given to this dreadful habit of cannibalism. The idea of eating others was that when a man ate another man he acquired the victim's qualities, physical strength, courage, cleverness, or cunning. Since the coming of the missionaries to the islands the Fijians have largely become Christians, and have given up cannibalism and almost all their other barbaric customs.[8]

There is no attempt to describe other ways of life in a total cultural context. All the book does is show how "inferior" they are to our "civilized" customs. The other side of the coin is never presented so that children could learn that values are relative. There is a description of the San, who "eat every creeping, running, and flying thing they can lay their hands on, including snakes and slugs." But nowhere is it mentioned how utterly repulsive it might seem to a San who shares all his food with his relatives and friends and other members of his society to see a rich yuppie paying astonishing prices for a nouvelle cuisine dinner, while other members of his society went to bed hungry. We are ethnocentric because we are not taught to question our own way of life, only to judge other practices against ours.

Here we must stop to make a very important point. We have been describing anthropology in such a way that the reader might

---

[5] Ibid., p. 309

[6] Until recently these hunting and gathering peoples were referred to as Bushmen, a term still commonly found in anthropological books. Today, however, many feel the term is inappropriate because of its sexist and racist overtones. Many contemporary researchers prefer to call them the San, the term that they use for themselves.

[7] Richard B. Lee and Irven De Vore, *Man the Hunter* (Chicago: Aldine-Atherton, 1968).

[8] *Our Wonder World*, p. 315.

conclude that by studying it he or she can avoid being ethnocentric. This is not true. Modern anthropology is moving away from ethnocentrism and is advocating acceptance of diverse cultural practices without culture-bound judgments. However, anthropologists, as human beings raised in a cultural setting, are and always will be ethnocentric. We can write whole books about how one must accept other ways as valid, but that does not mean that we can accept and practice them in our own lives. Anthropologists can learn to be more tolerant through long hours of training and fieldwork, but they will always be culture-bound to some extent. We can never completely get inside someone else's skin and live our lives according to the rules of their culture. Thus we cannot guarantee that by the time you finish this book you will no longer be ethnocentric, any more than the authors of this book can honestly say that they themselves have shed all the narrow-mindedness that was a part of their own upbringing. Ethnocentrism is not something human beings can will away—it constantly creeps back, as the following story illustrates.

A Colombian anthropologist was conducting field research among the Guajiro Indians in the northern part of her country, and in the course of her work she learned that a particular Indian group there practiced the custom known as bride price. According to this tradition, when a man took a woman as his wife, he or his family was obliged to offer a payment (in cattle, other goods, money, or a combination of them all) to the bride's family. Although this is a fairly common practice in many non-Western societies (and elements of it can be seen in our own marriage customs, if you look closely), the anthropologist was upset by it because she felt that it challenged the dignity of a woman to be bought and sold like any other possession. It never occurred to her that while it might rob a woman of her dignity in Western society, it could have the opposite effect in the culture she was studying. Allowing her own values to come through, she asked one recent bride if it didn't bother her to be

In parts of India where marriages are arranged, this young Hindu Indian bride would not meet her husband until the ceremony actually took place.

purchased like a cow. The woman replied by asking the anthropologist how much her husband had paid for her when they were married. Of course, the anthropologist explained that her husband had not paid anything, that people did not do such things in her society. "Oh, what a horrible thing," replied the Indian woman. "Your husband didn't even give a single cow for you? You must not be worth anything."[9]

Cultural Relativism

The widespread reaction against ethnocentrism in anthropology is fairly recent. In the

---

[9] George M. Foster, *Traditional Societies and Technological Change*, 2nd ed. (New York: Harper & Row, 1973), p. 87.

Franz Boas (1858–1942)

Franz Boas received his early training in mathematics and physics, but became interested in anthropology after a trip to Baffinland, in the Northwest Territories of Canada. In 1899 Boas became professor of anthropology at Columbia University, where he remained throughout his career. He was a leading figure in the attack against the theory of cultural evolution prominent in the nineteenth century. Most evolutionary scales ranked non-Western societies lower than Europeans because they did not have a pattern of monogamous marriage, a fully developed concept of private property, or a complex bureaucratic system. Instead, Boas argued strongly for a position of cultural relativism, meaning that one culture may not be judged or ranked according to the standards of another.

nineteenth century anthropology, like the other social sciences, was highly ethnocentric. The theory of Charles Darwin, which seemed harmless as long as it was applied to plants and animals, became a dangerous tool in the hands of social scientists who applied it to cultural differences among human populations. Of course, Darwin himself never meant his theory to be applied to social change—he is very clear on this point—but other scholars took some of the principles on which he based his theory and used them to explain the course of social evolution, usually without supporting their claims with facts. It was this **social Darwinism**, which really was not Darwin's theory at all, that twentieth-century anthropologists reacted against so strongly.

When Darwin's theory was applied to social evolution, the result was a number of ethnocentric doctrines, all of which were based on the belief that Western society was superior to that of the so-called primitives who were being studied by anthropologists and some sociologists. This view of evolution led to a racist theory that placed non-Western, nonwhite societies on a lower scale of cultural and physical development simply because they did not have the technological and military capacities of Western countries. It was felt that if we Westerners could subdue other societies through military strength, then the rest of our culture—our political system, our religious beliefs, our moral code—must also be superior. This in turn led to the belief that if we compared all societies to our own, we could set up a scale on which we could rank them; those most like ours were higher up the ladder, while those least like ours were at the bottom.

This view of social evolution tended to justify European colonialism and domination of non-Western countries. It was felt, for example, that if the forces of evolution were acting on whole societies, eliminating those that were unfit, the best thing to do was to let nature take its course. Colonizing a group of people was a way of helping them survive. Of course, the need to make them more like Westerners (in dress, language, religion, and the like) was hardly questioned. Before Franz Boas, few people challenged this theory. No one pointed out that there is a clear difference between societies and organisms, and that the mechanisms of change in one are not the same as those acting on the other. No one mentioned that societies struggle for survival in a completely different context than organisms do (i.e., in a physical battle rather than through adaptation). It was rarely recognized that social Darwinism was designed to maintain the status quo, which happened to be the domination of the world by the Western nations. Also, and perhaps most important to Boas, the racist aspects of this theory were not challenged.

Nineteenth-century theories of social evolution were racist because they were based on the assumed superiority of the Western world, which meant the white world; non-Western, nonwhite societies occupied the lower levels of the evolutionary sequence. As a newly developing science, anthropology had inherited the problem of classifying the peoples of the world, and it had to find a way to document obvious racial differences in a scientific manner. Of course, the political and economic situation in America had a strong impact on the directions that anthropologists took in their research and reporting. Despite the fact that the slaves had been freed and given equal rights in law after the Civil War (or perhaps because of that fact), many Americans sought scientific verifications of their racial prejudices. Anthropology, along with all other branches of science in the nineteenth century, undertook to soothe the troubled conscience of the American middle class by offering an acceptable proof of the inferiority of the nonwhite races.[10]

This was the background when Boas en-

tered the scene. Perhaps he had an advantage in his opposition to the previous half-century of American anthropology in that he was German by birth and had trained in German universities. Without the heritage of American culture and American history to influence his ideas and penetrate his values, he was able to reject the attempts that had been made to show a correlation between race and level of cultural evolution—that is, the superiority of Western, white cultures.[11] He was particularly vexed by the assumption that nonwhites were less intelligent, as the following passage indicates:

> It has often been claimed that the very primitiveness of human handiwork of early times proves organic mental inferiority. This argument is certainly not tenable, for we find in modern times isolated tribes living in a way that may very well be paralleled with early conditions. A comparison of the psychic life of these groups does not justify the belief that their industrial backwardness is due to a difference in the types of organism, for we find numbers of closely related races on the most diverse levels of cultural status. . . . It is safe to say that the results of the extensive materials amassed during the last fifty years do not justify the assumption of any close relation between biological types and form of culture.[12]

In his opposition to the enthnocentrism of nineteenth-century anthropology, Boas arrived at a position that is best described as **cultural relativism**. By this he meant that the anthropologist must remain neutral when describing and comparing other cultures, and make no judgments about the merits of one culture over another. For Boas, cultural relativism was an ethical position in which all cultures were taken as equal, each being a separate unit with its own integrity that should not be compared to our own culture

[10] For more detailed analysis, see the excellent summary of nineteenth-century scientific attitudes on the question of race in John S. Haller, *Outcasts from Evolution* (Urbana: University of Illinois Press, 1971).

[11] Boas was not immune to problems caused by bigotry and prejudice. As a German Jew, he had suffered as a result of anti-Semitism, which in part prompted him to emigrate to the United States.

[12] Franz Boas, *Race, Language and Culture* (New York: Free Press, 1966), pp. 249–250.

in terms of how it measures up to our standards. This position dominated anthropology in the early 1900s, and has been an important aspect of the field ever since.

Cultural relativism was a logical outcome of Boas's work, in which he showed that the history of each group was distinct. Thus whatever a culture is like today, it became that way as a result of its own development, and therefore cannot be ranked against another culture, with a different history. All cultures have changed over time, some more than others in certain areas, and some in response to pressures that others did not face. The point for Boas was that, because each culture has its own history, cultures cannot be compared on a scale of excellence in which the ranks are set according to the standards of one particular group. There could not be a model toward which all change had been directed in the past, for change had proceeded in many different directions at the same time.

Boas's position, which he passed on to his students, involves an attempt both to maintain neutrality in analyzing cultural differences and, at the same time, to be constantly aware of one's own cultural biases. If we are to make judgments about another culture, they should be based not on our own background but on our experience in that culture. In short, the anthropologist should put everything else out of his or her mind when describing another culture. One of Boas's students, Margaret Mead, tells how she came to this conclusion in the 1920s, during her first field trip to Samoa. Her autobiography, *Blackberry Winter*, from which the following passage is taken, offers the reader many insights into the nature of perhaps the most famous anthropologist of our time.

> Field work is a very difficult thing to do. To do it well, one has to sweep one's mind clear of every presupposition, even those about other cultures in the same part of the world in which one is working. Ideally, even the appearance of a house should come to one as a surprise that there are houses and that they are square or round or oval, that they do or do not have

walls, that they let in the sun or keep out the wind or rain, that people do or do not cook or eat in a dwelling house. In the field one can take nothing for granted. For as soon as one does, one cannot see what is before one's eyes as fresh and distinctive, and when one treats what is new merely as a variant of something already known, this may lead one far astray. Seeing a house as bigger or smaller, grander or meaner, more or less watertight than some other kind of house one already knows about cuts one off from discovering what this house is in the minds of those who live in it. Later, when one has come to know the new culture, everything has to be reassimilated into what is already known about other peoples living in that area, into our knowledge about primitive peoples, and into our knowledge about all human beings, so far. But the point of going to the field at all is to extend further what is already known, and so there is little value merely in identifying new versions of the familiar, when we might, instead, find something wholly new. But to clear one's mind of presuppositions is a very hard thing to do.[13]

Every culture proposes solutions to the problems people face. If the anthropologist is to look at these solutions—for example, to look at a house as a solution to the problem of shelter—he or she must consider it from the point of view of the members of the culture under study. If a solution seems impractical to us because we know a different solution, we must not overlook the fact that within its cultural context it may be very practical indeed. For example, Americans tend to be critical of societies that have high birth rates yet suffer from periodic famine and high death rates because of starvation or malnutrition. It seems "irrational" to us to have more children when there is not enough food for those who have already been born. We make a value judgment based on our view of the situation. We do not look at the context in which the people themselves make decisions. But if we look deeper, we will find that having large families is a logical survival

---

[13] Margaret Mead, *Blackberry Winter, My Earlier Years* (New York: Simon & Shuster, 1972), pp. 143–144.

Two young mothers—one living in Guatemala and the other in the United States—show how different cultures often arrive at similar solutions to the same problem.

strategy. In many parts of the developing world almost half of the children born within a given year are likely to die before they reach age 5. Although most families may not sit down and "rationally" or systematically plan out coping devices, experience has taught them that the chances of an infant's reaching adulthood are not very good—not just because of the danger of starvation but also because of the high rate of disease and the poor medical facilities available to them. Therefore if they wish to have a certain number of children survive to adulthood (perhaps enough to support them in their old age), then they need to have more than that number of infants.

Or take the example of a young man who works as a day laborer. He does not work every day, but only a few days a month, and he earns only as much as he has to in order to support his family at a minimal level. We might tend to think that he is lazy, has no ambition, and will never get ahead. Within our cultural context that might be an accurate judgment. But if we look more closely at the context in which the laborer makes his decisions, we may find that in his society it is customary for a man to open up his house to his relatives and never refuse them hospitality. If he lives at a subsistence level, he has nothing left over to offer his relatives, and they will probably leave him alone. However, if he earns more than he needs to survive and to feed his own family, his house is likely to be invaded by relatives who have a rightful claim to his hospitality. He knows this, and his decision to work only as much as he has to is very rational. He realizes that if he worked any more he would not be working for himself and that he would not be able to get ahead, and therefore he values his leisure according to what he knows about his own culture. To suggest that he is lazy would be to judge a member of another society by our society's standards.

Even one's view of the physical world is affected by culture. Earlier it was noted that languages do not contain the same number of basic words for colors. We might find a language in which blue and green and red were all called by one term. This may be hard for us to comprehend, but that does not make it less valid as a solution to the problem of describing the physical world. To turn the tables slightly, in many societies there are several words used to refer to relatives that we lump together under one term in the English language. We use the word *uncle* to describe several different kinds of relatives: father's brother, mother's brother, father's sister's husband, and mother's sister's husband, as well as great-uncles and sometimes even people who are not uncles in any biological sense but are close to us in a social sense. Yet in many societies there are distinct terms for each of these different types of uncle. If we find these societies strange because they call red and green and blue by the same term, think of how strange we must

come across to them when we can't even seem to tell the difference between our mother's brother and our father's brother, or between an uncle by birth and an uncle by marriage. How ignorant we must appear to be of the biological basis of reproduction!

Relative Values

One of the most fruitful discussions of cultural relativism is in the area of values and morals. This is an interesting topic because it is the strongest factor in culture shock, yet is the most ethnocentric area of our behavior. We tend to be much more defensive about our moral behavior than about most other aspects of our culture, perhaps because it is so strongly ingrained in us from early childhood. One's morals and values are based on the cultural and physical environment in which one grows up, and cannot be separated from it. Yet when anthropologists go into the field they are confronted with a totally new value system that most likely conflicts with their own in many ways. We may find many values totally unacceptable—and this is valid on a personal level—yet as anthropologists we cannot let this enter into our work. Rather, we must describe and analyze values in terms of how they fit into the culture of which they are a part. We may not approve of certain practices, and certainly will not engage in them ourselves, but if we are to translate the culture we are studying, then we must present its practices objectively, so that the reader can understand what they mean to the people of that culture, regardless of what they mean to the anthropologist.

Sexual practices that do not conform to our moral standards have often been the basis for labeling non-Western societies "primitive" or "barbaric." In the nineteenth century the American anthropologist Lewis Henry Morgan claimed that all of human social development pointed toward monogamy as the most perfect form of marriage. The closer to monogamy a society's marriage pattern was, the higher up the ladder of evolution it was. Conversely, the farther removed from monogamy a society's customs were, the more primitive it was. This view failed to take into account the fact that marriage practices and sexual behavior are tied in with the rest of the culture, and what may make sense in one context might not make sense somewhere else. Consider a society in which there is no advanced medical science and in which beliefs about how a child is conceived differ somewhat from our own. Whereas in our society monogamy may be necessary in order to determine the paternity of a child, in other societies this might not be the case. If it were thought that sperm contribute to a child's makeup throughout the pregnancy, rather than simply at the moment of conception (not an illogical belief, even though it is scientifically incorrect), then it might be proper for the mother to have intercourse with as many different men as possible during her pregnancy. In this way she could ensure that her child would have the best traits of all her lovers. In fact, not to do so might be considered immoral, in that she would be depriving a helpless child of its rights.

Suppose, instead, that it is believed that only the mother contributes to the makeup of the child. After all, the baby is born of the mother, not the father. In this case there would be a closer link between the mother and the infant than between the father and his child. To carry this argument further, because the father is unrelated to either the mother or the infant by birth, he would be even more distant from the child than the

Taste is a purely cultural matter, and, as you can see from the expression on several faces, beauty is truly in the eye of the beholder.

mother's brother, who is a blood relative of the mother, having been born of the same woman. Such a kinship system contradicts Western notions about the role of the father in the family, yet in a different setting it makes sense.

As you can tell from these examples, morality is not always as clear-cut as it might seem. While we can be firmly convinced of the validity of our own moral standards, we must recognize that they fit only one way of life. The lesson of cultural relativism is that we must always be on guard against applying our values and moral standards to other ways of doing things. There can be no absolute standards. Anything that is possible might be acceptable in a certain cultural context. Every society has a system of morals and values, even if they vary greatly from one to another. We may make judgments about whether that system is effective in any one society, but we may not make judgments about the content of such a system. For example, we might ask whether cultural relativism can be used to justify a practice such as cannibalism. We can explain it on the basis of conditions that affect the group. We can analyze it and find out whether it is effective and how it fits in with related practices. We can compare it to other practices in our societies, as long as we avoid judging one by the standards of another. As anthropologists it is our place to explain why certain cultural practices occur among a given group and others do not. Any justification we offer is based on our own private opinions, which are in part shaped by our own cultural background. This does not mean that if we feel that something is wrong we are not obliged to say so. We cannot sit back in our chairs and explain the extermination of the Jews in Hitler's Germany or the racism in the United States, and then claim that we have fulfilled our responsibility. We must speak out against injustice whenever and wherever we find it. But we must distinguish between our duty as objective observers of our cultures and our duty as human beings. Cultural relativism is a way of attaining objectivity. It is not a stopping point but a starting point.

Studying Culture

Anthropologists have often argued that culture is hard to study. To begin with, most of us simply are not used to analyzing what we do. "I just know what to do" or "It just comes naturally, without thinking" are responses we often get when we ask people why they do what they do. That's true because culture is learned from a very early age, in a number of contexts, and is often picked up in subtle ways. We are simply unaware of why we behave the way we do. How frequently have we become frustrated with someone who persists in asking us why something is done a certain way when all we can reply is "Because that's the way it's done!"

However, not all aspects of culture are difficult to explain. Most of you could expound with considerable ease and in great detail on the courtship patterns of North Americans between the ages of 17 and 23 so that someone from another culture could quite easily grasp the essential do's and don'ts. When in doubt we can rely on popular sages such as Ann Landers, Dr. Ruth, or Miss Manners, whose syndicated columns are designed to help us wade through sticky issues in a culturally appropriate fashion.

Dispensing culturally appropriate advice is a practice found in many parts of the world. In eastern and southern Africa a syndicated columnist writing under the byline of "Tell me, Josephine" assists her readers in a fashion not unlike our own "Dear Abby." In so doing, she bridges the rural-urban gap, as well as a variety of interethnic differences, an example of which appears below:

Q. My uncle who is a charcoal-burner was taken to Native Court and told to pay 15 pounds for damaging two virgins. He has written to me that according to our custom I must get money for him, and send it quickly to the Northern Province or he will go to prison. This will take all my savings which I had planned to use for marriage in two years. So must I send him the money?

A. If you wish to keep tribal custom, then you are obliged to help your uncle. If you do not care about tribal custom any more and do not intend to visit your family in the rural areas again, then no one can make you pay. Only you can decide. I presume that according to the same custom you will inherit your uncle's property when he dies.[14]

Still, studying culture can present problems for a number of reasons. First, there is the difficulty of maintaining objectivity—something we have already discussed. The student of culture must strive not to let her or his own personal biases color the description of the culture. Social scientists must work hard at being objective; it does not come easily or naturally.

Second, there is the difference between "ideal" and "real" behavior. At times *both* perspectives are necessary for really understanding a culture. As a young neophyte in anthropology, and as a participant in a field school in cultural anthropology, one of the authors was sent off to Mexico to study a peasant village. One of his exercises was to learn how individuals greeted each other in the villages where he worked. He interviewed women and men of different ages and essentially got the same story. When people greeted each other they would stand face to face, engage in a very soft double handshake, and make quiet, polite inquiries about the health of family members. It was expected that both parties would bow their heads a bit during this ritual. In discussing the subject people were consistent and pretty emphatic, so the anthropologist thought he understood the system. Then he began observing what *actually* took place when members of the community greeted each other. Almost always they shook hands, but rarely was it the quiet, dignified greeting that he had been led to expect. Where was the deference and the bowing of heads? They were nowhere to

be seen. Had he been lied to? He asked some of the people who had explained the "cultural rule" that he had yet to see verified. Sure, they said, what they had explained to him was *how it should be done*, and in some instances still was. More often, however, men would greet each other in the much more casual form he had observed. The exercise was a pretty good lesson in the difference between "real" and "ideal" culture. Both aspects are important to know if one wishes to understand a culture, but so is the distinction between them.

Perhaps an example closer to home will assist us in appreciating why the dichotomy between the "real" and the "ideal" complicates studying culture. Say you are explaining local driving habits to someone from another country who is staying with you. Among other things, you might suggest that the person pick up a driver's manual that details most of the rules necessary for driving in your state. This manual is actually a series of cultural rules that have been formalized and enacted into state law. Your guest notes that the speed limit for most roads outside of city limits is 55 miles per hour. How can that be, she asks, when so many people seem to go so much faster than that? She then asks whether similar guidelines for speed limits in urban areas can be ignored. How do you explain the difference between speeding in a congested city and speeding on a highway?

Studying culture can be difficult in other respects as well. Obviously, since we all have grown up in the same culture, there is quite a large body of common knowledge with which we're all familiar. However, no single individual knows everything about his or her culture. Depending on such factors as age, sex, and social position, each of us is privy to cultural information not always shared by others. It has been said that culture is a composite. To really understand a culture, then, it is important to visit with enough different people from various walks of life so that one can fit all the pieces of the cultural puzzle together.

[14] William Mangin, "Introduction," in W. Mangin, ed., *Peasants in Cities: Readings in the Anthropology of Urbanization* (Boston: Houghton Mifflin Company, 1970), p. xvi.

Summary

As anthropologists use the term, *culture* is the way of life shared by a group of people. It is what makes people similar to one another and unites them as a group, overcoming individual differences in personality. Culture is *acquired* behavior; it is learned rather than inherited genetically.

Culture is passed on from one generation to the next through the process known as *socialization*. Although the methods of teaching children the appropriate behavior patterns may vary from one society to another, all societies engage in some form of child training. We assume that early childhood experiences will have a lasting effect on an individual, and insofar as the same basic experiences are shared by most children in a society, a general personality pattern will be shared among most adults in that society.

Not too long ago anthropologists believed that culture was a uniquely human phenomenon, but as more was learned about the behavior of other primates, this notion was discarded. First we found that some primates use tools in their natural setting. Then it was discovered that they even manufacture the tools they use. More recently we have witnessed primates inventing new patterns of behavior (such as washing sweet potatoes in seawater) and then transmitting that behavior to others. Attempts to teach chimpanzees sign language have shown us that human beings are not the only animals capable of at least some level of language, or even conceptual thought. In other words, we have recognized that culture as a dividing line between the human species and other animals is not as clear-cut as we used to believe.

One way of understanding what it is that sets us apart from other animals is to look at the sheer amount of cultural behavior in human beings as opposed to other animals. Also, if we look at the kinds of behavior that are found in all societies, or what we refer to as *cultural universals*, we recognize many things that are not found in the behavior of any other species.

Our culture establishes a pattern of life for us that is very difficult to live without. When we travel to a foreign country and confront another way of life, we often become very uncomfortable. Our values no longer fit the situation, our expectations usually prove to be wrong, and it is difficult for us to fit in with other people and behave as they do. This creates a feeling of *culture shock*, something that is not limited to anthropologists who conduct fieldwork in another culture, but can be experienced by anyone.

In the process of learning our culture we also are taught to believe that our way of life is correct, that it is good, that it is indeed the best possible way to live. This attitude is known as *ethnocentrism*, a feeling of cultural superiority. It is found in our reactions to foreign customs, in our myths and proverbs, even in our dietary preferences. And ethnocentrism is perpetuated (not always consciously) through our educational system, which tends to put down other people's ways of doing things as bizarre or inferior.

Through our training in anthropology and the study of other customs, we attempt to overcome as much of our ethnocentrism as possible. We try to become more objective about cultural differences, to be tolerant of other people. This attitude is known as *cultural relativism*, and is based on the idea that all values are relative and that there are no absolute standards that are valid in all cultural settings. Before an anthropologist can be objective about another people's way of life, it is essential that he or she attain a degree of cultural relativism and learn to accept foreign customs for their own sake, rather than comparing them to their Western counterparts.

Studying culture is not an easy task. Normally we are not used to dissecting and analyzing our cultural patterns. We tend to do many things without thinking about why we act in specific ways. In looking at culture we must divorce ourselves from our preconceived notions about why people might act in the manner they do. We need to be able to distinguish between "ideal" and "real" modes of behavior. Finally, we must remember that culture is a composite. No two individuals have exactly the same perception of how their culture operates.

Glossary

cultural relativism The idea that every anthropologist must be strictly neutral in describing and comparing other cultures, and should avoid judgments concerning the merits of one culture over another.

cultural universals The basic solutions to the problems of living that are found in one form or another in all human cultures.

culture A way of life that is common to a group of people, including a collection of beliefs and attitudes, shared understandings, and patterns of behavior that allow those people to live together in relative harmony, but set them apart from other peoples.

culture shock The trauma experienced by people who enter a new cultural setting; the depression and frustration resulting from the confrontation of a way of life very different from one's own culture.

ethnocentrism The belief that one's own patterns of behavior are preferable to those of all other cultures. When used as a standard to judge outsiders, it becomes an attitude that one's own cultural patterns are correct and natural, while different patterns are wrong and unnatural.

social Darwinism A theoretical orientation prevalent in the nineteenth century, based on the erroneous application of Darwinian principles to social and cultural evolution.

socialization The process of learning to be a member of society, usually said of children learning the appropriate rules of behavior through interaction with other members of their society.

Questions for Discussion

1. In American society there are many smaller groups, which we refer to as *subcultures* (for example, black subculture, student subculture, drug subculture). What subcultures are present in your community? Which of these do you belong to? What type of values, attitudes, and beliefs are shared by the members of these groups, and how are they different from the general pattern in American society?

2. What are some common child-rearing practices found in American culture? How might you perceive their relationship to the adult personality type?

3. How does the United States government use ethnocentrism in its propaganda about other countries? How do these attitudes change according to official policy (for instance, Germany and Japan in the 1940s as compared to today)? What changes have you seen in recent years regarding such countries as China, Russia, and Iran?

4. There are changes in values and attitudes in every culture from one generation to the next.

How have our prejudices changed in recent years, and how can you measure this change in American society (for example, in the 1950s men were expected to be clean-shaven and wear their hair short, whereas in the 1980s even important public figures such as congressmen have beards and long hair)? What happened between those three decades? What other changes can you predict for the near future?

Suggestions for Additional Reading

MARSTON BATES, *Gluttons and Libertines: Human Problems of Being Natural* (New York: Vintage, 1967). A humorous study of eating and sexual practices in cross-cultural perspective, particularly valuable in light of the discussion in this chapter of relative values and ethnocentrism regarding foods and morals.

MICHAEL BRAKE, *Comparative Youth Culture* (London: Routledge & Kegan Paul, 1985). A comparative study of youth subcultures in Britain, Canada, and the United States with emphasis on minority youth and girls.

FRANZ BOAS, *Race, Language and Culture* (New York: Free Press, 1940). A collection of essays by the leading figure in the movement toward cultural relativism. The author argues that there is no causal relationship between race, language, and culture; that is, that nonwhite cultures are not inferior or inherently different.

WILLIAM M. KEPHART, *Extraordinary Groups*, 3rd ed. (New York: St. Martin's Press, 1987). A description of different American subcultures; included are chapters on the Old Order Amish, the Oneida Community, the Father Divine Movement, the Gypsies, the Shakers, the Mormons, and the Modern Communes.

ALFRED L. KROEBER and CLYDE KLUCKHOHN, *Culture: A Critical Review of Concepts and Definitions* (Papers of the Peabody Museum of American Archaeology and Ethnology, Harvard University, vol. 47, 1952). A collection of definitions of culture, with comments on their utility for anthropology.

ROBERT A. LEVINE and DONALD T. CAMPBELL, *Ethnocentrism: Theories of Conflict, Ethnic Attitudes and Group Behavior* (New York: John Wiley, 1972). A study of the causes and problems of ethnocentrism.

MARGARET MEAD, *Coming of Age in Samoa* (New York: William Morrow, 1928). A classical anthropological study comparing the process of growing up among Samoan and American adolescent girls.

HOWARD J. WIARDA, *Ethnocentrism in Foreign Policy* (Washington, D.C.: American Enterprise Institute for Public Policy Research, 1985). The author makes the compelling argument that at the root of U. S. problems with its foreign policy in the Third World is American ethnocentrism, which is perpetuated in the U.S. educational system, particularly through social science literature on development.

LESLIE A. WHITE, WITH BETH DILLINGHAM, *The Concept of Culture* (Minneapolis: Burgess, 1973). A short discussion of the anthropological view of culture by the leading cultural evolutionist in modern anthropology.

Shakespeare in the Bush

LAURA BOHANNAN

In the article that follows, Laura Bohannan describes her difficulty in trying to tell the Tiv the story of Hamlet. The problem involves different concepts of kinship and marriage and the family. She was telling her version of the story, based on her own cultural interpretation of what was the proper behavior for each of the characters. But her audience had different views on the subject, which led to an interesting reinterpretation of the story.

Just before I left Oxford for the Tiv in West Africa, conversation turned to the season at Stratford. "You Americans," said a friend, "often have difficulty with Shakespeare. He was, after all, a very English poet, and one can easily misinterpret the universal by misunderstanding the particular."

I protested that human nature is pretty much the same the whole world over; at least the general plot and motivation of the greater tragedies would always be clear—everywhere—although some details of custom might have to be explained and difficulties of translation might produce other slight changes. To end an argument we could not conclude, my friend gave me a copy of *Hamlet* to study in the African bush; it would, he hoped, lift my mind above its primitive surroundings, and possibly I might, by prolonged meditation, achieve the grace of correct interpretation.

It was my second field trip to the African tribe, and I thought myself ready to live in one of its remote sections—an area difficult to cross even on foot. I eventually settled on the hillock of a very knowledgeable old man, the head of a homestead of some hundred and forty people, all of whom were either his close relatives, or their wives and children. Like the other elders of the vicinity, the old man spent most of his time performing ceremonies seldom seen these days in the more accessible parts of the tribe. I was delighted. Soon there would be three months of enforced isolation and leisure, between the harvest that takes place just before the rising of the swamps and the clearing of new farms when the water goes down. Then, I thought, they would have even more time to perform ceremonies and explain them to me.

Reprinted from *Natural History*, 75(1966), by permission of the author.

I was quite mistaken. Most of the ceremonies demanded the presence of elders from several homesteads. As the swamps rose, the old men found it too difficult to walk from one homestead to the next, and the ceremonies gradually ceased. As the swamps rose even higher, all activities but one came to an end. The women brewed beer from maize and millet. Men, women, and children sat on their hillocks and drank it.

People began to drink at dawn. By midmorning the whole homestead was singing, dancing, and drumming. When it rained, people had to sit inside their huts; there they drank and sang or they drank and told stories. In any case, by noon or before, I either had to join the party or retire to my own hut and my books. "One does not discuss serious matters when there is beer. Come, drink with us." Since I lacked their capacity for the thick native beer, I spent more and more time with *Hamlet*. Before the end of the second month, grace descended on me. I was quite sure that *Hamlet* had only one possible interpretation, and that one universally obvious.

Early every morning, in the hope of having some serious talk before the beer party, I used to call on the old man at his reception hut—a circle of posts supporting a thatched roof above a low mud wall to keep out wind and rain. One day I crawled through the low doorway and found most of the men of the homestead sitting huddled in their ragged cloths on stools, low plank beds, and reclining chairs, warming themselves against the chill of the rain around a smoky fire. In the center were three pots of beer. The party had started.

The old man greeted me cordially. "Sit down and drink." I accepted a large calabash full of beer, poured some into a small drinking gourd and tossed it down. Then I poured some more into the same gourd for the man second in seniority to my host before I handed my calabash over to a young man for further distribution. Important people shouldn't ladle beer themselves.

"It is better like this," the old man said, looking at me approvingly and plucking at the thatch that had caught in my hair. "You should sit and drink with us more often. Your servants tell me that when you are not with us, you sit inside your hut looking at a paper."

The old man was acquainted with four kinds of "papers": tax receipts, bride price receipts, court fee receipts, and letters. The messenger who brought him letters from the chief used them mainly as a badge of office, for he always knew what was in them and told the old man. Personal letters for the few who had relatives in the government or mission stations were kept until someone went to a large market where there was a letter writer and reader. Since my arrival, letters were brought to me to be read. A few men also brought me bride price receipts, privately, with requests to change the figures to a higher sum. I found moral arguments were of no avail, since in-laws are fair game, and the technical hazards of forgery difficult to explain to an illiterate people. I did not wish them to think me silly enough to look at any such papers for days on end, and I hastily explained that my "paper" was one of the "things of long ago" of my country.

"Ah," said the old man. "Tell us."

I protested that I was not a storyteller. Storytelling is a skilled art among them; their standards are high, and the audiences critical—and vocal in their criticism. I protested in vain. This morning they wanted to hear a story while they drank. They threatened to tell me no more stories until I told them one of mine. Finally, the old man promised that no one would criticize my style "for we know you are struggling with our language." "But," put in one of the elders, "you must explain what we do not understand, as we do when we tell you our stories." Realizing that here was my chance to prove *Hamlet* universally intelligible, I agreed.

The old man handed me some more beer to help me on with my storytelling. Men filled their long wooden pipes and knocked coals from the fire to place in the pipe bowls; then, puffing contentedly, they sat back to listen. I began in the proper style, "Not yesterday, not yesterday, but long ago, a thing occurred. One night three men were keeping watch outside the homestead of the great chief, when suddenly they saw the former chief approach them."

Why was he no longer their chief?

"He was dead," I explained. "That is why they were troubled and afraid when they saw him."

"Impossible," began one of the elders, handing his pipe on to his neighbor, who interrupted. "Of course it wasn't the dead chief. It was an omen sent by a witch. Go on."

Slightly shaken, I continued. "One of these three was a man who knew things"—the closest translation for scholar, but unfortunately it also meant witch. The second elder looked triumphantly at the first. "So he spoke to the dead chief saying, 'Tell us what we must do so you may rest in your grave,' but the dead chief did not answer. He vanished, and they could see him no more. Then the man who knew things—his name was Horatio—said this event was the affair of the dead chief's son, Hamlet."

There was a general shaking of heads round the circle. "Had the dead chief no living brothers? Or was this son the chief?"

"No," I replied. "That is, he had one living brother who became the chief when the elder brother died."

The old man muttered: such omens were matters for chiefs and elders, not for youngsters; no good could come of going behind a chief's back; clearly Horatio was not a man who knew things.

"Yes, he was," I insisted, shooing a chicken away from my beer. "In our country the son is next to the father. The dead chief's younger brother had become the great chief. He had also married his elder brother's widow only a month after the funeral."

"He did well," the old man beamed and announced to the others, "I told you that if we knew more about Europeans, we would find they really were very like us. In our country also," he added to me, "the younger brother marries the elder brother's widow and becomes the father of his children. Now, if your uncle, who married your widowed mother, is your father's full brother, then he will be a real father to you. Did Hamlet's father and uncle have one mother?"

His question barely penetrated my mind; I was too upset and thrown too far off balance by having one of the most important elements of *Hamlet* knocked straight out of the picture. Rather uncertainly I said that I thought they had the same mother, but I wasn't sure—the story didn't say. The old man told me severely that these genealogical details made all the difference and that when I got home I must ask the elders about it. He shouted out the door to one of his younger wives to bring his goatskin bag.

Determined to save what I could of the mother

motif, I took a deep breath and began again. "The son Hamlet was very sad because his mother had married again so quickly. There was no need for her to do so, and it was our custom for a widow not to go to her next husband until she has mourned for two years."

"Two years is too long," objected the wife, who had appeared with the old man's battered goatskin bag. "Who will hoe your farms for you while you have no husband?"

"Hamlet," I retorted without thinking, "was old enough to hoe his mother's farms himself. There was no need for her to remarry." No one looked convinced. I gave up. "His mother and the great chief told Hamlet not to be sad, for the great chief himself would be a father to Hamlet. Furthermore, Hamlet would be the next chief: therefore he must stay to learn the things of a chief. Hamlet agreed to remain, and all the rest went off to drink beer."

While I paused, perplexed at how to render Hamlet's disgusted soliloquy to an audience convinced that Claudius and Gertrude had behaved in the best possible manner, one of the younger men asked me who had married the other wives of the dead chief.

"He had no other wives," I told him.

"But a chief must have many wives! How else can he brew beer and prepare food for all his guests?"

I said firmly that in our country even chiefs had only one wife, that they had servants to do their work, and that they paid them from tax money.

It was better, they returned, for a chief to have many wives and sons who would help him hoe his farms and feed his people; then everyone loved the chief who gave much and took nothing—taxes were a bad thing.

I agreed with the last comment, but for the rest fell back on their favorite way of fobbing off my questions: "That is the way it is done, so that is how we do it."

I decided to skip the soliloquy. Even if Claudius was here thought quite right to marry his brother's widow, there remained the poison motif, and I knew they would disapprove of fratricide. More hopefully I resumed, "That night Hamlet kept watch with the three who had seen his dead father. The dead chief again appeared, and although the others were afraid, Hamlet followed his dead father off to one side. When they were alone, Hamlet's dead father spoke."

"Omens can't talk!" The old man was emphatic.

"Hamlet's dead father wasn't an omen. Seeing him might have been an omen, but he was not." My audience looked as confused as I sounded. "It *was* Hamlet's dead father. It was a thing we call a 'ghost.'" I had to use the English word, for unlike

many of the neighboring tribes, these people didn't believe in the survival after death of any individuating part of the personality.

"What is a 'ghost?' An omen?"

"No, a 'ghost' is someone who is dead but who walks around and can talk, and people can hear him and see him but not touch him."

They objected. "One can touch zombis."

"No, no! It was not a dead body the witches had animated to sacrifice and eat. No one else made Hamlet's dead father walk. He did it himself."

"Dead men can't walk" protested my audience as one man.

I was quite willing to compromise. "A 'ghost' is the dead man's shadow."

But again they objected "Dead men cast no shadows."

"They do in my country," I snapped.

The old man quelled the babble of disbelief that arose immediately and told me with that insincere, but courteous, agreement one extends to the fancies of the young, ignorant, and superstitious, "No doubt in your country the dead can also walk without being zombis." From the depths of his bag he produced a withered fragment of kola nut, bit off one end to show it wasn't poisoned, and handed me the rest as a peace offering.

"Anyhow," I resumed, "Hamlet's dead father said that his own brother, the one who became chief, had poisoned him. He wanted Hamlet to avenge him. Hamlet believed this in his heart, for he did not like his father's brother." I took another swallow of beer. "In the country of the great chief, living in the same homestead, for it was a very large one, was an important elder who was often with the chief to advise and help him. His name was Polonius. Hamlet was courting his daughter, but her father and her brother . . . [I cast hastily about for some tribal analogy] warned her not to let Hamlet visit her when she was alone on her farm, for he would be a great chief and so could not marry her."

"Why not?" asked the wife, who had settled down on the edge of the old man's chair. He frowned at her for asking stupid questions and growled, "They lived in the same homestead."

"That was not the reason," I informed them. "Polonius was a stranger who lived in the homestead because he helped the chief, not because he was a relative."

"Then why couldn't Hamlet marry her?"

"He could have," I explained, "but Polonius didn't think he would. After all, Hamlet was a man of great importance who ought to marry a chief's daughter, for in his country a man could have only one wife. Polonius was afraid that if Hamlet made love to his daughter, then no one else would give a high price for her."

"That might be true," remarked one of the shrewder elders, "but a chief's son would give his mistress's father enough presents and patronage to more than make up the difference. Polonius sounds like a fool to me."

"Many people think he was," I agreed. "Meanwhile Polonius sent his son Laertes off to Paris to learn the things of that country, for it was the homestead of a very great chief indeed. Because he was afraid that Laertes might waste a lot of money on beer and women and gambling, or get into trouble by fighting, he sent one of his servants to Paris secretly, to spy out what Laertes was doing. One day Hamlet came upon Polonius's daughter Ophelia. He behaved so oddly he frightened her. Indeed"—I was fumbling for words to express the dubious quality of Hamlet's madness—"the chief and many others had also noticed that when Hamlet talked one could understand the words but not what they meant. Many people thought that he had become mad." My audience suddenly became much more attentive. "The great chief wanted to know what was wrong with Hamlet, so he sent for two of Hamlet's age mates [school friends would have taken long explanation] to talk to Hamlet and find out what troubled his heart. Hamlet, seeing that they had been bribed by the chief to betray him, told them nothing. Polonius, however, insisted that Hamlet was mad because he had been forbidden to see Ophelia, whom he loved."

"Why," inquired a bewildered voice, "should anyone bewitch Hamlet on that account?"

"Bewitch him?"

"Yes, only witchcraft can make anyone mad, unless, of course, one sees the beings that lurk in the forest."

I stopped being a storyteller, took out my notebook and demanded to be told more about these two causes of madness. Even while they spoke and I jotted notes, I tried to calculate the effect of this new factor on the plot. Hamlet had not been exposed to the beings that lurk in the forests. Only his relatives in the male line could bewitch him. Barring relatives not mentioned by Shakespeare, it had to be Claudius who was attempting to harm him. And, of course, it was.

For the moment I staved off questions by saying that the great chief also refused to believe that Hamlet was mad for the love of Ophelia and nothing else. "He was sure that something much more important was troubling Hamlet's heart."

"Now Hamlet's age mates," I continued, "had

brought with them a famous storyteller. Hamlet decided to have this man tell the chief and all his homestead a story about a man who had poisoned his brother because he desired his brother's wife and wished to be chief himself. Hamlet was sure the great chief could not hear the story without making a sign if he was indeed guilty, and then he would discover whether his dead father had told him the truth."

The old man interrupted, with deep cunning, "Why should a father lie to his son?" he asked.

I hedged: "Hamlet wasn't sure that it really was his dead father." It was impossible to say anything, in that language, about devil-inspired visions.

"You mean," he said "it actually was an omen, and he knew witches sometimes send false ones. Hamlet was a fool not to go to one skilled in reading omens and divining the truth in the first place. A man-who-sees-the-truth could have told him how his father died, if he really had been poisoned, and if there was witchcraft in it: then Hamlet could have called the elders to settle the matter."

The shrewd elder ventured to disagree. "Because his father's brother was a great chief, one-who-sees-the-truth might therefore have been afraid to tell it. I think it was for that reason that a friend of Hamlet's father—a witch and an elder—sent an omen so his friend's son would know. Was the omen true?"

"Yes," I said, abandoning ghosts and the devil; a witch-sent omen it would have to be. "It was true, for when the storyteller was telling his tale before all the homestead, the great chief rose in fear. Afraid that Hamlet knew his secret he planned to have him killed."

The stage set of the next bit presented some difficulties of translation. I began cautiously. "The great chief told Hamlet's mother to find out from her son what he knew. But because a woman's children are always first in her heart, he had the important elder Polonius hide behind a cloth that hung against the wall of Hamlet's mother's sleeping hut. Hamlet started to scold his mother for what she had done."

There was a shocked murmur from everyone. A man should never scold his mother.

"She called out in fear, and Polonius moved behind the cloth. Shouting, 'A rat!' Hamlet took his machete and slashed through the cloth." I paused for dramatic effect. "He had killed Polonius!"

The old men looked at each other in supreme disgust. "That Polonius truly was a fool and a man who knew nothing! What child would not know enough to shout, 'It's me!'" With a pang, I remembered that these people are ardent hunters, always armed with bow, arrow, and machete; at the first rustle in the grass an arrow is aimed and ready, and the hunter shouts "Game!" If no human voice answers immediately, the arrow speeds on its way. Like a good hunter Hamlet had shouted, "A rat!"

I rushed in to save Polonius's reputation. "Polonius did speak. Hamlet heard him. But he thought it was the chief and wished to kill him to avenge his father. He had meant to kill him earlier that evening. . . ." I broke down, unable to describe to these pagans, who had no belief in individual afterlife, the difference between dying at one's prayers and dying "unhousell'd, disappointed, unaneled."

This time I had shocked my audience seriously. "For a man to raise his hand against his father's brother and the one who had become his father—that is a terrible thing. The elders ought to let such a man be bewitched."

I nibbled at my kola nut in some perplexity, then pointed out that after all the man had killed Hamlet's father.

"No," pronounced the old man, speaking less to me than to the young men sitting behind the elders. "If your father's brother has killed your father, you must appeal to your father's age mates; they may avenge him. No man may use violence against his senior relatives." Another thought struck him. "But if his father's brother had indeed been wicked enough to bewitch Hamlet and make him mad that would be a good story indeed, for it would be his fault that Hamlet, being mad, no longer had any sense and thus was ready to kill his father's brother."

There was a murmur of applause. *Hamlet* was again a good story to them, but it no longer seemed quite the same story to me. As I thought over the coming complications of plot and motive, I lost courage and decided to skim over dangerous ground quickly.

"The great chief," I went on, "was not sorry that Hamlet had killed Polonius. It gave him a reason to send Hamlet away, with his two treacherous age mates, with letters to a chief of a far country, saying that Hamlet should be killed. But Hamlet changed the writing on their papers, so that the chief killed his age mates instead." I encountered a reproachful glare from one of the men whom I had told undetectable forgery was not merely immoral but beyond human skill. I looked the other way.

"Before Hamlet could return, Laertes came back for his father's funeral. The great chief told him Hamlet had killed Polonius. Laertes swore to kill Hamlet because of this, and because his sister Ophelia, hearing her father had been killed by the man she loved, went mad and drowned in the river."

"Have you already forgotten what we told you?" The old man was reproachful. "One cannot take ven-geance on a madman; Hamlet killed Polonius in his madness. As for the girl, she not only went mad, she was drowned. Only witches can make people drown. Water itself can't hurt anything. It is merely something one drinks and bathes in."

I began to get cross. "If you don't like the story, I'll stop."

The old man made soothing noises and himself poured me some more beer. "You tell the story well, and we are listening. But it is clear that the elders of your country have never told you what the story really means. No, don't interrupt! We believe you when you say your marriage customs are different, or your clothes and weapons. But people are the same everywhere; therefore, there are always witches and it is we, the elders, who know how witches work. We told you it was the great chief who wished to kill Hamlet, and now your own words have proved us right. Who were Ophelia's male relatives?"

"There were only her father and her brother." Hamlet was clearly out of my hands.

"There must have been many more; this also you must ask of your elders when you get back to your country. From what you tell us, since Polonius was dead, it must have been Laertes who killed Ophelia, although I do not see the reason for it."

We had emptied one pot of beer and the old men argued the point with slightly tipsy interest. Finally one of them demanded of me, "What did the servant of Polonius say on his return?"

With difficulty I recollected Reynaldo and his mission. "I don't think he did return before Polonius was killed."

"Listen," said the elder, "and I will tell you how it was and how your story will go, then you may tell me if I am right. Polonius knew his son would get into trouble, and so he did. He had many fines to pay for fighting, and debts from gambling. But he had only two ways of getting money quickly. One was to marry off his sister at once, but it is difficult to find a man who will marry a woman desired by the son of a chief. For if the chief's heir commits adultery with your wife, what can you do? Only a fool calls a case against a man who will someday be his judge. Therefore Laertes had to take the second way: he killed his sister by witchcraft, drowning her so he could secretly sell her body to the witches."

I raised an objection. "They found her body and buried it. Indeed Laertes jumped into the grave to see his sister once more—so, you see, the body was truly there. Hamlet, who had just come back, jumped in after him."

"What did I tell you?" The elder appealed to the others. "Laertes was up to no good with his sister's body. Hamlet prevented him, because the chief's heir, like a chief, does not wish any other man to grow rich and powerful. Laertes would be angry, because he would have killed his sister without benefit to himself. In our country he would try to kill Hamlet for that reason. Is this not what happened?"

"More or less," I admitted. "When the great chief found Hamlet was still alive, he encouraged Laertes to try to kill Hamlet and arranged a fight with machetes between them. In the fight both the young men were wounded to death. Hamlet's mother drank the poisoned beer that the chief meant for Hamlet in case he won the fight. When he saw his mother die of poison, Hamlet, dying, managed to kill his father's brother with his machete."

"You see, I was right!" exclaimed the elder.

"That was a very good story," added the old man, "and you told it with very few mistakes. There was just one more error, at the very end. The poison Hamlet's mother drank was obviously meant for the survivor of the fight, whichever it was. If Laertes had won, the great chief would have poisoned him, for no one would know that he arranged Hamlet's death. Then, too, he need not fear Laertes' witchcraft; it takes a strong heart to kill one's only sister by witchcraft.

"Sometime," concluded the old man, gathering his ragged toga about him, "you must tell us some more stories of your country. We, who are elders, will instruct you in their true meaning, so that when you return to your own land your elders will see that you have not been sitting in the bush, but among those who know things and who have taught you wisdom."

4

Aims and Methods
of
Cultural Anthropology

When a Western visitor to Songhay country rides a bush taxi, he or she is suddenly thrown into a social universe in which many of the advantages of being a "prestigious'" European are rudely pushed aside. No matter a person's status in the pecking order of Songhay society, riding a bush taxi in Songhay country is a rude initiation both to the uncomfortable conditions of public travel in the Republic of Niger and to the "hardiness" of Songhay social interactions.

I took my first bush taxi ride in the fall of 1969 when I had been in the Republic of Niger [in West Africa] a scant three weeks; I was going to depart for the town of Tera and my first teaching post. Arriving at the bush taxi depot early, I fully expected the taxi to leave on schedule. I waited impatiently for nearly 30 minutes before I asked someone in French about the hour of departure. He smiled at me and said, *"Toute de suite."* Reassured, I sat down under a tree and bought two oranges. One hour passed. City taxis came into the bush taxi depot and deposited more passengers bound for Tera. Young men took the baggage of these passengers and hoisted them atop the bush taxi. In my inchoate Songhay I asked the old woman sitting next to me about the hour of departure. "Who knows?" she said. "In a little while." After two hours of waiting I noticed that a man, who appeared to be working on the engine of the bush taxi, was leaving the depot. Beside myself, I asked him where he was going. "To the auto shop. We need a new part." When I asked him when he would be back, he said characteristically, *"Toute de suite."* Another hour passed before the Songhay mechanic returned from the auto shop. He looked at me and said, "You should buy some meat before we get started." About 30 minutes later, another man, who had been scurrying about the depot all morning, announced that the taxi was about to depart and that all the passengers for Tera should board the taxi.

Bush taxis in the Songhay view of things are either converted Peugeot 404 pickup trucks, the carriers of which have two wooden planks secured to the floor for passenger seating, or larger vehicles called *mille kilo*, which are more like buses. Our vehicle for the ride to Tera was of the *mille kilo* variety. Along with the other passengers, I picked up my bags and moved toward the vehicle that would transport us and our baggage to our destination. As I approached the *mille kilo* three or four young boys attempted to help me with my things. When I resisted their efforts, exclaiming that I could handle my own bags, they said something to me in Songhay that I did not comprehend and then attempted to help the elderly Nigerian gentleman just ahead of me with his things. He gave them his bags and gave each of them a few francs for their efforts. Inside the bus, the man who had announced our departure was telling people where they should sit. He suggested to the generous elderly gentleman that he sit next to the driver. When he saw me, he suggested that I sit next to the elderly gentleman. I said that it would be better for an old woman to sit in front of the taxi: "I'll sit in the back of the taxi like everyone else." The man looked at me strangely and told me to move on. The other passengers already seated in the back of the taxi greeted me and either giggled or laughed. Meanwhile, I squeezed myself between two young mothers, both of whom were nursing their children. The noontime heat made the air hot and stuffy in the crowded *mille kilo*, and the baby to my left vomited on me. The driver started the engine and we began our trek to Tera, a voyage of some 190 km which, due to frequent flat tires, engine breakdowns, social visits, and police stops along the way, took more than ten hours to complete.

I was too overcome by the heat, filth, and discomfort, not to mention my own ignorance of the Songhay sociocultural world, to understand what was occurring all around me. As in the case with the oracle of Delphi, no one was "speaking" to me, and no one was concealing anything from me; rather, I found myself immersed in an alien universe of signs that I did not comprehend."[1]

This very interesting story by Paul Stoller goes on to highlight many of the fundamental problems associated with doing fieldwork and studying culture: How does one explain the signs that constitute social action, ethnocen-

[1] Paul Stoller, "Signs in the Social Order: Riding a Songhay Bush Taxi," *American Ethnologist*, 9, no. 4(1982):750–751. Reproduced by permission of the American Anthropological Association. Not for further reproduction.

trism, the relativity of time, fieldwork, and the interpretation of the experience?

Cultural anthropology grew out of curiosity about the many and varied ways of life found among the peoples of the earth. From the very earliest records of anthropological studies until the nineteenth century, when the field developed into an academic discipline, the major area of interest was non-Western peoples and their cultures. The more bizarre or different their way of life, the more it attracted the attention of anthropologists.

There were some special problems in studying such peoples, however. The societies that presented the sharpest contrast to Western society could not be studied using the same methods that sociologists and others had used in looking at our own society. There are several reasons for this. Since almost all of these groups were nonliterate, they could not keep written records of their history or of their customs and daily practices. Historians tended to focus on the leaders of nations and not on the isolated, politically unimportant peoples anthropologists studied. Census figures and other statistics, so valuable to the sociologist in studying Western societies, were almost useless in areas where there were no accurate records. The languages spoken by most groups were not the national language of the literate elite but local languages known to few outsiders. As a result, anthropologists had to rely on information acquired from a variety of sources—some more reliable than others—but they almost always obtained most of their data from direct contact with the people they studied.

Revolutionizing Fieldwork

Throughout the nineteenth century anthropology was often a hobby of well-to-do scholars who were able to travel to out-of-the-way places and study exotic peoples. A number of anthropologists also analyzed accounts written by others, especially if they could not afford the time and expense of a field expedition. This "armchair" anthropology, based on travel diaries and missionary accounts rather than field research, led to a particular style of analysis that could not hope to capture the true nature of traditional societies. Even among those who could do field research there was no systematic attempt to meet strict research standards.

It was not until the twentieth century that anthropologists became really concerned with the quality of their research and began to develop a set of standards for the fieldworker. A leader in the movement toward controlled research methods for cultural anthropology was Bronislaw Malinowski. Born in what is now Poland, Malinowski was trained in mathematics, but early in life he became interested in anthropology. He studied in London and then went to the Pacific, where he was doing research when World War I broke out. He ended up in Australia, where, as a citizen of Germany, he was subject to internment for the duration of the conflict. He was, however, able to persuade the officials to let him stay in a small group of islands just to the north, the Trobriand Islands. Here, he argued, he

Bronislaw Malinowski, who established rigorous standards for conducting fieldwork, is shown here working with Trobriand Islanders.

could do no harm, yet he would be able to continue his research. Malinowski lived in the islands for several years, sharing the way of life of the natives. Isolated from "civilization," he was forced to live in native villages, learn their language, and take part in their way of life.

As a result of his lengthy field experience, Malinowski published a series of books and articles on the culture of the Trobriand Islanders. He described their economics, their forms of social control, their kinship and marriage patterns, and their religion and magic. In the course of his work he also laid out in detail his experiences in the field, showing how they differed from traditional anthropological **fieldwork** and pointing out the need for some of his novel approaches. In *Argonauts of the Western Pacific*, published in 1922, Malinowski offers one of the earliest statements of the problems and requirements of anthropological fieldwork.

First, he said that in order to be effective and produce valid results, the anthropologist must *live in the community being studied*. Until this time, though researchers had conducted field studies among native peoples, they had rarely lived with the people they were studying. In a typical research design the anthropologist worked out of a mission outpost or a colonial office, perhaps making short trips into the field for more thorough study, but never sharing the day-to-day life of the natives. Often interpreters were used, adding another filter through which information about native customs had to pass and removing the anthropologist still further from the object of study. Malinowski's experience on the Trobriand Islands convinced him that only by becoming part of the daily life of the community can the anthropologist hope to put together a valid picture of what the culture means to the members of the group. Today when anthropologists talk about "going to the field," they are usually referring to a period of residence lasting anywhere from a couple of months to more than a year.

Strangely enough, time is an important methodological intangible. Only long-term residence permits the fieldworker's picture of the community to develop accurately. In doing research in Colombia, South America, one of the authors was told by an informant that he had moved from the community where he was born in order to find work. But late in his stay this man told the author a long story about how, when he was young, he had gotten into a machete fight with a drinking companion whose family forced him to flee his village. Revelations like this, built on trust and occurring after a long period of time, demonstrate why fieldwork cannot be rushed.

Traditionally, anthropologists have studied relatively small, homogeneous communities. Increasingly, there are plenty of exceptions to this statement, and we will address that issue a little bit later, but for much of anthropology's history, most researchers worked in rural, out-of-the-way communities whose populations ranged from fewer than a hundred to no more than a couple of thousand residents. In most of these settings the divisions of labor were not terribly complex, being based primarily on age and sex distinctions. These were also communities where families had resided together for a number of generations. It was usually possible for an anthropologist, either working

Close relationships can develop as a result of fieldwork. Here one of the authors (Whiteford) poses with a colleague in Colombia, South America.

alone or with a spouse, to collect data on practically all aspects of life over a year's time.

Although anthropologists go into the field with a specific theme or research focus, they also try to do a *holistic study* that encompasses everything from birthing practices to religious rituals to the social organization of the community. Traditionally, the belief has been that whatever the anthropologist is studying can only be truly understood in the context of how the entire community functions. For example, an anthropologist interested in looking at the agricultural cycle will obviously need to gather information on what and how much is planted, how it is harvested, and what happens to the produce once it is cleared from the field. But if you truly want to understand agricultural practices in many traditional societies, you will need to go well beyond gathering those types of data. You will need to understand who participates at what points in the planting and harvesting processes. Do people call upon their relatives or neighbors to assist them? If so, how is their help reciprocated? Are there certain religious practices associated with the agricultural cycle? What specialists are called in and how are they compensated? After the harvest, is the produce distributed among nonagriculturalists in the village? What is received in return? How much is kept for the family to consume and to plant the following year, and is any of it actually sold for cash? In order to comprehend all the intricacies of the agricultural cycle, the anthropologist must look at many different facets of the entire community.

Second, Malinowski insisted that the anthropologist must *learn the native language*. If, as noted in Chapter 1, the goal of the anthropologist is to translate accurately one culture into another, he or she must first be able to comprehend it on its own terms. This requires thinking in the language of the natives, not just understanding what they say. Only when we are able to see the world as the natives do can we begin to translate their culture, and if language shapes the way we order our perceptions, then thinking in an-

other language is essential to sharing another culture. Again, this was a revelation to anthropologists when Malinowski first suggested it, since they were used to working with interpreters, especially when the native language was not widely known or was not part of a literary tradition that could have been included in the anthropologist's formal education. But interpreters not only translate; they can also take it upon themselves to edit material for one reason or another.

A poignant example comes to mind. A little more than a decade ago President Jimmy Carter went to Poland. When during his airport address he spoke of the traditional ties between the United States and Poland, the message came out so twisted that the audience response was almost hostile. When Carter mentioned that he had left the United States just that morning, his translator had him leaving the United States forever. When he said he was interested in learning about Poles' desires for the future, the remark was interpreted as expressing an interest in Poles' sexual desires. Needless to say, the State Department translator responsible for these gaffes was assigned to other tasks for the remainder of Carter's journey.

The point is that to meet today's exacting standards, the anthropologist has to be able to handle the language. Marjorie Shostak mentioned that in working with the !Kung San of southern Africa's Kalahari Desert, she spent the first three months doing practically nothing but learning the language.[2] Karl Heider, who has spent years studying the Dani of New Guinea, talks about the difficulties and frustrations of trying to communicate while he painstakingly learned the language.[3] The importance of learning the language of the people under study cannot be overestimated.

We emphasize the need to be able to

[2] Marjorie Shostak, *Nisa: The Life and Words of a !Kung Woman* (Cambridge, Mass.: Harvard University Press, 1981).

[3] Karl Heider, *Grand Valley Dani: Peaceful Warriors* (New York: Holt, Rinehart and Winston, 1979).

evaluate not only the literal meaning of a language but its idiomatic or local meaning as well, and this usually entails becoming fluent in the language. If researchers simply accept the literal meaning of an informant's statement, they can arrive at some very bad conclusions. For example, for many years anthropologists were puzzled by the fact that in some societies a child refers to many different male adults by the same term, which may be roughly translated as "father." They assumed that this meant that paternity could not be established and that there was a kind of group marriage, or "primitive promiscuity," in those societies. But this assumption was based on an incomplete understanding of the meaning of the term, derived from the fact that the analogous term in the English language refers to a biological relationship, but in some societies this is not the case. The term that was translated as "father" really meant "a male of the generation of my father."

You can see how important an accurate command of the language can be, for without it the anthropologist is in danger of accepting the literal meaning of someone's statement, even if it contradicts the meaning intended by the speaker. But the speaker will certainly not provide this information. For example, a speaker will not provide an explanation of an idiomatic phrase. It is up to the anthropologist to avoid such problems.

Finally, Malinowski urged anthropologists to use the method known as **participant observation**. Observation alone is not enough, he argued, for an observer cannot know the true meaning of the actions of others until he or she has a chance to take part in them. But participation alone is not enough, for without the ability to step back and observe objectively, people are unable to grasp the meaning of their actions. (This is clearly the case in our own culture, where we are often unaware of the meaning of many of our daily activities or the interrelationships between them, as the rest of this book will point out.) Therefore, anthropologists must both observe and take part in the daily rou-

tine of life in the native community in order to understand its culture. In addition, they must include in participant observation the special events that, while not part of the daily routine, are part of the total picture. Deaths, rituals, quarrels, and the like are just as important as topics for research as the routine activities of raising a family, making a living, maintaining social relationships, and so forth.

Participant observation is a part of the fieldwork process that most anthropologists enjoy thoroughly and it is an important part of becoming part of the community under study. One of our colleagues enjoys telling about participant observation and his initial field experience. He had gone to study a peasant Indian community located on the shores of Lake Atitlan in Guatemala. It was his first trip to the field, and after years of reading about what anthropologists did and hearing his professors and others talk about life in the field, he was exhilarated to become part of the process at last. His excitement peaked shortly after he arrived in the community when he was invited to participate with other men in a ceremony dealing with the reburial of the remains of the mother of an important man in the village. The observance took place early in the morning, as the sun was just beginning to come up over the shore of the lake. Shortly after the ceremony began, one of the leaders opened a bottle of locally made rum and proposed a ritual toast. The rum had a filmy appearance and was being poured from an old bottle into a rather large tumbler—both of which showed signs of considerable age and prior use. The thought of drinking an alcoholic beverage at that time of the morning from a container that appeared to have a life of its own was somewhat disconcerting to our friend. Nevertheless, he knew that once invited, he simply could not refuse to participate, since to do so would be interpreted as a great insult to his host and might jeopardize his ability to do fieldwork effectively in the community from that point on. He took a deep breath as he was handed about ten ounces of that potent brew. "This is participant observation!" he thought—an essential part of the data collection process and the anthropological experience. He drank the entire contents of the glass in one breath, handed the glass back to the pourer, wiped his lips, and stepped aside. As he stood there with his eyes watering, his throat and stomach burning, and wondering if he would live through the morning, the next man in line received the same full tumbler. Looking over at our friend almost in horror, he said, "How can you drink this so early in the morning?" took a small ritual sip, and poured the remainder of the contents on the ground.

People outside the field (and anthropology students) often think that anthropological field research is a romantic exploration of a far-off society; however, a closer look at Malinowski's experiences reveals much about the effects of this forced life style on the individual. Although Malinowski was clearly a master of objective research and a talented investigator, his life in the Trobriands was filled with anxiety and frustration. Many years after his death the diary he had kept in the Trobriands was published. It revealed a very different picture of the man from that contained in his formal work. People who regard fieldwork as an escape, in which the anthropologist can "go native" for a short time and then return to "civilization" relaxed and refreshed, are greatly mistaken. This romantic idea ignores the utter frustration of working in a foreign culture where one is unable to share the values and comfortable habits that one has grown up with. It does not take into account the normal human desire to communicate with others about topics of mutual interest. It overlooks the fact that every individual has needs that arise out of growing up in a particular cultural setting and these needs cannot be fulfilled in another. It forgets that we have ingrained expectations about how others will act, and that these expectations are not valid for members of another culture. In Malinowski's diary we read of a man who was constantly frustrated by his inability to overcome his cultural background. No matter how fine his analysis of

his experiences, it was no substitute for the familiar and reassuring culture that had been part of his life until then. We read of a man who was transplanted into another world, and of the trauma—we call it **culture shock**—that he endured throughout his field research. Yet while Malinowski's diary shows us the weaknesses of the man, it also confirms his greatness, for not everyone could have put up with the problems he faced daily and yet retain the objectivity shown in his later writing.

If you are still not convinced that fieldwork isn't always the romantic adventure it is cracked up to be, perhaps the following passage describing Napoleon Chagnon's first encounter with the Yanomamö, an Indian society in Venezuela, will cause you to reconsider:

> The excitement of meeting my first Indians was almost unbearable as I duck-waddled through the low passage into the village clearing. I looked up and gasped when I saw a dozen burly, naked, filthy, hideous men staring at us down the shafts of their drawn arrows! Immense wads of green tobacco were stuck between their lower teeth and lips making them look even more hideous, and strands of dark-green slime dripped or hung from their noses. We arrived at the village while the men were blowing a hallucinogenic drug up their noses. One of the side effects of the drug is a runny nose. The mucus is always saturated with the green powder and the Indians usually let it run freely from their nostrils. My next discovery was that there were a dozen or so vicious, underfed dogs snapping at my legs, circling me as if I were going to be their next meal. I just stood there holding my notebook, helpless and pathetic. Then the stench of the decaying vegetation and filth struck me and I almost got sick. I was horrified. What sort of a welcome was this for the person who came here to live with you and learn your way of life, to become friends with you?[4]

In addition to the intensive immersion process of long-term residence in the com-

---

[4] Napoleon A. Chagnon, *Yanomamö, the Fierce People* (New York: Holt, Rinehart and Winston, 1968), p. 5.

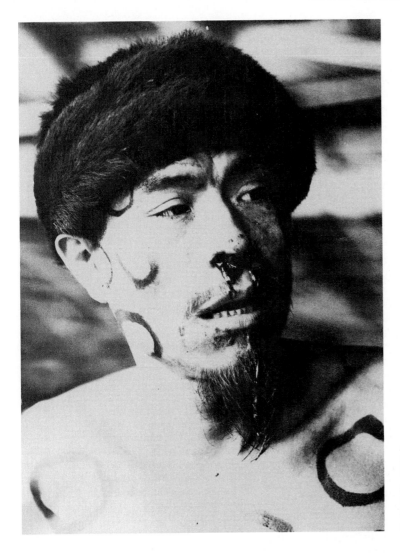

A Yanomamö Indian from the Amazon rainforest region of southern Venezuela. Their propensity for aggressive behavior and frequent use of various hallucinogenic substances have made them subjects of considerable interest to outsiders.

munity being studied, learning the local language, and employing methods of participant observation, anthropologists rely on a number of other data-gathering techniques as well. Open-ended, structured interviews may be constructed in order to gather information on any number of subjects. Here the anthropologist writes out a number of key questions that are then used to guide the conversation. The interview is structured in the sense that the questions are organized into a flow of topics with some internal consistency, and it

is open-ended to allow the informants to provide indepth information. It is from participant observation and open-ended interviews that an anthropologist is able to build a base of information on topics of interest, as well as gather essential data on how the community operates. Many anthropologists refer to information gathered in these ways as "qualitative data."

After the anthropologist has been in the field for a period of time, she or he often will put together a closed-response, structured interview schedule. This schedule has specific questions and fixed answers among which the respondent must choose. In order to construct a good survey schedule the anthropologist needs to understand the culture well enough to know what the possible appropriate answers would be. Because this approach is often used with a large number of people, all of whom are asked the same questions in the same fashion, generally the results are useful in constructing tables and the data can be employed in a variety of ways to demonstrate statistical importance. This type of information is referred to as "quantitative data."

For a long period of time anthropologists shied away from employing survey techniques except under certain circumstances, such as gathering demographic information on households. Part of the reason for this was the feeling that such an approach was unnecessary. When the anthropologist wrote, "Villagers are united in their feeling that the gods will certainly punish those who don't share with their neighbors," the statement was usually based on consultation with a number of people and resulted from a combination of direct questioning and observations. Increasingly, however, anthropologists utilize a healthy mixture of quantitative and qualitative data-gathering techniques in the field. This approach is particularly important when they work—as more and more anthropologists do—in complex societies.

Although, as we noted earlier, anthropologists who work among nonliterate peoples have no written historical records kept by the people themselves to draw on, in many instances they do have access to local statistical and archival materials. These materials can be very important sources of data on the communities being studied. For example, anthropologists working in rural Latin America routinely burrow through village church records. From these sources one can gather invaluable information on births, marriages, and deaths of community members. Attempts to reconstruct or understand community so-

cial organization are greatly enhanced by such data.

In addition, many anthropologists are assisted in their data-collection processes by the use of tape recorders to gather folk tales, songs, and other information in which exact wording and intonation are important. Movie and still cameras have long been indispensable for recording events, and today more and more video cameras are being taken into the field. Portable computers are also becoming an essential part of the anthropologist's tool kit, not only to use as word processors in which to enter ethnographic data, but also to analyze survey data, at least in part, while still in the field. Obviously, all this fancy equipment can greatly assist the anthropologist, but at a cost that earlier anthropologists who relied on pens, notebooks, and typewriters never imagined. Battery packs must be kept charged. Magnetic tapes, whether used for video or computer purposes, easily malfunction because of exposure to dust, excessive heat, moisture, or cold. Thus the new technologies, while immensely useful, make the anthropologist dependent on the outside world in a way that earlier anthropologists never were.

Finally, although it is never listed as a fieldwork technique, luck is often a key component of success. Some of the best data can come without planning, as one of the authors found out when he was working in southern Colombia. He asked some families to itemize their daily income and expenditures for a period of time, hoping to gain some insight into their economic life. Shortly after he began this project he noticed that some debits and credits for one family were being accounted for in a way he didn't understand. Although he thought the man who was doing the accounting was a cobbler, it turned out he was also a folk medicine practitioner. They became good friends and over the course of months the author learned a great deal about curing and healing. In another instance the author was collecting data on religious practices. Although he was successful in gathering information on church attendance and household religious paraphernalia, the nature of the people's beliefs remained a closed book. One weekend he took a trip that included a visit to the religious shrine of Las Lajas. When he got back and told some of his informants about the experience, they began telling him anecdotes about the miraculous acts of saints and the Virgin Mary—just the sort of information he had been unable to obtain before.

Maintaining Objectivity

Despite the distractions, pressures, and personal problems of fieldwork, the anthropologist must always remember the need for objectivity. It is hard to imagine how one could remain detached when faced with a scene like the one Chagnon described, but if the anthropologist cannot refrain from judging another culture, his or her work will be worthless. After overcoming his initial shock, Chagnon was able to describe and analyze Yanomamö culture objectively and thoroughly, leaving us with the impression that even if he did have some rather unpleasant and frightening experiences, he was still able to remain detached and avoid judging Yanomamö culture by comparing it to his own or to any other standards.

Of course, complete detachment is impossible. No one can escape the past, nor is it necessary to do so to become an anthropologist. The best solution is to remind oneself constantly that there are two cultures working at the same time: the culture of the observer, which lurks in the back of our mind, and the culture of the observed, which lies before us. Anthropologists must always try to keep these two worlds separate and to take their own cultural biases into account when writing about other cultures. The main point is to devote oneself to an understanding, and not a judgment, of the culture under study. And this is not always as easy as it sounds, for

deeply held values and preferences cannot be overcome by sheer willpower—it takes long hours of training and experience in the field, something for which no amount of lectures, readings, and classroom discussions can substitute.

In addition, the anthropologist must avoid going into the field with preconceived ideas about what he or she will find; there is no surer way to determine the outcome of a research project than to make up one's mind beforehand what the results are likely to be. An open mind and a willingness to change the research design to match the situation at hand are required if one is to obtain truly valid results. Fieldwork is the anthropologist's laboratory. Just as a scientist in a chemistry lab must be willing to accept the results of an experiment even if they disprove the law he or she is testing, so anthropologists must be willing to accept what they find at face value, whether it fits into the pattern or not. Although in high school chemistry most of us wrote up the results of an experiment before we performed it because we knew what they *should* be according to the textbook, a real scientist does not reach conclusions before he or she has finished the experiment.

The lesson of scientific objectivity can be seen in an important controversy between two famous anthropologists who studied the same community. In the 1920s Robert Redfield conducted research in the Mexican village of Tepoztlán.[5] Seventeen years later another anthropologist, Oscar Lewis, went to Tepoztlán to restudy the same community.[6] Lewis had read Redfield's work and was puzzled by its many inconsistencies with what he found. Redfield described Tepoztlán as an idyllic rural setting in which people were happy, healthy, and well integrated. When Lewis studied the same community he found the exact opposite: Tepoztlán was character-

[5] Robert Redfield, *Tepoztlán, A Mexican Village* (Chicago: University of Chicago Press, 1930).

[6] Oscar Lewis, *Life in a Mexican Village: Tepoztlán Restudied* (Urban: University of Illinois Press, 1951).

ized by constant suspicion and tension; there was no cooperation among the villagers; and the social relations were typically weak and strife-ridden.

The first question that comes to mind is: How can the village have changed so much in such a short period? A deeper look at the situation reveals that although the village certainly changed over the seventeen years, the outlook of the observer differed as well. Redfield favored the rural life style over that of the city. He considered the city a source of cultural decay, a center of disorganization where the "pure" character of the rural dweller breaks down under the pressures of the fast-paced urban routine. Thus Redfield had a preference for rural life, and when he lived and worked in Tepoztlán he was unable to overcome this bias. He saw everything that was good in the life of the villagers and overlooked much of what was bad. Lewis, on the other hand, approached his research from the opposite point of view. He felt that the peasant life was one of suffering, that poor people were disadvantaged, and that Redfield's view of the relative values of country and city life was backwards. Thus in his work in Tepoztlán he looked for—and found—suspicion and distrust where Redfield had seen harmony and cooperation. The point is that we must be aware not only of our culture and its impact on our perception of another way of life, but also of our own personality and preferences. We do not have to change in order to be good anthropologists, but we do have to suppress some of our stronger feelings while doing research if we are to be objective.

Several years ago a similar anthropological controversy spilled onto the public scene. "New Book Challenges Margaret Mead's Conclusions" was the headline of the *New York Times* article in January 1983 describing Derek Freeman's attack on Mead's classic work on Samoa.[7] In the mid 1920s Margaret Mead, a 28-year-old student of Franz Boas, set off for Samoa. One of her goals was to learn whether Samoan adolescents differed markedly from their counterparts in industrialized society. Which had the greatest effect, she and Boas wanted to know, nature (biological determinism) or nurture (culture)? Mead came down firmly on the side of nurture,[8] and that early bit of fieldwork brought her national attention and established her as one of anthropology's most famous and outspoken figures, a position she held for the remainder of her long and very productive life. Freeman's book, based on his own research in the area, disputes many of Mead's findings. He argues that Samoan culture, even at the time Mead was conducting her initial work, had many of the same problems and conflicts found in North American and European cultures. Freeman concludes that Mead was not rigorous in her collection of data, was naive, and did not thoroughly understand Samoan culture, and consequently presented a picture that was far from accurate.

Again the question is raised: How can individuals supposedly applying the same scientific methods reach such radically different conclusions? Although there are differences between the Redfield-Lewis and Mead-Freeman controversies, there are some interesting parallels. Mead appears to have focused on the factors that allowed Samoan culture to function in a rather harmonious fashion. Freeman, in contrast, emphasizes some of the negative aspects of Samoan culture—high levels of aggression, assault, competition, and authoritarianism. Although Freeman's results were published after Mead's death, the sensationalism generated by his allegations provoked a lively discussion. A number of anthropologists who did research in Samoa after Mead's pioneering work immediately took sides, most tending to support Mead's observations. Not surpris-

---

[7] Derek Freeman, *Margaret Mead and Samoa: The Making and Unmaking of an Anthropological Myth* (Cambridge, Mass.: Harvard University Press, 1983).

[8] Margaret Mead, *Coming of Age in Samoa: A Psychological Study of Primitive Youth for Western Civilization* (New York: William Morrow, 1928).

ingly, Freeman's research came under careful scrutiny. His critics argued that in addition to grandstanding (something regarded as unprofessional in academic circles), he was guilty of many of the same methodological and theoretical shortcomings that he laid to Mead. Although the debate still rages, Mead's work appears to have successfully withstood Freeman's attack.

Goals of Research

So far we have emphasized the requirements of anthropological fieldwork. But once these requirements have been met, how does the anthropologist do research? What do we look for when we do fieldwork in a foreign culture? What kinds of questions do we ask, and

how do we know whom to ask? Obviously, the anthropologist must structure research in some way; we cannot simply move into a village and expect its people to flock to our doorstep and give us a description of their way of life in tightly organized chapters.

Unwritten rules One way in which anthropologists try to understand another culture is by uncovering the rules that govern the behavior of members of that group. This is not limited to written laws covering acceptable behavior, but includes the culture's unwritten codes of conduct. Every society has such rules, and they are shared by almost all of its members. We are able to interact with other members of our society because we expect that in certain situations they will respond in a limited number of ways. Without such expectations, social interaction would be

Social behavior is predictable because people share understandings of what is proper in a given situation.

chaotic. For instance, if upon meeting someone for the first time you extend your hand, you do so with the understanding that the other person will do likewise and that the two of you will shake hands. You do not expect the other person to pour hot coffee on your hand or to grab it and give you a judo flip. Indeed, if something like that did happen, you would be shocked. Thus we have a basic rule that governs behavior in this kind of situation, and when we put together a collection of such rules for all situations we are able to behave as a native in American culture.

Anthropologists going into a foreign culture are at a disadvantage in that they do not know all of these rules. Furthermore, it is not always easy to uncover them. We cannot simply ask a native to tell us all the rules of behavior in his or her society. In many instances individuals simply are unable to recite cultural rules. Rather, we must learn these rules by watching how other people react in certain situations and piecing together whatever information we can get. The trouble is that at the same time we are trying to be a part of this group, to participate as well as observe, and in doing so we are likely to break many of the group's rules, making it more difficult for the members of the society to accept us as one of them and treat us as an equal.

Let us look at another example from our own culture in order to point out how hard it can be for an outsider to learn these rules. Suppose an international visitor comes here for the first time from a culture in which it is usual for a person to bargain with the seller over the price of an item, a practice found in many societies. Our visitor no sooner arrives than he realizes that he has forgotten his toothpaste. So he walks into a drugstore, picks up a tube of toothpaste marked 69 cents, and takes it to the counter, where he offers the pharmacist 50 cents for it. The pharmacist would probably stare at him in disbelief and think about calling the folks in the white coats to come and get him. No doubt this reaction would lead our foreigner

to conclude rather hurriedly that bargaining over the price of something is simply not done—he has broken an unwritten rule of behavior in American society, and the reaction to his bargaining over a paltry 19 cents was so strong that he would not be likely to do it again. Now let's put him in a different situation. Instead of buying a tube of toothpaste, he is shopping for a used car. He walks onto Honest John's "Quality" Used Car lot, where he sets his eyes upon a 1980 Plymouth, with only modest amounts of rust on the rocker panels priced at only $995. Remembering his escapade in the drugstore, and wanting very much to fit in with American culture, he doesn't think twice but simply forks over the money. Bargaining, he has concluded, is un-American. Imagine the look on Honest John's face!

Right away you can see the problem. Picture yourself in a foreign country not knowing the rules, and you can imagine how difficult it would be for you. One of the authors remembers his first trip to Europe. He didn't know how much to tip for which services, was afraid to ride the bus or use the telephone, and dreaded the look of disapproval that followed even the slightest mistake. The more intimate our interactions become, the more likely we are to make such mistakes, and until people get to know us well enough to overlook them, we are in for a lot of disapproving looks. One of the problems is that we are adults, and as such we are expected to know what the rules are. Children don't know what behavior is proper in all situations, and they are forgiven because they are children. But for adults to act like children, to be ignorant of what is expected of them, is an entirely different story. Perhaps this explains why an anthropologist often has a much easier time getting to know the children in a community than the adults—and in the end this can make it even harder to break into the adult world.

Once fieldworkers begin to uncover the rules of behavior, they must put them together into a system or code. The problem is that these rules are unrecorded; in contrast to written laws about what may not be done, there is no written handbook on the details of how one should behave in everyday interactions. Sometimes only a minor variation in style can have a major effect on meaning, changing an ordinary action into the most serious insult; yet nowhere will you find these variations described for an outsider. This brings to mind an experience in a department store in Switzerland in which one of the authors was embarrassed by an innocent mistake. We all know the symbolic meaning of various hand gestures. In our country, for example, holding up the middle finger of the hand conveys a certain meaning to the observer, a meaning strong enough in some cases to lead to arrest or a fist fight. In some parts of Europe this gesture is replaced by one in which you hold up both the index and the middle fingers, with the back of the hand facing the observer (not the front of the hand, as in the noted "V for Victory" sign made famous by Winston Churchill during World War II). If you want to use your fingers to count, the proper way is to begin with the thumb for "one," the thumb and the index finger for "two," and so on. But there he was in a department store in Geneva, asking the saleswoman for two pairs of socks. "How many?" she asked. "Two," he replied, holding up two fingers to emphasize his request.

In trying to uncover these rules of behavior, anthropologists are limited in the questions they can ask. It is much easier, for example, to suggest a particular situation and ask an informant to describe the proper behavior in that situation than it is to ask about correct behavior in abstract terms. For example, we might want to know about the philosophy of crime and punishment in a society; we could be interested in what crimes are taken most seriously, and for what reasons. This is not as simple as it sounds, for even if there is a written legal code that states the punishments for various crimes, it does not capture the variations in the way these crimes occur, the kinds of things that might influence a jury but do not become part of the formal legal code. Thus in doing research on crime and social control in a village, we

Chinese students in Tiananmen Square giving the V for Victory sign. (Or are they giving the sign of "cuckold" to their leaders?)

might sit down with informants and ask questions such as what they think is the most serious crime in that society. Their answer will probably parallel the legal answer for the society as a whole, but it will not necessarily help us understand how that legal code would be applied in a specific case. We might ask what would happen if A stole from B, using specific members of the community as examples. We could gain further insight by asking the same question about two other individuals and noting whether the answer is the same. Then we could change the situation somewhat. Suppose A's family needed food and A stole from B, who was wealthy. As you can see, such questions can become rather complicated. Only by collecting a variety of examples and observing behavior in many different contexts can we begin to understand the complexity of social life in a foreign culture. It is much like the example of bargaining over prices in our country: We cannot set a hard-and-fast rule for an outsider because so many different factors affect whether we bargain or whether we accept the price as stated.

Real versus ideal: Concealment and impression management   There are always many aspects of their way of life that informants cannot describe accurately. Most of people's daily routine is so much a part of themselves that they do not stop to analyze it but simply act it out without thinking. Thus a question about it might not bring any response because the informants do not perceive it as important or as fitting in with a set of rules governing their behavior. In other words, we are unaware of much of the meaning of our own behavior. This raises the distinction between what we call "real" and "ideal" behavior in a given culture. We all see ourselves as conforming to our culture's ideals, and there is often substantial agreement on what those ideas are. But when we observe a group of people performing the same activities, we find that there is not as much conformity with those ideals as we thought. It is here that the anthropologist must supplement

questions with observations; asking yields the ideal, while observing yields the real. Both are essential to understanding behavior in our society.

For example, if we were to inquire about driving an automobile in the United States, we would probably be told the basic rules on which all Americans agree: Stop for stop signs and red lights; do not exceed the speed limit; do not double park; etc. This yields the "ideal." But if we were to observe American driving practices, we would have a picture of the "real" behavior involved in driving a car. The next time you're out in traffic, watch how many people roll through a stop sign without coming to a complete halt. Or, better still, drive 65 miles per hour on the freeway and count the number of cars that pass you compared to the number you pass. You'll soon see why participation must go hand in hand with inquiries about a people's way of life.

In addition to the difference between real and ideal behavior, there are always some things that people conceal from observers, so that their actions correspond to the ideal in the presence of the observer though they do not at other times. As one colleague put it, "A group will behave differently if a stranger is present until the stranger is part of the group. That is one of the reasons anthropologists are supposed to live with the people they are studying." We all hide aspects of our behavior from some (but not all) observers in order to give them the impression we would like them to have of us. For example, if you are away at school and go home for Christmas, your parents may ask you how much you study. You will most likely exaggerate a bit, concealing some of your activities that cut into your study time. Students definitely keep certain things hidden from parents (and often from their professors as well).

The conscious effort to conceal deviations from ideal behavior is called **impression management**, for it involves people's attempts to manage the impressions others have of them. If you stop and think for a minute about the different kinds of clothes you wear on dif-

How can there be poverty, discrimination, and homelessness in an affluent society? There is often a difference between what people say is "ideal" behavior and what is "real" behavior.

ferent occasions, you can see this as a form of impression management. You probably don't wear a coat and tie or an expensive suit to anthropology class, but if you were going to a bank to ask for a loan, you wouldn't go in wearing torn Levi's and a sweatshirt. You would want to create the impression that you were stable and employed and could be counted on to repay the money, and grubby clothes do not convey that impression. So you "manage" your impression by dressing up, by concealing certain aspects of your life from the bank official. There is nothing dishonest about this, and we really don't feel guilty about doing it. It is just that our social life has many facets; we all fit into society in many different ways, and we control the way we fit in at any given time according to the impression we wish to create.

The importance of the concepts of concealment and impression management to the anthropologist is obvious. The people we observe, if they are aware of our presence, are managing the impression they create. While we want to get to know their "normal"

behavior, they want to conceal certain aspects of it from us.

Impression management also creates problems when we read accounts of foreign cultures written by people who were not trained in anthropology. Many early accounts of foreign peoples were written by missionaries who had been sent by their church to convert people to Christianity. Of course, the missionaries set themselves up in a particular role, demanding certain kinds of behavior from the people and rewarding them when their standards were met. But they were content to describe what they saw on the surface and did not look deeper into the native life. Thus they might recount how successful they were at getting the native women to wear halters and at teaching them the Christian virtue of modesty. But in reality, the women wore the halters only when they came to church services at the mission outpost; when they got back to their village the first thing they did was to take them off. Or the missionaries might write about how they persuaded the natives to give up practicing magic and accept the church's doctrines and belief in the power of the Christian God, even though the natives went on practicing their magic but simply didn't tell the missionaries because they knew it would upset them. In short, when we read descriptions of other cultures we must look closely at who wrote them, since many of these people were not always careful to get past the barrier of impression management and portray an accurate and objective picture of a total life style.

This leads us to the question of how we can evaluate the information we receive in the process of doing fieldwork. How do we know when we ask informants a question that they will tell us the truth? How can we evaluate their version of the truth as opposed to someone else's? One way to get around this problem is to obtain as much information about a particular question from as many different people as possible. In this way, we can put together a composite picture that will be more accurate, much as a jury weighs the conflicting evidence in a trial in an effort to come up with a more accurate picture of what happened.

Structuring behavior Another important technique in anthropological research is to contrast the way a structure is assigned to observed behavior by the researcher with the way it appears to be ordered by the people themselves. There is usually a difference between what we call the "folk image" in the minds of the natives of another culture and the "analytical image" in the mind of the anthropologist. Of course, neither one is right or wrong; both can be accurate in entirely different ways.

People perceive their behavior as fitting into a pattern according to what they have learned about their culture. Anthropologists are outsiders with knowledge about many different ways of life. They may view people's behavior in a completely different light, seeing different meanings in it or assigning a different structure to it than the people themselves do. For example, because of the way you were brought up in American culture you treat your brothers and sisters in a certain way, according to your **folk image** of what is proper within the family. However, an anthropologist might see your interactions with your siblings as an example of family structure and patterns of authority, and these would be tied in with patterns of inheritance, the relative importance of age and sex, the roles prescribed for various family members, and so on; this is an **analytical image** of the American family. This does not mean that the anthropologist ignores the folk image,

A gathering of important men of the Bilona group in the Solomon Islands, showing a mixture of indigenous and Western dress.

for it is our job to understand behavior not just as it would be explained to an outsider but also in terms of its meaning to a member of the culture being studied. But we do tend to look beyond specific events and try to form an overall pattern. People are not always aware of the implications of what they do. They act in a certain way because it is "natural" or because it is "the right thing to do." By using an analytical image the anthropologist can obtain a better understanding of these implications, even if the people themselves cannot confirm it. This distinction is explained very well by the anthropologist John Middleton in the following passage from his book about the Lugbara, a society in Uganda, East Africa:

> The reader may well wonder why it is necessary for the anthropologist to use these special terms to describe a society whose members do not themselves find it necessary to do so. The anthropologist is sometimes accused of building up a needlessly complex structural model, while the people he is studying seem to manage very well without it. In the case of a people like the Lugbara the reason is simple, but I think it is important to state it. The Lugbara "live" their society; they do not have to describe it or analyze it so as to make sense of it to outsiders. For a Lugbara, the range of everyday social relations, the context of his everyday life, is narrow. He is concerned with at the most about a score of small local groups and lineages. . . . But the anthropologist is in a different position. He is, in a sense, outside and above the society. . . . To describe this pattern, which is found throughout Lugbara, the anthropologist requires special terms which are not needed by the people themselves.[9]

We can see how conflicts between folk and analytical images can arise. Suppose we take the example of a funeral in American society. We might observe the rituals of a funeral, in which the family and friends of the deceased get together and perform certain acts that are intended to aid the dead person's spirit

[9] John Middleton, *The Lugbara of Uganda* (New York: Holt, Rinehart and Winston, 1965), p. 36.

in the afterlife. Prayers are said, holy water is sprinkled on the coffin, and a variety of similar acts are carried out for the benefit of the deceased. This is the folk image—the belief that this ritual aids the spirit of the deceased. The anthropologist offers another perspective. The outside observer sees the actions of the people at the funeral not only in terms of the spirit of the deceased but also in terms of the social context of the group. Thus the analytical image is based on the observation of the people who are united in a common cause. The funeral not only has religious significance but is also a way of promoting the solidarity of the group, and it can be seen in a social, nonreligious sense as well.

Studying world view So far we have discussed the way anthropologists study the structure of society and the rules that govern everyday behavior, both from the viewpoint of a member of the culture and from the objective, analytical viewpoint of an outsider. There is a third area of study that can be approached only from the insider's perspective, something we call **world view**. The world view of a culture is the basic outlook of most of the members of a society. It is not something that we can ask about directly; rather, we must learn about it through inference, by putting together various clues about what is in the minds of the people we are observing. Furthermore, we cannot be content to get inside one individual's head; we have to focus on the attitudes of the entire society. We may be able to ask a person how he or she feels about a particular question, but we are interested in the answer to the extent that it represents the outlook of the entire society, not that of a single person.

If we recall Robert Redfield's and Oscar Lewis's differing interpretations of life in the Mexican village of Tepoztlán, it was their differing world views that caused some of their disagreement. That is, Redfield's world view, including his attitudes toward rural life and his preference for it over city life, led him to seek a similar world view in the people he studied. The same might be said for Lewis. Obviously, a problem in studying the world view of another culture is to avoid imposing our own cultural or personal preferences on it. We must try to portray the outlook of the people in the other culture, to present the world as they see it. This is perhaps the most difficult part of the cultural translation for which the anthropologist is responsible, because those who read the anthropologist's description probably have a very different world view from the one he or she is writing about.

A common aspect of the world view of people who live closer to nature than we do in industrial society is that they perceive themselves to be a part of a natural system, whereas we see ourselves as being outside that system. Industrial societies have learned to control the environment, so we see ourselves as dominant over nature. People who live off the land, through hunting and gathering or cultivation or both, do not feel that they are the masters of the earth. They have a different world view, in that they feel closer to nature. When a San of the Kalahari Desert in southern Africa kills a giraffe, he feels a loss, for he recognizes that a living spirit has departed from the world. When a Plains Indian killed a buffalo, it was not part of his plan to dominate nature and exploit it; rather, it was part of his interaction with nature.

Perhaps the anthropological approach to the study of world view is best summed up by Malinowski:

> The final goal, of which an Ethnographer should never lose sight . . . is, briefly, to grasp the native's point of view, his relation to life, to realise *his* vision of *his* world. We have to study man, and we must study what concerns him most intimately, that is, the hold which life has on him. In each culture, the values are slightly different; people aspire after different aims, follow different impulses, yearn after a different form of happiness. In each culture, we find different institutions in which man pursues his life-interest, different customs by which he satisfies his aspirations, different codes of law and morality which reward his virtues or punish his defections. To study the institutions, customs, and codes or to study the behaviour and mentality without realising the substance of their happiness—is, in my opinion, to miss the greatest reward which we can hope to obtain from the study of man.[10]

Changing Directions in Anthropological Research

Anthropology's stress on the study of nonliterate peoples continued until World War II. The common pattern was for an anthropologist to spend a year or more living in an isolated community of hunters and gatherers, horticulturalists, or pastoralists, and then to return for shorter periods (usually summer vacations from teaching positions) to do specialized research. Much of the research conducted in this way focused on traditional areas of interest—religion, myth, kinship, social organization. A few pioneer studies dealt with peasant or even industrial societies; sometimes these were supplemented by studies of the changes that had taken place as a result of contact with the Western world. But for the most part anthropology in the first half of the twentieth century amounted to the study of non-Western, nonliterate peoples, using the traditional methods of research that had been developed earlier by researchers like Malinowski.

World War II saw a major break in this pattern and brought about an opportunity to study Western societies. Cut off from many of the areas of earlier research by travel restrictions and the fear of hostility, anthropologists began to look for new sources of information about cultural differences. One logical alternative was to turn inward, bringing their knowledge of world cultures to bear on Western ways of life. The result was that, while anthropology did not abandon the

---

[10] Bronislaw Malinowski, *Argonauts of the Western Pacific* (New York: E. P. Dutton, 1922), p. 25.

Margaret Mead (1901–1978)

Margaret Mead undertook her doctoral research in Samoa, designed to study the relationship between patterns of child rearing and adult personalities. An important early link between psychology and anthropology, Mead's study of women and children in foreign cultures was a pioneering effort. Until then, male field researchers had been relatively unsuccessful in gathering information about females in other cultures. She played a leading role in developing the field of applied anthropology, and during the Second World War she helped promote the study of the cultures of our allies and enemies. In her later years, as an author and a public figure, Mead did more than anyone else to popularize the field of anthropology in the United States.

study of nonliterate peoples, studies of modern societies gained legitimacy. The long-standing tradition of initiation into anthropology through fieldwork in a non-Western culture was no longer practical, and those anthropologists who were trained in the 1940s and later became accepted by working in their own "backyard."

Another event that occurred at about the same time had a lasting impact on the field of anthropology. The U.S. government, wishing to increase its understanding of both its allies and its enemies in the war, sought the aid of many leading anthropologists in making cultural surveys of those countries. Even though they were unable to conduct actual fieldwork, the anthropologists managed to put together descriptions of the cultures of modern industrial countries by analyzing literature, historical documents, films, and many other sources of information, including personal interviews with immigrants and refugees. This practice was called "the study of

culture at a distance," and because it involved the work of so many leading anthropologists it gave even greater legitimacy to the anthropology of the postwar era.

During the war a number of books were produced on cultural practices and values in countries like Germany, Russia, Japan, and even the United States. Shortly thereafter, anthropologists began a wave of studies of peasant societies in response to the changes brought about by the war. Countries with a high proportion of peasants in their population became more important both politically and economically—countries like India, China, and Mexico, as well as much of the rest of Latin America and the Middle East. Anthropologists saw that peasant populations had played a growing role in world affairs, not only in terms of their contribution to major revolutions such as those in Russia in 1917 and China in the 1940s, but also in terms of the massive change they were undergoing as a result of the modernization of agriculture, health, population control, and education.

But peasant studies presented a different set of problems for anthropologists, and the tried-and-true methods of the past had to be revised to fit the new research setting. Most research among hunters and gatherers or horticulturalists involved long-term, intimate contact with a small, isolated group of people. The result was usually a description of their way of life, perhaps comparing it to similar groups, but generally treating the group as an isolated unit unaffected by the outside world. If the question of change came up, it was often seen from the point of view of the breakdown of traditional patterns and their replacement by Western ones introduced through contact with the outside.

Peasant studies, however, forced anthropologists to stop looking at small communities as isolated units relatively unaffected by the outside world. Peasants could be understood properly only if they were seen as part of a larger social and political system, the bottom of a vast economic pyramid; they were producers who were exploited by an elite who lived in the cities yet controlled the rural economy. Peasants were tied to national political events and were affected by decisions made far away by people with little or no understanding of their way of life. They were tied to national and international market systems, if only indirectly, and their day-to-day decisions had to be seen in the context of what was happening outside their community.

Another factor contributing to the changing directions of anthropological research in the postwar era was the tradition of literacy in peasant societies. Even though many peasants are nonliterate, they are part of a historical tradition that cannot be ignored. Formerly, anthropologists could emphasize fieldwork and pay almost no attention to written information; now they had to spend much more time combing archives for references to villagers, reading and interpreting census data, and learning about the impact of national and international policies on a single rural village. They could no longer seek to master the traditions of a single community; instead, they had to view them in the context of a literate tradition with a long history and a vast number of local and regional variations. Clearly, the task of the anthropologist has changed greatly.

If the methods of cultural anthropology have changed in the past 30 years, so too have the goals of research. The emphasis on such topics as kinship, religion, and social organization that characterized cultural descriptions written a generation ago has been replaced by a more Western-oriented set of topics that take account of the changes that have taken place is most developing nations. As traditional agricultural practices have given way to modern industrial technology, patterns of village life have been transformed. In many places the typical self-sufficient peasant farmer of the past has been transformed into a commercial farmer who produces for a wider market. The introduction of modern media into the village has produced a more cosmopolitan attitude toward religion and led to the breakdown of many beliefs and practices that do not conform to the mass culture portrayed in radio and television programs. In short, anthropology has had to shift its focus from traditional topics to issues that are important today: political organization and participation, health and the effects of Western medicine, education, and urbanization. While it would be an exaggeration to say that in the 1990s anthropology is only interested in people in developing or industrialized nations, it is equally false to pretend that anthropology continues to study mainly non-Western traditional peoples, as it did for so much of its past.

Some Observations

To conclude our discussion of the methods of anthropology, it is important to note how difficult it is for anthropologists to fit into the society they are studying. We come to a community as strangers, not knowing the cues and rules of behavior there, yet wanting people to accept us and take us into their homes and their private lives and reveal to us the most intimate details of their behavior. Is it any wonder that they reject us or think we are crazy? Colby Hatfield has made an interesting analysis of the role of anthropologists in the field.[11] First, he says, anthropologists are seen as children. Often they speak the language poorly and make many mistakes, both serious and silly. They do not know the rules of behavior and are frequently rude or insulting. They are unable to perform even the simplest task, because they have not learned the techniques used by members of that culture. All of these things are true of children, whose experience in the culture is equally limited (although they master the language at a much earlier age and much more rapidly, a torturous fact for anthropologists whose language gaffes make them the butt of teasing by little children).

A second role an anthropologist may slip into in a community, especially if it is a poor rural village, is what Hatfield calls the Fort Knox syndrome. Western anthropologists on even the skimpiest of research grants generally have much more money than the average villager. Thus the villagers think of them as wealthy. Anthropologists are willing to pay for the services of villagers, and it looks as if they never run out of money. At the same time, they obviously do not have to work for a living, because all they do is walk around the village all day asking questions. Their money miraculously arrives by mail every month, but it is not clear who is paying them for what. Anthropologists constantly fight this image, but no matter how modest their research grant or how financially strapped they feel, they are going to be viewed as wealthy.

Third, the anthropologist is often assigned the role of "Sahib," as Hatfield calls it, the

expert in all things, the high and mighty foreigner with power and knowledge that the villagers can never hope to have. After all, anthropologists are literate, whereas the people they have traditionally studied are not. Anthropologists can deal with government bureaucracies, which in itself is a kind of power. They know about people and places in every corner of the world and can tell stories that challenge the imagination of any villager. Despite the fact that in some ways they seem like children in the culture they are studying, they obviously know things the villagers do not, so they are often given the artificial status of village expert.

The anthropologist's role presents problems to both villagers and anthropologists. On the one hand, they are often given the status of "insiders," although rarely is this an unqualified acceptance. After all, they are interested in thoroughly learning about the community they are studying—which makes them very different from the usual outsider—so their efforts and persistence are rewarded by quasi-acceptance. Sometimes anthropologists are "adopted" by a family, which gives them special access to certain people and a definite status. That was what happened to Jean Briggs when she became a "daughter" of an Inuit family.[12] As a single female doing fieldwork in the Canadian Arctic, she found a number of advantages in having a family. But she also discovered there were some trade-offs. At times she had trouble balancing the roles of dutiful daughter and objective and conscientious anthropologist. Still, her family role provided her with a clear-cut position in the community, and that is often very important for the anthropologist to have. While working in southern Colombia one of the authors noted that after a couple of weeks the attitude of the community residents toward him changed. While he had insisted from the beginning that he would be working there for about a year, many of the people thought that he would

[11] Colby R. Hatfield, Jr., "Fieldwork: Toward a Model of Mutual Exploitation," *Anthropological Quarterly*, 46, no. 1 (1973):15–29.

[12] Jean L. Briggs, "Kapluna Daughter: Adopted by the Eskimo," in Peggy Golde, ed. *Women in the Field* (Chicago: Aldine, 1970).

turn out to be like other outsiders who had shown up, spent a very short time conducting some type of investigation that no one in the community really understood, and then disappeared as quickly and quietly as they had arrived. After about a month people began to accept the fact that he was truly interested in their life styles, and this realization helped to integrate him further into the community.

In some sense, of course, the anthropologist will always be regarded as a nosy outsider, no matter how long his or her stay. But this fact of life can be turned to advantage if the anthropologist learns to make inquiries that insiders would be too polite or know better than to ask. During a period when one of the authors was doing fieldwork in the Swiss Alps, he could not get the farmers to let him help them with their tasks. They felt that a city fellow shouldn't get his hands dirty working in the fields. When he pointed out to them that he had put on his work clothes and actually wanted to help, they would respond by saying something like "Oh, what do you have work clothes for?" They would laugh at the silly questions he asked about farming and the way they raised livestock, much as if he were a naive young boy. And they were amazed at the fact that he bought all his food and did not even grow his own potatoes. On the other hand, they respected his ability to deal with aspects of the outside world with which they had had little experience. He was asked to translate for them, to type letters and reports, and to tell them the meaning of various happenings. Perhaps most important in their minds was the fact that he could explain the American programs that appeared on their TV screens dubbed in German. The experience confirmed Hatfield's description of the fieldworker as child/Fort Knox/Sahib, and it points out some of the problems the anthropologist faces.

We have said much about these problems, and about the kinds of situations the anthropologist encounters, but little about actual techniques of fieldwork. We have not, for example, discussed the proper way to phrase a question or write up an interview, or the best way to use a tape recorder or a camera. This is because we believe that each fieldworker and each situation is unique, and therefore flexibility is preferable to strict rules. Although academic practice is changing somewhat, graduate students trained in anthropology generally are not taught the methods they are to use in great detail because it is assumed that they will adjust to the demands of the community they live in, and any attempt to teach them hard-and-fast rules of how to do research would not be valid. Besides, anthropological research calls for a lot of personal qualities that simply cannot be acquired through training: the guts to stick it out, the ability to control your temper when people laugh at you and kids throw snowballs at you, the willingness to eat whatever you are given with a smile and to compliment the chef even if you don't like fried lizard, and perhaps above all the ability to cope with loneliness when you are so far away from home for so long. There is no standard technique for dealing with these aspects of fieldwork, and there is no way to train for them. Not everyone who starts out to be an anthropologist actually becomes one, but those who do usually develop their own ways of doing research, ways that fit both their own personality and the unique demands of the research setting.

Summary

The methods used by cultural anthropologists to conduct research have been one of the distinguishing features between anthropology and other, related disciplines. One of the leading figures in revolutionizing the field techniques of anthropology was Bronislaw Malinowski, who engaged in what is called *participant observation*. Malinowski recommended that all anthropologists live in the community being studied, learn the native language, and try to understand the culture from the native's point of view. While not abandoning the societal types traditionally studied by anthropologists, researchers in the past several decades have shown an increased concern for the investigation of urban societies. In the past, social anthropologists had also avoided working in their own cultures. Today attitudes toward both of these formerly held positions have changed, and anthropologists not only work in the city environments, but also in their own backyards.

A major difficulty in conducting research in a foreign culture is maintaining objectivity in the face of massive *culture shock*. If anthropologists are reduced to making value judgments about the way of life of the people being studied, then they will never be able to describe or analyze that culture without personal prejudices slipping in. An interesting controversy arose over the objectivity of two anthropologists who studied the same community and arrived at contradictory conclusions about the people who lived there. Robert Redfield and Oscar Lewis both conducted field research in the Mexican village of Tepoztlán. Redfield described the village as being harmonious and happy, while many years later Lewis found it to be characterized by suspicion and lack of cooperation. Much of the difference in these two views can be assigned to the different temperaments of the two authors, each of whom was looking for something different and managed to find what he sought. Several decades later a similar controversy arose over which description of Samoan character was correct—that of Margaret Mead or the interpretations of Derek Freeman.

In doing research in a foreign culture, the anthropologist tries to uncover the unwritten rules that govern people's behavior. Often it is difficult to do this simply by asking people why they act in a particular way. For this reason the anthropologist must combine several different methods, including actual participation in the culture, questioning informants who share the culture, and standing back and observing as an outsider. One of the problems the anthropologist must overcome is the universal tendency of people to create the desired impression of themselves by concealing certain aspects of their lives and emphasizing others, a process we call *impression management*. In uncovering the hidden behavior of people in another culture, the anthropologist must also engage in a bit of impression management, proving that it is just as natural a process for us as for anyone else.

As anthropologists, our role in another culture is often made difficult by the fact that although we are in many ways similar to children, in that we do not know all the rules of behavior and do not speak the language perfectly, we are nonetheless adults and cannot be treated like children. In addition, anthropologists are often in command of more resources—money, an automobile, knowledge, and so forth—than the people they are studying. This leads people to place all kinds of demands on them, and makes it difficult for the anthropologist to be accepted completely as a member of the community.

Glossary

analytical image The manner in which an anthropologist organizes or structures the behavior of a particular culture.

fieldwork In cultural anthropology, research conducted among a group of people, usually of a different culture from that of the anthropologist, for the purpose of describing their way of life and comparing it to that of other peoples.

folk image The manner in which the natives of a particular culture organize or structure their own behavior.

impression management The attempt to control the opinion that others have of us. We all do this, through the clothes we wear, the way we talk and act in a given situation, and in many other ways.

participation observation The method used by the anthropologist in conducting field research, aimed at an equal balance between actual participation in the activities of the community and objective observation of that community.

world view The basic outlook (relationship to nature, values, attitudes, morals, beliefs, and so forth) held in common by most members of a society.

Questions for Discussion

1. Have you ever been in a foreign country where you didn't speak the language, or have you ever had contact with a foreigner who had trouble speaking English? How did this language problem affect your interaction? What difficulties would this create for an anthropologist, and how could they be overcome?

2. What are some of the unwritten rules in American culture that a foreigner might have trouble learning? How would you, as an anthropologist, go about learning unwritten rules in a foreign culture?

3. What forms of impression management do you practice in your daily life? What are some of the impressions you try to create in different situations, and how do you vary your behavior (for instance, by varying the clothes you wear, the speech patterns you use, and so forth)?

4. Select a subculture within your community and design an anthropological research program to study it. What would be the most important methods you would use? What problems do you foresee in doing this research? What kind of information would be easiest or most difficult to obtain, and why?

Suggestions for Additional Reading

MICHAEL H. AGAR, *The Professional Stranger: An Informal Introduction to Ethnography* (New York: Academic Press, 1980). A delightful book on "doing" ethnography, this is a must for even the casual student interested in fieldwork.

SORAYA ALTORKI and CAMILLIA FAWZI EL-SOHL (Eds.), *Arab Women in the Field: Study Your Own Society.* (Syracuse: Syracuse University Press, 1988). Experiences by Arab female researchers which focus on a range of important issues related to gender and working in one's own society.

H. RUSSELL BERNARD, *Research Methods in Cultural Anthropology* (Beverly Hills, Cal.: Sage Publications, 1988). An important guide to research, this book covers everything from coding field notes to sampling and site selection.

GERALD D. BERREMAN, *Behind Many Masks*, Monograph no. 4 (Washington, D.C.: Society for Applied Anthropology, 1962). A description of impression management in a village in India, and how the author learned to deal with it during his research there.

ELENORE SMITH BOWEN (LAURA BOHANNAN), *Return to Laughter* (New York: Doubleday, 1954). A novel by a woman anthropologist based on her study of the Tiv, an African society. The author captures many of the problems and emotions involved in fieldwork and communicates them in a delightfully entertaining fashion.

ROBERT B. EDGERTON and L. L. LANGNESS, *Methods and Styles in the Study of Culture* (San Francisco: Chandler and Sharp, 1974). A brief handbook covering a wide variety of techniques used by anthropologists, and explaining how they can be combined in both ethnographic and cross-cultural analysis.

GEORGE M. FOSTER and ROBERT V. KEMPER (Eds.), *Anthropology in Cities* (Boston: Little, Brown, 1974). Collection of essays written by anthropologists engaged in urban research.

MORRIS FREILICH (Ed.), *Marginal Natives: Anthropologists at Work* (New York: Harper and Row, 1970). This was one of the first books in which a group of anthropologists talked about the trials and tribulations of conducting fieldwork. It is still very worthwhile reading.

PEGGY GOLDE (Ed.), *Women in the Field: Anthropological Experiences* (Chicago: Aldine, 1970). As the title indicates, the volume not only deals with conducting ethnographic research, but also examines the roles of women as field researchers.

MARTYN HAMMERSLEY and PAUL ATKINSON, *Ethnography: Principles in Practice* (London: Tavistock Publications Ltd., 1983). A short book, accessible to those with little or no knowledge of ethnographic techniques, on the theory and methods of ethnography, containing an annotated bibliography of texts on ethnographic method.

NANCY HOWELL, *Surviving Fieldwork: A Report of the Advisory Panel on Health and Safety in Fieldwork* (Washington, D.C.: American Anthropological Association, Number 26, 1990). A rather sobering account of perils facing anthropologists in the field, this book is designed to help us learn from our past experiences.

BRONISLAW MALINOWSKI, *A Diary in the Strict Sense of the Term* (New York: Harcourt Brace Jovanovich, 1967). The private notes taken by Malinowski during his fieldwork in the Trobriand Islands and published after his death. This book is particularly revealing of the stresses and strains of research in a foreign culture and the problems of culture shock.

MARGARET MEAD, *Blackberry Winter, My Earlier Years* (New York: Simon & Schuster, 1972). The autobiography of one of the leading anthropologists of the century, which includes lengthy descriptions of her experience in the field in a wide variety of cultural settings.

PERTTI J. PELTO and GRETEL H. PELTO, *Anthropological Research: The Structure of Inquiry*, 2nd ed. (New York: Cambridge University Press, 1978). One of the more detailed books treating the various research techniques and approaches used by anthropologists, this book is especially valuable for its blend of the humanistic and scientific elements of fieldwork.

HORTENSE POWDERMAKER, *Stranger and Friend: The Way of an Anthropologist* (New York: W. W. Norton, 1966). A personal account of the author's research in four societies and the different approach she adopted in each.

GEORGE D. SPINDLER (Ed.), *Being an Anthropologist: Fieldwork in Eleven Cultures* (New York: Holt, Rinehart and Winston, 1970). Eleven anthropologists describe their experiences in conducting research in other cultures.

JAMES P. SPRADLEY, *The Ethnographic Interview* (New York: Holt, Rinehart and Winston, 1979). A detailed examination of one of the most important research techniques used by cultural anthropologists.

JAMES P. SPRADLEY, *Participant Observation* (New York: Holt, Rinehart and Winston, 1980). An up-to-date discussion of some of the major problems and research methods in participant observation in cultural anthropology.

PHILIP R. DEVITA, (Ed.) *The Humbled Anthropologist: Tales from the Pacific.* (Belmont, Cal.: Wadsworth Publishing Co., 1990). A delightfully interesting humanistic collection of "stories from the field" which focus on unexpected quirks of fate and the fascinating lessons learned from these experiences.

TONY WHITEHEAD and MARY ELLEN CONWAY (Eds.), *Self, Sex, and Gender in Cross-Cultural Fieldwork* (Urbana: University of Illinois Press, 1986). A good, contemporary, well-balanced volume on gender and fieldwork.

Assault on Paradise

CONRAD P. KOTTAK

This is a delightful retelling of a well-respected anthropologist's first foray into the field. How was the community chosen, and what sorts of accommodations did it have? As a neophyte anthropologist, what expectations did he bring to the field regarding what he could realistically accomplish? Kottak retraces the steps that led him to become an anthropologist, at the same time putting his experiences into a perspective that is instructional for other novices interested in conducting field research.

This anthropological study of rapid change in a formerly isolated and tranquil Atlantic coastal community in Brazil covers nearly twenty years. The story of Arembepe (Ah-*raim*-beppy), once just a small fishing village in Bahia state, north-central Brazil, is worth telling in its own right. But it also has a larger significance. Although far more dramatically than most, Arembepe has met the increasingly common fate of the little community in the Third World. As a result of their poverty and powerlessness, the people of Arembepe, or Arembepeiros (Ah-raim-bep-*pay*-roos), have been compelled by external forces to give up a large part of their previous autonomy, egalitarianism, and peace of mind. Like a thousand other places, Arembepe has grown increasingly dependent on, and vulnerable to, a world political economy of which its inhabitants have little understanding, and over which they have even less control. And provincial folk who once were impressed by, yet dared only gently probe, the novelty and strangeness of foreign ways have become eager initiates into a mass-mediated world culture.

It Began Quite by Accident

This is a story of change, but it did not start out to be that. In fact, it began quite by accident. I first lived in Arembepe during the (North American) summer of 1962. That was between my junior and senior years at New York City's Columbia College, where I was majoring in anthropology. I went to Arembepe as a participant in a now defunct program designed to

Conrad P. Kottak, *Assault on Paradise* (New York: Random House, 1983), pp. 3–28. Copyright © 1983 by Random House Inc. Reprinted by permission of the publisher.

provide undergraduates with experience doing ethnography—firsthand study of an alien society's culture and social life. The program's cumbersome title, the Columbia-Cornell-Harvard-Illinois Summer Field Studies Program in Anthropology, reflected participation by four universities, each with a different field station. The others were in Peru, Mexico, and Ecuador. The area around Salvador, Brazil, had just been chosen for the Columbia field station, and that is where I was sent.

The field team leader was Professor Marvin Harris, who was later to become my adviser and doctoral dissertation committee chairman during my graduate work in anthropology at Columbia University, which began in 1963. Also in Salvador that year was Professor Charles Wagley, another Columbia anthropologist, who had worked with Harris and others to establish the program. Through their links with Bahian social scientists, Harris and Wagley chose two villages that were sufficiently remote to be anthropologically interesting but close enough to Salvador to maintain contact with the undergraduates. The two communities lay along the same road. Abrantes, the agricultural village, nearer to Salvador, was district seat for Arembepe, the more remote fishing village. Liking the coast, I expressed a preference for Arembepe, where I was assigned, along with fellow team member David Epstein. Harris arranged for us to rent the dilapidated three-bedroom summer house of a city man who sometimes vacationed in Arembepe.

In the meantime, Professor Wagley's daughter, Betty, a Barnard College student who was considering majoring in anthropology, arrived to spend the summer with her parents in Salavador. She went along with us to visit Abrantes and Arembepe and decided that she, too, would like some fieldwork experience in the latter. Betty arranged lodging with a local woman, but since David and I had hired a cook, she ate with us and shared the cost of food and supplies. Betty's mother is Brazilian, and Betty, who was herself born in Brazil, is bilingual in Portuguese, which made her more adept at fieldwork than either David or I. She was also kind enough to translate for us on many occasions.

Having taught anthropology now for fifteen years, I retrospectively realize how unusual my first field experience was. Most anthropologists begin fieldwork, which is required for the doctorate, after a few years of graduate study and not as undergraduates. Furthermore, they usually determine for themselves the part of the world they want to work in and the kind of problem they will investigate there. For example, my own most lengthy ethnographic project came at the end of graduate school. Having taken courses about several world areas, I became particularly interested in Madagascar. I read as much as I could about the cultures of Madagascar and settled on a problem—the social implications of an economic change, the expansion of irrigated agriculture—that could be investigated there.

In the case of Arembepe, however, someone else—the directors of the summer field program, for which I was chosen competitively—selected the general area, and even the specific village, for me. I did not have time to do the extensive background reading that normally precedes fieldwork, nor did I have much time to study the language that I would be using in the field. I therefore had no control over the initial choice of Arembepe, though I did decide to keep on studying it, particularly when, by 1973, it became apparent that Arembepe was changing more rapidly in a decade than some communities have changed in centuries—which is why I decided to write this book.

Most of my preparation for my 1962 fieldwork was in a prefield seminar that Harris offered at Columbia, and in another seminar about ethnographic field techniques taught by Professor Lambros Comitas. In Harris's class, students talked about the kinds of research we planned to do when we got to Brazil, and Harris urged us to do microprojects, focusing on limited aspects of community life that we could investigate easily in three months. The program's founders did not intend for this to be traditional holistic ethnography—intensive study of all aspects of life through long-term residence and participant observation. Comitas's seminar, on the other hand, had introduced me to techniques used in long-term, in-

depth ethnography. As I describe later on, one of my problems in doing fieldwork in Arembepe in 1962 was the conflict between my own desire to do a holistic study and the program's preference for a microproject.

The program's goals were limited, and I now realize that this was realistic, since we were novices. Harris and the other leaders intended for us to get our feet wet—to see if we actually liked fieldwork enough to pursue a career in cultural anthropology and to give us an experience that would help prepare us for subsequent, longer-term field research. As preparation for our microprojects, the prefield seminar assignment was to do background reading and a research paper on the topic we planned to investigate in Brazil. Harris suggested that I study race relations, which already had a large literature. Comparisons of race relations in Brazil and the United States are in order because both countries have a heritage of slavery and plantation life, and in both there has been considerable mixture of Europeans, Africans, and (to a lesser extent) Native Americans. For the seminar, I read extensively. I learned the main differences between the role of race in Brazil and the United States and wrote a research paper on my findings. Harris and I later worked out a specific microproject on Brazilian racial classification for the field, which is discussed later in this chapter.

Although I prepared myself adequately to investigate Brazilian race relations, my preparation in Brazilian Portuguese was insufficient, and language turned out to be my biggest barrier in the field. The only Romance language I had ever studied was Latin, for two years in high school. I had taken German in college, which was no help at all. I had never been abroad before and had no experience actually speaking a foreign language: high school and college had barely taught me how to read one. As a result, I spent most of the summer of 1962 asking Brazilians to repeat everything they said to me, which led Arembepeiros to call me a *papagaio* ("parrot")—because I could only echo words that someone else had originated. I discovered that it is difficult to gain profound insight into native social life when you can't converse even as well as a five-year-old.

The Sixties

In June 1962, when I first visited Arembepe, the 60 kilometer trip from Salvador was neither simple nor certain. It required about three hours in a vehicle equipped with four-wheel drive. I first arrived, and indeed have always visited, Arembepe during the austral winter. Located some 13 degrees south of the equator and at sea level, Arembepe is never cold, but June and July are rainy months, making travel difficult. The clay-surfaced road was usually muddy, and we always got stuck at least once in any round trip. Since the field team used a large and heavy jeep station wagon, the task of getting unstuck usually required a work group of field team members and a dozen helpful onlookers. Friendly natives would do most of the work, we learned to hope, particularly when we were headed into Salvador for occasional "rest and recreation." Otherwise we would have to walk into the lobby of a city hotel covered with red mud, raising doubts about whether we should be given lodging.

On the road to Arembepe, sand, lagoons, and more sand came after the mud. Following a heavy rain, crossing the freshwater lagoons that bound Arembepe on the west made the jeep seem like a motorboat, as high water washed onto the cabin floor, and occasionally stalled the engine. After the lagoons came the dunes, with their closely planted coconut trees—posing another traffic hazard. Making it into the village required finding another vehicle's tracks, flooring the accelerator, and for some, exhorting deities for assistance. Once, as a particularly frustrating trip from the city seemed to be coming to an end, I pulled up in front of the house I was renting to find that the brakes had failed; only frantic pumping kept me from crashing through the kitchen wall.

But Arembepe was worth the trip. I can't imagine an anthropologist finding a more stereotypically beautiful field setting. The village was strung along a narrow strip of land (less than a kilometer) between ocean and lagoons. More spectacular than any South Seas island I later visited, Arembepe's houses—many brightly painted in tones of blue, pink, peach, and orange—stood under lofty coconut palms. To the east, stretches of smooth white sand and protected swimming areas alternated with jagged rocks and churning Atlantic waves. In the heat of a clear, sunny day in August, Arembepe was alive with color: the green-blue hues of ocean and lagoon, orange-reds of bricks and roof tiles, pinks and blues of painted houses, greens of palms, and white of sands. Arembepe's colorfully painted fishing boats were anchored each evening and on Sunday in the port located just east of the central square and the small, white, attractive Roman Catholic chapel. The harbor is formed by a rugged, partially submerged reef; the boats rowed out each morning through its narrow channels, then raised their sunbleached sails to travel to their destinations for the day.

Arembepe in 1962 belonged in a movie. (In fact, a team of French photographers did use the chapel as a background for fashion advertisements that appeared in *Vogue* in 1966.) This conjunction of natural beauty with the middle-class appeal of a "quaint," remote village subsisting on a wind-powered, hook-and-line fishing industry had already attracted a handful of tourists and summer (dry season, December to February) residents to Arembepe in 1962. However, the poor quality of the road made it a lengthy and difficult trip from Salvador even in the dry season, and only a few residents of the capital—primary middle-class and lower-middle-class people—had summer houses in Arembepe. Limited bus service began in 1965, but it attracted few visitors until the condition of the road improved around 1970.

Poverty and poor public health were the most obvious blights that made Arembepe of the 1960s—despite the title of this book—something less than paradise. In theory, Arembepeiros got their drinking water from Big Well, a tiny settlement about 2 kilometers away. An entrepreneur who resided there made money selling barrels of water in Arembepe. In fact, however, when well water was not immediately or readily available, Arembepeiros occasionally drank water from the freshwater lagoon. Some mothers even used lagoon water in the powdered milk they mixed for their children. Considering these traditional uses of water—and the fact that the bushes where Arembepeiros relieved themselves were just on the edge of the lagoon, which rises during the rainy season—it is easy to understand why most children in Arembepe in the 1960s showed symptoms of intestinal disorders and of extreme malnutrition (the latter partly caused by the presence of enervating parasites in their bodies).

Malinowski and Microprojects

I entered this romantic yet imperfect setting as a fledgling ethnographer with ambitious goals and a huge linguistic impediment. Two dimensions of the work I did in Arembepe beginning in 1962 bear discussion here. One involves my scientific and professional aims. The second has to do with my personal reactions to an alien setting. First the scientific goals.

As a conscientious anthropology major, I very much wanted to put into personal practice some of the lessons I had learned in my classes. I wanted to do the kinds of things, for example, that Bronislaw Malinowski describes as the ethnographer's work in the first chapter of his well-known book *Argonauts of the Western Pacific*, which is a study of fishermen and traders in Melanesia. We had read this classic in Comitas's seminar.

During the summer of '62 I often compared my own experiences with Malinowski's; the settings of our fieldwork struck me as similar. He had also worked in what seemed a romantic, tropical South Sea setting (the Trobriand Islands). Despite the fact that Arembepe is on the mainland, the phrase "South Sea island" kept running through my head during my 1960s field trips. As I read Malinowski's description of the moment when the ethnographer "sets foot upon a native beach, and makes first attempts to get in touch with the natives" (Malinowski, 1961, p. 4), I imagined myself in his sandals. He had talked of trying to get to know the natives by observing them making things and writing down names of tools. Like me, Malinowski initially had trouble communicating with the natives. "I was quite unable to enter any more detailed or explicit conversation with them at first. I knew well that the best remedy for this was to collect concrete data, and accordingly I took a village census, wrote down genealogies, drew up plans and collected the terms of kinship" (Malinowski, 1961, p. 5).

I was eager to do these things that Malinowski had done, especially to census the village. However, field leader Harris discouraged me, offering another lesson: before I could hope to gather the kind of detailed and accurate data that ethnography demands, I would have to establish rapport within the community. People would have to get to know and trust me. I would have to convince them that I was not dangerous and that it would not be to their disadvantage to answer my questions. Furthermore, I did not yet know enough about village life to devise pertinent questions to ask during a census. Accordingly, but regretfully, I put the census on hold and set about "building rapport." David Epstein and Betty Wagley, my associates in the field, were doing the same thing, as did Marvin Harris, when he eventually moved in with David and me to spend the month of August in Arembepe.

How does one establish rapport? "Get to know the men," I was told. To do this I started joining the fishermen for their evening bath in the freshwater lagoon. I developed my first doubts about the wisdom of this kind of participant observation when I accidentally swatted a floating piece of donkey dung (I like to think I identified the correct mammal) during my third bath. I abandoned lagoon bathing once and for all, however, when I learned of the lagoon system's infestation by schistosomes—liver flukes. Thereafter, I was careful to avoid the lagoon and followed the advice of public health officials to rub exposed body parts with alcohol whenever I came into contact with lagoon water. Arembepeiros found these precautions laughable: Not to worry, they said—there were small fish in the lagoon that ate the liver flukes (and germs in general) so that there was no health threat to people.

If the lagoon was now off-limits, there was still the chapel stoop, where each evening, after the fishing fleet had returned, baths had been taken, and the day's main meal consumed, men would gather to talk. This area was male territory. Only small girls and old women dared approach. David and I would sit and try to talk. My Portuguese remained rudimentary; I resented David because he spoke and seemed to understand better than I did. Still, villagers tossed questions my way. They were curious about the United States, and their questions were scintillating: "Were there camels in the United States? . . . Elephants? . . . Monkeys?" They went through a litany of animals they had seen on the lottery tickets that people brought back from Salvador. "Look! Up in the sky. It's a jet from the United States heading for Rio," they observed every other night, reflecting the airline's schedule. Whenever, after minutes of laborious mental rehearsal, I managed to find the proper Portuguese words to ask a question about Arembepe, I would get an incomprehensible reply, followed by some such query as "Have you even seen a bear, Conrado?"

"Bear, bear," I parroted.

"Parrot, parrot," they guffawed.

"Yes, I have seen a bear. I have seen a bear in a zoo."

Rapport building was fascinating indeed.

Visions of Malinowski danced in my head as I came to resent this kind of activity as a waste to time. I was eager to do something "more scientific." The microproject that Marvin Harris and I had planned for me involved testing a difference between race relations in Brazil and the United States. In the United States one's racial identity is determined by a rule of descent. If an American has one black parent and one white one, he or she is assigned, automatically at birth and without regard for physical appearance, to "the black race." In Brazil, it seemed that several factors determined racial identity and that no descent rule operated. Since, however, the absence of such a rule had never been investigated systematically, we decided that a genetically and phenotypically (physically) diverse and mixed community such as Arembepe would be a good place to test it.

When a descent rule operates, full siblings are assigned to the same descent group. Thus in the United States, siblings cannot belong to different races. In Arembepe, Harris and I set out to find full siblings who were physically very different, to see if they were assigned to different races. We soon found three sisters with widely varying skin shades, hair types, and facial features. After we had photographed them, I finally got to do something that seemed more professional than answering questions about what animals were to be found in the United States. I chose a sample of 100 villagers and showed the photo of the sisters to all, asking them to tell me each girl's race. Sure enough, I found that many different terms were employed, that full siblings could indeed belong to different races in Brazil.

Some interesting new questions about Brazilian race relations were stimulated by that first survey, and Harris and I devised another set of questions about drawings of individuals who contrasted phenotypically. As a result of questioning another sample of villagers, I found that Arembepeiros used far more racial terms (over forty) than had previously been reported for a Brazilian community. More interestingly, they used them inconsistently, so that the racial term used for another person might vary from day to day, as might even self-identification. By the time my three months in Arembepe were up, I had developed a specialized linguistic proficiency in Brazilian racial terminology, and Harris and I had the basis for a couple of innovative journal articles. Although I still felt guilty that I had not managed to do a Malinowskian village census, I did think that I had accomplished something during my first field experience.

If I was ever to work again in Brazil, I knew that I would have to improve my Portuguese. I could get only so far, I realized, talking about race relations. Therefore, I spent the next summer taking an intensive course in Brazilian Portuguese at Columbia University while another field team lived in Arembepe. Also in that summer of 1963, Betty Wagley and I, whose romance had begun under Arembepe's full moon, got married; and I began graduate school in the fall.

I was delighted, in the spring, to be offered the job of assistant leader of the program's 1964 team, and I returned to Arembepe in June of that year determined finally to do my census. And not just a census. By then I had studied more anthropology and my Portuguese had improved dramatically; I felt that I was ready to do a full-fledged interview schedule. Peter Gorlin, who now holds a Ph.D. in anthropology and an M.D. degree, was an undergraduate field team member stationed in Jauá, the next fishing village south of Arembepe. Peter had read Malinowski, too, and he was as eager as I to employ Malinowski's "method of concrete, statistical documentation" (1961, p. 24), in order to satisfy the ethnographer's "fundamental obligation of giving a complete survey

of the phenomena, and not of picking out the sensational [and] the singular" (1961, p. 11).

I felt ready to do a survey of all the households in Arembepe, and Peter wanted to do the same in Jauá. But we needed "an instrument." The field team leader, Bahian physician and anthropologist Thales de Azevedo, supplied us with one—an interview schedule that had been previously used in southern Bahia. We modified the schedule for the fishing villages and had it printed up.

An *interview schedule* contrasts with a questionnaire in that respondents fill our questionnaires, whereas with an interview schedule the interviewer, in this case the ethnographer, asks informants a set of questions and then fills in the answers on the form. Like other social scientists, many anthropologists like to gather comparable quantifiable information about people in the group they are studying, as I wanted to do in Arembepe. However, sociologists normally work with literate people, who can fill out the answer sheets or questionnaire forms themselves. Anthropologists, on the other hand, have not usually worked in places where most people are literate; so we have to record the answers ourselves. Because we are in charge of pacing, we can also choose to digress temporarily from the scheduled questions to follow up intriguing bits of information that emerge during the interview. Thus the researcher can keep the interview open-ended and exploratory while also asking all respondents the same basic set of questions. I learned as much about Arembepe through such open-ended questioning as I did from the formal queries.

Yet another difference between the research techniques of anthropologists and sociologists is illustrated by our interview in Arembepe and Jauá. Since sociologists normally deal with large and complex societies, such as the contemporary United States, they must use *sampling techniques*, which enable them to make inferences about larger groups on the basis of a detailed study of smaller ones. However, like most anthropologists, we did not need to do sampling in Arembepe and Jauá, since both were sufficiently small for us to do total samples—that is, to complete the schedule with all the households in each community. Arembepe, it turned out, had 159 households and Jauá about 40.

A final contrast between cultural anthropology and sociology is worth mentioning. Sociologists often enjoy the luxury of distributing their questionnaires by mail or having graduate-student research assistants administer them as well as code and analyze them. But the anthropologist works right in the community and thereby faces a hundred real-world obstacles. My main problem doing the interview schedule in Arembepe was not the few villagers who slammed doors and windows in my face, or even the snot-nosed children who used my pants as a handkerchief. Rather, it was fleas. I still recall my third or fourth interview, in a sand-floored hut in northern Arembepe. As I asked the set of questions to a dozen cooperative, smiling, hospitable members of an extended family, I began to itch, particularly in the crotch. For the good of science I made it through to the end of the form, but I did not tarry for open-ended inquiry. Instead I ran home, through the house, out the back door, and right into the harbor at high tide. I quickly removed my shorts and let the salt water burn into the flea wounds. Fleas bothered most of us, particularly Betty, that summer. The remedy for the men, we discovered, was to wear pants with cuffs liberally sprinkled with flea power. In this way we managed to interview in virtually all of Arembepe's households, despite the predatory sand fleas with their seemingly special thirst for North American blood.

Our interview schedule was eight pages long and included questions (for each household member) about age, sex, racial identity, diet, employment, religious beliefs and practices, education, political preferences, possessions, consumption patterns, and ownership of livestock, boats, coconut trees, land, and farms. As the field leader who worked most closely with Peter, I encouraged him not to do a microproject but to follow the Malinowskian path that I had always wanted to tread. He did it with gusto; in two months he had finished the schedule with all the households in Jauá, and he hiked up the beach to spend August helping Betty and me complete the schedule in Arembepe.

There are advantages, I now realize, in both models for brief fieldwork. A microproject is easily manageable and offers the promise of a modest scientific paper. Yet the holistic Malinowskian approach is also valuable. I am convinced that my Portuguese would have gotten much better if I had done the interview schedule the first summer, rather than limiting my talk to rapport building and race relations. I later found this to be true, when I used a simple interview schedule fairly soon after I began working among the Betsileo people of Madagascar in 1966. The first interview schedule does not have to be as detailed as the one we used in Arembepe. In Madagascar I used a succession of schedules, about different subjects and of increasing complexity. All provided me with comparable information about a group of people, and all increased my ability to discuss a range of topics significant to the Betsileo. Similarly, Peter Gorlin's work with the interview schedule in

Jauá and Arembepe in 1964 helped him improve his Portuguese much more quickly than I had done in 1962.

There was an added benefit from doing the interview schedule that I did not fully realize in 1964: it got at least one member of the field team into every home in Arembepe. Years later I was to hear from many villagers that they remembered these visits warmly. Our questions, asked in their homes, had communicated our personal interest and had shown villagers that we were not the kind of outsiders who disdain Arembepeiros, considering their own life style incomparably superior.

I found Arembepeiros to be open, warm, and hospitable people, much less wary of outsiders than the Betsileo I studied for fourteen months in 1966–1967. Most Arembepeiros welcomed us into their homes and gladly answered our questions. A handful, however, played hard to get, slamming windows and doors as I approached, telling neighbors that they would not answer our questions. I had to settle for sketchier information about them and could only make estimates of their incomes and consumption patterns, on the basis of public information and behavior. Fortunately, since the 1964 interview schedule data are the basis for much of this book's comparison of Arembepe of the 1960s with that community today, fewer than a dozen households, scattered throughout the village, refused to let us do the schedule.

The interview schedule was not the only thing I did in Arembepe in 1964. Soon after my arrival, I met an excellent informant, Alberto, whose name figures prominently in the story that follows. A forty-year-old fisherman, Alberto was the eldest brother of our cook. He felt free to visit our house almost every night, and he was eager to instruct me about the fishing industry. I got additional information about fishing by talking to fishermen and fish marketers on the beach, and by going out in several boats, including that of Tomé, Arembepe's most successful boat captain and owner. Tomé's name, too, is a prominent one in Arembepe's recent history.

In 1965 I had my third chance to study Arembepe. The results of analyzing the interview schedules and my information on fishing had been so promising that both Marvin Harris and I felt that I might, with one more summer, amass sufficient data to write my doctoral dissertation about Arembepe, which I did. This time Betty and I were not part of a field team but on our own. A graduate fellowship and grant supported my work, and living was still cheap in cash-poor Arembepe. That summer, I again followed the Malinowskian plan, but I already had much of the statistical and observational data needed for the "firm, clear outline" of my community's organization and the "anatomy of its culture" (Malinowski, 1961, p. 24). Now I needed flesh for the skeleton. So I spent the summer of 1965 gathering data on the "imponderabilia of actual life . . . collected through minute, detailed observations . . . made possible by close contact with native life" (Malinowski, 1961, p. 24). By this time, however, I didn't really have to harken back to Malinowski to know that although I had the bare bones, I still needed to find out more about native opinions, values, and feelings; to listen to stories, examine cases, and gather intimate, basic details about everyday life. Like Napoleon Chagnon, the principal ethnographer of the Yanomamo Indians of Venezuela, I knew "how much I enjoyed reading monographs that were sprinkled with real people, that described real events, and that had some sweat and tears, some smells and sentiments mingled with the words" (Chagnon, 1977, p. xi). I wanted to add such dimensions—feeling tones—to my ethnography of Arembepe.

It Was an Alien Place

Those were some of my professional goals and scientific procedures. The other aspect of doing ethnography is more personal. No matter how objective and scientific they fancy themselves, anthropologists are not mechanical measuring instruments. We are inevitably participant observers, taking part in—and by so doing modifying, no matter how slightly—the phenomena we are investigating and seeking to understand. Not recording machines but people, anthropologists are raised in particular cultural traditions, possess idiosyncratic personality traits and experiences, have their own motivations, impressions, values, and reactions. Nor are our informants all alike, and we come to appreciate them differently. Some we never appreciate; an occasional one we detest.

Brought up in one culture, intensely curious about others, anthropologists nevertheless experience culture shock, particularly on the first field trip. *Culture shock* refers to the whole set of feelings about being in an alien setting, and the ensuing reactions. It is a chilly, creepy feeling of alienation, of being without some of the most ordinary, trivial—and therefore basic—cues of one's culture of origin.

As I planned my departure for Brazil in 1962 I could not know just how naked I would feel without the cloak of my own language and culture. My sojourn in Arembepe would be my first trip outside the

United States. I was an urban boy who had grown up in Atlanta, Georgia, and New York City. I had little experience with rural life in my own country, none with Latin America, and I had received only minimal training in the Portuguese language.

New York City direct to Salvador, Bahia, Brazil. Just a brief stopover in Rio de Janerio; a longer visit would be a reward at the end of fieldwork. As our propjet approached tropical Salvador, I couldn't believe the whiteness of the sand. "That's not snow, is it?" I remarked to a fellow field team member. Marvin Harris had arranged our food and lodging at the Paradise Hotel, overlooking Bahia's magnificent, endlessly blue, All Saints' Bay. My first impressions of Bahia were of smells—alien odors of ripe and decaying mangoes, bananas, and passion fruit—and of swatting ubiquitous fruit flies I had never seen before, although I had read extensively about their reproductive behavior in genetics classes. There were strange concoctions of rice, black beans, and gelatinous gobs of unidentifiable meats and floating pieces of skin. Coffee was strong and sugar crude, and every table top had containers for toothpicks and manioc (cassava) flour, to sprinkle, like parmesan cheese, on anything one might eat. I remember oatmeal soup and a slimy stew of beef tongue in tomatoes. At one meal a disintegrating fish head, eyes still attached, but barely, stared up at me as the rest of its body floated in a bowl of bright orange palm oil. Bearing my culture's don't-drink-the-water complex, it took me a few days to discover that plain mineral water quenched thirst better than the gaseous variety. Downstairs was the Boite Clock, a nightclub whose rhythmic bossa nova music often kept us from sleeping.

I only vaguely remember my first day in Arembepe. Unlike ethnographers who have studied remote tribes in the tropical forests of interior South America or the highlands of New Guinea, I did not have to hike or ride a canoe for days to arrive at my field site. Arembepe was not isolated relative to such places, only relative to every other place *I* had ever been. My first contact with Arembepe was just a visit, to arrange lodging. We found the crumbling summer house of a man who lived in Salvador, and arranged to rent it and have it cleaned. We hired Dora, a twenty-five-year-old unmarried mother of two, to cook for us, and another woman to clean house and do our laundry. My first visit to Arembepe didn't leave much of an impression because I knew I'd still have a few more days at the Paradise Hotel, with a real toilet and shower, before having to rough it "in the field."

Back in the city, using her almost native fluency in Brazilian language and culture, Betty Wagley bargained for our canvas cots, pots, pans, flashlights, and other supplies from small stores in Salvador's least expensive commercial zones. I don't remember our actual move to Arembepe or who accompanied us. There were field team members to deposit in Abrantes, on the road to Arembepe, and Harris had employed a chauffeur for the program's jeep station wagon. But I do recall what happened when we arrived. There was no formal road into the village. Entering through southern Arembepe, vehicles simply threaded their way around coconut trees, following tracks left by automobiles that had passed previously. A crowd of children had heard us coming, and they pursued our car through the village streets until we parked in front of our house, near the central square. Our first few days in Arembepe were spent with children following us everywhere. For weeks we had few moments of privacy. Children watched our every move through our living room window. Occasionally one made an incomprehensible remark. Usually they just stood there. Sometimes they would groom one another's hair, eating the lice they found.

Outcasts from an urban culture, David and I locked our doors. Once he went into Salvador and I stayed the night alone.

"Conrado's scared," said Dora. "He's afraid of the *bichos* [beasts, real and imaginary] outside." There was really nothing to be afraid of, she assured me; a dangerous *bicho* had never bothered anyone in Arembepe, and most people didn't even have locks on their doors.

Our most annoying intruders were a few drunks who occasionally paid us nighttime visits, seeking alcohol or money to buy it. Fairly late one night (around nine or ten o'clock, after most villagers were in bed) two men pounded on our door. From their slurred speech and loudness it was apparent that both had been drinking. One was a young villager, who said that he wanted to introduce us to the other man, a visitor from Camaçari, the county seat.

"Some Americans in Camaçari taught my friend how to speak English," said the villager.

"Oh, yeah," we said. "Let's hear him."

"John Wayne," said the visitor.

"Very good," observed David. "Do you know anything else?"

"Yes," the man responded. "Fucky, fucky." (My subsequent travels throughout the world have revealed several permutations of this common but stigmatized four-letter English word.)

The sounds, sensations, sights, smells, and tastes of life in northeastern Brazil, and in Arembepe, slowly grew familiar. I gradually accepted the fact that the only toilet tissue available at a reasonable price had almost the texture of sandpaper. I grew accustomed to this world without Kleenex, in which globs of mucus habitually drooped from the noses of village children whenever a cold passed through Arembepe. A world where, seemingly without effort, women with gracefully swaying hips carried 18-liter kerosene cans of water on their heads, where boys sailed kites and sported at catching houseflies in their bare hands, where old women smoked pipes, storekeepers offered *cachaça* (common rum) at nine in the morning, and men played dominoes on lazy afternoons when there was no fishing. I was visiting a world where human life was oriented toward water—the sea, where men fished, and the lagoon, where women communally washed clothing, dishes, and their own bodies.

Arembepe was a compact village, where the walls of most houses touched those of their neighbors, where, through gossip, the peccadillos of individuals and families instantaneously became community property. Privacy was one of the scarcest commodities. No wonder villagers didn't lock their doors—who could steal anything and have it stay a secret? Young lovers found what privacy they could at night.

Even more obviously than in other places without electricity, Arembepe's night life was transformed when the moon was full. Reflected everywhere by the sand and water, moonlight turned the village by night into almost day. Young people strolled through the streets and courted on the beach. Fishermen sought octopus and "lobster" (Atlantic crayfish) on the reef. Accustomed to the electrified, artificial pace of city life, I was enhanced by the moonlight and its effect on this remote village. Moonless nights impressed me, too; for the first time I could understand how the Milky Way got its name. Only in a planetarium had I previously seen a sky so crammed with stars. Looking south, Salvador's electric lights could only slightly dim the contrast of white stars against the coal-black sky, and for the first time in my life I could view the Southern Cross in all its magnificence.

Even the most devout believer in astrology would have been impressed with the extent to which human activities were governed by the phases of the moon. This was a slower and more natural epoch in Arembepe's history than the years that were to follow. People awakened near sunrise and went to bed early. Moonlight and a calm sea permitted occasional nighttime fishing, but the pattern was for the fleet to leave in the early morning and return in the late afternoon. Boats generally went out five or six days per week; as Christians, Arembepeiros took Sunday as a day of rest. But generally, life in Arembepe followed the availability of natural light and the passing of day and night.

Another force of nature, the weather, affected the rhythm of life. My visits to Arembepe came during the season of rain and rough seas. Sailboats were especially vulnerable to high winds and stormy weather; it was dangerous to negotiate the narrow channels in Arembepe's rocky reef when racing home to escape a sudden squall. Storms usually lasted no more than a week, but I remember one three-week lull, in 1964. People speculated incessantly about when the weather would improve; of course they had no access to weathercasters. Villagers lamented that they couldn't work, and eventually they began to complain of hunger. Cattle were brought in from farms to be butchered and sold in Arembepe, but many households were too poor to buy beef. Villagers complained that they were hungry for fish, for something meaty to complement a diet of coffee, sugar, and manioc flour. The weather even forced us to let up on doing our interview schedule. There was a whole section on diet—the quantities of the various foods that people bought or ate per day, week, or month. We soon felt embarrassed asking people what they ate in normal or good times when they were virtually starving for animal protein and, indeed, for all items whose purchase required cash.

The tropical rainy season meant constant high humidity, a perfect climate for the growth of molds. My black leather dress shoes turned white with mildew. Peter Gorlin had bought a navy blue drip-dry suit before his trip to Bahia in 1964. Since we attended few formal affairs in Salvador, Peter let his suit hang in a wardrobe in Jauá until he finally needed it. Discovering, a few hours before a party, that it was covered with mildew, Peter checked into a Salvador hotel, took a shower with his suit on, lathered it, and then dripped dry for the next few hours.

The tile roofs of the houses we rented in Arembepe were never completely effective in keeping the moisture (and bats) out. Whenever it rained, we had to avoid the large leaks, but there was no place where we could be completely dry. One rainy day during the three-week fishing lull, Dora told us that lately, smelling the moist walls of her wattle-and-daub (stick-and-mud) hut, she had remembered her intense desire as a child to lick, and even eat, dirt from her home's mud walls. Many Arembepeiros did sometimes eat earth, she told us. This geophagy may have been a symptom of iron deficiency during the leanest times of year.

In addition to the everyday sensations and experiences of a foreign land and culture, there were also the special occasions. A few women held prayer sessions in their homes to honor their household saints and pray for deceased relatives. July's big event was the *Chegança*, when, in the building in the central square that served as the seat of the Fishermen's Society, fishermen went through a few hours of formal dancing and singing intended to reenact some historical event—the village had forgotten exactly what! (I believe that it was the arrival of the Portuguese in Brazil.) Saint John's night, June 24, was the lesser of Arembepe's two main annual festive events. (The ceremony for Saint Francis took place in February, the time of Arembepe's most productive fishing, and because of this was much more elaborate.) In Arembepe of the 1960s, following Iberian traditions for Saint John's night, villagers lit bonfires, drank special *cachaça* (rum) concoctions, and cooked such delicious confections as *cocada* (sweetened coconut candy) and such disgusting ones as *canjica* (a manioc flour cake, whose flavor, when prepared properly, approximates that of pencil eraser.) Childbirth brought forth other barely tolerable mixtures, most notably a drink combining cachaça, onion, garlic, and various exotic berries and herbs.

I can summarize my feelings about living in Arembepe during the 1960s by saying that I had a profound sense of being away from everything. In those days, virtually no one other than a fish buyer from Salvador ever drove a car into Arembepe. I felt cut off from the external world. Only a few villagers owned radios, which rarely brought news of the rest of the world anyway. I remember poring over every work of *Time's* Latin American edition on each visit to Salvador. In fact, in later years we sometimes planned our trips into Salvador to coincide with the day the new *Time* came out.

Even for Betty Wagley Kottak, who had previously lived in Brazil, Arembepe was something special, far removed from the sophistication, stratification, and style consciousness of Rio de Janerio and São Paulo. Social class governs interpersonal relations in Brazilian cities, and urban Brazilians, with whom Betty had spent most of her previous time in Brazil, have little direct contact with even the urban poor, whom they encounter mainly as servants and menials. Betty had been exposed to much of Brazil's "Great Tradition" (to use Robert Redfield's term for the culture of literate, mainly urban, elites) but not the "little traditions" of its peasants and rural poor. For both of us, then, as for other field team members, Arembepe's relative isolation, simplicity, autonomy, tranquillity, and "naturalness" contrasted with every previous setting in our lives. Such a reaction to first fieldwork is very common among cultural anthropologists.

I believe that our work in Arembepe also provided us with a more accurate understanding of rural America as recently as the 1930s and 1940s, when in many isolated pockets, especially among the poor, night life still went on by candle and lantern light—and before the twin forces of state and corporation had fully introduced backwoods folk to the modern world's vast inventory of benefits and costs.

In Arembepe we got to know firsthand about the values and habits of poor people, how they attempted to make ends meet, how they dealt with fortune and adversity. We got to know many people as individuals and as friends. Characters such as Alberto, Dora, and Tomé, whose words, stories, and experiences are laced through this chronicle of a changing Arembepe, are much more to me than informants. They are people I value as I do my friends and special colleagues in the United States. Yet they are the kind of people that few outsiders will ever have a chance to meet. The anthropologist's special obligation is to tell their story for them.

5

Language
and Communication

Anyone who has lived in another country and had to speak a foreign language for a long time knows that there is much more to language than putting words together in the proper order. Learning a new language means learning a culture as well. It is no wonder, then, that the study of language is an important part of anthropology, and an appropriate topic for students of cultural anthropology. In previous chapters we considered the importance of social behavior in humans and in closely related animals, and how the use of language has led to increased emphasis on learning rather than instinct. In this chapter we will look at some of the main areas of linguistic anthropology, particularly as they relate to the question of what makes human behavior unique.

The Origin and Evolution of Language

One question that is of interest to anthropologists concerns how and when language came about and how it reached its present form. Language is one of the most important results of human evolution, one that makes culture possible and contributes to social behavior and learning. All higher animals communicate with one another through vocal signs and gestures. But human language is unique in many ways. In this section we will discuss five aspects of human language in order to show the relationship between language and culture: the evolution of the ability to produce speech, including increased intelligence and memory as well as changes in the vocal tract; theories about the origin of language; an analysis of the content of human communication and how it is different from that of other animals; misconceptions about so-called primitive languages; and how language continues to change today.

The capacity for language We can assume that there is a genetic or biological basis for language among humans. This can be seen in the unique shape of our vocal tract, which

is different from that of similar animals such as the chimpanzee. Our vocal tract is somewhat bent, and the **larynx** or voice box exits into the **pharynx** rather than directly into the mouth. This allows for more resonance, more control over the sound produced, and a wider range of sounds. Yet at the same time it has some drawbacks: It increases the danger of choking on food or suffocating if the breathing passages are blocked. We must assume that the capacity for speech makes up for these disadvantages.

We should distinguish between the capacity for speech and the capacity for language. Several researchers have tried to teach chimpanzees to talk. In the 1940s Keith and Catherine Hayes tried to teach a chimp named Viki to speak. Viki learned three words—*mama, papa,* and *cup*—but only with great difficulty. It was clear from her interactions with the Hayeses that she knew what a number of other words meant, but she could not learn to speak them. As a result, the researchers concluded that her vocal tract was simply inadequate for speech.

Further experiments with chimps showed how important it is to distinguish between speech and language. Twenty years after the Hayeses' experiment with Viki, Allen and Beatrice Gardner took another approach, trying to teach a chimpanzee named Washoe to communicate using **American Sign Language** for the deaf. This language system uses signs for words in an arbitrary way, so that anyone who communicates in this way must have mastered the elements of symbolic communication.

The Gardners were quite successful, and Washoe eventually had over 200 words in her vocabulary. She learned to use them in a grammatically correct way, and she was also able to generalize. For example, she learned the word for dog by being shown a picture of a dog. Since that time she was able to apply that word to a live dog and then to the sound of a dog barking, even when she could not see it! She was also able to express abstract ideas, as in her use of the word *dirty* to refer to a monkey that she did not like.

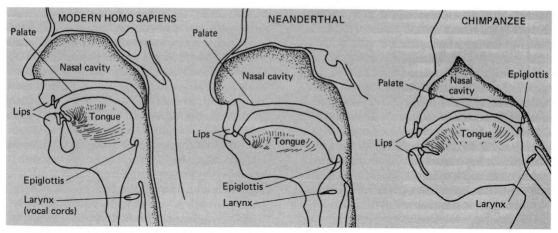

FIGURE 5.1 A Comparison of Speech Apparatus.

Recently, however, much of the research on chimps' language use has been challenged by a study showing different results. Herbert Terrace has argued that apes may learn words, but they can't produce new sentences, as the Gardners and others claimed. Terrace also suggests that most of the chimps' use of language results from prompting by a human trainer, and is not a spontaneous effort to communicate. Whether Terrace is correct or not, it is clear that there is a wide gap between even the most advanced chimp and an average 3-year-old human child. In the last 20 years we have made great advances in un-

Nim the chimpanzee "communicating" with his trainer using the American Sign Language.

derstanding the human capacity for language. The current controversy raises some important questions about how much we have been able to teach chimps; it is hoped that future research will tell us much about language and how it is produced by the human brain.

At this point it seems safe to conclude that chimps are capable of using a rudimentary humanlike language, even though they cannot speak. This tells us two very important facts about human evolution. First, our prehuman ancestors probably were intelligent enough to engage in some kind of symbolic communication, however limited. Second, the ability to speak is crucial in that it allows for much more communication about many more topics, and at a greater speed. Anthropologists are currently debating the question of what stage of human evolution was the one in which speech became possible. According to some, reconstructions of the vocal apparatus and oral structure of Neanderthal skeletons indicate that Neanderthals could not pronounce many of the sounds commonly found in modern languages. Others disagree, claiming that the cultural advances of the Neanderthals could have been achieved only with the use of speech, which would have been needed in order to organize and carry out the cooperative hunting ventures that were the main source of food for some groups. While this debate may never really end, we do know that only through speech have we been able to reach present levels of technological and cultural advancement.

The origin of language   Studies of language learning, both in humans and in nonhuman primates such as chimpanzees, have led us to ask when and how language evolved among early humans. One factor in this evolution was intelligence, for it is clear that language ability is closely linked to intelligence. If we look at the fossil remains of our prehuman ancestors, we note that during the evolution of the first humanlike species, dating from about 3 to 4 million years ago, into modern humans, the size of the brain more than doubled. A major reason for this increase might have been the need for a larger memory to contain the sounds and meanings of language.

However, the link between brain size and intelligence is not absolute. Although modern human brains average about 1,350 cc in size, they may range anywhere from under 1,000 cc to over 2,000 cc without any difference in intelligence or linguistic ability. According to one account, the nineteenth-century Russian author Ivan Turgenev had a **cranial capacity** of 2,012 cc, as measured after his death, whereas Anatole France had barely 1,000 cc of head space! The brains of human females tend to be on average 100–150 cc smaller than those of human males, a difference that is related to the difference in their body size, but this does not result in a difference in intelligence. By itself, cranial capacity does not determine the intelligence of an individual; rather, it is the development of different areas of the brain that determines intelligence, language ability, and related capacities.

If brain size does not determine language ability, we might ask what other factors led to the first attempts at language. Of course, this is a matter of speculation, since we have no records of early speech. One theory is that natural sounds used as interjections began to take on more generalized meanings. For example, the English word *ouch* may be uttered by someone who has just been hurt but may then be used to mean "pain" or "the act of hurting oneself" or even "Watch out!" Early languages might have been formed through such expansions of meaning. Natural sounds might have been added to interjections, and these sounds might have developed into a vocabulary that was shared by a group of people.

But this theory barely touches on the real question of the origin of language. The more important question is how arbitrary sounds took on meanings that were shared by an entire group of people, and how they were tied to a particular thing or event. A second theory suggests that language might have been derived from children's games. For example, children involved in a make-believe battle or hunt may have created new sounds. These sounds could have taken on special meanings for the children, just as you and your playmates probably had what you called "secret codes" used as signals for certain activities or objects. As the children grew up, the sounds would have become more useful in actual hunting or in battle, and their use would have spread to other members of the group, gaining standardized meanings in the process. Although this is just a guess, it is a plausible explanation of how meanings were assigned to sounds. It is easy to imagine how, once the usefulness of this type of communication was evident, it would have been expanded to include a large number of sounds with different meanings.

Another recent theory deals with a **call system**—a series of calls with which most primates communicate. In most cases these calls form a "closed" system; that is, each one has a separate meaning, and they cannot be combined to form new meanings. Thus there may be a call indicating danger and a different call indicating the presence of food, but there is no way of combining parts or all of the two calls to indicate the presence of food in a dangerous situation. But suppose, whether by accident or on purpose, these two calls were mixed or blended so that they took on a double meaning. This change to an "open" call system could be the beginning of a more complex form of verbal communication. From there, we can see how a call could be developed for the meaning "food without danger" as opposed to the earlier call "food" or the derived call "food with danger." Logically, then, if there is a call that means "danger," another call might mean "no danger," thus adding to the system the concept of absence or negation. As the system grew larger, a set of rules would be required to organize the sounds so that meanings could be agreed upon. This would lead to the development of grammar. Although this theory is only speculation and, like all theories of language origin, cannot be proved, it does open new areas of study in human evolution.

The content of language One of the major advantages of human language over other forms of animal communication is **displacement**, the ability to communicate a message when either the sender or the receiver is not directly in contact with the conditions or events involved in the message—in other words, being able to talk about a time or place other than here and now. We can talk about what we ate for dinner last night, about what is going on in another room or another part of town, or about what will happen in the future. This contrasts with most nonhuman communication, which can deal only with events in the present. A chimp's cry of fear can refer only to the immediate present, not to something that happened yesterday or that might happen tomorrow.

We know that chimps can think about other times and places because they sometimes make tools for getting termites before they actually arrive at the termite nest. This means they can anticipate the need for the tool and take action without the stimulus of seeing the termite nest. But as far as we know, they cannot communicate this message to other chimps. If they ever became able to teach other chimps displacement, using language abilities learned from humans, this would be a major step toward humanlike communication.

Our ability to use displacement is a major reason why we have been able to build up cultural traditions. Because we can talk about the past, we do not have to learn or invent everything ourselves; instead, we can rely on the learning and inventions of our ancestors. As we look at human evolution, both biological and cultural, we must recognize the importance of language in this regard. In terms of how we got to be the way we are, there is clearly a great advantage in being able to learn in the absence of personal experience. By using displacement to build on the past, humans were better able to compete with other animals. Thus the evolution of the brain, which allowed for the increase in memory that went along with the expanded use of language, must have provided a new basis for interaction among human groups. Somewhere between our earliest prehuman ancestors and modern *Homo sapiens*, speech and language content became so important for human survival that they led to changes in the vocal apparatus and in the brain. These changes testify to the growing interaction between biological and cultural evolution as the two processes continued to affect each other and together led to modern human culture.

"Primitive" languages For a long time there has been a misperception that the languages spoken by certain groups are not "fully developed" or lack the ability to express emotion. Let's set the record straight: There is no such thing as a truly "primitive" language. All human languages are systematic, regular, highly developed, and complex. In other words, there is no known society whose adult members speak anything that could be considered a "baby language." However, for many years most Westerners believed that "primitive" languages existed that were incapable of expressing motion or distinguishing between hues of colors. This notion was quite common toward the end of the nineteenth century. At that time concepts of social evolution were widely held among Western social scientists and were just as popular with government officials in colonial areas. In writing about the Twi of Ghana a century ago, A. B. Ellis stated, "There is, as is commonly the case with languages of the lower races, a great paucity of abstract terms in [Twi], and the language is entirely deficient of such terms as space, tone, species, quantity, sex, degree, etc.... Terms of endearment are ... few in number.... At a rough calculation, there are from three hundred and fifty to four hundred different words."[1] Unfortunately, this type of world view—although not widely subscribed to now—is still believed by some. Karl Heider writes that when he first went to study the Dani of New Guinea in the early 1960s he was told by a government official that the "Dani language had no grammatical structure at all, and therefore no European could ever really learn it."[2] Heider, of course, knew this could not be true, and came to appreciate just how complex and difficult it is to learn the Dani language. Still, the idea that some cultures have languages that are not fully "developed" is a concept that dies hard.

Linguistic change When we use the phrase *evolution of language*, we generally mean change over a long period, perhaps thousands or even hundreds of thousands of years. But we may also be interested in linguistic change over a much shorter period. Patterns of language within any society differ now from those that prevailed a few centuries ago or even a generation ago. As you know if you have read an old text such as Chaucer's *Canterbury Tales* (common fare in high school English classes) or even an older version of the Bible, speech patterns can change rather drastically in a relatively short time. In the jargon of today, how do you describe something that is spectacular? The slang of the authors' generation included such words as *groovy*, *neat*, and *keen*. This is linguistic archeology and evokes laughter among today's teenagers.

The following example shows how fast language can change. When one of the authors came home after being in the field, he had trouble understanding certain slang phrases. One day a classmate told him that his apartment had been "ripped off," and he asked why the landlord hadn't told him that the building was going to be destroyed!

Mass media and compulsory education, combined with the mobility of teachers and pupils alike, tend to reduce differences in speech patterns. Few national radio and television personalities or actors speak with a noticeable regional accent. The result is a kind of standardized American English that is at least familiar to almost all Americans,

---

[1] A. B. Ellis, *The Tshi-Speaking Peoples of the Gold Coast of West Africa: Their Religion, Manners, Customs, Laws, Language, Etc.* (Oosterhout N. B.; The Netherlands: Anthropological Publishing, 1966 [first printed 1887]).

[2] Karl Heider, *Grand Valley Dani: Peaceful Warriors* (New York: Holt, Rinehart and Winston, 1979), p. 8.

even if it is not spoken by them. But by the same token, the speed with which we can communicate also increases the rate of change in our language. A word can be invented on one coast and, if it catches on, spread across the country within a few days or weeks. Newspaper columnists, authors, TV and radio announcers, politicians—almost any public figure can contribute to change in our language.

A warning is in order, however: Do not think that language never changes in societies that lack advanced technology and communication systems. We learn our language in the process of learning our culture, from parents, peers, and others. But we never learn our language or culture exactly as it is taught because there is no single version to

Two young passengers, seemingly oblivious to their surroundings, ignore the subway graffiti, which is regarded by some as a form of folk art, and often reflects aspects of linguistic change.

be learned. Instead, we learn parts of many different versions of a language—street slang, classroom English, patterns of speech reflecting the accents of immigrant groups, and, as some commentators are fond of pointing out, a host of "incorrect" usages that are widely shared. People in other cultures are no different. They make up new words, mispronounce old ones, give new meanings to old words, and in the process change their languages too.

Glottochronology and Historical Reconstruction

It is fairly easy to tell that certain languages are related; you simply compare words that have the same or similar meaning. For example, if you have studied German, you know that many words are easy to remember because they are so much like the English words for the same thing. Such words are called *cognates*. The German word for "father" is *Vater*, and since the V is pronounced like our *f*, the sound of the two words is almost identical. (The letter V is capitalized in German to indiciate that the word is a noun.) Likewise, in German "mother" is *Mutter*, "sister" is *Schwester*, and "brother" is *Bruder*. In French the comparable words are *père* for father, *mère* for mother, and *soeur* and *frère* for sister and brother. In many cases we can show by comparing words from different languages that one language is related to another, and that both are descended from a common parent language.

But knowing that two languages are traceable to a single parent language might not tell us very much. For example, we know that the western hemisphere was settled by people who migrated from Asia and crossed the land bridge over what is now the Bering Strait. We also know that this land bridge did not exist for very long (it was possible to cross only during the most recent ice age, when the sea level was low enough). Therefore we can probably assume that the people who made the crossing spoke the same language or at least very similar languages. If we follow this logic to its conclusion, all Indian languages are related, since they are all descended from a common ancestor language.

Yet anthropologists who have worked with Native American groups and are familiar with more than one language are aware that some Indian languages are much more closely related than others. Indian tribes did not simply settle in one place and stay there for thousands of years; instead, they migrated and intermingled, moving back and forth from one area to another, so that their languages grew more similar in some places and less so in others in a constantly changing pattern. We could not draw a map of North America and place the different Indian tribes on it, and then claim that the closer one tribe lived to another, the closer their languages would be. How, then, can we reconstruct the relationships between these languages, and how can we judge how related they are?

One way that has been proposed by anthropological linguists is based on a method that uses a mathematical formula for estimating the amount of time that has passed since two languages developed from a common ancestral tongue. This involves counting the number of similar or cognate words and applying the formula to estimate the rate at which such words could be expected to change. This method is called **glottochronology** (from two Greek words, *glotta*, meaning "tongue," and *chronos*, meaning "time").

Glottochronology is possible because there are a number of things for which all languages have words, for example, certain colors, aspects of the physical environment, qualities of objects such as hot or cold, and so on. Because this is so, we can usually find words with roughly the same meaning in different languages, whether they are related languages or not. The task then becomes one of making a list of words from one language and seeking cognates in another. Such lists need not be long; they rarely contain more than 200 items. The next task is to determine the number of words that are cognates, that is, the number of words similar in meaning and in the way they sound. Using a formula developed by the anthropological linguist Morris Swadesh, we can estimate that on the average a single language will lose or change about 19 percent of its basic words every 1,000 years, or, to put it another way, it will

FIGURE 5.2 The seven languages compared in this chart are members of the Indo-European family of languages. English, German, and Swedish belong to the Germanic branch, while Spanish and French are both derived from Latin and belong to the Italic branch. Russian and Eastern Slavic languages belong to the Balto-Slavic branch. Using techniques of glottochronology, linguists would compare words such as these to estimate the amount of time that has passed since two or more languages split off from a common parent language. For example, the Spanish and French words for *father* and *mother* are quite similar, but words for *sister* and *brother*, *son* and *daughter* are less like each other.

ENGLISH	GERMAN	SWEDISH	SPANISH	FRENCH	LATIN	RUSSIAN
father	Vater	fader	padre	père	pater	ahtyets
mother	Mutter	moder	madre	mère	mater	mahtch
sister	Schwester	syster	hermana	soeur	soror	syestra
brother	Bruder	broder	hermano	frère	frater	braht
son	Sohn	son	hijo	fils	filius	seehn
daughter	Tochter	dotter	hija	fille	filia	doch

keep about 81 percent. Thus, for example, English of today retains roughly 81 percent of the vocabulary of English of a thousand years ago. However, if we are looking at two different languages and want to estimate how long ago they were the same, we must multiply the 81 percent rate of correlation for one language by the 81 percent rate of correlation for the second (since both languages have changed at that rate over a 1,000-year period). This means that for two languages that have been apart for 1,000 years we should expect to find 66 percent agreement in vocabulary.

In the few cases in which we know what a parent language was like (because it was written) 1,000 years ago, we can test this formula to prove that it is accurate. For example, it has been estimated that English and German share about 59 percent of their basic vocabulary, which would mean that they separated about 1,500 years ago; this we know from historical evidence to be fairly accurate. But in most cases we don't know when a parent language began to split into divergent languages, so we must apply the formula after establishing similarities between key words.

There are a number of problems with this approach, however. For one, there is the question of what constitutes a basic element of vocabulary—a key word. Another problem arises when two unrelated languages borrow a word from the same source; this might be taken as an indication of relatedness, when in fact it is not. Then there is the question of whether all languages change at the same rate. Groups that are in contact might share some changes, while groups that are completely isolated would not. And what is the effect of literacy on change? Some linguists have argued that writing makes a language more conservative—that is, slower to change—because it creates a single accepted form that is written in only one way regardless of the many different ways in which it might be pronounced by speakers of that language.

Glottochronology developed as a tool for measuring time depths involved in linguistic change. More important perhaps, it has been combined with other measures of cultural change, since anthropologists are concerned with language as a part of culture rather than as an entity in itself. It may not appear useful when studying American English and Western European languages beause we have accurate historical records and glottochronology does not seem to add much to what we already know. But it is quite valuable in reconstructing culture histories for groups that lack written histories and whose past is not familiar to us.

Elements of Language

An anthropologist who goes into the field faces many of the same problems that any student of a new language faces. Anthropological linguistics tries to overcome some of these problems by looking at language in general rather than at specific languages. In this approach there are three main areas of concern: *sound, meaning*, and *structure*.

Human beings are able to make a wide range of sounds. If you have heard people speaking other languages, you know that they sound different from English, not just because the words are unfamiliar but because some of the sounds used are not used in the English language. Hebrew, for example, has many sounds made deep in the throat that are unlike anything that occurs in English. Chinese may have a "sing-song" effect when spoken by a native, a pattern quite different from that of English speech. Some African languages use clicks as part of their speech, sounds like those you might use in calling a horse or those you might produce when making idle (but meaningless) sounds with your tongue.

The study of the sounds of languages is called **phonetics**. If you were suddenly placed in a situation in which you could not understand what was being said, the first thing you would do is try to recognize the sounds people were making. The important or critical sounds of a language are called **phonemes**. The study of phonemes also includes such factors as stress or accent (for example, the difference between *preSENT*, a verb, and *PRESent*, a noun or adjective), and pitch and tone (which are very important in Chinese but much less so in English). One of the reasons that we have so much trouble pronouncing foreign words is that they include phonemes that are not part of our own language.

One way we can tell the phonemes or important sounds in a language from ones that are not is by recognizing **minimal pairs**. This is a way of separating those sounds that change meaning from those that do not. For instance, you can recognize where certain people come from by the way they speak English. Some people have what we call a British accent, and they sound different from people raised in New England, New York City, or Georgia. Yet even though they sound different, we can still understand what they say because their use of sounds does not change the meaning of their words. The use of minimal pairs allows us to see what range of sounds can be used in a word without changing its meaning.

We do this by saying pairs of words in which just one sound has been changed and noting whether the meaning stays the same or not. For example, we could compare the sound of the letter *b* in *bat* with the sound of a *b* with a puff of breath, or *aspiration*, after it, as in *b^hat*. In English these two words have the same meaning, even though they do not sound exactly the same. We could conclude that, at least in this situation, the two initial sounds *b* and *b^h*, are not significantly different in English and do not signal different meanings. However, if we compare the word *bat* with the word *cat*, we do have a change of meaning, indicating that the sounds of the letters *b* and *c* are significantly different in English. To cite another example, many people from Chicago (and other places as well) would say *dat* rather than *that* or *trew* rather than *threw*. We recognize this as a different accent rather than as signals for different

meanings. By constructing minimal pairs like these, we can identify sounds as significantly different or not in a language, and thereby recognize the phonemes of that language.

Once we have identified phonemes, the next step is to put those sounds together into meaningful units. A unit of meaning is called a **morpheme**, and it may include one phoneme or several. It may also include such things as pitch and tone, which can change the meaning of a sound—every child knows from the tone of his or her mother's voice whether she is angry or happy! Not all sounds have meaning in all languages and not all sounds are considered important. For example, in Chinese the sounds represented by the English letters *l* and *r* are not distinct phonemes; hence the jokes about Chinese waiters bringing in "flied lice." In Spanish the sounds indicated by the letters *v* and *b* are not significantly different, and to a Spanish speaker who is unfamiliar with English the words *very* and *berry* would be the same. In all, there are about 45 phonemes in English.

A morpheme, then, is a meaningful unit of sound or sounds in a particular language. We must remember that language is a form of symbolic communication and that the meaning of the sounds in a language are arbitrary, being whatever the people who speak them have agreed upon. We say *water* while the French say *eau* (pronounced "oh") and the Spanish say *agua*. All three words mean the same thing because the people who use them have agreed that they do. On the other hand, we say *knee* (in which the *k* is silent) while the Germans say *nie*—which means "never," not "knee." Even though both words are pronounced in the same way, the sound is not important to the meaning. Language is a purely cultural product because it must be learned in the process of becoming a member of a group, must be shared by other members of that group, and must be transmitted to new members.

Morphemes should not be thought of in terms of written words; they are more than just the sounds those words represent. There

Robert Russell taping the unwritten language of the Amahuaca Indians of Peru.

are morphemes in languages for which there is no writing. And some morphemes can have several forms, both written and spoken. For example, the English word *cat* is a single morpheme, but the word *cats* is two morphemes—one means "small, furry animal" and the second means "more than one." This plural morpheme can take any of a number of forms in English, depending on the sound added to a particular word. For example, the sound in the word *hugs* is different from that in *cats*; the former is like the sound of the letter *z* and the latter is like the sound of the letter *s*. Then there is the plural word *kisses*, which is different from either *cats* or *hugs*, as are the plural forms of *goose* (*geese*), *ox* (*oxen*), *child* (*children*), *woman* (*women*), or even *fish* (*fish*). These are all called **allomorphs**, a term

referring to the fact that different phonemes all serve as the same morpheme, in this case the plural form of a word.

Once we have solved the problems of sound and meaning, the next area of language that we need to consider is the structure, or the way morphemes are put together to form words and sentences that are both meaningful and correct. We use the term **syntax** to refer to the way words are put together into phrases and sentences. The term **grammar** refers to the overall set of rules for speaking and writing a given language.

Every language has syntactic rules that govern how words are put together. In English we say "the blue hat," while in French one would say "the hat blue." It is not that one way is any better than the other but, rather, that one way is agreed upon as "correct" in each language and the other is not. We can all accept the statement "I sat on the chair," but we know that a similar statement, "The chair sat on I," is incorrect. The words are the same, but the difference in order makes the second example nonsensical. Using the same reasoning, we can accept a statement as correct even if we have never heard it before in exactly that way.

This fact led a linguist named Noam Chomsky to develop a new area of linguistic study called *generative* or **transformational grammar**. Chomsky reasoned that if a native speaker can create an infinite number of grammatically correct statements without ever having heard them, there must be a set of underlying linguistic rules that allow a person to *generate* his or her language. The process of moving from those underlying rules (which Chomsky called **deep structure**) to the actual statement (**surface structure**) is termed a *transformation*. In the same way, a native speaker can reject any statements that are not correct without ever having heard them before and usually without even having to think about them (as in the case of "The chair sat on I"). Chomsky argues that the deep structures of all languages are the same, and that all people are born with an innate knowledge of deep structure. They are also born with the capacity for making transformations, regardless of the deep and surface structures of their language. We might say that this capacity to generate linguistic utterances according to a set of rules is an inborn trait of all human beings—and research with chimpanzees is beginning to tell us that this trait is not limited to humans.

Language and Cognition

A fascinating aspect of the relationship between language and culture is the impact of language on the way we organize our thoughts (cognition) and perceive our environment. The anthropologist Edward Sapir first brought the problem of language, culture, and perception into the open, and one of his students, Benjamin Lee Whorf, developed this idea further in his own research and writing. Together, they were responsible for the **Sapir-Whorf hypothesis**, which focuses on the relationship between language and culture.

One important question in this regard is: Are we really free to express anything and everything through language? The answer is: Maybe not. To some extent our language structures—and hence limits or directs—our communication. If you have studied a foreign language, you know that there are some ideas or ways of thinking that are language-specific, or unique to that language. If you speak a particular language, you might use different terms to refer to older brothers and younger brothers. This forces you to think of your brothers differently than if you speak English, where all brothers are called by the same term regardless of age. Or, to use another example, not all languages have the concepts of past, present, and future built into their verbs. For native English speakers, it is natural to think about time and to structure thought in terms of a linear view of time. (In fact, we cannot speak of an event without saying when it occurs, since we must use a tense when we use a verb, and every sentence must have a verb.) However, if we all assume that an infant can learn any language in the world (that is, that there is no genetic predisposition to a specific language), then we can see that it is not some inborn trait that directs a person's way of thinking but, rather, something contained in the structure of the language.

Another question anthropologists ask about the relationship between language and culture is whether we see the environment differently because of our language. Here the answer is probably a qualified yes. As we pointed out in Chapter 1, different languages emphasize different concepts. People who live in the Arctic region have many words for snow because snow is an important part of their environment. Speakers of American English have words for many different types of cars because cars are important to them. Does this mean that we see things differently? The answer depends on how you define the word "see." If by "see" we mean the physical act of visual perception, then we do not see snow any differently than a native Alaskan does. We can, through experience and instruction, learn the differences among dry, powdery snow; wet snow; snow driven by winds from the north; and so on. Certainly we learn very quickly the difference between snow that packs well, so that it is good for making snowballs, and snow that is dry and powdery and falls apart in our hands when we try to make a snowball.

On the other hand, not everything that we perceive is reflected in our language, because not all the fine distinctions that we are capable of making are important. For most of us, it probably is not important whether a four-door sedan that pulls up beside us at a traffic light is made by Chrysler, Ford, or General Motors. Unless it is a police car, we would be hard put to say later whether it was red or green or blue, or whether it was missing a hubcap or had a dent in its right front fender.

What we perceive is a function of how important it is for us. For an automobile sale-person, the model of the car might be important. For a police officer, the license plate number might be worth noting so that it can be checked against the "hot sheet." Thus it is not a physiological difference but a cultural difference that dictates how much our language allows us to say about various aspects of our existence, and then a situational difference that dictates what distinctions we make.

Whorf also showed how words can be misleading. While working as an inspector for a fire insurance company, he found many examples of how perceptions can lead to false conclusions. For example, in a wood distillation plant an insulation material called "spun limestone" was used. Workers in the plant often exposed this insulation to heat, and one day it caught fire. During his investigation Whorf learned that the workers had been surprised by the fire because they assumed that anything with the word *stone* in it would not burn. In another case he found that in places where full gasoline drums were stored workers tended to be very careful with cigarettes, whereas around empty drums they

The large number of English words for different kinds of cars indicates their importance to us, and leads us to make distinctions in our speech that people of another culture normally would not recognize.

were not careful. Yet as Whorf pointed out, the fumes in the empty drums were more dangerous. However, the word *empty* conveyed the meaning "harmless," which in this case was incorrect.

Although Whorf's attention to these questions led to modern studies of the relationship between language and culture, recent research suggests that Whorf's linguistic determinism is not valid. That is, we can profit from his work by looking at ways in which language *influences* thought, but language does not *determine* thought. We may accept Whorf's belief that speakers of different languages experience the world differently, without suggesting that it is language itself that causes these differences. The fact that languages can and do change in response to changes in the social and physical environment indicates that people's thoughts are not limited to the language they speak. We can create new words to express our thoughts, even though we tend not to do so. This is what we mean by language *influencing* but not *determining* thought.

Sociolinguistics

Up to this point we have concentrated on the study of language and its relationship to culture and cognition in an abstract sense. Recently, however, a new branch of anthropological linguistics has emerged that has as its primary concern the social context in which language is used. This area of study is known by a number of terms, of which the most common is **sociolinguistics**.

We all use different forms of our language, depending on the way we define a situation and what we feel is proper in that situation. If you were applying for a bank loan, you would not begin with a string of curses—instead, you would be very polite and would try to use what you think is "proper" English. On the other hand, if you were going out for a beer with some friends, you would not use "proper" English because if you did, you

would probably be considered snobbish and your friends might think you were trying to show that you were better than they are. The point is that we adjust our language to fit the social situation we are in.

Similarly, we can define a social situation partly by the way language is used. Every time we enter a new social setting, the first think we do is try to judge it in terms of what we know from past experience. We try to pick up clues about the other people involved, so that we will know how to behave. Some clues come from such things as the age of the other people, their clothing, and their general appearance. But much of what we learn comes in the form of language. If we meet a friend who is talking to an older man, and the friend says, "Thank you, sir," right away we think of the man as socially superior in some way. If, on the other hand, we enter a conversation and hear a person speak with a heavy foreign accent, we define that person differently and speak a different form of our language; we may speak louder or more slowly, using shorter words and simpler sentences. We tend to classify people according to the way they speak our language, and regardless of where you come from, you would have no trouble agreeing that people fall into certain categories based on their speech patterns. That is, after all, how characters in movies are defined—by their dress and speech. If you were directing a film about a gangster, it would not be enough to dress him in "gangster clothes" if he spoke with a very proper British accent!

Sociolinguistics includes understanding the social cues regarding what subjects may be discussed with which individuals. For example, all of you can think of topics that you might talk about to a good friend of your age and sex but that you would not regard as appropriate for discussion with your parents. Whom we talk to about what subjects and in what fashion are matters that to a certain extent are guided by cultural rules and personal preferences. U.S. business people learn that when working in Latin America it is appropriate to inquire about their colleagues' spouses. In contrast, the U.S. representative working in the Middle East would be ill-advised, no matter how well-intentioned, to inquire about the wife of his Arab counterpart. That would be culturally inappropriate behavior.

The notion of how we communicate through the use of time clearly falls under the rather broad umbrella of sociolinguistics. U.S. culture places a great deal of importance on punctuality. Clocks on the walls of public buildings attest to the fact that Americans feel a need to check the time frequently. Being late for a meeting without a good excuse is often interpreted as an indication that you are not taking the occasion seriously. But here there are some exceptions. Bosses can walk in late to a gathering of underlings and either not say anything about their own tardiness—a benefit of rank—or apologize and expect to hear a chorus of "That's okay, we just got here." However, pity the poor individual who casually trots into the office of his or her employer twenty minutes after a meeting was supposed to begin.

The American obsession with time is by no means a cultural universal. Flexible scheduling is as much the norm in other parts of the world as punctuality is in the United States. In much of Africa and Latin America if you showed up at nine o'clock for a meeting scheduled to begin at that time, you might be the only one around. Fifteen or twenty minutes after nine is considered a more appropriate time to commence the meeting. When one of the authors first went to Mexico, he tried to arrange times when he could conduct interviews and quickly found that his notion of noon or two o'clock differed dramatically from that of his informants. Although most of the men wore wristwatches, they had a far more flexible concept of time than he was used to. After a while he learned to schedule interviews using the more culturally appropriate way of dividing up the day by arranging gatherings shortly before or just after certain daily activities.

Basically, what is important is learning the unwritten rules of the culture and accom-modating to them. In Costa Rica some good friends of the family of one of the authors planned a birthday party for their young daughter that was to include a mixture of several Costa Rican and North American families. The hostess wanted all the guests to come around the same time, so she handled the situation of different cultural perceptions in an innovative fashion. The festivities were scheduled to "start" at 3:00 P.M. To ensure that everyone would arrive close together, she invited the Americans to come at 3:00. knowing how punctual they would be, and asked the Costa Ricans to come at 1:30, knowing that they would think it highly appropriate to arrive 90 minutes after the time stated on the invitation. Everyone showed up within a 15-minute period, and the party was a smashing success.

The field of sociolinguistics is much more diverse than it may seem from these few pages, and it is one of the fastest-growing areas of cultural anthropology. It is important mainly because it signals a new direction for anthropological linguistics: away from the description of language for its own sake and toward the study of language in its social and cultural context. It certainly will not replace traditional linguistics, but it will add a new and dynamic dimension to the study of language.

Nonverbal Communication

A final area of linguistics deserves brief mention, and that is the growing interest in **nonverbal communication**. Studies of chimpanzee language learning have focused on communication through sign language. Other studies have looked at the way we communicate through gestures, facial expressions, body positions, and even such aspects of our daily life as clothing styles or automobiles.

Often the first clues you get about a social situation are not verbal but visual. A person standing with his hands on his hips is probably impatient. One who looks at her watch is bored and wants to get out. A smile indicates happiness; tears show sadness. All these clues may be clear to people who share a particular culture, but we must remember that they are culturally defined and are not necessarily shared by members of other cultures. For example, in American culture waving the hand usually indicates "good-bye," but in Chinese and Latin American cultures it means "come here."

Nonverbal communication may include posture and facial expressions, which convey a clear meaning.

Gestures are a very important method of communicating. In regular conversation most North Americans are taught not to wave their hands about. Hand waving is reserved for emphasis, to indicate that something important and maybe urgent is being discussed. In much of the rest of the world, however, hands and arms play a far more active and visible role in everyday communication. This is not because these cultures lack a sufficient vocabulary and therefore must fill in with gestures, but simply because they consider the use of hands a natural and regular part of the communication process. Even the particular hand used in gesturing can communicate a great deal. In the United States it is common for left-handed persons to use that hand to eat, to hold up the appropriate number of fingers to indicate numbers, and to do a variety of other things. In much of Asia and Africa it is culturally inappropriate to eat with your left hand, to touch someone with it, or to gesture—however innocently—to someone with your left hand. The reason for this is that the left hand is used to clean oneself after going to the bathroom and therefore is felt to be dirty and polluted. Touching someone or gesturing with that hand is regarded as a defiling act and would constitute a gross insult.

In comparison to people in many other cultures, most Americans tend to refrain from touching the person they are talking to. The obvious exceptions are those romantically interested in one another, who might hold hands, put their arms around each other, or otherwise signal that they enjoy more than a casual relationship. Individuals involved in athletic activities can hug each other and pat each other on the back or on the fanny, but the contexts in which those actions are culturally permissible are rather strictly defined. Some exceptions to this rule involve the elderly and the infirm, who for reasons of age or injury can support each other while walking.

In contrast, in a number of cultures it is not only permissible but expected that individuals will engage in touching while talking. In Latin America and parts of Mediterranean Europe, men often greet each other with affectionate hugs (abrazos), combined with good-natured slaps on the back. Talking men often pat each on the shoulder or one might gently grasp the other's upper arm while explaining something. Women, too, will exchange abrazos, but will refrain from the back slapping and instead give each other kisses on the cheeks. In contrast to most North Americans, Latin Americans are very tactile or touching individuals. These acts have no sexual connotations, but are regarded as a proper way of communicating. One of our colleagues joined the Peace Corps upon graduating from college and within a few months was teaching science in West Africa. Two events within a couple of days impressed upon him the differences in nonverbal communication between the United States and Ghana. On the day of his arrival one of his local co-workers offered to show him around town. The offer was gladly accepted and the two of them started off through the center of town. They had not gotten very far when the other man reached over and took hold of our colleague's hand. For the American, this was totally unexpected; it made him very uncomfortable and he had a hard time knowing how to react. That evening the newly arrived American went with a few local people to a beer hall for some entertainment. Once again, he was quite unprepared when another man asked him to dance. And as he says, "It was a slow dance, too!" Upon looking around he saw that the request was not unusual. From the perspectives of the Ghanaians, both incidents were culturally appropriate for heterosexual men. However, for someone from a culture where this kind of behavior communicates something totally different, such experiences required a bit of adjustment.

Nonverbal gestures are also used in many cultures to indicate levels of respect as well as deference and demeanor. In Japan, for example, instead of shaking hands, it is customary for men to bow when they meet. Often just a generic tilt from the waist, with hands at the side and eyes pointing to the floor suffices. Under certain circumstances, when more than a modicum of protocol is necessary, bowing form communicates a great deal. As a sign of respect, business or social "inferiors" always bow deeper and hold it for a longer time than do those who outrank them.

In addition to sign language and body movement, nonverbal behavior is concerned with the way people use space. From the viewpoint of anthropology, the use of space can vary greatly from one culture to another. This applies to the way people stand, the way they use their eyes, the distance they keep between themselves and others, and many other aspects of personal space.

In the United States it is generally regarded as polite behavior to look at the person you are addressing. How many of us remember parents or teachers instructing us to "Look at me when you're talking to me"? Yet doing this could be highly insulting in some other societies.

Stories are often heard regarding the unfortunate cultural binds in which individuals may find themselves. Children of Hispanic background may find non-Latin teachers insisting children look them in the eye when spoken to. This behavior gets drummed into the child's head as an aspect of proper etiquette; yet, when he or she gets home it is made clear that it is *not* appropriate behavior in dealing with one's father. In the rules of this culture, unless you are of the same social rank, you would not look directly at the person you are speaking to.

Interpersonal space is also culturally defined. Under normal circumstances, when communicating with others, Americans seem to need about 18 inches between the faces of those who are having the conversation. If the distance is reduced much more than that,

Violating someone's personal space can be a hostile gesture, adding to the verbal communication. Are Tommy Lasorda and Whitey Herzog having a friendly conversation?

one or both parties are likely to feel uncomfortable and to commence evasive action. This might involve backing up to reestablish the amount of space deemed comfortable, or averting eye contact—a common way of signaling that one is uncomfortable with the situation and simultaneously an attempt to create greater distance between oneself and the other. There are culturally appropriate exceptions, of course. The foot-and-a-half barrier can be reduced when the speakers are romantically interested in one another;

in this case they are using a culturally acceptable standard for communicating. And in situations where there is a lot of noise or one of the parties cannot hear, it is also culturally permissible to reduce the 18-inch distance. Once again, many other cultures have quite different standards. In the Middle East, for example, people commonly stand much closer when conversing together. Abiding by our own culture's unwritten guidelines in the Middle East would communicate aloofness and a feeling of disinterest in the other person.

These rules, like other cultural codes, are things we learn. They not only vary from culture to culture, but tend to change as people move from one stage in the life cycle to another. Observe young children at play in our society. They very often touch each other while talking, stand very close together, and in general show themselves to be oblivious of many of the patterns of nonverbal communication that they will learn by the time they are 9 or 10.

Studies of nonverbal communication have added a new dimension to anthropological linguistics. Of course, we could argue about whether language includes nonverbal communication. But we all recognize the importance of the subtle aspects of communication that accompany speech, and of the way those nonverbal aspects of communication are patterned. The fields known as **kinesics** (the study of body movement) and **proxemics** (the study of the use of space) have attracted much attention in recent years and probably will become even more important in the future. From a cross-cultural point of view, they can make an important contribution to anthropological linguistics.

Summary

Language is an important part of culture, and the study of cultural behavior involves an understanding of the process of human communication through language. All higher animals communicate with one another through vocal signs and gestures, but human language is unique in many ways. Our vocal tract is different from those of other primates, so that we are able to speak rapidly and clearly. Our greater intelligence allows for a larger vocabulary than chimps, for example, and it also provides us with a better memory, to add to the importance of language in the learning process.

Human language is constantly changing. One way of reconstructing this historical relationship between two different languages is *glottochronology*, a method of counting the number of similar words in two languages and applying a formula to estimate the amount of time that has passed since the two languages diverged from a common parent language.

In analyzing a language the anthropological linguist looks at three main areas of concern: sound, meaning, and structure. The study of sounds is called *phonetics*. The important or critical sounds of a language, called *phonemes*, can be obtained by recognizing *minimal pairs* of words in which only one sound is different, but which have different meanings. The study of meaning focuses on the simplest meaningful units of a language, called *morphemes*. The structure of a language involves the way morphemes are put together to form words and sentences that are meaningful and correct. *Syntax* is the way words are put together into phrases and sentences, while *grammar* is the overall set of rules for speaking and writing a given language. The fact that people know the rules of their language and can apply them to words and sentences that they have never heard before led Noam Chomsky to develop the theory of *transformational grammar*, which states that every person is able to generate his or her language by transforming an underlying rule (called a *deep structure*) into an actual statement (called a *surface structure*).

Language strongly influences the way we think and perceive our environment. Edward Sapir and Benjamin Lee Whorf together developed the idea that language structures our perceptions of the environment, and that speakers of different languages will react to the same environmental stimulus differently, based on their language. For example, if a language requires that a verb be in the past, present, or future tense, speakers of that language will think in terms of linear time sequences from the past to the future.

Two relatively recent areas of interest in anthropological linguistics are *sociolinguistics* and *nonverbal communication*. Sociolinguistics is concerned with the way different forms of a language are used in different situations, an important aspect of the interaction of language and culture. The interest in nonverbal communication has arisen partly as a result of experiments with teaching language to nonhuman primates, but in a broader sense it is also concerned with the culturally patterned ways that people define personal space (*proxemics*) and use body movements (*kinesics*) in communicating with others.

Glossary

allomorph   One of the number of phonemes that may serve as the same morpheme.

American Sign Language   A communication system that uses signs for words; the form of communication used by many deaf people in the United States.

call system   A series of specific noises with which most primates communicate. May be closed, so that each call has a separate meaning, or open, so that calls can be combined to form new meanings.

cranial capacity   The volume of the skull, often used in the nineteenth century as a hypothetical measure of intelligence.

deep structure   The set of underlying rules for language, from which a speaker makes transformations to arrive at correct statements. (See *transformational grammar*.)

displacement   The ability to communicate a message when either the sender or the receiver is not directly in contact with the conditions or events involved in the message.

glottochronology   A method for reconstructing the historical relationship between two languages by applying a mathematical formula based on the number of key words that are similar in the languages.

grammar   The overall set of rules for speaking and writing a given language.

kinesics   The study of body movement, sometimes associated with the anthropological interest in the area of nonverbal communication.

larynx   The "voice box" at the top of the trachea, containing the vocal cords that vibrate to produce sounds. (See Figure 5.1.)

minimal pair   Two words in which only one sound is different, but which have different meanings, enabling the linguist to determine which sounds are significant in changing the meaning in a language.

morpheme   A unit of meaning in a language, which may include one or more phonemes, or such things as pitch or tone.

nonverbal communication   Communication through gestures, facial expressions, body positions, and any other means besides speech or calls.

pharynx   The cavity between the larynx and the mouth, which, in humans, allows for more resonance, more control over the sound produced, and a wider range of sounds than is possible in other animals. (See Figure 5.1.)

phoneme   An important or critical sound of a language.

phonetics   The study of sounds of languages.

proxemics   The study of the use of space, often in culturally established patterns, as part of the area of nonverbal communication.

Sapir-Whorf hypothesis   The idea that language influences the way we organize our thoughts and perceive our environment.

sociolinguistics   A branch of anthropological linguistics that studies the way people use language or communicate in different social situations.

surface structure   The actual statements generated by a speaker of a language, resulting from transformations of the underlying rules, or deep structure. (See *transformational grammar*.)

syntax   The way words are put together into phrases and sentences in a language; the word order of a language.

transformational grammar   The theory proposed by Noam Chomsky that there is an underlying set of linguistic rules (deep structure) that allow a person to generate correct statements (surface structures) by applying "transformations" to those rules.

Questions for Discussion

1. In a country like the United States where mass communications media reach into almost every home, why do we still have regional speech patterns that are so different from one another?

2. To get an idea of how important written language is in the evolution of culture, try to conduct a conversation with a friend in which neither of you may refer to anything you have learned by reading—that is, you can only talk about things you have personally experienced or heard about from others.

3. The example of different kinds of cars was given to illustrate how language reflects what is important in a culture. Choose a few more areas where you would expect the vocabulary to be particularly well developed (e.g., sports, medicine) and list as many words as you can think of.

Suggestions for Additional Reading

ROBBINS BURLING, *Man's Many Voices: Language in Its Cultural Context* (New York: Holt, Rinehart and Winston, 1970). A good analysis of the many facets of the anthropological approach to language.

JOHN B. CARROLL, *Language and Thought* (Englewoods Cliffs, N.J.: Prentice Hall, 1964). A brief look at the role of language in thought patterns, including how people learn language and how it influences their behavior.

NOAM CHOMSKY, *Syntactic Structures* (The Hague: Mouton, 1957). The original discussion of transformational grammar.

R. ALLEN GARDNER and BEATRICE T. GARDNER, "Teaching Sign Language to a Chimpanzee," *Science*, 165 (1969): 644–672. A description of the experiments with Washoe and her success in learning American Sign Language.

EDWARD T. HALL, *The Silent Language* (Greenwich, Conn.: Fawcett, 1959). A fascinating study of the nonverbal communication that accompanies all social interaction in culturally patterned and predictable ways.

DELL H. HYMES (Ed.), *Language in Culture and Society: A Reader in Linguistics and Anthropology* (New York: Harper & Row, 1964). A thorough collection of articles on many different areas of anthropological linguistics, designed for the more advanced student.

PHILLIP LIEBERMAN, *On the Origins of Language: An Introduction to the Evolution of Language* (New York: Macmillan, 1975). A discussion of various theories of the evolution of language, including the controversial question of when speech first became possible.

PHILIP LIEBERMAN, *The Biology and Evolution of Language* (Cambridge, Mass.: Harvard University Press, 1984). A detailed, lengthy study of the biological genesis of human language, drawing data from neurology, linguistics, developmental psychology, primatology, and anthropology.

HERBERT S. TERRACE et al., "Can an Ape Create a Sentence?" *Science*, 206 (1979): 891–902. A report on an experiment with teaching language to a chimp that challenges the conclusions of the Gardners and earlier scholars, who claimed that apes could be taught to use language.

The Laws of Looking

MICHAEL ARGYLE

In this amusing contribution Michael Argyle reminds us of the many communication clues we generate with our eyes. How we look at one another can communicate messages every bit as strongly as our spoken words. Lest we unwittingly assume that certain types of glances mean the same thing in every culture, Argyle provides a number of examples suggesting that assumptions true for one culture might have very different consequences in another.

Residents of big cities quickly learn the laws of looking. Never make eye contact with a panhandler, or you will be pursued for handouts; with a religious fanatic, or you will be caught in a diatribe; with a belligerent loner, or you will become the object of a menacing tirade; with a lost visitor, or you will feel responsible to help. Never stare back at a stranger who stares relentlessly at you, or your life may be in danger.

There are happier laws, of course. Ovid, wise in the ways of sexual seduction, advised the lover to "Let your eyes gaze into hers, let the gazing be a confession: Often the silent glance brings more conviction than words." The woman was to keep her eyes "gentle and mild, soft for entreating of love. . . . If he is looking at you, return his gaze, and smile sweetly." Ovid understood that gaze is a sensual signal of sexual intention.

What poets suspected, researchers have demonstrated. Patterns of gaze are neither aribitrary nor accidental, but follow definite rules—some apparently innate and others specific to culture. We use vision not just as a channel for collecting information about the world around us, but also as a signal that directs conversation, conveys silent messages, and expresses personality. Gaze is closely coordinated with speaking and listening; it provides feedback, for example, that tells a speaker when to be quiet and the listener when to start talking. You will know from your companion's sullen glare that she is peeved, or from her misty gaze that she is smitten.

Gaze emerged as a social signal early in evolutionary time, as soon as vision developed. Eyes and eyelike designs often acted as protective coloration or a warning to predators. Some butterflies have eye designs on their wings, for instance, and if these patterns are experimentally removed, the butterflies are more likely to be attacked by birds. Some fish have eye spots that expand during attack; small eye spots apparently provoke attack and large ones inhibit it. In primates, eye patterns such as eyebrows and eye rings may play a similar role. Many human societies have believed in the power of the eye to inflict harm (the evil eye), and tribal masks with elaborate eye displays are common devices to ward off danger and assert authority.

The most common meaning conveyed by gaze is a threat signal. Ralph Exline and Absalom Yellin found that if an experimenter stared at a caged monkey, the monkey attacked or threatened to attack on 76 percent of the trials; if the experimenter looked away almost at once, the monkey responded aggressively about half the time. We have much of the monkey in us. Phoebe Ellsworth and her colleagues found that when they got motorcyclists or pedestrians to stare at car drivers stopped at intersections, the drivers moved off more rapidly from stoplights. Peter Marsh found that a mere glance from a member of a rival group of football supporters is enough to start a fight; the recipient of the glance justifies his attack with cries of "He looked at me!"

Conversely, to avoid or break a stare has a shared meaning among many animal species—appeasement. During battle or courtship, gaze cutoffs reduce the opponent's aggression or the urge to flee. I heard of one man who discovered the appeasement meaning of gaze cutoff just in time. He was riding a New York subway one afternoon when he inadvertently

Michael Argyle, "The Laws of Looking," *Human Nature* 1 (1) 1978, pp. 32–40. Copyright © 1977 by Human Nature, Inc. Reprinted by permission of the publisher.

caught the eyes of a large, nervous man sitting opposite, reading about the art of self-control. At once they were locked in a deadly stare-down. My friend soon capitulated, smiled, broke the gaze and offered the V sign. The nervous giant laughed, strode across the aisle and, magnanimous victor he, embraced my friend warmly.

The further a species travels up the evolutionary ladder, the greater the range of significance of the eye. Reptiles, birds, and mammals use their eyes and eye rings (such as the raccoon's mask) for many social purposes; territoriality, courtship, dominance, withdrawal. At the primate level, however, gaze takes on a unique capacity to indicate attachment. Only primates—monkeys, apes, and human beings—use gaze to attract as well as attack, to make friends as well as enemies, to seduce as well as repel.

Primates can use gaze to threaten, but they are just as likely to gaze fondly. Psychologists have found that couples in love and individuals who are mutually attracted gaze longer at each other than couples who are indifferent. This may not be news to songwriters and lovers, but it is a special talent of primates that should be celebrated.

My colleague Mansur Lalljee suggests that the reason primates use gaze for affiliation is that primate infants and mothers are able to look at each other during breast-feeding. Human babies, for example, are able to focus to a distance of 20 to 30 cm, roughly the proximity of the mother's face when she holds the infant to nurse. Primates are the only mammals in which nursing fosters eye-to-eye contact.

Gaze emerges as a social signal early in the life of infants. By the third week of life babies smile at a nodding head, and by the fifth week they can exchange mutual gazes. Further, babies respond positively to eyes and eye patterns—they smile and their pupils dilate, indicating that they are attending to the stimulus. During the infant's first year, parent and child typically play many mutual-gaze games, such as peekaboo, that seem to delight both players and are among the first forms of social communication.

The physiological underpinning of the meaning of gaze has been established mainly by studies with monkeys. We know, for instance, that one effect of staring eyes is arousal. Various measures of physiological arousal—galvanic skin response, EEG, brainstem activity—show that organisms can tolerate a certain amount of stimulation and find it interesting, but that overstimulation becomes unpleasant. Too much arousal is unsettling and causes the animal— wolf, bird, or human being—to avoid the prying eyes by fleeing, fighting, or threatening. This is true

whether the eyes are those of one's natural predator or those of a stranger on a subway.

When two people like each other there is more gaze and more mutual gaze. Too much gaze, however, is uncomfortable. Janet Dean and I postulated that there are tendencies to approach or to avoid other people, to look or not to look, resulting in an equilibrium level of intimacy. This balance is based on a combination of proximity, gaze, smiling, and other affiliative signals. It would follow that if two people moved away from each other, they would maintain their intimacy level by increasing their gaze, and a number of experiments have confirmed this. Mark Patterson has extended the theory, proposing that signals a person interprets favorably lead him to respond in kind; if he finds the same signals unpleasant or disquieting, he will retreat or look away, thereby restoring equilibrium.

Human beings are able to use the additional cues of context and body language to interpret a gaze. Most people find a steady gaze to be pleasant if they like the gazer and want to be liked by him; the same gaze will be irritating if they think the gazer has undue sexual interests or is seething with anger. If the gazer's stare seems meaningless and vacant, and no other cues allow one to interpret his intentions, the gaze will be even more disturbing.

Usually, though, people within a culture show an excellent ability to decode the message sent in a look. They can readily distinguish affectionate gazes that say "I like you," worried gazes that request help, or threatening gazes that say "Lay off." Although the specific meaning of a look may shift across cultures, people everywhere recognize that a gaze means that the other person is attending, and therefore requires a reaction. The experience of being looked at has a special subjective quality—the feeling of being observed, of being an object of interest for another. Mutual gaze also has such a quality—based on the realization that each person is open to signals from another.

Some meanings and rules of gaze seem to be universal, possibly a result of our biological heritage or the nearly universal experience of being held closely while being fed. Generally, people convey positive attitudes and emotions, such as affection and happiness, with more and longer gazes; they convey negative feelings, such as dislike or depression, with less gazing. In all cultures people notice if a look or stare is done incorrectly. Too much or too little gaze creates an unfavorable impression. A person who gazes too much is usually regarded as disrespectful, threatening, insulting, or supercilious; a person who looks too little is regarded as impolite, inattentive, dishonest, or submissive.

But apart from these universal aspects of gaze, each culture tends to have its own specific variations on the main rules. Sometimes the lessons are taught specifically: "Don't stare, it's impolite," or "Don't look back at him, dear, you'll only encourage him." More often the lessons are indirect, acquired in the course of experience; they remain subtle but strong influences on action.

For example, Navaho children learn not to gaze directly at another person during a conversation. Among the Wituto and Bororo Indians of South America, both the speaker and the listener look at irrelevant objects during conversation, and a storyteller turns *away* from his audience to face the back of the hut. Japanese speakers focus on the listener's neck rather than the eye. A Luo man of Kenya must not look at his mother-in-law. The Mende of Sierra Leone believe that the dead reappear in human guise—but that the dead can be recognized because they never look a live person in the face. Naturally, the Mende are suspicious of people who avert their eyes during a conversation; a Mende would think that America and England are nations of zombies.

The language of the eye is, of course, only one part of a culture's communication system. Variations occur depending on the other communication channels a culture has adopted. Among the Tuareg of North Africa, gaze is an especially important way to send and receive messages, partly because the whole body, apart from the eyes, is covered with clothes and veils. Tuaregs stare steadily at each other while they are conversing in order to glean as much information as possible. In contrast, the Japanese make little use of the facial-visual channel, either to send or receive information; much of their communication takes place through nuances of spoken language and body position. (Possibly the Japanese pay less attention to eyes because Japanese infants are carried on their mothers' backs much of the time, and thus have less visual contact with the mother's face.)

An extensive study of cultural variations in the rules of gaze comes from O. Michael Watson, who worked with male foreign students at the University of Colorado. The students participated in the experiment in pairs, talking about anything they wanted to in their native language while the researchers observed them behind a one-way mirror. Each man's visual style was scored on a scale from one (sharp focusing directly on the other person's eyes) to four (no visual contact at all; looking down or gazing into space). Watson found that young men from contact cultures, where people typically stand close together and frequently touch each other, were far more likely to make eye contact and gaze at each other directly than the men from noncontact cultures:

	Number of Men	Average Score
Contact cultures:		
Arabs	29	2.57
Latin Americans	20	2.47
Southern Europeans	10	2.19
Noncontact cultures:		
Asians	12	3.25
Indians-Pakistanis	12	3.59
Northern Europeans	48	3.51

Watson also found that these cultural differences in gaze held up no matter how much time each student had spent in the United States or in big cities. Apparently styles of gaze, once learned in childhood, are relatively unaffected by later experience.

Roger Ingham observed how 22 pairs of Swedes and 22 pairs of Englishmen conversed with each other. The Swedish speakers looked at their listeners less often than the English did, with longer glances, and the Swedish pairs had a greater amount of mutual gaze. Swedes, Ingham found, dislike being looked at if they can't look back. This custom differs sharply from other traditions. Indeed, Greek friends have told me that Greeks traveling in Europe feel rejected and ignored because, they say, people do not look at them enough.

Such cultural clashes can provoke unexpected problems when a person from one society moves to another that has different rules. Anthropologist Judith Herbstein explains that in Latin America it is considered rude and disrespectful to gaze too long at one's superior. When a Puerto Rican child in an American school is admonished by a teacher, the child will lower his eyes as a sign of respect and obedience. But what do American teachers and parents demand of the child they are scolding? "Look at me! Pay attention!"

Researchers have found individual differences within cultures as well as broad differences across them. Everyone knows the hearty salesman who looks you in the eye and the shy violet who can barely raise his head high enough to look at your nose. Some people look directly at their companions and prefer a few long gazes to frequent darting glances; their characteristic style transcends situation. Individual differences are related to personality traits, though a given person will vary his gaze patterns in different situations.

Richard Christie devised a scale some years ago to measure a person's "Machiavellian" qualities—skepticism about human nature, willingness to use deceit to get one's way, belief in manipulation. In an ingenious experiment on the connections between cheating, lying, and gaze, Ralph Exline and his colleagues arranged to get students implicated in cheating on a project. They managed this by having another subject, who was actually a confederate, pretend to cheat. Then Exline questioned them about the cheating. He found that low-Machiavellian students looked away when lying to protect the subject who cheated; the high Machiavellians looked squarely at him, as much when lying as when telling the truth. Other studies show that most people will look down and otherwise avoid eye contact when they feel guilty or embarrassed, but not psychopaths, high Machiavellians, or, we infer, some used-car dealers. One explanation is that these exceptions do not feel as guilty about lying as most people do, and they probably realize that gaze avoidance indicates lying.

Individual styles can be quite distinctive. Gerhard Nielsen observed pairs of students in conversation and found, as is typical, that people look at their partners less when they are speaking than when they are listening. But individuals varied considerably. Some students looked at their partners only 8 percent of the time, others as much as 73 percent. Extroverts gaze more than introverts, women more than men, adults more than adolescents. Some experiments find that the gaze levels of adolescents may reflect the lower self-esteem or uncertain self-image of many teenagers. It should be emphasized again that a person's gaze level is quite different in different situations. For instance, people tend to look most at people they like, when they are some distance away, and when there is nothing else to look at.

People at the atypical extremes—those who stare too much or who avoid eye contact altogether—may have serious psychological problems. Schizophrenics and depressives tend to avert their gaze (at least when interviewed about their problems), as do some neurotics. Autistic children gaze least. In fact, they are so fearful of looking at others that gaze aversion is one criterion of diagnosis. Autistic children peek at others in abrupt glances, only one half second long, often through their fingers. Or they avoid looking at people by turning their backs or pulling hats over their heads. They avoid looking at eyes and faces, but they do not shun all social contact; they will sit on an adult's lap but avert their gaze.

Corinne Hutt theorizes that autistic children have an abnormally high level of cortical arousal, possibly caused by a genetic defect. Because mutual gaze is arousing, they avoid eye contact to keep their high levels of arousal tolerable. Other researchers, however, think that the overarousal is a consequence, not a cause, of the autism.

At the other end of the spectrum, people with certain psychiatric problems may stare inappropriately for extended minutes. One consequence of the research on gaze is that patients can be taught how to look at other people properly without making them feel uncomfortable or threatened. The patient role-plays an encounter with the therapist. The scene is videotaped and played back to the patient, while the therapist comments on what was correct or incorrect about the patient's gaze level. Practice ensures that the patient learns to get the visual information that he or she needs without excessive staring.

So far I have discussed general patterns of gaze, but in fact we have identified gaze rules to a precise degree. The glances exchanged during a conversation are used to send and to collect information; they are central to the encounter. In conversation, the gazes of speaker and listener are closely linked to the spoken words, and aid in the timing and synchronizing of speech.

We look at people primarily to collect information, to open a channel for observing their expressions and other cues. But the act of looking also becomes a signal for others, and the same glance may serve two purposes. For example, the long glance at the end of an utterance collects feedback and also serves as a full-stop signal to the listener.

The earliest studies of gaze required an observer to watch two speakers through a one-way mirror, recording on a stopwatch how many seconds each participant gazed at the other during a three-minute conversation. Technology has relieved the experimenter of this tedious task. Today we can keep a permanent record of the interaction by using two video cameras, one trained on each speaker, that shows us precisely how gaze is synchronized with speech. Pen recorders keep track, on a moving strip of paper, of continuous gaze sequences—how often speaker A looks at speaker B, how many seconds mutual gazes last, who gazes most, and so on. The reliability of these recordings is very high; two observers agree with each other on the timing and length of gaze sequences virtually all the time.

Gaze provides feedback to the speaker when it is

most needed—at the ends of long statements, at grammatical breaks. Adam Kendon studied the timing of gaze in relation to speech for 10 people. He found that the speaker gazes at the listener before the end of an utterance, and the listener looks away. The speaker seeks feedback on whether the listener understands, agrees, is paying attention, or daydreaming. If the speaker does not end an utterance with a full-stop gaze, there is likely to be an awkward delay before the listener realizes it is time to reply. The listener's gaze, in turn, indicates interest, acknowledgment, or impatience. Thus, while the speaker is sending verbal signals, the listener is returning nonverbal signals. This balance of communication permits the conversation to continue with a surprising minimum of overlap and interruption.

Other studies show that there are many nonverbal ways a speaker can keep (or yield) his turn. A raconteur who wants to hold the spotlight does not pause at the end of a sentence, gives no terminal gaze, and keeps a hand in mid-gesture. If interrupted he speaks more loudly, drowning out the interrupter.

The speaker uses gaze for purposes other than feedback and full stops. As Walker recently found, speakers may emphasize a point with an eye flash, a sudden widening of the eye. The speaker can even direct which of several listeners should speak next, simply by a steady look at his choice. Conversely, a listener can get the speaker's attention and good will by looking at him supportively, smiling, and nodding.

If gaze is so important in social exchange, what happens when people do not see each other? If negotiators cannot read visual messages between the spoken lines, what difference does it make? Dozens of experiments have compared face-to-face communication with communication by television video and by voice only (telephone). By and large, the loss of visual signals is not as disastrous as people think. People *prefer* to meet face to face; they prefer videophone to telephone; but the phone is not the antisocial creature that many people think it is. With practice, speakers have adapted beautifully to the nonvisual disadvantage. Most of our phone conversations are well synchronized because we have learned to replace visual signals (gaze, head nods, facial expressions) with audible ones (uh-huhs and hmmms). For the exchange of factual information, the telephone is no worse than face-to-face exchange. Its only disadvantage is that one cannot convey spatial material, such as maps, graphs, and spiral staircases.

There are, in fact, some situations in which the telephone is the best medium. John Short, in a series of studies, showed that it is easier to change someone's opinions over the phone than face to face, especially if the opinion is not a personal attitude but based on official policy or factual data. Ian Morley and Geoffrey Stephenson carried out a series of management-union bargaining simulations to see whether face-to-face or telephone encounters were the more effective. They gave one side or the other a clearly stronger case to defend, and indeed the stronger case was much more likely to win—*but only when it was presented on the telephone!* If the negotiators could see each other, the weaker side won quite often, probably because the participants became more concerned about being thought well of by the opposition. Telephone encounters allow a person to ignore the distracting information of gaze and other nonverbal signs and concentrate on business. This result augurs well for potential negotiators: Keep to the telephone if you are in a strong position, or your strength may be dissipated by the blandishments of an attractive opponent.

However, face-to-face communication is better for making friends than the telephone is. All things being equal, people who are meeting for the first time will like each other more and be more cooperative if they meet in person than if they meet on the telephone. We know this from experiments that required people to play the Prisoner's Dilemma Game, a task that offers players a choice of competitive or cooperative strategy, either face to face or over the telephone. When the players could see each other, they were much more likely to cooperate and come to early agreement.

Such research has produced a wealth of practical applications. The development of the picture-phone, for instance, may be regarded not just as an extravaganza on the part of Bell Telephone, but as an important aid to diplomacy, business relationships, friendships, and love affairs. Telephones will still do nicely for most business dealings, but people want the benefits of nonverbal language for first contacts, for negotiations when they have a weaker case, for the social signals that make routine conversation work smoothly.

Architects, decorators, and designers are becoming more aware of the subtle ways in which the design of a room or building, and the location of chairs and desks, affect how and whether people interact, even how they feel about each other. Care should be taken, for example, to arrange office furniture so that workers are not forced to stare at each other every time they look up. Otherwise, much time will be wasted in provoked but irrelevant conversation, or in unexpected seductions.

Training in gaze rules is not useful simply for psychiatric patients. Teachers, interviewers, social workers, managers, diplomats, and people who move to another culture have all benefited from learning the cultural rules of the people they meet. Englishmen who learn Arabian gaze customs, for example, do better and are better liked by Arabs than Englishmen who unconsciously follow their own customs.

Looks speak as clearly as the voice. Like speech, gaze is part of our biological heritage, yet wears many cultural disguises. For all the emphasis on spoken words, we would do well to pay more attention to the messages of gaze. The eyes, as often as not, have it.

6

Hunting and Gathering Societies

This chapter and the following one serve as introductions to several major societal groups studied by anthropologists. The categories of hunting and gathering, pastoralism, horticulture, and agriculture are generic ones because there are important common denominators or adaptive strategies within each group. Categorization makes it possible for anthropologists to talk about similar features that, for example, all hunting and gathering societies have. One of the major themes we will examine is food acquisition. How do people obtain food? Do they gather or hunt for it in the wild state, or do they plant or cultivate it? What types of social organizations are related to the particular method of food procurement? What are the multiple roles that food plays within the societal context?

Perhaps you are thinking that it is obvious what is important about food—nutrition. To a certain extent that is true. Food is crucial to the maintenance, growth, and development of the body. Young people require food in certain types and amounts in order to grow and develop. Specific foods are necessary to prevent certain diseases, such as goiter, which can result from too little iodine in the diet, or scurvy, the plague of sailors in centuries past who did not get enough fruit with vitamin C while on the high seas. But food has a number of functions besides nutrition.

Studying food habits can tell you a great deal about a society. If you learn about how a group of people obtain their food, who prepares it, and when, how, and with whom it is eaten, you will come to understand a lot about how that society functions and the interrelations of the group's members. Culture and food are very intertwined. Every culture begins by defining what it regards as food. No group would ever consider eating all of the potential food possibilities. For example, there are a number of things normally not eaten in the United States that would be regarded as standard fare in many parts of the world. With some exceptions, Americans do not regard dogs, rats, horses, insects, and lizards as acceptable dietary choices. We would not dream of walking into a fast-food restaurant and asking for a nine-pack of Kitten McNuggets, although that possibility might be rather tempting to some groups in other parts of the world. Not surprisingly, many of the foods we regard as part of the all-American diet would not be eaten under any circumstances elsewhere. Beef is avoided by millions of Hindus, and pork is not an acceptable food choice for most people living in the Middle East. These last two examples are called **general food taboos** because they represent restrictions that prohibit an entire society from eating certain things. In addition, many societies withhold an item from a particular group of individuals or restrict members from consuming certain things during particular times in their life cycle. These prohibitions are called **specific food taboos** because they are not directed at the entire society. For example, among traditional Yoruba of Nigeria, eggs are denied small children because of the belief that their consumption would delay the closure of the fontanel—the soft area on the top of a baby's head. Pregnant women of the Mbum Kpau of Chad in West Africa are cautioned against eating chicken since it is believed this food complicates childbirth. In much of rural Malaysia women who have just given birth refrain from eating many types of fruits and vegetables because these are felt to interfere with the recovery process.

Food plays other important roles in every society. Often it is an essential part of initiating and maintaining relationships. In our society having people over to dinner or going out to drink a beer or a bottle of pop with friends are prime ways of establishing and preserving friendships. What is consumed is not so important. Rather, it is the act of eating and drinking together, the feeling of camaraderie and good cheer, that are important. Food may also serve to define membership in a group. Religious prohibitions not only spell out what group members should not eat, but also reinforce group unity. Looking at what people eat and how they eat it can also tell the careful observer of culture something about sex roles and social status.

Who is served first? Are men given the choicest and largest portions, are they reserved for women, or are no distinctions made? When hunters or fishermen bring home the catch, how is it divided? What share goes to one's brother's family? Does the hunter's mother's brother get a larger share of the allotment? These are important questions in many societies, and just how they are addressed explains a great deal about how that culture operates.

Food serves still other functions. Some foods enjoy certain status—perhaps because they are expensive or otherwise not generally available to the entire society. When the San of the Kalahari kill a giraffe, the liver is divided and eaten on the spot. It is considered the hunters' share, and they enjoy the fact that their success in the hunt entitles them, and only them, to eat it. Truffles and caviar are high-status foods in the United States mainly because their cost puts them out of reach of most people. In parts of the developing world such items as commercially prepared soft drinks and powdered infant formula have taken on high status, often with negative financial and nutritional consequences. Food, then, plays a multiplicity of roles in many societies.

In this chapter we begin to look at the evolution of culture, starting with the earliest way in which people obtained food—*hunting and gathering*. We will see how this type of adaptation provided early humans with a distinct advantage over their competitors. Toward the end of the chapter we will take a brief look at an example of a hunting and gathering society in order to see how these characteristics fit together. Finally, we will look at some of the evolutionary limits on hunting and gathering, limits that led to more complex forms of social organization and more productive **subsistence strategies.**

Hunting for food dates back to our prehuman ancestors, although the earliest humanlike hunters were primarily scavengers and probably killed only small game or the young of larger animals. Over the years advances in skills and tools, increased intelli-

gence, and the development of cooperation and communication led to greater success in hunting. This enabled the hunters of the Ice Age, for example, to survive by eating large game, such as mammoths and mastodons, at a time when there was little vegetation to add to their diet.

Studies of hunting and gathering societies are based on two sources of information. First, there are archeological records of extinct hunting and gathering societies. These help us fill in the record of the past, but they give only a limited amount of information. Remains of tools and weapons may tell us something about advances in technology, and the bones of dead animals may add some valuable information about diet. But aside from interpreting the few physical remains that have survived to the present, archeology cannot tell us much about hunting and gathering in prehistoric times.

The second source of information is the observation of hunting and gathering societies that exist today. By studying such people as the San of the Kalahari Desert in southern Africa, the Pygmies of the Congo region of central Africa, and the Aborigines of Australia, we can learn about some of the ecological limits on hunting and gathering and perhaps see some patterns in these peoples' social organization. Of course, there is a danger in assuming that early hunting and gathering societies were just like those of today, and any conclusions we might come to regarding the earliest forms of human society are simply conjectures based on what we observe in the present. But in the absence of written records, and given the limitations of archeology for this type of study, information about present-day hunters and gatherers is the best we have to go on.

Evolutionary Implications of Hunting and Gathering

We assume that hunting and gathering were the main sources of food for the earliest human populations, and in this sense these early populations were not much different from nonhuman primates. However, once human culture took over in the process of gaining a living from the environment, humans became increasingly different from other primates.

It is important to understand how hunting and gathering societies are organized and how they are similar in spite of variations in climate, food sources, and the environments in which they are found. For not only are hunting and gathering societies the key to our prehuman past, but they represent the subsistence strategy that has supported the human species for more then 99 percent of its existence.

As recently as 10,000 years ago the entire population of the earth—estimated at roughly 10 million people—consisted of hunters and gatherers. Eight thousand years later, about the time of Christ, half of the population had become agricultural or pastoral, but the other half still lived by hunting and gathering. By the time of the discovery of the New World some 500 years ago, only about 15 percent of the world's population were hunters and gatherers. And today, with the earth's population at about 4 billion, fewer than 300,000 (or less than 1/1000 of 1 percent) are hunters and gatherers. They are found in a few isolated pockets scattered around the world in the most barren and forbidding environments, where they are allowed to remain because they pose no threat to their neighbors and do not occupy land that could be used for anything else.

However, because hunting and gathering was such a long and important phase in our cultural evolution, it is worth some attention. Remember, too, that we can understand biological as well as cultural evolution only in the context of hunting and gathering as a way of life. Physically, we evolved the way we did as an adaptation to hunting and gathering. The past few hundred years may have produced major changes in our societies, and it may seem that the biological effects have been enormous, but the impact of the last

ten generations of human evolution cannot compare with that of the thousands of generations that preceded them.

Division of labor In an earlier chapter we touched briefly on the role of hunting in early human culture and on the similarity between human beings and nonhuman primates in this regard. The evolution of human societies is related to hunting (and, to a lesser extent, gathering as well) in a number of ways. One of these is the **division of labor,** or the assigning of different tasks to different members of the group.

Hunting usually requires more territory than gathering, because animal food is more widely distributed. Even before the invention of farming, a family or larger group could survive on much less land by relying solely on plant foods. But because hunting requires frequent long trips for extended periods, it probably led to a simple division of labor in which the adult men took over the bulk of the hunting while the women and other members of the group remained closer to the home base and did more gathering of plant foods. This would allow the women to care for the children and remain in a larger group for mutual protection.

The division of labor put a premium on cooperation and communication. Everyone would benefit from the ability to share information about where and when to meet or who would perform which task. Thus even though hunting might not produce as much food as gathering (which is usually the case), it is important from the standpoint of human evolution because it required cooperation.

Also, when work is divided up, people must share in order to survive. If they want to take advantage of the nutritional value of different kinds of food, they must have a home base where they can meet after a day's work and share out the food. Also, as mentioned earlier, a home base allows ill or injured individuals to recover. Many diseases force people to lie down and rest for long periods, which is impossible without a home base. When meat was introduced into their

Arunta men hunting with boomerangs and spears. In this group, hunting is primarily a male activity.

diet, humans became liable to the diseases and parasites transmitted by the flesh of the animals they hunted. But they developed a new cultural pattern—caring for the sick—and thereby extended the life span of most members of the population. As a result, learning and experience had a greater impact on evolution, and social bonds between members of the group were strengthened as well.

Ownership and transportation of goods
Hunting and gathering also led to the technological advances required to transport goods. If hunting meant frequent movement of the home base in pursuit of animal food, then it was necessary to transport the group's possessions and whatever food and water there was. While large amounts of meat can be carried fairly easily, especially when it has been dried, vegetables are heavy and bulky and cannot be carried far without containers. Thus humans were under pressure to invent both weapons and tools, including baskets or some other means of carrying food.

Moving around a lot also means that possessions must be kept to a minimum. This fact tends to reduce the differences in wealth among members of a group since it is impossible for any one person to accumulate much property. In hunting and gathering societies whose environment was rich enough to permit people to live in one place, differences in wealth played a more important role in the social life of the group. But such situations are rare today, and probably were rare in prehistoric times as well.

As a result of the environmental pressures on hunters and gatherers—at least those that we observe in such societies today—the absence of social levels based on wealth extends to the concept of private property. Groups usually do not maintain exclusive rights to natural resources, and frequent movement in search of food keeps any group from becoming attached to a single territory. If one group claims exclusive rights to a water hole and it dries up, that group may not survive if it does not have the right to use water holes owned by other groups. The fact that hunters and gatherers live in relative harmony with the environment, but without putting much labor or capital into its development, seems to have led to a fairly universal

In traditional Inuit society, transportation by dogsled limited personal possessions. Modern technology, included ownership of snowmobiles, has contributed to a changing way of life, more permanent settlements, and increasingly uneven distribution of wealth.

pattern in which the concept of ownership of natural resources had no place.

Group size and life style Our estimate of the "average" size of a hunting and gathering group is based on present-day populations. Since, as noted earlier, all groups that live this way today occupy marginal areas, they can hardly be considered typical of those that existed during the vast majority of human history. In present-day populations the nature of the food supply tends to keep such groups small; they usually have fewer than 50 members. Smaller bands may join together for ceremonies on a seasonal basis, when enough food is available in one centralized location. In general, however, the size of the group varies with the availability of food.

If we were to make a guess about how similar pressures might have affected hunting and gathering populations in the past, we might expect that because they occupied more fertile land they could support somewhat larger groups. But group size would still be likely to vary with seasonal changes in the food supply, and only a few environments would offer a stable enough resource base to support a fairly constant, dense population. Membership ties would remain loose, and conflicts would probably be resolved by splitting the group into two or more parts. This, at any rate, is a pattern that has been observed in modern hunting and gathering societies.

Kinship and Reciprocity in Hunting and Gathering Societies

Although specific adaptations among hunting and gathering groups may differ according to the environment, there are certain similarities among all present-day societies of this type. Two patterns emerge that are clearly related to hunting and gathering as a subsistence strategy, and might therefore have occurred in similar societies in the past. These two patterns are (1) cooperation or **reciprocity** in obtaining food; and (2) a loose-knit social organization based primarily on **kinship** ties, that is, family relationships created either by birth or by marriage.

Reciprocal exchange of food is common, but other items may be exchanged as well. A large animal may be enough to supply food for a sizable group of people. Since it is not usually possible for such groups to store meat, reciprocity serves the same purpose. A hunter gives meat away, knowing that if he does not do so it will rot. In return, he can expect a portion when another hunter is successful. Even the most skillful hunter may have a run of bad luck, and reciprocity works to everyone's advantage in overcoming the dry spells that every family will experience at one time or another.

Close family ties often serve as the basis for reciprocity. A hunter's main obligation is to his immediate family, but beyond that, he is expected to share the food he obtains with close kin, more distant kin, and so on, in decreasing amounts. In many societies it is expected that a person will be generous and will not try to take more than his or her fair share. Gifts are not given—one has a right to expect a share of someone else's success. If a member of the group does not live up to this code, it is enforced through informal social sanctions, such as gossip or avoidance or, in extreme cases, banishment.

Kinship is at the root of almost all relationships in hunting and gathering societies. Because there is little specialization, people are not identified with their jobs, as they often are in our society. Instead, they are identified by their kinship, either by blood or by marriage, to other members of the group. Thus the family forms the basis of religious, economic, and political activity, along with almost every other aspect of community life. This is illustrated by the case of

an anthropologist who went with a native guide to visit a group of Australian Aborigines. During the day they talked with the people, and the guide acted as interpreter. But at night the guide would not stay in the camp but slipped off into the desert. When the anthropologist asked why, he learned that the guide had not been able to establish a kinship relationship with anyone in the group, and therefore had felt that his life was in danger. It seems that, to his mind, there were but two classes of people—relatives and enemies. Since the guide had no relatives in the group, he was defined as an enemy and feared that he would be killed.

The Band as a Form of Social Organization

Kinship is also closely tied to the organization of members of a hunting and gathering society into what anthropologists term a **band.** This term describes a small, loose-knit group that is based on the relatedness of its members—there are usually no formal leadership roles, no formal exchange systems such as a marketplace, and no distinct legal institutions. Those who lead in a political sense are also leaders in a family sense. Exchange is based on reciprocity, which follows family lines. Informal rules of behavior are enforced through consensus rather than by courts or police. In short, while the band is very different from our complex forms of social organization, it is well adapted to the life style of hunting and gathering peoples and appears to be almost universal among them.

The most common type of band organization is formed around a core of related males married to females who were born and raised in other bands, but moved into their husbands' group upon marriage. Anthropologists use the term **patrilocal** to describe this type of social organization; this term comes from the Latin words *pater*, meaning "father," and *locus*, or "place"—in other words, living in the place of the father. Sons remain in or near the households of their fathers and bring their wives into their community, while daughters marry outside the community and go to live in the households of their husbands' fathers. (The opposite arrangement is termed **matrilocal**, meaning that the men leave their parents when they marry and go to live with their wives' families, while the women remain where they grew up and bring their husbands to live with them.)[1]

These marriage and residence patterns create a group of people who are all related to one another, either by birth or by marriage. If the group is small enough, everyone may be no farther apart than cousins and their spouses, while in a larger group the relationships may be more distant. The important point is that the members recognize that they are related, and this imposes certain obligations on them in their interactions with others—we all feel that relatives are special people to whom we owe more loyalty and devotion than we owe to people who are not related to us.

Because there is a special feeling of relatedness between members of a patrilocal band, there are rules against marriage between band members (just as we have rules against marriage with close relatives). This practice is termed **exogamy,** from the Greek *exo*, meaning "outside," and *gamos*, meaning "marriage." Such a rule forces people to look outside their own band for marriage partners—a man brings a wife into his group, while a woman moves into her husband's group. Marriage thus not only provides spouses and creates a setting in which reproduction may occur; it also creates alliances among bands and widens the network of relationships that tie different groups together. In other words, it performs economic

and political functions as well as kinship-related functions. Exogamous marriage helps explain how hunting and gathering groups can share the same territory and even cooperate in hunting parties and religious rituals. When, as a result of many intermarriages, the members of two groups share a large number of relatives, either through birth or through marriage, it is much easier for them to work together toward a common goal.

But why are most bands patrilocal rather than matrilocal? Why isn't it more common for men to move in with the woman's group rather than the other way around? Obviously, there is no single answer to this question, since marriage practices have roots in the past and we can never hope to know how they got started. But we can make an educated guess on the basis of our observations of the benefits of patrilocal marriage patterns in hunting and gathering societies today.

Patrilocality is sometimes explained by the fact that the male's knowledge of the hunting territory must be preserved. If the male moved into his wife's territory, he would not be familiar with the habits of the animals there or the best places to hunt. But this does not explain the presence of patrilocality in societies in which most of the food is supplied by gathering. Also, in most cases marriages occur between neighboring bands whose territories are not very different and may even overlap. Then, too, not all hunting and gathering bands are patrilocal—some Australian Aborigines are matrilocal, and some groups of San in the Kalahari Desert of South Africa are matrilocal until the wife has had at least one child. There are many other examples from around the world, showing that it is not necessary for a band to be patrilocal.

Probably the reason most hunting and gathering societies are patrilocal is that hunting requires cooperation, and gathering does not. A team of brothers or male cousins can be maintained if the men remain in the same group. Thus hunting, though less important in terms of the amount of food produced, is still a major factor in the social organization of hunters and gatherers.

---

[1] Kinship is often said to be the most complicated and confusing topic in anthropology, but at the same time the most unavoidable one. If we are to understand how a society can be organized on the basis of kinship, it will be necessary to learn some elementary concepts. Kinship as an institution will be discussed in more detail in Chapter 9, and the reader may wish to look ahead at this point, or else to look back at this chapter later on.

The kinship systems of hunting and gathering societies are not as simple or as uniform as we have indicated here—if they were, they would not have such a bad reputation among anthropology students. We will go into kinship in more detail in Chapter 9, but for now it is important to understand how kinship serves as the basis for almost all social interaction among hunting and gathering societies. A second type of band organization, found much less often, is the **composite band.** This type does not follow the regular customs of exogamy and residence with either the husband's or the wife's family. Instead, the immediate family unit is more important, and the rest of the band plays a lesser role in social interaction. In some areas each family is an economic unit, and cooperation is limited to those few times when a group of families might join in a common venture. Such a pattern is found among such groups as the Algonkian-speaking Indians of the sub-Arctic areas of North America, and among some Inuit (Eskimo) groups. There hunting and trapping are individual male activities, and cooperation would not greatly increase the yield.

Composite bands are arranged more for convenience and companionship than for joint economic activities. Marriage is based on the circumstances of each family, and since not all band members consider themselves related, there is no rule of band exogamy.

It has been suggested that the composite band is a product of contact and change that occurred after the white settlement of North America and other parts of the world. It is possible that most, if not all, hunting and gathering peoples were either patrilocal or matrilocal before contact with the Western world, but that in later times their populations were reduced by either hostility or disease. In many cases the survivors were forced to migrate to new lands, which further broke up family patterns. This upset the traditional order and threw together people who were not related. During such a rapid change the "logic" of the patrilocal (or matrilocal) band could have been lost, and the rules that governed marriage and social interaction among relatives would no longer have applied. But this is only a guess, since we do not know how hunting and gathering societies were organized before contact with the Western world.

Politics, Law, and Religion in Hunting and Gathering Societies

The nature of hunting and gathering has led to a special type of economic and family relationship that is common to most hunters and gatherers. The same limitations apply to their political organization, as well as their religious organization and many other aspects of their lives. Unlike contemporary industrial societies, in which religious, political, and economic institutions are distinct, hunting and gathering societies blend these institutions, and all of them are based on kinship relations. For example, in our society we can distinguish between an economic act, such as spending eight hours at work earning money, and a political act, such as voting, or a religious act, such as saying a prayer before eating dinner. For most of us there is nothing political about prayer, any more than there is anything religious about voting. Among hunting and gathering peoples, by contrast, all of these activities are fused. The exchange of food—basically an economic act—may have political overtones in that it creates an alliance between members of two separate groups. It may have religious meaning in that the food is from an animal that plays a major role in the belief system of the people. It may be legal behavior in the sense that it follows informal, but very strict, rules about the sharing of meat by a cooperative hunting party. Or it may tie in with the kinship system in that food is distributed according to how closely various people are related. Thus in looking at other spheres of activity among hunters and gatherers, we must not forget that distinctions among economic, political, and religious acts are artificial ones that we make for the sake of analysis—they are not made, on a conscious level, by the people we are describing.

Control over property We have already noted that there is little or no control or ownership of property among hunters and gatherers. This is because the resources that support them are sometimes scarce, often unpredictable, and clearly not controllable. A small group could not hope to defend a territory that is large enough to support it and still have time to feed itself—nor would there be any need to do so as long as there was enough land to permit the population to spread out as it increased. Even somewhat more predictable resources, such as a water hole or a grove of trees, are not controlled by the groups that use them. Hunter-gatherer groups generally will not locate their campsite right at a water hole but will make camp a few hundred yards away. They do this partly to avoid scaring off any game that might want to use the water hole, but also because it allows other people to use the water hole and thus prevents tension.

The same is true with regard to other resources. Among the Shoshone Indians of the Great Basin in what is now Utah, Nevada, and part of California, large groves of nut trees provided plenty of food when the trees yielded a heavy harvest. But the groves did not produce evenly each year. Bands of Shoshone scattered throughout the territory would scout out the more productive groves in advance, and several bands would meet at these groves when the time came to harvest the nuts. This precluded ownership of any one grove, an advantageous custom, for if

In traditional Inuit society, seal hunting is a solitary activity not requiring communal effort.

the grove did not bear well in a given year, no one would go hungry. The same applies to hunting territory: After a very successful season the game population might not be enough to support the entire group for several years. By cooperating and moving from one area to another, several bands could survive with much more security than if each remained in a smaller territory over which it claimed ownership rights.

The absence of warfare The absence of private property among most hunting and gathering peoples removes one of the main causes of organized warfare. Warfare is usually carried out for a purpose, such as seizing land or other valuable property. But among most hunting and gathering groups ownership of territory was not important and their nomadic life style limited the amount of property they could carry with them. In addition, a hunting and gathering way of life does not allow for long periods of fighting, because while food may be plentiful, it cannot be stored very long. A farmer who produces grain by working eight or ten hours a day for six months can store the grain and engage in other activities. But even though a hunter-gatherer may have to spend only two or three hours each day to get enough food, that food must be obtained almost every day.

Some anthropologists have suggested that warfare can be broadly defined as armed combat between territorially or politically defined groups. Using this definition, we can readily see why hunting and gathering societies rarely engage in war. Most such societies are organized into small, loose-knit bands without sharp territorial boundaries. Because there is no strong political organization, their membership may fluctuate, and as people move about or intermarry, they form alliances with neighboring bands. This open type of social organization keeps them from identifying closely with any single group, and their group ties are not strong enough to sustain a long and bloody battle. This does not mean that there is no violence; rather, conflict tends to occur on an individual or family level rather than pitting two whole groups against each other.

For groups that cover a wide territory and move about freely, warfare does not make sense. What would you do if you won? You could not defend your territory, and you would not gain much personal wealth. You might have more land in which to hunt, but as long as the population was small you could achieve the same results simply by moving into new, unpopulated areas. Not until we find permanent villages do we see the beginnings of group efforts to defeat opponents and take over their territory. And such settlements are rarely found among hunting and gathering peoples. Life in a permanent village represents an investment of time and labor in a house, a cultivated field, or other possessions that take on value, such as tools or domesticated animals. But once a group reaches the level of technology at which labor is invested in the environment to change it rather than simply to gain a living from it the way it is, they are no longer a hunting and gathering people.

Flexible social organization Hunting and gathering societies are noted for their flexible social organization. If a quarrel arises, it can often be settled by the group's dividing up into separate bands rather than fighting. There are no political barriers to such division because there is no centralized control over the group. No leader can force people to submit to his or her wishes; the group acts together only by consensus. The lack of formal laws means that everyone has a voice in the legal system. If the unwritten rules of behavior are violated, everyone in the group helps to enforce the penalty, which, again, is a matter of consensus. But it is important to note that in a society in which cooperation is important for survival there can be a great deal of pressure to conform to group standards.

The structure of most hunting and gathering bands does not include social stratification or political hierarchy. Everyone in the society is more or less equal; if a person does gain high status, it is because of age or wisdom or some talent or ability. However, higher status does not free that person from his or her obligations to the group, and the abilities or talents that led to that status must be used for the good of the group. For example, a good hunter may become a leader, but only if he shares his meat with the rest of the group—if he keeps it all for himself and lets some of it go to waste, his talents will not help him gain a higher status among his fellow band members.

Since the group has no permanent leader, leadership roles may shift from one activity to another. In a hunting party, one man may be a leader because of his skill as a hunter. In a ceremony performed to cure a sick member, another person may take over the leadership role because of his or her knowledge of healing practices. Since skills vary from one activity to another, so do the people who act as leaders.

Settling disputes   Because there is no leader to enforce a code of law, control over social behavior is achieved largely by the weight of tradition. Accepted practices, or **social sanctions,** are applied instead of formal laws. Punishment may be light, consisting of nasty gossip or ridicule, or may go as far as actual violence. A person who behaves in an antisocial way and does not respond to mild sanctions may be exiled from the group; in some environments this could amount to a death sentence.

An interesting way of settling disputes is found in Inuit society. Two men who are involved in a dispute will engage in a **song duel.** Singing ability is more important to the Inuit than physical strength in settling disputes, and it certainly is less harmful and dangerous to the parties involved. The parties create songs designed to insult each other, and in so doing they gain the support of various members of the audience that gathers around them. As the duel proceeds, the audience begins to take the side of one of the parties and abandons the other. The main

goal is prestige for the winner and the satisfaction of having shamed or insulted the loser—there is often no other penalty for the loser

Another interesting form of dispute settlement is found among the Tiwi of northern Australia. Disputes often arise between older and younger men, with the older men accusing the younger ones of seducing their wives. While it is common knowledge that the young men do this, it is also against the group's rules of behavior, since marriage gives the husband exclusive rights over his wife or wives.

When a man accuses another of some wrongdoing, they may enter into a spear-throwing duel. Again the audience is important: It judges the claims of the contestants and puts pressure on one or the other to end the duel. The accuser, usually an older man, throws spears at the accused until he either wounds him or gives up. The audience will communicate, by means of cheers and comments, its opinion about the guilt or innocence of the accused. If the audience feels that the accused is guilty, he will get the message and, instead of dodging the spears, let one hit him in a relatively harmless place and draw blood, thereby ending the duel. If the audience sides with the accused, he may continue to dodge the spears until the thrower gives up. In this way public pressure is brought to bear and the ritual is carried out so that "justice" prevails, much the same as the song duel works for the Inuit.

Religious specialization   As in other areas of social life, there are few specialists in religious activities. An exception is the **shaman,** or medicine man. The shaman is usually a male who has some special talent for curing the sick, for example, by falling into a trance so as to communicate with the spirits that are thought to be causing the illness. The shaman does not usually receive formal training. He is not a full-time specialist, but an amateur who cures the sick in addition to his regular role in the community.

Emile Durkheim (1858–1917)

Emile Durkheim, a noted French sociologist, is also an important figure in the history of anthropology. In *The Division of Labor in Society*, his first major book, he compared the social organization of hunting and gathering societies with that of industrial societies. In his last great work, *The Elementary Forms of the Religious Life*, he looked at the religion of the Australian Aborigines in an attempt to reconstruct the early history of religious institutions in human society.

The main job of the shaman is to diagnose and cure illnesses that are thought to be caused by the supernatural. Unlike the treatment of illness in our society, the activities of the shaman are usually carried out in front of the entire group. This type of religious treatment can be very effective, especially when there is a psychosomatic element in the illness or when the psychological support received by the patient can help in the curing process.

Shamans provide a number of other services linked to their contact with the supernatural. These include weather forecasting, predicting future events, and similar activities. Their religious activities represent a certain amount of specialization, but again, it is worth noting that shamans do not hold a formal position in their society. Rather, they achieve their special status because of the talents they show in one area of social behavior.

Stratification in Hunting and Gathering Bands

Hunting and gathering as a way of life tends to keep social differences to a minimum. As a result, there is usually little social stratification, and anthropologists sometimes refer to hunting and gathering bands as **egalitarian,** meaning that the members are more or less equal in rank. There are many reasons why this might be true.

In hunting and gathering societies we find little division of labor. Most men engage in hunting and most women in gathering. Although one man might be a better hunter than another, or one woman a better gatherer, still there are no status distinctions based on economic specialities. The emphasis is on sharing with the group rather than increasing the wealth of one's family. The few status differences that exist are usually based on achievement—there are few ascribed status positions in hunting and gathering bands. While it is true that age and sex may be considered in assigning status, the differences within the band are not very great—men are not so dominant over women, nor are older people dominant over younger ones. Each person contributes to the survival of the family and the group, and decisions are made by consensus rather than by a strong leader.

Because of the size of most bands, there is a close personal relationship among members. In a large society like ours, in which we cannot know every other member personally, we tend to identify people according to occupation or some other defining feature. In a small group, in which everyone knows everyone else, personal qualities can determine social relationships. What ranking there is, is usually on the basis of known abilities, such as the curing powers of a shaman, the hunting skill of a young man, or the storytelling ability of an older member of the group.

Another factor that limits social stratification in most hunting and gathering societies is the inability to amass personal wealth. The combination of a nomadic life style and a limited technology means that a person usually owns no more than a few items that can be carried from place to place. Ownership is therefore a rather loose concept, and the tools or weapons or artwork that a person produces are likely to be given away, since they cannot be stored or saved. Giving such things away is a means of impressing others with one's generosity. Likewise, there is usually no concept of private property—the environment is free for all to exploit, and while one group may stake out a territory as its own, it will probably allow neighboring groups to have access to game or other resources in the area simply for the asking. Thus the features of social organization that lead to stratification—specialized roles, wealth, control over the environment, and control over other people—are missing from hunting and gathering bands.

Comparing Political Institutions

Band organization We have discussed the band as a form of social organization in hunting and gathering societies and described in detail how it reflects the features and limitations of that way of life. In this section we will look more closely at the political scope of band organization so that we may compare it with other forms of political organization.

We can better understand how band organization works if we consider it in the context of the problems that hunters and gatherers must face and the environment in which they live. People who live off the land without practicing agriculture, raising livestock, or in some other way increasing the amount of food available require a great deal of land. They soon exhaust the food supply in a given area and are forced to move to a new source of food. Sometimes they follow migratory animals (which are moving to new sources of food and water for themselves), but more often the movements of a hunting and gathering band are based on the availability of a combination of animal and plant food. Various fruits ripen in different seasons, and the rainy season lasts longer or comes later in one area than it does in another. All of these factors make for a unique life style, to which the band seems well suited.

Hunting and gathering bands tend to be rather small throughout most of the year, consisting of about 25 to 40 people. Of course, the size of the group fluctuates, so that when food is plentiful several bands might join together for a feast, while when food is scarce a number of splinter groups will spread out over a larger area seeking water, animals, and edible plants. Each band thinks of a certain area as its own, and while there are no specific boundaries that limit the movement of the group, members rarely go beyond what they consider to be their territory. Territories may overlap slightly, so that two groups might come into contact when each is on the fringe of its own territory, but for the most part a band is isolated from its neighbors.

Two elements of political organization operate to maintain the band: the internal organization of the small group, and the external set of regulations governing the organization of a large number of neighboring groups when they come into contact. On the level of the small group, we can see how the combination of environment and life style would lead to a loose-knit structure. Little in this way of life is permanent. Groups often split up; some families join another group, or a larger faction forms a new band. Sometimes the group becomes too large to be supported by the surrounding area, and new land must be found. At other times disputes may be solved by the division of a band into two or more groups. Moreover, a necessary aspect of hunting and gathering as a way of life is that each person must contribute something to the support of the group. There is little room for nonproductive individuals when the food supply is so limited. As a result, each family tends to be self-sufficient and does not rely as heavily on the rest of the society as we are used to doing. (Consider where you would be today if you had to grow your own food, make your own clothes, and even manufacture your own automobile!)

The ties that bind people together in a band are different from those that bind people together in a contemporary industrial society. If a disagreement occurs, each party feels free to leave the group if the solution is not satisfactory. Thus membership in a band is like membership in a club. We are free to drop out and join another club if we do not get along with other members or if we disagree with changes in the club's rules or activities. But few of use would go so far as to drop out of American society just because we disagree with some of its laws or because the candidate we voted for lost the election. We have become so specialized that we rely on others to keep us alive, whereas the typical !Kung San or Australian Aborigine or Inuit—all of whom are members of bands—can survive by himself or with his family, despite living in a far more hostile environment.

Within such a group, all members are basically equal. This is not to say that there are no differences among them—every member is ranked according to his or her skill as a hunter, storyteller, curer, or whatever. But when decisions are made that affect the group as a whole, they are made on the basis of consensus and are not imposed by a dominant king or chief. Cooperation is the best way to ensure survival. If a hunter is successful, he shares his kill with the rest of the group, for he knows that the time will come when his luck will be down and someone else will share with him. This form of cooperation affects not just the distribution of food but the concept of ownership itself. The resources of the band belong to everyone equally and are to be shared by all. In such a society the status of leader, or **headman,** is based on personal qualities and the respect of others. Such leaders cannot impose their own desires on the rest of the group against their will; should they attempt to do so, they will probably lose their position as leaders.

A second type of political relationship regulates interactions among two or more small bands. As mentioned earlier, two groups may come into contact in areas where their territories overlap. Or several groups may gather to celebrate a special event, usually at a time of year when the food supply is abundant—when migratory animals return, wild grains or other plants ripen, or the rainy season begins. In such a setting the bonds that hold these groups together in a political alliance can be most important, for they not only guard against warfare but also help integrate the groups and give them a basis for interaction.

Although they are self-sufficient in the sense that they can obtain enough food to support themselves, bands cannot exist in total isolation from one another. A group of fewer than 40 or 50 people contains only a few families, so that the number of potential mates is very limited. As we will see in the chapter on kinship, every society has some form of incest taboo that limits the choice of a mate to someone outside the immediate family. In a group the size of a band inbreeding would soon lead to a situation in which there were no eligible marriage partners. If the group remained isolated and continued to obey the incest taboo, it would die out. On the other hand, the incest taboo, which forces people to look beyond their own group, leads to cooperation and interdependence with neighboring groups. It is interesting to ask whether the incest taboo arose as a way of forcing hostile neighbors to cooperate and overcome their differences in order to find marriage partners. Surely it is one of the most effective means of preventing warfare at the band level, for each person has ties with many other groups through the marriages of his or her relatives, and who would want to do battle with relatives?

The !Kung San

In concluding, it is helpful to look at an example of a hunting and gathering society in detail to see how it reflects some of the patterns of social organization discussed in this chapter. We should stress again, however, that although our discussion has been divided into sections on politics, law, religion, economics, and kinship, this is an artificial division. In reality, hunting and gathering societies do not show the degree of specialization that we are used to in these various spheres of activity. This should become clear in the following description.

A few hunting and gathering societies, such as the Inuit or the Indians of the northwestern coast of North America (prior to white contact), lived in an environment so rich in fish and game that they could get most of their food by hunting and fishing. However, most hunting and gathering peoples obtain the vast majority of their food by gathering roots, berries, nuts, and other vegetable products. The importance of hunting is often due to its role in the group's religious

rituals and in the cooperation it requires, and not to the amount of meat it contributes to the diet. This is especially true of the !Kung San of the Kalahari Desert in Botswana, who rely mainly on gathering for their subsistence.

Many in-depth studies have been done of the San way of life. Among other things, they have found that the San need to spend very little time to obtain enough food. This is somewhat surprising, since we tend to think of hunting and gathering as a precarious way of life in which one never knows whether there will be enough food. But the San do not fit this "feast or famine" image. They need only a few hours each day to get enough food to live quite comfortably, and they have a great deal of leisure—much more than we do.

The San also contradict the common belief that hunting and gathering peoples rely heavily on meat for survival. One of the most thorough studies of San life was done by the anthropologist Richard Lee among a group called the !Kung.[2] In addition to describing many of their customs, Lee studied their diet and nutrition. He estimates that a San spends about one-third of his time in camp; the rest of the time he visits neighbors and relatives in nearby areas. Because travel is a major part of the normal life style, there are few chances to accumulate and store food, and there is rarely more than two or three days' worth of food on hand. This means that, while there is no danger of starvation, frequent short periods of labor are needed to obtain food, since it cannot be stored for long. On the average, the San collect food every third or fourth day throughout the year and go on extended hunting trips less often.

Vegetable foods make up between 60 and 80 percent of the San diet by weight, depending on the season and the availability of

---

[2] The sign in front of the name is used to indicate a click sound, which is made by flicking the tongue against the roof of the mouth. Although English contains no such sounds, a number of languages use clicks of various kinds.

Richard Lee interviewing a !Kung San hunter about a recent kill.

meat. Most of the gathering is done by women and involves two or three days of work each week. Men also do some gathering, but their major contribution to the diet is hunting large and medium-sized animals. Although they are not as successful at hunting as the women are at gathering, they put in about the same amount of time. Lee estimates that the women provide two to three times as much food by gathering as the men do by hunting.

The most important food in the !Kung diet is the mongongo nut, which is both plentiful and nourishing, and accounts for about half of the vegetable diet by weight. It contains five times as many calories and ten times as much protein as cereal; an average daily ration of mongongo nuts yields about 1,260 calories and 56 grams of protein. Also,

the mongongo nut is resistant to drought and abundant even in dry years—which occur often in the Kalahari Desert. The nut's hard shell protects it from rotting, so it can be harvested and eaten up to a year after it has fallen to the ground.

In addition to mongongo nuts, the San eat 84 other species of plants, including 20 species of fruits, berries, and melons and 30 species of roots and bulbs. This gives their diet a broad base and provides them with a margin of safety during the dry season, when many foods are unavailable. Lee also counted 54 different species of animals that were classified by the San as edible, including a wide variety of birds and reptiles as well as mammals such as antelope, wart hog, porcupine, and rabbit. Smaller animals are usu-

A San woman and child cracking roasted mongongo nuts.

ally trapped in snares, while larger ones are hunted with bows and poison-tipped arrows.

In addition to observing the time spent getting food, Lee analyzed the amount of food consumed during a two-month period. He estimated that meat amounted to 37 percent of the diet, mongongo nuts 33 percent, and other vegetables the remaining 30 percent. The average weight of the food consumed per day was about 1.5 pounds (630 grams), including 93 grams of protein, and this diet provided a total of 2,140 calories. Lee also calculated the Recommended Daily Allowance for people of the size and stature of the San and with their level of physical activity, and estimated it to be 1,975 calories

and 60 grams of protein. Thus the San are well above the minimum in both categories.

Lee's figures are all the more startling because his study was conducted during the third year of one of the most severe droughts ever recorded in southern Africa. The United Nations organized a famine relief program to assist 180,000 residents of the region who were not able to support themselves through pastoralism or agriculture, but the San needed no help.

Another indicator of the relative ease of the San life style is their life span. Of the 466 people in Lee's census, 46 were over 60 years old. Old people are respected in San society. They are cared for and fed even after they are no longer able to provide food for others. Even blind, senile, and crippled people take part in the social life of the group and are called on to assist at special occasions such as religious rituals.

The group of !Kung San observed by Lee included several bands and covered a territory of about 1,000 square miles during one year's wandering. When they are in camp the San exploit an area of about 100 square miles, that is, the area within a 6-mile radius of the camp. The 466 people in Lee's census were divided into a number of bands that came together and then split up again, depending on the season and the availability of food. Lee observed one such campsite for three weeks in order to see how much time was spent collecting food. The group contained from 23 to 40 individuals, depending on how many visitors were in camp. On the average, each adult spent 2.5 days per week either hunting or gathering, with an average workday of about 6 hours. Thus the average work week was about 15 hours. The maximum work week was that of a hunter who spent 32 hours on an extended trip; for much of this time he was tracking an animal that he had shot and waiting for it to die from the poison in the arrow.

In comparing the San life style with that of other peoples, we should consider the fact that the San have no seasons of intensive work such as plowing or harvesting. Extended hunting trips are about the only exception to the 15-hour work week. The rest of the time is generally spent in camp or visiting other camps. Women do odd jobs such as embroidery, cooking, and collecting firewood, while men spend much of their leisure entertaining visitors. A popular event is trance-dancing, in which men fall into trances around the campfire, an event that often lasts well into the night. Lee concludes that the San could be called the original "leisure class" and that, despite their lack of control over their environment, they lead a stable and secure existence.

The Limits of Hunting and Gathering

Hunting and gathering has been the main pattern of subsistence for more than 99 percent of human existence. Although all of the remaining hunters and gatherers occupy marginal areas of the earth that are not productive enough to support agriculture, this has not always been the case. Until fairly recent times—that is, 15,000 years ago—all human groups supported themselves by hunting and gathering. And if today's San can survive in the Kalahari Desert, we can assume that previous hunters and gatherers had an equally easy life in areas where both animal and vegetable foods were much more abundant.

If this is the case, why do we find so few hunters and gatherers in the world today? If it is such a successful subsistence strategy, why did changes occur? And what were the causes of those changes?

These questions are not easy to answer. The archeological record supplies us with dates but not with reasons. Again remembering that anything we say about the shift from hunting and gathering to other ways of obtaining food is only an educated guess, we can at least identify some of the factors that might have led to new subsistence strategies. More important, from what we know about hunting and gathering societies today, we can

identify some of the limitations on the life style of these peoples, factors that would have affected their ability to compete for survival in the more desirable areas of the world.

Almost all known hunting and gathering societies are small, loose-knit groups, rarely numbering more than 100 people. Larger groups often come together at various times, but then they divide up and go their own ways. The crucial factor that determines the size of such a group is not the maximum amount of food available at the peak season of the year but the minimum amount available in the off-season. If a river provides water for thousands of people for ten months out of the year but dries up during the summer, the maximum population that can survive is limited to the amount of water available from springs, wells, or water holes. If a herd of wild animals provides meat for several hundred people during the spring, summer, and autumn but then migrates to another area in the winter, the maximum year-round population is limited by the amount of food available during the winter. Thus we can refer to the population **carrying capacity** of the land.

Hunting and gathering as a subsistence strategy does little if anything to change the environment in such a way as to increase the amount of food and water available. People make their living by gathering vegetable foods and hunting animals, but they rely on nature to replace what they have taken. In other words, hunters and gatherers do not increase the carrying capacity of the land. The population of such groups is therefore limited by the amount and stability of the food in a given area. As a result, group size is likely to fluctuate widely from one season to the next. Group boundaries will be weak, and the group will lack a strong, centralized authority. The *band* type of organization typically found in hunting and gathering societies is characterized by this kind of loose-knit political, social, and economic organization, in which the family is the most important tie that binds people together.

In contrast, the Indians of the northwestern coast of North America show what can happen to population size and stability in the hunting and gathering way of life when the carrying capacity is much greater than in the Kalahari Desert. The environment along the northwestern coast provides a stable and plentiful food supply; both fish and game are available throughout the year. In fact, food was always available in such large quantities that people could live in permanent settlements without domesticating plants or animals. The inhabitants of the region lived in large, well-built houses and, unlike the San, showed great variation in personal wealth. Unlike other hunting and gathering societies, they engaged in limited warfare with their neighbors; this, too, was due to the stability and amount of their food supply. But these groups were the exception rather than the rule, even thousands of years ago when they occupied more fertile lands, because large populations could live in permanent year-round settlements and did not have to break up into smaller groups in response to seasonal changes in the environment.

Unlike most other hunting and gathering societies, the Northwest Coast Indians did not have a loose-knit social and political organization. Private property was clearly defined and protected, and differences in

Unlike most hunting and gathering societies, the Northwest Coast Indians lived in permanent settlements, like this Kwakiutl village.

wealth created differences in rank. The various tribes were divided into groups headed by a formal leader who could exercise authority over the members of the group and organize them into raiding parties or command them to cooperate in other community-based activities. This shows how, in the right conditions, a hunting and gathering society can develop a more complex political system much like those that are typical of pastoral or horticultural groups that live by raising animals or growing their food.

Thus the decline of hunting and gathering and the shift to different subsistence strategies were due not only to technological advances but also to the ability of the environment to support a large and stable population. In analyzing the rise and spread of horticultural and pastoral societies and the decline and increasing marginality of hunting and gathering societies, a trend that began around 15,000 years ago, we can point to the role of domesticated plants and animals in supporting a larger population throughout the year. More people can occupy a given area if they raise vegetable foods that can be harvested in what was formerly the lean period of the year or if they produce a surplus that can be stored until a shortage occurs. By domesticating animals, human societies gained the ability to store food "on the hoof," keeping animals alive until other sources of food ran out. Hunting and gathering of locally available foods could be used to sup-

plement the diet and could even provide the greater part of the food consumed. But the crucial factor was the ability to get through the lean months without having to divide up into smaller groups. With this ability, a larger population could take over a more desirable territory and, because of its size, defend it and even expand into surrounding areas. Loosely organized hunters and gatherers would be no match for the strength and organization of such a group.

As noted earlier, we cannot identify the exact time and place at which people first advanced beyond hunting and gathering. All we can do is point to some features of hunting and gathering societies that set limits on the amount of cultural evolution that could take place under those conditions. This is not to say that hunting and gathering is a less effective strategy for staying alive—if anything, the opposite is true, since the San need to work only a few hours a day to get by in one of the most forbidding environments in the world. Rather, by its very nature hunting and gathering cannot compete with other cultural systems. This illustrates how the introduction of cultural variation into the natural environment brings about rapid change. In the next chapter we will look more closely at some of the cultural systems that replaced hunters and gatherers as the dominant type of society. We will also identify some of the factors that enabled them to do so.

Summary

The acquisition of food and the forms of social organization that develop in response to the food procurement process have long been of interest to anthropologists. This chapter looks at the varied roles food plays. The earliest human beings obtained food by hunting and gathering—only in the last few thousand years have human societies relied on the domestication of plants and animals for their survival. Hunting and gathering requires very little in the way of technology, and even in the harshest environment it can supply small groups of people with enough food while demanding only a few hours of work each day.

Anthropologists have found many similarities in hunting and gathering societies, despite the wide range of environments in which they live. Hunting and gathering became important in human evolution because of changes in the life style of early humans. It requires some division of labor, with the men doing most of the hunting and the women most of the gathering. This means there must be a home base for hunters and gatherers to meet and distribute the food they have obtained at the end of each day. There is little opportunity to acquire great wealth, because the home base is not permanent, and there is no way to store personal goods or carry them from one campsite to another. As a result, social inequality is almost entirely absent from most hunting and gathering groups.

Hunting and gathering societies tend to be organized around two major spheres of activity: the kinship activities of the group and the pattern of reciprocity among its members. Kinship forms the basis for most social interaction, and most members are related either by blood or by marriage. Marriages are often used to create alliances with neighboring groups, and there is usually a rule that says a man and a woman from the same band may not marry each other.

Politically, the band is a loose-knit organization of people without strong, centralized leadership. The band does not exercise exclusive control over property, nor does it have enough authority to force people to act against their will. Instead, it has a flexible social organization that allows it to grow or shrink, and often the size of the group will vary according to the time of year, the availability of food, or the tensions among its members.

The !Kung San of the Kalahari Desert in southern Africa are one of the few remaining hunting and gathering societies. They live mainly by gathering plant foods, and add to their diet whenever possible with meat obtained from hunting. In spite of their desert surroundings, they lead a secure life with plenty of food and leisure. They tend to live in small groups of fewer than 100 people, moving often in search of food. Although the environment is not particularly favorable, they are able to survive because their population does not increase rapidly and their life style does not significantly alter the environment or use up its resources. In the past there were hunting and gathering societies in areas that could support larger and more permanent settlements, such as were found among the Native Americans on the northwestern coast of North America at the time of first white contact. However, as these areas became more desirable for settlement by technologically superior populations, the hunters and gatherers were either killed off or pushed into marginal areas such as deserts or the sub-Arctic region.

Glossary

band   A form of sociopolitical organization found primarily among hunting and gathering peoples. These groups, usually made up of between 25 and 40 people, are loosely organized and tend to be organized on a principle of equality.

carrying capacity   The maximum population that can be supported by a given environment.

composite band   A sociopolitical group found in some hunting and gathering societies in which the normal patterns of kinship and reciprocity are weaker than in a patrilocal or matrilocal band, possibly as a result of severe depopulation, which forced unrelated families together into a group.

division of labor The degree of differentiation of tasks in society and their performance by different groups of specialists. Contrasts to situation in which everyone does the same work.

exogamy The prohibition against marriage within a group, however that group is defined.

general food taboos Restrictions that prohibit an entire society from eating certain things.

kinship The system of defining and organizing one's relatives.

matrilocal residence The pattern in which a married couple resides in the bride's mother's household after marriage.

patrilocal residence The pattern in which a mar-ried couple resides in the groom's father's household after marriage.

reciprocity In hunting and gathering societies, the pattern of sharing food and personal wealth, so that each member of the group has the right to expect gifts from others.

shaman A religious specialist considered to have contact with spirits, and whose powers come directly from those supernatural forces.

social sanction Rewards or punishments that are imposed on members of a society in order to maintain social control—for example, in the settlement of disputes.

song duel A contest in Inuit society used to settle disputes without resorting to violence.

specific food taboos Food prohibitions directed only at a specific group in a society.

subsistence strategy A way of making a living from the environment, including the techniques used and the resources exploited.

Questions for Discussion

1. Human beings have existed on the earth for millions of years as hunters and gatherers, and only in the last few thousand years have most people given up that way of life in favor of some form of domestication of plants and animals. Thus, biologically speaking, we are adapted to hunting and gathering as a way of life, since most of our biological evolution took place during that period of our history. Looking at human societies today, what features seem to fit better with a hunting and gathering life style than with the way of life we tend to follow in industrial society?

2. What kinds of biological changes would you expect to occur as a result of human adaptation to life in an industrial society? Would people tend to get larger or smaller, stronger or weaker, smarter or less smart—or would they change at all? How could you measure to see if there were any such change?

3. What are some of the major differences between the way people are organized into social groups in the United States and how they are organized in a hunting and gathering society such as the !Kung San? Are there any similarities?

Suggestions for Additional Reading

CARLETON S. COON, *The Hunting Peoples* (New York: Penguin, 1976). A broad survey of hunting and gathering cultures, including references to both past and present societies.

A. P. ELKIN, *The Australian Aborigines*, 3rd ed. (Garden City, N.Y.: Doubleday, 1964). A detailed analysis of one of the few remaining hunting and gathering societies, providing a fascinating view of their way of life.

D. R. HARRIS and G. C. HILLMAN (Eds.), *Foraging and Farming* (London: Unwin Hyman, 1989). Forty-five chapters dealing with the latest evidence on the origin and early development of agriculture in all the main geographical regions of the world.

ELEANOR LEACOCK and RICHARD LEE (Eds.), *Politics and History in Band Societies* (Cambridge, Eng.: Cambridge University Press, 1982). Presented are ways in which modern hunter-gatherers organize to solve problems and settle disputes among themselves, with neighboring farmers, and within nation-states.

RICHARD B. LEE, *The Dobe !Kung* (New York: Holt, Rinehart and Winston, 1984). An excellent summary of the author's extensive work among the !Kung. Includes a nice discussion of doing fieldwork as well as a very important final chapter on changes taking place in the Kalahari.

RICHARD B. LEE and IRVEN DEVORE (Eds.), *Man the Hunter* (Chicago: Aldine, 1968). A collection of articles covering a wide range of interests in hunting and gathering, both in the present and in the past.

ELMAN R. SERVICE, *The Hunters,* 2nd ed. (Englewood Cliffs, N.J.: Prentice Hall, 1979). A brief survey of hunting and gathering societies, with short ethnographic summaries of a few selected groups.

MARJORIE SHOSTAK, *Nisa: The Life and Words of a !Kung Woman* (Cambridge, Mass.: Harvard University Press, 1981). A nice presentation of the woman's world among the !Kung.

ELIZABETH MARSHALL THOMAS, *The Harmless People* (New York: Vintage, 1959). An entertaining ethnographic account of the San of the Kalahari, providing many insights into their day-to-day activities.

Eating Christmas in the Kalahari

RICHARD BORSHAY LEE

The earlier discussion of hunting and gathering societies pointed to many cultural practices that help maintain a sense of balance and equality within the group. Sharing, or reciprocity, is expected of everyone, and a person's generosity is thought of as normal and not a cause for special praise. For someone from another culture where these values are not commonly held, it may be difficult to understand the behavior of hunting and gathering people, as Richard Lee illustrates in the following article.

The !Kung* Bushmen's knowledge of Christmas is thirdhand. The London Missionary Society brought the holiday to the southern Tswana tribes in the early nineteenth century. Later, native catechists spread the idea far and wide among the Bantu-speaking pastoralists, even in the remotest corners of the Kalahari Desert. The Bushmen's idea of the Christmas story, stripped to its essentials, is "praise the birth of white man's god-chief"; what keeps their interest in the holiday high is the Tswana-Herero custom of slaughtering an ox for his Bushmen neighbors as an annual goodwill gesture. Since the 1930s, part of the Bushmen's annual round of activities has included a December congregation at the cattle posts for trading, marriage brokering, and several days of trance-dance feasting at which the local Tswana headman is host.

As a social anthropologist working with !Kung Bushmen, I found that the Christmas ox custom suited my purposes. I had come to the Kalahari to study the hunting and gathering subsistence economy of the !Kung, and to accomplish that it was essential not to provide them with food, share my own food, or interfere in any way with their food-gathering activities.

Reprinted with permission from *Natural History*, 78 (1), December 1969. Copyright 1969, the American Museum of Natural History.

* The !Kung and other Bushmen speak click languages. In the story, three different clicks are used:

1. The dental click (/), as in /ai/ai, /ontah, and /gaugo. The click is sometimes written in English as tsk-tsk.
2. The alveopalatal click (!), as in Ben!a and !Kung.
3. The lateral click (//), as in //gom.

Clicks function as consonants; a word may have more than one, as in /n!au.

While liberal handouts of tobacco and medical supplies were appreciated, they were scarcely adequate to erase the glaring disparity in wealth between the anthropologist, who maintained a two-month inventory of canned goods, and the Bushmen, who rarely had a day's supply of food on hand. My approach, while paying off in terms of data, left me open to frequent accusations of stinginess and hard-heartedness. By their lights, I was a miser.

The Christmas ox was to be my way of saying thank you for the cooperation of the past year; and since it was to be our last Christmas in the field, I determined to slaughter the largest, meatiest ox that money could buy, insuring that the feast and trance dance would be a success.

Through December I kept my eyes open at the wells as the cattle were brought down for watering. Several animals were offered, but none had quite the grossness that I had in mind. Then, ten days before the holiday, a Herero friend led an ox of astonishing size and mass up to our camp. It was solid black, stood five feet high at the shoulder, had a five-foot span of horns, and must have weighed 1,200 pounds on the hoof. Food consumption calculations are my specialty, and I quickly figured that bones and viscera aside, there was enough meat—at least four pounds—for every man, woman, and child of the 150 Bushmen in the vicinity of /ai/ai who were expected at the feast.

Having found the right animal at last, I paid the Herero £20 ($56) and asked him to keep the beast with his herd until Christmas day. The next morning word spread among the people that the big solid black one was the ox chosen by /ontah (my Bushman name; it means, roughly, "whitey") for the Christmas feast. That afternoon I received the first delegation. Ben!a, an outspoken sixty-year-old mother of five, came to the point slowly.

"Where were you planning to eat Christmas?"

"Right here at /ai/ai," I replied.

"Alone or with others?"

"I expect to invite all the people to eat Christmas with me."

"Eat what?"

"I have purchased Yehave's black ox, and I am going to slaughter and cook it."

"That's what we were told at the well but refused to believe it until we heard it from yourself."

"Well, it's the black one," I replied expansively, although wondering what she was driving at.

"Oh, no!" Ben!a groaned, turning to her group. "They were right." Turning back to me she asked, "Do you expect us to eat that bag of bones?"

"Bag of bones! It's the biggest ox at /ai/ai."

"Big, yes, but old. And thin. Everybody knows there's no meat on that old ox. What did you expect us to eat off it, the horns?"

Everybody chuckled at Ben!a's one-liner as they walked away, but all I could manage was a weak grin.

That evening it was the turn of the young men. They came to sit at our evening fire. /gaugo, about my age, spoke to me man-to-man.

"/ontah, you have always been square with us," he lied. "What has happened to change your heart? That sack of guts and bones of Yehave's will hardly feed one camp, let alone all the Bushmen around /ai/ai." And he proceeded to enumerate the seven camps in the /ai/ai vicinity, family by family. "Perhaps you have forgotten that we are not few, but many. Or are you too blind to tell the difference between a proper cow and an old wreck? That ox is thin to the point of death."

"Look, you guys," I retorted, "that is a beautiful animal, and I'm sure you will eat it with pleasure at Christmas."

"Of course we will eat it; it's food. But it won't fill us up to the point where we will have enough strength to dance. We will eat and go home with stomachs rumbling."

That night as we turned in, I asked my wife, Nancy: "What did you think of the black ox?"

"It looked enormous to me. Why?"

"Well, about eight different people have told me I got gypped; that the ox is nothing but bones."

"What's the angle?" Nancy asked. "Did they have a better one to sell?"

"No, they just said that it was going to be a grim Christmas because there won't be enough meat to go around. Maybe I'll get an independent judge to look at the beast in the morning."

Bright and early, Halingisi, a Tswana cattle owner, appeared at our camp. But before I could ask him to give me his opinion on Yehave's black ox, he gave me the eye signal that indicated a confidential chat. We left the camp and sat down.

"/ontah, I'm surprised at you; you've lived here for three years and still haven't learned anything about cattle."

"But what else can a person do but choose the biggest, strongest animal one can find?" I retorted.

"Look, just because an animal is big doesn't mean that it has plenty of meat on it. The black one was a beauty when it was younger, but now it is thin to the point of death."

"Well I've already bought it. What can I do at this stage?"

"Bought it already? I thought you were just considering it. Well, you'll have to kill it and serve it, I suppose. But don't expect much of a dance to follow."

My spirits dropped rapidly. I could believe that Ben!a and /gaugo just might be putting me on about the black ox, but Halingisi seemed to be an impartial critic. I went around that day feeling as though I had bought a lemon of a used car.

In the afternoon it was Tomazo's turn. Tomazo is a fine hunter, a top trance performer and one of my most reliable informants. He approached the subject of the Christmas cow as part of my continuing Bushmen education.

"My friend, the way it is with us Bushmen," he began, "is that we love meat. And even more than that, we love fat. When we hunt we always search for the fat ones, the ones dripping with layers of white fat: fat that turns into a clear, thick oil in the cooking pot, fat that slides down your gullet, fills your stomach and gives you a roaring diarrhea," he rhapsodized.

"So, feeling as we do," he continued, "it gives us pain to be served such a scrawny thing as Yehave's black ox. It is big, yes, and no doubt its giant bones are good for soup, but fat is what we really crave and so we will eat Christmas this year with a heavy heart."

The prospect of a gloomy Christmas now had me worried, so I asked Tomazo what I could do about it.

"Look for a fat one, a young one . . . smaller, but fat. Fat enough to make us //gom ('evacuate the bowels'), then we will be happy."

My suspicions were aroused when Tomazo said that he happened to know of a young fat, barren cow that the owner was willing to part with. Was Tomazo working on commission, I wondered? But I dispelled this unworthy thought when we approached the Herero owner of the cow in question and found that he had decided not to sell.

The scrawny wreck of a Christmas ox now became the talk of the /ai/ai water hole and was the first news told to the outlying groups as they began to come in from the bush for the feast. What finally convinced me that real trouble might be brewing was the visit from u!au, an old conservative with a reputation for fierceness. His nickname meant spear and referred to an incident thirty years ago in which he had speared a man to death. He had an intense manner; fixing me with his eyes, he said in clipped tones:

"I have only just heard about the black ox today, or else I would have come here earlier. /ontah, do you honestly think you can serve meat like that to people and avoid a fight?" He paused, letting the implications sink in. "I don't mean fight you, /ontah; you are a white man. I mean a fight between Bushmen. There are many fierce ones here, and with such a small quantity of meat to distribute, how can you give everybody a fair share? Someone is sure to accuse another of taking too much or hogging all the choice pieces. Then you will see what happens when some go hungry while others eat."

The possibility of at least a serious argument struck me all too real. I had witnessed the tension that surrounds the distribution of meat from a kudu or gemsbok kill, and had documented many arguments that sprang up from a real or imagined slight in meat distribution. The owners of a kill may spend up to two hours arranging and rearranging the piles of meat under the gaze of a circle of recipients before handing them out. And I also knew that the Christmas feast at /ai/ai would be bringing together groups that had feuded in the past.

Convinced now of the gravity of the situation, I went in earnest to search for a second cow; but all my inquiries failed to turn one up.

The Christmas feast was evidently going to be a disaster, and the incessant complaints about the meagerness of the ox had already taken the fun out of it for me. Moreover, I was getting bored with the wisecracks, and after losing my temper a few times, I resolved to serve the beast anyway. If the meat fell short, the hell with it. In the Bushmen idiom, I announced to all who would listen:

"I am a poor man and blind. If I have chosen one that is too old and too thin, we will eat it anyway and see if there is enough meat there to quiet the rumbling of our stomachs."

On hearing this speech, Ben!a offered me a rare word of comfort. "It's thin," she said philosophically, "but the bones will make a good soup."

At dawn Christmas morning, instinct told me to turn over the butchering and cooking to a friend and take off with Nancy to spend Christmas alone in the bush. But curiosity kept me from retreating. I wanted to see what such a scrawny ox looked like on butchering, and if there was going to be a fight, I wanted to catch every word of it. Anthropologists are incurable that way.

The great beast was driven up to our dancing ground, and a shot in the forehead dropped it in its tracks. Then, freshly cut branches were heaped around the fallen carcass to receive the meat. Ten men volunteered to help with the cutting. I asked /gaugo to make the breast bone cut. This cut, which begins the butchering process for most large game, offers easy access for removal of the viscera. But it also allows the hunter to spot-check the amount of fat on the animal. A fat game animal carries a white layer up to an inch thick on the chest, while in a thin one, the knife will quickly cut to bone. All eyes fixed on his hand as /gaugo, dwarfed by the great carcass, knelt to the breast. The first cut opened a pool of solid white in the black skin. The second and third cut widened and deepened the creamy white. Still no bone. It was pure fat; it must have been two inches thick.

"Hey /gau," I burst out, "that ox is loaded with fat. What's this about the ox being too thin to bother eating? Are you out of your mind?"

"Fat?" /gau shot back, "You call that fat? This wreck is thin, sick, dead!" And he broke out laughing. So did everyone else. They rolled on the ground, paralyzed with laughter. Everybody laughed except me; I was thinking.

I ran back to the tent and burst in just as Nancy was getting up. "Hey, the black ox. It's fat as hell! They were kidding about it being too thin to eat. It was a joke or something. A put-on. Everyone is really delighted with it!"

"Some joke," my wife replied. "It was so funny that you were ready to pack up and leave /ai/ai."

If it had indeed been a joke, it had been an extraordinarily convincing one, and tinged, I thought, with more than a touch of malice as many jokes are. Nevertheless, that it was a joke lifted my spirits considerably, and I returned to the butchering site where the shape of the ox was rapidly disappearing under the axes and knives of the butchers. The atmosphere had become festive. Grinning broadly, their arms covered with blood well past the elbow, men packed chunks of meat into the big cast-iron cooking pots, fifty pounds to the load, and muttered and chuckled all the while about the thinness and worthlessness of the animal and /ontah's poor judgment.

We danced and ate that ox two days and two nights; we cooked and distributed fourteen potfuls of meat and no one went home hungry and no fights broke out.

But the "joke" stayed in my mind. I had a growing feeling that something important had happened in my relationship with the Bushmen and that the clue lay in the meaning of the joke. Several days later, when most of the people had dispersed back to the bush camps, I raised the question with Hakekgose, a Tswana man who had grown up among the !Kung, married a !Kung girl, and who probably knew their culture better than any other non-Bushman.

"With us whites," I began, "Christmas is supposed to be the day of friendship and brotherly love. What I can't figure out is why the Bushmen went to such lengths to criticize and belittle the ox I had bought for the feast. The animal was perfectly good and their jokes and wisecracks practically ruined the holiday for me."

"So it really did bother you," said Hakekgose. "Well, that's the way they always talk. When I take my rifle and go hunting with them, if I miss, they laugh at me for the rest of the day. But even if I hit and bring one down, it's no better. To them, the kill is always too small or too old or too thin; and as we sit down on the kill site to cook and eat the liver, they keep grumbling, even with their mouths full of meat. They say things like, 'Oh this is awful! What a worthless animal! Whatever made me think that this Tswana rascal could hunt!'"

"Is this the way outsiders are treated?" I asked.

"No, it is their custom; they talk that way to each other too. Go and ask them."

/gaugo had been one of the most enthusiastic in making me feel bad about the merit of the Christmas ox. I sought him out first.

"Why did you tell me the black ox was worthless, when you could see that it was loaded with fat and meat?"

"It is our way," he said, smiling. "We always like to fool people about that. Say there is a Bushman who has been hunting. He must not come home and announce like a braggard, 'I have killed a big one in the bush!' He must first sit down in silence until I or someone else comes up to his fire and asks, 'What did you see today?' He replies quietly, 'Ah, I'm no good for hunting. I saw nothing at all [pause] just a little tiny one.' Then I smile to myself," /gaugo continued, "because I know he has killed something big.

"In the morning we make up a party of four or five people to cut up and carry the meat back to the camp. When we arrive at the kill we examine it and cry out, 'You mean to say you have dragged us all the way out here in order to make us cart home your pile of bones? Oh, if I had known it was this thin I wouldn't have come.' Another one pipes up, 'People, to think I gave up a nice day in the shade for this. At home we may be hungry but at least we have nice cool water to drink.' If the horns are big, someone says, 'Did you think that somehow you were going to boil down the horns for soup?'

"To all this you must respond in kind. 'I agree,' you say, 'this one is not worth the effort; let's just cook the liver for strength and leave the rest for the hyenas. It is not too late to hunt today and even a duiker or a steenbok would be better than this mess.'

"Then you set to work nevertheless; butcher the animal, carry the meat back to the camp and everyone eats," /gaugo concluded.

Things were beginning to make sense. Next, I went to Tomazo. He corroborated /gaugo's story of the obligatory insults over a kill and added a few details of his own.

"But," I asked, "why insult a man after he has gone to all that trouble to track and kill an animal and when he is going to share the meat with you so that your children will have something to eat?"

"Arrogance," was his cryptic answer.

"Arrogance?"

"Yes, when a young man kills much meat he comes to think of himself as a chief or a big man, and he thinks of the rest of us as his servants or inferiors. We can't accept this. We refuse one who boasts, for someday his pride will make him kill somebody. So we always speak of his meat as worthless. This way we cool his heart and make him gentle."

7

Horticultural, Pastoral, and Agricultural Societies

In the last chapter we saw how, as new methods of exploiting the environment were invented, large populations could be supported. This led to the decline of hunting and gathering societies. With the domestication of plants and animals, human societies gained much greater control over their food supply. With improved techniques, they could increase production, and hence population size. Instead of following the nomadic life style typical of most hunting and gathering bands, they could live in permanent settlements, which grew from small villages into towns and even cities. And as the size of the group grew, its social organization changed. Whereas the band is an adaptation to the conditions found in most hunting and gathering societies, it does not work well for larger, more permanent populations. Instead, after the domestication of plants and animals we find new types of social organization.

In this chapter we will discuss several different subsistence strategies that represent important changes from the hunting and gathering way of life. We will pay special attention to the types of social organization that are linked to these different ways of making a living from the environment.

Horticulture

Horticulture refers to small-scale cultivation of fruits and vegetables. Whereas agriculture usually involves domesticated animals and the use of more advanced tools such as a plow in the cultivation of a variety of field crops, horticulture requires much less in the way of technology—often nothing more than a sharpened digging stick and an ax. Horticultural societies usually engage in **swidden** or **slash-and-burn** cultivation, in which an area is cleared of trees and brush, which are then burned and the ashes used as fertilizer. The land is cultivated as long as it remains fertile; depending on soil conditions and the crops that are planted, this might be for only

a few years. Once the land has become infertile or the infestation of weeds has become too great, it is abandoned and left fallow until it recovers. New land is then burned off and used in a similar way.

This type of cultivation requires a large amount of land, is characteristically found throughout lowland, humid, tropical rain forest areas, and is usually effective only where there is low population density. Depending on the number of people, the settlements can be permanent, but usually they have to be moved from time to time as new land is cleared.

Generally a swidden plot is cultivated for only three or four years before gardening is discontinued and the ground is reclaimed by the jungle. Under normal conditions a field would not be used again for 10 to 20 years. The reason slash-and-burn cultivation usually requires low population density is that so much land is either in the process of recovery or has not yet been converted into fields. Although in some of the drier zones seed crops such as corn, rice, and beans are grown, the major swidden areas in the world are used for the cultivation of root crops such as yams, sweet potatoes, and manioc. While these plants are good sources of carbohydrates (sugars and starches), they are low in proteins and do not constitute the type of nutritional balance more often found in seed crop complexes. The result is that people who practice swidden cultivation are more dependent on noncultivated sources of food, such as pigs or other domesticated animals, or they engage in hunting or the gathering of other plants to ensure a suitable diet.

Most of the horticultural societies that we know about today are divided up into villages containing at most a few hundred people, but we have evidence of past societies that were able to support cities with populations of up to 100,000 using horticultural techniques. The Yoruba, living in what is now Nigeria, had large cities that served as religious centers, and most people made daily trips to the fields surrounding the city to tend their gardens. Of course, the land did not remain fertile for long, so the cities often had to be moved to new sites, which was a major inconvenience in establishing any kind of permanent settlement.

The contribution of horticulture to the diet can vary greatly, ranging from as little as 10 percent to as much as 100 percent. Horticulture may be combined with the herding of animals, making both hunting and gathering unnecessary. In such a case larger settlements are possible, since the normally scarce animal population of the area does not limit the food supply. However, most groups that practice horticulture today still hunt and fish to supplement their food supply. When hunting is common, the garden work is done mainly by the women. If warfare is common, women may tend the gardens while the men stand guard. Usually, however, the gardening tasks are divided, with the men doing the heavy digging at planting time and the women doing most of the tending and harvesting of the crops.

In tropical South America most horticultural tribes do quite a bit of hunting as well. Many such groups inhabit the jungle areas of northern Brazil and Venezuela, where they grow bananas, plantains, manioc, sweet potatoes, and other crops. In addition, they hunt wild pigs, deer, turkeys, and other birds and mammals. They live in small, semipermanent villages surrounded by their gardens. While there are a few domesticated animals, all of the work is done by humans.

An interesting contrast to the tropical horticulturists is found in the practices of the Pueblo Indians of the American Southwest prior to their contact with white people. The Pueblos used mountain streams and springs for irrigation and planted their gardens below their villages, where they could divert the water as it was needed. In addition to their main crop, maize, they planted several varieties of squash, beans, melons, and gourds, and supplemented their diet with wild game. Their villages were relatively permanent, consisting of square houses built into the sides of cliffs.

Horticultural societies include most of the rural peoples of tropical Africa, Melanesia, and parts of tropical South America, and, prior to white contact, many native North American groups. The introduction of Western technology has led to rapid change in these societies. They now use more modern techniques to raise cash crops for an international market system. Lands that were formerly planted in gardens have been turned

Land being worked at a tea plantation in China.

into coffee plantations in South America and commercial farms in North America. The few societies that continue to live the way they did in the past are usually isolated, like the horticultural tribes in the South American jungles.

Despite the wide range of environments in which they live, horticultural societies share several features. These similarities are closely tied to the technology and life style of this subsistence strategy. In contrast to hunters and gatherers, horticulturists tend to live in semipermanent settlements close to their gardens, a condition that both results from and allows for their greater investment of labor in the land they cultivate. Living in a semipermanent settlement allows them to have more material possessions—houses, tools for working the land, weapons for hunting or defending themselves, and other handmade goods such as religious objects, artwork, and household goods.

With horticulture, we often see the beginning of private ownership of land as well as other possessions. And, of course, private ownership leads to social inequality based on differences in wealth. In horticultural societies, since it is not possible to store wealth in some compact form (such as money in the bank), such differences are usually expressed in terms of whether a person can control the labor of others and how large a family a person can support. Therefore wealth is often a quality of the family rather than of a single person. In most horticultural societies it is the male head of the family or household who attains the highest status. This, again, is in contrast to hunting and gathering societies, in which men and women often have equal status.

Horticultural societies are also more specialized. This is made possible partly by the predictability of the food supply and partly by the production of a surplus, which permits some members of the group to perform tasks that are not directly related to feeding themselves and their families. The most frequent area of specialization is religion, but we may

Peasant women harrowing a plot of land in the highlands of Peru.

also find people who specialize in producing artworks, tools, and weapons, or occasionally filling full-time leadership positions. In most cases these specialists gain power and prestige as a result of being set apart from the rest of the group.

Finally, horticulturists are different from hunters and gatherers in that they sometimes engage in warfare, both to acquire more territory and simply to plunder or avenge themselves on another group that attacked them. Because slash-and-burn cultivation requires a constant supply of new land, it is not surprising that neighboring groups would fight over boundaries. And since such groups can amass large amounts of personal possessions, it is not surprising that they would raid other villages to steal whatever they could. Thus the very nature of horticulture as a way of life creates new problems for human societies at the same time that it allows larger and more diverse groups of people to live together in semipermanent settlements.

Sociopolitical organization in horticultural societies As we saw in the last chapter, the band is not an efficient form of social organization for large groups, since their survival often requires joint efforts and the interests of individual members must sometimes be put aside in favor of those of the group. In a hunting and gathering band a dispute can split the group without any serious effects, but in a horticultural society, in which each member has a great deal of labor invested in the land, the group cannot be divided, since no one is willing to leave all that labor behind. Thus in the shift from hunting and gathering to horticulture, and later to agriculture, different types of social organization replaced the band, types that were more appropriate to the size of the group and the way its members lived.

Anthropologists use the word **tribe** to refer to the type of social organization that unites many bands into a larger, more centralized political unit. Whereas a band might be a loose grouping of between 25 and 100 people, a tribe is much larger and contains a number

of smaller units that are usually related through kinship ties. When plants and animals were first domesticated, some 15,000 years ago, tribal organization was probably a limited extension of band organization, a set of alliances between bands to provide mutual protection and security as people began to settle down in one spot and acquire more wealth. As competition for land increased, these alliances became more important, and the stronger the alliance, the better its chances of success against other groups.

A tribe is a group of people who are related to each other in many ways. They share the same language and usually have a common ethnic heritage. A tribe also shares a territory, which it defines as its own, not in an individual sense, but as the property of the group as a whole. Most important, all the members of the tribe believe they are descended from a common ancestor, and therefore that they are related by blood, even if they cannot trace their descent that far back.

Tribe members may be scattered throughout a territory and may not be in constant contact with each other. In fact, most of the time the organization of the tribe may not be much more formal than that of a band. The difference is that the potential for cooperation and joint action is much greater. The tribe may unite in battle against a common enemy or come together to share in a celebration, a religious festival, a major work project, or some other, similar event. Otherwise the tribe exists as a number of separate villages or communities.

These communities are not isolated, however; they are tied together in a number of ways. Family members may be dispersed among several villages, and kinship ties serve as the basis for interaction between different communities. Age sets that unite people of the same age from different villages can also be a strong unifying force, as can other types of associations, such as religious groups, secret societies, or groups organized around special events such as sports or hunting. Compared with a band, in which each group is a self-contained unit tied to the others

Melanesian boys and men taking part in a dance ceremony.

mainly by marriages between the members, in a tribe a person's membership in the wider society is equally important as membership in the community for defining who he or she is, as well as his or her relations with others. While a tribe is like a band in that it is based on a network of kinship relations, it differs in that the network is wider and group loyalty is stronger, even among more distant relatives. It is probably best to think of a tribe not as something different from a band but simply as a group that is larger than a band, slightly more complex, and more centralized—that is, able to bring people together in a common cause.

Although tribal society is a more effective adaptation to increased population pressure and more intensive exploitation of the environment, it lacks a strong central authority. Tribal organization works well in relatively small areas, but as the group spreads out and increases in size, the ties that bind people together become weaker. However, if power is in the hands of a single individual, giving him or her the right to command others to act—a right that is usually backed up by the

military strength to enforce it—more people can be brought into a single society and their activities controlled and directed toward the good of all members of the group. This type of society is called a **chiefdom.** In a tribal society there are no people with the legal right to enforce their will, and leaders can use only their personal influence to get people to do certain things. A chiefdom represents a greater concentration of power, and hence a different pattern of social organization from that of a tribe.

Chiefdoms usually have greater population density than tribes and often are more productive as well, yielding a surplus that can support a larger number of specialists. In a society in which people work only for themselves and their families, there is little reason to produce a surplus. A chiefdom is different in that the power of the leader allows him or her to force people to produce more than they need and to give the surplus to the leader for distribution to others who are not food producers. In this way the leaders of the society can pay an army, a labor force, religious specialists, and other types of nonagricultural specialists. Hence in the chiefdom we begin to see a greater separation of economic activities from other areas of life, such as religious, political, and kinship institutions.

Chiefdoms differ from bands and tribes in that they are not based on the equality of all members. Instead, there is a definite leadership *office* occupied by an individual; usually this office is inherited. Thus the power of the office is vested in the position, not necessarily in the person who occupies it. A person may perform the duties of the chief well or poorly but that person is still chief. If the position is passed on to another family member, it does not always go to the most qualified person; instead, it goes to the next person in the line of succession.

Along with the position of chief goes the power to command people to act in certain ways, for example, to collect and redistribute food and other goods. This type of authority may be backed up by force, but it is also supported by myths, customs, and social values. The people believe in the power of the chief, and the stories they tell about the supernatural, the origins of their society, and its great heroes tend to reinforce that power. It is this belief system that enables the chief to coordinate the work of the society's members and unite them in a way that would not be possible in a tribal type of social organization.

A chiefdom is more complex than a band or a tribe. In hunting and gathering societies a band is linked to other bands only through the alliances created by exogamous marriages. A tribe is more firmly integrated because it contains groups that cut across village lines, such as lineages and age sets. But a chiefdom is more centrally organized than a tribe. It has a line of authority that ties all the members of the society directly to the leader. It also has a stronger bond to its territory, with more clearly defined boundaries.

Chiefdoms are different from tribal societies in other ways, too. Greater specialization allows for greater emphasis on new technol-

A traditional high chief and his retainers in Ghana.

ogy as well as artistic creativity. The ability to direct labor may lead to major public works projects such as irrigation systems, as well as large monuments like the pyramids of Egypt. Also, religion may be used to increase the power of the chief. Religious specialists sometimes gain the status of priest. No longer are they part-time specialists like the shaman or medicine man of a tribal society; now they are trained religious specialists who hold institutionalized offices. In some cases the offices of priest and chief are combined, creating a priest-king theocracy. This was the case in ancient Egypt, where the pharaoh was not only the political leader but the religious leader as well.

A chiefdom differs from a tribe or a band in that it is a stratified society with a great deal of potential for specialization and division of labor on a massive scale. At the same time, there is a higher degree of centralization. This can even go so far as to place ownership of property entirely in the hands of the chief, who then allocates the land among his or her subjects to be used—but not owned—by them. The office of chief also results in unequal control over goods and production, since the chief has the power to tap surplus production and allocate it to nonproducing members of the population.

In sum, horticulturists tend to be organized into tribal societies or chiefdoms. The distinction between these two social types is not always clear, but it is mainly related to the size of the group, the amount of land it occupies, and the quantity of food produced. If a group is large and its territory is densely populated, then we might expect to find a chiefdom with a greater degree of central control to maintain order. However, if the land is not productive enough to support a dense population, settlements will be scattered, people will have less contact with others outside their own village, and the need for social control will be less. In such a case we would expect a tribal form of organization.

Political organization among tribes and chiefdoms   There are very few hunting and gathering societies in the world today, and much of our knowledge about band organization is based on reports of early contacts with such groups. Most non-Western peoples live in larger groups and obtain their living by other means, which creates an entirely different set of problems that require political solutions. One such form is the tribe.

A tribe may contain hundreds or even thousands of people, making its patterns of authority much more complex than those of a band. Yet even at the tribal level politics is not separate from other institutions but is closely tied to the rest of the social organization. A family might have control over a piece of land and thus might engage in behavior that we would call *economic*. It might also be part of an alliance with other families, to which we would apply the term *politics*. Or it might be the center of a religious activity such as **ancestor worship.** Thus when we consider political organization on the tribal level we are really looking at political behavior in a wider social context, and not at political institutions that stand apart from the rest of society (the way a political party is set apart in our society).

A tribe can be defined as a confederation of groups (with a minimum of central authority) that are related to one another by a common ethnic origin, a common language, or a strong pattern of interaction based on intermarriage or presumed kinship. Each tribe is divided into smaller segments, such as villages or regional groups, which in turn are divided into clans or lineages and, on the lowest level, families and households. The tribe is "political" in the sense that it is the broadest base on which joint activities can be organized and carried out by the group and in the name of the group.

Tribal organization can be important in controlling behavior within the tribe and in organizing the tribe's opposition to outside groups. Of course, it can also coordinate economic activities, such as trading networks, or religious activities, such as the worship of a tribal deity—but these are part of the political process as well. Within the tribe any dispute among smaller groups can be settled on the next higher level. If two families argue, a settlement can be reached by appealing to the elders of the clan, whose authority comes from and is backed by the tribe itself. If two clans engage in a feud, the solution may be handed down by the village headman. On the other hand, if there is a conflict with some group outside the tribe, then the entire tribe acts in unison. This form of political organization is called **segmentary opposition,** and it is not unique to tribal societies. We have it in our own political system. For example, southern Democrats and northern Democrats might disagree over whom to nominate for the presidency, but once a nominee has been chosen, both groups will support that candidate against the rival Republican candidate. Yet on a higher level both Republicans and Democrats will support the president, regardless of party, in a disagreement with the leader of another country. And if the earth were invaded by creatures from outer space, we would probably overcome our differences with the Soviet Union and join forces against our common enemy. Segmentary opposition is merely a way of defining allegiance in terms of the scope of the problem.

The tribe is perhaps the simplest type of political system other than the egalitarian band. In a tribal system behavior is organized on different levels, but because it is so decentralized there is no way to force different groups to cooperate unless they themselves want to. As power becomes more centralized, the political organization of the group becomes more complex. Such a system, in which regional or tribal groups are organized under a single official, is a chiefdom. The chief can call upon the members of the group not just for political purposes but usually for economic or religious ones as well. Thus the chief tends to be a strong force in bringing together the segments of the tribe, uniting them in a single group while retaining a greater degree of authority over each member.

The chiefdom is considerably different from a tribal political organization because it is the first political system in which power is centralized—an important step in the evolution of the state-based society that is so familiar to us. Also, along with the chiefdom comes a system of ranking, or social stratification. In a band all people are basically equal; while greater skill in hunting might give a man a greater voice in the organization of the hunt, it does not give him the right to more than his share of the kill. In a small tribal society the same holds true. A person might be recognized for some achievement or skill and obtain a certain amount of power or influence as a result, but such a position is not permanent and can change with the fortunes of the individual.

In a chiefdom the leader is entitled to

special treatment because of his position. His family, lineage, and village share in his prestige and high position. The chief may be in a position to tax the people or collect and allocate goods. Such power can easily increase differences in rank within the society, for the power to allocate goods will entrench the chief and other high-ranking members in their positions by giving them greater wealth and control over resources. It can also lead to an increase in the size of the society controlled by the central authority. For example, before the arrival of Europeans, Hawaii was a chiefdom with a population over 100,000.

A good example of the difference between a tribe and a chiefdom is provided by Marshall Sahlins in a comparison of leadership in two areas of the Pacific Islands. Western Melanesia is characterized by tribal organization. The Melanesian tribes contain fewer members and have less control over them than the chiefdoms of Polynesia to the east. The typical Melanesian leader is described as a **"big man"** whose authority is based on his ability to influence others. "Big man" thus is not a political office but an achieved position of informal leadership. The overall political structure of Melanesia is one of small, separate, fairly equal units; because it depends on the personal qualities of its leaders, it is unstable over time. In contrast, Polynesia has a type of chiefdom in which leadership is vested in a formal position, not in the personal influence of the holder of that position. The Polynesian political structure affects a much larger population than the Melanesian political structure, and it integrates larger units into a pyramid of groups headed by a paramount chief. In this way whole islands or even groups of islands could be united in a common cause.

Tribal horticulturists: The Dani of highland New Guinea The Dani are a tribal people who live in the central highlands of New Guinea, a large island north of Australia. They are horticulturists who live mainly from the food produced in their gardens. They also raise pigs, but the pigs are more important for prestige than as a source of food; it has been suggested that the pigs supply less energy than is spent raising them. The main crop is sweet potatoes, which make up 90 percent of the people's diet. Other vegetables, such as taro and cucumbers, and fruits, such as the banana, add to the diet. However, the importance of the sweet potato is seen in the fact that there are over 70 different terms used to refer to it. Land is cultivated with crude tools of wood and stone, although recently metal tools have been acquired in trade with outsiders.

The Dani live in small settlements of about 350 people on up to one square mile of land. At the center is a tight cluster of small houses, surrounded by a high fence; beyond lie the gardens belonging to the residents. But between the settlements there is much uninhabited field and forest, so that the population is actually rather sparse. There is plenty of space between the villages where new land can be cleared for gardens when the old ones lose their fertility. The residential compound or village consists of several families. It includes a long house where everyone gets together for cooking, eating, and other social activities; a large round house where all the men and boys sleep and work; a number of small round houses where women sleep with their daughters and infant sons; and many small pig sties where the pigs belonging to each family are kept.

Groups of neighboring villages are organized into a larger political unit, called an *alliance*. Alliances are formed for mutual defense and protection, and the members share the duties of guarding their territory against intruders from other villages. This is necessary because the Dani are constantly at war, and live in fear of raids from neighboring alliances. Two types of violence occur most frequently: surprise attacks by raiding parties designed to catch the enemy off guard, and formal battles in which all the men of the alliance join together. The formal war is a ritual that involves little loss of life or conquest of new land. Instead, it is carried out

to appease the ghosts—the Dani believe that when a person dies, his or her ghost returns to haunt that person's relatives, particularly if the death was caused by an act of violence. Therefore a death at the hands of the enemy calls for revenge. Since the score is never considered even, the Dani are always on guard.

Secret raids are often effective in killing the enemy. Raiding parties made up of from a dozen to as many as 50 men lie in wait for a single individual or a small group and ambush them. It does not matter whether the victims are women or children. However, raiding parties can be dangerous to the aggressors as well, because if they are trapped behind the enemy lines, they may all be killed by a counterambush.

When a raiding party is successful, the members of the victim's alliance begin a formal battle to appease the ghosts of their dead. The battle is very different from the secret raid. Both sides meet at the boundary between the alliances—in fact, if one side gets there before the other, they will wait rather than cross into the neighboring alliance's territory. The men dress up in elaborate costumes with shell ornaments and jewelry, and paint on their faces and bodies. Much taunting and joking occurs between the two groups, and the fighting consists mainly of men running up to the front and shooting arrows at the enemy, then retreating to the back of the group while others take their place. This goes on until someone is seriously injured, whereupon the battle ends and the victim's relatives take him home. But whether he lives or dies, the cycle of raids and warfare goes on. The interesting thing about this practice is that it does not lead to all-out warfare in which many people are killed; raiding rarely occurs, because each group's defenses are so effective, and formal battles are also rare and do not cause many deaths.

The Dani represent an interesting way of life in a horticultural society, and there is much that we can learn from looking at their practices in detail. In some ways they are like a hunting and gathering band: They have a

Dani tribesmen of New Guinea engage in ritual battle with a neighboring tribe. The rules of warfare are carefully laid out and help keep fatalities to a minimum.

flexible social organization and disputes within a village may lead to a split, with some members setting up a new village on the edge of the garden plots. They do not have great differences in wealth, and all members of the community have equal status. They do not have a formal legal system, but rely instead on group consensus to control behavior.

At the same time, in some ways they are clearly different from hunting and gathering bands. They live in permanent settlements where they can accumulate personal property and possessions. They have more clearly defined territorial boundaries, which separate them from neighboring groups. They form political alliances that are much stronger than those of hunters and gatherers and include many more people. And they engage in organized activities together, such as warfare and religious rituals, feasts, and other celebrations.

But the extent of cooperation among the Dani is limited to the group of villages that form an alliance. Two or more alliances do not join together to fight a common enemy, perhaps because the occasion has never arisen when they had to do so. In this sense, the Dani are clearly not a chiefdom, since there is no central authority that can bring them together and no single leader that all Dani would obey. They produce only what they need to survive, and because they live in an area that is not of much value to a technologically more advanced society, they have not had to worry about expanding their production to pay taxes or provide a surplus for a market economy. However, we can be certain that as the Indonesian government extends its authority into these areas, people like the Dani will be forced to change their way of life, for better or worse.

Pastoralism

Societies that depend to a large extent on domesticated animals for their survival represent a different kind of adaptation to the environment. In many ways pastoral peoples have the same degree of control over their food supply as horticultural peoples, only they do it by keeping animals for food rather than raising vegetables and fruits in gardens and orchards. But there are some major differences between the life styles of pastoralists and horticulturists. Again, these result from the different requirements of the two subsistence strategies.

Perhaps the chief difference is that **pastoralism** generally leads to a nomadic way of life, in contrast to the relatively permanent settlements of horticultural societies. All animals require large amounts of food and quickly use up the vegetation in an area if they are allowed to graze heavily without giving the land a chance to recover. The larger the animal population, the greater the tendency toward a nomadic way of life, since the herd must be moved to new pastures more often. As a result, the ties to the land that are commonly found in horticultural groups are absent from pastoral groups, and property and wealth are measured in terms of animals rather than land. The need for constant movement keeps other material possessions to a minimum, another important difference.

Archeological remains of prehistoric settlements show that domesticated animals have been kept by humans for many thousands of years. Animals were probably first domesticated by people living in the river valleys of what is now China, India, Egypt and Mesopotamia. The remains of domesticated sheep, goats, pigs, cattle, and chickens have been found in association with those of humans in Asia, northern Africa, and the Middle East. Sometimes the early pastoralists also cultivated plants; in other cases domesticated animals were the main source of food for a wandering pastoral group. In the New World there were no animals that could be domesticated for use as a food source—although the dog and llama were domesticated, neither was adequate as a basis for subsistence. The horse, cow, and sheep were all introduced from Europe, and although buffalo were plentiful, they were not domesticated.

A variety of pastoralism that is still found today in the northern parts of Europe and Asia is based on reindeer herding. The reindeer is used as a pack animal, and both its milk and its meat form a basic part of the diet; the hides and bones are used for clothing and tools. Many formerly nomadic herders now live in permanent settlements for part of the year and move to a grazing area during the summer. This type of herding requires a large amount of land, especially in the sub-Arctic regions, where food for the animals is scarce. However, as with so many nonagricultural peoples, there is little competition for these marginal areas.

In some ways pastoral societies are similar to horticultural societies, yet different from hunting and gathering groups. For example, among reindeer herders animals are an important form of wealth. Since a sizable group of males is needed to protect them, the reindeer often are not the property of one individual or family, but belong to a larger kinship group. Where raids occur often, especially in the summer when heavy snows no longer prevent travel over long distances, the size of the group increases and herds are combined for mutual defense. Thus the herd-

A Rendille man from northern Kenya, where pastoralists make up much of the population, tends his herd of camels.

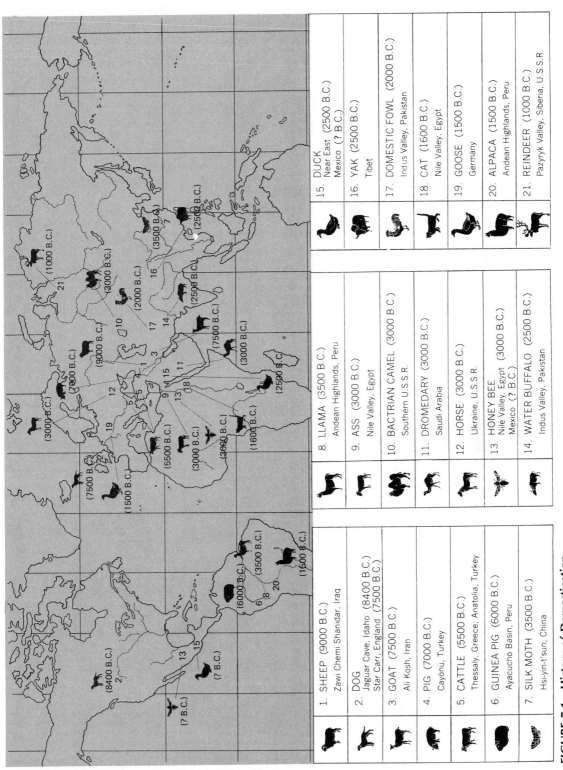

FIGURE 7.1 History of Domestication.

SOURCE: Marvin Harris, *Culture, People, Nature: An Introduction to General Anthropology*, 4th ed. Copyright © 1985 by Harper & Row, Publishers, Inc. Adapted with the permission of HarperCollins Publishers.

ers live in small groups during the winter but often form larger communities for the rest of the year.

A different pattern of pastoralism is found among a number of the East African tribes who raise cattle as their main source of food. (Most of these tribes also raise a few sheep and goats, but these animals do not play the same role as cattle in the economy or social life of the people.) The milk from the cattle is used for food, as is the blood, which is either consumed straight or mixed with milk. However, a cow is rarely killed for meat but is eaten only after it has died a natural death. This seemingly unhealthy practice must be understood in the context of the role cattle play in other areas of the lives of their owners.

Cattle are the main economic force in the lives of East African pastoralists. They are a measure of a man's prestige and wealth. A man will use cattle to "buy" a wife, a custom known as *bride price*. To show just how important cattle are, among the Baganda (a tribe in what is now Uganda), when a couple is married, the man builds a hut for his wife next to the cattle stalls and she spends the first three days after the wedding learning to recognize her husband's family's cows.

In most of the East African pastoral societies the males are at the center of the family. A child is automatically a member of its father's kin group but not of its mother's—a pattern called **patrilineal descent** (from the Latin *pater*, "father"), because the child is descended from relatives only on the father's side. (It is like our practice of taking only our father's surname and not our mother's, except that they carry it further and count relatives only on the father's side.) The basic economic unit is the patrilocal family, which consists of a man, his wife, his sons, and their families. The daughters, on the other hand, move into their husbands' households when they marry. Thus each household is formed around a core of related males who bring in unrelated females from outside the family.

Another common feature of the social organization of pastoral peoples in East Af-rica is the **age set.** This is a group of males (in rare cases, females as well) of about the same age who go through life experiencing the same major events—they are initiated into adulthood together, enter military service together, and generally marry at the same time as well. Although households tend to be dispersed because of the amount of land needed for grazing the cattle, the age sets tie the members of the society together, bringing men from different villages to communal events and reinforcing social bonds between families. In this way alliances are created for both mutual defense and social solidarity.

In sum, pastoralism as a subsistence strategy creates new possibilities and new restraints that are not present among hunting and gathering peoples. In some ways pastoralists are like horticulturists, while in other ways they differ as a result of their different way of making a living. Compared to hunting and gathering peoples, both pastoralists and horticulturists are able to amass personal wealth, support larger populations, live in at least semipermanent settlements during much of the year, and engage in warfare with other groups in order to obtain land (for grazing or planting) and other material goods.

When compared to horticulture, however, pastoralism usually does not lead to the accumulation of material wealth in the form of houses or large, heavy household goods. Because most pastoralists must move at least once a year to get to their grazing lands, their goods are limited to the amount they can transport. In modern times pastoralists, like horticulturists, tend to be found in areas that are of marginal value for agriculture. This is a result of the greater ability of agriculture to support a large, dense population with greater military strength.

Pastoralism does not often lead to strong, centralized political organization. Because they tend to move about, pastoral peoples are often independent and form only loose alliances for mutual defense. They usually engage in trade with more settled agricultural peoples, but may also prey upon them as raiders—something they can do quite effectively in areas where transportation is difficult.

Finally, pastoral peoples tend to have more highly stratified social systems than either hunters and gatherers or horticulturists. Wealth, power, and prestige are measured in terms of animals, and it is easier for a family to own and defend a large group of animals than to own and work a large amount of land. While the animals can be kept close together and maintained by a relatively small group, a large land holding cannot be defended by a small group, nor can it be worked efficiently without added labor. Therefore among pastoralists we often see a greater disparity of wealth, even though there are fewer specialized positions held by individuals who are not also food producers. In most cases pastoral societies are patrilineal and male dominated, although this pattern is not universal.

Sociopolitical organization in pastoral societies Like horticulturists, pastoral peoples tend to be organized into tribal societies or chiefdoms. Through domestication of animals, pastoralists gain the same kind of control over their food supply as horticulturists have, and this enables them to live in larger groups than hunters and gatherers. But the size of the community and the existence of animals as a form of wealth and property calls for a greater degree of control than is found in the hunting and gathering band. Mutual defense of the animals and sharing of grazing lands are better dealt with in societies that have a stronger form of social and political organization than the band.

Some pastoral societies are self-sufficient and have little contact with people outside their territorial boundaries. If they raise animals mainly for food and clothing, and the animals do not have much commercial value to outsiders or cannot be raised in large enough numbers to be profitable, then it is likely that a loose-knit tribal organization will

Reindeer in Lapland still constitute a major source of livelihood.

be enough to meet the political needs of the society. Disputes that arise can be settled locally by informal leaders, peace can be maintained within the society, and the limited threat from outsiders can be met by a joint effort of many smaller communities.

However, if animals provide more than just food and clothing and have an important market value, the threat from outsiders will be greater, and tribal organization may not be strong enough to protect the members of the society, either from outsiders or from each other. As a result, some pastoral peoples have been known to form chiefdoms, in which strong central authority is vested in a leader who controls much of the wealth and military strength of the society. In fact, many societies that still practice pastoralism today are strongly linked to market economies and state organizations, an even stronger political unit than the chiefdom (see pp. 186–187). This is true in Iran and throughout the Middle East, where rural pastoral tribes grew so powerful that they became a major political force. The

former Shah of Iran was able to gain power in part because he created a strong political alliance among the major pastoral groups; the inability of the Ayatollah Khomeini's successors to maintain that alliance continues to weaken their control over the outlying areas of the country.

In sum, pastoralists, like horticulturists, tend to be organized into tribal societies or chiefdoms, depending on the size of the group, the amount of land they occupy, the amount of food produced, and the contact they have with surrounding populations. A densely populated pastoral society may require greater internal control than tribal organization can provide, while a sparsely populated and isolated society may not be able to produce enough wealth to support a chiefly office. The number of animals that the land can support and the market value of those animals may also influence the type of political organization in pastoral societies according to the need to defend the herds and the territory against outside aggressors. The

The mobility of pastoral peoples, such as the Tuareg of Morocco, leads to a different form of social and political organization.

more marginal the land occupied, the sparser the population, and the fewer economic resources a society has, the less centralized authority we are likely to find. Again, however, we should remember that there is no clear distinction between a tribe and a chiefdom, and that pastoral societies exist with a wide range of types of social and political organization.

East African pastoralists: The Nuer of the Upper Nile   The Nuer of the Upper Nile River Valley are a pastoral people of East Africa who combine cattle raising with a small amount of horticulture. The total population of Nuer is estimated at about 300,000, but politically they are divided into smaller groups and there is no central authority that unites all people who call themselves Nuer into a single large tribe. Even though all the Nuer speak similar languages and share many cultural features, the Nuer population is divided into regional tribal groups.

Cattle are the mainstay of the Nuer way of life. They cultivate a few crops like sorghum and maize and raise a few sheep and goats, but these are much less important than the cattle in terms of both diet and prestige. The Nuer do not hunt other animals for meat, since in their eyes a man who hunts is too poor to support himself.

Nuer villages contain from 50 to several hundred people, depending on the availability of grazing land in the area. The settlements often are not permanent, since the cattle must be moved from one grazing area to another as the seasons change. During the wet season the people tend their gardens, and in the dry season they migrate in search of water and pasture for their animals. As a result, individuals have no permanent land rights, and the land around a village is available to everyone. Only cattle and other animals and household goods are owned by individuals, and a person's wealth is measured by the number of cows he has.

The main economic unit among the Nuer is the household, which consists of a married couple, their unmarried daughters, and their sons' families. That is, when a son marries, his wife moves into the household, while when the daughter marries, she moves out of her parents' home and into her husband's. This type of family structure, which includes several married couples and usually consists of three generations, is called an **extended family.** In Nuer society, as in many horticultural and pastoral societies, it functions well as an economic unit because it combines several families into a larger work force united by strong kinship ties.

A village is composed of a number of extended families that are all related either by blood or by marriage. Marriage rules do not require that a person marry outside his or her village, but the marriage partner cannot be a close relative. Since the Nuer trace their descent only through the father's side, their descent system is patrilineal. Such a group of relatives is called a **lineage,** a term that refers to the people who can trace their ancestry to a common source by going back through the father's side of their family (or the mother's side, in which case it would be a **matrilineage**). The Nuer marriage rules prevent a person from marrying anyone in the same lineage.

A Nuer marriage includes a payment by the husband's family to the wife's. This payment, or bride price, is almost always made in the form of cattle, and is a way of solidifying the economic alliance between the two families. The bride remains in her parents' household and her husband visits her periodically until a child is born. The husband then goes to live with his wife, and when the child has been weaned they move in with his family. Not until this first child is born has the marriage contract been fulfilled. If the wife does not bear a child or the marriage breaks up before she becomes pregnant, the bride price must be returned.

The political organization of the Nuer is normally rather loose. There are no actual "chiefs" whose orders are obeyed by the rest of the tribe, but there are people who are respected and asked for advice. The closest thing to a political office is that of the **leopard**

skin chief, so called because only he is allowed to wear a cloak made of leopard skin, a highly prized possession. The main function of the leopard skin chief is to mediate when villagers become involved in feuds. For example, if one man kills another, the victim's family may try to retaliate. But the man who committed the murder can go to the leopard skin chief and receive sanctuary until the problem is resolved without further bloodshed. Usually the chief acts as a go-between and arranges for the victim's family to be paid a certain number of cattle as compensation. Other disputes, such as conflicting claims of ownership or accusations of theft, are mediated by the leopard skin chief in a similar way.

Much of the culture of the Nuer people has changed since they came into contact with the Western world. Diseases introduced by the whites have decimated their cattle, and as a result the Nuer have had to rely on horticulture to survive. Today they are more settled, both because they must spend more time raising crops and because the government of Sudan has more control over the movement of people within its boundaries. This has changed the Nuer life style drastically, and in a sense the tribal loyalty of the past is being replaced by a growing awareness of membership in a regional and national government that cuts across the boundaries of the tribe and unites many people who were formerly enemies.

Agriculture

With the introduction of **agriculture,** including dependence on cereal crops and the use of animal power for cultivation, human societies were able to support larger and denser populations than ever before. Grain is a nutritious, high-calorie food, but more important, it can be cultivated intensively so that relatively little land can yield large amounts of food. When animal power is used as well as human labor, a lower percentage of the population is needed to provide enough food for everyone. Thus with agriculture comes more specialization as well as a considerable increase in inequality. Land takes on much greater value, as do animals that can be used to cultivate the fields. The services and products of nonagricultural specialists also take on added value, increasing the potential for differences in wealth and status.

Anthropologists refer to rural cultivators who engage in subsistence agriculture as **peasants.** Numerically, peasants probably constitute the largest category of people in

A Nuer chief serving as a mediator of disputes.

the developing world. They differ in many ways from horticulturists. Horticulturists rarely are able to produce enough of a surplus to be of value to anyone outside the family. Peasants, on the other hand, have the potential to be exploited, because they are engaged in agriculture and thus are capable of producing a surplus that can be used to support others. The result is that peasants are not as independent as horticulturists—indeed, they are integrated into the economy of their society. In fact, anthropologists commonly argue that one of the key factors distinguishing peasants from horticulturists is the historical link that peasants have with the nation-states in which they reside. They may own their land and pay taxes to a government that has some control over them, or they may simply work land owned by someone else and pay either a rent or a portion of their harvest or both. Although the primary goal of peasants is to produce enough food to feed their family, they must always produce something extra for rent or taxes.

There is, then, an economic mutual dependency, or symbiosis, between the nation and these agriculturalists, as the peasant feeds the urban areas and in return obtains needed goods not locally produced. Peasants stand in marked contrast to the traditional horticulturists, like the Dani or the Yanomamö,

or pastoralists, like the Masai, who historically have not had or felt the need for linkages with the outside world. Although the connection of peasants with the urban areas has always existed, until two decades ago most peasants were generally self-sufficient. They grew or raised all of their own food, made their own clothes, and crafted most of their own tools. Today's peasants have a greater dependence on the outside world than their parents, or certainly their grandparents, did. Machine-made clothes have replaced homespun and locally woven garb, and rubber boots or synthetic work shoes are used instead of hand-crafted traditional footwear.

Peasants also differ from farmers like those found in our society in that they are not commercial businessmen producing crops for cash—their activity is oriented toward their own subsistence and only marginally integrated into a market system. Whereas a farmer might produce large crops of soybeans, field corn, and wheat, none of which he expects to consume himself, the peasant is likely to grow food mainly for his own family, and only enough of a cash crop to meet his other obligations. In spite of the problems American farmers currently face, we nevertheless think of them as individuals who engage in agriculture for a profit, whereas the primary goal of the peasant is

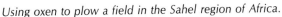

Using oxen to plow a field in the Sahel region of Africa.

still to feed off of the land and have a little left over.

We also tend to think of peasants as a social class. They are often contrasted with the nobility or the merchants who live in towns, or the military, or a number of other groups. In many ways this view reflects a basic difference between peasants and horticulturists or pastoralists. Peasants are part of a larger society and are integrated into that society through a market system (economics) and a regional government (politics). In contrast, pastoral and horticultural peoples are separate from the larger society. The horticultural tribes in the jungles of South America are unaffected by market conditions and remain untouched by political processes at the national or regional level. The same is true for many pastoral peoples in the world today.

Because of their integration into the larger society, peasants cannot be viewed as a separate group. That is, while a peasant village might be fairly homogeneous in that most of its residents have the same life style and engage in the same agricultural activities, there is a great deal of diversity and specialization in the wider society, and this affects the lives of the peasants.

Still, there are certain features shared by peasant communities throughout the world, regardless of the political, economic, or religious differences between the countries in which they are found. Thus anthropologists, while recognizing important regional differences, often talk about peasants as a distinct generic group or class of people. Although this is changing, peasants everywhere engage in simple forms of agriculture, using animal power but little or no mechanical power. There is little specialization within the community; that is, there is little division of labor. Everyone does much the same tasks, and most work is duplicated many times over. The productive unit is usually the household, which consumes most of what it produces. And because of the long tradition of permanent settlement associated with most peasants, there is a strong bond that ties them to the land. This is not typical of horticulturists and pastoralists, whose settlements often are not permanent.

Changes in peasant agricultural practices—such as the use of tractors, hybrid crops, commercial fertilizers, and pesticides—reflect a change from a subsistence to a market-oriented economy.

The chief goods of the peasants are land and labor. If the peasant is healthy and can work, and has some land, that is enough. If there is good year and a surplus is produced, it will probably be consumed or shared rather than reinvested. Ties to the community can be strengthened in this way, since peasants often identify strongly with their fellow villagers and much less strongly with their national government.

Although peasant economies and technology tend to be fairly similar throughout the world, other aspects of their social organization may vary greatly. For example, there is no uniform rule of descent—membership in a kin group may be inherited from the father's side or from both sides equally, although it is rarely inherited from the mother's side in a peasant society. Land is the one thing without which peasant agriculture could not exist. Yet even when it comes to inheriting land there is no single practice that is common to all peasant societies. In some cases land is divided equally among all the heirs, while in others it may all go to one heir—often the eldest son, but sometimes the youngest son. In still other cases the land is divided equally among all the sons, while the daughters receive other types of wealth and property or even a cash payment for the land they do not receive. In short, while land is very important, there are many different ways of passing it from one generation to the next.

Marriage in peasant societies, as in the types of societies discussed earlier, is not just a product of the mutual love of two people. Rather, it is often an economic arrangement that creates a bond between two families, perhaps even two villages. Marriages may even be arranged by parents without the consent of the couple. Although this might be rare, it illustrates the role of marriage as an economic and political alliance, not just the union of two people and the beginning of a family.

It is common for a couple to reside with the husband's family after marriage, either in the same household or nearby in the same village. Arrangements depend on how land is passed from one generation to the next. If males receive most of the land, daughters are expected to leave the household when they marry, while the sons' wives will move in with them if there is enough land to support them. However, if both sons and daughters inherit equally, other approaches are possible. For example, when a daughter moves out she can trade her land for land closer to her husband's home. Or she can marry someone who lives close by in order to combine their land holdings and still be close enough to the land so that they can work it without spending a lot of time going back and forth. Thus where land is inherited equally by both sexes we might expect to find a higher rate of marriage within the community (this is called **endogamy,** from the Greek words *endo*, meaning "inside," and *gamos*, meaning "marriage"). Where land is inherited only by males, we would expect more *exogamy*, or marriage with outsiders, and the splitting up of groups of siblings.

In sum, agriculture as a subsistence strategy is very different from both horticulture and pastoralism. It creates a completely different type of social organization because of its potential for intensive cultivation and the production of a large surplus. In agricultural societies we find larger and more densely populated villages, but in addition we find towns and cities in which large numbers of nonagricultural residents practice specialized trades and skills. Political and economic power is centered in these towns and cities, and the rural cultivators are controlled from them. Although peasant agriculturalists have a strong sense of local identity, they are integrated into the region and the nation economically and politically, often without their consent. Thus, while we might look at hunting and gathering bands and many tribal horticultural and pastoral societies as isolated, homogeneous groups with clear cultural boundaries, in studying peasants and rural agricultural people in general, we must recognize that they share in a wider cultural tradition.

As we mentioned earlier, one of the important features that traditionally distinguished peasant groups from the other major societal types that have been the focus of anthropological attention has been the historical links with the nation states in which they reside. For much of their histories hunter-gatherers, horticulturalists, and pastoralists have had relatively little continuous meaningful contact with the state system, and their view of the society outside their immediate confines generally did not include being part of some larger political entity; the same has generally not been true for peasants. For example, it was probably not until the past decade or two that most members of Dani society knew that they were part of a nation called Indonesia, or that the Yanomamö, depending on the exact location of their particular village, knew or much less cared that they were residents of either Venezuela or Brazil. This ignorance of and ambivalence toward a larger and greater political entity has never been a luxury afforded to peasant groups.

One of the defining characteristics of peasants is a symbiotic relationship with urban areas. From a political perspective, in addition to producing the food that feeds the urban populations and supplying the cheap labor to help cities function, peasants often find themselves subject to the dictates of rules and authority emanating from the outside. Community leaders often are appointed from the outside and are responsible for enforcing laws, mediating disputes, and resolving conflicts according to rules imposed by larger and more powerful political entities. In this context, as well as in setting the prices for their goods, peasants often find themselves subject to the control of outsiders.

Peasant leadership is normally weak for several reasons. First, in many instances the state simply is concerned that not too much power reside at the local level. Decisions might then be made that could challenge the traditional and uneven balance of power. The state would not want to have its authority questioned. Second, many peasant communities appear to be reluctant to let their members acquire too much power, as this might be seen as a way of selfishly furthering one's own needs.

Because there is often ambivalence, if not outright hostility, toward political intervention from the outside, it is not unusual to see dual or parallel systems for settling disputes or dealing with minor litigation. Often the first avenue for handling grievances is to take complaints to a group of elders who, by virtue of wisdom and savvy acquired by age, are able to understand the pulse of the community. For example, what does one do when Villager X's cow keeps wandering into Y's cornfield and destroying the crops? Taking the complaint to the legally appointed authorities is likely to bring in outsiders to mediate, which could cause lingering hard feelings, and at the very least result in seemingly unnecessary bureaucratic procedures. Consulting the unofficial, although highly regarded, community leaders might resolve the problem quickly, quietly, and in a fashion that is amenable to community consensus and norms.

In the Mexican peasant village where one of the authors worked, there were many instances in which community members went to considerable efforts to *avoid* involving municipal authorities in what villagers felt were truly internal or local matters. Clearly they knew that they needed to cooperate with state authorities in order to have certain needs met, like obtaining electricity for the community. Community residents knew who the key actors in elections were and dutifully appeared at rallies to demonstrate their unwavering allegiance. At the same time they wanted to take care of problems among community members and to prevent matters that took place in the village from going any further, even if this meant ignoring whenever possible contradictory and potentially more powerful rules being imposed from the outside.

Sociopolitical organization in agricultural societies Rural agriculturalists usually exist within the type of social organization that we

Julian Steward (1902–1972)

Julian Steward spent his early career studying the archeology of American Indian societies, and later turned to ethnographic work as well. His background in archeology led him to consider the importance of the environment in the development of culture, which formed the basis of his concept of multilinear evolution. Steward noted striking similarities in the historical sequence of the rise of civilizations in river valleys surrounded by arid hinterlands, and believed that this environmental setting, given the right circumstances, would favor a particular line of cultural evolution. As a result of his work, Steward became a leading figure in the field of cultural ecology.

call the **state**. A state differs from a chiefdom or tribe in several ways. First, it is defined solely on the basis of the territory to which it has a claim, and not on the basis of a group of people who claim to be related to one another and to their leaders. Bands and tribes are kinship-oriented societies, and even the chiefdom is based on the belief of common descent among all the members of the group. But a state is defined in terms of legal membership in a group that is not based on kinship. For example, you are legally French if you are a citizen of France. Having French relatives, or living in America while being loyal to France, is not enough by itself. You may choose to become a member of the French state by giving up your American citizenship, moving to France, and applying for French citizenship. Such is the nature of the relationship between the state and the individual. But in a tribe or a chiefdom this would not be possible—a Crow Indian could not choose to become a Sioux, because both

Crow and Sioux group membership are based on descent, not just place of residence and legal duties.

States differ from chiefdoms to the extent that the government has the power to force its members to act in certain ways. While it is true that a chief also has such power, it is often expected that he or she must act according to kinship obligations. In contrast, a state can compel people to act according to its laws, and personal relationships play no role in the enforcement of these laws—at least in theory. Consensus or common agreement, which is so important in tribes and chiefdoms, is less important in a state.

Another special characteristic of the state is its tendency to develop a complex *bureaucracy*, a separate political institution set up to govern the people. Also, because states are usually linked with the growth of towns and cities, they require more complex economic and social institutions to satisfy the needs and interests of their citizens.

Most states were formed to support larger and denser populations, when agriculture took over from horticulture or pastoralism as the society's main subsistence strategy. Intensive use of land, reliance on greater amounts of nonhuman labor, and increased ability to amass a surplus and gain personal wealth created a need for a more complex form of social and political organization to maintain control. Some anthropologists have argued that early states arose out of the need for some way of managing the irrigation systems of river valleys where population growth had led to dense settlements of agriculturalists. As the land was worked more intensively, irrigation became more important, and some form of regulation was needed to protect the interests of the cultivators. In the end the problem grew beyond the local level to include the region as a whole, and government became centralized as a result. Although this is just one of several theories about the origin of states, it is valuable for pointing out how states differ from other forms of social organization. States are founded on public issues and laws rather than based on kinship ties among the members of the society. With each locality promoting its own interests, the state represents an efficient way of bringing these potentially conflicting interests together and promoting the programs that are best suited to the society as a whole.

State organization   A state is a territorial government with the power to organize and carry out activities aimed toward the achievement of group goals. It is the most common form of political organization in Western societies, although it is by no means the only one. There is no sharp distinction between a chiefdom and a state, just as there is no clear line dividing a chiefdom from a tribe. Indeed, there can be simple forms of state organization headed by someone whom we might call a chief, in that his position is not merely that of secular leader (such as a president or prime minister), but is also religious and perhaps even based on kinship as well.

What makes a state different from other forms of political organization is the extent to which it can force people to act in certain ways. Its authority can be defined on religious grounds, or it can be secular, as it is in our society, where the power of government rests with "the will of the people." Along with this power goes a division of the population into classes and, in more highly developed states, a bureaucracy that sets political institutions apart from the rest of the society.

Higher levels of economic and social organization are usually associated with a state. One such feature is *urbanism*, the concentration of people in towns and cities. Some anthropologists have argued that the sheer size of cities requires a statelike political system. Moreover, the specialization of economic tasks in a large society not only creates a more complex social organization but also leads to a hierarchy of social classes or castes.

Peasant agriculturalists: South Indian villages   The southern Indian landscape is dotted with thousands of small villages where peasants follow an agricultural way of life not very different from that of their ancestors a thousand years ago. Grain and other crops are produced with the help of an ox-drawn plow, and much manual labor is required for tasks for which the animals cannot be used. Although in most places the land has the potential to be fertile, production is generally low, not much above the level needed to survive, because of limited use of technology and scientific methods. The typical peasant produces enough for his or her own family, and a surplus to use in paying for the services of nonagricultural villagers such as the carpenter who makes and repairs tools, the potter who makes cooking utensils, and the village priest.

It would seem at first glance that the peasant village of southern India is a self-sufficient community with no ties to the outside world. However, a closer look reveals a wide variety of ties to the local region as well as to the national government. On an economic level, for example, the peasants must obtain products that are not available in their own village, such as metal for tools and utensils; salt, sugar, and other foods that are not native to their region; and a variety of items made in nearby villages by specialists in a trade that is not represented in their own village. In return for these goods the peasants may pay cash, but more likely they will trade something of value that they have produced themselves—food, if they are farmers, other things if they are craftsmen. Suppliers from these regional markets deal in larger market systems that link the peasant to national and international markets.

Thus peasants are tied economically to the state in that the nature of the products they trade can be controlled by a government agency or even regulated on the village level. The state may be able to dictate what crops will be grown in a certain region, if not through direct orders to the cultivators, then by taking actions that will affect the market prices of various products. It can arrange for agricultural advisers to visit each village to help the peasants increase their production, thereby tapping a larger surplus for itself. In short, while peasants may appear to be self-sufficient cultivators, they are affected either directly or indirectly by the government in terms of the amount and kinds of crops they produce.

The state makes its presence known in other ways as well. It levies taxes on each household and sends a tax collector to each village on a regular basis. It may also extend its bureaucracy into the village by setting up public health clinics, schools, agricultural development programs, and a police force and a representative of the legal system. In all of these cases government institutions are not based on kinship; in fact, the representatives of the state may be strangers who come from other parts of the country.

Politically, the peasant is tied to the state through a series of political institutions. In India peasants elect village representatives to a council called a *panchayat*. In some cases

the elected leaders may also be salaried government officials, so that they represent both the villagers and the state at the same time. The panchayat, in turn, is integrated into a regional governmental system that represents the interests of many villages and carries out the policies of the government on a wider scale.

Still another major difference between peasants in a state and members of other kinds of societies has to do with the extent to which they are integrated into a wider cultural system. In tribal societies the members are united by a common language, a common cultural heritage, and a shared system of beliefs. A chiefdom likewise is a culturally unified group based on the relatedness of its members, either actual or figurative. Even though a chiefdom might include many thousands of individuals, all share in a single cultural tradition, and it is this common bond that backs up the authority of the chief. But in a state organization the power of the government is not derived from the relatedness and shared beliefs of its members— it is derived from the state's ability to enforce its will on its citizens. People obey the commands of the state because they believe its power is legitimate, not because they feel obliged to out of kinship or religious belief in the divine nature of the ruler.

The peasants of southern India are members of a state that is much larger than their own region. India includes many different people with diverse ethnic backgrounds who speak different languages and worship different gods. They share some of these traditions with other people throughout the country—the Hindu peasants of southern India follow the same religious practices as those of northern India. Yet each village and each region has its own local traditions that are not shared with outsiders, traditions that are unique to them. This combination of shared traditions and cultural diversity is typical of the state and makes it different from a chiefdom. For the state cannot rely on the sacredness of its leadership the way a chiefdom can, and the state has no hold over its citizens through bonds of kinship or cultural similarity.

The Growth of Social Inequality

With the rise of horticulture and pastoralism, social inequality becomes possible. There have even been some hunting and gathering societies in which the food supply was large and stable enough to support dense permanent settlements, and under these conditions stratified societies emerged. So it is not simply the way people obtain food that is important—it is the size of the group and the ability to acquire wealth and control resources.

In the discussion of horticultural societies in Chapter 7, it was pointed out that as people begin to invest labor in land, there is more incentive to own private property. Because horticulture does not allow for the storage of large amounts of wealth, social inequality in horticultural societies is often based on the ability to command a large labor force and support a large family. Horticulture can also support specialists in such areas as religion, thereby raising their social standing in the group. In tribal societies we begin to see the development of a separate political office, but it is not as clearly defined as it is in a chiefdom, in which one person is recognized as a full-time leader whom all the members of the group must follow.

Pastoral societies also permit ownership of private property, but in the form of animals rather than land. However, ownership beyond what is needed to support one's family requires control over a larger labor force to help feed and defend the herds. Pastoral societies often show greater stratification than horticultural societies because a family or group of families can acquire more wealth as measured in animals than would be the case if they measured their wealth in land that must be cultivated as well as defended. Differences in wealth among pastoralists may lead to the ranking, not of individuals, but of families, since animals tend to be the property of a group of related families.

Tribal societies, whether horticultural or pastoral, are held together by a common language, ethnic heritage, and territory. They share a sense of equality; if they have leaders, the leaders cannot force the members of the group to behave in a certain way without the support of group consensus. It is in chiefdoms that we begin to see social stratification in which the chief and his or her close relatives command respect and obedience from the rest of the group. The concentration of power in the office of the chief and the uneven distribution of power throughout the society form the basis for greater specialization, which itself adds to social inequality.

Peasant societies offer more opportunities to form dense, permanent settlements. The use of animal power, irrigation, or other technological aids to transform the environment allows for the investment of large amounts of labor in the land and produces a greater yield from a given piece of land. As a result, the distribution of wealth and status can become more uneven. Peasants are exploited by urban-based nonagricultural elites who control their labor and production either directly, through ownership of the land, or indirectly, through taxation or control over market outlets.

State organizations, of which peasant societies are a part, have the greatest potential for social stratification, since they contain not only rural communities but cities and towns as well. Differences in wealth and status on the village level may be large or small when compared to such differences in a similar-sized community of horticulturists or pastoralists, but in the context of the state the peasant community represents the lowest rung on the social ladder. Specialists living in towns and cities rank above the agricultural peasant and may, in turn, rank below political or religious elites who exercise control over land and labor. Because the state is not bound by the kinship ties and duties of a chiefdom or a tribal organization, it can obtain and redistribute wealth in a highly uneven fashion. In contrast to a chiefdom, in which families are ranked according to how closely they are related to the royal lineage, in a state society there are large stratified groups ranked not on the basis of kinship but according to their power over those below them.

The Evolution of Adaptive Strategies

In the last chapter we discussed the concept of a band and how it fits in with the life style of hunting and gathering peoples. The small, loose-knit residence group lacks clear lines of leadership and authority and comes close to being a group of equals. There is little specialization, little division of labor, little difference in wealth, and a great deal of similarity in beliefs, experiences, values, and general life style. The band is well adapted to a society in which the level of technology and the way of obtaining food do not allow for large, dense, permanent settlements. It can grow or shrink according to the season and the availability of food without major rifts among its members. It creates just enough of an alliance to allow groups to come together for special ceremonies or to obtain husbands and wives, but it does not create strong alliances that might result in warfare with other groups. Because there is so little material wealth in hunting and gathering societies, the band tends to foster equality and prevent the domination of some members by others.

In this chapter we have dealt with several different types of society as they evolved over the past 15,000 years. Hunters and gatherers were limited by their way of exploiting the environment. We can understand band organization as an adaptation to hunting and gathering as a way of life, and we can also see why it is not found in societies with some form of agriculture or domestication of animals. Tribal societies are a more complex

form of social organization and tend to be found in association with a more productive type of technology—horticulture, pastoralism, or a combination of the two. Chiefdoms are an even more complex form of social organization, and again, they generally have a more productive technology and can support large, dense, more or less permanent settlements. In looking for an evolutionary reason for the development of chiefdoms, we can consider several possibilities. Warfare could have played an important role because the chiefdom can both support a full-time army and coordinate its activities. If this gave one society an advantage over the other groups, it may explain how a chiefdom could become dominant in a given area. A related explanation has to do with the increased amount of specialization that is possible in a chiefdom. This results in more productivity, which in turn can lead to a larger and denser population. Thus we can understand how a chiefdom could have spread out and grown through conquest, given the increased political, economic, and military strength that allowed it to rule more land and people more effectively.

In horticultural societies we find that the proportion of the food produced directly affects the type of sociopolitical organization. If relatively little food is grown, and most is hunted or gathered, then the society may be bandlike in its organization. As the amount of food obtained from horticulture increases, so does the density of the population. And as the basis of group membership broadens from the residence group to the larger society, so does the political affiliation—ultimately leading to a chiefdom.

In pastoral societies, because of the mobility associated with seasonal migration or nomadism, there is little chance for centralized political authority to develop. As a result, most pastoral peoples are internally organized along the lines of tribal societies. However, many pastoral groups are not totally self-sufficient, but depend on wider economic networks in which they trade animal products for food, weapons, and other important items. As a result, they are often integrated into a more complex form of political organization, while still keeping their political autonomy as tribal units.

With the development of agriculture, people were able to combine the domestication of plants and animals, leading to many other changes in their life style. No longer did they have to move around in a wide area to find enough food. The size of the group could grow, since the land could support many more people through agriculture. Equally important was the fact that agriculture allowed a family to produce more food than it could consume, and this surplus could be used to feed other people, who were thus freed for occupations other than food producing. Surplus food could also be stored for future use, or exchanged in trade networks, or used in many different ways. Agricultural surplus was crucial to the development of civilization; for the first time a class of people emerged who could turn their attention to other aspects of life without worrying where their next meal was coming from.

The next step was the formation of urban centers. Although most of the early urban centers were so small that they would barely deserve the name "city" in today's meaning of the term, they were important in the process of culture change. The concentration of people in cities was a natural outgrowth of the increase in population that resulted from agriculture, combined with the growing number of people who no longer had to engage directly in food production. These people congregated in a single community where they could perform other crafts and services, which at first they exchanged directly with the agriculturalists of the region. In fact, early cities were small enough to accommodate both farmers and nonfarmers. But as the size of the city grew, it became a center for specialists in other activities, and its population became increasingly heterogeneous—that is, composed of people who were unlike one another.

As cities grew, more and more power became concentrated in the hands of people who lived in them. They dominated the coun-

Using a technique several thousand years old, a Sudanese youth winnows rice.

Using a combine and other modern technologies illustrates an important difference between commercialized agriculture for profit and peasant cultivation for subsistence.

tryside and controlled the economies of peasant villages. The final step in the transition to a state form of political organization was made when the leaders in the cities gained the power to force the rest of the population to cooperate to achieve the economic and political goals of the state. Political leaders increased their control over internal production and trade, over economic relations with neighboring societies, and over the day-to-day activities of the members of the population, usually at the expense of the peasants, who had to produce a surplus to pay taxes and fight in wars far from home over issues of little importance to them personally.

These changes in subsistence strategies from hunting and gathering to horticulture, pastoralism, and agriculture, and in sociopolitical organization from band to tribe, chiefdom, and state, occurred together, but not in any single series of stages. That is, there was no single line of progression from hunting and gathering band to horticultural tribe to pastoral chiefdom to agricultural state. In some areas of the world where conditions favored stronger centralized government, chiefdoms arose more quickly than elsewhere. Some pastoral peoples still live in tribal societies, while others are part of larger state organizations. A few agricultural societies existed before the development of the state.

In short, we cannot say that one type of adaptive strategy necessarily means a corresponding type of sociopolitical organization. Instead, many different lines of cultural evolution have occurred, depending upon the environment and social conditions in a particular place and time.

Summary

Horticulture, pastoralism, and agriculture represent significant changes from a hunting and gathering way of life. Once humans domesticated plants and animals, they were able to transform their environment and thereby support larger and denser populations. But in doing so, they created new demands for social and political organization beyond the capacity of the hunting and gathering band.

Horticulture is the cultivation of fruits and vegetables using primitive tools. Most horticultural societies today have only a few hundred people, but in the past some had the capacity to support extremely large, dense populations up to 100,000 or more. Horticulturalists live in semipermanent settlements close to their gardens. They are able to have more material possessions and thus tend to be more stratified than hunters and gatherers. Some horticultural societies are organized into loose-knit confederations known as *tribes*, while others are more centrally organized into *chiefdoms*, where power is in the hands of a single individual who holds a political office. In a chiefdom there is more control over the distribution of goods within the society and individual members may be called upon to turn over some of their production or give up some of their labor to the chief.

Pastoralism depends on domesticated animals for the subsistence needs of people, although there is usually a set of reciprocal trade relationships with neighboring agriculturalists. Pastoralism usually leads to a nomadic life style, with wealth measured in terms of the size of one's herd rather than other kinds of material possessions. Because they are more mobile, pastoralists often engage in raiding or warfare. Like horticulturalists, they tend to be organized into tribes or chiefdoms, depending on the size of the group, the population density, the need for mutual protection, and a number of other factors.

Agriculture represents a more productive economic activity, in that a smaller percentage of the population is needed to produce enough food for all. The intensive cultivation of grain crops allows a large nonagricultural population to live in cities by exploiting the rural cultivators, or *peasants*. These peasants are not really independent, but are controlled by forces outside their community; they have little economic or political power of their own. Peasants usually are part of a political system called a *state*, which is defined in terms of territorial authority rather than kinship or religious-based authority.

As human groups have expanded their technological capacity and improved their ability to control their environment, they have been able to form larger and denser settlements. These, in turn, have led to more elaborate sets of political relationships in order to reduce hostility and promote cooperation. Horticulture and pastoralism represent the first major advances over hunting and gathering as an adaptive strategy, and in these kinds of societies we find more complex forms of social and political organization, such as tribes and chiefdoms. Intensive agriculture represents yet another technological advance, and it is often found in association with even more complex political organizations, called *states*. While there is no direct relationship between a particular type of adaptive strategy and a specific form of sociopolitical organization (which is influenced by many other important factors besides technology and the size of the group), we can recognize a general trend in the course of cultural evolution. Julian Steward's concept of *multilinear evolution* describes this process of change, with many different lines of cultural evolution occurring, depending on the environmental and social conditions in a particular place and time.

Glossary

ancestor worship A religious system based on the belief that one's dead ancestors can have an effect in determining the events of one's life.

age set A group of people of the same sex and roughly the same age who remain close throughout their lives and go through the same experiences together, such as initiation ceremonies, military service, or marriage.

agriculture Cultivation of the land using animal or mechanical power and relying mainly on grains, often combined with the domestication of animals for food and labor.

"big man" The typical Melanesian leader, whose authority is based on his ability to influence others; an achieved position of informal leadership.

chiefdom A type of sociopolitical organization in which a central leader occupies a definite political office, rather than ruling by consensus. This type of society is usually characterized by a system of ranking or social stratification.

endogamy The practice that restricts marriage to another member of an individual's group; a rule against marrying someone outside that group.

extended family A family group consisting of several generations, usually including a married couple, their unmarried children, and one or more nuclear families of their married children. (See Chapter 9.)

headman In band societies, the leader of a group in which the authority is based on the personal qualities of the individual, rather than a formal position of authority.

horticulture Cultivation of fruits and vegetables using primitive tools and usually a slash-and-burn technique for clearing the land.

leopard skin chief In Nuer society, a man who mediates village disputes, and who represents the closest thing to a political official by virtue of the respect he commands from his fellow tribesmen.

lineage A descent group in which the members can trace their relationship to an actual common ancestor.

matrilineal descent The system of tracing membership in a kinship group only through the mother's side of the family.

pastoralism An adaptive strategy based on raising domesticated animals, although it usually involves trade with neighboring agricultural peoples to meet some of the group's subsistence needs.

patrilineal descent The system of tracing membership in a kinship group only through the father's side of the family.

peasant A rural agriculturalist who cultivates the land primarily for his or her own consumption, but who is tied into a wider economic and political system that controls and exploits his or her activities.

segmentary opposition A form of political organization in which a society is divided into groups, each subdivided into hierarchical units. Alliances are formed within each unit, and they provide a mechanism for settling disputes either within the group or between groups.

slash-and-burn cultivation A technique associated with horticulture in which vegetation is cut down and burned to clear the land, which is then used until it loses its fertility.

state A territorially based government characterized by a centralized authority, a specialization of economic tasks, and social stratification. The state is usually associated with urbanism, which in turn means a large, dense population.

swidden See slash-and-burn cultivation.

tribe A loose-knit organization of groups that recognize a relationship to one another, usually in the form of common ethnic origin, common language, or a strong pattern of interaction based on intermarriage or presumed kinship.

These groups provide the broadest base in the society upon which joint activities can be organized and carried out.

Questions for Discussion

1. What is the future likely to hold for the horticultural and pastoral peoples of the world? Are they likely to be able to adapt to the changing political and economic environment, or will they disappear? Why?

2. What is the difference between a peasant in southern India and a farmer in the United States?

3. Some anthropologists have suggested that in a

totalitarian society where the government has control over the agricultural labor and the crops produced, the rural population is no longer a peasantry but instead is more like a group of factory workers. What are some of the important differences between peasant cultivators and agricultural laborers that would lead you to such a conclusion?

Suggestions for Additional Reading

ALAN R. BEALS, *Village Life in South India* (Chicago: Aldine, 1974). A survey of peasant villages in southern India, describing their peasant agricultural practices, their ties to the wider society, and their general life style.

JULIET CLUTTON-BROCK (Ed.), *The Walking Larder* (London: Unwin Hyman, 1989). An archeological exploration of 40,000 years of human-animal relationships.

JULIET CLUTTON-BROCK, *Domesticated Animals* (London: Heineman Ltd., 1981). An illustrated survey of common domestic mammals with archeological and historical evidence about their domestication.

E. E. EVANS-PRITCHARD, *The Nuer* (New York: Oxford University Press, 1940). A classic ethnography of this East African pastoral people by one of the leading British anthropologists of the twentieth century.

FREDERICK C. GAMST, *Peasants in Complex Society* (New York: Holt, Rinehart and Winston, 1974). A brief survey of peasant societies, their common characteristics, and their relationships to the wider societies of which they are a part.

KARL HEIDER, *Grand Valley Dani: Peaceful Warriors*, 2nd ed. (New York: Holt, Rinehart and Winston,

1991). An ethnographic description of the Dani, a horticultural people in highland New Guinea.

WILLIAM J. PETERS and LEON F. NEUENSCHWANDER, *Slash and Burn* (Moscow, Idaho: University of Idaho Press, 1988). A brief, concentrated study of the use of fire in shifting cultivation in the world's tropical forests, including a fascinating chapter on the social, cultural, economic, and political aspects of clearing fields by burning.

Journal of Peasant Studies (London: Frank Cass & Co., Ltd.). This journal contains articles dealing with peasants from every part of the world.

JACK M. POTTER, MAY N. DIAZ, and GEORGE M. FOSTER (Eds.), *Peasant Society: A Reader* (Boston: Little, Brown, 1967). A sampling of ideas about peasant society and culture by prominent authors from fields of anthropology, sociology, economics, philosophy, and social psychology.

MARSHALL D. SAHLINS, *Tribesmen* (Englewood Cliffs, N.J.: Prentice Hall, 1968). A brief survey of tribal peoples, with contrasting descriptions of tribal organizations in groups with different adaptive strategies.

ERIC WOLF, *Peasants* (Englewood Cliffs, N.J.: Prentice Hall, 1966). A short but important discussion of anthropological views on peasant societies.

India's Sacred Cow

MARVIN HARRIS

In this now-classic article Professor Harris argues that Hindu prohibitions against eating beef are based on pragmatic ecological considerations that were implemented a thousand years ago. This practice appears irrational to many Westerners, and even to many Indians. Yet the use of cattle as draft animals, beasts of burden, providers of milk, and major contributors of dung for fertilizer and cooking fuel underscores the significance of these animals in Indian life.

News photographs that came out of India during the famine of the late 1960s showed starving people stretching out bony hands to beg for food while sacred cattle strolled behind them undisturbed. The Hindu, it seems, would rather starve to death than eat his cow or even deprive it of food. The cattle appear to browse unhindered through urban markets eating an orange here, a mango there, competing with people for meager supplies of food.

By Western standards, spiritual values seem more important to Indians than life itself. Specialists in food habits around the world like Fred Simoons at the University of California at Davis consider Hinduism an irrational ideology that compels people to overlook abundant, nutritious foods for scarcer, less healthful foods.

What seems to be an absurd devotion to the mother cow pervades Indian life. Indian wall calendars portray beautiful young women with bodies of fat white cows, often with milk jetting from their teats into sacred shrines.

Cow worship even carries over into politics. In 1966 a crowd of 120,000 people, led by holy men, demonstrated in front of the Indian House of Parliament in support of the All-Party Cow Protection Campaign Committee. In Nepal, the only contemporary Hindu kingdom, cow slaughter is severely punished. As one story goes, the car driven by an official of a United States agency struck and killed a cow. In order to avoid the international incident that would have occurred when the official was arrested for murder, the Nepalese magistrate concluded that the cow had committed suicide.

Marvin Harris, "India's Sacred Cow," *Human Nature*, 1 (2) 1978, pp. 28–36. Copyright © 1978 by Human Nature, Inc. Reprinted by permission of the publisher.

Many Indians agree with Western assessments of the Hindu reverence for their cattle, the zebu, or *Bos indicus*, a large-humped species prevalent in Asia and Africa. M. N. Srinivas, an Indian anthropologist, states: "Orthodox Hindu opinion regards the killing of cattle with abhorrence, even though the refusal to kill the vast number of useless cattle which exists in India today is detrimental to the nation." Even the Indian Ministry of Information formerly maintained that "the large animal population is more a liability than an asset in view of our land resources." Accounts from many different sources point to the same conclusion: India, one of the world's great civilizations, is being strangled by its love for the cow.

The easy explanation for India's devotion to the cow, the one most Westerners and Indians would offer, is that cow worship is an integral part of Hinduism. Religion is somehow good for the soul, even if it sometimes fails the body. Religion orders the cosmos and explains our place in the universe. Religious beliefs, many would claim, have existed for thousands of years and have a life of their own. They are not understandable in scientific terms.

But all this ignores history. There is more to be said for cow worship than is immediately apparent. The earliest Vedas, the Hindu sacred texts from the Second Millennium B.C., do not prohibit the slaughter of cattle. Instead, they ordain it as a part of sacrificial rites. The early Hindus did not avoid the flesh of cows and bulls; they ate it at ceremonial feasts presided over by Brahman priests. Cow worship is a relatively recent development in India; it evolved as the Hindu religion developed and changed.

This evolution is recorded in royal edicts and religious texts written during the last 3,000 years of Indian history. The Vedas from the First Millennium B.C. contain contradictory passages, some referring to ritual slaughter and others to a strict taboo on beef consumption. A. N. Bose, in *Social and Rural Economy of Northern India, 600 B.C.–200 A.D.*, concludes that many of the sacred-cow passages were incorporated into the texts by priests of a later period.

By 200 A.D. the status of Indian cattle had undergone a spiritual transformation. The Brahman priesthood exhorted the population to venerate the cow and forbade them to abuse it or to feed on it. Religious feasts involving the ritual slaughter and consumption of livestock were eliminated and meat eating was restricted to the nobility.

By 1000 A.D., all Hindus were forbidden to eat beef. Ahimsa, the Hindu belief in the unity of all life, was the spiritual justification for this restriction. But it is difficult to ascertain exactly when this change occurred. An important event that helped to shape the modern complex was the Islamic invasion, which took place in the Eighth Century A.D. Hindus may have found it politically expedient to set themselves off from the invaders, who were beefeaters, by emphasizing the need to prevent the slaughter of their sacred animals. Thereafter, the cow taboo assumed its modern form and began to function much as it does today.

The place of the cow in modern India is every place—on posters, in the movies, in brass figures, in stone and wood carvings, on the streets, in the fields. The cow is a symbol of health and abundance. It provides the milk that Indians consume in the form of yogurt and ghee (clarified butter), which contribute subtle flavors to much spicy Indian food.

This, perhaps, is the practical role of the cow, but cows provide less than half the milk produced in India. Most cows in India are not dairy breeds. In most regions, when an Indian farmer wants a steady, high-quality source of milk he usually invests in a female water buffalo. In India the water buffalo is the specialized dairy breed because its milk has a higher butterfat content than zebu milk. Although the farmer milks his zebu cows, the milk is merely a by-product.

More vital than zebu milk to South Asian farmers are zebu calves. Male calves are especially valued because from bulls come oxen, which are the mainstay of the Indian agricultural system.

Small, fast oxen drag wooden plows through late-spring fields when monsoons have dampened the dry, cracked earth. After harvest, the oxen break the grain from the stalk by stomping through mounds of cut wheat and rice. For rice cultivation in irrigated fields, the male water buffalo is preferred (it pulls better in deep mud), but for most other crops, including rainfall rice, wheat, sorghum, and millet, and for transporting goods and people to and from town,

a team of oxen is preferred. The ox is the Indian peasant's tractor, thresher and family car combined; the cow is the factor that produces the ox.

If draft animals instead of cows are counted, India appears to have too few domesticated ruminants, not too many. Since each of the 70 million farms in India requires a draft team, it follows that Indian peasants should use 140 million animals in the fields. But there are only 83 million oxen and male water buffalo on the subcontinent, a shortage of 30 million draft teams.

In other regions of the world, joint ownership of draft animals might overcome a shortage, but Indian agriculture is closely tied to the monsoon rains of late spring and summer. Field preparation and planting must coincide with the rain, and a farmer must have his animals ready to plow when the weather is right. When the farmer without a draft team needs bullocks most, his neighbors are all using theirs. Any delay in turning the soil drastically lowers production.

Because of this dependence on draft animals, loss of the family oxen is devastating. If a beast dies, the farmer must borrow money to buy or rent an ox at interest rates so high that he ultimately loses his land. Every year foreclosures force thousands of poverty-stricken peasants to abandon the countryside for the overcrowded cities.

If a family is fortunate enough to own a fertile cow, it will be able to rear replacements for a lost team and thus survive until life returns to normal. If, as sometimes happens, famine leads a family to sell its cow and ox team, all ties to agriculture are cut. Even if the family survives, it has no way to farm the land, no oxen to work the land, and no cows to produce oxen.

The prohibition against eating meat applies to the flesh of cows, bulls, and oxen, but the cow is the most sacred because it can produce the other two. The peasant whose cow dies is not only crying over a spiritual loss but over the loss of his farm as well.

Religious laws that forbid the slaughter of cattle promote the recovery of the agricultural system from the dry Indian winter and from periods of drought. The monsoon, on which all agriculture depends, is erratic. Sometimes it arrives early, sometimes late, sometimes not at all. Drought has struck large portions of India time and again in this century, and Indian farmers and the zebus are accustomed to these natural disasters. Zebus can pass weeks on end with little or no food and water. Like camels, they store both in their humps and recuperate quickly with only a little nourishment.

During droughts the cows often stop lactating and become barren. In some cases the condition is per-

manent but often it is only temporary. If barren animals were summarily eliminated, as Western experts
in animal husbandry have suggested, cows capable
of recovery would be lost along with those entirely
debilitated. By keeping alive the cows that can later
produce oxen, religious laws against cow slaughter
assure the recovery of the agricultural system from
the greatest challenge it faces—the failure of the
monsoon.

The local Indian governments aid the process of
recovery by maintaining homes for barren cows.
Farmers reclaim any animal that calves or begins to
lactate. One police station in Madras collects strays
and pastures them in a field adjacent to the station.
After a small fine is paid, a cow is returned to its
rightful owner when the owner thinks the cow shows
signs of being able to reproduce.

During the hot, dry spring months most of India
is like a desert. Indian farmers often complain they
cannot feed their livestock during this period. They
maintain the cattle by letting them scavenge on the
sparse grass along the roads. In the cities cattle are
encouraged to scavenge near food stalls to supplement their scant diet. These are the wandering cattle
tourists report seeing throughout India.

Westerners expect shopkeepers to respond to
these intrusions with the deference due a sacred animal; instead, their response is a string of curses and
the crack of a long bamboo pole across the beast's
back or a poke at its genitals. Mahatma Gandhi was
well aware of the treatment sacred cows (and bulls
and oxen) received in India. "How we bleed her to
take the last drop of milk from her. How we starve
her to emaciation, how we ill-treat the calves, how
we deprive them of their portion of milk, how cruelly
we treat the oxen, how we castrate them, how we
beat them, how we overload them."

Oxen generally receive better treatment than
cows. When food is in short supply, thrifty Indian
peasants feed their working bullocks and ignore their
cows, but rarely do they abandon the cows to die.
When cows are sick, farmers worry over them as they
would over members of the family and nurse them
as if they were children. When the rains return and
when the fields are harvested, the farmers again feed
their cows regularly and reclaim their abandoned animals. The prohibition against beef consumption is a
form of disaster insurance for all India.

Western agronomists and economists are quick to
protest that all the functions of the zebu cattle can
be improved with organized breeding programs, cultivated pastures, and silage. Because stronger oxen
would pull the plow faster, they could work multiple
plots of land, allowing farmers to share their animals.

Fewer healthy, well-fed cows could provide Indians
with more milk. But pastures and silage require arable land, land needed to produce wheat and rice.

A look at Western cattle farming makes plain the
cost of adopting advanced technology in Indian agriculture. In a study of livestock production in the
United States, David Pimentel of the College of Agriculture and Life Sciences at Cornell University
found that 91 percent of the cereal, legume, and vegetable protein suitable for human consumption is
consumed by livestock. Approximately three quarters
of the arable land in the United States is devoted to
growing food for livestock. In the production of meat
and milk, American ranchers use enough fossil fuel
to equal more than 82 million barrels of oil annually.

Indian cattle do not drain the system in the same
way. In a 1971 study of livestock in West Bengal,
Steward Odend'hal of the University of Missouri
found that Bengalese cattle ate only the inedible remains of subsistence crops—rice straw, rice hulls,
the tops of sugar cane, and mustard-oil cake. Cattle
graze in the fields after harvest and eat the remains
of crops left on the ground; they forage for grass and
weeds on the roadsides. The food for zebu cattle costs
the human population virtually nothing. "Basically,"
Odend'hal says, "the cattle convert items of little direct human value into products of immediate utility."

In addition to plowing the fields and producing
milk, the zebus produce dung, which fires the hearths
and fertilizes the fields of India. Much of the estimated 800 million tons of manure produced annually
is collected by the farmer's children as they follow
the family cows and bullocks from place to place.
And when the children see the droppings of another
farmer's cattle along the road, they pick those up
also. Odend'hal reports that the system operates with
such high efficiency that the children of West Bengal
recover nearly 100 percent of the dung produced by
their livestock.

From 40 to 70 percent of all manure produced by
Indian cattle is used as fuel for cooking; the rest is
returned to the fields as fertilizer. Dried dung burns
slowly, cleanly, and with low heat—characteristics
that satisfy the household needs of Indian women.
Staples like curry and rice can simmer for hours.
While the meal slowly cooks over an unattended fire,
the women of the household can do other chores.
Cow chips, unlike firewood, do not scorch as they
burn.

It is estimated that the dung used for cooking fuel
provides the energy-equivalent of 43 million tons of
coal. At current prices, it would cost India an extra
1.5 billion dollars in foreign exchange to replace the
dung with coal. And if the 350 million tons of manure

that are being used as fertilizer were replaced with commercial fertilizers, the expense would be even greater. Roger Revelle of the University of California at San Diego has calculated that 89 percent of the energy used in Indian agriculture (the equivalent of about 150 million tons of coal) is provided by local sources. Even if foreign loans were to provide the money, the capital outlay necessary to replace the Indian cow with tractors and fertilizers for the fields, coal for the fires, and transportation for the family would probably warp international financial institutions for years.

Instead of asking the Indians to learn from the American model of industrial agriculture, American farmers might learn energy conservation from the Indians. Every step in an energy cycle results in a loss of energy to the system. Like a pendulum that slows a bit with each swing, each transfer of energy from sun to plants, plants to animals, and animals to human beings involves energy losses. Some systems are more efficient than others; they provide a higher percentage of the energy inputs in a final, useful form. Seventeen percent of all energy zebus consume is returned in the form of milk, traction and dung. American cattle raised on Western range land return only 4 percent of the energy they consume.

But the American system is improving. Based on techniques pioneered by Indian scientists, at least one commercial firm in the United States is reported to be building plants that will turn manure from cattle feedlots into combustible gas. When organic matter is broken down by anaerobic bacteria, methane gas and carbon dioxide are produced. After the methane is cleansed of the carbon dioxide, it is available for the same purposes as natural gas—cooking, heating, electricity generation. The company constructing the biogasification plant plans to sell its product to a gas-supply company, to be piped through the existing distribution system. Schemes similar to this one could make cattle ranches almost independent of utility and gasoline companies, for methane can be used to run trucks, tractors, and cars as well as to supply heat and electricity. The relative energy self-sufficiency that the Indian peasant has achieved is a goal American farmers and industry are now striving for.

Studies like Odend'hal's understate the efficiency of the Indian cow, because dead cows are used for purposes that Hindus prefer not to acknowledge. When a cow dies, an Untouchable, a member of one of the lowest ranking castes in India, is summoned to haul away the carcass. Higher castes consider the body of the dead cow polluting; if they do handle it, they must go through a rite of purification.

Untouchables first skin the dead animal and either tan the skin themselves or sell it to a leather factory. In the privacy of their homes, contrary to the teachings of Hinduism, untouchable castes cook the meat and eat it. Indians of all castes rarely acknowledge the existence of these practices to non-Hindus, but most are aware that beefeating takes place. The prohibition against beefeating restricts consumption by the higher castes and helps distribute animal protein to the poorest sectors of the population that otherwise would have no source of these vital nutrients.

Untouchables are not the only Indians who consume beef. Indian Muslims and Christians are under no restriction that forbids them beef, and its consumption is legal in many places. The Indian ban on cow slaughter is state, not national, law and not all states restrict it. In many cities, such as New Delhi, Calcutta, and Bombay, legal slaughterhouses sell beef to retail customers and to the restaurants that serve steak.

If the caloric value of beef and the energy costs involved in the manufacture of synthetic leather were included in the estimates of energy, the calculated efficiency of Indian livestock would rise considerably. As well as the system works, experts often claim that its efficiency can be further improved. Alan Heston, an economist at the University of Pennsylvania, believes that Indians suffer from an overabundance of cows simply because they refuse to slaughter the excess cattle. India could produce at least the same number of oxen and the same quantities of milk and manure with 30 million fewer cows. Heston calculates that only 40 cows are necessary to maintain a population of 100 bulls and oxen. Since India averages 70 cows for every 100 bullocks, the difference, 30 million cows, is expendable.

What Heston fails to note is that sex ratios among cattle in different regions of India vary tremendously, indicating that adjustments in the cow population do take place. Along the Ganges River, one of the holiest shrines of Hinduism, the ratio drops to 47 cows for every 100 male animals. This ratio reflects the preference for dairy buffalo in the irrigated sectors of the Gangetic Plains. In nearby Pakistan, in contrast, where cow slaughter is permitted, the sex ratio is 60 cows to 100 oxen.

Since the sex ratios among cattle differ greatly from region to region and do not even approximate the balance that would be expected if no females were killed, we can assume that some culling of herds does take place: Indians do adjust their religious restrictions to accommodate ecological realities.

They cannot kill a cow but they can tether an old or unhealthy animal until it is starved to death. They cannot slaughter a calf but they can yoke it with a large wooden triangle so that when it nurses it irritates the mother's udder and gets kicked to death. They cannot ship their animals to the slaughterhouse but they can sell them to Muslims, closing their eyes to the fact that the Muslims will take the cattle to the slaughterhouse.

These violations of the prohibition against cattle slaughter strengthen the premise that cow worship is a vital part of Indian culture. The practice arose to prevent the population from consuming the animal on which Indian agriculture depends.

During the First Millennium B.C., the Ganges Valley became one of the most densely populated regions of the world. Where previously there had been only scattered villages, many towns and cities arose and peasants farmed every available acre of land. Kingsley Davis, a population expert at the University of California at Berkeley, estimates that by 300 B.C. between 50 million and 100 million people were living in India. The forested Ganges Valley became a windswept semidesert and signs of ecological collapse appeared; droughts and floods became commonplace, erosion took away the rich topsoil, farms shrank as population increased, and domesticated animals became harder and harder to maintain.

It is probable that the elimination of meat eating came about in a slow, practical manner. The farmers who decided not to eat their cows, who saved them for procreation to produce oxen, were the ones who survived the natural disasters. Those who ate beef lost the tools with which to farm. Over a period of centuries, more and more farmers probably avoided beef until an unwritten taboo came into existence.

Only later was the practice codified by the priesthood. While Indian peasants were probably aware of the role of cattle in their society, strong sanctions were necessary to protect zebus from a population faced with starvation. To removed temptation, the flesh of cattle became taboo and the cow became sacred.

The sacredness of the cow is not just an ignorant belief that stands in the way of progress. Like all concepts of the sacred and the profane, this one affects the physical world; it defines the relationships that are important for the maintenance of Indian society.

Indians have the sacred cow; we have the "sacred" car and the "sacred" dog. It would not occur to us to propose the elimination of automobiles and dogs from our society without carefully considering the consequences, and we should not propose the elimination of zebu cattle without first understanding their place in the social order of India.

Human society is neither random nor capricious. The regularities of thought and behavior called culture are the principal mechanisms by which we human beings adapt to the world around us. Practices and beliefs can be rational or irrational, but a society that fails to adapt to its environment is doomed to extinction. Only those societies that draw the necessities of life from their surroundings without destroying those surroundings, inherit the earth. The West has much to learn from the great antiquity of Indian civilization, and the sacred cow is an important part of that lesson.

8

Social Structure
and Social Organization

In its simplest sense, a society is an organized group of people who interact with one another and form a cohesive unit. This definition would include not only humans but also baboons, bees, ants, and other nonhuman "social" animals. The definition of society does not include culture, for we can talk of baboon "social organization" without saying that baboons have culture. It is only when we speak of human societies that we refer to the concept of culture, for among people we find that the basic principle around which the group is organized is the way of life that its members share—their culture. The society is a cohesive unit because its members share the same language, values, knowledge, and beliefs. In short, the society is unified by its members' way of life and the fact that they tend to think of themselves as belonging to the same group. Societies range from a complex civilization like "American society" to a small unit such as an army company or a ship's crew. There need not be political boundaries to set it off from other societies; although when we speak of societies we tend to think in terms of nation-states, a society can exist below the national level or across national boundaries. For example, we might speak of Jewish society or Chinese society as existing within many separate political units.

A Definition of Society

The term **society** refers to an association of individuals. When we speak of social relations, we are referring to interactions among members of that group. Further, when we speak of social organization, we are referring to patterns of interaction. We assume that the personal interactions within a society have some sort of structure, and in analyzing that structure we tend to assign behavior to certain categories. In doing so we divide the people of the society into various groups, such as families, clans, classes, clubs, and so on. Further, we can analyze behavior in political, economic, or religious terms, although people

might not keep these categories separate in their everyday life.

Society, then, is an artificial construct that is used by anthropologists to see patterns in people's behavior. As we group these patterns together they take on a structure, and the units of that structure are called **institutions.** An institution is simply a pattern of behavior that focuses on a central theme. We may speak of a market as an economic institution, but there is more to a market than a place where people buy and sell things. By *market* we also mean the activities involved in production, distribution, selling, and consumption. We refer to the patterns of behavior involved in exchanging goods, and the values and preferences and other factors that affect the exchange. Thus a market as an economic institution is much more than a matter of supply and demand or a set of sales figures—it is the whole set of behaviors involved in any exchange of goods.

The same is true for religion. When we speak of a religious institution we are referring to much more than a church and what goes on inside it. We include all behaviors that might be considered religious, such as the extent to which behavior is controlled by religious beliefs or the extent to which belief systems serve to integrate the community. When we combine all these patterns of behavior, we can begin to see how various institutions are tied together and how they affect one another. This tells us the basic structure of the society.

Structure and Function

Anthropologists seek to understand the structure of a society—how its institutions fit together and how each element in the structure functions to maintain the whole. We sometimes speak of the "functional integration" of society because the concepts of structure and function are intertwined and interdependent. Every society is an integrated unit made up of many different parts, each of which is related to the others and each of which contributes something different by functioning in its own way to keep the system intact. As an institution changes, the others react to that change and compensate for it, thereby changing themselves in the process. But all the parts remain integrated into a single unit.

We can see how this principle of functional integration operates on a number of levels in our society. For example, on a rather general level we can discuss the relationship among three different institutions—religion, economics, and politics—in American society. The American political system is basically democratic, offering a certain amount of freedom to each person to act as he or she wishes within certain limits. The economic system is a free-enterprise system in which each individual can engage in whatever economic activities he or she chooses (again,

within certain limits). Personal achievement is fostered by political freedom. Finally, the Judeo-Christian ethic emphasizes hard work, saving, and achievement, so that a religious person is not expected to devote all of his or her time to worship but instead is encouraged to work hard for the sake of family and community. In the process he or she is encouraged to take advantage of the economic and political freedoms of American society. In this way the political ideology of democracy, the economic system of free enterprise, and the religious ideology of the Judeo-Christian ethic combine to form an integrated unit centered on a basic theme. We could also assume that if one of these basic institutions were to change, it would affect the others. If Americans suddenly adopted a religious outlook that stressed withdrawal and prayer rather than work, or if the political system became less democratic, the

Markets like this one in Chichicastenango, Guatemala, are much more than physical structures; they bring people together for purposes of selling surplus goods, purchasing necessities, and for a variety of social reasons.

free-enterprise system would no longer be effective and would probably be replaced by something else. But in the long run a new way of integrating the parts of the social structure would be found.

We can also look at functional analysis on a smaller scale: We can search for direct links between certain aspects of the social structure and the immediate results they produce. Government economists do this all the time when they talk about the relationship between inflation and unemployment or the cost of living and the balance of trade. Criminologists make the same kinds of functional links between different parts of the social structure when they relate a major drug arrest in Marseilles to a rise in street crime in New York City. As the drug supply diminishes, the demand cannot be met; hence the cost rises, and the crime rate rises, because people who need money to support a drug habit must find a way to get more money.

It is important to point out that we cannot observe social structure any more than we can observe culture. Both are abstractions. What we observe is the behavior of human beings in a social context. As we do so, it becomes obvious that this behavior is predictable and that it follows some sort of pattern. From this we conclude that there is a structure that guides social relations, even though it is an abstract structure that we apply as observers rather than as actors. This structure is just as real as the structure we apply to organisms or to language; it is a generalization about the relationships among parts. Just as all organisms are unique, all societies are unique, and we can compare them only by making generalizations about the similarities in their structures. Without concepts such as structure and function, we could not have a science dealing with human behavior any more than we could have a science of anatomy or physiology.

The American auto industry is part of a larger economic and social structure that extends to the OPEC countries of the Middle East and the auto producers of Europe and Japan.

Manifest and Latent Functions

Another aspect of the concept of function is what the sociologist Robert Merton calls manifest and latent functions. Merton points out that an activity may have more than one function, and one or more of its functions may be unintended or at least not obvious to those who practice it. The **manifest function** of a pattern of behavior is the effect or result that is apparent to the members of the society. If you ask people why they do a certain thing, the reason they give will be the manifest function of that behavior—the agreed-upon value of the action, the ideal as opposed to the real. The **latent function** of the behavior is the effect or result that is not apparent to the members of the society who engage in it.

An example may make this concept easier to grasp. In American society, when a person dies we often follow a pattern of behavior called a funeral. This can include a religious service, a meeting of family and friends either before or after the service, and a service in which the body is buried. If we were to ask Americans who engage in this practice what its functions were, we would probably get some of the following answers: (1) The funeral serves to dispose of the body of the deceased, an obvious necessity; (2) the gathering of friends and relatives at the funeral helps console the family of the deceased, supporting them and comforting them in their time of sorrow; (3) the religious service, in which prayers are offered for the deceased, is designed to aid the soul or spirit in its journey to whatever awaits in the afterlife; (4) in addition, part of the funeral service can be devoted to the achievements of the deceased, and thus can serve as a memorial to that person, which also comforts the family. All of these functions are fairly obvious and can be termed *manifest* because they are known to the participants.

But what about some of the less obvious functions of the funeral, those that might be apparent to the anthropologist looking at it from the outside but not to the participants?

The wide variety of tombstones in this cemetery indicates that they do more than just identify the grave site.

For one thing, the funeral service is a way of displaying wealth. The family may not want to admit it, but their actions are clearly part of a pattern that is commonly called **conspicuous consumption:** The things that we buy (consume) and then openly (conspicuously) display are designed not just for our own enjoyment but also for the impression they will make on others. This pattern may be seen in many aspects of funerals. The size, shape, and material of the casket are important, not because we are concerned about whether the deceased will be comfortable in the grave, and certainly not because we are worried about how long the casket will last under the ground, but simply because for the few minutes that it will be seen by those who attend the funeral it will serve as an indicator of wealth and social position. Surely no one would claim that the deceased is more likely to be admitted to heaven in a metal casket than in a pine box!

Other aspects of the funeral also reveal the wealth and social position of the members of the family who have been left behind. The car at the head of the funeral procession is a good example. The head car is usually a Cadillac limousine, not because it gives a smoother ride than a Ford or a Chevy, although it might, but because it is a high-prestige car. Other ways of exhibiting wealth include the type of funeral home used, the way it is decorated, and the number and type of floral arrangements displayed. In addition, there is the cemetery itself, which offers another chance for conspicuous consumption. The location of the grave, the neighborhood in which the cemetery is located, even the view from the grave site (as if the deceased could enjoy it!)—all are examples of how the family uses the funeral to exhibit its wealth. Finally, the tombstone will vary in size and quality according to how much the family wishes to spend. Again, this expense is not so much for the deceased as for those left behind.

Another latent function of a funeral is to provide a break in the routine for those who attend, although most people will argue that they would rather have the deceased back among the living than use the funeral as an excuse to have a family reunion. In the process of bringing people together, a funeral also serves the latent function of reinforcing the solidarity of the group. Members of the typical American middle-class family often are scattered throughout the city, state, and even the country, making close contact difficult and family gatherings a relatively rare occurrence. However, the funeral offers the family a chance to get together (weddings serve the same purpose). A funeral can also have the latent function of raising another person to a higher social position. When someone dies, the position he or she held is vacated and must be filled by someone else. A son, for example, might be called upon to take an active role in the funeral, or he might

at least be mentioned by the clergyman who performs the ceremony—a subtle hint that he has a new role to fill.

Finally, a funeral can help alleviate the fear of death. Those who participate in the ceremony become aware of their concern for the deceased, and in the process they convince themselves that, as they have not forgotten the deceased, they will not be forgotten by their friends and relatives when they are gone.

Of course, it might be difficult to get most people to admit they had any of these feelings when they attended a funeral, which is one reason anthropologists stress the importance of studying the latent functions of social behavior as well as its manifest functions. Only by analyzing what, to the objective and impartial observer, people appear to be doing, as well as what they think or say they are doing, can we get a full and clear picture of how a society works. The functions of various institutions cannot be limited to those listed by the people involved, for as we have seen in the example of a funeral, there are many more functions that are obvious to outside observers. To ignore these functions would be to ignore a large portion of the structure of society. If our goal is to understand human behavior, then we must examine it from all points of view and not limit ourselves to what the members of a particular group want us to see or to the functions that they consider important.

Status

The concept of social structure in general, or the structure of any given society, really refers to the typical behavior of members of the society. If every person behaved differently and every situation were completely new and unexpected, there would be no way to predict how people will act. Thus if we are to arrive at this kind of abstraction, social behavior must be consistent. People must act pretty much the same way in similar situations, even though, technically, no two sets of events are exactly the same. As participants in society, therefore, we must be able to generalize about social interaction; that is, we must be able to say that even though the interaction we are now engaging in is unique, it is similar enough to one we engaged in in the past that we can expect others to recognize it as such and to act in a predictable way. In other words, social interaction is based on two factors: *expectation* and *reciprocation*.

The fact that we can predict what others will do in a certain situation is basic to the structuring of social behavior. Without the ability to predict behavior, social interaction would be disorderly and chaotic. Imagine what it would be like if you never knew how anyone would act toward you. As we saw in Chapter 3, every society has a set of unwritten rules that governs people's behavior; part of the socialization process involves learning those rules and becoming comfortable with them. If you went into a restaurant, and instead of giving you a menu or asking you what you would like to eat the waiter simply told you what he had chosen for you, you might be upset. But that doesn't happen because in our society, as in all others, there is a way of defining most situations so that the expected behavior is clear. Behavior is structured and orderly because we send out signals that define situations and place them in categories that we and those with whom we interact can relate to.

The definition of the situation rests in part on the **status** of those involved. The term comes from the Latin word for position, and, in general, refers to the social position a person holds relative to a particular situation. A status can be either **ascribed**, if a person is born into it, or **achieved**, if it requires competition or special effort. "Sister," "male," and "king of England" are all ascribed statuses, since the individual has nothing to say about whether he or she occupies such a position. Examples of achieved statuses include "student," "bricklayer," and "husband." In all societies the majority of statuses are ascribed. Even in our own society most of the positions we hold were determined for us at birth. Besides age and sex, over which we have no control, being born into a particular ethnic and social group largely determines our place in society.

We can arrive at the structure of a society by assigning statuses or social positions to all of its members as actors in a social setting. For example, when two individuals meet for the first time and are introduced, they immediately assign the status of "newcomer" both to themselves and to the other person. The situation then takes on structure; in fact, we could describe it with a mathematical formula: (newcomer + newcomer) × introduction = handshake. This formula applies to all situations governed by the same rules, so that even though we have never seen a given person before, we are reasonably sure that he or she will reciprocate and shake our hand. If this does not happen, we immediately assign the other person a new status, something like "different kind of newcomer," and make a mental note of all that we know about him or her so that we can predict the behavior of others more accurately in the future.

We are constantly assigning statuses to the people with whom we come into contact in our daily lives. Often we have clues about what status to assign people we have not met before. Then, as we get to know them better, we change our views of them, and hence their social position. When we meet a policeman in uniform, for example, we immediately know what his social position is because the uniform gives us the cue we need. However, if we meet an off-duty policeman socially and he is not introduced as such, we probably will not immediately know that he is a policeman (although some people might disagree with this), and we would assign him to the category of strangers who are not yet defined.

A status is associated with a collection of rights and duties. In terms of social interaction, if behavior is to have structure, we must be able to expect certain things of others (rights) and they must be able to expect certain things of us (duties). Obviously, not

Ralph Linton (1893–1953)

Ralph Linton began his career as an archeologist, but later turned to cultural anthropology. His ethnographic fieldwork took him to Polynesia and Madagascar, as well as on archeological expeditions in Latin America and the United States. He developed the concepts of status and role in his classic book *The Study of Man* (1936). Linton was a leading figure in the development of the subfield of psychological anthropology in the 1930s and 1940s, and published widely on the topic of culture and personality. He also was instrumental in promoting the study of culture change, and published several studies on the acculturation of Native Americans (see Chapter 13).

every status entails the same collection of rights and duties. The rights and duties attached to the status of police officer are quite clear. Police officers, by virtue of the authority vested in them by law, are entitled to strict obedience. In return, as private citizens, we are entitled to fair and impartial enforcement of the law and protection from violations of the law. The fact that this ideal situation is not always achieved, and that there are varying interpretations of what is fair and how far the law extends, does not negate the fact that the status of the police (and those of private citizen, criminal, etc.) defines a situation in which we can predict behavior with reasonable success. Remember, status is a combination of ideal situation and real behavior. We are always revising our views of people in the light of their behavior and the behavior of others in similar positions, so that the structure we assign to society changes as the statuses of various groups of people change.

Role

If a status is a position with certain rights and duties, then we can refer to the behaviors that are appropriate to that position as a **role**. A role refers to the behavior that is expected in a particular situation. Thus the position of professor means that the person's role is to act as teacher and scholar. The traditional position of father entails the role of breadwinner, decision maker, and general head of the household. This role is changing rapidly, showing that the concept of social structure is not static.

Role and status cannot be separated. Just as statuses combine to form the social structure, roles combine to form the behavior patterns that we call institutions. The concepts of status and role are meaningful only in relation to other statuses and roles, and therefore they cannot exist by themselves. Every person occupies a number of different statuses, each with its own appropriate role behavior, and usually these positions operate in harmony with one another. A man might occupy the statuses of bank president, churchgoer, country club member, upper-class suburban dweller, husband, father, lodge member, and so on. All of these positions fit together, and we would not be surprised to find a person who occupied all of them at once. On the other hand, we would be shocked to find a person occupying such an unlikely combination of statuses as bank president, race car driver, ex-convict, ghetto dweller, and country club member. The behaviors expected in some of these positions would conflict with those expected in others, and while it would not be impossible for one person to occupy all of these positions, it would certainly be unlikely.

If this sounds like an obscure theory intended to make life more confusing, it is not; it is exactly the model you yourself follow every day, only you do so unconsciously. Every time you interact with other people you are following the model that you have constructed in your mind as to how society is structured and what your position in that structure is. While it might not be necessary to know the structure of your own society to be a functioning member of that society, it is essential to know how another society works if you want to understand that society. Just as many of you learned to speak English long before you studied grammar and learned the formal structure of the language, so do you learn the rules of social behavior without being aware of their structure. If, as an anthropologist, you want to learn the rules for another society, it helps to know what their basis is and how your own society works. Thus anthropology teaches us not only about other people, but, most important, about ourselves.

Changes in Status and Role

The concepts of status and role are fairly stable for society as a whole, although they are constantly changing for the members of the society. The social structure is based on a certain number of positions, which are filled by various individuals. In terms of the overall structure of the society, it does not matter who fills what positions. Thus although the new army recruit is likely to spend only a few years in the service, making for a rapid turnover of personnel, the army itself remains intact over time. Likewise, although the makeup of Congress changes every two years, the present session of Congress is not too different from the last one, nor will the next one be too different from the present one.

On the other hand, for the individual member of society status and role are dynamic; they change often and sometimes drastically. Our statuses and roles change throughout our lifetime. They change with age, from child to adult to senior citizen; they change with generation, from child to parent to grandparent; and they change as we learn new skills and achieve new social positions. In addition, one's status and role can change in relation to the social situation, in that people can retain the same level of skills and the same income, yet their relative status will change as others pass them by.

Throughout life we are constantly learning new roles. We learn our first roles through the training we receive as children. We are taught what is appropriate in each situation, not according to an absolute standard, but on the basis of our ascribed characteristics. Thus we are taught one thing if we are male, another if we are female; we learn different limitations based on our social position. Later in life we may reject the position assigned us and seek a different one, in which case we have to learn new patterns of behavior to go with our new status.

A role must be validated if we are to achieve the status to which that role is attached. Once we have in mind what that status is, we set out to gain the right responses from people, to convince them that we are entitled to the status we seek. If we want to achieve the status of student, we dress the

In recent years women have moved into jobs that were traditionally regarded as "men's work."

way a student would dress, carry books under our arms, attend classes (sometimes), and engage in the behaviors appropriate to students. On the other hand, if we want to achieve the status of "deviant," we simply act in a way that we think will convince people we are different and do not follow the rules. The degree to which we do this depends on just how deviant we want to be considered. Curiously enough, even the path to deviance is predictable in our society.

The movement from one status to another is called **social mobility**. We usually speak of mobility in terms of movement from a lower to a higher position, such as from the lower class to the middle class or from a working-class, blue-collar job to a middle-class, white-collar job. As we move from one status to

another, we seek to have our new position validated by society. For example, we usually think of membership in the middle class as being mainly a function of income. Yet in recent years many members of the working class, especially those who belong to strong unions, have experienced a rise in income that places them in the middle class by income standards. However, if you were to place two individuals—a schoolteacher earning $25,000 per year and a truck driver earning $35,000 per year—on a scale of social standing, you would probably distinguish between them on the basis of factors other than income. You might consider, for example, the fact that the teacher has had five years of college and wears dress clothes to work, while the teamster probably has not gone to college, might not have finished high school, and does not wear dress clothes when working. In fact, the teamster himself would probably recognize these differences and would have higher hopes for his children, including a college education.

In such cases social mobility is obviously based on more than income. If the teamster wants to move into the middle class, he will have to change in many ways. Some of these changes can be made simply by earning a higher income. With more money, one can move to a better neighborhood, but a more expensive car, and wear better clothes. But other changes cannot be made without great difficulty, and often only by the next generation. Thus the teamster sends his children to college, not because education is important to him in making a living, but because it is an important part of his effort to validate his role as a member of the middle class. While he may not be able to return to school himself, he wants to be sure that his children will have their middle-class membership validated. Likewise, the speech patterns that identify the teamster as less educated—frequent use of double negatives or such words as *ain't*—cannot always be dropped in a single generation, but they can be avoided by future generations. Again, this is not because one needs to speak "textbook English" to communicate but because middle-class status is more likely to be validated if one speaks the way an educated person would.

For many years peasant villagers in Mexico, Central America, and parts of the South American Andes have relied on a system designed to keep the political and religious activities of the community operating. At the same time, this system, called the **civil-religious hierarchy**, allows individuals to validate their status in the community while participating in a process of society-approved social mobility.

In the most traditional form of the system the process of community service began when a boy became a man, and lasted intermittently until he was a village elder. The status of manhood was usually conferred when he got married, although in some communities it was deferred until he fathered a child. Working for the village meant that for one-year periods he would perform certain jobs for which he received no financial remuneration, but instead acquired status and respect. These tasks were hierarchically ranked, the high-status jobs being those that required not only lots of time but also considerable financial burdens. The positions were divided between religious and civil jobs, and over the course of several decades men would rotate or alternate between them while simultaneously working their way up through the hierarchy. At the bottom of the system on the religious side might be serving as the maintenance man of the church. Its equivalent on the civil side might be to serve the community as the town crier. Neither of these posts was very demanding in terms of time or resources and the status that went with them was correspondingly low. Increasingly the individual assumed jobs that took more and more time and that brought him higher status in the eyes of the community, though there might be fairly long interruptions between service. When a man was in his 40s or 50s he periodically held posts that were practically full-time occupations and that were financially quite burdensome for his family. These might include sponsorship of a major

religious festival or serving as the village judge. By the time he was an elder, he would have served in a number of these posts and could expect to be left alone during his remaining years.

It should be noted that there are a number of variations on the civil-religious hierarchy as it is actually played out. While the male household head might be listed as the sponsor of a particular religious festival, in many places the job is performed by the couple. In some communities even the title that accompanies the task is shared equally between the male and female household representatives.

Although the civil-religious hierarchy is an institution designed to keep the important activities of the community going without resorting to taxing the residents, it has many other components and functions, and these are what interest anthropologists. It serves to strictly identify community membership, because only those born in the village may hold office and only those who participate can fully achieve proper status in the eyes of their fellow villagers. In addition, it often has an economic leveling effect. As an individual becomes more established as an adult and has a greater opportunity to improve his economic situation, he finds himself taking on more and more expensive community service jobs. The tradeoff is the acquisition of status in exchange for financial loss. Of course, there are exceptions to this. In some communities it is possible to serve the community in various capacities without incurring a big financial burden. In fact, a number of recent studies have shown that the civil-religious system may result in the further stratification of communities where the custom is for rich families to assume sponsorship of costly fiestas, while poor families are relegated to the less expensive, and less prestigious, undertakings.

Over the past 50 years the civil-religious hierarchy has been transformed by outside interference and changes in community attitudes. No longer do men and their families always feel an obligation to serve the community unquestioningly, and many do not.

Also, civil jobs that used to be part of the community service are now often filled by political appointees or elected officials. On the religious side, the Roman Catholic Church has regulated some of the ceremonial activities that were traditionally performed by males seeking to obtain and validate their status in the community.

Role Conflict

Sometimes we occupy several different positions at once and the behavior that is appropriate to one is not in harmony with the behavior that is appropriate to another. This creates a situation called **role conflict**. Role conflict is often the theme of soap operas in which the plot centers on a person who is torn between two duties; no matter which one he or she chooses, someone will be hurt or some duty will be violated. One of the basic problems with role conflict is that other people hold conflicting expectations of you and your behavior, and no matter how you act in a given situation, you cannot satisfy everyone. This problem is described quite well by the anthropologist Lloyd Fallers, who discusses the plight of the African chief under British colonial rule.[1]

The setting of this study is among the Basoga, a tribal group located in East Africa. Prior to the arrival of the British, the chief had a clearly defined set of rules to guide his interaction with members of his society. The Basoga chiefdom was not a secure position, and constant warfare and threats of revolt checked the ruler's power. Thus, if the chief was to remain in office, he had to balance opposing factions, and the lack of a stable leadership position shows that such a balance was hard to maintain for long periods.

When the British took over, they wanted to set up a stable system through which to administer their colonies. In order to do this, they made the position of chief more secure, giving him both economic and military support. The chief received a fixed salary from the native treasury and was granted civil service status, complete with a pension. All of these changes strengthened the chief's ties to the British, but at the same time they weakened his ties to his own people. The salary he received lowered his prestige in the eyes of his fellow tribesmen, for it made him dependent on others. The chiefdom became an achieved status based on education rather than an ascribed status based on royal birth, and the fact that the chief was not required to have royal blood cheapened the office in the eyes of the natives. Thus the men who held the position of chief were torn between two worlds as their ties with the British strengthened and they moved farther away from the traditional role of the Basoga leader.

Also, the duties of the two roles came into conflict. As a member of the British civil service, the chief had to take on a new set of values that often conflicted with the values he held as a Basoga tribesman. As a Basoga, the chief owed loyalty to members of his own family or tribe and responded to the requests of his subjects according to how closely they were related to him and how obligated he felt toward them. However, as a civil servant, he was obliged to be impartial and not grant favors to anyone for any reason. The result is that at different times, depending on the individual and the situation, both systems of values functioned. When the chief was impartial, he alienated his friends and relatives and went against his own values. On the other hand, when he gave in to his tribesmen's demands, he failed in his duty as a civil servant and stood a good chance of losing his job. One result of this role conflict was a rapid turnover among chiefs. Either the chief was caught breaking civil service rules, or else he applied them strictly and was framed by his own family and friends, who resented his violation of traditional obligations.

---

[1] Lloyd A. Fallers, "The Predicament of the Modern African Chief: An Instance from Uganda," *American Anthropologist* 57, no. 2 (1955): 290–297.

Social Stratification

In addition to holding a particular status in many different social circles, we all have a more general position in our society that is based on the sum of all of our statuses. Every society ranks its members according to their overall position. In larger groups such as the population of the United States, this ranking is inexact, but in small groups in which all the members know and interact with one another as individuals, the entire population can be ranked, with each person occupying a separate rung on the social ladder. The status ranking of the members of a group is called **social stratification**. It is based on both ascribed and achieved statuses: People are ranked according to ascribed characteristics such as age, sex, and family background, and according to achieved characteristics such as occupation, wealth, or special talents.

Every society assigns people to different positions on the basis of sex, and women are almost always given a lower status than men. Age is also used as a basis for assigning people to various positions on the social ladder; when

Traditionally many cultures assigned tasks by gender. It is the women in rural Mongolia who harvest the hay.

combined with sex, it forms a concrete set of standards by which people are ranked. In traditional China, for example, two general principles operated in determining each person's rank: Maleness was ranked above femaleness, and age was a positive value. Thus the oldest man in the village was usually the highest-ranking member of his lineage, even though he might not have special skills or above-average wisdom and experience. This is not to suggest that in traditional China only age and sex mattered—obviously, people were respected for their achievements as well. However, in any social setting age and sex were taken into account.

The universal distinction between the sexes is usually backed up by a myth or folk wisdom that justifies the social order as somehow divine, correct, or in accord with the order of the universe. Though women work as hard as or harder than men in most societies, there is always a division of labor by sex, a division over which the women have little control. Each culture has developed its own ideas about the nature of women, and often these ideas are quite different. For example, we have traditionally seen women as ministering angels. This "Florence Nightingale" image is not at all like the traditional ideas about the nature of women among the Iroquois Indians, who, when they captured a prisoner in a battle with another tribe, would turn him over to the women for torture because women were thought to be much more sadistic than men. Only a foe who had shown exceptional bravery would be granted mercy: He would be killed by the men as a reward for his courage.

Because of the image different societies have of women, they are assigned certain jobs as "fitting." This is an important element of social stratification in our culture, and one against which the women's movement has reacted strongly. Thus we traditionally viewed women as suited for various kinds of jobs that required "feminine skills." Women should be librarians, secretaries, or waitresses, but not construction workers, bank presidents, or professors, according to traditional American cultural values. Fortunately, these views are changing, and with this change comes a realization of the fact that our system of social stratification, like everyone else's in the world, is culture-bound.

In other cultures occupations are also assigned to different sexes on the basis of commonly accepted views about what is appropriate to each sex. Among the Arapesh of New Guinea, for example, women are expected to carry heavier loads than men because their heads, on which they balance their baskets, are thought to be so much harder and stronger. In Tasmania seal hunting is women's work. They swim out to the seal rocks, stalk the animals, and kill them. They also hunt opossum, an activity that requires them to climb large trees. Men would not think of performing these tasks because it is agreed that they are "women's work." In Madagascar men make seed beds and terraces where rice is to be planted, while women do the backbreaking work of transplanting the rice. Such division of labor is typical of most societies, and there is no apparent logic to the way in which jobs are assigned that can explain this practice in cross-cultural terms.

Also, the division of labor by sex can change over time as the demands on one or both sexes change. One of the authors found in his study of a Swiss peasant village that in earlier times men and women had shared the agricultural tasks according to a fairly clear division of labor. Certain jobs were considered appropriate for men because they required more physical strength, while others were reserved mainly for women. Thus agricultural duties were shared, but clearly divided. After World War II, however, men began to take jobs in factories, and this prevented them from doing farm work. At the same time, they wanted to keep their farms going so that they would have something to fall back on if their new jobs did not prove to be stable. As the men spent more of their time in the factories, the women began to take over more of the agricultural labor, including what had formerly been defined as male jobs, such as harvesting and carrying the hay to the barns. The men helped out after work and on weekends, but the women had to bear the brunt of the agricultural labor if the farm was to be maintained. As it stands now, cultural views about what is appropriate for each of the sexes have changed to match the new economic situation—factory

In a number of societies, not only are men and women assigned different tasks, but they are also set apart by their dress, as illustrated by these veiled women from India.

jobs are for men, and household tasks (including farming) are for women. Even this pattern is changing, however, as young girls are finding jobs on assembly lines where they work side by side with men.

Stratification by sex is found in almost all societies—there may be exceptions, but we cannot think of one. This stratification may be expressed in many ways. For example, in some societies married women wear veils, a sign that a woman is looked on as a man's property and no other man should see her face. In a typical peasant society one rarely sees a woman in a bar or a coffee house; these places are reserved for males. Women gather in places associated with females tasks, or in the home, itself the domain of the woman much of the time. Most, if not all, societies link all sex-derived status distinctions to the biological differences between men and women. We should recognize, however, that just because this biological difference is invoked to justify sex discrimination does not mean that it is a valid basis. In fact, stratification by sex is a cultural practice based on cultural values, not biological factors.

Stratification on the basis of age is a different matter. There is no denying the validity of at least some of the biological and cultural arguments in support of inequality among age groups. There is no substitute for experience as far as certain skills or abilities are concerned. This does not mean that there is a biological reason to assign all of the privileges of high status to older members of the population. We would not want all 80-year-old Americans to be allowed to drive simply because of their supposed maturity and good judgment, any more than we would want 12-year-olds to drive because their reflexes are quick. We compromise by requiring minimal amounts of both maturity and quick reflexes, in that we set age limits on who may drive, but also require people to pass a performance test in order to obtain a driver's license. Again, not all societies would treat stratification on the basis of age the same way we do, and this too shows that stratification on any basis is mainly a cultural question, not a biological one.

Caste

One of the most extreme forms of social stratification is the organization of society into highly separate groups known as **castes**. A caste can be defined as a group of people who are jointly assigned to a certain position in the social hierarchy. Each person is born into a caste and cannot change it throughout his or her life. Caste membership is based on ascribed characteristics such as the caste membership of one's parents, which is passed down from one generation to the next. It can also be based on physical features such as skin color, again an ascribed characteristic that is inherited. The boundaries of a caste are maintained through the practice of endogamy; that is, a person may marry only someone from his or her own caste. Thus if there are genetic factors that determine caste membership, such as skin color, these tend to be maintained by the ban on marrying outside the group.

The best-known caste system was found in traditional India. Vestiges of the system remain, especially in rural areas, although it was formally outlawed when India became independent from Great Britain. In this system caste membership carries with it a total social ranking. Every aspect of a person's life is limited by his or her caste. Because of the ascribed nature of caste membership, each local caste group is made up of related individuals, usually a set of families within the same village. Traditionally, each caste is linked with an occupation, at least ideally. A person's occupation is based on the caste into which he or she was born. A carpenter's son becomes a carpenter, just as a farmer's son becomes a farmer. Of course, in a small village there will be some occupations for which a member of the appropriate caste is not available. In such cases someone else will take the job. Such people do not change their caste, however; if a man is a member of the carpenter caste, he will remain in that caste even though his job might now consist of weaving rather than carpentry.

The caste system in India operates according to customs established by the Hindu religion. Each caste is ranked in a hierarchy according to Hindu principles that value certain kinds of behavior, especially the avoidance of acts that are thought to be polluting. For example, according to Hindu teachings it is polluting to eat meat, to come into contact with dead animals, and to engage in occupations that deal with death either literally or symbolically (such as those of a barber or a leather worker). Members of the various castes are expected to follow these teachings to a degree that depends on their level in the social hierarchy. The lowest rank, commonly called the outcastes or Untouchables, is made

up of people who eat meat and engage in polluting occupations such as sweeping or butchering. They are Untouchable because they are considered so polluted that mere contact with them would defile a member of a higher caste.

Thus in traditional India a village consists of a number of castes, each with many members. Each caste performs a certain function; each occupation is linked to a caste and limited to its members. With each caste performing a special function, all are able to survive, but they are dependent on one another. The ranking system that places castes in a social hierarchy ensures that this system will operate in a stable manner by forcing some people into occupations that they might not choose for themselves. And the entire system is supported by Hindu teachings, which stress the fact that different behaviors are appropriate for each social level and hold

In India tasks are divided not only on the basis of age and sex, but also according to caste.

that it is wrong to avoid doing what is prescribed for one's station in life. Hindu teachings also say that if one performs the duties of one's caste well, through reincarnation one will be born into a higher caste in the next life.

The caste system in India survived for so long because of a number of factors. First, it enjoyed religious blessing. To deviate from one's ascribed role was regarded as religious blasphemy. To the true believers, challenging one's position in this life might result in reincarnation into a lower position in the next life. Second, one of the manifest functions of the caste system was to keep society functioning with a minimum of disruption. If everyone performed her or his hereditary tasks, the daily life of the village continued to operate. The system of redistribution of goods and services ensured that all would be provided for adequately—that is, according to their station in life. Finally, and very importantly, if an individual was unhappy with his or her position in the caste system, until relatively recent times there was really no alternative but to accept the situation as ungrudgingly as possible. Should someone whose hereditary role was that of a potter entertain notions of being a landowner, it simply was not possible to achieve that position. Moving to another community and declaring that you were from a caste different from the one into which you were born probably wouldn't work either. Sooner or later the truth would be learned, and the consequences for deception were severe.

If the caste system was restrictive in many ways, it also provided a type of security. Unlike many individuals in our own society who agonize over what career to choose and who sometimes regret their decisions, participants in India's caste system derived some comfort in knowing from a very early age what their role in life would be. They probably realized—and in traditional rural India still do—that there was little or nothing that they could or should try to do to change it. In other words, it could plausibly be argued that people did not feel deprived or frus-

trated at not being able to do something or be someone else when they and others around them firmly and sincerely believed that these were not possible options. However, it would be wrong to convey the impression of a caste-ridden traditional India as always harmonious. Historically, the caste system was exploitative and the chief beneficiaries were—and are—the members of the upper castes. The work of social scientists has shown that where the caste system still operates very often lower-caste individuals recognize and resent the religiously-sanctioned positions in which they find themselves.

The term *caste* is not limited to India and can be applied to other stratified groups in which membership is hereditary and permanent. For example, consider the racial situation in the United States. The relationship between the higher castes and the Untouchables in India is similar to that between blacks and whites, since they form separate social groups that are arranged in a hierarchy and maintained through endogamy. Membership in either group is both hereditary and permanent. In traditional India caste also limits occupational choice, or at least bars certain people from engaging in certain occupations. The same situation used to apply in the United States, and can still be found to a certain degree throughout the country: Certain jobs are commonly held by blacks, while others are considered suitable only for whites.

In both traditional India and the Old South there were rigid rules separating the castes, and certain types of contact were felt to be polluting. Note that the taboos against intercaste contact are symbolic rather than literal, as is shown by the fact that they are applied inconsistently. For example, sexual contact is supposedly polluting, but in both India and the Old South there was a double standard. Upper-caste men (either high-caste Indians or white slave masters) were permitted to have sexual contact with lower-caste women, while sexual contact of the opposite sort (low-caste men with high-caste women, or black men with white women) was forbid-

Until a little more than two decades ago, laws preventing interracial contact in public places in the American South reflected a situation similar to the caste system in traditional India.

den. Again, in both cases the high and low castes were interdependent, and the rules governing other kinds of contact between them did not cut into the upper caste's demand for lower-caste products and services.

In other words, the distinction between whites and blacks in the United States, and between the higher and lower castes in India, was made strong enough to maintain clear social boundaries but not so strong as to cause

Although change is occurring slowly in South Africa, apartheid helped maintain the dominance of the white minority by creating a caste system based on race.

total isolation and thus reduce the economic and social advantages to be gained by the higher castes at the expense of the lower ones. The high caste stood to gain not only in economic terms, by exploiting low-caste labor, but also in social terms, for example, by gaining prestige and a higher position in the social hierarchy.

The parallels between India and some aspects of our own society illustrate one of the most positive values of cross-cultural studies. Americans, who tend to have little experience in studying foreign cultures, have a limited perspective toward their own way of life. By bringing in outside models like the caste system of India—models that provide clearer examples of social situations that we can find in our own society—anthropology can broaden our perspective. The study of other cultures enables us to see similarities between those cultures and our own, rather than viewing everything around us as "American." Indeed, the parallels between caste in India and the racial situation in the United States are striking, whether we accept them or not.

Class

Another form of social stratification is the division of society into groups that we call **classes**. Class membership is based on a number of factors, including wealth, education, and occupation. To a much greater extent than a caste system, a class system ranks people on the basis of achieved as well as ascribed characteristics. Class membership is largely subjective; members of the lower classes tend to place themselves slightly higher, while those in the higher classes tend to look down on those below them and to rank them lower than they would rank themselves. Outsiders' rankings are equally subjective, since they are based on characteristics that seem important to the outsider but might not be important to the people themselves. There is no single way of defining a person's class, because class is a combination of factors, any one of which can take on greater or lesser importance relative to the others. For example, the "upper crust" of American society might be much less wealthy than some of the

The only hunting permitted in Ohio on Sundays is fox hunting, typically an upper-class activity. This offers a good illustration of how the law reinforces the inequities of the class system.

nouveau riche, those business tycoons who have made a fortune in recent years but still lack the sophistication of the older, more established families.

Classes tend to be endogamous, but the rules against marrying outside one's class are by no means rigid. We tend to seek out partners from the same class, not because there are rules that guide us in that direction, but because similarities in income, education, and general life style create similar tastes and preferences among members of the same class. In fact, in our own society there are many pressures, some of them not very subtle, that dictate whom we may choose as mates, and these pressures are based mainly on a combination of class and caste characteristics—race and social position. Of course, the system is not rigid, as is shown by the occasional rise of a young man or woman out of the lower class and into the limelight, and thus into a higher class, where he or she can seek out its members as friends and even as mates. But the fact that such stories are newsworthy shows that they are exceptional, and that they happen in spite of the barriers between the classes. We enjoy reading a "rags to riches" story and admire people who achieve success even though they dropped out of school in the eighth grade. On the other hand, we are far less surprised—indeed, we are not surprised at all—when we read about Richard Nixon's daughter's marriage to Dwight Eisenhower's grandson, because it matches our expectations of class endogamy.

Caste versus Class

Although a caste system is more rigid than a class system, it is not completely closed, any more than a class system is completely open. Although ideally there is no mobility in a caste system, the rules that govern the interactions of members of different castes can be bent and often are. At the same time, in a class system it is supposed to be possible for

anyone to move up the social ladder. In reality, however, there is little class mobility, for there are unwritten rules that keep people from moving out of a lower class and into a higher one. The businessman who rose from the ghetto to become a millionaire can send his children to exclusive schools, drive a fancy car, and live in an expensive house, but none of these things will gain him entry into the upper-class elite, who reject him because of his original social background.

In contrast to a caste, a class is not a clearcut group. People are not fully aware of their class and therefore are not united by a feeling of class membership. In a caste system the members of a caste are united by close personal ties, and each caste has definite boundaries. In view of the connection between caste and occupation, it is difficult *not* to be aware of one's caste as one performs the daily tasks and ritual behaviors attached to that caste. Likewise, a black person in the United States must live with the fact that he or she is a different color from the majority, just as a sweeper in an Indian village is constantly reminded of his Untouchable status.

Another contrast between caste and class lies in the fact that a caste is based on kinship whereas a class is a collection of people who are similar in many ways but are not assumed to be related. Strict caste endogamy maintains the kinship basis of caste membership, while looser marriage rules in a class system, as well as the possibility of mobility, prevent classes from developing a kinship base. If classes are basically endogamous, it is for different reasons than those used to enforce and justify caste endogamy.

Finally, caste is often viewed as if it were accepted by everyone in the system because it is justified by religious or other doctrines. However, both in India and in the United States this is not the case, especially among members of the lower castes, who must do most of the "dirty work" for a small share of the social and economic rewards. Neither lower-caste people nor lower-class people accept the doctrines that justify their being where they are. In a society like ours people in the lower social levels are thought to be where they are because of their own failings. The argument is that there is free social mobility and therefore anyone with ability and ambition can get ahead, so the only reason some people are at the bottom is that they lack either talent or ambition. As we have seen, however, this doctrine is false. Unlimited mobility does not exist, and our open class system is superimposed on a closed caste system that keeps some people at the bottom of the social hierarchy because of ascribed characteristics, regardless of their talent or ambition. The suggestion that all people accept the social or religious doctrines used to justify this situation, either in American society or in Indian society, is a naive attempt by members of higher castes or classes to avoid feeling guilty about their large share of society's economic and social rewards.

Summary

A *society* is an organized group of people who interact with one another and share a common way of life or a culture. We think of the interaction between members of a society as being structured, and we can organize it into categories, or what we call *institutions*. For example, we may speak of economic institutions such as a marketplace, or legal institutions such as a court, or political institutions such as a political party.

Because behavior follows predictable patterns, we may speak of a *social structure*, or the relationship between these different patterns. For example, we may consider the relationship between religion and law in American society, noting the basis for our laws in our religious teachings. We may then speak of the *function* that an institution has in relation to this structure, such as the function of religion in providing the basis for our legal system.

Not all functions of our behavior are evident to us. Those aspects that are obvious to us are called *manifest* functions, while those that are not so obvious are called *latent* functions. In a typical American funeral manifest functions would include getting rid of the body, consoling the family, offering prayers for the deceased, and commemorating the achievements of the deceased. All of these are carried out consciously by the participants. But many other functions are also carried out, even though the people themselves might not be aware of them. These latent functions might include exhibiting wealth and social standing, providing a break in everyday routine, reinforcing the solidarity of the group, elevating a person to a higher social status, and coping with the fear of death.

We can get along with other people because we know what to expect from them in certain social situations, and in the same way they can rely on us to act in a predictable manner. In other words, social interaction is based on *expectation and reciprocation*. Part of the way we decide how to behave is determined by the *status* we assign people in a given situation. A status can be *ascribed*, based on characteristics that a person is born with or has no control over, such as age or sex or race, or it can be *achieved*, based on personal actions or abilities. For each status there is an appropriate pattern of behavior, which we call a *role*.

In the course of a lifetime an individual's social position may change, through the process known as *social mobility*. Movement from a lower to a higher social position may be associated with such changes as an increase in income or education, advance in age, development of new skills, or any other aspect of a person's life that causes others to reassess their evaluation of that person.

Every individual occupies a number of different statuses, each with its own appropriate form of behavior. Occasionally a situation arises where the different expectations are incompatible, a situation known as *role conflict.*

Every society ranks its members according to their overall position, or what we call *social stratification.* This can occur on the basis of both ascribed and achieved characteristics, including such factors as age, sex, occupation, wealth, or special abilities or talents. All societies recognize a social distinction based on sex, the women usually being given a lower status. Age is also a universal factor in social stratification, although not always in the same way. The justification for using age and sex as the basis for stratification is usually culturally derived, and although people might claim a biological reason for assigning different positions to women or to old or young people, cross-cultural research indicates that such justifications are generally incorrect.

Some societies have a system of stratification known as *caste.* A caste is a group of people jointly assigned a position in the social hierarchy, and it is usually a permanent grouping that an individual cannot change. Caste membership is based on ascribed characteristics: A person inherits membership in a caste based on the caste affiliation of one or both parents. Caste boundaries are maintained through restricted marriage patterns, or *endogamy.* The most common form of the caste system is found in India, and although it has been officially outlawed, some aspects of it still persist in many areas of that country.

In contrast to the caste system is a type of stratification known as *class.* A class is a more open grouping, less clearly defined than a caste. It is often based on such factors as wealth, education, and occupation. People can move in and out of a class, unlike a caste. Although marriage tends to occur within the limits of a class, there is no absolute rule that it must. And although people's class affiliation is at first based on that of their parents, it ultimately becomes more of an achieved position. Aspects of both caste and class can be found in American society.

Glossary

achieved status   A social position that a person holds by virtue of individual effort or competition (e.g., schoolteacher, husband, football player).

ascribed status   A social position that a person holds because of inherited characteristics, rather than obtains through individual effort (e.g., the king of England is an ascribed status, while the president of the United States is not).

caste   A group of people jointly assigned a position in the social hierarchy based on inherited characteristics; in its extreme form caste does not allow an individual to change this position.

civil-religious hierarchy   A system of holding community positions in which, over time, family representatives alternate between civil and religious offices. As one works one's way up through the hierarchy, each position extracts greater costs from the family, but in exchange the domestic unit receives increasing amounts of prestige.

class   A group of people assigned a position in society based on a combination of inherited characteristics and those traits earned through individual effort and competition. Individuals usually marry within this group but are generally able to move to a different ranking group.

conspicuous consumption The buying and open display of goods and services as a means of demonstrating one's wealth and social position.

egalitarianism A condition of social equality for all members of a society, regardless of social and biological position at birth.

institution A pattern of behavior that focuses on a central theme (e.g., economy: marketplace; politics: a political party; religion: a church).

latent function The effect or result of a pattern of behavior that is not apparent to the members of society who are engaging in it (e.g., funeral: to exhibit wealth).

manifest function The effect or result of a pattern of behavior that is apparent to the members of a society (e.g., funeral: to comfort the mourning family).

nouveau riche Describes people who have recently acquired great wealth, but have not yet developed the social characteristics to allow them entrance into the very highest level of society.

role The appropriate and expected behavior attached to a social position in a particular situation.

role conflict The condition of an individual occupying several different positions in society, in which the appropriate behaviors do not coincide in a given situation.

social mobility The process of moving from one position to another in society, and adopting the appropriate behaviors attached to the new social position.

social stratification The ranking of the members of a group according to the sum total of an individual's inherited characteristics and those traits earned through individual effort and competition.

society An organized group of individuals engaging in social interaction and forming a unit bound together by their shared way of life or culture.

status The social position a person holds relative to a particular situation; it is associated with a particular collection of rights and duties.

Questions for Discussion

1. Pick a common activity in American culture, such as a football game, a business meeting, or a wedding. What are the manifest functions of this activity? What might an anthropologist, as an outside observer, see as the latent functions of this activity?

2. What personal characteristics combine to determine your own status? Which of these characteristics are ascribed, and which are achieved? Which are more important in determining your overall status?

3. Give an example of role conflict from your own experience. What were the expected patterns of behavior in the particular situation, and how did they conflict with each other? How did you resolve the conflict?

4. What are the most common means of achieving social mobility in American society? Are these avenues for mobility equally available to all members of our society? What restrictions do you see, and whom do they affect most?

Suggestions for Additional Reading

ROBERT R. BELL and MICHAEL GORDON (Eds.), *The Social Dimension of Human Sexuality* (Boston: Little, Brown, 1972). Frank, scholarly discussions of how people's social roles reflect their sexual attitudes, including cross-cultural comparisons.

GERALD D. BERREMAN, *Caste and Other Inequities: Essays on Inequality* (Meerut, India: Folklore Institute, 1979). A collection of essays on social inequality and social stratification, with major emphasis on the caste system of India.

JOHN BROOKS, *Showing Off in America* (Boston: Little, Brown, 1979). An entertaining analysis of conspicuous consumption in the United States.

STEPHANIE COONTZ and PETA HENDERSON (Eds.), *Women's Work, Men's Property* (London: Verso, 1986). Essays on the origin and development of sex role differentiation and sexual inequality.

JOHN DOLLARD, *Caste and Class in a Southern Town*, 3rd ed. (Garden City, N.Y.: Doubleday, 1957). An analysis of social stratification in the American South, applying the concepts of caste and class.

RALPH LINTON, *The Study of Man* (New York: Appleton-Century-Crofts, 1936). One of the earliest attempts at a synthesis of anthropological theory, particularly valuable for its discussion of the concepts of status and role.

ROBERT K. MERTON, *Social Theory and Social Structure*, 2nd ed. (Glencoe, Ill.: Free Press, 1957). A modern-day classic in sociology, this volume includes a thorough discussion of the concepts of structure and function as used in the social sciences.

ASHLEY MONTAGU, *The Natural Superiority of Women*, rev. ed. (New York: Collier Books, 1968). A noted anthropologist debunks the myth of male superiority by drawing upon cross-cultural examples to present contradictions to the misconceptions about women.

TED POLHEMUS and LYNN PROCTER, *Fashion and Anti-Fashion* (London: Cox & Wyman Ltd., 1978). An amusing pictographic anthropology of clothing and adornment.

ANDREW H. WHITEFORD, *Two Cities in Latin America: A Comparative Description of Social Classes.* (Prospect Heights, Ill.: Waveland Press, 1990). A comparison of the class system in the cities of Popayán, Colombia, and Querétaro, Mexico, as they existed in the middle of this century.

R. RICHARD WOHL, "The Function of Myth in Modern Society," in Walter Goldschmidt (Ed.), *Exploring the Ways of Mankind* (New York: Holt, Rinehart and Winston, 1960), pp. 619–25. An analysis of the Horatio Alger myth in American culture, and the assumptions and misunderstandings about the process of social mobility that Alger portrays.

Society and Sex Roles

ERNESTINE FRIEDL

As a strong believer in the equality of women, Professor Friedl explores the social relationship between men and women, while asking why male domination is so prevalent cross-culturally. Although she notes that there are a number of societies in which male domination does not exist, these examples are more the exception than the rule. In this article she examines hunting and gathering societies as a means of determining the social and cultural conditions that produce equality or inequality between the sexes. Friedl argues that the source of male power in many groups is the males' control of scarce resources. Among hunters and gatherers this is animal protein. Where food or some other scarce resource is not exchanged, near equality of the sexes is likely to occur. In observing industrial societies, Friedl notes that equality takes place when both sexes control the exchange of resources.

"Women must respond quickly to the demands of their husbands," says anthropologist Napoleon Chagnon describing the horticultural Yanomamö Indians of Venezuela. When a man returns from a hunting trip, "the woman, no matter what she is doing, hurries home and quietly but rapidly prepares a meal for her husband. Should the wife be slow in doing this, the husband is within his rights to beat her. Most reprimands . . . take the form of blows with the hand or with a piece of firewood. . . . Some of them chop their wives with the sharp edge of a machete or axe, or shoot them with a barbed arrow in some nonvital area, such as the buttocks or leg."

Among the Semai agriculturalists of central Malaya, when one person refuses the request of another, the offended party suffers *punan*, a mixture of emotional pain and frustration. "Enduring *punan* is commonest when a girl has refused the victim her sexual favors," reports Robert Dentan. "The jilted man's 'heart becomes sad.' He loses his energy and his appetite. Much of the time he sleeps, dreaming of his lost love. In this state he is in fact very likely to injure himself 'accidentally.'" The Semai are afraid of violence; a man would never strike a woman.

The social relationship between men and women has emerged as one of the principal disputes occupying the attention of scholars and the public in recent years. Although the discord is sharpest in the United States, the controversy has spread throughout the world. Numerous national and international conferences, including one in Mexico sponsored by the United Nations, have drawn together delegates from all walks of life to discuss such questions as the social and political rights of each sex, and even the basic nature of males and females.

Whatever their position, partisans often invoke examples from other cultures to support their ideas about the proper role of each sex. Because women are clearly subservient to men in many societies, like the Yanomamö, some experts conclude that the natural pattern is for men to dominate. But among the Semai no one has the right to command others, and in West Africa women are often chiefs. The place of women in these societies supports the argument of those who believe that sex roles are not fixed, that if there is a natural order, it allows for many different arrangements.

The argument will never be settled as long as the opposing sides toss examples from the world's cultures at each other like intellectual stones. But the effect of biological differences on male and female behavior can be clarified by looking at known examples of the earliest forms of human society and examining the relationship between technology, social organization, environment, and sex roles. The problem is to determine the conditions in which dif-

Ernestine Friedl, "Society and Sex Roles," *Human Nature* 1(4): 68–75. Copyright © 1978 by Human Nature, Inc. Reprinted by permission of the publisher.

ferent degrees of male dominance are found, to try to discover the social and cultural arrangements that give rise to equality or inequality between the sexes, and to attempt to apply this knowledge to our understanding of the changes taking place in modern industrial society.

As Western history and the anthropological record have told us, equality between the sexes is rare; in most known societies females are subordinate. Male dominance is so widespread that it is virtually a human universal; societies in which women are consistently dominant do not exist and have never existed.

Evidence of a society in which women control all strategic resources like food and water, and in which women's activities are the most prestigious has never been found. The Iroquois of North America and the Lovedu of Africa came closest. Among the Iroquois, women raised food, controlled its distribution, and helped to choose male political leaders. Lovedu women ruled as queens, exchanged valuable cattle, led ceremonies, and controlled their own sex lives. But among both the Iroquois and the Lovedu, men owned the land and held other positions of power and prestige. Women were equal to men; they did not have ultimate authority over them. Neither culture was a true matriarchy.

Patriarchies are prevalent, and they appear to be strongest in societies in which men control significant goods that are exchanged with people outside the family. Regardless of who produces food, the person who gives it to others creates the obligations and alliances that are at the center of all political relations. The greater the male monopoly on the distribution of scarce items, the stronger their control of women seems to be. This is most obvious in relatively simple hunter-gatherer societies.

Hunter-gatherers, or foragers, subsist on wild plants, small land animals, and small river or sea creatures gathered by hand; large land animals and sea mammals hunted with spears, bows and arrows, and blow guns; and fish caught with hooks and nets. The 300,000 hunter-gatherers alive in the world today include the Eskimos, the Australian aborigines, and the Pygmies of Central Africa.

Foraging has endured for two million years and was replaced by farming and animal husbandry only 10,000 years ago; it covers more than 99 percent of human history. Our foraging ancestry is not far behind us and provides a clue to our understanding of the human condition.

Hunter-gatherers are people whose ways of life are technologically simple and socially and politically egalitarian. They live in small groups of 50 to 200 and have neither kings, nor priests, nor social classes. These conditions permit anthropologists to observe the essential bases for inequalities between the sexes without the distortions induced by the complexities of contemporary industrial society.

The source of male power among hunter-gatherers lies in their control of a scarce, hard to acquire, but necessary nutrient—animal protein. When men in a hunter-gatherer society return to camp with game, they divide the meat in some customary way. Among the !Kung San of Africa, certain parts of the animal are given to the owner of the arrow that killed the beast, to the first hunter to sight the game, to the one who threw the first spear, and to all men in the hunting party. After the meat has been divided, each hunter distributes his share to his blood relatives and his in-laws, who in turn share it with others. If an animal is large enough, every member of the band will receive some meat.

Vegetable foods, in contrast, are not distributed beyond the immediate household. Women give food to their children, to their husbands, to other members of the household, and rarely, to the occasional visitor. No one outside the family regularly eats any of the wild fruits and vegetables that are gathered by the women.

The meat distributed by the men is a public gift. Its source is widely known, and the donor expects a reciprocal gift when other men return from a successful hunt. He gains honor as a supplier of a scarce item and simultaneously obligates others to him.

These obligations constitute a form of power or control over others, both men and women. The opinions of hunters play an important part in decisions to move the village; good hunters attract the most desirable women; people in other groups join camps with good hunters; and hunters, because they already participate in an internal system of exchange, control exchange with other groups for flint, salt, and steel axes. The male monopoly on hunting unites men in a system of exchange and gives them power; gathering vegetable food does not give women equal power even among foragers who live in the tropics, where the food collected by women provides more than half the hunter-gatherer diet.

If dominance arises from a monopoly on big-game hunting, why has the male monopoly remained unchallenged? Some women are strong enough to participate in the hunt and their endurance is certainly equal to that of men. Dobe San women of the Kalahari Desert in Africa walk an average of 10 miles a day carrying from 15 to 33 pounds of food plus a baby.

Women do not hunt, I believe, because of four

interrelated factors: variability in the supply of game; the different skills required for hunting and gathering; the incompatibility between carrying burdens and hunting; and the small size of seminomadic foraging populations.

Because the meat supply is unstable, foragers must make frequent expeditions to provide the band with gathered food. Environmental factors such as seasonal and annual variation in rainful often affect the size of the wildlife population. Hunters cannot always find game, and when they do encounter animals, they are not always successful in killing their prey. In northern latitudes, where meat is the primary food, periods of starvation are known in every generation. The irregularity of the game supply leads hunter-gatherers in areas where plant foods are available to depend on these predictable foods a good part of the time. Someone must gather the fruits, nuts, and roots and carry them back to camp to feed unsuccessful hunters, children, the elderly, and anyone who might not have gone foraging that day.

Foraging falls to the women because hunting and gathering cannot be combined on the same expedition. Although gatherers sometimes notice signs of game as they work, the skills required to track game are not the same as those required to find edible roots or plants. Hunters scan the horizon and the land for traces of large game; gatherers keep their eyes to the ground, studying the distribution of plants and the texture of the soil for hidden roots and animal holes. Even if a woman who was collecting plants came across the track of an antelope, she could not follow it; it is impossible to carry a load and hunt at the same time. Running with a heavy load is difficult, and should the animal be sighted, the hunter would be off balance and could neither shoot an arrow nor throw a spear accurately.

Pregnancy and child care would also present difficulties for a hunter. An unborn child affects a woman's body balance, as does a child in her arms, on her back, or slung at her side. Until they are two years old, many hunter-gatherer children are carried at all times, and until they are four, they are carried some of the time.

An observer might wonder why young women do not hunt until they become pregnant, or why mature women and men do not hunt and gather on alternate days, with some women staying in camp to act as wet nurses for the young. Apart from the effects hunting might have on a mother's milk production, there are two reasons. First, young girls begin to bear children as soon as they are physically mature and strong enough to hunt, and second, hunter-gatherer bands are so small that there are unlikely to be enough lac-

tating women to serve as wet nurses. No hunter-gatherer group could afford to maintain a specialized female hunting force.

Because game is not always available, because hunting and gathering are specialized skills, because women carrying heavy loads cannot hunt, and because women in hunter-gatherer societies are usually either pregnant or caring for young children, for most of the last two million years of human history men have hunted and women have gathered.

If male dominance depends on controlling the supply of meat, then the degree of male dominance in a society should vary with the amount of meat available and the amount supplied by the men. Some regions, like the East African grasslands and the North American woodlands, abounded with species of large mammals; other zones, like tropical forests and semideserts, are thinly populated with prey. Many elements affect the supply of game, but theoretically, the less meat provided exclusively by the men, the more egalitarian the society.

All known hunter-gatherer societies fit into four basic types: those in which men and women work together in communal hunts and as teams gathering edible plants, as did the Washo Indians of North America; those in which men and women each collect their own plant foods although the men supply some meat to the group, as do the Hadza of Tanzania; those in which male hunters and female gatherers work apart but return to camp each evening to share their acquisitions, as do the Tiwi of North Australia; and those in which the men provide all the food by hunting large game, as do the Eskimo. In each case the extent of male dominance increases directly with the proportion of meat supplied by individual men and small hunting parties.

Among the most egalitarian of hunter-gatherer societies are the Washo Indians, who inhabited the valleys of the Sierra Nevada in what is now southern California and Nevada. In the spring they moved north to Lake Tahoe for the large fish runs of sucker and native trout. Everyone—men, women, and children—participated in the fishing. Women spent the summer gathering edible berries and seeds while the men continued to fish. In the fall some men hunted deer but the most important source of animal protein was the jack rabbit, which was captured in communal hunts. Men and women together drove the rabbits into nets tied end to end. To provide food for the winter, husbands and wives worked as teams in the late fall to collect pine nuts.

Since everyone participated in most food-gathering activities, there were no individual distributors of food and relatively little difference in male and female rights. Men and women were not segregated from each other in daily activities; both were free to take lovers after marriage; both had the right to separate whenever they chose; menstruating women were not isolated from the rest of the group; and one of the two major Washo rituals celebrated hunting while the other celebrated gathering. Men were accorded more prestige if they had killed a deer, and men directed decisions about the seasonal movement of the group. But if no male leader stepped forward, women were permitted to lead. The distinctive feature of groups such as the Washo is the relative equality of the sexes.

The sexes are also relatively equal among the Hadza of Tanzania but this near-equality arises because men and women tend to work alone to feed themselves. They exchange little food. The Hadza lead a leisurely life in the seemingly barren environment of the East African Rift Gorge that is, in fact, rich in edible berries, roots, and small game. As a result of this abundance, from the time they are 10 years old, Hadza men and women gather much of their own food. Women take their young children with them into the bush, eating as they forage, and collect only enough food for a light family meal in the evening. The men eat berries and roots as they hunt for small game, and should they bring down a rabbit or a hyrax, they eat the meat on the spot. Meat is carried back to the camp and shared with the rest of the group only on those rare occasions when a poisoned arrow brings down a large animal—an impala, a zebra, an eland, or a giraffe.

Because Hadza men distribute little meat, their status is only slightly higher than that of the women. People flock to the camp of a good hunter and the camp might take on his name because of his popularity, but he is in no sense a leader of the group. A Hadza man and a woman have an equal right to divorce and each can repudiate a marriage simply by living apart for a few weeks. Couples tend to live in the same camp as the wife's mother but they sometimes make long visits to the camp of the husband's mother. Although a man may take more than one wife, most Hadza males cannot afford to indulge in this luxury. In order to maintain a marriage, a man must supply both his wife and his mother-in-law with some meat and trade goods, such as beads and cloth, and the Hadza economy gives few men the wealth to provide for more than one wife and mother-in-law. Washo equality is based on cooperation; Hadza equality is based on independence.

In contrast to both these groups, among the Tiwi of Melville and Bathurst Islands off the northern coast of Australia, male hunters dominate female gatherers.

The Tiwi are representative of the most common form of foraging society, in which the men supply large quantities of meat, although less than half the food consumed by the group. Each morning Tiwi women, most with babies on their backs, scatter in different directions in search of vegetables, grubs, worms, and small game such as bandicoots, lizards, and opossums. To track the game, they use hunting dogs. On most days women return to camp with some meat and with baskets full of *korka*, the nut of a native palm, which is soaked and mashed to make a porridge-like dish. The Tiwi men do not hunt small game and do not hunt every day, but when they do they often return with kangaroo, large lizards, fish, and game birds.

The porridge is cooked separately by each household and rarely shared outside the family, but the meat is prepared by a volunteer cook, who can be male or female. After the cook takes one of the parts of the animal traditionally reserved for him or her, the animal's "boss," the one who caught it, distributes the rest to all near kin and then to all others residing with the band. Although the small game supplied by the women is distributed in the same way as the big game supplied by the men, Tiwi men are dominant because the game they kill provides most of the meat.

The power of Tiwi men is clearest in their betrothal practices. Among the Tiwi, a woman must always be married. To ensure this, female infants are betrothed at birth and widows are remarried at the gravesides of their late husbands. Men form alliances by exchanging daughters, sisters, and mothers in marriage and some collect as many as 25 wives. Tiwi men value the quantity and quality of the food many wives can collect and the many children they can produce.

The dominance of the men is offset somewhat by the influence of adult women in selecting their next husbands. Many women are active strategists in the political careers of their male relatives, but to the exasperation of some sons attempting to promote their own futures, widowed mothers sometimes insist on selecting their own partners. Women also influence the marriages of their daughters and granddaughters, especially when the selected husband dies before the bestowed child moves to his camp.

Among the Eskimo, representative of the rarest type of forager society, inequality between the sexes is matched by inequality in supplying the group with food. Inland Eskimo men hunt caribou throughout the year to provision the entire society, and maritime Eskimo men depend on whaling, fishing, and some hunting to feed their extended families. The women process the carcasses, cut and sew skins to make clothing, cook, and care for the young; but they collect no food of their own and depend on the men to supply all the raw materials for their work. Since men provide all the meat, they also control the trade in hides, whale oil, seal oil, and other items that move between the maritime and inland Eskimos.

Eskimo women are treated almost exclusively as objects to be used, abused, and traded by men. After puberty all Eskimo girls are fair game for any interested male. A man shows his intentions by grabbing the belt of a woman and if she protests, he cuts off her trousers and forces himself upon her. These encounters are considered unimportant by the rest of the group. Men offer their wives' sexual services to establish alliances with trading partners and members of hunting and whaling parties.

Despite the consistent pattern of some degree of male dominance among foragers, most of these societies are egalitarian compared with agricultural and industrial societies. No forager has any significant opportunity for political leadership. Foragers, as a rule, do not like to give or take orders, and assume leadership only with reluctance. Shamans (those who are thought to be possessed by spirits) may be either male or female. Public rituals conducted by women in order to celebrate the first menstruation of girls are common, and the symbolism in these rituals is similar to that in the ceremonies that follow a boy's first kill.

In any society, status goes to those who control the distribution of valued goods and services outside the family. Equality arises when both sexes work side by side in food production, as do the Washo, and the products are simply distributed among the workers. In such circumstances, no person or sex has greater access to valued items than do others. But when women make no contribution to the food supply, as in the case of the Eskimo, they are completely subordinate.

When we attempt to apply these generalizations to contemporary industrial society, we can predict that as long as women spend their discretionary income from jobs on domestic needs, they will gain little social recognition and power. To be an effective source of power, money must be exchanged in ways that require returns and create obligations. In other words, it must be invested.

Jobs that do not give women control over valued resources will do little to advance their general status. Only as managers, executives, and professionals are women in a position to trade goods and services, to do others favors, and therefore to obligate others to them. Only as controllers of valued resources can women achieve prestige, power, and equality.

Within the household, women who bring in income from jobs are able to function on a more nearly equal basis with their husbands. Women who contribute services to their husbands and children without pay, as do some middle-class Western housewives, are especially vulnerable to dominance. Like Eskimo women, as long as their services are limited to domestic distribution they have little power relative to their husbands and none with respect to the outside world.

As for the limits imposed on women by their procreative functions in hunter-gatherer societies, childbearing and child care are organized around work as much as work is organized around reproduction. Some foraging groups space their children three to four years apart and have an average of only four to six children, far fewer than many women in other cultures. Hunter-gatherers nurse their infants for extended periods, sometimes for as long as four years. This custom suppresses ovulation and limits the size of their families. Sometimes, although rarely, they practice infanticide. By limiting reproduction, a woman who is gathering food has only one child to carry.

Different societies can and do adjust the frequency of birth and the care of children to accommodate whatever productive activities women customarily engage in. In horticultural societies, where women work long hours in gardens that may be far from home, infants get food to supplement their mothers' milk, older children take care of younger children, and pregnancies are widely spaced. Throughout the world, if a society requires a woman's labor, it finds ways to care for her children.

In the United States, as in some other industrial societies, the accelerated entry of women with preschool children into the labor force has resulted in the development of a variety of childcare arrangements. Individual women have called on friends, relatives, and neighbors. Public and private childcare centers are growing. We should realize that the declining birth rate, the increasing acceptance of childless or single-child families, and a de-emphasis on motherhood are adaptations to a sexual division of labor reminiscent of the system of production found in hunter-gatherer societies.

In many countries where women no longer devote most of their productive years to childbearing, they are beginning to demand a change in the social relationship of the sexes. As women gain access to positions that control the exchange of resources, male dominance may become archaic, and industrial societies may one day become as egalitarian as the Washo.

9

Kinship, Marriage, and Family

In previous chapters we surveyed the field of anthropology and some of the concepts used by cultural anthropologists in their work. We looked at the origins of culture among humans and then at the evolution of culture through various stages of technology and social organization. We also dealt with the methods anthropologists use in doing research in other cultures, and the means by which they seek to remain objective when analyzing other peoples and their ways of life. And we have defined and discussed the concepts of culture and society, showing how each is related to the other and how each is structured so that its parts fit together into a unified whole. We are now ready to look at some of the specific elements of culture in order to see how, in the course of studying a culture or comparing two or more cultures, an anthropologist can piece together the puzzle of life and better understand the vast differences and surprising similarities among cultures throughout the world.

Kinship Systems

For a number of reasons we begin our discussion of the elements of social organization with kinship. **Kinship** is another word for a way of defining and organizing one's relatives. It is the basis of social structure in all societies, but in the traditional, non-Western societies on which anthropologists have long focused, it is the guiding principle of social relations. In contemporary industrial societies this is less true; a person fills a given position not because of who he or she is, but because of what he or she can do. But this is the exception rather than the rule; in most societies a person occupies a social position mainly on the basis of his or her relationships to other members of the group.

The most basic forms of social organization are domestic groups that historically developed to meet certain fundamental needs. Among these needs are reproduction of the species, care of newborn infants, and protec-

tion of the very young. Domestic groups also developed out of the need for cooperation in obtaining food, securing proper shelter, socializing young members of the group into their roles, as well as caring for those members of the group who could not adequately take care of themselves. Thus domestic groups were formed as an important human strategy for adaptation.

Every culture has its own system of relationships for dealing with reproduction, training, and passage from one generation to another. There are two main types of relationships: those between people who are related biologically or genetically, whom we call blood relatives; and those between people who are related by marriage. Of course, anthropologists have special terms for these relationships (it seems that we never pass up a chance to create a new scientific term, and kinship offers many such chances). We call blood relatives **consanguineal** relations, while those who are related by marriage are called **affinal** relations. People who are related by blood are descended from a common ancestor, although they may not be the same number of generations removed from that ancestor. Thus, according to the American system, we would include anyone who was descended from a common ancestor on any generational level, such as brothers, sisters, aunts, uncles, cousins, and so forth. Relatives by marriage usually are not descended from a common ancestor but have "married into" the family. They include husband or wife, "in-laws," and the spouses of "blood" aunts and uncles.

When we speak of kinship in any society, we generally refer to it as a *system*. This implies that the relationships that are considered important by the members of the group are arranged systematically so that they are regular and predictable. To the degree that a society is kinship oriented, this system of relationships can serve as the basis for economic interactions such as distribution of food and assignment of tasks; for political interactions such as the distribution of power over other members of the society; and for

Lewis Henry Morgan (1818–1881)

Lewis Henry Morgan is perhaps the best known American anthropologist of the nineteenth century. Trained as a lawyer, Morgan developed an interest in anthropology through his experiences with the Iroquois Indians near his home in upstate New York. He began studying other Indian tribes, and in *Systems of Consanguinity and Affinity* (1871) he compared the kinship systems and terminologies of many societies throughout the world. As an outgrowth of his kinship studies, Morgan began to contemplate these differences in terms of an evolutionary sequence—he believed that the differences in kin terminologies could be explained by the fact that some societies represented an earlier stage of cultural evolution, and therefore their kinship systems were older, or in some cases simpler.

many other aspects of group life. In addition, kinship can define the relationships between a group of people and the land they occupy, or the way in which land and other goods are transferred from one member of the group to another. It can determine who may marry whom as well as who may not marry whom. It provides the context within which new members are trained in the society's culture. In short, kinship can and does affect every aspect of social behavior in some societies, and even in our own society, which deemphasizes blood relationships in most contexts, the kinship system is an important part of our way of life.

Kinship terms Since most people marry and most married couples have more than one child, we are related to a very large number of people, both living and dead. You may come from a large family yourself and know

as many as 100 living relatives by name. Even if you come from a small family and have only a few close relatives, you still have a huge number of more distant relatives who are descended from a common ancestor. If, for example, your great-great-grandfather had two children, each of whom had two children, and so on down to your generation, you would have one brother or sister, two first cousins, four second cousins, and eight third cousins, all in your generation, not to mention aunts and uncles, first and second cousins once removed, and so on. And remember, you had eight great-great-grandfathers! As you can see, the number of relatives grows rapidly with each new generation.

In every culture there is a set of terms that are used to describe relatives. But it is important to note that not every society uses the same categories or makes the same distinctions. What is considered important in one culture could well be completely ignored in another. In fact, individuals who are regarded as close or intimate kin in one culture may not be viewed as even being related in another. For example, in American culture there is a category of relatives described by the term *uncle*. This group includes four kinds of relatives: (1) the brother of our father, (2) the husband of our father's sister, (3) the brother of our mother, and (4) the husband of our mother's sister. These relationships are shown in Figure 9.1. In this diagram a triangle stands for a male, a circle for a female, and a square for a person of either sex. In addition, an equal sign stands for marriage, a vertical line for descent, and a horizontal line for a sibling (brother-sister) relationship. We use these symbols to show how individuals are related to a central reference point, which we call **Ego**. All relationships are calculated from Ego's point of view. It helps if you put yourself in Ego's place when looking at the diagram, and in this case it does not matter whether you are male or female.

Now, we may ask why it is that we put these four types of relationship into the same category and call them by the same term. Does this happen in all cultures? The answer, of course, is that it does not, for as we will see shortly, while for Americans the distinction between different kinds of uncles is not very important, for members of another culture this distinction can be crucial to the way people organize their lives and their social interaction.

The reason kinship terms vary from one culture to another (beyond obvious differences in language) is that the system for organizing relations differs. Each category is based on the patterns of behavior expected of people in that category. In other words, *kin terms are role terms;* that is, they indicate not only a biological relationship but a social relationship as well. They vary from one culture to another because the behavior expected of certain individuals varies in different cultures.

Let us return to our "uncle" example to see how this works. In our culture we generally expect the same treatment from all four kinds of uncles. For one thing, we do not make a legal distinction between our mother's brother and our father's brother. They are expected to act toward us the same way. While the husbands of our parents' sisters are not related by blood, they are married to people who are and are expected to follow the behavior patterns of their spouses. This is not to say that every uncle will treat us in exactly the same way—we all have favorites—only that in our system we *expect* the same treatment from all.

In another society the situation might be quite different, however. Suppose, for example, that instead of tracing our line of descent through both parents equally, we tend to favor one over the other. This is not as far-fetched as it might sound, for after all, in our society we usually take our father's name and not our mother's, although one can find a number of exceptions to this nowadays. In some societies inheritance is even more one-sided, and each child becomes

FIGURE 9.1

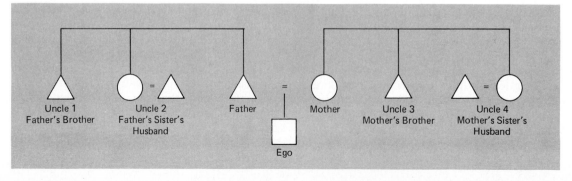

a member of a kinship group only through one side of the family—either the mother's (*matrilineal*) side or the father's (*patrilineal*) side. Let us assume, for the sake of simplicity, that there are two groups in a society, the Smiths and the Joneses. A Smith may not marry another Smith, and a Jones may not marry another Jones. Finally, let us assume that the child inherits not only its surname but also its kin group membership from its father. We can see why there might be a tendency to differentiate among various types of uncles in such a society; such a distinction would be important because of the rules for defining relationships. This point is illustrated more clearly in Figure 9.2, in which the dark shapes stand for Smiths and the light ones Joneses.

What makes one kind of uncle different from another kind? Uncle 1 is a Smith, like Ego; his children will be Smiths too. Uncle 2 is a Jones, a member of a different kin group from that of Ego, and his children will also be members of a different kin group; thus he is very different from uncle 1, both because of his own group membership and because his children belong to the pool of potential marriage partners for Ego, while the children of uncle 1 do not. Uncle 3 is also a Jones, and in terms of group membership he is in the same category as uncle 2. Note, however, that while 3 is a blood relative because he is the brother of Ego's mother, 2 is not a blood relative but is related to Ego by marriage. Finally, uncle 4 is a Smith, and

in terms of kin group membership is of the same type as uncle 1. Again, however, note that while uncle 1 is a blood relative, uncle 4 is not.

How does kinship operate in real life? Again, an example may help. The Yanomamö, a tribe living along the Orinoco River in Venezuela, are a patrilineal society; a child inherits its kin group membership from its father and not from its mother. The different types of uncles are important in that they are not all related to Ego to the same degree, and this difference is reflected in the **kinship terminology.** Ego calls his father *Hayä;* he uses the same term for his father's brother, who belongs to the same clan, having inherited his kin group membership from Ego's father's father. But Ego calls his mother's brother *Shoaiyä,* which shows that he is different in some way from Ego's father and father's brother.

The Yanomamö word for father also means father's brother. This does not mean that people don't see any difference between the two—only that the kin term stresses group membership rather than biological parentage.

In a few societies in East Africa there are not only separate terms for father and father's brother but a third term for mother's brother. Thus three terms are used in these societies, whereas the Yanomamö use only two, as does our own culture (*father* and *uncle*).

There is an important lesson to be learned

FIGURE 9.2

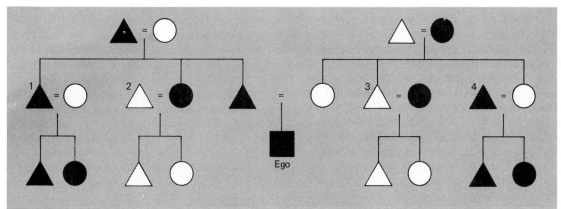

from the fact that different societies categorize people in different ways. We tend to assume that because we classify relatives in a certain way in our own society, there is a universal principle of kinship organization, and that cultures in which this principle does not operate are backward. However, this is clearly not the case. A kinship system can be based on any set of principles, and there is no right or wrong way to do it. The beliefs that a group of people share about what is important in their kinship system do not have to be based on some absolute rule. Otherwise, how could we lump all of our uncles into one category and not distinguish between uncles by blood and uncles by marriage?

In our society cousins generally do not marry each other. In fact, marriage between cousins is against the law in some states. However, in some societies such marriages are not only allowed by encouraged. If we look again at Figure 9.2, we can see why this is so. If Ego is a member of his father's kin group but not his mother's, then he will have two types of cousins (in our sense of the term): those who belong to his own group and those who belong to another group. Which cousins belong to which group (in this example) can be determined by a simple rule: **Parallel cousins** are members of the same group, but **cross-cousins** are not. By parallel cousins we mean those who are related to Ego through relatives of the same (parallel) sex, namely, *mother* and *mother's sister* or *father* and *father's brother*. Cross-cousins are related to Ego through relatives of the opposite sex: *mother* and *mother's brother* or *father* and *father's sister*. This distinction is illustrated in Figure 9.3.

In our society, with its millions of people and many different kinship groups, we have no trouble finding suitable marriage partners who are not related to us. But in many smaller societies, in which the number of potential marriage partners is limited, it can be difficult to find a husband or wife. Hence, in many societies a rule that makes a cross-cousin the ideal marriage partner ensures that every person will marry someone from a different

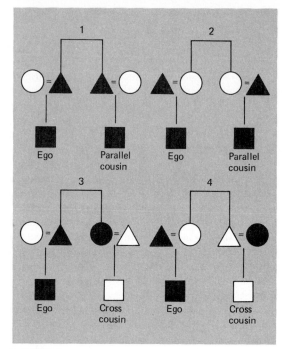

FIGURE 9.3

kin group. Of course, such a system never works exactly, because not every married couple has exactly two children, one of each sex, who grow up to marry and repeat the process. But if the ideal is present in the minds of the people, it places a high value on marrying outside the kin group. This promotes interaction between kin groups through the exchange of marriage partners, and thus promotes the solidarity of the society as a whole.

Although not nearly as commonly practiced as cross-cousin marriage, in parts of the Middle East parallel-cousin marriage is regarded as a preferred method of obtaining a spouse.

The basis of kin terms In American culture we use four criteria in assigning kinship terms to individuals. First, we sometimes make a distinction based on sex; for example, we call a male sibling a brother and a female sibling a sister. Note that this is not true in all cases, since we have only one term for cousins, regardless of sex. But we make this distinction in many other categories (e.g., mother/father, aunt/uncle, nephew/niece).

Second, we make a distinction based on *generation*. Thus we have a different term for members of different generations, such as daughter, mother, and grandmother. Technically, this distinction also exists for cousins, although it is not always made in everyday conversation. We tend to lump cousins of different generations together, especially as they grow more distant, although we could distinguish between "first cousin," "first cousin once removed," "second cousin," and so on.

Third, we make a distinction based on whether or not a relative is related to us in a direct line of **descent** from a common ancestor. Thus we distinguish between our father and our father's brother (i.e., our uncle). Other such distinctions include mother and aunt, son and nephew, grandfather and great-uncle. This distinction is between **lineal** relatives (because they are in the direct line of descent) and **collateral** relatives (because they are lateral branches of Ego's family tree, not part of the main trunk or line).

Finally, we sometimes distinguish between relatives who are related by blood (*consanguineal*) and those who are related by marriage (*affinal*). This distinction includes such categories as brother and brother-in-law, mother and mother-in-law, and so forth. But note that it is not valid for all categories: We use the same terms for consanguineal and affinal uncles or aunts.

Different factors are sometimes used in other cultures, although they do not come into play in the American system. One of these is the sex of the linking relative, an approach called **bifurcation.** Using this system, we would distinguish between a relative related through a female and the same general type of relative related through a male. For example, we would have one term for mother's brother and another for father's brother, or we might have separate terms for brother's children and sister's children. We do not make these distinctions in our society (in the first case, all are uncles; in the second, they are all either nephews or nieces), but in many societies they are important in determining kinship categories.

Another factor that we do not use in our society is the sex of the speaker. Many kinship

A father and child from Afghanistan. Kinship patterns may differ, but children are important in all societies.

An extended family of Laplanders gathers together to enjoy a moment of relaxation.

systems have a different structure and a different set of categories, depending on whether the person speaking (Ego) is a male or a female. In our society the sexes are basically equal (this may not seem true, but when our society is compared to some non-Western societies the difference is astounding), and therefore it does not make much difference whether it is a girl or a boy who uses the term *uncle*. But in many societies it is important to show whether the speaker is male or female, and hence girls are taught one set of kin terms and boys another set. Such a distinction could reflect inequality between the sexes. If a girl calls her uncle by a different term from that used by a boy, it might indicate that the relationship between the uncle and the boy is different—with a different set of rights and duties—from the relationship between the uncle and the girl. Thus in a cultural context this practice makes sense.

Another factor used in defining a kinship system is the relative age of the speaker, that is, relative to the person being referred to. Thus a boy might use one kin term to refer to his older brother and another to refer to his younger brother. Again, while this would not make much sense in American culture, it would be meaningful in a society in which age is an important aspect of social relationships.

At this point you may ask: Why is it necessary to know about all of these kinship factors? We have stressed throughout this book that one of the best ways to understand your own culture is to look outside it. If we accept the fact that there is a structure to our way of life, the task of uncovering that structure is made easier by knowing what we are looking for.

Also, it is valuable to know just how important kinship can be in ordering the lives of people in other cultures. In American society we put little emphasis on kinship because many of its functions have been taken over by other institutions—the work group, the church group, the school, and so forth. But in many non-Western societies kinship is still a major force in the lives of the people, and for them almost everything is seen in the context of the kinship system.

Finally, terms carry social as well as biological meanings, and as such, they stand for the patterns of behavior that are appropriate to each situation. Often a kin term can be used as a cue to the kind of interaction that is about to occur. The anthropologist Paul Bohannan gives an example from his fieldwork among the Tiv in Africa. He reports that if an informant wanted to give him a gift, he would call him "my father," because one gave gifts to people whom one respected and honored. If the informant wanted to correct Bohannan's grammar or manners, he called him "my child," because children were not expected to know all the rules of proper social conduct and were still learning the language. Thus, even though Bohannan was clearly an adult, his role in Tiv society sometimes coincided with that of a child. On the other hand, if the informant wanted to include him on the same side in an argument, he would call him "son of my mother." This term showed that they were obliged to defend one another and to stick together—the type of behavior that is called for in an argument. Finally, if the informant wanted to offer Bohannan a drink, he would use a non-kin term meaning "my age mate" (i.e., a member of the same peer group but not a blood

relative). This term indicated that there was a common interest that held the two together, and that the behavior called for in the situation was not kinship-oriented behavior but the interaction of friends. Drinking was appropriate for men of the same age but was not related to kinship, so the correct term was used, not only to inform Bohannan of the speaker's expectations, but more generally to define the situation for everyone involved.

American kinship terms We have already mentioned some aspects of the American kinship system and the standard terms for relatives in the English language. But here we will look at the subject in more detail and show that kinship in the United States is, in fact, a system, and that it is only one of many different systems found in the world today.

In the American kinship system relationships are traced equally through both sides of the family rather than through either the mother's side or the father's side. This means that we tend to treat people related to us through our mother and those related to us through our father in similar ways, and that we use the same terms to designate relatives no matter which side of the family they are on. The formal system of terms used by Americans is similar to the general type that anthropologists call the **Eskimo kinship terminology.** In this system there are separate terms for "father" and "mother," while the categories "father's brother" and "mother's brother" are merged in one term (*uncle*) and likewise "father's sister" and "mother's sister" are merged in the term *aunt*. Further, the children of parents' siblings are all members of a single category and are referred to by the same term (*cousin*).

But American kinship is more than a set of terms; a variety of informal words are used to address or refer to people in different situations. For example, although we have the formal term *mother*, we may use any of a number of alternate terms, such as *mom, mommy,* or, *ma,* or we may use a first name, a nickname, a diminutive, or some other

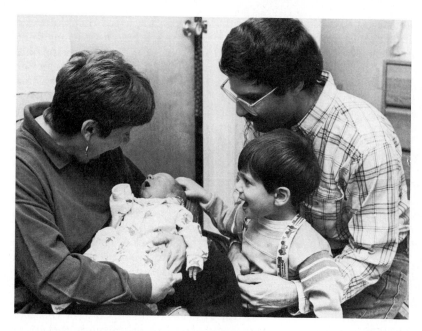

An American nuclear family—mother, father, and offspring—share a time of joy with the newest member of the family.

descriptive or joking term such as *old woman* or *old lady*. The same holds true for the term *father*, which can be replaced by such terms as *pop, daddy,* or *old man*. The last term tends to be used in reference rather than in address; that is, we might refer to our father as "old man" when talking about him to someone else out of his hearing, but we would be unlikely to use that term to address him. In other words, different kinds of terms are used, depending on whether the individual is being addressed, referred to in his or her presence, or referred to in his or her absence. Thus we might use the term *mother* when talking about her with our father, the term *ma* or *mom* when speaking to her, and the term *my mother* when speaking to a friend about her when she is not there. These forms of reference and address vary greatly from one situation to another.

From this variation in the use of kinship terms, we can see that each term has two basic functions: to organize relatives into categories, or classify them; and to define or describe a role. When we use the term *uncle*, we are both categorizing the person in terms

of his relationship to us and defining the general set of behaviors that that person is expected to follow in interacting with us. It is important to note that these alternate terms are not synonyms. Father and Daddy do not mean the same thing. One is formal, while the other implies a closer, more informal relationship.

This use of kin terms to define behavior rather than biological relationship points to another aspect of kinship systems. In social situations we behave toward others in a way that corresponds to kinship behavior, even though we are not related to them. Sometimes people formalize such behavior by creating artificial, or **fictive,** kinship ties. For example, the anthropologist Elliot Liebow, in a book (*Tally's Corner*) about an African-American ghetto in Washington, D.C., described a relationship called "going for cousins," a close nonsexual relationship between two people of the opposite sex. By invoking the cousin relationship, which in American culture implies a taboo against sex, the two people can avoid the disapproval of the rest of the community. The important aspect of this rela-

I WANT YOU

for the U.S. ARMY ENLIST NOW

Kinship terms are sometimes used to create a particular image, as in the case of "Uncle Sam."

tionship from the anthropologist's point of view is that it exists in a kinship context and thus shows how crucial kinship is to the overall pattern of social relationships.

Descent

Having discussed the various relationships between members of a society and the meaning of those relationships, it remains to be shown how people determine who their relatives are. In every culture there are rules that govern how one defines one's kin and who is to be included or excluded from the kin group. The categories of relatives are arbitrarily limited by these rules.

One of the features that defines the various categories of kin is *descent,* the way in which two blood relatives trace their relationship to a common ancestor. This is not a biological factor but a social one, for if the culture does not consider the biological link between two individuals important, then, according to the rules of that culture, those individuals are not related. It is not a question of how many physical traits they share as a result of having a common genetic heritage. It is simply a social fact.

Descent relationships can be reckoned through one line (either male or female) or through both. If descent is reckoned only through the mother's line, it is *matrilineal;* if only through the father's line, it is *patrilineal;* if through both lines, it is **bilateral.** As we noted earlier in this chapter, by excluding people related through one parent, we divide our biologically related relatives into two groups, only one of which is recognized as part of our kin group. Often people who are related to a common ancestor have a common name and are considered a corporate group with certain shared rights and privileges. Perhaps the group holds land in common for its members, or it might be associated with a religious shrine or the possession of a common fund of knowledge, such as a family ritual or myth. A **clan** is such a descent group, as is a **lineage;** the major difference between them is that a lineage consists of members who can trace their relationship to an actual common ancestor, while the members of a clan assume that they are related but cannot actually trace their lines all the way back to a common ancestor.

In many cases a particular descent system is explained in a way that makes sense to the people themselves, as well as to the anthropologist. For example, the prevailing theory of conception might have something to do with whether descent is traced through the male line, through the female line, or both. Of course, in American culture we recognize the role of each parent in conception, and we consider a child to be equally close to both parents in biological terms. Thus it seems logical to us for descent to be traced equally through both the male and female lines.

Among the Ashanti in West Africa people believe the blood of the child is contributed only by the mother, while the child's spiritual makeup comes from the father. Since the Ashanti distinguish between two aspects of the self—physical and spiritual—the descent of each part of the individual is traced by different principles. Therefore among the Ashanti biological descent is matrilineal, since it is the mother who gives the infant its physical essence. Spiritual descent, on the other hand, is patrilineal, and the child becomes a member of its father's spiritual kin group.

Another example is found in the Trobriand Islands of the Western Pacific, where it is believed that the child's spirit enters its mother's uterus by itself. The only roles the male plays are to widen the path to the womb through intercourse, and to ensure that the woman is married, since only married women may legitimately bear children. The biological role of the father is not considered. Thus the mother's line is the important one in reckoning descent since the child is born of the mother and not of both parents. Furthermore, the mother's brother is thought to have a closer relationship to the child than its biological father because of his relationship to the mother through a common ancestor.

Most societies reckon descent through the male line, a fact that proves the dominance of social factors over biological factors. Even though it is obvious that the child is a part of its mother in a biological sense, in male-dominated societies (the vast majority) it is the male line that wins out. Where men own property and hold power, they seek to maintain exclusive rights to that property and power. They can do this only to the extent that they are able to exclude women from positions of power, and it is through the descent system that they make sure that their children will carry on the tradition of male dominance.

Along with the prevailing theory of conception or male dominance, there may be obvious economic reasons why a particular descent system exists in a particular society. Residence patterns are sometimes tied in with descent. In a matrilineal society the husband often comes to live in his wife's home village, thus reinforcing the pattern of descent; the opposite holds true for a patrilineal society. If property is owned and distributed by women (as it is in some societies), then matrilineal descent is more likely. On the other hand, if a skill usually found in males, such as hunting, is based on close knowledge of the area, then patrilineal descent is likely because in that way men can retain their rights over the territory and keep their place of residence for many generations. This allows the group to benefit from the experience of elders, who can pass along their specialized knowledge of the region and their skill in hunting the local game.

Marriage and the Family

If kinship is the basis of social organization in all societies, then marriage is the basis of kinship. Of course, strictly speaking, marriage is not necessary. Societies could produce and train new members without creating the institution of marriage and without organizing themselves into family units. Yet in no society is this the dominant cultural rule; marriage and the family are found in some form everywhere in the world. Marriage functions to control sexual activity within the society, following the rules by which the group is organized. The family functions as a primary group, the most important influence in the socialization of the young, and it also defines the channels through which membership in a kinship group is transferred (descent) and material and nonmaterial possessions are passed from one generation to the next (inheritance).

Actually, there are several functions that marriage can perform in different societies. To the extent that society is concerned about the legitimacy of its new members, marriage creates a set of legal parents. To the extent that society is concerned about restricting sexual activity among its members, marriage provides guidelines for such activity. In some societies marriage can be used to control an individual's labor power—usually that of a woman who comes to live with her husband and his family. In many societies marriage includes a transfer of property, so that the rights to that property—land, money, material goods, or whatever—are given over to the family of one of the spouses.

An important element in any marriage is the relationship it creates between two groups. A marriage is not simply an agreement between two people that they want to live together (although this is becoming more common); rather, in most societies it is a contract that binds two families or even larger groups together socially and sometimes economically. In Europe, for example, marriage was formerly used as a way of tying two countries together. The marriage of Philip II of Spain and Mary Tudor, the daughter of King Henry VIII and Catherine of Aragon, created a social, economic, and military bond between Spain and England. In addi-

tion, inbreeding among the nobility was encouraged so as to prevent the division of royal estates; if the wealth was kept within a small group, there was less danger of spreading the royal fortunes and power too thin.

Likewise, in non-Western societies marriage can be more of an economic contract than a bond between two individuals. Among the Tiwi in northern Australia a man acquires a wife by promising his first-born daughter to his future father-in-law or to the latter's close relatives. The more wives he can obtain, the more daughters he can promise, and thus the stronger his ties to other groups in the society. As he grows older, he begins to reap the rewards of his shrewd economic transactions by acquiring more younger wives who will produce more daughters whom he can trade for promises of future wives—a kind of primitive social security system, at least from the male's point of view.

In traditional China a wealthy family might acquire a wife for a son when she was still a child. They would bring her into the household at an early age, so that she could be trained to work with her mother-in-law, and when she reached the proper age she would

Benazir Bhutto, former Prime Minister of Pakistan, and her husband—a political marriage. In many parts of the world marriages are still arranged for political, economic, or social interests of the two families.

be married to the son. However, the main function of the wife was to work in the household and provide sons for her husband's lineage. Her role as a companion was minimal, as is shown by the fact that marriages were arranged by the families and did not require the consent of either party.

This list of the possible functions of marriage is not complete. Its purpose is to indicate some of the basic ways in which marriage can be viewed: sexual access, parentage, labor, property, and alliance. It is interesting to note that even though we assume that for us marriage is based on the free choice of the two people involved, very strong pressures operate against this freedom. Our society sets up barriers to limit opportunities for children to meet other children whose families do not have a great deal in common. As a result, the chances that one will marry someone very much like oneself are very high. Segregation in housing and schools is an effective way of making sure children spend their time with "their own kind." Social functions arranged by a group, such as a religious organization, or a social club, are another way of putting subtle pressure on people to interact with others with whom they have much in common. Even the fraternity and sorority systems at colleges and universities serve to channel their members into the "right" social crowd.

The Family: Variations on a Theme

In every society the family is an important unit, but in each society different members of the family are considered important and the family unit is structured in different ways. Thus the makeup of the family differs from one culture to another. In the United States, as in most industrial countries, the family has grown smaller. Mobility, both social and geographic, has trimmed the family to a small unit that can move about easily and is not a heavy economic burden for the breadwinner.

While on the farm extra hands are helpful, in the city the presence of uncles and aunts, grandparents, and cousins under one roof is inefficient. As a result, the typical family in our culture has become what we call the **nuclear family,** a family formed around a nucleus of parents and their unmarried children with few, if any, other members.

In contrast to the American nuclear family, in many societies the family is a residential unit that includes a wider circle of relatives. When more than two generations are represented, and especially when collateral as well as lineal relatives are included in the household (for example, aunts, uncles, cousins), we speak of an *extended family*. This family type is usually found in peasant or tribal societies, and tends to disappear as a country becomes urbanized. A variant of the extended family is what is called the *joint family* (or joint extended family), which consists of a married couple, their unmarried sons and daughters, and the nuclear families of their married sons.

Usually we think of the family not only in terms of biological and marital relationships but also as an economic unit, a unit for socializing the young, and in general as having a number of different functions. However, this is not always the case. In some societies the biological family is not the basic social unit; that is, satisfaction of sexual needs is separated from other functions of the family. Such was the case among the Nayar, a people of southern India, where until the late nineteenth century marriage existed in a very different form from what we would consider normal. Around the time of puberty each Nayar girl was ritually married to a boy selected by her family. After the ceremony the couple were secluded for a few days, during which sexual activity might take place but was not necessary. The couple then separated, with the boy returning to his home village and the girl to hers. After that point the girl had no further obligations to her husband until he died, when she and her children (by whatever man) had to perform a death ritual for him.

After the ritual marriage and separation each party went his or her own way. The woman was free to engage in sexual activity with whomever she chose (provided that he had the proper social standing), and the man was likewise free to do so. The functions of satisfying sexual desires and producing new members of the society thus were fulfilled through a series of informal love affairs that created no permanent bond between a woman and her lover. A woman could have as many lovers as she wished at any one time, or she could limit herself to one man. They could be short affairs or long-term relationships. The lover would visit after supper and stay until early the next morning, leaving his weapons outside the door as a sign to others. Anyone who arrived and found another man's weapons there was free to sleep on the woman's porch.

The children of such unions called their mother's lovers by a term meaning "lord" or "leader," and that term did not imply either biological or legal paternity. Even when paternity was definitely known, the man had no duties toward his children other than paying for the expense of their birth. The children became members of the mother's kinship unit, or matrilineage. This female-centered kinship unit included men, such as the brothers of the woman or her mother's brothers, and those men were obliged to contribute to the care and raising of the children born into the group, although they had no such obligation toward their own "biological" children born into another woman's matrilineage.

The explanation for this type of marriage—surely one of the most curious types found anywhere in the world—lies in the social organization of the Nayar. As we saw in the last chapter, traditional Indian society was divided into a number of distinct social groups called *castes*. Each caste was ritually linked with a specific occupation, and along with it went a whole set of rules and a way of life that applied only to that caste. The Nayar were a warrior caste, and it is thought that the lack of obligations toward their bio-

logical children left the men free to follow that occupation. Of course, the men were responsible for the children in their own matrilineage, but the matrilineage as a whole took care of the children and could take over in the man's absence. At the same time, the pattern of courtship and sexual activity seemed to fit in with the life style of the warrior caste, enabling men who were away from home (and women whose husbands might be away much of the time) to engage in a normal sex life with the approval of their society. As the need for warriors decreased and the caste system was ended, this pattern disappeared.

It has also been suggested that the Nayar marriage pattern helped to maintain the unity of the matrilineage. If a man became devoted to one wife, his ties to his sisters and their children would be weakened. With marriage separate from sexual activity and reproduction, the biological father is legally removed from his children's matrilineage and, at the same time, closely tied to his own matrilineage. Thus, while reproduction is necessary to continue the matrilineage, husbands are not. The Nayar form of marriage is one way of seeing that this distinction is maintained.

Nayar society shows how much marriage and the family as social institutions can vary. Therefore the Nayar are of great interest to the anthropologist. They have a woman-centered family in a male-centered society, for while the matrilineage is the basic unit of social organization, the male-dominated warrior caste is the central focus of the group. Another variant of the family is a woman-centered family in a woman-centered society. Malinowski describes this type of society in his account of the Trobriand Islanders.

In the Trobriands descent is reckoned only through the mother's line. This fits in with the theory of conception discussed earlier. it is thought that the mother alone determines the makeup of the child, while the father is only a passive agent. Therefore the child is a member of its mother's kinship group, or matrilineage, and is not considered to be in the same group as its father, who belongs to another matrilineage. This pattern results in a different set of statuses and roles, and different kinds of behavior between family members. For example, the term for "father" means "husband of my mother." The father is an outsider with regard to family affairs, and it is the mother's brother who heads the family.

Even so, the father is a companion to his children, and the relationship between them is a warm one. However, the role of the father as disciplinarian and head of the household, which is so common in Western society, is not filled by the father in Trobriand society. Instead, the mother's brother is the authority figure because of his membership in the family group. He gives his sister's son permission to do things, a role that would be filled by the father in other societies. A boy inherits property from his mother's brother, not from his father.

The Incest Taboo: A Universal Puzzle

Malinowski's description of family structure in the Trobriands raises another interesting question regarding the institution known as the **incest taboo.** In every society there are rules that prohibit incest, that is, sexual relations between certain relatives. The most basic of these incest taboos is the universal restriction on marriage between members of the nuclear family. Historically, there have been only a few known exceptions: Incan, Egyptian, and Hawaiian royalty approved brother-sister marriages, but even in these cases that option was not permissible for the rest of the society. Beyond this basic taboo, the same rules are not found everywhere— what is important is that *some* such rules exist in all societies. A number of theories have been proposed to explain why this is so, but anthropologists have not yet arrived at a final answer to this question.

The reason for Malinowski's interest in the incest taboo can be traced to the work of Sigmund Freud, the noted founder of psychoanalysis. In *Totem and Taboo* Freud suggested that the incest taboo arose out of the jealousy and range of early man, who was denied access to the women of his group by a domineering father. He and his brothers banded together and killed the father, ate him, and then engaged in sexual relations with their mother and sisters. But guilt caught up with them, and once they realized how horrible their crime had been, they renounced their sexual rights to the women of their family, thus creating the incest taboo. Freud argued that this was the first truly cultural act, for it represented increased awareness and careful structuring of social (in this case sexual) relations as a result of that awareness.

Malinowski reacted strongly to Freud's view of the incest taboo on the basis of his field experience in the Trobriands. Against Freud's theory that the incest taboo was the result of an early struggle between father and sons—a question of power and authority—Malinowski argued that it was a way by which society could prevent tension between members of the family and the wider kinship unit. By banning sexual relations between members of the nuclear family, the incest taboo ensures that the jealousies and conflicts that could lead to the breakup of the family will be avoided. It has nothing to do with some long-forgotten act of early men, but rather can be seen in purely functional terms as a way of enabling society to operate effectively.

A number of other theories have been proposed to account for the incest taboo, but each fails as a total explanation. According to some theorists, the incest taboo is a way of avoiding the harmful effects of inbreeding. But this argument does not explain why the incest taboo exists in nonliterate, non-Western societies in which the science of genetics is unknown. Early human beings did not know enough about reproduction and genetics to make a law like the incest taboo for purely scientific reasons. The reason must lie elsewhere.

More recently, it has been suggested that the incest taboo is what permits human beings to form a society. The argument is that if men and women who are related by blood also form the family unit (through marriage and reproduction), then the result is a small, self-sufficient group. The only way for that group to grow and become allied with others is to exchange marriage partners with another group, and thus form a bond with them. But in order to do this, the members of a group must be forbidden to take mates among their blood relatives—hence the incest taboo.

It has also been suggested that exchange is a basic part of human nature; that is, that the human species is basically social and has a built-in need to give and receive. When early men were able to exchange women with other groups, the social bonds that arose between the two groups gave them an advantage. As this practice spread, it was so successful that the rules against intercourse between members of the same family were made stronger. Thus, according to this theory, we can view the incest taboo as resulting from cultural evolution; that is, a cultural practice gave a strong advantage to those who adopted it. This theory of incest seems more believable than the others, but the trouble is that we have no way of proving it. And it does not completely explain why the incest taboo includes different relatives in different societies (or even different degrees of relationship in our own society, as is shown by differences in the laws found in various states in the United States).

In an interesting and somewhat provocative argument the anthropologist Robin Fox states that incest taboos developed almost by default, as inbreeding simply wasn't possible among early human populations because of several interrelated factors. First, life expectancy was much shorter than it is today. People probably could not expect to live more than 35 years. Second, because of nutritional or dietary factors, women might not have reached puberty, and thus become fertile, until they were 15 or 16 years of age. Third, rates of infant mortality were probably very high, exceeding 50 percent, and the survivors were breast-fed for quite some time. While breast-feeding is not a sure form of birth control, it often inhibits ovulation. All these factors probably resulted in relatively few births, widely spaced. Fox argues that by the time a boy reached puberty, his mother was past breeding age, or perhaps even dead, and any older sisters would already have mated. Conversely, by the time a younger sister was old enough, the boy would have the equivalent of a wife. This explanation suggests that early human populations usually lacked the opportunity to commit nuclear family incest.

Marriage

The question of incest taboos brings us to another major subject, the institution of marriage. Just as there are a number of different types of family structure, there is a great deal of variation in the structure of marriage and the rules that govern whom one may or may not marry. But we should not confuse rules about marriage with rules about incest. Marriage rules deal with the formation of a conjugal unit, while the incest taboo deals strictly with sexual relations. A prohibition against marrying someone is not the same as a prohibition against having intercourse with that person, although both could be applied to the same individual. However, in many cases rules against marrying a certain type of person go along with the expectation that one is entitled to, or at least allowed to, have intercourse with such individuals. In traditional India, for example, one could not marry a person who belonged to a lower caste than one's own. Thus a member of the farmer caste was not allowed to marry a member of the sweeper caste, and doing so would mean being expelled from the caste and probably

A wedding party outside a church in the United States.

from the village as well. Yet it was expected that some men from the higher farmer caste would engage in sexual intercourse with some women of lower castes such as the sweeper caste (the opposite—men from a lower caste having intercourse with women from the higher caste—was not tolerated). This is clearly similar to the situation in some other societies, ours included.

The institution of marriage is not easy to define in such a way as to allow for all the forms in which it is found. The Nayar are an example of one extreme of marriage, in which the couple remain together for only a few days and sex is not a necessary part of the relationship. There are a number of factors that can vary in any marriage, and each society has its own set of rules to govern what forms these factors will take.

Number of mates A marriage can include any number of people of either sex. One

man can be married to one woman. This form is known as **monogamy,** derived from two Greek words, *mono-,* "one," and *gamy,* "marriage." Of course, this is the marriage form required in our country. A number of years ago the anthropologist George Peter Murdock compiled information on types of marriages found cross-culturally. You might be surprised to know that monogamous unions are regarded as the preferred marriage form in only one-quarter of the almost 600 societies for which information was gathered. Lately in our society a new variant of monogamy has become common, in which an individual of either sex has a series of spouses in succession. This pattern has been termed **serial monogamy,** and except for the legal marriage ceremony, it resembles the Nayar pattern described earlier.

The alternative to monogamy is the pattern in which an individual has more than one spouse at the same time. This is called **polygamy,** from the Greek *poly-,* "many." A man can have more than one wife (**polygyny,** from the Greek *gyn-,* "woman"), or a woman can have more than one husband (**polyandry,** *andr-* is related to *anthro-,* the Greek stem for "man"). Polygyny is more common than polyandry. Especially where the family is an economic unit and the women are called on for much of the labor, the addition of another wife can be seen as a contribution to the well-being of the entire family. Wives are not added merely for their sexual attributes or their childbearing capability, but for their labor power as well. Polygyny as a desired marriage form is widespread throughout much of Africa and the Middle East, as well as in parts of South and Southeast Asia. According to the Murdock analysis, it is the preferred marriage form in approximately 70 percent of those societies for which data were gathered. However, information such as this should be viewed in terms of ideal and real behavior. In reality, monogamous unions generally are more common, even in societies where multiple marriages are the ideal form of union.

In traditional China we find an interesting

example of polygyny. In some areas it was acceptable for a man to bring a second wife into his household, usually with the first wife's permission and only after the man had become wealthy enough to support two wives. The second wife was a welcome addition to the family from the point of view of both the husband and the first wife. The husband was glad to have her as a sexual partner. The first marriage had been arranged by the families, and the couple had not chosen each other as mates. Their sex life was secondary to the woman's role in the man's household and in his lineage, and there was no guarantee that they would be compatible. Thus, if the husband chose a second wife, she would be someone who appealed to him in different ways and for different reasons. At the same time, the first wife would be glad to have another person around to share the household chores, and since the second wife was usually much younger than the first one, the patterns of authority within the family would be clearly defined.

In many African societies where polygyny is common it is not unusual for sisters to marry the same man. These sororal polygynous arrangements are felt to reduce friction among wives. Polygynous unions would appear to be more conveniently adapted to a rural, farming environment. In West Africa co-wives tend their own fields and have separate apartments in the family compound or living area. Is this type of institution transferrable to urban settings? To a certain extent, yes, but unless each of the wives is self-supporting—and in many cases they are—economics is a much more inhibiting factor in cities. Also, in urban areas there are strong attitudinal and social pressures militating against having multiple wives.

Polyandry, which occurs only in several isolated areas of Asia, is the practice of one woman being married simultaneously to several men. Among the Toda of South India, fraternal polyandry (or the marriage of brothers to the same woman) often takes place. Questions of fatherhood are resolved when, after the wife becomes pregnant, one

A Zulu bride decked out in her wedding regalia.

of the husbands presents her with a toy bow. This symbolically signifies that he intends to assume the role of father for that child. The question of actual biological paternity is not an issue. Polyandry is the preferred form of marriage in less than 1 percent of those groups examined in the Murdock survey.

Patterns of authority   Since a marriage creates ties between two or more individuals and set up new roles, these must be new patterns of authority to go along with those roles. In the Chinese example described earlier, the society is male dominated. Men make all the important decisions and are the center of attention. A woman can be divorced and returned to her family if she does not produce a male heir for her husband. (Ironically, we know now that it is the sperm cell contributed by the male and not the egg cell contributed by the female that determines the sex of the infant.) The woman is the head of her household and has authority over her children, but outwardly the marriage is based on the principle of male dominance and authority.

Another example of a society with a male-dominated family type is the Sarakatsani of Greece, who have been described by J. K. Campbell. Among these rural pastoral people it is important for a man to have many sons, for as Campbell says: "Sons bring prestige, daughters do not. When the husband enters the hut for the first time after the birth of a daughter, his wife turns her head away and lowers her eyes in shame."[1]

The opposite case, in which authority rests mainly with women, is much less common. In societies in which descent is through the female line, such as the Trobriand Islanders or the Nayar, females tend to have more authority simply because the children are members of their mother's kin group and not their father's. Yet even in such cases we find that men have not given up all of their authority, for the role of the mother's brother becomes more important as that of the father becomes less so.

One of the clearest cases of authority resting with the woman is found in the so-called **matrifocal family** that is typical of lower-class ghetto life in the United States and other industrial countries. In this situation, because of the economic and social strains on the family, the role of the father is minimal. Men often cannot find work to support a family, and for a woman to receive welfare the husband must be absent. As a result, the marriage bond becomes weak or nonexistent, and the woman is not in a secure position as the wife of a single man but must form

alliances with a series of men for varying periods. The result is that the father is often absent and the family unit consists of the mother and her children; family life, therefore, centers on the mother rather than on the father.

Place of residence Where a couple lives after they are married varies from one culture to another. In American society newlyweds are expected to go out and find a place of their own rather than move in with the parents of either partner. This pattern is called **neolocal residence** (from *neo,* "new"), and it is typical of most industrial nations. It fits an economic system that demands mobility, so that the family is not tied to one place or to a larger group of people. It also fits in well with the nuclear family type, although it should be pointed out that while nuclear families and neolocal residence might exist as ideals in Western nations, they are not practical in a country with an acute housing shortage. In the nations of Eastern Europe, such as Czechoslovakia, Poland, and even Russia, the movement from the country to the city has been so rapid that there simply is not enough housing to take care of all the newcomers to the city. As a result, people are forced to live with relatives in small apartments until they can find a place of their own.

Another pattern is that in which newlyweds live with the family of either the bride or the groom, a practice that is required in some societies. If the couple moves into the household of the groom's father, the residence pattern is *patrilocal;* this practice is common in patrilineal societies. If the new family is set up in the household of the bride's mother, the residence pattern is *matrilocal.* This practice is less common and is usually found in matrilineal societies.

Choice of mate In no society do people have complete freedom in choosing a mate. Even in our own society, in which there are almost no restrictions in this area, there are clearly defined laws barring a person from marrying

---

[1] J. K. Campbell, *Honour, Family, and Patronage* (New York: Cambridge University Press, 1972), p. 56.

a close relative. In addition, there are social rules that do not carry the weight of law but have the effect of limiting the choice of a mate. Thus, despite the fact that laws prohibiting interracial marriages have been struck down in recent decades, to most Americans such marriages are still unacceptable. The idea of a marriage between people of different religions is equally unpopular to some. Whether we realize it or not, we are very likely to marry someone of the same social class, the same race, and the same basic religion as ourselves—in short, someone just like us in almost every way. We may think we are choosing freely, but we are really acting within the limits that are imposed on us by our culture and are instilled in us while we are growing up.

Not all cultures allow for freedom in the choice of a mate. The rules about whom one can or cannot marry may exclude or include a variety of people, which immediately sets limits on the choices an individual can make. Usually there are rules that force an individual to marry *outside* of a certain group (at least the nuclear family), while other rules define a different set of limits for a group *within* which that person should seek a partner. As we noted earlier, when marriage is *prohibited* within a group (however that group is defined), we call it *exogamy;* when it is *confined* to a specific group, it is called *endogamy.* Sometimes these two principles operate together to limit the choice of a mate, while at other times only one of the two is in force. For example, in American culture we don't have strict rules of exogamy—except for the laws that govern what is defined as incest. (Note that marriage and incest are separate topics. Incest deals with sexual relations, whereas marriage deals with conjugal relations; they are considered together because marriage and sex usually go together.) However, as noted, in our society there are such strong social barriers to interracial marriage that we could say the United States practices racial endogamy. We can all probably think of other examples of endogamy. Members of the same social class are encouraged to marry

The marriage of Caroline Kennedy and Edwin Schlossberg is a classic example of class endogamy.

within that group, and pressures to marry within one's religion can be very strong.

Marriage and economic exchange Not every society expects an economic exchange to occur at the time of marriage. In the United States a couple may marry without any such exchange. However, in many societies marriage includes an economic transaction, indicating that for most people marriage is much more than a social ceremony uniting two people. The exchange may take the form of a payment from the groom's family to the bride's (**bride price**), or it may consist of a payment from the bride's family to the groom's (**dowry**). A marriage may be accompanied by either or both of these forms of exchange, and the payments may be equal or unequal.

The payment of a bride price seems to imply that a woman is viewed as a commodity; however, this is not always true. In general, when the woman comes to live with her husband in his father's household or at least in the same village, her labor power is transferred from the household in which she was born and raised to the one in which she will live for the rest of her life. Thus the bride price can be seen as a way of compensating the woman's family for the loss of her services. In addition, the new role of the woman is to produce heirs for her husband's kin group, and her own family has no legal claim to her children.

The idea behind the payment of a dowry is that the man brings into the marriage whatever wealth he has inherited, plus his labor and earning power. The woman, on the other hand, probably will not inherit much, if anything, from her parents, and her earning power is greatly reduced by the fact that she will be expected to bear and raise children and take care of the household chores. In some societies the dowry is used to attract a more prestigious or higher-class husband. In traditional Greek peasant society, for example, a girl's family would save for many years to provide her with a suitable dowry with which to attract a man who had some education, or worked in the city, or owned a great deal of land. According to an old Greek saying, a man with many sons has been blessed, while a man with many daughters has been cursed and faces a life of poverty and ruin. Although not a widespread practice, in some farming areas of the American Midwest daughters acquire a dowry in the form of land when they marry. Often the land remains in the woman's name, although both she and her husband receive its economic benefits.

While not a payment from one family to the other, the trousseau, or hope chest, is another example of an economic transaction that occurs at the time of marriage. From an early age, girls in many families start to acquire items they will need during their married life and store them in a cedar chest.

Thus when she marries, the woman has many of the essentials for beginning an independent life with her spouse. Today's version of this custom differs from grandma's because of the substitution of such things as microwaves, food processors, and designer sheets for the traditional quilts and embroidered towels, napkins, and linen.

A third system is an equal exchange so that the dowry and the bride price have the same value. One might think that such an exchange is unnecessary, except that once again it shows that marriage is an economic arrangement, not just a social ceremony. Also, through such an exchange a family can make sure their children marry spouses of equal social standing: By putting up a dowry or bride price of a certain value, they eliminate anyone whose family cannot match that value. Equal exchange is therefore another way of limiting the choice of a mate by unwritten rules.

Age at marriage The age at which individuals of either sex are expected to marry varies greatly from one culture to another. Men usually are not supposed to marry until they are self-supporting, although here we must distinguish between the marriage ceremony and setting up a household. In some areas of India, for example, a boy is married before he reaches puberty, but his young bride returns to her parents' home and the couple do not live together for several years. At the other extreme is the male in traditional Irish peasant society. A man was not supposed to marry until he had taken over his father's farm. This meant that until the father died or retired, the son was subject to his authority and did not have the means to support his own family. In many cases this situation lasted until the son was well into his 40s, and his position in the family was emphasized by the fact that other men in the community continued to refer to him as "boy" even though he was an adult.

For women, marriage is more closely tied to childbearing. Obviously, any society that forced women to wait until they were 40

Having completed a ceremony that marks her transition from a child to an adult, a young Masai woman from Kenya is ready to be married.

before allowing them to marry would soon die out. However, it is not unknown for women to postpone marriage (or for society to put pressure on women to marry later) for purposes of population control, especially when artificial means of birth control are unavailable or unreliable. Since a woman's fertile period usually lasts from her early teens until her 40s, by postponing marriage until her late 20s or 30s a woman can limit the number of children she bears.

A rare case is found among the Tiwi, who have already been mentioned because of their unusual marriage practices. The Tiwi believe that a woman can become pregnant at any time (the fact that young girls and old women do not become pregnant does not seem to matter). They also believe that it is a very serious offense for a woman to become preg-

nant if she is not married. Therefore a girl is betrothed before she is born; that is, if an infant is a girl, she already has had a husband chosen for her by her father, and she is married from the day of her birth. If her husband dies, the woman is immediately married to another man, so that she is never unmarried at any time in her entire life. Other societies choose future marriage partners for young children, but Tiwi girls surely are the youngest in the world at the time of their marriage.

Strength of the marriage bond   In some societies, marriages can be ended rather easily while in others they can be ended only by the death of one of the spouses. In Hollywood marriage has all but lost its meaning, while in Italy divorce was out of the question until a few years ago; even today, under the "liberalized" divorce law, the couple must be separated for five years before a divorce can be granted. In some cases the possibility of divorce and the strength of the marriage bond have to do with the economic exchange involved in the marriage. If the dowry or bride price must be returned, the bond is stronger because the families do not want to give up what they have received.

In other cases the strength of the marriage bond is one-sided, depending on who has power and authority in the society. In Islamic culture it is easier for a man to divorce his wife than the other way around. Usually, the right to end a marriage is part of the male dominance found in most societies. However, in U.S. divorce courts the majority of cases are filed by women. This may reflect different economic roles of men and women in the United States, since divorce often entails the payment of alimony by the man. For women in other countries divorce may be difficult if not impossible. The following item from a newspaper column tells how an Iranian woman managed to end her marriage:

> When Farideh Ghayebi, 22, of Tehran, found herself hoist on the wrong point of a marital triangle, she sold her husband to her rival for 700,000 rials (about $9,000). Divorce isn't easy

in Iran, it seems, but when both parties reach a financial agreement, it is usually granted. "My husband wasn't such an extraordinary dish after all," said Mrs. Ghayebi. "I'm sure I'll find a better man later."[2]

Remarriage Whether a marriage is ended by divorce or by the death of one of the spouses, the question of remarriage for one or both partners also varies from one culture to another. At one extreme, remarriage is impossible. Among the high castes in India a custom known as **suttee** dictated that when a man died, his wife was supposed to throw herself on his funeral pyre and burn to death as he was being cremated. This practice, of course, is most effective in eliminating any possibility of the wife remarrying, although there is (not surprisingly) no similar custom for men.[3] In other cultures, when a woman's husband dies his brother or brothers are expected to provide for her, and she is married to one of them. It can also happen that when a woman dies her husband obtains marital rights to one of her unmarried sisters, if she has any. In both cases the custom reflects the economic side of marriage, for the payment of a bride price or dowry entitles the family to the services of the man or woman, and a premature death does not remove that obligation.

Other cultures have different rules governing remarriage that vary according to the age of the individual and whether the marriage was ended by death or by divorce. For example, in Swiss peasant villages it was very rare for a woman to remarry if she was widowed after her childbearing years were over, but if she was still young it was acceptable for her to marry again. In the United States we generally expect people to go through a period of mourning—usually about a year—for a deceased spouse, but we

have no such expectation when a marriage ends in divorce. In fact, we are not very surprised when a man or woman remarries within a short time after being divorced; it has been known to happen on the same day.

The nature of the marriage union The rights and duties of each partner in a marriage differ widely from one culture to another. Henry VIII justified at least one of his divorces by the fact that his wife had not given him a male heir. Likewise, in traditional China having a child was not enough. It had to be a male heir to carry on the tradition and name of the patrilineage. In our own society the rights and duties of each spouse have been changing rapidly, and the expectations of a generation ago are no longer agreed upon by all members of society. For example, a man can no longer expect his wife to take the traditional role of "housewife," which includes cooking, cleaning, and raising a family. With the introduction of birth control, equal rights, and more jobs for women, the traditional female roles are no longer clearly defined; women have opportunities that they did not have a few decades ago. What this means for the future of marriage in the United States is that the rights and duties of each partner will have to be redefined to suit the wishes and preferences of both. Many more people are choosing to postpone having children, to have fewer children than their parents had, or not to have children at all. The increase in the number of working wives has made it necessary for husbands to take on more responsibility for household tasks. Also, with the role of sexual partner no longer limited to a marriage partner (the pill had a lot to do with this), many couples are living together without going through the official marriage ceremony. This is a much more flexible, if somewhat less "stable," living arrangement.

Actually, recent statistics show that more people are getting married than ever before. More couples may be living together before (or without) marriage, but in the long run most of them get married, though not always

---

[2] *International Herald Tribune*, 1972.

[3] The suttee has been abolished today in India. However, there are still some isolated instances when it occurs, but if a woman is caught before she dies, she faces police charges because suttee is considered a crime. While the law allows widows to remarry, in many parts of India it is not a socially acceptable practice.

to each other. What is really changing is attitudes about premarital sex, which in turn changes the nature of marriage as an institution and people's expectations about it.

Not long ago one of the authors was interviewed by a local radio station concerning his thoughts on whether the institution of marriage was breaking down in the United States. His answer was that it was not breaking down but going through a period of rapid adjustment to the many changes that have occurred in the last few decades. It may be that if fewer people choose to have a formal marriage ceremony before they begin to live together, we will have to redefine what we mean by marriage. But as long as men and women have to interact in order to reproduce, and as long as they seek each other's company in any kind of permanent or even semipermanent relationship, there will be something that we can call marriage.

Ritual Kinship

Thus far the focus of this chapter has been on the establishment and maintenance of kinship ties. But in many societies close bonds are often formed between individuals who are not part of the same kin group. These relationships take on many features commonly found in families, include incest prohibitions among participants, and entail using special kinship terms by people united by these bonds to refer to each other. **Ritual** (or **fictive,** as it is frequently known) **kinship** ties involve mutually recognized rights, duties, obligations, and expectations. Usually, the unions are established through public acclamation with the blessing of some religious entity.

In Latin American this institution is known as *compadrazgo* or ritual godparenthood. As a result of participating in the rituals of baptism, confirmation, first communion, and marriage, over time an individual acquires a series of godparents. The godparents are the ceremonial sponsors of these events who from that time on theoretically assume certain mutual obligations with their godchildren. Children are expected to be respectful and helpful to their sponsors and to refer to them as "godfather" or "godmother," and it is anticipated that this behavior will be reciprocated. In much of rural Latin America this institution is quite elaborate. Not only do individuals acquire a number of godparents while growing up, but as adults these same people will become godparents as well. As the years go by, people develop quite an extensive network of ritually sanctioned **dyadic** (two-person) bonds. In addition to the obvious ties between godparent and godchild, a most important connection exists between the child's biological parents and the godparents. As a result, these adults enter into a reciprocal relationship that extends well beyond mutual concern over the spiritual welfare of the child. *Compadres,* as they are called, are obligated to help each other in the same fashion that siblings might assist one another. When families need aid in sponsoring a religious festival, bringing in the harvest, getting the planting done, or obtaining a loan, in addition to calling upon members of their immediate family, they can tap these sources of their fictive kin.

Similar institutions, all enjoying religious blessings that give the ties additional importance, are found throughout southern Europe and the Balkan states. Thus ritual kinship serves as a means of extending one's network of social obligations beyond what can normally be expected through family ties.

Summary

Kinship is the system of defining relationships and organizing relatives into different categories. Although in American society it is relatively unimportant as a determinant of how we organize the rest of our life, for most people in the world kinship provides the basis for all other social relations. By studying kinship in other societies we are better able to understand our own system and the role it plays in our lives.

Kinship terms are a way of categorizing relatives. Such terms are based not only on biological relationships among individuals, but on social relationships as well—that is, kinship terms designate certain patterns of behavior expected from individuals. Which person a culture places in any particular category can vary, depending on what the members of that culture think are significant factors in determining relationships. In American culture we use the factors of sex, generation, descent, and consanguinity in establishing kinship categories; other cultures do not necessarily follow the same pattern, but instead rely on other features of kinship.

Marriage and the family are institutions that exist in every human society, although the form they take can differ greatly. Within the limits of what we consider to be a family, there can be anything from a nuclear family (parents and children) to a residential group, called an extended family, that includes many other relatives. The Nayar of India provide an example of the minimal family unit, where the family is centered around the woman and the husband exists only in a formal sense. Among the Trobriand Islanders, a matrilineal society, the mother's brother takes over what we would consider to be the father's role as authority figure, and the father is cast in a more friendly and informal role comparable to that of an uncle in our society.

Not only do all societies have proscribed rules regarding the choice of marriage partners, but all groups maintain certain restrictions regarding the choice of mates. Cross-culturally, the most fundamental of these prohibitions is marriage between members of the nuclear family. With only a few historically known exceptions among certain groups of royalty, sibling marriages or marriages between parents and offspring constitute the minimum basis for incest taboos. However, as shown in this chapter, beyond these basic prohibitions, what one group may regard as incestuous behavior may be regarded as perfectly acceptable by another.

Marriage differs from one society to another in a number of ways. A man or woman can have more than one spouse. Authority can be equal or it can be vested in the male or (less frequently) in the female side. Residence after marriage can be with the husband's family, the wife's family, or in a new place independent of either. Mates can be selected by the parents (an arranged marriage), or there can be varying degrees of free choice. Economic exchange can occur with the marriage, in the form of dowry, bride price, or both. Age at marriage can range from infancy to delayed marriage in one's 30s or 40s. The marriage bond can be strong, or it can be broken relatively easily; remarriage may be allowed (and in fact required), or it can be forbidden. And the rights and duties of each spouse can differ as the roles are defined by society.

In many societies ties are formed between individuals that resemble kinship bonds. These fictive or ritual kin relationships often involve explicit or implicit reciprocal obligations similar to those expected among members of the same kin group.

Glossary

affinal Kinship relationships between people through marriage.

bifurcation The distinction of kinship relationships on the basis of the sex of the linking relative. For example, Ego uses one term for father's brother and a different term for mother's brother, based on the difference in sex of the linking relatives (father and mother). American kinship terms do not use this distinction, and we would refer to both individuals as "uncle."

bilateral descent The system of tracing descent (inheriting kin group membership) through both parents equally, that is, through both the male and female line.

bride price A payment made from the groom's family to the bride's as part of the marriage contract.

clan A descent group in which the members assume that they are related but cannot actually trace their links back far enough to reach a common ancestor.

collateral Individuals who are related to Ego but are not on the direct line of descent (e.g., mother's brother is a collateral relative of Ego, while mother's mother is a lineal relative).

consanguineal Biological or genetic relationships between people; "blood" relatives.

cross-cousins Those cousins who are related to Ego through relatives of the opposite sex, such as father's sister's children or mother's brother's children.

descent The rules by which kin group membership is defined, and the way in which two blood relatives trace their relationship to a common ancestor.

dowry A payment made from the bride's family to the groom's as part of the marriage contract.

dyadic contract Two-person bond or tie.

Ego The central reference point from which all relationships can be calculated on a kinship diagram.

Eskimo kinship terminology A general type of kinship terminology; the pattern of formal terms used in American kinship. In this system there is a separate term for "father" and "mother," while the categories of "father's brother" and "mother's brother" are merged under one term (uncle), and likewise "father's sister" and "mother's sister" are designated by a single term (aunt). The children of parents' siblings are merged into a single category, designated by the same term (cousin).

fictive kinship An artificial category of relationships that have been formalized in a kinship system between individuals who are not biological or affinal relatives.

incest taboo A set of rules found in some form in every society, which prohibit sexual relations between certain relatives.

kinship The system of defining and organizing one's relatives.

kinship terminology The set of terms people use to distinguish between different categories of relatives; these terms may stand for both a biological and a social relationship at the same time.

lineage A descent group in which the members can trace their relationship to an actual common ancestor.

lineal A term referring to individuals who are related to Ego through the direct line of descent.

matrifocal family The family unit in which the strongest bonds are those between the mother and her children. Family life may be centered around the mother or the father and mother together.

monogamy The marriage of one man and one woman.

neolocal residence The residence pattern in which the couple, after marriage, establish a household of their own, rather than moving in with the parents of either the bride or groom.

nuclear family The family unit composed of a married couple and their unmarried offspring.

parallel cousins Those cousins who are related to Ego through relatives of the same (parallel) sex, such as father's brother's children or mother's sister's children.

polyandry The marriage practice whereby a woman has more than one husband at the same time.

polygamy The marriage practice whereby an individual has more than one spouse at the same time (includes both polyandry and polygyny).

polygyny The marriage practice whereby a man has more than one wife at the same time.

ritual kinship See *fictive kinship*.

serial monogamy A variant of monogamy, in which an individual of either sex takes a succession of spouses, one at a time, divorcing in between.

suttee A custom formerly found among the high castes in India in which a woman would throw herself upon her husband's funeral pyre and burn to death as he was being cremated.

Questions for Discussion

---

1. In American culture we consider nepotism (using family ties as the basis for handing out favors, especially desirable jobs) to be wrong. In a business setting, when the president's son is appointed vice president over other more qualified candidates, there is grumbling about the favoritism being shown. Why has kinship become so unimportant in our society? Is there something in our economic or political system that makes nepotism unacceptable?

2. In Japan a factory is organized as one big, happy family. Workers and management feel a close relationship, and the strike is unthinkable in many Japanese factories. The owner and the executives take a very paternalistic attitude toward the workers, and try to promote personal relationships that seem quite contrary to the impersonal nature of American businesses. If there is something about modern business that fosters impersonality and promotes individual achievement rather than nepotism, how can we explain the success of Japanese industry in recent years?

3. Can you think of some examples of fictive kinship in your own life? Do you use kin terms for people who are not really related to you? What kind of behavior do you expect from them? Does it parallel the behavior you expect of those who are your actual kin?

4. What are some of the consequences for marriage in American culture caused by the women's movement, improved birth control, abortion, affirmative action programs for hiring more women, and other changes that have led to greatly equality?

Suggestions for Additional Reading

PAUL BOHANNAN, *Social Anthropology* (New York: Holt, Rinehart and Winston, 1963). A basic introductory textbook containing an excellent section on kinship and marriage.

NAPOLEON CHAGNON, *Studying the Yanomamö* (New York: Holt, Rinehart and Winston, 1974). In this companion volume to the author's ethnography of the Yanomamö, Chagnon describes in detail how an anthropologist goes about discovering the kinship system in the course of fieldwork.

ANTHONY CLARE, *Lovelaw* (London: BBC Publications, 1986). Originally produced as a television series, this book is an engaging, richly illustrated exploration of love, sex, and marriage around the world.

ROBIN FOX, *Kinship and Marriage: An Anthropological Perspective* (Baltimore: Pelican, 1967). A more advanced analysis, dealing in greater detail with the major aspects of kinship and marriage.

SIGMUND FREUD, *Totem and Taboo: Resemblances Between the Psychic Lives of Savages and Neurotics* (New York: Vintage, 1918). This classic work presents Freud's evolutionary theory of the incest taboo. Although much of the theoretical import of the book has since been discredited, it can still be read as an enlightening chapter in the history of anthropology.

ROGER M. KEESING, *Kin Groups and Social Structure* (New York: Holt, Rinehart and Winston, 1975). This is an excellent book for the serious student interested in kinship.

BURTON PASTERNAK, *Introduction to Kinship and Social Organization* (Englewood Cliffs, N.J.: Prentice Hall, 1976). A brief survey of the anthropological approach to kinship and marriage.

DAVID M. SCHNEIDER, *American Kinship: A Cultural Account* (Englewood Cliffs, N.J.: Prentice Hall, 1968). An interesting account of American kinship, with many insights into American culture, as well as some interesting and humorous perspectives about our kinship system.

ERNEST L. SCHUSKY, *Manual for Kinship Analysis*, 2nd ed. (New York: Holt, Rinehart and Winston, 1972). A short but thorough handbook for understanding kinship systems and terminologies, with explanation in simple language.

ERNEST L. SCHUSKY, *Variation in Kinship* (New York: Holt, Rinehart and Winston, 1974). An introduction to the concepts and terminology of kinship anthropology.

THOMAS R. TRAUMANN, *Lewis Henry Morgan and the Invention of Kinship* (Berkeley, Calif.: University of California Press, 1987). The story of how Morgan wrote *Systems of Consanguinity and Affinity of the Human Family*, a pioneer study in kinship which was published by the Smithsonian Institution in 1871.

PIERRE L. VAN DEN BERGHE, *Human Family Systems* (New York: Elsevier North Holland, 1979). A readable analysis of family from the perspective of evolutionary biology, comparing kinship not only cross-culturally, but also across species.

When Brothers Share a Wife

MELVIN C. GOLDSTEIN

In this intriguing article, Professor Goldstein examines fraternal polyandry, the practice whereby several brothers share a common wife. Although polygamy (the practice of a man having more than one wife at the same time) is an accepted form of marriage in much of the world, the practice of several men simultaneously marrying the same woman is unusual—except in Tibet. The author examines the cultural conditions and attributes that encourage this form of marriage and then speculates about under what conditions this ancient tradition might change or disappear.

Eager to reach home, Dorje drives his yaks hard over the 17,000-foot mountain pass, stopping only once to rest. He and his two older brothers, Pema and Sonam, are jointly marrying a woman from the next village in a few weeks, and he has to help with the preparations.

Dorje, Pema, and Sonam are Tibetans living in Limi, a 200-square-mile area in the northwest corner of Nepal, across the border from Tibet. The form of marriage they are about to enter—fraternal polyandry in anthropological parlance—is one of the world's rarest forms of marriage but is not uncommon in Tibetan society, where it has been practiced from time immemorial. For many Tibetan social strata, it traditionally represented the ideal form of marriage and family.

The mechanics of fraternal polyandry are simple. Two, three, four, or more brothers jointly take a wife, who leaves her home to come and live with them. Traditionally, marriage was arranged by parents, with children, particularly females, having little or no say. This is changing somewhat nowadays, but it is still unusual for children to marry without their parents' consent. Marriage ceremonies vary by income and region and range from all the brothers sitting together as grooms to only the eldest one formally doing so. The age of the brothers plays an important role in determining this; very young brothers almost never participate in actual marriage ceremonies, although they typically join the marriage when they reach their midteens.

With permission from *Natural History,* 96, no. 3 (March 1987): 39–48. Copyright the American Museum of Natural History, 1987.

The eldest brother is normally dominant in terms of authority, that is, in managing the household, but all the brothers share the work and participate as sexual partners. Tibetan males and females do not find the sexual aspect of sharing a spouse the least bit unusual, repulsive, or scandalous, and the norm is for the wife to treat all the brothers the same.

Offspring are treated similarly. There is no attempt to link children biologically to particular brothers, and a brother shows no favoritism toward his child even if he knows he is the real father because, for example, his other brothers were away at the time the wife became pregnant. The children, in turn, consider all of the brothers as their fathers and treat them equally, even if they also know who is their real father. In some regions children use the term "father" for the eldest brother and "father's brother" for the others, while in other areas they call all the brothers by one term, modifying this by the use of "elder" and "younger."

Unlike our own society, where monogamy is the only form of marriage permitted, Tibetan society allows a variety of marriage types, including monogamy, fraternal polyandry, and polygyny. Fraternal polyandry and monogamy are the most common forms of marriage, while polygyny typically occurs in cases where the first wife is barren. The widespread practice of fraternal polyandry, therefore, is not the outcome of a law requiring brothers to marry jointly. There is choice, and in fact, divorce traditionally was relatively simple in Tibetan society. If a brother in a polyandrous marriage became dissatisfied and wanted to separate, he simply left the main house and set up his own household. In such cases, all the children stayed in the main household with the remaining brother(s), even if the departing brother was known to be the real father of one or more of the children.

The Tibetans' own explanation for choosing fraternal polyandry is materialistic. For example, when I asked Dorje why he decided to marry with his two brothers rather than take his own wife, he thought for a moment, then said it prevented the division of his family's farm (and animals) and thus facilitated all of them achieving a higher standard of living. And when I later asked Dorje's bride whether it wasn't difficult for her to cope with three brothers as husbands, she laughed and echoed the rationale of avoiding fragmentation of the family and land, adding that she expected to be better off economically, since she would have three husbands working for her and her children.

Exotic as it may seem to Westerners. Tibetan fraternal polyandry is thus in many ways analogous to the way primogeniture functioned in nineteenth-century England. Primogeniture dictated that the eldest son inherited the family estate, while younger sons had to leave home and seek their own employment—for example, in the military or the clergy. Primogeniture maintained family estates intact over generations by permitting only one heir per generation. Fraternal polyandry also accomplishes this but does so by keeping all the brothers together with just one wife so that there is only one *set* of heirs per generation.

While Tibetans believe that in this way fraternal polyandry reduces the risk of family fission, monogamous marriages among brothers need not necessarily precipitate the division of the family estate. Brothers could continue to live together, and the family land could continue to be worked jointly. When I asked Tibetans about this, however, they invariably responded that such joint families are unstable because each wife is primarily oriented to her own children and interested in their success and well-being over that of the children of the other wives. For example, if the youngest brother's wife had three sons while the eldest brother's wife had only one daughter, the wife of the youngest brother might begin to demand more resources for her children since, as males, they represent the future of the family. Thus, the children from different wives in the same generation are competing sets of heirs, and this makes such families inherently unstable. Tibetans perceive that conflict will spread from the wives to their husbands and consider this likely to cause family fission. Consequently, it is almost never done.

Although Tibetans see an economic advantage to fraternal polyandry, they do not value the sharing of a wife as an end in itself. On the contrary, they ar-

ticulate a number of problems inherent in the practice. For example, because authority is customarily exercised by the eldest brother, his younger male siblings have to subordinate themselves with little hope of changing their status within the family. When these younger brothers are aggressive and individualistic, tensions and difficulties often occur despite there being only one set of heirs.

In addition, tension and conflict may arise in polyandrous families because of sexual favoritism. The bride normally sleeps with the eldest brother, and the two have the responsibility to see to it that the other males have opportunities for sexual access. Since the Tibetan subsistence economy requires males to travel a lot, the temporary absence of one or more brothers facilitates this, but there are also other rotation practices. The cultural ideal unambiguously calls for the wife to show equal affection and sexually to each of the brothers (and vice versa), but deviations from this ideal occur, especially when there is a sizable difference in age between the partners in the marriage.

Dorje's family represents just such a potential situation. He is fifteen years old and his two older brothers are twenty-five and twenty-two years old. The new bride is twenty-three years old, eight years Dorje's senior. Sometimes such a bride finds the youngest husband immature and adolescent and does not treat him with equal affection; alternatively, she may find his youth attractive and lavish special attention on him. Apart from that consideration, when a younger male like Dorje grows up, he may consider his wife "ancient" and prefer the company of a woman his own age or younger. Consequently, although men and women do not find the idea of sharing a bride or a bridegroom repulsive, individual likes and dislikes can cause familial discord.

Two reasons have commonly been offered for the perpetuation of fraternal polyandry in Tibet: that Tibetans practice female infanticide and therefore have to marry polyandrously, owing to a shortage of females; and that Tibet, lying at extremely high altitudes, is so barren and bleak that Tibetans would starve without resort to this mechanism. A Jesuit who lived in Tibet during the eighteenth century articulated this second view: "One reason for this most odious custom is the sterility of the soil, and the small amount of land that can be cultivated owing to the lack of water. The crops may suffice if the brothers all live together, but if they form separate families they would be reduced to beggary."

Both explanations are wrong, however. Not only has there never been institutionalized female infanticide in Tibet, but Tibetan society gives females considerable rights, including inheriting the family estate in the absence of brothers. In such cases, the woman takes a bridegroom who comes to live in her family and adopts her family's name and identity. Moreover, there is no demographic evidence of a shortage of females. In Limi, for example, there were (in 1974) sixty females and fifty-three males in the fifteen- to thirty-five-year age category, and many adult females were unmarried.

The second reason is also incorrect. The climate in Tibet is extremely harsh, and ecological factors do play a major role perpetuating polyandry, but polyandry is not a means of preventing starvation. It is characteristic, not of the poorest segments of the society, but rather of the peasant landowning families.

In the old society, the landless poor could not realistically aspire to prosperity, but they did not fear starvation. There was a persistent labor shortage throughout Tibet, and very poor families with little or no land and few animals could subsist through agricultural labor, tenant farming, craft occupations such as carpentry, or by working as servants. Although the per person family income could increase somewhat if brothers married polyandrously and pooled their wages, in the absence of inheritable land, the advantage of fraternal polyandry was not generally sufficient to prevent them from setting up their own households. A more skilled or energetic younger brother could do as well or better alone, since he would completely control his income and would not have to share it with his siblings. Consequently, while there was and is some polyandry among the poor, it is much less frequent and more prone to result in divorce and family fission.

An alternative reason for the persistence of fraternal polyandry is that it reduces population growth (and thereby reduces the pressure on resources) by relegating some females to lifetime spinsterhood. Fraternal polyandrous marriages in Limi (in 1974) averaged 2.35 men per woman, and not surprisingly, 31 percent of the females of child-bearing age (twenty to forty-nine) were unmarried. These spinsters either continued to live at home, set up their own households, or worked as servants for other families. They could also become Buddhist nuns. Being unmarried is not synonymous with exclusion from the reproductive pool. Discreet extramarital relationships are tolerated, and actually half of the adult unmarried women in Limi had one or more children. They raised these children as single mothers, working for wages or weaving cloth and blankets for sale. As a group, however, the unmarried woman had far fewer offspring than the married women, averaging only 0.7 children per woman, compared with 3.3 for married women, whether polyandrous, monogamous, or polygynous. While polyandry helps regulate population, this function of polyandry is not consciously perceived by Tibetans and is not the reason they consistently choose it.

If neither a shortage of females nor the fear of starvation perpetuates fraternal polyandry, what motivates brothers, particularly younger brothers, to opt for this system of marriage? From the perspective of the younger brother in a landholding family, the main incentive is the attainment or maintenance of the good life. With polyandry, he can expect a more secure and higher standard of living, with access not only to this family's land and animals but also to its inherited collection of clothes, jewelry, rugs, saddles, and horses. In addition, he will experience less work pressure and much greater security because all responsibility does not fall on one "father." For Tibetan brothers, the question is whether to trade off the greater personal freedom inherent in monogamy for the real or potential economic security, affluence, and social prestige associated with life in a larger, labor-rich polyandrous family.

A brother thinking of separating from his polyandrous marriage and taking his own wife would face various disadvantages. Although in the majority of Tibetan regions all brothers theoretically have rights to their family's estate, in reality Tibetans are reluctant to divide their land into small fragments. Generally, a younger brother who insists on leaving the family will receive only a small plot of land, if that. Because of its power and wealth, the rest of the family usually can block any attempt of the younger brother to increase his share of land through litigation. Moreover, a younger brother may not even get a house and cannot expect to receive much above the minimum in terms of movable possessions, such as furniture, pots, and pans. Thus, a brother contemplating going it on his own must plan on achieving economic security and the good life not through inheritance but through his own work.

The obvious solution for younger brothers—creating new fields from virgin land—is generally not a feasible option. Most Tibetan populations live at high altitudes (above 12,000 feet), where arable land is extremely scarce. For example, in Dorje's village, agriculture ranges only from about 12,900 feet, the lowest point in the area, to 13,300 feet. Above that altitude, early frost and snow destroy the staple barley crop. Furthermore, because of the low rainfall caused by the Himalayan rain shadow, many areas in Tibet and northern Nepal that are within the appropriate altitude range for agriculture have no reliable sources of irrigation. In the end, although there is plenty of unused land in such areas, most of it is either too high or too arid.

Even where unused land capable of being farmed exists, clearing the land and building the substantial terraces necessary for irrigation constitute a great undertaking. Each plot has to be completely dug out to a depth of two to two and half feet so that the large rocks and boulders can be removed. At best, a man might be able to bring a few new fields under cultivation in the first years after separating from his brothers, but he could not expect to acquire substantial amounts of arable land this way.

In addition, because of the limited farmland, the Tibetan subsistence economy characteristically includes a strong emphasis on animal husbandry. Tibetan farmers regularly maintain cattle, yaks, goats, and sheep, grazing them in the areas too high for agriculture. These herds produce wool, milk, cheese, butter, meat, and skins. To obtain these resources, however, shepherds must accompany the animals on a daily basis. When first setting up a monogamous household, a younger brother like Dorje would find it difficult to both farm and manage animals.

In traditional Tibetan society, there was an even more critical factor that operated to perpetuate fraternal polyandry—a form of hereditary servitude somewhat analogous to serfdom in Europe. Peasants were tied to large estates held by aristocrats, monasteries, and the Lhasa government. They were allowed the use of some farmland to produce their own subsistence but were required to provide taxes in kind and corvée (free labor) to their lords. The corvée was a substantial hardship, since a peasant household was in many cases required to furnish the lord with one laborer daily for most of the year and more on specific occasions such as the harvest. This enforced labor, along with the lack of new land and ecological pressure to pursue both agriculture and animal husbandry, made polyandrous families particularly beneficial. The polyandrous family allowed an internal division of adult labor, maximizing economic advantage. For example, while the wife worked the family fields, one brother could perform the lord's corvée, another could look after the animals, and a third could engage in trade.

Although social scientists often discount other people's explanations of why they do things, in the case of Tibetan fraternal polyandry, such explanations are very close to the truth. The custom, however, is very sensitive to changes in its political and economic milieu and, not surprisingly, is in decline in most Tibetan areas. Made less important by the elimination of the traditional serf-based economy, it is disparaged by the dominant non-Tibetan leaders of India, China, and Nepal. New opportunities for economic and social mobility in these countries, such as the tourist trade and government employment, are also eroding the rationale for polyandry, and so it may vanish within the next generation.

10

Economic Systems: Gifts, Obligations, and Other Exchanges

The anthropological approach to economics, politics, and social control raises entirely different questions from those raised by other social scientists. In this chapter we will face the problem of deciding exactly what falls under the heading of economics.

In a broad sense, an economic system refers to the allocation of goods and services, and we might begin our discussion by asking why this is necessary. Undoubtedly, some responses quickly come to mind. For most of us, being part of an extensive economic distribution system is essential in order to acquire things not locally produced or to obtain things for less than it would cost us to make them. Most of us couldn't make our own automobiles, tools, or clothing, but even if we could, we would probably find it cheaper to buy most of these items. In addition, participating in an economic system is an essential part of the establishment and maintenance of political alliances. When members of different Yanomamö tribes get together, one of the first things they do is to exchange goods. Often these are items that the other group already has. One family will exchange spun cotton yarn with another. Men will trade almost identical arrows. Trading is done in order to establish the basis for other activities, including forming alliances through intermarriage. Sometimes feasting and trading provide the basis for agreeing to mount a joint raiding party on a third village.

People also participate in economic systems of distribution in order to meet certain ritual expenditures. The process might involve borrowing funds or goods to help allay the costs of religious ceremonies or to meet the more mundane, but nevertheless important, expenses associated with obtaining seed for the spring planting.

Anthropologists feel that the study of economic systems should be done in a holistic perspective because there are often no clear distinctions among the various areas of social life. What may look like political behavior can also be a setting for economic exchange or an affirmation of existing patterns of power and authority. In this section we will review several different types of economic systems found in non-Western societies, showing how they are fused with other types of behavior. Because of this fusion, these economic systems can be studied only in the context of the total social system.

Tribal, Peasant, and Industrial Economic Systems

The anthropological approach to economics tries to show that, for economic theory to be considered valid, it must apply not only to Western industrial society but to all societies. In the discussion that follows we will first distinguish among *tribal, peasant*, and *industrial* economies. Then we will discuss three different modes of exchange: *reciprocity, redistribution*, and *market exchange* (based on supply and demand). Finally, we will show how the study of these topics can lead us to a better understanding of the nature of social organization and the integration of culture.

Western economic theory is based on the premise that people will try to become as wealthy as they can, that is, to maximize their economic gain. However, anthropologists do not accept this as a universal guiding force in economic activity. In many non-Western societies (and often in our own) other values affect the way people act. Prestige, the obligations of kinship, or any of a number of other factors might lead a person to disregard monetary gain and make an economic decision that seems "irrational" to us. This is possible because economic activity is not always separated from other aspects of life to the extent that it appears to be. For example, Americans believe there is no place for favoritism in a competitive business situation. The boss' son has to earn his promotion like anyone else. (In reality, of course, we can easily cite cases in which the boss' son or daughter received special treatment.) Yet in many societies this belief would be considered ridiculous. The son is entitled to special treatment, and it would be foolish *not* to expect him to be favored over others.

The blending of economics with other aspects of social life, such as religion, marriage, or kinship, is typical of traditional societies. What we call **traditional economies** are found in many of the non-Western societies studied by anthropologists, not only hunters and gatherers, but some agriculturalists and horticulturists as well. These small-scale economies exist among relatively isolated, self-sufficient groups. There is little division of labor within the society, which means that almost everyone performs the same economic activities. What little surplus the people are able to produce goes into their own fund to be used for ceremonies and special occasions; nothing is exported or marketed. In sum, the traditional economy is controlled entirely by the local community.

It is based on a fairly simple technology that relies on human and animal power.

In contrast to the traditional system of production and limited consumption stands the modern **industrial economy** with its advanced technology. Production in an industrial economy is almost entirely for exchange, which means that communities are not self-sufficient. The division of labor is carried to an extreme, with specialists taking over almost every aspect of the economy. The economy is controlled on the national or even international level, and the individual producer is subject to outside pressures. Typical of the industrial economic system is our concept of the farmer as a businessman—a cultivator who produces crops for sale in a market system in return for a cash profit.

Midway between these two types of economy is the peasant economy. Peasants are

The New York Stock Exchange. In American society, economic activities are clearly separated from religion, politics, and kinship.

partly self-sufficient, and while they resemble traditional producers in many ways, they also share certain characteristics with the modern farmer. There is no great division of labor in a peasant community; almost every member is engaged in the production of food for consumption. Peasants rely on a simple technology with tools made from locally available materials and animal power providing most of the energy. But unlike traditional producers, peasant producers are tied to a wider market system. The means and the results of their production are controlled to some extent by an outside elite group, and they are forced to rely on a town or city for their subsistence. They may be taxed, or their land and labor may be controlled in some other way.

We turn now to a discussion of the various types of exchange. Note that most anthropological studies have focused on tribal and peasant economic systems; only recently have anthropologists paid any attention to modern industrial economies, and even then it has been with the idea of pointing out the elements of tribal and peasant economics that can be found even in a modern economy.

Reciprocity   In his book *The Great Transformation* the economic historian Karl Polanyi has defined three patterns of exchange that can serve as the basis for an economic system: **reciprocity, redistribution,** and **market exchange.** Whereas Western economists tend to focus on market exchange, anthropologists have found the other two types equally important in their studies of non-Western societies. Market exchange implies the law of supply and demand, which dictates who exchanges what with whom. Redistribution entails the collection of goods by a central authority, which allocates those goods to members of the society. Reciprocity exists when people exchange goods without a market system or any outside authority. Although aspects of all three patterns are present in most societies, historically many societies relied principally on one form.

Whereas redistribution implies stratifica-

tion, with those in power able to control the society's wealth, reciprocity can occur in both highly stratified and basically egalitarian societies. It can be concerned with the exchange of goods, such as agricultural products or handicrafts, or it can involve other items, such as potential mates. Often there are reciprocal arrangements among members of a family or a wider kin group, and these arrangements are part of the obligations of kinship. Among the !Kung San of the Kalahari Desert, when a hunter or a group of hunters is successful in a big kill, the meat brought home is divided among the hunter's kin, with the expectation that when someone else makes a kill the debt will be repaid. It is not important for the amounts of meat to balance exactly, as long as the obligations of reciprocity are fulfilled.

Malinowski describes a complex set of reciprocal relationships among the different groups with which the Trobriand Islanders trade. One aspect of this economic system is the **Kula ring,** in which a series of island groups exchange shell ornaments and other ritually important items. The trading ring is organized so that different items travel in different directions (see Figure 10.1). For example, the Trobrianders trade arm bands for necklaces with the people from Dobu. This exchange would never be reversed; that is, the Dobuans would never give the Trobianders arm bands, and the Trobrianders would never give the Dobuans necklaces. In addition, each *Kula* trader has a number of formal trading partnerships with which he may exchange these items.

The necklaces, arm bands, and other treasures to be exchanged are held in very high esteem. They are used only in special ceremonies, and each piece is well known to all of the traders, having its own name and history. Furthermore, these items cannot be used to buy anything other than ritual trade items. In other words, a *Kula* trader could not use a necklace to buy food, but only to buy an arm band. The value of each piece depends on its special qualities and is generally agreed upon by all the members of the

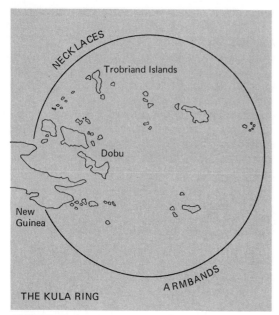

FIGURE 10.1

trade ring. It has been suggested that the *Kula* ring employs a primitive form of currency, for the ritual items are used in much the same way that we use money.

On the surface it would seem that there is no rational explanation for the exchanges that occur among members of the *Kula* ring. The trading expeditions require long canoe trips across open seas and are very dangerous. We can see why certain items might be given ritual value, especially when they are made of materials that are not locally available and can be acquired only by trading with other island groups. But it is hard to understand why these expeditions continue once a sufficient supply of these items has been obtained. It looks as if the Trobrianders and the others in the ring are inveterate traders who would go to any lengths to get together for an exchange.

Upon closer analysis, however, the reason for the trade expeditions becomes clear. The Trobriand Islanders distinguish between the trading of ritual items, such as arm bands and necklaces, and the trading of practical items such as food and tools. When they set off on a trading expedition, their main purpose is to exchange ritual items. Yet this activity is actually less important in another sense. The canoes used for *Kula* trade are laden with practical items as well as ritual ones, and those items are exchanged as a preliminary to the *Kula* trade. The practical items do not have a ritual value and are the subject of much haggling among the traders. But as long as all of the participants recognize that the mission really revolves around the *Kula* trade, this kind of haggling can occur, although the traders may not argue over the value of a *Kula* item. Trading partners who have a firmly established *Kula* relationship may not trade practical items with each other, and this prevents them from haggling with each other over anything.

In other words, although the Trobrianders may not admit it, the *Kula* trade is really important for two reasons: Not only does it bring about the exchange of ritual items, but it also brings people together for the "incidental" exchange of more important subsistence items. Thus we can see two types of exchange operating at the same time: the *Kula* system, which is basically a type of reciprocity, and the incidental trading, which is a type of market exchange with values that depend on supply and demand.

Insight into the functioning of the *Kula* ring and into Trobriand life in general has benefitted considerably by the recent publications of Annette B. Weiner.[1] Working among the Trobrianders 60 years after Malinowski had been there, Weiner noted that while Malinowski noted the high status of women in this matrilineal society, he underestimated the importance of women's wealth and importance in the operation of the *Kula* ring. Given Malinowski's interest in and attention to exchange systems, it is really quite amazing that he neglected this important aspect of Trobriand society. Women control a considerable amount of wealth and thus have direct access to items that are being

[1] Annette B. Weiner, *The Trobrianders of Papua New Guinea* (New York: Holt, Rinehart and Winston, 1988).

exchanged. In some instances they are directly involved in the trading process. More often they remain in the background, but are still important players in the process. Thus, Weiner's recent work emphasizes the importance of women's work and wealth in ascertaining how Trobriand society, including the *Kula* transactions, function.

The San and Trobriand patterns of reciprocity are examples of a traditional economic system in which small-scale, isolated societies control their own economies and are basically self-sufficient.

Redistribution   Redistribution generally refers to a type of economic system that differs from reciprocity principally in having some central authority that collects available goods and services for redistribution, and then requires the participation of all members of the society. Often this system is intended to support a nonproducing elite, which keeps the largest share for itself so as to maintain its power. In his book *Oriental Despotism* Karl Wittfogel has argued that this form of exchange was characteristic of irrigation societies such as that of ancient Egypt. According to his theory, societies grew up along the river beds in otherwise arid regions. The rivers provided the water and fertile soil necessary to support a fairly dense population. Eventually, however, the population outgrew the land, and to support more people irrigation was required. As the irrigation system grew more complex, more regulations and greater power to enforce those regulations were needed. The end result was the emergence of an elite group that maintained its power through laws and religious edicts.

Such was the case among the pharaohs of ancient Egypt. Originally their power was based on the regulation of irrigation along the Nile River. Later it was justified by religious doctrines that were accepted by the common people. The pharaohs forced the agricultural population to produce a surplus, which was turned over to them and redistributed to non-agricultural workers and the elite. In this way they were able to support the tremendous number of workers whose labor was devoted to the construction of the pyramids.

Like reciprocity, redistribution is often embedded in a complex set of kinship relations. In some cases the central authority who collects and redistributes goods might be the head of a large extended household; in others, the central figure has only a fictive relationship to the producers. The pharaoh was believed to be divine and thus was symbolically related to every member of the society. Likewise, a tribal chieftain who represented the spirit of all the ancestors of the tribe could invoke his position as head of the tribe and symbolic leader of the people in collecting and allocating the tribe's resources.

Redistribution need not always involve the collection and allocation of goods by the head of state. It can also take the form of a codified exchange of goods and services among many groups in a stratified society. To illustrate redistributive exchange in a peasant society, we turn to the *jajmani* system found in many peasant villages in India.

In a highly stratified society like India, redistribution is carefully calculated. In the **jajmani** system traditional payments are made for services. This is not a market system of exchange, however, because the values of the services are not based on supply and demand but are fixed by tradition. The *jajmani* system is based on the caste system, with its division of the population into groups according to occupation.

Although most of the peasant villages in India depend mainly on **subsistence agriculture,** some families in those villages do not till the soil. Because of the complex system of stratification, only certain members of the community are landowners and farmers. These are the families that enjoy roles of power and that, because of their position in the hierarchy, have the authority to ensure that the system of redistribution functions. Those who belong to different castes have different occupations. Some families practice specialized crafts: Carpenters make the farmers' tools, and water carriers bring water from

Bronislaw Malinowski (1884–1942)

Bronislaw Malinowski spent six years studying the peoples of the Australian territories during World War I. His contribution to the field of anthropology rests not only with his emphasis on field research and the method of participant observation; from his work in the Pacific, he produced many accounts of the economic, religious, and sexual lives of the people he studied. His analysis of the *Kula* ring as an economic institution among the Trobriand Islanders offers a valuable insight into the function of trading expeditions for the people within the island ring. He also offered the view of a people's mythology as an explanation and justification for their social order—in his words, myth serves as a charter for society.

the well for the other villagers. Each person receives payment for his or her services in the form of agricultural produce from the farmer caste and other services or products from members of the other castes. Thus the landowner commands the services of a wide group of lower-caste specialists. The *jajmani* system is the means that enables each specialist, including the cultivator, to obtain the goods and services of others, in order to have the variety necessary for existence. As such, it is an institutionalized form of redistribution.

It is impossible, however, to separate the *jajmani* system as an economic institution from other institutions of Indian society. The Hindu religion provides the basis for the *jajmani* system in the philosophy on which the caste system is based. Clearly, without the stratification imposed by the caste system and the religious rules prescribing specific tasks for specific groups, the *jajmani* system could not operate, since all the members of the

village could cultivate their own land and provide their own products and specialized services. Thus the *jajmani* system fuses economics, social class, caste, and religion. Likewise, the Hindu religion provides clear rules of behavior for each caste and therefore serves as a basis for social control on the village level. Political and legal authority are based partly on religious beliefs and partly on economic power, both of which are supported by the *jajmani* system. Although the *jajmani* system is an economic institution, it is defined mainly in social terms, as a network of alliances between groups of people with different occupations. It enables those groups to exchange their goods and services, but these exchanges can be understood only in the context of Indian society as a whole.

Money is rarely important in the *jajmani* system. It is the exchange of goods and services, with values defined by tradition, that maintains the system. Traditional customs keep this system closed, unlike our competi-

A village market in Bahri, India. Market exchange exists along with a system of redistribution in the traditional jajmani system.

tive open-market system. In fact, when local village economies become more dependent on cash, the *jajmani* system begins to break down. Consider, for example, what would happen if a carpenter's payment of grain was translated into a cash payment. Under the *jajmani* system, in return for making and repairing a farmer's tools, a carpenter would receive a certain amount of grain, which, in terms of feeding a family, has a fixed value over time. The grain payment will feed the same number of people today that it would have fed 100 years ago. If we translate this into a cash payment, again at a fixed amount, the carpenter's payment will vary in terms of how many mouths it can feed as the value of the cash varies. And if the payment in cash is designed to rise and fall with the value of the currency, so that the relative value of the carpenter's payment is maintained, the traditional system of payments no longer holds.

There are many cases of redistribution and reciprocity operating together, in the sense that one person might collect and give away goods with the expectation that those

to whom he or she has given something will reciprocate in some way. The **potlatch** of the Kwakiutl Indians is an example of such a system.

During the winter, when little productive activity could be carried out, the Kwakiutl turned to ceremonial activities in which redistribution took the form of festivals and ritual gift giving. Vast feasts were held, and these were sometimes accompanied by a potlatch, in which a man would give away his possessions. A potlatch was an important ceremonial occasion used to validate a life-crisis ceremony or rite of passage. A man would give a potlatch after being initiated into a secret society, after getting married, or on any of a number of other important occasions. In the course of the potlatch he would seek to prove that he was worthy of the position he claimed and to increase his prestige. The actual redistribution of his possessions was designed to shame his guests and flaunt his own status. A man would spend months or even years preparing for this occasion, borrowing and saving all he could

Kwakiutl Indians from British Columbia display objects to be given away at a potlatch.

in order to have enough to give away. The purpose of the potlatch was to show that he could give away more than his guests could give him. By doing this he proved his importance and validated his higher status. As a result, the guests at the potlatch felt obligated to reciprocate with an even bigger gift-giving festival.

Even more degrading to the guests than giving away wealth was destroying it. A man who gave a potlatch might end with a grand finale in which he literally burned blankets, canoes, valuable copper items, and even food. Then, having achieved the ultimate in status, he would pay off the debts he had incurred while storing up all his wealth, certain that he would be invited to the potlatches of others and would receive payments from them. At the same time, he would begin to build up a new fortune to be spent on his next potlatch, for he must always seek a higher status. The higher the status he could achieve, the better off he would be at the potlatches of others; one did not gain status by simply inviting a group of people to a potlatch, secure in the knowledge that they could be easily shamed.

Situations like the potlatch are not uncommon in our own society. We all know of peole who build up fortunes and then give much of their wealth to charity in return for pres-

tige, high social status, and perhaps even an important position in government or business (consider what it takes to become an ambassador). A debutante ball is similar to a potlatch in some ways. First, it is only for the wealthy; it is used to maintain or elevate their high status in society. Not everyone can have a coming-out party—it takes social position, not just money. By throwing such a party, one is actually redistributing wealth to other members of the society. And this is done with the expectation that others will reciprocate. If they don't, they will not be invited to the next party. The point is that the "strange" economic behavior found in other societies is not too different from our own.

We might also look at redistribution as a form of savings institution. A man gains prestige by distributing a surplus. The prestige is shared by his clan or his family. Then if he or his family should have a bad year or a river should run dry or a herd disappear, he can rely on others who are indebted to him. In this sense, distributing a surplus, by whatever means, serves the same purpose as putting money in the bank.

Market exchange Ever since the advent of cities there have been markets where peasants and other producers or manufacturers of goods bought and sold their wares. Many of us are familiar with Saturday morning farmers' markets where during the summer months people bring in their fresh fruits and vegetables for sale. Large cities in this country often have sections with permanent stands or shops where such items are sold on a regular basis, not by the producers or growers, but by intermediaries. While these examples approximate the markets found in small towns and large cities throughout much of the developing world, they are not identical to them.

In the big cities of the Third World there are sometimes areas the size of several city blocks in which hundreds or even thousands of vendors peddle everything from fresh flowers to pots and pans to horses and camels to the dried fetuses of animals and rhinoceros horns that are meant for medicinal purposes. To the outsider these markets seem chaotic, and the senses are almost overwhelmed by the blur of colors, the amalgamation of smells, and the cacophony of sounds. Yet beneath the chaos there is some semblance of order. Metal tools are sold in one section, fish and meat in another, and woven goods in a third. Large cities have markets operating every day of the week. Perhaps one or two of these days are special market times when outside vendors are permitted to peddle their wares in specific areas on the fringes of the regular marketplace. During these periods the markets become swollen to twice their normal size as extra participants jostle one another to buy and sell. In contrast, small towns and villages may have market days just once a week. The rest of the time only a few merchants operate small stores or stands.

Markets serve a number of functions besides the economic one. Historically, market settings have provided rural people with diversity and excitement compared to the humdrum existence of their daily lives. Musical groups wander through the crowds, accepting requests from passersby. Food stands offer up steaming hot soups, cooked meats, fried vegetables, and many other things to those who are hungry or thirsty. Markets are very social places. The process of buying goods in itself provides opportunities for social exchanges. Suppose you want to buy some beans. The vegetable section might have a number of merchants selling what looks like identical produce. You walk through the area, stopping quickly to look at what is available. Finally, you approach one vendor and ask the price of a quantity of beans. You are given an answer, whereupon you are expected to make a counteroffer. If the merchant accepts, you make your purchase. If the seller feels the reply is close but not good enough, a counterproposal is made and you accept it or leave. Bargaining sessions similar to this would characterize virtually every encounter you have that day in the market. Usually, when you purchase something like a small amount of fruit or vegetables, the exchanges are quick and not much time is spent dickering. However, if you are buying a larger item, a locally made rug, for instance, the bargaining might go on for quite a while. You would comment on the condition of the piece, pointing out all of its real or imagined flaws, while the vendor would vigorously protest that the item is in excellent condition and that the price you are offering is so ridiculously low that it would take an entire day of selling for him or her to make up for the loss. A good bargaining session consists of repartee and lots of mutual kidding, and should be a very social occasion. Once a price has been reached, all parties should feel they have gained much more than just a sale or a purchase.

From this discussion we can see that economic behavior in many market settings is not designed simply to maximize profits by calculating or estimating the return for labor and products. In the Haitian market, for example, trade is bound up with a personal relationship between intermediaries. This relationship, called **pratik,** refers to the personal ties between an intermediary and those with whom she deals.

A *pratik* is a relationship between a woman trader and her customer. On one side are the producers, who use her as an interme-

In the peasant village of San Lázaro, Mexico, peasant production is primarily for family consumption. Surplus agricultural products and crafts are sold in markets in order to purchase necessities. (Top) Peasants loading an ox cart with goods to be sold in regional market. (Bottom) A family making cane baskets.

diary in getting their goods to market, and on the other are the retailers in the market, who get their products from her. Bonds are formed between the woman and her clients in various ways, but they are always based on a personalized relationship such as granting a "baker's dozen," giving credit, or lowering prices. The *pratik* bond sets up obligations among all the participants and tends to lower profits while providing greater security. The reason for *pratik* can be seen in the nature of

the rural economy of Haiti. Production is fairly high, yet relatively few people are engaged in agriculture. As a result, there are thousands of women who make a small living by trading. This could be a high-risk occupation, since the competition is so keen and the profit margin so low. In order to reduce the risk and increase security, the women form personal bonds with both producers and retailers. For example, if you consistently sell to a retailer at a lower price, you reduce your profit, but you have a hold on that person when the supply is such that she could go elsewhere for an even lower price. Or suppose that as a trader you pay the producer slightly more than is necessary when the supply is high and the demand is low. When supply becomes scarce, the producer will hold some back for you and you will not be shut out of the market.

Thus *pratik* relationships tend to stabilize what would otherwise be a highly unstable market situation owing to the unstable nature of the Haitian agricultural economy. *Pratik* modifies pure competition by giving certain people priority in the market. As such, it turns out to be a highly practical, rational arrangement based on the economic context in which it is found.

Inheritance Up to this point we have been talking about types of exchanges among the living, but as we all know, most societies have rules to ensure that goods and property can be transferred from one generation to another. Many societies have rather specific regulations about **inheritance.** Are the goods divided among a number of heirs or do they all pass to one of the survivors? If the latter, does everything go to the eldest son, in which case other offspring realize from a very early age they must take care of themselves? Or does the youngest child inherit everything? In much of Africa and Asia the youngest son is expected to remain at home and take care of his parents. In return, he is assured of receiving the house. In the United States the general rule is that the spouse has first claim, and all children inherit equally. This rule can be overridden by a legal instrument, or will, which determines how goods and properties will be transferred. In the absence of a will, most states have laws defining how property passes and determining who gets what, and these laws follow the culturally approved rules granting all or most of the estate to the surviving spouse, and equal shares to close lineal relatives (parents and children). Of course, even a legal document does not ensure that all the heirs will be satisfied. News-

papers continually entertain their readers with accounts of the squabbling among the very rich over just how many millions each heir should receive.

Economic and Social Organization

So far we have surveyed several basic economic types and three modes of exchange that can occur in these economic systems. We have also seen that it is incorrect to characterize the economy of any society as based solely on reciprocity, redistribution, or market exchange. Any economy combines all of these types of exchange, although one type may dominate. We must also be aware of the relationship between economics and other basic institutions. We pointed this out in our discussion of the *jajmani* system, indicating how it is reinforced by religious doctrines and how it fits into the system of social stratification that defines all social relations in Indian villages. In the previous chapter we saw how marriage can be viewed as an economic exchange rather than a social activity, and in fact in most rural areas of non-Western societies the notion of love as a basis for a marriage runs counter to basic values.

We must also recognize that what appear to us to be basic principles of economic activity in Western society are not followed by every society and in fact are not universal values. Our notion of making the greatest individual profit, for example, is foreign to many people, who would prefer to engage in transactions that promote solidarity (such as *pratik* relationships), calculating their profit in social as well as monetary terms. We Westerners are used to calculating and weighing alternatives when we engage in economic transactions. However, many values cannot be calculated, and many objects cannot have a value assigned to them. In a small, isolated community in which everyone knows everyone else and people interact on a close, personal basis, getting ahead is rarely as important as fitting in with the group. Prestige and approval of one's actions can be much more important than a higher standard of living, and these factors will enter into any calculations made by a member of the community. Coming from another culture, we tend to view such calculations as irrational because they violate our ideas about what is "rational" according to our system of values. But we must take into account the nonmaterial, intangible values that the people themselves assign to things. When we do this, their actions almost always turn out to be just as "rational" in the context of their culture as ours are in the context of our culture.

Summary

In studying economic behavior the anthropologist recognizes that different principles govern the decisions people make in other societies. While maximization of profit is the driving force in our own society, in another cultural context other factors might be more important: the obligations of kinship, the feelings one has about the environment, or the sentimental attachment one develops to the land or to cultural traditions. Interestingly enough, in recent years many critics of American society have cited some typically "American" values as being the source of many of our current problems. We have long ignored family obligations in our emphasis on achieved status over ascribed status; we have depleted our resources and polluted our environment with little concern for anything but the almighty dollar; we have fought off all the ways of the past that held us back from expanding our economy. Now we are beginning to appreciate the values that other people have followed, values that a few years ago we called backward and primitive. We have gained a new respect for the native American's interaction with the environment, and for the close family ties that the children of immigrants used to have but gradually lost in their attempt to get ahead in industrial society.

Glossary

industrial economy An economy based on advanced technology in a society where tasks are specialized and production is primarily for exchange rather than self-sufficiency.

inheritance The means by which material and nonmaterial possessions are transferred from one generation to the next.

jajmani An economic system found in many peasant villages in India, based on the caste system and its implied occupational specialization.

Kula ring A pattern of exchange found in some of the islands of Melanesia, combining an exchange of both ritual trade items and practical items.

market exchange A pattern of exchange based on the law of supply and demand in which each individual attempts to maximize profits by placing a value on labor and products.

potlatch A form of exchange combining redistribution and reciprocity, found among the aboriginal populations of the Pacific Northwest coast of North America, involving the giving away of gifts and the destruction of material goods in order to increase prestige and status.

pratik The special personal relationship between a trader and her customers in the rural market system of Haiti.

reciprocity The exchange of goods and services between individuals or groups taking place without a market system and without a law of supply and demand dictating behavior.

redistribution A pattern of exchange in a stratified society in which there is a collection of goods by a central authority and then a reallocation of these goods to members of the society.

subsistence agriculture The production of food for one's own consumption.

traditional economy A small-scale economy found among relatively isolated, self-sufficient groups in which a small surplus goes toward ceremonial occasions, and in which production is not tied into the wider market system of the country.

Questions for Discussion

1. One of the characteristics of economic behavior in a small-scale society is the importance of personal relationships over the attempt to gain every last penny of profit from a transaction. Can you think of situations in your own society where personal factors enter in to reduce profit (such as the difference between the neighborhood grocer who throws in an extra item to make a "baker's dozen," as opposed to the formal and impersonal climate of a large supermarket)?

2. In what respects are aspects of redistributive exchange found at the national level in our society?

Suggestions for Additional Reading

CYRIL S. BELSHAW, *Traditional Exchange and Modern Markets* (Englewood Cliffs, N.J.: Prentice Hall, 1965). A short survey of different types of exchange and the impact of modernization on traditional peasant market exchange.

RHODA H. HALPERIN, *Economies Across Cultures* (London: The MacMillan Press, Ltd., 1988). A short book explaining the theory and methodology for explaining pattern and variation in economies across time and cultures.

EDWARD E. LECLAIR, JR., and HAROLD K. SCHNEIDER (Eds.), *Economic Anthropology* (New York: Holt, Rinehart and Winston, 1968). A collection of articles dealing with the major issues of economic anthropology.

ELLIOT LIEBOW, *Tally's Corner* (Boston: Little, Brown, 1967). A study of an African-American ghetto in Washington, D.C., with a valuable perspective on the economics of ghetto life from an insider's point of view.

J. PARRY and M. BLOCK (Eds.), *Money and the Morality of Exchange* (New York: Cambridge University Press, 1989). A collection of essays on the subject of how money is symbolized cross-culturally.

Guelaguetza: Reciprocal Exchange in a Mexican Peasant Village

MICHAEL B. WHITEFORD

How do members of tribal or peasant societies, where the accumulation of capital goods is difficult, deal with the occasional need to make significant expenditures? In this contribution Michael Whiteford examines a process of reciprocal exchange in a Mexican peasant village. To offset the costs of festivals, sponsors call upon certain members of the community to assist them through an institutionalized procedure called the guelaguetza. Villagers comply because they know that at some point in the future they will benefit from the contributions of those they have helped.

The members of technologically simple societies, peasant or tribal, usually find it difficult to accumulate economic surpluses. Yet these people, like those in more complex societies, are periodically faced with the need to make significant capital expenditures. Some of the needs are ritual: sponsorship of a religious festival, a funeral feast, a marriage celebration, and the like. Other expenses are more mundane, but still inevitable, such as those resulting from serious illness and economic adversity. The question is: How are members of such societies able to meet these peak periods of need? "Saving for a rainy day" is not practical in a subsistence economy; banks and other savings organizations are not readily available to these people. A very different process, which is played out in a variety of forms, must be utilized.

This process involves recognized exchange obligations and expectations. The person in temporary need of more capital calls upon other members of the community, or outside the community, to make available small amounts of their resources. In so doing, the individual invokes claims on a number of people. That is, recognized, institutionalized systems of borrowing permit an individual, as the need arises, to control more capital than he or she needs in daily life.

One such method of marshalling resources is through loans. These may be straight borrowing, or they may involve securities, depending on how much is being borrowed and the relationship between the participants. The rotating credit system offers yet another means of accumulating capital in a short period of time. In this system all of the participants meet periodically and contribute a set sum of money to a communal pool. At each meeting the money in the pool is given to a different member, so that eventually every member has access to a relatively large sum of money. There are still other recognized exchange institutions that are social and ritual as well as economic. These methods are not mutually exclusive and often are used simultaneously. Thus an individual may tap many available resources in a time of need.

In the Oaxaca Valley of southern Mexico a socioeconomic institution frequently used to muster resources for specific occasions is called the *guelaguetza*. The short discussion of this institution that follows is based on work conducted in San Lázaro Etla, a farming and dairying peasant community of 495 inhabitants located about 30 kilometers from Oaxaca City.

The word *guelaguetza* comes from a Zapotec Indian kinship term, but in Oaxaca it is used to denote a ritual exchange, centering around the act of "donating" the food, drink, money, or labor needed for social events. For most religious celebrations, such as feast days, wedding parties, and funerals, the sponsor (in this community it is generally a male role) requests help from certain individuals. Through blood and fictive kin relationships, people in San Lázaro have formed a series of dyadic (two-way) ties. By invoking them the sponsor can mobilize help. The request is phrased: "Can you make *guelaguetza*?" meaning "Can you help me at this time?" *Guela-*

guetza, therefore, is the activation of recognized reciprocal relationships.

The persons included in someone's network of *guelaguetza* ties are related to him by kinship, both fictive and real. There is a hierarchy of importance regarding which individuals are called upon first and when the line is drawn, after which no more guests are asked. Members of the immediate family are the first to be invited to a fiesta. Next the sponsor approaches members of his or her extended family, such as cousins, uncles, and aunts. After informing one's blood relatives of the impending fiesta, the sponsor seeks out fictive kin (called *compadres*) asking them to come.

Several years ago Soltero Hernandez's[1] *compadre*, Maclovio Arboleda, was responsible for the festival in honor of Our Lady of Perpetual Help. About two weeks before it was to take place Mr. Arboleda approached Mr. Hernandez and asked him to "make *guelaguetza*." Mr. Hernandez agreed. Nothing more was said regarding the occasion. Three days before the festival was to take place Mr. Hernandez contributed a sum of money to its cost. For portions of the next three days Mr. Hernandez worked without pay for Mr. Arboleda, at times cutting alfalfa and feeding his *compadre's* cow so Mr. Hernandez could devote all his time to preparing for the festival. Twice Mr. Hernandez and another *compadre* of Mr. Arboleda, Arnulfo Vasquez, made trips to the neighboring town for supplies. In preparing for and carrying out this festival Mr. Arboleda created or reaffirmed thirteen other *guelaguetza* relationships.

Non-*guelaguetza* guests are also invited to most fiestas of any size. These are people who do not recognize a bond with the sponsor and from whom no "donation" is expected. People of recognized status in the village, such as the Roman Catholic priest and the village officials, are invited to most festive gatherings. If they have been included because of their status rather than because of kinship ties, they assume no *guelaguetza* obligation. Another type of non-*guelaguetza* guest includes individuals that the sponsor is cultivating socially and with whom he would like to establish fictive kinship ties at a later date. For instance, Aurelio Gonzalez invited Rafael Narvaez to a fiesta. This set the stage and a month later Mr. Narvaez became the confirmation godfather of Mr. Gonzalez's daughter, Lola.

The sponsor invites the intended participants by asking them to take part in the activities. Relatives and *compadres* realize their social obligations to the sponsor, and will assist with the festivities by bringing fare and helping with the mechanics.

The people of San Lázaro keep no written records of gifts exchanged in *guelaguetza*, although most of them claim they remember all of their *guelaguetza* debits and credits.[2] In reality, however, while individuals know to whom they owe *guelaguetza* and who is in debt to them, they frequently do not agree on the items or amounts exchanged. In any case, record keeping is not necessary to the effective operation of the *guelaguetza* and may even be detrimental to it. What is important is that relationships continue. Some people argue that if individuals know their exact balance of *guelaguetza* credits and debits, they might choose to repay all their debts in full, thus jeopardizing the continuance of the relationship. One defense against such a possibility, participants claim, is for people to return double what they have received. The geometric progression would soon prove economically infeasible, so the double return is more a theoretical defense than an actual one. Nevertheless, it indicates the importance residents place on maintaining a *guelaguetza* relationship.

The *guelaguetza* relationship is significant in a number of ways. First, it enables an individual to call upon various members of his community for help in sponsoring a festive event. In this manner families are able to carry out preparations for important festivities without going so deeply into debt that it would take them years to recoup their losses. (In contrast, among peasants in many communities elsewhere in Mexico—and for that matter, throughout Central America—this is exactly what happens.) Soltero Caicedo has never held a major festival but will probably begin to sponsor religious celebrations within a few years. When the time comes, he is confident that any event he hosts will be a success because he will be able to call in his outstanding *guelaguetza* debts accumulated over the years. Second, being able to call in *guelaguetza* debts enhances the sponsor's prestige. It is a way of flexing social muscles. More debts to be called in and more new *guelaguetza* relationships formed mean a larger fiesta, which in turn signifies the preeminence of the sponsor. Third, *guelaguetza* implies at least tacit cooperation among participants, a factor of considerable importance in many peasant societies.

Guelaguetza relationships are utilized in other ways as well. The debits and credits thereby created

---

[1] All of the names used here are pseudonyms.

[2] In contrast, in one of the neighboring communities all *guelaguetza* transactions are carefully recorded to ensure that reciprocity is carried out and that exchanges are of equal worth.

may serve as collateral against which money can be borrowed. Filongonio Acevedo loaned some money to his *compadre* Ignacio Jiminez for funeral expenses when Mr. Jimenez's daughter died. Mr. Acevedo considers Mr. Jiminez a good risk. Not only will Mr. Jiminez recognize his obligations as a *compadre*, but he also has a *guelaguetza* relationship with Mr. Acevedo. This was the basis on which the loan was made. Having various *guelaguetza* relationships, then, makes people feel secure. It strengthens previously existing ties with relatives and *compadres* by adding a debtor-creditor relationship to the matrix.

Finally, the *guelaguetza* is a means of narrowing the number of people with whom a villager must interact closely. It permits the creation of solid bonds among relatively few individuals.

Although the *guelaguetza* has all these advantages, there are some problems and inequities in the system. Old people no longer sponsoring fiestas are still called on to make *guelaguetza*. Widows are expected to recognize the sometimes costly *guelaguetza* obligations incurred by their husbands. Once a *guelaguetza* obligation has been established, it is difficult to sever the tie. Even when incapacitated because of illness or economic misfortunes, heads of households must continue to fulfill their expected roles in the *guelaguetza* network. Acts of reciprocity are expected from relatives or *compadres* who may not want to "contribute." This may lead to bad feelings.

In summary, *guelaguetza* provides these peasant villagers with convenient and community-sanctioned means of controlling resources needed for specific events. It is a reciprocal institutionalized system that permits the individual to borrow from a circle of people who have acknowledged a bond of solidarity.

11

Dispute Resolution and Social Control

We tend to look at politics as a separate aspect of life. If you were asked to describe American politics, you would probably begin with the structure of our system of government, the nature of political parties, free elections, and so forth. It is quite unlikely that you would bring in other institutions such as the family, the church, or the school system. Yet in most societies political behavior, like economic behavior, is fused with many other aspects of social organization.

In its simplest sense, **politics** is the legitimate use of force or authority within a society. We all engage in some sort of political behavior, for a necessary part of living with other people is an agreed-upon pattern of authority based on special abilities, wisdom and experience, physical superiority, or anything else we choose. Politics is the means by which people define their group in relation to the outside world. Usually we define a group by linking it with a geographic unit like a nation or a state, but this need not always be the case.

Dispute Resolution

In every society there are times when people are unhappy with one another. Problems may arise out of anything from being snubbed in the grocery store to being mugged in an alley. Obviously, the range of potential social transgressions is great and covers many possibilities. Often the result is a *dispute*, which refers to a type of interaction stemming from a problem of a social relationship between two or more individuals. What is important is that every society has methods of managing, defusing, or settling these disputes, called **dispute resolution**. The ultimate resolution of grievances can be handled in a number of ways, and the course of action depends, among other things, on such factors as how severe the parties involved regard the infraction and how badly they wish to continue the relationship. For example, one could handle hurt feelings coming from not being "recognized" in the grocery store by ignoring from that point on the presence of the offending party. In contrast, the resolution of a dispute arising from a mugging that involved a black eye, wounded pride, and the theft of a wallet is usually handled in another fashion.

Nader and Todd[1] outline a series of mechanisms for resolving disputes outside of the formal legal system. Most of us have experienced a number of these procedures on a firsthand basis. They include:

1. *Lumping it.* We simply ignore the issue that created the problem in the first place. All of us have found at times that it is not worth the emotional energy or financial cost to pursue a resolution to a problem. In this type of situation the relationship with the offending party is not terminated, so "to forgive and forget" might best sum up the attitude associated with this process.

2. *Avoidance.* This procedure involves simply withdrawing from the situation and breaking off the social relationship.

3. *Coercion.* In this situation one party forces an outcome on the other. "Pay up or I'll beat the stuffing (or an expletive of your choice) out of you" is an example of how coercive dispute resolution occurs. Force or the threat of force is the important factor here.

4. *Negotiation.* This approach results in both parties sitting down and trying to resolve their differences by themselves.

5. *Mediation.* This procedure differs from negotiation in that it involves a third party who intercedes in an effort to reach an outcome mutually satisfactory to the antagonists.

6. *Arbitration.* A third party is also involved here, with the difference that both individuals agree to accept that party's

[1] L. Nader and H. F. Todd, Jr. (Eds.), *The Disputing Process—Law in Ten Societies* (New York: Columbia University Press, 1978), pp. 9–13.

judgment before it is rendered. The salary disputes of professional sports stars are often resolved by bringing in an arbitrator who listens to both parties and then offers a binding resolution.

7. *Adjudication.* Like the preceding two forms, adjudication involves a third party. What is different about this type of resolution is that the outside intervener is an uninvited authority who enters into the dispute, offers a resolution, and sees to it that the decision is enforced.

Obviously, these mechanisms are not all equally good or appropriate for every type of conflict resolution. In many instances several of these procedures may be required to resolve a single dispute.

The anthropologist who studies dispute resolution is interested in several things. First, how are problems managed and resolved? What types of decision-making processes are involved? Second, what are the stages of development of the dispute process? Once again, Nader and Todd offer some suggestions. The initial stage is a grievance or preconflict one in which one person is unhappy and feels wronged. Your neighbor's cattle have trampled your vegetable patch. The next step may involve going next door and communicating this resentment or unhappiness. You visit with members of that household and confront them with your version of what has happened. The issue may be resolved satisfactorily at that point; for example, the neighbor may tie up the cow and reimburse you for damages. Perhaps

In many societies social control takes on very formal procedures. In the United States, for example, we rely upon a judicial system complete with powers to carry out punishments for those who violate norms that have been codified into law.

there is some negotiation; you get paid for some of the lost crop, but receive nothing for the damaged tomatoes because, as it turns out, you have already eaten most of them. Or the dispute may escalate until it becomes a public matter and a third party is brought in. If you are members of the same kinship group, lineage or clan elders will attempt to resolve the issue. If not, the dispute might be taken to a different forum for resolution.

Law and Social Control

Anthropologists interested in politics and dispute resolution are also interested in **social controls** that societies place on their members. The anthropologist who studies this area of social behavior is concerned not only with formal rules, but also with the way people actually behave—that is, whether they conform to the rules or not. We assume that the rules of a society reflect its basic values, but at the same time we observe that those rules are not always followed. Since a society's cultural rules are a guide to the behavior that is acceptable in that society, we can learn from them what kinds of actions people consider contrary to their values; the punishments called for often indicate the seriousness of those actions. In our own society we can get a clear picture of American values by looking at the actions that are defined as illegal and comparing the punishments for those actions. A minor traffic offense calls for a small fine, while petty theft might land the culprit in jail for a short time. Armed robbery would probably lead to a stiffer sentence than embezzlement, even though the armed robber might net only a few dollars while the embezzler could get away with millions. Right away, this tells us something about American attitudes toward violence.

Anthropologists frequently distinguish between two major categories of approaches for social control: *formal* and *informal* mechanisms. Formal controls are sanctions that use some type of legitimized authority to

In American society, law enforcement is usually carried out by formally designated police officers, and is distinguished from informal control.

enforce compliance with norms and societal rules. Often they are based on **laws,** the breaking of which results in a formal procedural response that involves a community-recognized means of assessing blame and then enforcing sanctions.

Not all rules are formal or written down in a code of laws. There are many other rules that people are expected to follow, and if they do not, they are punished in some way. Social control can work in very subtle ways to mold the behavior of the members of a group. Informal mechanisms for social control include such practices as exclusion from group activities, gossip, or even open criticism. The offense can be as simple as failure to observe proper table manners—which is not a violation of the law but an offense against the values of the society. We are all subject to group pressure, as you will recognize if you look at the clothes you wear, the way you speak, the places you go, and the people with whom you associate.

An example of how informal sanctions operate in another society will illustrate the assumptions anthropologists make about the role of laws in social control. Among traditional Inuit groups there are no specialized legal institutions such as courts, police departments, and the like. When someone violates your rights, you must take the law into your own hands and seek to correct the situation yourself. No matter who is "right," the outcome usually depends on who has greater power and strength. This does not mean that the biggest and toughest person can bully everyone else, because if the offense is too blatant or is repeated too often, the victim's relative will step in and the offender's kin will quietly turn the other way.

If a member of an Inuit community is considered undesirable by the rest of the group, he or she may be removed either by exile or by execution. But there is no legal institution to deal with such a situation, and the injured party cannot act alone. Instead, the injured party gathers support for his or her cause, and the offender's own family is

asked to impose the sentence. This avoids feuds between families—an important factor in an environment in which people must cooperate if they are to survive. Thus, if we look closely at legal behavior in Inuit society, we can see how the basic values of ruggedness and individuality are reinforced by the way the community deals with behavior that violates the rules.

As in Inuit society, in the Trobriand Islands most minor violations are corrected by self-help; that is, the individual must right any wrong that has been done to him or her. If a feud develops, there are agreed-upon ways to end it without a great deal of bloodshed. The community can enforce a solution by first ending the fighting and then mediating between the parties involved. One solution is a **bloodwealth** to be paid by the offender; if the victim is unwilling to accept such a payment, the community may force him or her to do so.

Another option is a harmless contest in which the disputants can settle their grievance without bloodshed. The Inuit song duel, in which each party tries to outdo the other in inventing songs that shame and ridicule the

An elderly peasant leader in San Lázaro, Mexico. Although such peasants are subject to the political control of the nation states in which they reside, informal mechanisms at the local level generally are relied upon for resolving disputes and settling grievances within the community.

opponent, was described earlier. Other communities resort to wrestling matches or similar contests of strength in which no lasting damage is done. If the feud is allowed to continue, the entire society may be split into warring camps.

While most Americans dismiss the notion of witchcraft and the existence of witches, these attitudes are not shared by much of the world. Many societies cannot accept the idea that people get sick and die of natural causes, so they attribute illness to witchcraft. Further, practically every other misfortune, from having chickens that don't lay eggs or crops that wither to losing a prized possession or fighting with one's spouse, is attributed to malevolent witchcraft. Who are witches? Depending on the society, they may be either male or female. What is more important, anyone

can seek out a witch to have a curse placed on another person. Witchcraft accusations or threats of employing witchcraft are not taken lightly. Just the possibility of being accused often serves as a means of social control. Among other things, it is generally believed that witchcraft denunciations are used to get rid of individuals who deviate too much from expected social norms. Suspected witches or people who rely on them can be dealt with by banishment, cutting them off from kin support, or in some instances by killing them. Charges of witchcraft are not made without what is culturally felt to be good cause. People who quarrel, who can't get along with their neighbors, who refuse to participate in community activities, who decline to reciprocate in the expected fashion, or who do not enjoy strong kin support are good candidates for

Several centuries ago, witch trials were an extremely effective method of ensuring social control. The fear of being accused of being a witch made people behave in a very circumspect fashion.

such accusations. Obviously, the charge of witchcraft can be a very effective means of enforcing proper behavior.

Divination, conditional curses, oaths, and ordeals are other devices that employ the supernatural for social control.[2] Divination is the process of extracting information by manipulative means. Asking questions of a Ouija board is one example. The Azande of the southern Sudan will feed poison to a chicken, asking that the chicken die if the charge is true. Almost as a scientific confirmation, a second chicken will be given the same substance, although this time the request will be to spare its life if the charge is false. If the first chicken dies and the second lives, the indictment is validated.

A conditional curse calls upon the supernatural to intervene if someone is lying. As children, how many of you proclaimed your innocence by saying, "Cross my heart and hope to die, stick a needle in my eye"? Whether or not you really thought it through, what you were doing was calling upon supernatural forces to strike you down if you were lying.

Oaths are another way people proclaim that they are acting in a socially acceptable fashion. The oathtaker calls upon the supernatural to intervene should he or she not be telling the truth. Placing one's hand on the bible or some hold article is a common example of an oath.

Finally, the ordeal is a method whereby defendants are put through some torturous test in which the supernatural intercedes to save the innocent and punish the guilty, and in so doing reinforces the social order. In parts of West Africa an ordealist is brought in to resolve disputes. The hot-knife technique is a favorite method of determining who is telling the truth. Suppose there is a disagreement between two individuals about who has stolen a cow. Each claims he is innocent. The ordealist presses a glowing hot

knife against the bare legs of both. The one whose leg burns and blisters is declared guilty. Among traditional Ifugao, a tribal group in the Philippines, litigants were asked to reach into a pot of boiling water, pull out some rocks, and then *replace* them gently into the caldron. The innocent party was believed to be able to accomplish this without injury. Several tribes from approximately the same area had the habit of trussing up the defendants and tossing both into a river. The one who came up first would then be judged guilty. You might ask: What if the hot knife or pebble-and-boiling-water ordeals burned both parties or neither, or if the innocent party wound up with a seared leg or parboiled hand or surfaced first? Obviously, an injustice would be done. But the real point of these proceedings is not to ensure justice but to reduce pressure at the stress point of the social system and to ritually mediate conflict. To that end, the proceedings are designed to unite the community and ensure compliance with the decision.

An interesting situation occurs when two cultures whose legal systems do not mesh come into contact. Such a case was described by the columnist Anthony Lewis in a story reported in the *International Herald Tribune* several decades ago. A man from a rural village in what used to be British East Africa (now Tanzania) was charged with murdering an old woman. He pleaded self-defense, claiming that she was a witch and had threatened to kill him through her use of magic. The man told the court how one of his children had become ill and had died. The woman, a relative of the man, had been assigned the task of preparing the boy's funeral, but she had refused to do so, claiming that she had cast a spell on the child. Instead, she had threatened to kill the man and his entire family. Shortly thereafter another child died, but when the man demanded that the woman cease her witchcraft, she laughed at him and told him that he would be next. He fetched an ax and killed her; then he turned himself in.

Two things are important to note here.

[2] E. A. Hoebel and E. L. Frost, *Cultural and Social Anthropology* (New York: McGraw-Hill, 1976), pp. 294–95.

First, the old woman openly claimed she had cast a spell on the child. Second, as we have already discussed, accusations of witchcraft are pretty serious business in some cultures. Unfortunately, there are a couple of things we don't know about the case from the newspaper account that might be very illuminating in judging guilt or innocence by virtue of "extenuating circumstances." Although the defendant claimed to be acting in justifiable self-defense, it is entirely possible that he was carrying out the culturally sanctioned wishes of his entire village when he killed the "witch." This would not be a vigilante action, but rather a time-honored way of handling group conflict and disputes. Usually when someone is accused of being a witch there is some factual reason for suspicion. In this instance a man's children died. Often the person singled out as being a witch has a history of conflict with neighbors and is disruptive to the point of upsetting the equilibrium of the community. Perhaps the woman accused here was guilty of severe antisocial behavior. If so, informal sanctions, such as gossip, ostracism, or public humiliation, might not have produced the desired result. We might also assume that the woman did not enjoy the strong backing of family members who could deter her antisocial behavior or could have prevented her from being killed by intervening in some fashion. While we might regard the man's action as inexcusable, this sort of murder might be considered entirely appropriate in his culture.

The question for the anthropologist, or any student of comparative law, is how to reconcile two legal systems based on different sets of values. From one standpoint, the man was clearly justified in killing the old woman, for his belief in witchcraft was genuine and his fear was supported by the deaths of two of his children. However, from another point of view, there is an important difference between the violent act of killing someone with an ax and the comparatively passive—and to some minds impossible—act of killing someone with witchcraft. Before reading about the way the judges decided the case,

ask yourself what you would have done if you had been on the jury.

At his trial the man was convicted and sentenced to death. When the case was appealed to a panel of three judges, each offered a different opinion. The first judge held that while the man's beliefs were unquestionably sincere, the law of the land had to be based on reason, and belief in witchcraft was unreasonable. Such beliefs, the judge argued, would have to be discouraged. The new law of the land was English common law, and witchcraft was unacceptable in that context. The second judge held that what was important was not English law but the motives that drove the defendant to commit the murder. By that standard the man's act was justifiable, and he should be judged not guilty. The third judge rejected the opinions of the other two and offered an opinion that pulled the whole case together. Although traditional beliefs might be sincere, the country could not move ahead on that basis. And while English traditions might be more "rational," they could not be strictly applied outside the cultural context in which they arose. Instead, the solution should be a compromise: The man should be judged guilty, to emphasize the wrong he had done, but he should be given a lighter sentence in recognition of the motives for his crime.

The important lesson for students of anthropology is that law and social control are culture-bound and reflect the system of which they are a part. There are no absolute truths that can form the basis for a legal system, and there are no rights or wrongs that can be argued in all cultural contexts. In traditional Inuit society, when people became too old and could no longer take care of themselves, they might be left out on the ice to die. We may look at this as nothing less than murder, a cruel way to treat a close relative or a lifelong friend. But for the Inuit, who face a difficult and tedious struggle for survival in a forbidding environment, feeding an extra mouth can mean the difference between survival and death. Remember, too, that it is easier to accept such a fate if you grow up knowing that it is a customary and accepted practice. Indeed, it is not very different from euthanasia, or "mercy killing," which has been widely debated and is supported by many people in our society.

We can learn much about the inequities in our own legal system by studying law in other cultures. If we recognize that American society is made up of many different subcultures, it follows that the values and moral codes of Americans differ depending on the group to which they belong. The resident of an inner-city ghetto, the middle-class suburbanite, and the rural farmer face different problems and must solve those problems in different ways. Yet many of our laws do not take these cultural differences into account.

Finally, if we are to study social control and the nature of law cross-culturally, we must recognize that conflict has a positive side. Opposition to an outside force can unite a group by strenghtening its members' feelings of identity with the group. Conflict with outsiders can preserve the group by acting as a safety valve for feelings of aggression and hostility. In fact, the absence of conflict does not always result in stability, because there may be the potential for a major upheaval (as in a society ruled by a strong military dictatorship that allows no dissent). Moreover, conflict can unite people who might otherwise never come together in a joint venture. Every four years people find themselves working in support of a political candidate with others who are quite unlike them; they are united in opposition to the rival candidate. An even stronger example occurs in wartime, when men and women

Political conventions are a way of promoting unity among party members with conflicting interests, joining them together in support of a single candidate.

from all walks of life are brought together in the armed services, where they share a common life style and depend on each other for survival. In such situations the solidarity that results from conflict is perhaps the strongest possible bond.

Summary

Law and politics can be distinguished in that law is a way of organizing society to deal with internal matters, whereas politics organizes the society to deal with outside groups. The anthropologist who studies law is concerned with how disputes are settled. This involves studying mechanisms that exist for resolving grievances between individuals, what alternatives are available, and what considerations individuals take into account as they attempt to resolve differences. In addition, anthropologists are interested both in formal rules defining appropriate behavior and in informal or unwritten rules, which can be just as powerful and effective in regulating the way people act. We recognize that while all societies have some form of law, there are no absolute laws that exist in every society throughout the world. A law is a statement about culturally determined values, and it can exist on a formal level or through the more subtle means of social control that are acted out in countless situations in everyday life. In our own society, where there is a great deal of cultural diversity, we find many problems in our written legal system, which ignores cultural differences. The cross-cultural perspective of the anthropologist offers us a better understanding of these problems, and the hope of finding a workable solution.

Glossary

bloodwealth   A social sanction found in Trobriand society to settle disputes and avoid feuding between individuals or groups.

dispute resolution   Forums for obtaining satisfaction in the resolution of problems involving two or more individuals.

law   A formal system of rules that are a guide to the appropriate behavior in a particular society, backed by the threat of force.

politics   The legitimate use of force or authority by which people maintain peace within a group and define their group relative to the outside world.

social control   The legal sanctions of a particular society that ensure conformity to the values of that society. These sanctions may be in the form of laws or less formal and unwritten rules.

Questions for Discussion

1. In American political thinking, many activities that would be unacceptable if done to a fellow American are praiseworthy if done to an outsider. For example, in war we condone the killing of others, and even in peacetime we promote spying against other countries, but deny the right of foreign agents to pry into our own affairs. How does such behavior reflect the notion of segmentary opposition in a tribal society?

2. Your neighbor and longtime friend, who is also a professional housepainter, offers to paint your garage. A color is selected and you reach a verbal agreement on how much the job will cost. You are pleased with this arrangement, especially because the painter and your sister are engaged to be married in the near future. When you return from work you see the color is not the one chosen. The painter explains the store was out of the color you wanted and that the substitute is, in his estimation, a pretty close match. You receive the bill and are shocked to find that it is quite a bit higher than the price he quoted you. In response to your inquiry, your future brother-in-law tells you that the original estimate was for labor only and did not include the price of the paint. Furthermore, the job took two hours longer than he originally thought it would. The situation is not a happy one. How do you plan on resolving the dispute? What types of factors and considerations will you take into account as you review your strategies for dealing with this problem?

3. A classic hypothetical legal case, called "The Case of the Spelunkean Explorers," describes a group of scientists trapped in a cave. They calculate the amount of air available, and the time it will take for the workers on the outside to rescue them, and determine that there is not enough oxygen for all to survive. Accordingly, they draw lots and the loser is killed. In the end, their calculations prove accurate. They are rescued just in time, and had they allowed one additional person to live, all would have suffocated. Are the survivors guilty of murder? Why or why not? How does the anthropological approach to law contribute to your understanding of this problem?

Suggestions for Additional Reading

Dispute Resolution

LAURA NADER and HARRY F. TODD, JR. (Eds.), *The Disputing Process—Law in Ten Societies* (New York: Columbia University Press, 1978). A series of cross-cultural case studies focusing on conflict resolution and dispute management.

RICHARD L. ABEL, "A Comparative Theory of Dispute Institutions in Society," *Law and Society Review*, 8, no. 2 (1973). A very comprehensive review of why dispute institutions operate the way they do.

Law and Social Control

PAUL BOHANNAN (Ed.), *Law and Warfare: Studies in the Anthropology of Conflict* (Garden City, N.Y.: Natural History Press, 1967). A collection of articles on law and warfare in non-Western societies.

E. ADAMSON HOEBEL, *The Law of Primitive Man* (Cambridge, Mass.: Harvard University Press, 1954). One of the earliest studies of legal anthropology, a survey of different forms of legal institutions around the world, emphasizing non-Western societies.

Law and Order

JAMES P. SPRADLEY and DAVID W. McCURDY

When we consider American law, we are likely to think of formal written statutes, police, courts, lawyers, strict rules of evidence, the determination of guilt, and punishment. In our large society the system seems technical and impersonal. In this selection, Spradley and McCurdy discuss the structure of law in the context of fieldwork conducted by anthropologist Laura Nader, who did research in the Zapotec community of Ralu'a. They discuss several legal cases to illustrate such concepts as substantive and procedural law, legal levels, and legal principles. They conclude with Nader's argument that Zapotec law seeks "to make the balance," to attempt a settlement between disputants that will promote social harmony.

The land rover disappeared in a cloud of dust on its way back to Oaxaca City. The anthropologist adjusted the shoulder straps on the backpack, turned away from the end of the road, and began to follow the two Zapotec Indian guides. The trail led north, climbing along the edge of steep valleys, crossing over mountain ridges, and winding back and forth to make a steady gain in altitude. Accustomed to living at 5000 feet above sea level, the two guides walked rapidly, oblivious to the hard breathing of their American companion. In every direction, scattered over much of the 36,000 square miles of Oaxaca State in southern Mexico, the anthropologist knew there were small Zapotec villages. The three of them headed toward the Rincon district, which means "the corner," calling attention to the fact that the area is partially encircled by three high mountain peaks. As they walked, the anthropologist could see the distant and formidable Zempoateptl Mountain reaching to more than 10,000 feet; Maceta and El Machin, the two other peaks, would come into view before they reached their destination, the pueblo of Ralu'a. One of the Zapotec men spoke Spanish and had told the anthropologist as they started, "We are called the people of the corner, *Rinconeros*, because we live between the peaks." The sun was high on this day in early May 1957 and the sky clear; it was several

weeks before the rainy season would begin. Wild orchids were in bloom everywhere. The mountains had a kind of awesome beauty for the anthropologist, particularly since she had anticipated the sight for many months. As she walked behind the guides, she wondered why no other social scientist had ever come before to this place, to live and study among these people.

The Zapotec guides pushed on, stopping only for water now and then at the edge of fast-flowing mountain streams. During the first hour they had passed scattered fields of coffee plants in bloom and sugarcane, evidence that a pueblo or homestead was nearby, enfolded in some mountain niche. The anthropologist would like to have stopped to inquire about these settlements and to rest, but the two guides never hesitated, pressing on toward their destination. The sun had already disappeared behind the highest peak when, after a 3½-hour walk, they came to Ralu'a, a pueblo of 2000 people. Unexpectedly, as they came over a rise, houses appeared everywhere; children played on the paths, and women could be seen carrying firewood. The anthropologist felt a sense of excitement as she looked down on the town that would be her home for many months to come. Here she would live and work and make friends; from here she would travel to other villages and nearby settlements in her efforts to discover the cultural ways of the Zapotec; and here she would try to understand Zapotec law, to describe the cultural rules these people used when settling disputes.

As they entered the edge of the pueblo, she won-

James P. Spradley and David W. McCurdy, "Law and Order" (abridged) in *Conformity and Conflict* (Boston: Little, Brown, 1987). Reprinted by permission of Random House, Inc.

dered how these people would receive her. Would they understand why she had come? In Oaxaca City she had met an engineer, a government employee who had friends in Ralu'a. He had made tentative arrangements for her to stay with a family while she conducted her field study. All was excitement at the home of her hosts, for a fiesta was in progress to celebrate the return of religious pilgrims from the Sanctuario in Veracruz. Her hosts seemed polite but not enthusiastic as they invited her to join them in the fiesta meal of special foods. After they had eaten, the head of the household came to her and asked, "Are you a Catholic? If you are not a Catholic, you cannot stay here. We do not want Protestants in our town." Surprised by this question, she explained her role and assured him that she belonged to the original Catholic church (Eastern Orthodox).

It would be many weeks before she would fully appreciate what lay behind this simple question about her religion. She was to discover that it concerned authority, conflict, and the process of law and dispute settlement, the very areas she had come to investigate. Before two weeks had elapsed a message came from the priest: she was to come to his house immediately. She entered and, after a brief exchange in Spanish, he said, "You are a Protestant missionary! Why have you come to our pueblo?" Nothing would convince him that it was not so; even the letter of recommendation that she brought from a priest in Oaxaca was dismissed as a fake, and a wire of confirmation from that priest that she was an anthropologist and a good Christian did not convince him. Although others would eventually accept her, the priest in Ralu'a would remain unconvinced, spreading the word from the pulpit and in the streets that she was really a Protestant missionary. Several years earlier some missionaries had come to Ralu'a and, as a result of winning converts, conflicts erupted that led to burning of Protestant homes. The dispute reached enormous proportions for this small pueblo and was only settled through the process of law when the state government forced the town to pay heavy fines for damage inflicted.

When the anthropologist was called to the home of the priest in the Zapotec pueblo of Ralu'a, she became a party to a dispute. He accused her of being a Protestant missionary; she denied it. Although she appealed to another priest to confirm her identity, he did not have the authority to settle the dispute. Like many troubles that beset human interaction, this dispute was never settled, and the anthropologist had to work around the difficulties it created with other individuals in the village. The dispute remained below the level of the law, but it is conceivable that the priest or the anthropologist could have appealed to some agent whose authority was recognized and who could settle the case. It would then have become a legal matter.

One of the earliest disputes that came to the anthropologist's attention occurred at a Ralu'a well several months after she arrived among the Zapotec. She awoke as usual one morning to the sound of the women in the household getting ready to go to the mill. It was 5:00 A.M., and each morning at this time the women in Ralu'a arose to take their corn to nearby mills. The men were still asleep as the anthropologist dressed and prepared to go with the women. It was not yet light at this hour of the morning, but the daily walk to the mill was exhilarating. Other women greeted them and, at the mill, while they waited to have their corn ground, they visited with each other. Soon each would return home to prepare tortillas, fix breakfast for the family, and make lunches for the men who must walk many miles to their fields for a day of work. But now they caught up on the local news and enjoyed visiting.

This morning two women were earnestly discussing an argument that had occurred on the previous day at Los Remedios, one of the town wells. Carmen had gone to the well to wash the family clothes, and instead of using the flat slab of stone that belonged to her, she selected one near a friend so they could visit as they worked. Like other women she looked forward to this task because it enabled her to visit and gossip with others in the neighborhood, a pleasant change from working alone inside her house. But hardly 20 minutes had passed when the owner of the washing stone appeared, and instead of taking another place she angrily asked Carmen to move. As Carmen began to gather her wet clothes together, she loudly commented on the other woman's generosity. Insults began to fly, and the situation became especially tense when Carmen "accidentally" splashed water on the newcomer's dress as she went off to finish washing on her own slab. Some said Carmen should have moved to her own stone without comment; others declared that the second woman was wrong and should have gone quietly to another place to wash. Someone recalled a similar conflict several years earlier when a woman had taken the matter to the *municipio*, or town hall, where the *presidente* had settled the dispute. Some of the women wondered whether the trouble of yesterday would go that far.

It was the end of the summer before the dispute over washing stones reached the boiling point and became a case of law, but it did not happen in the way the anthropologist had expected, for no one took the dispute to the *municipio*. The incident at the well did not die down; the two women continued to make insulting remarks in public, and others began to take sides. Then a similar conflict arose between several other women who were not using the stones that belonged to them. At night in the *cantina* as the men drank *mescal*, an alcoholic drink made from the fermented juice of agave plants, they talked of the disputes they had learned about from their wives. Some men reported that at the wells where their wives washed clothes no such fights had occurred; everyone agreed that the problem was primarily at Los Remedios.

The bickering and fighting continued until one day people noticed that the water at Los Remedios had begun to dry up. Some said this was caused by the fighting. The men who belonged to the Well Association, a group that worked to maintain the wells, called a special meeting and decided that they must take action to save the water. They formed a work party and improved the well to ensure more water, but they also removed all the slabs of stone used for washing. In place of these privately owned washing places they constructed 24 shallow tubs from cement and announced that no one could own or reserve one of these spaces. They belonged to the well and were to be used on a first-come, first-serve basis. The priest blessed the new well, and the disputes were settled. Although some women complained that they liked the old way better, everyone recognized the authority of the men's Well Association, and the change was accepted. . . .

The ethnographer who investigates the process of law in a non-Western society must collect data on all kinds of disputes. Since any conflict can be transformed overnight into a legal dispute involving some agent with recognized authority, it is important to examine the range of ways that people handle such troubles. By means of various ethnographic discovery procedures, one begins to focus more and more on legal cases, those that are settled by people or groups with authority.

The Structure of Legal Culture

By examining dispute cases, observing their outcome, and questioning the parties involved, one can describe a goodly portion of the law ways of a community. Such legal knowledge can be analyzed into three different aspects. First, the most explicit aspect of legal knowledge includes *substantive law* and *procedural law*, which are interrelated. At a more implicit level, underlying these rules, are the fundamental *legal principles* that determine the shape of the law in a particular society. Finally, there is a common core of *cultural values* that influence the legal principles and link the law of any culture to other domains of that culture. . . .

Substantive law. The term "law" is most often used in our own society to refer to substantive law, the legal statutes that define right and wrong. Phrases such as, "He broke the law" or "It is illegal to bring liquor across the state line," refer to substantive law. It is easy for us to assume that substantive rules can be equated with written statutes, but this is not always the case in our own society, and most of the world's cultures do not have written laws at all. But all people have agreed-on substantive rules. Let us look at an example of an unwritten law from our own society.

Until recently every city in the United States had passed legislation that made it a crime to appear drunk in public. For many years in the city of Seattle this substantive rule was used to make more than 10,000 arrests each year. Although the law against public drunkenness seems clear and simple, ethnographic investigation of individual cases in Seattle shows that many other substantive rules of a complex nature were actually being used. In practice, the police used their own discretion to arrest some drunks but not others. The unwritten rule was, "If you see a poor man on skid row who is drunk, arrest him; those of the middle and upper class who are drunk in other parts of town need not be arrested." A tramp from skid row who had been arrested many times reported the following experience. Standing outside the University Club located several blocks from skid row, he observed men coming out of the club in states of obvious intoxication. A policeman not only saw the same men, but assisted them into cabs for transportation home.

The substantive law of Ralu'a contains many specific rules. Some are part of a written legal code, others must be inferred from what people say and do in dispute cases. Many cases end up in the town hall, the *municipio*, a two-room, adobe building in the center of town. Here certain officials hold a kind of court to settle disputes. Thirteen respected men make up an advisory group for the pueblo, the *principales*. Each year this group nominates three men for the position of village chairman, or *presidente*, one of whom is elected by the village to serve 1 year. The *presidente*, in turn, appoints these same *principales* for another 1-year term. Working closely with the *presidente* is a man elected to the office of *sindico*, who runs the communal work program of the pueblo and is also head of the town police. There are 12 *policia* who serve under two lieutenants and a chief of police. Each year the outgoing men of this police force nominate other men, generally those who have been the biggest troublemakers during the year, to take over as replacements. They are then elected by the village as a whole, and the roughest man of all becomes the chief of police for the year. The *presidente* and the *sindico*, working together, handle minor disputes such as drunkenness, fighting, flirting, slander, boundary trespass, and theft. There is a third elected official, the *alcalde*, a kind of justice of the peace, who presides over more serious disputes. The *presidente* will often pass more serious cases as well as any cases that he cannot resolve directly to the *alcalde*. More serious cases or those that the *alcalde* cannot resolve are passed on to the district court. While the *presidente* and the *sindico* have various duties, the *alcalde* deals only with legal matters. We can see substantive law in action among the Zapotec if we examine two specific cases.

The case of the flirting husband. The first dispute involves a violation of rules that prohibit flirting. An unmarried woman, Señorita Zoalage, came to the *presidente* early on a Tuesday morning. She complained that a married man, Señor Huachic, had flirted with her. He appeared outside her house and made the equivalent of American wolf-calls shortly after dark on Monday night on his way home from the market. The *presidente* talked over the matter with the *sindico*, and someone was sent to notify Señor Huachic to appear in court that afternoon. It was now 2:00 P.M. and the *presidente* sat behind a long table at the front of the *presidencia*, one of the rooms in the town hall. Both Señor Huachic and Señorita Zoalage sat before him. After presenting the complaint to Señor Huachic, the *presidente* waited for his response. "Yes," he admitted, "I did what she said, but only because this woman here, Señorita Zoalage, flirted with me last week! She even invited me to come with her to collect firewood!" After some discussion about the particulars of the case the *presidente* said, "Señorita Zoalage, I am going to fine you 30 pesos for flirting with Señor Huachic. And Señor Huachic, you are fined 60 pesos for flirting with Señorita Zoalage. You are a married man and should have been at home with your wife." After warning them to refrain from further exhibitions of such behavior he dismissed them, they paid their fines, and returned to their homes. Each had violated a substantive rule that holds flirting to be illegal. In some cases individuals refuse to pay fines and, as a result, may be detained in jail or compelled to work on a community project.

The case of the disobedient son. The second case sheds light on substantive rules involving the relationships between parents and children. It was rela-

tively easy to elicit cultural rules for this relationship. For example, one evening after the anthropologist had been in Ralu'a for 8 months, she was having dinner with a Zapotec family. The father had just told the others about a son who had been sent to jail in the district capital because when his father had beat him he had struck back, hitting his father. The anthropologist asked quizzically, "And for this they sent him to jail?"

"Of course," he said, looking rather surprised that she would ask such a stupid question.

"But," she said, seeking to enlarge on the discussion, "many men beat their wives, and they never go to jail for that!"

"Yes," the father responded, "but wives are one thing, fathers another."

It seemed a good place to introduce a hypothetical question and so she asked, "But what if the father beats his son harshly, and the father is in the wrong? Is it still wrong for the son to strike his father?"

The son in the family spoke up, entering the discussion with a serious tone. "Fathers are never in the wrong for beating their sons. They always do it for their own good."

Still not satisfied, the anthropologist asked one last question, "All right, but sons grow up and become men. Under your law could a father ever be proved guilty for doing wrong to a son, even if he is a grown man?"

The father's answer brought looks of agreement from the others, "A father cannot do wrong with his children." There the discussion ended, but several days later she observed a case in the *presidencia* that underscored this substantive rule of Zapotec law.[1]

Señor Benjamin Mendoza Cruz had complained to the court about his son, Clemente Mendoza, who was 25 years of age. Because the complaint had been made several days earlier, both men were sitting before the *presidente*. Señor Cruz repeated his charge. "I have coffee planted on my land near one of the neighboring *ranchos*. Someone harvested some of my ripe coffee beans, and I thought the thief was from the neighboring pueblo, but a woman who has the land next to mine said she saw my son harvesting the coffee. I demand that he repay me for the coffee he has stolen."

The *presidente* turned to the son, Clemente Mendoza, waiting for him to speak. His eyes were on the

---

[1] This case is presented in the excellent ethnographic film *To Make the Balance* (Berkeley: University of California Extension Media Center), and also in "Styles of Court Procedure: To Make the Balance," in Laura Nader, ed., *Law in Culture and Society* (Chicago: Aldine, 1969).

floor; he did not look at the *presidente* or his father as he spoke. "Yes," he said, "I admit that I went to his field and cut some coffee. A year ago he allowed me to cut some coffee on his property, and I was confident he would give the coffee to me, but I am at fault, and now he can decide how to punish me. I have committed a crime against him and now I wish he would forgive me." There was a long pause when the son finished speaking. The *presidente* sat silently as the secretary continued writing. Then the father spoke slowly. "I am, as his father, very sad that my son Clemente should have done this wickedness to me. I did not believe that it was he until the woman told me. Now I will leave it to his *Municipio Presidente* to decide what is suitable. As his father I have to help him and look after him, but he should not act this way, disposing of the fruit of my harvest without my consent."

Another period of silence followed; flies buzzed noisily around the room. It was warm and the *presidente* thought about the man and his son, how he would settle the case. He recalled that fathers should provide for their sons when they came asking for a bride price, but Señor Cruz had already given more than once to his son for his purpose; Clemente had spent it on other things. Yes, it was the son who was at fault. He turned to him now. "Now you heard what your father said, and I will tell you that your father does not have an obligation to give you, his son, *anything.*" He raised his voice on the last word as if to emphasize the great distance between fathers and sons. He continued, "Nor is a father obliged to give you what is his. If a father loves his son very much, he may give him something, but nobody can force him to do so. Now, you have abused him and, as you have admitted, there is no reason why your father should help you because you committed this wrong." Clemente Mendoza had been afraid of his father all of his life. After his mother died, his father remarried, and he found it even more difficult to get along with the old man. Now he sat in silence, his eyes shifting nervously, focused on the floor most of the time as he listened to the *presidente* ask, "Are you now both ready to come to an agreement?" They would accept his settlement.

"Clemente Mendoza," the *presidente* addressed the guilty son, "you shall repay your father for the coffee that you took without permission. Without delay you have to deliver the 25 pounds of dried coffee to your father, and the deadline is Friday, the 21st of this month, and for the wrong you have committed I impose on you a 200-peso fine, which you have to pay today." The secretary prepared an agreement that finalized the ending of the dispute, and it

was soon ready for signing. More than an hour had passed since they first appeared before the *presidente*. The agreement showed the amount Clemente would repay his father as well as the fine payable to the *municipio*. The agreement was shown to both parties, and the *presidente* addressed them one more time.

"Clemente Mendoza, you should realize that both you and your father are bound by this agreement; you should not inflict reprisals on your father or stepmother, and you must realize that your father has the right, as a father, to correct any of your faults. You, as his son, must ask him for full permission to harvest some coffee or give you anything else, to avoid being offensive to your father. You should now go and behave as a good son should behave."

Turning to the father he said, "Señor Cruz, whenever you desire you can dispose of your property and give it to your son, you can help him in mutual agreement, but the father does not have any obligation to give his son anything; on the other hand, the son cannot demand his father to give him any of his property. It is entirely in the hands of the father whether he wants to give or not."

The two men, father and son, signed the agreement and turned to walk out of the *municipio*. It had been a rare occurrence for a father to bring his son to court. Most disputes of this sort are easily settled by the authority of the father. Although all sons feel the constraints of the father's authority, they know they will one day marry and have sons of their own and, like their father, require total obedience.

Procedural law. When a dispute moves into the settlement stage, numerous procedural rules come into play. Procedural law refers to the agreed-on ways to settle a dispute. They guide not only the *presidente*, the *sindico*, the *alcalde*, or other authority agent, but also the parties to a dispute. Take, for example, the unwritten procedural rule about *who* should bring family disputes to the court. Although a large number of family cases are brought to the *presidente's* court, only certain classes of persons would think of settling such disputes in the court. The *principales*, for example, are some of the most respected men in Ralu'a, and they take pride in their respectable families. Undoubtedly their authority in the pueblo enhances their authority within their families, giving them the power to arbitrate and settle any disputes that may arise. If any member complained about family problems in court, it would bring shame and dishonor to the entire family. There is, therefore, considerable social pressure to keep members abiding by the unwritten procedural rule that says that *principales and their families should not use the court to settle family disputes*. If the wife of a *principale* were to appear in court making a complaint against her husband, the *presidente* would be greatly surprised, and news of this event would quickly spread throughout the pueblo. Everyone would know that she had violated an implicit procedural rule of Zapotec law.

Procedural rules in U.S. society. Procedural rules in our own legal system are not always clearly specified. The ethnographer seeks to make these rules explicit, thereby shedding light on substantive rules and the entire process of law. The ethnographic research among the tramps in Seattle, Washington, mentioned earlier, revealed an implicit procedural rule that held enormous significance for this population. It involves a procedural rule for sentencing that can be stated as follows.

> *If a man is poor and has been arrested many times for being drunk in public, he shall be sentenced with greater severity than those with money or with no record of previous arrests for drunkenness.*

On the basis of this rule, two men could be arrested at 10:00 P.M. on Monday on the same block in Seattle and plead guilty in court to public drunkenness. One would be given a 2-day suspended sentence and would walk out of the courtroom a free man. The other would be given 90 days in jail. Why this difference? The first man had not been arrested for this crime during the preceding 6 months, whereas the other had been arrested seven times.

The most significant part of this procedural rule, however, involves differences in wealth. Take two men, for example, who were arrested 10 to 15 times each year for public drunkenness. Each time they were picked up by the Seattle police they had to spend several hours in the jail "drying out." Then both men were allowed to post a $20 bail, *if they had the money*. Only one of the men had this amount, and he alone was immediately released from jail. He might be arrested again within a few days or weeks and repeat the process. Over the course of 15 or 20 years such a man might spend several thousand dollars for bail, each time walking away from jail after a few hours of sleep. Although a man who posted bail was expected to appear in court for his arraignment, no one did, choosing instead to forfeit this money than face a judge and possible jail sentence. The man who could not post bail, on the other hand, waited several days in the drunk tank, appeared in court, pleaded guilty, received his sentence, and then returned to the jail to serve his time. Thus violation of the same *substantive rule* can lead to enormously different consequences, depending on the nature of related *procedural rules*. . . .

Legal Levels

In every culture the existence of different kinds of authority agents means that disputes can be settled at different levels. In our own society a dispute between a teacher and a student can be settled by the school principal. If the dispute continues, it could go to the town board of education. If still unsettled, it might go to the local court and even be appealed to a series of higher courts.

Among the Zapotec, several levels for settling disputes exist. Disputes can be settled by family elders, witches, local officials, the priest, supernatural beings, or officials in the *municipio*. If all else fails, the dispute can be taken to the district court in Villa Alta. Consider the following case.

Mariano's son Pedro married the only daughter of a family in the pueblo and went to live with her family. Mariano was pleased with the arrangement because he had helped decide the marriage. But soon trouble began to develop between his son and the new wife. It came to his atttention directly when his daughter-in-law came to him and complained, "Your son Pedro is always drunk, he does not work now, and he argues with me all the time in the home of my parents." Mariano talked with her for some time and, on the following day, he warned Pedro that he should drink less and live at peace with his new wife. Like any son in Ralu'a, Pedro promised his father that he would change his behavior. However, within a month Mariano's daughter-in-law was back again with the same complaint. This time Mariano was angry. "She is back again so soon," he thought. "This son of mine does not learn from words." Mariano found his son and this time, amidst stern warnings, he whipped Pedro harshly.

The weeks passed and still Pedro did not change. His wife now turned to tthe *padrinos de pano*, the godparents of the marriage. But their warnings to Pedro were to no avail, and so she went to the priest. He talked to Pedro several times, and it seemed the penitent husband might change with his intervention. Then one night Pedro came home very drunk and began cursing at his wife and threatening her. Then he beat her, and she lay awake most of the night wondering what to do next. The fact that he had beat her was less important than that it was another stage in their deteriorating relationship and evidence that Pedro had not changed. Early in the morning while Pedro was still asleep she went to the *municipio* and made a complaint to the *presidente*. Pedro was cited and appeared in court later that same afternoon. He told the *presidente* that he had been drunk and did not know what he was doing, that he would change his ways, and that he would begin to work regularly in his fields. Pedro paid a fine of 50 pesos and signed an agreement that he would live at peace with his wife.

Disputes such as this can be resolved at various levels and through various remedy agents such as male family heads, church officials, village officials, and even by appeals directly to supernatural beings and individuals who are witches. For example, a man who is having trouble with his wife may go to a witch and say, "Somebody is gossiping about me and every time I come home my wife is after me because she is so upset. Can you do something about this person who is spreading bad tales about me?" The witch will reply, "Pay me 5 pesos and I'll find out who it is and do something about it." But whether a man goes to a witch or to the *presidente*, or whether a woman goes to her father-in-law is not left to happenstance. The procedural rules of a culture's law help define which authorities should be employed for various kinds of disputes.

Legal Principles and Cultural Values

Underlying the settlement of disputes in every society we find legal principles based on the fundamental values of a culture. A legal principle is a broad conception of some desirable state of affairs that gives rise to many substantive and procedural rules. The witness is asked, "Do you promise to tell the truth, the whole truth, and nothing but the truth, so help you God?" We accept the value of telling the objective truth, getting at the facts, and we believe that humans are capable of telling the truth. In some societies, however, people hold different assumptions, asserting that it is not possible to tell objective truth. In other cultures the value placed on the facts is small when compared to the importance of restoring amicable relationships. In order to understand the decisions authorities make to settle disputes, we need to grasp the legal principles of a culture.

When the Zapotec talk about the characteristics of those wise men who have settled disputes in the proper way, they say, "He knows how to *make the balance.*" This principle means that fault-finding in a particular trouble case is not as important as balancing the demands of all parties and restoring conditions of peaceful coexistence. The men's Well Association did not concern itself with seeking culprits who had violated rules about the use of private prop-

erty. Instead, they sought to restore peace and prevent future conflicts at Los Remedios. Their goal—*hacer el balance*—to make the balance, was achieved.

The principle of balance does not mean people are never at fault, never violate substantive rules. Instead, it means that disputes are not settled merely by establishing the facts of the case, finding the guilty party, and administering punishment. When Clemente Mendoza harvested his father's coffee without permission, he was clearly in the wrong. But the *presidente*, acting as a kind of father to the citizens of Ralu'a, sought to restore the balance, to mend the relationship between father and son, eliciting a signed agreement from them that they would not hold grudges and continue the dispute.

The case of fright. To the Zapotec, making the balance means settling disputes with an eye to the future of the relationships involved, not merely an examination of past events. Disputes create difficulties for pepole, financial losses, bitter feelings, and disrupted relationships. It would be possible to settle disputes without rectifying any of these conditions, but for the Zapotec this would not be sufficient, although the guilty person were given a life sentence for his or her crime. Take the case of Señora Juan. She complained to the *presidente* that she had been working, cutting coffee in the field of Señora Quiroz, when a young boy, Teodora Garcia, had picked on her 6-year-old boy, hitting him. The experience had been so disconcerting to the smaller boy that he had come down with *susto*, or magical fright, an illness involving the loss of one's soul. "My little boy got frightened," she told the *presidente*, "and now he yells during the night and has diarrhea because of the fright. I am asking the *presidente* to help me make my little son well again." The *presidente* asked Teodoro Garcia about the dispute, and he answered that the son of Señora Juan was always calling him names and taunting him while he worked. Back and forth the discussion went, but the *presidente* did not seek to discover what really happened; *his goal was not to find out the facts.* He allowed people to express their feelings in the matter. It was difficult to tell who was at fault, but he could easily see that this upset had disturbed the equilibrium in social relationships of all those involved. A boy had *susto* as a result, and the *presidente* knew he could do something about that, restoring the balance required. The poor mother said she needed 30 pesos for the curer. After negotiation, Teodoro Garcia offered to settle for 20 pesos. The case was resolved, the boy taken to a curer, and the balance restored.

Cultural values. Underlying the legal principles of

a society are the values that form the basis of social life. Making the balance in settling disputes is based on a widely held Zapotec cultural value of maintaining equilibrium. Direct confrontation between individuals in which one loses and another wins is unsettling to Zapotecans. As expressed by Laura Nader:

> This concern for equilibrium is evident through Ralu'a. Upon my making inquiries as to the motives for witchcraft in Ralu'a an informant reported the following as causes: "because one works too much or not enough; because one is too pretty or too ugly or too rich; for being an only child; for being rich and refusing to lend money; for being antisocial—for example, for refusing to greet people." These are all situations that somehow upset the balance as Ralu'ans see it. It is no wonder that the zero-sun game (win or lose) as we know it in some American courts would be a frightening prospect to a plaintiff, even though all "right" might be on his side. The plaintiff need not worry, however, for the *presidente* is equally reluctant to make such a clear-cut zero-sum game decision for a variety of reasons—among them that witchcraft is an all too possible tool of retaliation for such behavior. If a plaintiff wanted to play the zero-sum game he would go to a witch and not to the courts, where behavior is far too public.[2]

No doubt on that first day when the anthropologist entered the pueblo she had somehow upset some unseen sense of equilibrium in this Zapotec pueblo. A strange woman, dressed in strange clothes, with a strange reason for being there, asking strange questions; she must be a Protestant missionary, a person with supernatural power, at least someone to arouse suspicion. However, after weeks of persistently defining her role and participating in the daily round of life, she had overcome most of the suspicion and fear. Then one warm day when the excitement of a fiesta filled the air of Ralu'a, she had purchased a large barrel of *mescal* and donated it to the pueblo celebrations. It was a simple token, but the citizens of Ralu'a responded with enthusiasm. Public officials lauded her generosity and declared that she was now a true member of the pueblo. Others apologized for their suspicions and unfriendliness as they drank and laughed together. Without calculation she had *hacer el balance*. . . .

[2] "Styles of Court Procedure: To Make the Balance," in Laura Nader, ed., *Law in Culture and Society*, (Chicago: Aldine, 1969), pp. 73–74.

12

Magic, Witchcraft, and Religion

To the newcomer to anthropology, it seems that most anthropological studies include at least one chapter on the religion of the people being studied, and often a whole book is devoted to the subject. Why should this be the case? Are non-Western peoples more religious than we are? The answer lies in the fact that in non-Western societies religious institutions are more closely tied to other aspects of life than they are in our own society, making it difficult, if not impossible, to study any aspect of the people's life without touching on their religious behavior. Our advanced technology has removed us from the problems of wresting a living from the land. We have gained some degree of control over the natural environment, a control that does not exist in many non-Western societies, and we are now dealing with an artificial, cultural environment. The problems that we face in our daily life are problems of a human-made cultural system. In other words, we are farther removed from nature than people in many non-Western societies, and our religious institutions reflect this fact. The effect of religion on economic, political, legal, and other institutions is therefore less in our society.

As we will see, religion is not easy to study cross-culturally. It is especially hard to understand the "why" of religious beliefs and practices in other societies. Compare the study of religion, for example, to the study of agricultural practices in another culture—an equally interesting topic to the anthropologist. The variety of agricultural practices and the reasons behind them cannot differ too much from one culture to another because of the limits imposed by the environment. In contrast, with religion the opportunity for variation is almost unlimited. Anything we can imagine is possible. And while we have scientific answers for the "why" of agriculture, we have no such answers for the "why" of religion.

Religion was first defined by Sir Edward Tylor more than 100 years ago as belief in spiritual beings. However, in our discussion of the anthropological approach to religion we will not be limited to his definition, for we also wish to include the basic assumptions that people make about other forces in the universe and the place of humans in nature, and the rituals they perform in an attempt to control their environment.

In its broadest context religion comprises a wide assortment of supernatural spirits, beings, forces, behaviors, and beliefs. Religion includes everything from somber and humble communication with one omnipotent creator deity, to the belief in a pantheon of gods or spirit helpers, to the practice of magic and sorcery. When anthropologists talk about religion, their concept is very sweeping and reflects the extensive dimensions of human beliefs. It is important to realize that the religious world views of many people do not reflect the sharp distinctions between the natural and the supernatural that are common to the thinking of most Westerners. For example, in many African and Asian cultures there is a firm conviction that an ongoing, regular communication exists between the living and the dead. Furthermore, ghosts of the deceased, spirits, and deities are believed to play a role in the everyday affairs of people. Thus, if you do well on your next test, it is because the ghost of a dearly departed uncle assisted you in completing the answers. Should you lose your notes just before the final exam, this would be attributed to the magical activities of enemies and probably the intervention of spirits. In the culture of the United States people might shake their heads and pity Aunt Matilda because she sits and rocks while talking out loud to her deceased husband; that type of behavior would not be regarded as one bit strange in much of the world.

Let us consider the relationship among religion, magic (which includes witchcraft), and science. Although these three categories seem quite distinct in our own culture, we find that for many non-Western peoples they tend to be fused, and it is hard or impossible for the observer to separate them. **Religion** is basically a belief system that includes myths explaining the social and religious order and rituals through which the members of the religious community express their beliefs. **Magic** is the attempt to manipulate the forces of nature to obtain certain results. Magic can be religious in some contexts, since it is part of a belief system that relates humans to nature. The main difference is that magic assumes that humans have supernatural power over the forces of the universe, whereas religion generally does not. **Science,** on the other hand, is different from both religion and magic in that it is based on observed relationships in the knowable universe; its attempts to manipulate natural forces are based on experiment and do not call on supernatural powers, as magic does.

Magic, science, and religion exist together in all societies. In American culture science is dominant, and we have great faith in our ability to control the environment through natural (as opposed to supernatural) forces. American farmers, for example, use fertilizers to increase yield, irrigation to overcome lack of rainfall, pesticides to kill insects, and many other scientific methods to ensure success. They probably also resort to magic, but in our science-oriented culture they call it **superstition.** "Don't plant on Friday the 13th," for example, is a superstitious dictum

that is not unlike the magical practices of many non-Western peoples. The main difference is that when we bend to such superstitions it is usually not with the same degree of conviction that others apply to their magical practices.

In a society in which people do not have the ability to control the environment, they must resort to magic and religion. They perform a rain dance to bring on the rain that is vital to survival, whereas we would never perform a rain dance because we "know" that rain is a natural phenomenon and is not subject to supernatural control. In some societies people might also use magic to ensure a good yield; for example, they might not plant under a full moon and might forbid a menstruating woman to help with the harvest. Such practices are ways of manipulating or appeasing the supernatural forces that are thought to govern success in agriculture. But whether religion, magic, or science is dominant, there are elements of each in all cultures. While American farmers might resort to cloud seeding as a scientific solution, they also pray for rain. If we asked why they thought prayer would help, even though they understood the natural causes of rain, we would probably get an answer like: "Well, it won't hurt, will it?" And there is an element of "science" in practices that appear magical to us. People probably would not perform a rain dance at a time when rain was not normally expected, showing that a certain amount of observation and "scientific" prediction goes into magical practices.

In this chapter we will first discuss religion as a cultural universal. We will pay special attention to the relationship between religion and other aspects of the social order. We will then discuss magic and witchcraft, showing how they, too, are related to the social context in which they exist.

Comparative Studies of Religion

People tend to take their religious beliefs for granted. They learn them as they grow up,

Members of the Gururumba Tribe in New Guinea prance beside a display of magical herbs and other botanical remedies used in curing.

as part of their culture. You will recall that in discussing the definition of culture we pointed out that much of what we learn is on an unconscious level and that we never really analyze our behavior. Thus, if we call upon people to state their religious beliefs, the results tend to be unrewarding. Imagine a non-Western anthropologist asking an American Christian to explain how God could be one and three at the same time, or to describe God. We have the same problem when we try to study religion in another society. We are always bound by our own beliefs and concepts about religion, and even the questions we ask are limited by our own religious framework.

The French sociologist Émile Durkheim stressed three aspects of religion: (1) the social context of religious systems; (2) the sacred aspects of religion; and (3) the moral basis of religion in society.[1] Let us discuss each of these in order.

The real purpose of religion, according to Durkheim, is to express people's beliefs about the universe. Religion structures the universe, puts things in order, relates what is unknown to what is known. Other anthropologists have stated this principle in different ways. Sir James Frazer noted the relationship between the religious order and the political structure of many societies, pointing out many parallels between them.[2] Such a relationship might be harder to see in our own society because of the separation of church and state, but elsewhere it is quite clear. In traditional China, for example, the emperor was the incarnation of God, and the Imperial City was thought to be an earthly duplication of the Heavenly City. In ancient Egypt the pharaoh was descended from God. And in medieval Europe the church supported the divine right of kings and maintained the feudal order through the operation of its land holdings. In each case the holy order and the earthly order were one

and the same, and religion was the link between them. As Malinowski pointed out, the nature of the social order is justified by the myths that people create and in which they believe.[3] Thus myths not only explain things that cannot be understood otherwise, but also tell people why the world is the way it is and why it should stay that way. They serve, in Malinowski's words, as a charter for the social system.

Second, Durkheim divided things into the two categories of **sacred** and **profane.** Some things in every society are set apart and considered special—dangerous or powerful or imbued with a mystical aura. These things are sacred. In contrast, the rest of the world is ordinary, or profane. Every society considers different things sacred, but the setting apart of certain things as sacred is a cultural universal.

The third point made by Durkheim is that religion requires people to act in a certain way. As part of the system of beliefs about the nature of the universe, religion offers a guide to behavior, including a system of rules. Furthermore, because religious beliefs are so deeply ingrained in people by their cultural training, religion is a means of social control. When people violate a religious rule governing behavior, they feel guilty whether or not they are caught and punished. At the same time, when they follow the rules, they feel good and their beliefs are reinforced. We are all familiar with this notion in Western religions, in which belief in salvation and an afterlife is directly linked to conformity with a code of behavior during one's earthly life.

Religion meets basic, universal human needs by helping people cope with the unknowable and the uncontrollable. It is hard for us to understand many of these functions, for in American culture we do have some control over our environment, and there is little that happens in our everyday life that science cannot explain. In the United States, therefore, religion has become more **secular** in recent years. It still performs the same

[1] Emile Durkheim, *The Elementary Forms of the Religious Life* (London: George Allen & Unwin, 1915).

[2] James G. Frazer, *The Golden Bough* (New York: Macmillan, 1922).

[3] Bronislaw Malinowski, *Myth in Primitive Psychology* (London: Routledge & Kegan Paul, 1926).

functions, but only to a limited extent. For example, Western religions have become more concerned with the path to salvation and less concerned with the control of supernatural power. Since we have no scientific knowledge about the concepts of soul and afterlife, these have become the primary concerns of our religion, replacing more mundane (to us) problems such as climate, illness, and the like.

It is also interesting to note that in recent years we have heard much about a "crisis" in religion in the United States; that is, the drastic changes that have taken place in the function of religion in our society. At the same time, in some groups there has been a revival of religious fervor. One explanation for this revival can be found in the rapidly changing morality of American society, which has led some people to call for a return to a stronger moral order. Religion thus is trying to provide some stability in a time of change. Religion provides rules of behavior so that human interaction can be based on predictable responses and patterns of behavior. The

A Guatemalan peasant praying inside of a Roman Catholic church in rural Guatemala, where beliefs and ceremonies combine elements of Christianity and indigenous religious beliefs.

religious response to current trends in American culture is basically conservative: It seeks a return to an old morality rather than the creation of a new one.

In studying religion from a comparative standpoint, it is helpful to keep Durkheim's threefold definition in mind, both to guide our study and to avoid being subjective in our analysis of non-Western religious behavior. We should concentrate on how religion is integrated with the rest of the social order, the elements of the culture that are set off from the rest and treated as sacred, and the extent to which the community is unified by shared religious values and rules of behavior.

Types of Religious Beliefs

The most basic religious belief is that there is a spirit or soul in all living things, a belief that Edward Tylor called **animism.** Tylor found this type of belief to be universal, and it is easy to see why all peoples would arrive at the same basic kind of belief in trying to deal with the unknown. Belief in spirits or souls may arise out of experiences such as dreaming or hallucinogenic trances, in which, despite the person's seemingly normal outward appearance, some inner "thing" leaves the body and engages in its own activities. What better way to explain the fact that a person can awake from a deep sleep, without having moved, and talk about an adventure that occurred just then in a dream? How else can you explain the unconscious and unremembered actions of a person in a trance? Likewise, in death the body remains behind, yet obviously something within the body—that "inner spirit"—has left it. Sometimes the spirit is thought to dwell in the shadow of a person during the day, but to leave and wander about at night while he or she sleeps. At other times the spirit is not connected with the physical being; this is especially true in death. If a person's wandering soul meets (in a dream) the spirit of a dead ancestor, then there must be some kind of life after death, for despite the death of the physical part of the relative, there is a part that lives on.

Such experiences make sense if one believes that each person is two separate beings—one tangible and earthly and the other intangible and spiritual. Tylor considered this the most basic of all religious beliefs and proposed it as a minimal definition of religion. Animism is religious in that spirits are worshiped and are thought to have some kind of supernatural power. The attribution of a spirit and a supernatural power to animate and inanimate objects alike is a way of explaining the unknown and relating humanity to the universe.

The concept of animism implies the presence of power, a special kind of power that cannot be controlled because it is supernatural. It can be observed and in some cases manipulated, but it cannot be created or destroyed. Belief in such power is found in many different religious systems, and anthropologists use the term **mana** in referring to it. Mana is a supernatural force that is neither good nor bad in itself but simply exists in nature. It can be manipulated for good or bad purposes, but at the same time it is often capricious, acting in different ways at different times without any clear reason. It is the nature of mana to be unpredictable and uncontrollable.

Closely tied to the concept of mana is **taboo** (also spelled *tabu*), a set of restrictions on the behavior of humans the purpose of which is to prevent them from coming into contact with mana. (The words *mana* and *taboo* are derived from a Polynesian language.) Taboo is based on the notion that power can be dangerous and that people need to follow a set of rules that define their behavior toward sacred beings and objects. (A good way of understanding these concepts is to think of mana as a form of electricity. A person may have so much mana that to touch him or her would be dangerous; hence the taboo against such contact.)

The concept of a special power such as mana can have many functions in a society. It can explain why some people are different from others—better hunters, farmers, lovers, artists. The power can lie within the individual or in a physical object controlled by that person. A brave and successful warrior can

Wig men from New Guinea invoking the supernatural.

excel because he himself has mana or because he possesses objects that transfer their power to him, such as a magic charm worn around the neck, or a powerful bow or spear. Mana can also explain why much of nature is so unpredictable. If a garden produces a larger crop than the one next to it, its cultivator may have more mana. If a normally successful curer or healer is unable to cure a patient, the reason may be that he has lost his mana or that there is a stronger force working against him.

A taboo prohibits certain kinds of behavior. Often the authority behind this prohibition is supernatural power, along with the danger inherent in the behavior itself. The taboo can be arbitrary, with no "logical" explanation to back it up, or it can be based on commonly understood and accepted principles. For example, in the Garden of Eden no reason was given as to why the fruit of one tree could not be eaten. It was an arbitrary rule set forth by God and was to be followed without question. Other taboos may have clearer explanations. In native Hawaiian culture, and also in ancient Egypt, it was customary for people of royal blood (kings or pharaohs) to marry only relatives, preferably sisters. Furthermore, it was taboo for the ruler to have sexual intercourse with a commoner. The reason for this taboo was that these individuals were of divine origin, and as such possessed a great deal of mana. While another member of the royal family also inherited this divine power, a commoner did not. Thus, producing offspring with a commoner would defile the power. Only by producing children within the royal line could the purity of the ruler's mana be guaranteed. However, since there was no need to worry about the purity of the divine lineage among commoners, incest was prescribed for the royal family but not for the rest of society; instead, there were strong prohibitions against it.

A taboo, thus, is a kind of sacred law that replaces secular law in maintaining some form of social control. As Marston Bates points out in *Gluttons and Libertines*, our taboo against incest is much stronger than our laws might imply.[4] Although the punishment for incest is less severe than that for rape, it is often assumed that the legal penalty will be accompanied by divine retribution. The main difference is that the penalties for violating a taboo come mainly from supernatural agents, whereas violations of the law are punished by society.

Mana and taboo can also explain things that cannot be explained in any other way. A predictable event does not occur, and this requires an explanation. A formerly successful warrior falls in battle, and the men sitting around the campfire recall that he violated a taboo and was not able to purify himself. His death was not at the hands of the enemy but was caused by supernatural power.

In analyzing these various types of religious beliefs, we might ask what creates and sustains them in a society. The answer can be found in the study of **myth.** Like animism and the belief in supernatural power, myth is a cultural universal. Myths are the vehicles through which a society expresses its beliefs about the things it holds sacred. They are sacred stories that contain explanations of how things came to be the way they are and how they should be maintained. There are creation myths that relate the story of the origin of society, and there are tales that state how people must act and explain why they must act that way. Thus, as Malinowski pointed out, myths present a charter for society, and as such they not only deal with the sacred but are themselves sacred.

Historical verification of the "truth" of a myth is unimportant and generally impossible. Since most myths are oral legends passed down from one generation to the next, after a short time they can no longer be verified anyway. When myths have been written down, they often deal with a time or an event for which there are no written records. The importance of a myth is in its "social truth," not its historical accuracy. Myths explain

---

[4] Marston Bates, *Gluttons and Libertines* (New York: Vintage Books, 1967).

things that cannot otherwise be understood; their validity is maintained through the practices they prescribe, which are carried out according to instructions contained in the myth itself.

Earlier we discussed the Indian caste system as a form of social organization with a rigid hierarchy of social groups, or castes. This system is justified by Hindu mythology. According to Hindu teachings, when a person dies, he or she goes on to another life through the process of **reincarnation** or rebirth. Since a person is born into a particular caste and remains in it throughout life, a change in status comes about only through reincarnation—being born into a higher or lower caste in the next life. Furthermore, the way to achieve a higher status in the next life is not to strive for a high-caste life style in this life, but to follow the rules of behavior for the caste into which one was born. Any attempt to leave one's caste and achieve a higher status within one's own lifetime is a violation of this rule and will result in reincarnation into a lower caste (or possibly in a subhuman form; this is called *transmigration*).

We can see how the myth of reincarnation serves as a charter for the caste system in India. In effect, it justifies the way things are and seeks to keep them that way in the future. Throughout Hindu mythology there are stories of how these rules came to be and why they must be followed. There are also tales about individuals who either broke the rules and were punished or followed them and were rewarded. The same is true for every culture. For example, in the United States we have, among others, the series of stories told by Horatio Alger in which a young boy or girl of humble origins "makes it" in the outside world through individual effort and initiative. These stories reflect the widespread myth that anyone can achieve success up to the limits of his or her ability. Yet, as we all are aware, opportunities are not equal in our society, for there is discrimination on the basis of race, sex, religion, and many other factors. The "equal opportunity" myth justifies the free-enterprise system, but it does

not describe reality. Nevertheless, the notion that theoretically anyone can be a success has some very positive implications regarding what people should be able to do on their own.

Another example of the role of mythology in the organization of society is "The Dreaming," a myth of the Australian tribes known as the Arunta. As described by W. E. H. Stanner, The Dreaming refers to the time when the mythical ancestors of the Arunta were alive. It includes both the act of dreaming or meditation and the mythology on which the people meditate. The Dreaming is difficult for Westerners to understand because it does not conform to our notions of time. To quote Stanner:

> Although, as I have said, The Dreaming conjures up the notion of a sacred, heroic time of the indefinitely remote past, such a time is also, in a sense, still part of the present. One cannot "fix" The Dreaming *in* time: it was, and is, everywhen. . . . Clearly, The Dreaming is many things in one. Among them, a kind of narrative of things that once happened; a kind of charter of things that still happen; and a kind of *logos* or principle of order transcending everything significant for aboriginal man.[5]

The Dreaming is the Arunta attempt to explain the unknown. It is the means by which one attains unity with one's own spirit and with the world in which one lives. It provides continuity between the past and the present, between the spiritual and the here and now. The Dreaming provides an explanation for creation, for how things come to be the way they are. It deals with a moral order, with rules of conduct for how things are to be carried out in the present. It states the punishment for breaking the rules and offers a logical explanation for why people should act a certain way. It carries with it a

---

[5] W. E. H. Stanner, "The Dreaming," T. A. G. Hungerford, Ed., in *Australian Signpost*, (Melbourne: F. W. Cheshire, 1956), pp. 51–65. Reprinted in William A. Lessa and Evon Z. Vogt, Eds., *Reader in Comparative Religion*, 2nd ed. (New York: Harper & Row, 1965).

sacred authority—Arunta society is the way it is because The Dreaming says so. Perhaps most important, The Dreaming is the means by which the Arunta become one with nature. Through it they are spiritually united with their environment and all its inhabitants, and they carry out this philosophy in their daily activities.

Types of Religious Practices

If myth is the "why" of religious life, then **ritual** is the "how" by which those concepts are put into practice. A ritual is a prescribed way of carrying out a religious activity, such as a prayer, an act of worship, or a sacrifice. Rituals can be tied to regular events, such as the seasons in the agricultural cycle, or they can accompany birth, marriage, illness, or any other unique or unplanned event. Rituals are important not only for their spiritual value but also for their symbolic meaning. They signify that the proper actions have been performed, so that the deities or spirits will be satisfied. At the same time, they have a deeper meaning to the members of the group, for they mark group boundaries by setting off those who perform the ritual, and

therefore are part of the group, from those who do not. By comparing several different types of rituals, we can see how they reinforce the belief system of a society and how a wide variety of rituals can perform the same basic functions.

A familiar set of rituals marks off different stages of life: birth, entry into a religious community, adulthood, marriage, death. At each stage there is a ritual that signifies the change in the individual (as much for society's benefit as for the individual's). In our society the attainment of adulthood is accompanied by secular rather than religious rituals, and the status of adult is not as clearly defined as it is in other societies. The rituals of entry into adulthood include obtaining a driver's license, becoming eligible to vote, the twenty-first birthday, and graduation from high school or college. In some cases even the wedding ceremony can serve to confirm a person's adult status.

Rituals of this type, which confer a new status on an individual, are called **rites of passage;** they involve a passage from one stage of the life cycle to another. Although cultures define these stages in different ways, all cultures celebrate the passage from one stage to another with rites of passage. It is interesting to note that in some cultures the

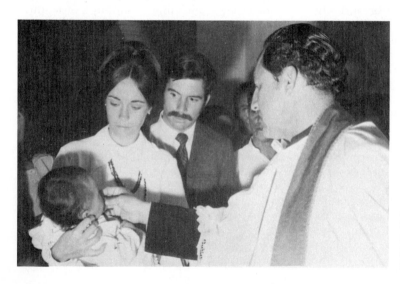

Baptism into the Roman Catholic Church in Popayán, Colombia. In many societies baptism, or some formal naming ceremony, is the first in a series of rites of passage.

passage from one stage of life to the next is a relatively informal, gradual process without much pressure or ceremony, while in others it can be an abrupt change surrounded by anxiety, mystery, and even fear. As noted before, in our culture the achievement of adulthood is a relatively gradual process. A young man or woman obtains certain rights at several different points along the way, so that by the time he or she is 21 much of the activity defined by society as "adult" is already commonplace.

In contrast to the American pattern of achieving adulthood, in some societies this transition is much more abrupt and is marked by an important ceremony. Among many tribal societies a boy's passage from childhood to adulthood is marked by ritual circumcision at puberty. As children, boys are taught to fear this ritual, and the closer they come to it, the more intense their fear becomes. Yet they are also taught that only as adult males can they take part in the meaningful religious activities of their tribe, so there is no alternative to the rite of passage. During the ceremony itself the boys' fears are intensified even further by the older men who perform the circumcision. They may dance and sing of the "killing" they are about to do, or offer their sympathy to the boys' mothers. The

A Hausa tribesman from Nigeria. His facial scars signify a ritual passage into adulthood.

boys are often forced to fast and go without sleep for some time prior to the ceremony. During the circumcision they are removed from their families and from the rest of the group and taken to an isolated place where the sacred operation is performed.

In many ways this type of ceremony is similar to the old-fashioned fraternity initiation, with its hazing and its ways of building up anxiety. A "pledge" spends a year or more seeking admission to the chosen group. During this time he is taught the basics of fraternity life but is never allowed to share the group's "sacred" secrets. The initiation itself is built up by the members, so that while the pledge becomes more eager to gain this new status, he also becomes more anxious about what will be involved in the initiation ceremony. Rumors of corporal punishment, personal embarrassment, and other forms of hazing add to his concern. When the time finally arrives for him to undergo the initiation, he does so with a mixture of pride and anxiety, eagerness and hesitation. Once the ceremony is over and he has been accepted into the group, he usually guards the secrets and sacred knowledge that he has obtained as jealously as his predecessors did before him.

Rites of passage exist in a number of societies to mark the transition from girlhood to womanhood. Unlike the circumcision ritual, which is frequently a group event, the female rite of passage is often a rather solitary affair, often coinciding with the onset of menstruation. At that time the girl is segregated from the rest of the group and attended to by older women, who instruct her in the ways of being an adult. When she emerges from her period of seclusion and instruction, she is considered a woman. Frequently this is made clear by her appearance—she might dress differently, display her hair in a new manner, show the facial scarification she was lately subjected to, or wear a veil. If she is not already betrothed, this ritual signifies that she is now ready to marry.

Another type of rite of passage is the **vision quest.** In some Plains Indian tribes a boy

Members of the Hare Krishna sect chanting on a public street. Religious groups sometimes dramatize their beliefs by a symbolic separation from the rest of society.

could become a man only by acquiring spiritual power through a hallucinatory vision. Throughout his childhood a Crow Indian boy constantly heard from his peers and his elders that the only way he could acquire power in his society was by having a vision. As he grew older his desire for the good things in life—many horses, a wife from an important family, and recognition from his fellow tribesmen—led him to seek a vision. First he would go off alone, perhaps deep into the woods or to the top of a mountain. There he would beg the spirits to send him a vision that would give him some of their supernatural power for his own use. He might fast for many days, induce exhaustion, or inflict pain upon himself in order to gain the sympathy of the spirits. When this finally happened, he would have a vision in which he obtained valuable information to be used when he returned to the tribe. The benefits of the vision were of many kinds; they might include the supernatural power of a curer or medicine man, or economic power, or perhaps some special ability as a warrior or a tribal leader.

Not only young boys but mature men and women would seek visions in time of emergency or stress. A woman with a sick child would seek a cure through a vision; a man who had lost a close relative would seek revenge through a vision. Thus vision quests existed both as rites of passage and as rituals designed for specific occasions that did not involve a change of status. The concept of a unique personal revelation was based on belief in the transfer of supernatural power through hallucinatory visions, and the vision often included instructions in how to keep the power through special magic or further rituals. The occurrence of religious visions in contemporary Western society, as is said to have taken place at Lourdes or Fatima, shows that such things are not limited to so-called primitives but may play a similar role in industrial societies.

The vision quest is an individual act performed in isolation, away from the rest of the group. Other rituals involving the transmission of supernatural power through a human agent can occur in a group situation. One such ritual is **spirit possession,** in which a person becomes possessed by a supernatural spirit, usually in a state of trance. That person

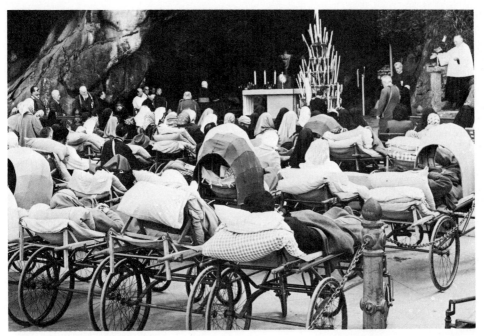

Believing in the supernatural powers associated with the site, individuals seek miracle cures at Lourdes, France.

then acts as a medium through which the spirit communicates to others. The trance can be induced by drugs or other substances, or by dancing or some other physical activity. The messages that are transmitted may concern future events, the nature or cure of an illness, the cause of some evil event, and so forth. Spirit possession often spreads throughout the group, for the excitement and frenzied activities of such rituals are contagious.

The examples given here illustrate only a few of the types of religious activities found throughout the world. However, they show how important ritual is to the religious life of a society, as well as to the individuals who practice it. In the following section we will try to pull together the elements of religion that we have discussed so far in order to show how a particular belief system, coupled with a mythology and a set of rituals, can act as a principle around which people organize their lives and interact as members of a social group. For this we turn to a discussion of the religious system known as *totemism.*

Totemism

The term **totem,** which is derived from the Chippewa Indian language spoken in the Great Lakes area, refers to a natural item, either animate or inanimate, that an individual or a group identifies itself with. Although totemism is found among American Indian tribes, the best examples of religions based on the relationship between a group of people and their totem are found in Australia. While the form of totemic religions varies greatly from one society to another, it is possible to speak of totemism in general terms, and to define some of its basic characteristics.

A totem can be an animal, a plant, or an inanimate object, such as a rock, that is used as a symbol of the unity of the group. A society may be divided into many totemic groups, each of which identifies with a different totem. In its most extreme form—for example, that found among Australian Aborigines—the totem is not merely a symbol of the unity of a group of people; instead, the identification is so complete that if a man says "I am a wallaby," he does not mean he is a member of the wallaby totemic group or clan, but rather that he is of the same species as the wallaby—that there is a blood tie between him, the wallaby, and all the members of his group.

Totemism can be seen as a form of nature worship in which the spirit of the human and the spirit of the totem animal or plant are merged. Usually there are a number of taboos associated with totemism. It is common, for example, for people to be strictly forbidden to kill or eat any member of the totemic species, except in rituals that celebrate the unity of the group. Another common rule states that it is incestuous for a person to have sexual relations with another member of his or her totemic clan. The mystical relationship among all the members of the clan is so strong that it overrides any blood relationship. Thus the totemic clan usually sets the limits of the incest taboo.

Totemism is not only the basis of the moral code of Australian Aborigines but also the principle by which their society is organized. A person inherits membership in a totemic clan from his or her parent (from the mother in a matrilineal society, from the father in a patrilineal society). The relationship between an individual and other members of the clan is clearly spelled out by their joint membership in the group. Likewise, the relationship between an individual and members of other totemic groups is also part of the knowledge gained through membership in his or her own group. Thus the totemic system of classifying not only people but also nonhuman elements of the environment is a way of creating harmony between the social system and the universe and defining each person's place in that system.

We are all familiar with the symbolic aspect of totemism in our own culture. While we might not attach religious significance to the identification of a group with a particular animal, plant, or other natural object, we do use it as a principle of organization. Our sports teams, for example, are not referred to simply by location or hometown, which would be enough to allow us to tell them apart, but also by a mascot of some sort. The mascot can be human (San Francisco 49ers, Kansas City Chiefs, Cleveland Indians); an animal (Boston Bruins, Baltimore Orioles, Detroit Lions); a force of nature (Iowa State Cyclones, Miami Hurricanes); a plant (Ohio State Buckeyes, Toronto Maple Leafs); or

A totem pole of the Northwest Coast Indians. These poles were used to commemorate important events, such as the naming of a chief's son or the elevation of a chief.

some kind of inanimate object that serves as a unifying symbol (Chicago White Sox, Detroit Pistons, New York Jets). Ralph Linton described the development of totemic groups in the U.S. Army during World War I, showing that although a totem may lack religious significance, the tendency to organize the universe and divide it into categories is found in all societies and is not a sign of a "primitive mentality."

Linton described the "Rainbow Division," the 42nd Division of the U.S. Army.[6] Shortly after the name was assigned to the division (in 1918), members began to use the term *Rainbow* to refer to themselves, rather than using the formal name *42nd Division.* Furthermore, the members of the division developed the idea that the appearance of a rainbow in the sky was a good omen for them (but not for anyone else). This notion gained popularity until it became so strong that members of the division claimed to have seen rainbows just before going into battle or after a victory, even though weather conditions did not support their claims. The men in the division began to use the rainbow as their symbol, painting it on their equipment and even wearing it on their shoulders—despite official regulations forbidding them to do so. The idea spread to other divisions, which adopted different "totems" for themselves.

Religious Specialists

While religious beliefs and practices differ a great deal from one society to another, in all societies certain individuals act as **religious specialists.** The position of religious specialist is based on the belief that people have unequal amounts of knowledge and ability, and that those with more than their share are in a better position to relate to the supernatural. Such specialists can be religious, in that they seek help from the divine or

[6] Ralph Linton, "Totemism and the A. E. F.," *American Anthropologist,* 26 (1924): 296–300.

spiritual world, or magical, in that they try to manipulate the spirits or supernatural forces.

In our society we have training programs to prepare religious specialists for their work. A clergyman or -woman is a person who has had such training. The clergy's authority is based on their religious office, not on their personalities. On the other hand, some religious movements have lay preachers whose authority is based more on their ability than on their education. Thus we have two kinds of religious specialization—one in which the power is in the office, and another in which the power is in the individual. This holds true for religious specialists in other societies as well.

In contrast to the priest, who acquires religious knowledge through formal training, in many societies there are religious specialists whose powers come directly from supernatural forces, spirits, or gods. Of course, both types of specialists can exist in the same society. The latter type is sometimes called a **shaman,** a term derived from the language of the Siberian societies in which such specialists are found. Among the Plains Indians, a person who wished to become a shaman had to seek the necessary power through a vision. In other societies, however, a shaman can be anyone who comes into direct contact with a spirit. Often this involves being possessed by the spirit, in which case the individual loses (or seems to lose) control of himself, and acts as if directed by the spirit.

A person can become a shaman as a result of a mystical experience, such as a vision, or a period of special training, or both. Many anthropologists are skeptical about shamans, noting that they use such tricks as ventriloquism, sleight of hand, and optical illusions to achieve their results. Thus, in a practical sense, a shaman requires training not in religious doctrines, which he interprets as a priest would, but in the methods he uses. Shamans are known in many societies as indigenous healers or curers. They help their clients by using supernatural powers to suck out the poison that is harming them, pull

A Zulu shaman sucking out a foreign spirit through the ear of a patient.

foreign matter from their "soul," or advise them as to what rituals to perform in order to rid themselves of the evil infesting their body or spirit. But the main difference between a shaman and other religious specialists, such as priests, is that the shaman is not an actor but a medium for the supernatural spirit that performs the act of curing.

Among the Yanomamö, the shaman actually works in several capacities. One of his roles is to keep his people healthy. This he does through the use of herbal potions and spirit helpers. The other major function he must perform is directing spiritual warfare, in which he commands the supernatural forces under his control to eat the souls of enemies in other villages. When Yanomamö die, their deaths are usually attributed to supernatural causes.

In most societies shamans are males, although there are some important exceptions. Among the Mapuche, an Indian group in southern Chile, for instance, the role of shaman is typically a female one.

Shamans can also act as **diviners,** individuals who can foresee future events or uncover the causes of past events. A diviner may try to learn the will of the gods so that the group can control future events or plan around them. He can also discover the supernatural cause of an illness when no other cause is apparent. He may do this by viewing some natural event, such as the flight of a flock of birds, the entrails of a slaughtered animal, or the design created by tea leaves in the bottom of a cup. Or he may act as a medium for a spirit that speaks through him to the members of the group. Divination thus takes many different forms, but in most societies it can be considered a religious activity because it deals with the supernatural and involves an attempt to control the forces of nature.

Priests, shamans, and diviners are but a

few of the many types of religious specialists found throughout the world. The important point is not the variety of religious specialists, but rather the fact that in most cases they perform many of the same functions. Whether we call him a guru, a priest or minister, a shaman, a medicine man, or a witch doctor, the religious specialist occupies his position because he is believed to have some special knowledge or talent that carries with it a higher religious authority. His role is more important in societies in which religious beliefs and practices are the basis for social behavior, as is the case in most of the non-Western societies studied by anthropologists. When religion is fused with economic and political power, the religious specialist takes on added importance as a leader and as an interpreter of custom and morality. In the United States there are a few individuals—people like Jerry Falwell, Pat Robertson, or Jesse Jackson—who combine their religious position with a certain amount of political power. But their influence is not nearly as great as that of a political leader whose position is grounded in religious tradition, such as the pharaohs of ancient Egypt or, in modern times, politico-religious leaders like the late Ayatollah Khomeini of Iran.

Magic and Witchcraft

As noted earlier, all people seek to control their environment. They do this by manipulating the supernatural through the practice of magic; through the explanation of how or why things happened the way they did, which is related to witchcraft; and through the prediction of future events, or divination. We discussed divination in the last section. We turn now to witchcraft and magic.

Magic is manipulative. It is like science in the sense that it seeks control over the forces of nature, but unlike science it uses supernatural means to gain that control. Magic can be good or bad; it can be directed against an individual or a group; and it can be practiced

by an individual or by a group. When it succeeds it is proof that the magic is effective, that the spirits exist, and that they can be manipulated. When it fails, however, it does not prove the opposite. Rather, a failure means that the proper rituals were not performed correctly, that an important rule was broken, or that someone else used stronger magic. It is never the supernatural power that is at fault, but always the human practitioner.

Sir James Frazer isolated two basic principles of magic: (1) Like produces like (the **law of similarity,** or sympathetic magic). (2) Things that have been in contact with each other continue to affect each other after they have become separated (the **law of contact,** or contagious magic).[7]

One of the best-known examples of the law of similarity is **voodoo.** A person makes a doll in the image of the intended victim, then injures the doll (for instance, by sticking a pin in it) or destroys it. According to the law of similarity, the magic will be carried from the doll to the victim, producing the same degree of injury or death. Voodoo is very successful in some cases, and people have actually died after being exposed to voodoo magic. Walter Cannon has shown that such results are caused by the strength of the victim's beliefs about voodoo.[8] When belief is deeply ingrained, the fear of voodoo is enough to cause death. Cannon traces the physical effects of voodoo magic: The body is stimulated by the initial fear; when this condition is prolonged, shock sets in, causing reduced blood pressure, deterioration of the heart, and similar effects. Lack of food and water adds to the debilitation, and if it continues for more than a few days, it can be fatal. Cannon gives two reasons why voodoo might have this effect on believers. The first is that if you've seen the effect of voodoo on others throughout your life, you're more likely to respond as you've seen them respond

---

[7] Frazer, *op. cit.,*chap. 3.

[8] Walter B. Cannon, '"Voodoo' Death," *American Anthropologist,* 44 (1942): 169–181.

in the past. Second, often the people around you isolate you completely—they act as if you were already dead, and leave you with no source of emotional or personal support. This is bound to be fairly devastating under the circumstances.

The law of similarity can also be used for good purposes. The Inuit of the Bering Strait region make dolls in the image of young babies and give them to barren women to help them conceive. This law can also help prevent or cure illness, as in the use of a yellow substance to prevent jaundice, or something red to prevent bleeding. In medieval Germany ashes were rubbed on the forehead of a person with a high fever in the hope that just as the ashes had cooled, so would the patient's fever. Among the Dyak in Borneo a medicine man lies down and pretends to be dead. His fellow villagers wrap him in mats and take him out to be buried, whereupon he rises up, fully recovered and restored to life. The magic is supposedly transferred to the patient, who lies near death yet should (if the magic is successful) recover

A houngan, a voodoo priest, possessed by a voodoo spirit during a ceremony. Note the severed head of a rooster in his mouth.

and return from death as the medicine man did.

There are also negative practices or taboos based on the law of similarity. These taboos tell us what not to do to bring about a desired event or avoid an unfavorable one. For example, among the Inuit of Baffin Land boys are forbidden to play cat's cradle because their fingers might later become entangled in their harpoon lines. The game is taboo for boys despite the fact that it is popular among girls. Among the Ainu of the Sakhalin Islands north of Japan, pregnant women may not spin thread for two months before the baby is born lest the child become entangled in its umbilical cord.

The second kind of magic (the law of contact or contagion) is based on the principle that things that have been in contact can affect each other afterward. A common example of this is the belief that any magic worked on a severed portion of a person will affect that person. For example, the Navajo bury their hair and nail clippings far away from the settlement because they fear that these items could be used against them. Among some Australian tribes it is believed that one can cause a person to become lame by placing a sharp piece of glass or bone in his or her footprint, which is considered part of that person. This notion carries over to hunting, as may be seen in the old German practice of pounding a nail into the footprint of an animal that is being tracked in order to prevent it from escaping.

Witchcraft is an explanation of how or why certain events occurred, and it usually involves the application of magic by a person to bring about a desired result. Witchcraft can have many functions in society. It provides an outlet for aggression and hostility; it is a way of resolving tensions and conflicts; and it provides a scapegoat for society. It can regulate the hostility that arises in any social situation. And it can explain such things as failure, disease, or misfortune. As we pointed out in the last chapter, witchcraft can act as a mechanism for social control by regulating the behavior of certain members of the group. People can be forced to follow certain patterns of behavior either because they are afraid of becoming the victims of a witch or because they are afraid of being accused of witchcraft. Thus, in studying the social effects of witchcraft, we must also study the way a society deals with witches.

E. E. Evans-Pritchard, an anthropologist known for his studies of African societies, discusses witchcraft among the Azande, an African group living near the Congo River.[9] Witchcraft is an important aspect of the social life of the Azande. Accusations of witchcraft prevent some people from striving for success at the expense of others. A man who is too successful is likely to be accused of being a witch, and because men fear such accusations, members of the group tend to be about equally successful.

Evans-Pritchard points out that most of the Azande take witchcraft for granted. They expect to find it in their daily lives and are not surprised when it occurs, for it is a natural outgrowth of living with other people in a social setting. Witchcraft is especially useful in explaining events that could not otherwise be explained. How does an action that is repeated day after day suddenly produce an unfortunate result? For example, one day you are walking along a path and you bump into a stump, cutting your foot in the process. The next day the cut is infected. Here are several clear signs of witchcraft. First, you have walked along the path every day for years and never bumped your foot before. Why now? Second, you have bumped yourself many times before, but rarely did such a bump produce a cut. Why now? Third, you have had cuts before, but rarely did they become infected. Why now? Clearly, some evil force caused you to suffer this mishap by making you blind to the stump and then causing the cut to become infected.

In a thorough study of the relationship between witchcraft and other aspects of the social order, S. F. Nadel compares witchcraft among four African societies.[10] He groups the societies into two pairs, the Nupe and Gwari in northern Nigeria and the Korongo and Mesakin in the Nuba Mountains of central Sudan. Within each pair there is a great deal of cultural similarity, but witchcraft beliefs differ.

In comparing Nupe and Gwari witchcraft beliefs, Nadel points out that while beliefs about the nature of witchcraft are similar (it is evil and destroys life), Nupe witches are always women, while among the Gwari witches and their victims can be members of either sex. This can be explained by the strong antagonism between the sexes in Nupe society, and by the fact that only women are accused of witchcraft and only men have the power to defeat witchcraft. Among the Gwari no such antagonism exists. Digging deeper into the social factors involved, Nadel stresses the economic and social independence of women in Nupe society. Women generally work as traders, and their husbands, who are agriculturalists, are often in debt to them. Women also sometimes refuse to have children, thus freeing themselves for their jobs. This creates a role reversal so strong that it is reflected in Nupe witchcraft patterns.

In comparing witchcraft among the Korongo and the Mesakin, Nadel again points out how similar they are in many ways—environment, language, economics, political organization, religious beliefs, kinship system. However, he says, to understand witchcraft we must understand the age grading that occurs in both societies. Males are divided into age groups focused on the display of virility in athletic activities. At puberty this virility is formalized in a ceremony, and during the celebration each boy receives an animal from the herd of his mother's brother. Since the boy will inherit the entire herd later, this pattern of gift giving is normal in both societies.

Regarding witchcraft in these groups, Nadel notes that the Korongo have no witch-

[9] E. E. Evans-Pritchard, *Witchcraft, Oracles and Magic Among the Azande* (Oxford: Clarendon Press, 1937).

[10] S. F. Nadel, "Witchcraft in Four African Societies: An Essay in Comparison," *American Anthropologist*, 54 (1952): 18–29.

James Frazer (1854–1941)

Sir James Frazer was one of the most influential an- thropologists of his time, primarily because of his monumental work *The Golden Bough.* In this work Frazer traced the evolution of human culture through the successive stages of reliance upon magic, reli- gion, and science. It is one of the most detailed and complete accounts of various practices among human cultures, as well as one of the last truly classic evolutionary works of the period. One of Frazer's many important contributions to anthropology con- cerned the distinction between different types of magic—imitative magic, such as the use of a doll to imitate a desired result upon a person, and conta- gious magic, where a severed portion of a person could be used to practice magic upon that person.

craft beliefs at all, while the Mesakin are obsessed by fears of witchcraft and accusa- tions of being a witch. Such accusations often lead to violent quarrels and attacks. Among the Mesakin witchcraft usually operates be- tween a boy and his mother's brother. Since witchcraft is seen as occurring only if there is some reason for resentment or anger, it is usually caused by an argument over the gift received by the boy at the initiation ceremony.

The distinction between these two societies seems to lie in the fact that while among the Korongo the mother's brother never refuses to give his sister's son an animal, among the Mesakin the mother's brother always refuses at first, and often the animal must be taken by force. Thus quarrels are frequent, and if something happens to the youth during such a quarrel, the mother's brother is usually accused of witchcraft.

Nadel attributes the difference between these two groups to cultural differences in adult attitudes toward life, and especially toward growing old. Both groups fear aging. Yet the Korongo men accept it, whereas the Mesakin try to avoid it, even to the point of concealing and denying sexual intercourse, which is believed to be the major cause of aging. In both societies the mother's brother sees the demand for a gift as a reminder that he is growing old. The gift anticipates the death of the donor, since upon his death the entire herd will be turned over to his heir, the sister's son. In Korongo society the men are prepared for a gradual decline, so it is more acceptable, but for the Mesakin there is no gradual transition from youth to old age, and it is harder to accept when it arrives.

Clearly, then, there is more hostility to- ward the sister's son and toward the whole process of gift giving in Mesakin society, and this helps explain their beliefs about witch- craft. Every man projects his own frustrations into accusations of witchcraft by others, and in punishing them he works out these feelings. Nadel also points out that the Korongo, who have no witchcraft, have a full mythology that explains the important things in the world in another way, whereas the Mesakin do not have a well-developed mythology.

In conclusion, Nadel suggests that witchcraft beliefs are related to specific anxieties and stresses in social life. These anxieties can arise from childhood experiences, but they can also result from adult experiences, as among the Mesakin. Nadel also suggests that accusations of witchcraft tend to maintain the existing structure of society by identifying the witch as the one who breaks its rules. And finally, while it may be true that witchcraft beliefs serve to reduce hostility, they may also create tension. The hostility may be reduced only in the sense that it is directed toward a few scapegoats.

If we follow this line of reasoning, we can learn a great deal about the way our own society operates. For example, during the early 1950s the United States went through a period of "witch hunting" known as McCarthyism in which an influential senator and his followers tried to cleanse American society of communism. They found communists everywhere they looked, and in many cases the punishment suffered by the victims of this witch hunt was completely out of line with their alleged crimes. Today we have the same kind of witch hunt, in which a scapegoat is created to absorb the hostility of various groups in our society. Senator Proxmire used to single out the monthly recipient of his "Golden Fleece" award as a scapegoat for waste and bureaucratic mismanagement that can be found throughout the government. A floundering sports team fires its manager rather than its players, making him a scapegoat for the team's lack of success. The president fires his advisers when his public image declines in the popularity polls. In each of these cases, to blame one individual for a complex problem is like blaming an old woman for the outbreak of an epidemic.

The Evolution of Religious Systems

There is no series of stages in the evolution of religion that can be neatly linked to stages in food-producing technology (hunting and gathering, horticulture and pastoralism, agriculture) or in political organization (band, tribe, chiefdom, state). Nothing in the way people gain their living or the way they are organized into a social group determines their religious beliefs. Therefore, if we want to look at long-term changes in religious systems, we must do so with the understanding that they do not fit automatically into the evolutionary framework outlined in earlier chapters of this book.

Anthropologists have suggested various theories to explain the evolution of religion, and many of them conflict with one another. Edward Tylor thought the earliest form of religious belief was the concept of a spirit or soul. According to Tylor, this stage preceded belief in a god or deity. However, a criticism of this view was presented by Tylor's student Andrew Lang, who pointed out that many traditional peoples believed in important deities as well as spirits, and that this contradicted Tylor's view that belief in spirits and belief in deities were two different stages in the evolution of religion.

Wilhelm Schmidt, a Jesuit priest as well as an anthropologist, drew upon Lang's study in developing another theory of the evolution of religion. Schmidt claimed that monotheism was the original form of religion and that all other belief systems represent a falling away from this early state of true belief. Unfortunately, this view was based on a limited understanding of religion in non-Western societies, for the high gods are not the only ones worshiped, nor are they the all-powerful deities of monotheistic belief systems. Gods can often be manipulated, and they are not always thought of as good or wise.

Yet another theory of the origin of religion was presented by Max Müller, who thought that deities arose from the attempt to personify natural forces such as wind and fire and rain. Like the theories already discussed, Müller's view takes into account only a limited view of traditional religion, and does not explain all the various types of beliefs found in non-Western religions.

More recently, Robert Bellah[11] has tried to link religion to economic and political institutions. In its most basic stage religion is not separate from the rest of social life but is tied in with all other aspects of daily life. Religious beliefs stress harmony with the environment, and ideas about life after death are often vague, based on a concept of a single world that is not divided into heaven, hell, and earth. There is no worship in the sense of praying to powerful deities; rather, there is an acting out of a sense of the unity of humans and nature.

A later stage in the evolution of religion is the emergence of more distinct concepts of gods and rituals, including worship, sacrifice, and the development of a priesthood. A clearer distinction is made between humans and deities, and this distinction is reinforced by rituals of worship and sacrifice. Such a religious system tends to be linked with the change from a society in which people see themselves as equal to one another and in harmony with the spiritual world to one in which there are two classes, with power concentrated in the upper or priestly class. Thus the religious belief system mirrors political reality.

In the next stage of religious evolution the concept of life after death emerges, and the goal of religion becomes salvation. The emphasis shifts from life in this world to actions aimed at attaining life in the next world. Related to this change is the development of a four-class social system; the upper class splits into independent political and religious classes, and the lower class splits into a population of rural peasants and an urban lower-status population. This four-class division reflects changes in the political and economic

realm; literacy plays a major role in defining the religious elite's power as separate from the military-political leadership. Likewise, the urban lower class has higher status because of its closeness to the centers of religious activity, while the peasantry is felt to be beyond salvation. But the most important change that occurs during this stage is the separation of religion from government. This enables religion to provide a standard for judging political acts and, in some cases, to serve as a basis for rebellion and social change.

In later stages of religious evolution the notion of salvation changes somewhat. Instead of being based on rejection of and withdrawal from the world, it becomes based on participation in worldly affairs. After the Protestant Reformation it was no longer necessary for a person to attain salvation through the priestly class; rather, the individual gained direct access to the supernatural. Religion thus became an activity of the individual rather than a plan acted out by a deity. The old religious hierarchy with its dominant elite group was replaced by a new two-class system stressing the division between the saved and the damned. Thus the system of social classes in which peasants and townspeople were divided from religious and political elites broke down. Bellah links this change to the introduction and development of a system of common law in which political and religious domination of the masses is no longer permitted; the power of the church and the state is limited, and individual rights are guaranteed.

According to Bellah, these changes lead to a situation in which religious institutions no longer control the system of religious beliefs. Instead, there is a shift toward interpretation by the believer. Whereas in earlier times the search for meaning and the place of humanity in the universe were religious questions, in modern religions they have become personal, secular questions that extend beyond the realm of religion to that of social philosophy. Individual solutions become interwoven with religious doctrine, and the church reflects

[11] Robert N. Bellah, "Religious Evolution," *American Sociological Review*, 29 (1964): 358–74.

the variability of its members rather than imposing an inflexible dogma on them. Bellah sees this trend as reflecting the increasing diversity of society, in which many different groups are included in a single political system. As religion must represent this diversity, it becomes more flexible and open to individual differences and varying interpretations. Our technology gives us more control over our environment, and science gives us more answers to questions that formerly were religious in nature. Modern religion is a response to these changes.

Bellah himself calls his evolutionary scheme a "risky enterprise." Yet, unlike those of the nineteenth- and early twentieth-century anthropologists, his view is holistic. It looks at religion in a social context by relating it to the economic and political order. Whether Bellah's stages can be clearly outlined or merely seen as part of a gradual, overall transition, they help us understand the role that religion has played in cultural evolution. We can see from Bellah's scheme the kinds of religious beliefs and practices that are likely to arise in hunting and gathering societies, in which a group of people of equal social and economic status live together in harmony with nature. We can also see that as social inequality increases and technological advances give humans greater control over the environment, religious beliefs and practices will change to reflect the new social order. Likewise, as power becomes more concentrated and political institutions more centralized, religion can be expected to play a different role in the society. It is in this sense, rather than as a series of clear-cut evolutionary stages, that Bellah's outline of religious change is most helpful.

Revitalization Movements

In the 1940s and 1950s anthropologists turned their attention to a specific result of culture contact that often had an important religious or supernatural component to it. As

Western culture reached into the far corners of the world, bringing with it great wealth and impressive technology, many isolated and unknown people saw their way of life threatened. Helpless against the pressure exerted by their new masters, people who had been free and proud found that their traditions were no longer effective. Frustration became a widespread social problem. One response was to give up the old ways and try to be like the Westerners in the hope of gaining the desirable elements of Western culture. Another response was to reject everything that was new and to preach a return to the "pure" culture of the good old days. Such efforts have been called **revitalization movements** because they often take on a religious character as their leaders try to breathe new life into old cultural patterns and traditions.

The earliest studies of revitalization movements focused on such phenomena as the Ghost Dance of the North American Indians in the late nineteenth century and the cargo cults of Melanesia in the twentieth century. Both types of movement arose mainly in response to the breakdown of a way of life as a result of contact with white culture. One of the earliest discussions of these movements as a kind of response to specific conditions all over the world was offered by Anthony Wallace, who coined the term *revitalization*. He brought together a variety of movements and described them in similar terms, showing that such varied events as the rise of Christianity, the Ghost Dance of 1890, the Taiping Rebellion in China, and the Russian Revolution were all variations of the same process of social change.

The process of revitalization is based on dissatisfaction with the current way of life, and is an attempt to create more satisfactory conditions. Wallace sees revitalization as a reaction to stress. When individuals are faced with a problem, they must either change themselves in order to live with it, or else change the stress at its source, the problem itself. When a group of people are subject to the same stress, and choose to do something about it, they are in effect seeking to revitalize

Amish culture represents an attempt to retain many traditional ways of life in the midst of a changing society. Tractors and automobiles may be more efficient, but the Amish prefer horse-drawn plows and buggies.

their culture. They can do this by changing either the physical reality or the psychological reality (that is, either the problem itself or their perception of the problem). In this way we can see basic similarities in such seemingly different responses as a religious movement (which offers a new doctrine to change the psychological reality of the problem) and a revolution (which seeks to change the physical reality of the stress through violent means).

Although the various revitalization movements showed great diversity in philosophical or ideological meaning and ritual expression, most of them emerged out of similar causes and progressed though an almost predictable pattern of development. While some anthropologists have suggested that it is possible to distinguish major types of revitalization movements, it is important to note here, at the risk of adding confusion, that a movement categorized as one type may be quite similar in a number of respects to a movement placed in another category.

Nativistic movements Nativistic movements seek to eliminate alien persons, customs, values, and materials from the culture. The term *nativism* refers to the attempt to return to traditional or native cultural patterns and expel everything foreign from the culture. In such a movement certain aspects

of the traditional culture are selected as being especially important and are given symbolic value; rarely does the movement embrace *all* elements of culture.

The Ghost Dance: Return to the good old days The Ghost Dance of the North American Indians is an example of a nativistic movement. It arose out of the frustration many Indian tribes experienced in their contacts with the westward-moving whites. Forced to give up their traditional ways of life and stunned by the drastic change in their environment caused by the intrusion of white culture (such as the elimination of the buffalo, which had been so important to Plains Indian culture), the Indians did not know where to turn. Many were forced onto reservations and began to adopt white culture. They soon found that this was not the answer, for they encountered more negative than positive elements of that new way of life. They experienced alcoholism, racial discrimination, poverty, and illiteracy—not wealth, power, or freedom. In short, the time was ripe for a new solution, one that did not require submission to the authority of the white man.

An Indian prophet named Wovoka provided the answer. He had a religious vision in which he saw into the future. The answer he gave to his people, which spread throughout the Great Plains, was that they should reject the ways of the white man, return to their old traditions, and practice the new ritual of the Ghost Dance. When this task had been accomplished—that is, when Indian culture had been purified of the evil ways of the white man—the buffalo would return and the dead ancestors of the Indians would ride out of heaven into battle to help them drive the whites from the earth. In more radical versions of this prophecy it was claimed that those who kept the faith would be immune to the bullets of the white man's gun and could ride into battle without fear of injury or death. It must have been a tragic event for a band of Indians to ride up to a cavalry troop, armed only with bows and arrows, yet secure in the belief that they would not be harmed.

Cargo cults: Imitating the new ways Cargo cult is a term applied to a series of cults found in the Pacific Islands during and after World Wars I and II. Natives on many of these islands saw huge amounts of cargo being delivered to the military bases and missions of Western nations, and realized that they were not sharing in this new wealth. They came to believe that if they adopted the ways of the foreigners, they, too, would receive the cargo. Obviously, they did not correctly perceive the relationship between foreign customs and the delivery of the cargo, and the result was that they adopted Western dress, built imitation airstrips and boat docks and waited in vain for the planes and ships to come and deliver their reward.

Cargo cults are different from nativistic movements in that they seek to revitalize their culture by adopting new cultural patterns rather than by returning to traditional ways of life. The earliest anthropological study of cargo cults was Francis Williams' 1923 report of such a movement among the native people in New Guinea. The movement was named the Vailala Madness after a town on the southern coast of New Guinea, where it began in 1919. Faced with the technological and military superiority of the white culture, the people sought to adopt many of the alien ways. They destroyed sacred objects and discontinued their ritual practices, substituting Christian elements for them. The actual "madness" was a dance involving frenzied, uncontrolled excitement along with the destruction of religious and art treasures.

The Vailala Madness centered on two main themes. First, there was the expectation that the dead would return on a cargo ship similar to the steamers that were seen bringing goods to the whites. Second, probably because they saw the white culture as superior, the natives adopted the belief that their ancestors had been white and that therefore the deceased who would return on cargo ships would be white. There were also many Christian ele-

ments in the movement; several leaders claimed that they were Jesus Christ and that the heavenly state they were expecting would be Jehovah's Land, as described in the Christian teachings.

From descriptions of this and other cargo cults in the Pacific Islands, we can understand many of the forces that seem to lead people to join such movements. A number of similar movements have occurred in widely scattered places and many years apart, leading us to conclude that, rather than resulting from the diffusion of an idea, they arise out of similar conditions. An element common to all of these movements is that they occur in areas where there has been considerable contact with Western culture. In addition, they occur where people have not been able to participate in the higher standard of living that they have seen in the white community. Thus in port towns, where the standard of living actually *is* higher, such movements have not arisen. Nor have they occurred in the more isolated areas of the Pacific, such as the interior of New Guinea, where European influence has not spread.

Cyril Belshaw, an anthropologist who has studied such movements throughout Melanesia, has concluded that the cults are caused by a change to a position halfway between the old and the new, coupled with the inability to change further. In other words, the people experience enough of the benefits of Western culture to want more, but just as their expectations rise, they are cut off. One result is that they imitate the ways of the white man, either out of respect or out of jealousy or hatred. It is interesting to compare this type of movement with the concept of nativism in order to see how opposite responses can be generated by culture contact and the prospects of rapid change.

Millenarian movements: Looking to the future Millenarian movements look to a transformation of the world designed and carried out by a supernatural power. Such movements are based on belief in the coming of the millennium, a time when all wrongs will be set right. The idea of a millennium is most often associated with the Christian tradition of the second coming of Christ, when he shall reign for 1,000 years. In a wider sense, however, it can be applied to any concept of a future time or place that will be free from the evils of the present. Millenarian movements often take on a messianic quality, being inspired by a charismatic leader who generates emotional involvement among followers. Most radical millenarian movements occur among oppressed peoples, indicating that there is a connection between social and economic conditions and this type of revitalization movement.

The functions of these movements, as pointed out by the Italian anthropologist Vitorio Lanternari, tend to be quite varied. They serve as powerful agents of change, creating a bridge between the future and the past. They connect religion and politics, for they often serve as models for modern revolutionary movements. Revolutions, like millenarian movements, are brought about by a combination of deprivation and frustration on the part of a large number of people who have seen their culture disintegrate. In many cases what started out as a local and small-scale millenarian movement mushroomed into a full-scale revolution.

Millenarian movements usually demand that their followers undergo some ordeal that will make them worthy, such as a difficult journey or pilgrimage, a ritual purification, or an act of violence. The idea of a millennium that will bring with it a golden age is especially popular in situations of culture contact, but it can be the basis of a movement that arises in a crisis situation of any kind. Famines, plagues, and other natural disasters can lead to a religion-based movement seeking to revitalize the culture, as can a major political upheaval.

Millenarian movements often believe that new age lies in the near future, and although they are vague about exactly how it will become a reality, they offer a plan for those who wish to bring it about. Millenarianism is an element of many political movements in this century. Communism, with its utopian view of the future, fits this model, and the Communist movement can be seen as the plan by which utopia will be achieved. Likewise, Nazism called for a ritual purification that would lead to a new golden age. In these and other cases there are a number of similarities: the importance of charismatic leaders (Lenin, Hitler); reliance on magical properties or symbolically important beliefs (the German army's belief that it was invincible parallels the Indian notion of immunity to white men's bullets); the elimination of foreign or unwanted elements from the culture, especially groups that were important in symbolic terms (for instance, the Russian aristocracy, the German Jews), and the internal political and economic problems that threatened the people with unwanted change.

To a certain extent nativistic movements, which tend to focus on the revival of a lost way of life, and the cargo cults of Melanesia, which seek to change believers' lives through the acquisition of European material items, share some important characteristics with millenarian movements. Some anthropologists regard the socioreligious movement in contemporary Iran and elsewhere in the Middle East as possessing traits from all three of the categories presented here. The goal of reviving traditional Islamic culture, purged of selected ("satanic") Western elements, is clearly nativistic or revivalistic. The movement's reliance on outside technologies and material culture items, such as video tape decks, computers, petroleum engineering techniques, and sophisticated military hardware, is characteristic of cargo cults. And the charismatic and messianic role of the late Ayatollah Khomeini, who was able to rally a large segment of the population around the belief that Iran's political and religious transformation will usher in a new and better age, suggests millenarianism.

Relative deprivation: A cause of revitalization movements   It is interesting to reflect on the causes of revitalization movements. What must happen to a group of people, or to their way of life, before they will actively seek to change things? How severely must their traditions be challenged and their values weakened before they are moved to act? One of the most plausible answers to this question has been presented by David Aberle, who suggests that revitalization movements can be understood as a reaction to what he calls **relative deprivation.** He defines this as "a negative discrepancy between legitimate expectation and actuality"—that is, a change over time that leads a group of people to feel deprived in relation to some other standard. We can measure relative deprivation by comparing the past and present circumstances of a single group of people, such as the Indians before and after the disappearance of the buffalo. The Indians of the late nineteenth century felt their way of life was deprived compared to the conditions in which they had lived not so many years earlier. Or we can compare the present situation of one group to that of another group, noting any differences that cause the disadvantaged group to feel deprived.

It is important to stress the notion of relativity, for as Aberle notes, it is not so much the difference itself as dissatisfaction with the difference that causes revitalization movements. For a hunting and gathering society that expects (on the basis of experience) to go without meat one day out of four, failure to find game is not relative deprivation. However, for middle-class Americans not to be able to eat meat every day is relative deprivation—not compared to the hunters and gatherers, but compared to what they're used to in American society. For multimillionaires to lose all but their last million in a stock-market crash would be relative deprivation, for even though they would be able to live like many other millionaires, they would be comparing their situation to their past, not to their present or to the situation of others around them. A more powerful example is the situation of poor people in the United States. The standard of living of the poorest people in the United States is probably higher than that of 75 percent of

all the people in the world. Yet there is a very strong feeling of relative deprivation among America's poor, for what is important to them is not how peasants live in India or China, but how the rest of the American people live. The poor feel deprived because, while they receive a relatively large slice of the *world's* pie, they receive a relatively small slice of the American pie.

Relative deprivation can occur not only in a material sense but also in a symbolic sense. Thus when a group feels itself to have higher status than it is ascribed by the rest of the society (as was true of Indians after they had come into contact with whites), this is a case of relative deprivation. In a study of dissatisfaction in the U.S. Army, for example, it was found that men in lower-ranking groups were more content with their status than men

A homeless man—poverty in the land of plenty.

in higher-ranking groups. This confusing result can be explained in terms of relative deprivation. Promotion was much less frequent on the lower levels (that is, proportionately fewer low-ranking men were promoted) than on the higher levels. If a low-ranking solider was passed over for promotion several times, he might be disappointed, but he did not feel deprived relative to the rest of the men on his level. On the other hand, the higher a man rose in the system, the greater his expectation of promotion, and thus the greater his feeling of relative deprivation when he was not promoted. This was expressed as dissatisfaction with the system, jealousy, anxiety, and frequent complaining.

Note that relative deprivation must exist on a group level for it to be an important force in bringing about a revitalization movement. If we as individuals feel that we are not given a high enough status or are denied our fair share of the things we strive for, we might feel deprived, but this is not a solid basis for a social movement. However, when conditions that create dissatisfaction are widespread enough so that the feeling is shared by a large part of the population, the potential exists for a strong movement calling for social change. The concept of relative deprivation is a useful tool for understanding many of our own social problems, and we should be able to apply it, along with other concepts derived from the study of culture, to the solution of those problems.

Summary

Religion has been one of the most studied aspects of non-Western societies, not because other people are more religious than we are, but rather because their religious behavior is not clearly divided from other aspects of their life, and thus it is hard to study any aspect of their life without touching on religion. We usually distinguish between *religion,* which is a belief system that explains the social and spiritual order; *magic,* an attempt to manipulate the forces of nature; and *science,* which is based on experiment and does not call on supernatural powers. Religion, magic, and science exist together in all societies.

Religion exists in a social context—that is, religious beliefs are an expression of the way people order their lives. It is also a way of dividing up the universe into things *sacred* and things *profane,* and thereby setting apart those elements that are considered special. Religion also imposes a moral pressure on people to act in accordance with what is believed to be right or proper.

One of the most basic religious beliefs is the attribution of a spirit or soul to all living things, called *animism.* Usually this takes the form of a belief in two separate beings, one tangible and earthly, the other intangible and spiritual. Another common belief is in the concept of supernatural power, often uncontrollable, which we call *mana.* This concept is linked to that of *taboo,* a restriction on behavior to avoid contact with such power or to avoid certain actions that would cause the power to work against oneself. Religious beliefs are created and sustained by *myths,* or sacred stories that contain explanations of how things came to be the way they are and how they should be maintained. Myths are accepted on faith and need not be proved in order to be considered valid.

A *ritual* is a set way of carrying out a religious activity, such as a prayer, an act of worship, or a sacrifice. Rituals surrounding the different stages of life, such as birth, marriage, or death, are called *rites of passage.* In some societies an individual could gain entry into adult status only by acquiring spiritual power through a hallucinatory vision, a ritual known as a *vision quest*. Another religious ritual is known as *spirit possession,* in which an individual is possessed by a supernatural spirit, usually in a state of trance.

Totemism is a religious system found among many peoples throughout the world. A *totem* is a natural item with which an individual or a group identifies. A society may be divided into many different totemic groups, each with its own totem. Totemism can form the basis for a moral code for the society by setting up rules about eligible marriage partners, guidelines for interaction among members of the society, and even rules involving the interaction between people and their natural environment.

All societies include people who are *religious specialists*. In some cases these are people who have undergone special training for their position, while in others a person attains such a position as a result of innate personal qualities. A *priest* is an example of a religious specialist who must undertake a period of formal training. In contrast, a *shaman* is a religious specialist whose powers come directly from the supernatural forces; while there may be a training period involved in becoming a shaman, that in itself is not enough. A third type of religious specialist is a *diviner,* an individual who can foresee future events or uncover the causes of past events.

Magic is a practice designed to manipulate the supernatural forces, whereas *witchcraft* is used as an explanation of how or why things happened as they did. Magic can be good or bad, designed to benefit or harm a person or group of people. Sir James Frazer discussed two principles of magic: the *law of similarity,* which states that an action will produce a like effect; and the *law of contact,* which states that things that have been in contact with each other continue to have an effect on each other after they have become separated. An example of the law of similarity is *voodoo,* in which a doll is made in the image of the intended victim and actions taken against the doll are believed to have a similar effect on the victim. An example of a belief in the law of contact or contagion is found among people who follow the custom of burying hair or nail clippings so that nobody can use them to cause the person harm.

Witchcraft can be used to explain unfortunate events. If an accident occurs in an otherwise normal activity, it can be explained by witchcraft. Also, witchcraft can function as a way of relieving tensions that arise in a society. Nadel compared witchcraft in four African societies, and showed how in each case the pattern of witchcraft accusations could be understood by uncovering sources of tension between various groups within the society, such as antagonism between the sexes or between two groups of relatives. We can also see elements of witchcraft accusations operating to relieve tensions in our society, by creating a class of scapegoats who can be blamed for various problems or otherwise inexplicable events.

Many evolutionary sequences have been proposed to explain religious change. Recently, Robert Bellah has linked religion with economic and political institutions in an attempt to reconstruct an evolutionary sequence. As the concept of a god and the practices of worship and sacrifice develop, religion becomes more distinct from other activities, and a separate priestly class emerges. Next the concept of life after death arises, and the goal of religion becomes salvation. At the same time, a four-class social system develops, with the upper class divided into political and religious leaders, and the lower class split into a population of rural peasants and urban dwellers. In later stages this social class distinction based on religious beliefs disappears, as religion becomes an individual activity rather than a divine plan. In modern religions doctrine reflects the variability among members and the increasing diversity of society, becoming more accommodating to individual differences. *Revitalization movements* often resulted from acculturation, because of dissatisfaction people felt at seeing their old way of life become ineffective in a new environment. Some societies tried to return to their old way of life, while others sought to adopt a new way of life by imitating the culture of those who dominated them. In most cases the revitalization attempt was associated with a widespread feeling of *relative deprivation,* a gap between what people felt they could rightfully expect and what they were actually getting.

Glossary

---

animism   A religious belief in which a spirit or soul is attributed to all living things, and sometimes even to inanimate objects. The spirits are worshiped and, at times, thought to have supernatural power.

cargo cult   An attempt to adopt new cultural patterns as part of a revitalization movement based on imitation of Western culture; so named because this kind of cult arose in the Pacific islands where cargo was shipped to Western military bases.

diviner   A religious specialist who is able to foresee future events or uncover the causes of past events. Divination reflects an attempt to control the forces of the universe through the prediction of future events.

law of contact or contagion   A principle in the use of magic stating that things that have been in contact with each other continue to exert an effect on each other after they have become separated. (Also known as *contagious magic.*)

law of similarity   A principle in the use of magic that involves manipulation of symbolic objects to produce the same effect upon an actual person.

magic   An attempt to manipulate the forces of nature to get certain desired results.

mana   A concept found in many religious systems of a supernatural force or power in nature that is neither inherently good nor bad, and is both unpredictable and uncontrollable.

millenarian movement   A revitalization movement in which an oppressed and frustrated people believe in the coming of a new age. Such a movement relies on symbolically important beliefs, usually has a charismatic leader, and attempts to eliminate foreign or unwanted elements from the culture.

myth   A sacred story that serves as an explanation for the natural environment, a group's relationship to the supernatural or spirit world, and their cultural customs and rituals. In nonliterate societies these elaborate stories are part of an oral tradition passes on from one generation to the next, and they function as guidelines to explain how and why rituals are performed.

nativistic movement   An attempt to return to traditional cultural patterns and to eliminate alien persons, customs, values, and materials from the culture.

profane   Those aspects of society that are considered ordinary, having no special religious significance.

reincarnation   A concept found in the Hindu religion that refers to the rebirth of an individual into a higher or lower social position in the next life.

relative deprivation   A change over time that leads a group of people to feel deprived relative to another group or to their own past situation, with a revitalization movement the potential result.

religion   A belief system, which includes myths that explain the social and spiritual order, and rituals through which the members of the religious community carry out their beliefs and act out the myths.

religious specialist A position held in society by the individual considered most able to relate to the supernatural. Depending on the society, the position may be filled by a person who has undergone specialized training, or by a person considered to have inherited ability.

revitalization movement A conscious process on the part of a people designed to produce change through the renewal of their old cultural patterns and traditions, which have disintegrated because of contact with Western culture.

rite of passage A ceremony marking the change from one period or stage of life into another (also called *life-crises rite*).

ritual A prescribed way of carrying out a religious activity, such as a prayer, an act of worship, or a sacrifice. Rituals reinforce the belief system of a society, and function both in terms of spiritual value and in terms of symbolic meaning for the group.

sacred Those aspects of society that are considered special (such as dangerous or powerful) and are thought of as having a certain mystical quality.

science A system of beliefs based on observed relationships in the knowable universe, and attempts to manipulate natural forces based on experiment.

secularization The process by which a society becomes more reliant on civil attitudes and explanations than on religious attitudes and explanations.

shaman A religious specialist considered to have contact with spirits, and whose powers come directly from the supernatural forces. Communication with spirits usually takes place through possession, and the individual serves as a vehicle of contact for the rest of the group.

spirit possession A religious practice involving the transmission of supernatural power through a human agent. The ritual occurs in a group situation in which a person becomes possessed by a spirit through trance, induced by drugs or some physical activity, and then acts as a medium through which the spirit communicates to other people.

superstition A belief based on supernatural explanations, but held with less conviction than a religious belief.

taboo A ritual prohibition against a specific behavior, punishable by supernatural sanctions.

totemism A religious system based on the concept of totem, which may be an animal, a plant, or a natural inanimate object signifying the symbolic unity of a group.

vision quest A ritual, sometimes a rite of passage, in which an individual seeks the support of a spirit during a hallucinatory vision, usually induced through fasting or self-multilation.

voodoo A form of magic based on the law of similarity, in which a symbolic representation is made of a person and is then manipulated to produce a similar effect on the person.

witchcraft An explanation of how or why certain events occurred. Witchcraft functions as an outlet for aggression and hostility, resolves tensions and conflicts, explains otherwise inexplicable events, and acts as a mechanism of social control by regulating the behavior of certain members of society.

Questions for Discussion

1. Émile Durkheim emphasized three aspects of religion: (1) the social context of religious systems; (2) the sacred aspect of religion; and (3) the moral basis of religion in society. How can you relate each of these features to your own religion?

2. How does religion influence the other institutions of American society? What are some of the sacred objects or concepts in our culture, and what is it that makes them sacred?

3. Under what conditions in American society do we rely on supernatural help or support? What makes these situations different from those in which we rely on science and technology?

4. There are certain behaviors surrounded by taboo in our society (for instance, talking about sex with one's parents). What are some examples of these behaviors or objects? What makes them taboo?

Suggestions for Additional Reading

MARY DOUGLAS, *Purity and Danger* (New York: Frederick A. Praeger, 1966). A lucid explanation of how ritual serves as a means to create and maintain order in perceived chaos.

NEVILL DRURY, *The Shaman and the Magician* (London: Routledge & Kegan Paul, 1982). A comparative study written for the general reader of the contents and techniques of shaman trance.

ÉMILE DURKHEIM, *The Elementary Forms of the Religious Life* (London: Allen & Unwin, 1915). A classic study of traditional religion, in which the author looks at Australian totemism in an attempt to reconstruct the origins of religion in human society.

A. P. ELKIN, *Australian Aborigines*, 3rd ed. (Garden City, N.Y.: Doubleday, 1954). A thorough analysis of totemism is included in this study of the cultures of native Australians.

E. E. EVANS-PRITCHARD, *Witchcraft, Oracles and Magic Among the Azande* (Oxford: Clarendon Press, 1937). A classic account of religious beliefs and practices in this African society.

SIR JAMES G. FRAZER, *The Golden Bough: A Study of Magic and Religion*, abridged ed. (New York: Macmillan, 1922). Originally published in 12 volumes, now available in abridged form, this is one of the best known works in anthropology, valuable for its wide range of examples and sources.

WESTON LABARRE, *They Shall Take up Serpents: Psychology of the Southern Snake-Handling Cult* (New York: Schocken, 1962). A study of a snake-handling Pentecostal church in the American South.

MICHEL S. LAGUERRE, *Voodoo Heritage* (Beverly Hills, Calif.: Sage Publications, 1980). A systematic study of the syncretic evolution of voodoo from French Catholicism and West African religion in the ecology of Haiti.

ARTHUR C. LEHMANN and JAMES E. MYERS (Eds.), *Magic, Witchcraft, and Religion; An Anthropological Study of the Supernatural* (Palo Alto, Cal.: Mayfield, 1985). A nice combination of readings dealing with Western and non-Western topics.

WILLIAM A. LESSA and EVON Z. VOGT (Eds.), *Reader in Comparative Religion*, 4th ed. (New York: Harper & Row, 1979). An excellent collection of articles on the anthropology of religion.

BRONISLAW MALINOWSKI, *Magic, Science and Religion, and Other Essays* (Glencoe, Ill.: Free Press, 1948). A collection of Malinowski's papers, including the famous article distinguishing magic, science, and religion.

MERIDITH B. McGUIRE, *Ritual Healing in Suburban America* (London: Rutgers University Press, 1988). An interesting study documenting beliefs and practices in nonmedical healing that exist among well-educated, economically comfortable U.S. suburbanites.

NINIAN SMART, *The World's Religions* (Englewood Cliffs, N.J.: Prentice Hall, 1989). A broad examination of religions in historical and geographical perspective.

SIR EDWARD B. TYLOR, *Primitive Culture: Researches into the Development of Mythology, Philosophy, Religion, Language, Art, and Custom* (London: John Murray, 1871). Includes an early anthropological view of religion, and Tylor's analysis of animism as the most basic form of religious belief.

ANTHONY F. C. WALLACE, *Religion: An Anthropological View* (New York: Random House, 1966). One of many modern-day texts dealing with the anthropological approach to the study of religion.

Baseball Magic

GEORGE GMELCH

North Americans too often think that magical practices occur only in the non-Western settings generally studied by anthropologists. In this humorous contribution Professor Gmelch discusses some of the interesting rituals that baseball players go through in an effort to ensure good luck and success.

On each pitching day for the first three months of a winning season, Dennis Grossini, a pitcher on a Detroit Tiger farm team, arose from bed at exactly 10:00 A.M. At 1:00 P.M. he went to the nearest restaurant for two glasses of iced tea and a tuna fish sandwich. Although the afternoon was free, he changed into the sweat shirt and supporter he wore during his last winning game, and one hour before the game he chewed a wad of Beech-Nut chewing tobacco. During the game he touched his letters (the team name of his uniform) after each pitch and straightened his cap after each ball. Before the start of each inning he replaced the pitcher's rosin bag next to the spot where it was the inning before. And after every inning in which he gave up a run he would wash his hands.

I asked him which part of the ritual was most important. He responded, "You can't really tell what's most important so it all becomes important. I'd be afraid to change anything. As long as I'm winning, I do everything the same. Even when I can't wash my hands [this would occur when he had to bat], it scares me going back to the mound. . . . I don't feel quite right."

Trobriand Islanders, according to anthropologist Bronislaw Malinowski, felt the same way about their fishing magic. Among the Trobrianders, fishing took two forms. In the inner lagoon, fish were plentiful and there was little danger; on the open sea, fishing was dangerous and yields varied widely. Malinowski found that magic was not used in lagoon fishing, where men could rely solely on their knowledge and skill. But when fishing on the open sea, Trobrianders

George Gmelch, "Baseball Magic," *Human Nature*, 1 (8), 1978: 32–39. Copyright 1978 by Human Nature, Inc. Reprinted by permission of the author, and revised and updated especially for this volume.

used a great deal of magical ritual to ensure safety and increase their catch.

Baseball, the American national sport, is an arena in which the players behave remarkably like Malinowski's Trobriand fishermen. To professional baseball players, baseball is more than a game. It is an occupation. Since their livelihood depends on how well they perform, they use magic to try to control or eliminate the chance and uncertainty built into baseball.

To control uncertainty, Chicago White Sox shortstop Ozzie Guillen didn't wash his underclothes after a good game. The Boston Red Sox's Wade Boggs ate chicken before every game (that's 162 meals of chicken per year). Ex-San Francisco Giant pitcher Ron Bryant added a new stick of bubble gum to the collection in his bulging back pocket after each game he won. Jim Ohms, my teammate on the Daytona Beach Islanders in 1966, used to put another penny in the pouch of his supporter after each win. Clanging against the hard plastic genital cup, the pennies made an audible sound as the pitcher ran the bases toward the end of a winning season.

Whether they are professional baseball players, Trobriand fishermen, soldiers, or farmers, people resort to magic in situations of chance, when they believe they have limited control over the success of their activities. In technologically advanced societies that pride themselves on a scientific approach to problem solving, as well as in simple societies, rituals of magic are common. Magic is a human attempt to impose order and certainty on a chaotic, uncertain situation. This attempt is irrational in that there is no causal connection between the instruments of magic and the desired consequences of the magical practice. But it is rational in that it creates in the practitioner a sense of confidence, competence, and control, which in turn is important to successfully executing a specific activity and achieving a desired result.

I have long had a close relationship with baseball, first as a participant and then as an observer. I devoted much of my youth to the game and played professionally as a first baseman for five teams in the Detroit Tiger organization over three years. I also spent two years in the Quebec Provincial League. For additional information about baseball magic, I interviewed twenty-eight professional ballplayers, scouts, and sportswriters.

There are three essential activities in baseball—pitching, hitting, and fielding. The first two, pitching and hitting, involve a great deal of chance and are comparable to the Trobriand fishermen's open sea; in them, players use magic and ritual to increase their chances for success. The third activity, fielding, involves little uncertainty, and is similar to the Trobriander inner lagoon; fielders find it unnecessary to resort to magic.

The pitcher is the player least able to control the outcome of his own efforts. His best pitch may be hit for a home run, and his worst pitch may be hit directly into the hands of a fielder for an out or be swung at and missed for a third strike. He may limit the opposing team to a few hits yet lose the game, or he may give up a dozen hits and win. Frequently pitchers perform well and lose, and perform poorly and win. One has only to look at the frequency with which pitchers end a season with poor won-lost records but good earned run averages (a small number of runs given up per game), or vice versa. For example, in 1990 Dwight Gooden gave up more runs per game than his teammate Sid Fernandez but had a won-lost record nearly twice as good. Gooden won 19 games and lost only 7, one of the best in the National League, while Sid Fernandez won only 9 games while losing 14. They pitched for the same team—the New York Mets—and therefore had the same fielders behind them. Regardless of how well he performs, on every outing the pitcher depends upon the proficiency of his teammates, the inefficiency of the opposition, and caprice.

An incredible example of bad luck in pitching occurred some years ago involving former Giant outfielder Willie Mays. Mays intentionally "dove for the dirt" to avoid being hit in the head by a fastball. While he was falling the ball hit his bat and went shooting down the left-field line. Mays jumped up and ran, turning the play into a double. Players shook their heads in amazement—most players can't hit when they try to, but Mays couldn't avoid hitting even when he tried not to. The pitcher looked on in disgust.

Hitting is also full of risk and uncertainty—Red Sox outfielder and Hall of Famer Ted Williams called it the most difficult single task in the world of sports. Consider the forces and time constraints operating against the batter. A fastball travels from the pitcher's mound to the batter's box, just sixty and one half feet, in three to four tenths of a second. For only 3 feet of the journey, an absurdly short two-hundredths of a second, the ball is in a position where it can be hit. And to be hit well, the ball must be neither too close to the batter's body nor too far from the "meat" of his bat. Any distraction, any slip of a muscle or change in stance can throw a swing off. Once the ball is hit, chance plays a large role in determining where it will go—into a waiting glove, whistling past a fielder's diving stab, or into the wide-open spaces. While the pitcher who threw the fastball to Mays was suffering, Mays was collecting the benefits of luck.

Batters also suffer from the fear of being hit by a pitch—specifically, by a fastball that often travels at speeds exceeding 90 miles per hour. Throughout baseball history the great fastball pitchers—men like Sandy Koufax, Bob Gibson, Nolan Ryan, and currently Red Sox Roger "Rocket" Clemens—have thrived on this fear and on the level of distraction it causes hitters. The well-armed pitcher inevitably captures the advantage in the psychological war of nerves that characterizes the ongoing tension between pitcher and hitter, and that determines who wins and loses the game. If a hitter is crowding the plate in order to reach balls on the outside corner, or if the batter has been hitting unusually well, pitchers try to regain control of their territory. Indeed, many pitchers intentionally throw at or "dust" a batter in order to instill this sense of fear (what hitters euphemistically call "respect") in him. On one occasion Dock Ellis of the Pittsburgh Pirates, having become convinced that the Cincinnati Reds were dominating his team, intentionally hit the first three Reds batters he faced before his manager removed him from the game.

In fielding, on the other hand, the player has almost complete control over the outcome. Once a ball has been hit in his direction, no one can intervene and ruin his changes of catching it for an out. Infielders have approximately three seconds in which to judge the flight of the ball, field it cleanly, and throw it to first base. Outfielders have almost double that amount of time to track down a fly ball. The average fielding percentage (or success rate) of .975, compared with a .250 success rate for hitters (the average batting percentage), reflects the degree of certainty in fielding. Compared with the pitcher or the hitter, the fielder has little to worry about. He knows that in better than 9.7 times out of 10 he will execute his task flawlessly.

In keeping with Malinowski's hypothesis about the relationship between magic and uncertainty, my research shows that baseball players associate magic with hitting and pitching, but not with fielding. Despite the wide assortment of magic—which includes rituals, taboos, and fetishes—associated with both hitting and pitching, I have never observed any directly connected to fielding. In my experience I have known only one player, a shortstop with fielding problems, who reported any ritual even remotely connected with fielding.

The most common form of magic in professional baseball is personal ritual—a prescribed form of behavior that players scrupulously observe in an effort to ensure that things go their way. These rituals, like those of Malinowski's Trobriand fishermen, are performed in a routine, unemotional manner, much as players do nonmagical things to improve their play: rubbing pine tar on the hands to improve a grip on the bat, or rubbing a new ball to make it more comfortable and responsive to the pitcher's grip. Rituals are infinitely varied since ball players may formalize any activity that they consider important to performing well.

Rituals usually grow out of exceptionally good performances. When a player does well he seldom attributes his success to skill alone. Although his skill remains constant, he may go hitless in one game and in the next get three or four hits. Many players attribute the inconsistencies in their performances to an object, item of food, or form of behavior outside their play. Through ritual, players seek to gain control over their performance. In the 1920s and 1930s sportswriters reported that a player who tripped en route to the field would often retrace his steps and carefully walk over the stumbling block for "insurance."

The word *taboo* comes from a Polynesian term meaning prohibition. Failure to observe a taboo or prohibition leads to undesirable consequences or bad luck. Most players observe a number of taboos. Taboos usually grow out of exceptionally poor performances, which players often attribute to a particular behavior or food. Certain uniforms may become taboo. If a player has a poor spring training season or an unsuccessful year, he may refuse to wear the same number again. During my first season of professional baseball I ate pancakes before a game in which I struck out four times. Several weeks later I had a repeat performance, again after eating pancakes. The result was a pancake taboo—I never ate pancakes during the season from that day on. Another personal taboo, against holding a baseball during the national anthem (the usual practice for the first basemen, who must warm up the other infielders), had a similar origin.

In earlier decades some baseball players believed that it was bad luck to go back and fasten a missed buttonhole after dressing for a game. They simply left missed buttons on shirts or pants undone. This taboo is not practiced by modern ballplayers.

Fetishes or charms are material objects believed to embody supernatural powers that aid or protect the owner. Good-luck fetishes are standard equipment for many ballplayers. They include a wide assortment of objects: horsehide covers from old baseballs, coins, bobby pins (Hall of Fame pitcher Rube Waddell collected these), crucifixes, and old bats. Ordinary objects acquire power by being connected to exceptionally hot batting or pitching streaks, especially ones in which players get all the breaks. The object is often a new possession or something a player finds and holds responsible for his good fortune. A player who is in a slump might find a coin or an odd stone just before he begins a hitting streak, attribute an improvement in his performance to the influence of the new object, and regard it as a fetish.

While playing for Spokane, a Dodger farm team, Alan Foster forgot his baseball shoes on a road trip and borrowed a pair from a teammate. That night he pitched a no-hitter, which he attributed to the borrowed shoes. After he bought them from his teammate, they became a prized possession.

During World War II, American soldiers used fetishes in much the same way. Social psychologist Samuel Stouffer and his colleagues found that in the face of great danger and uncertainty soldiers developed magical practices, particularly the use of protective amulets and good-luck charms (crosses, Bibles, rabbits' feet, medals), and jealously guarded articles of clothing they associated with past experiences of escape from danger. Stouffer also found that prebattle preparations were carried out in a fixed "ritual" order, much as ballplayers prepare for a game.

Because most pitchers play only once every four days, they perform rituals less frequently than hitters. The rituals they do perform, however, are just as important. A pitcher cannot make up for a poor performance the next day, and having to wait three days to redeem oneself can be miserable. Moreover, the team's win or loss depends more on the performance of the pitcher than on any other single player. Considering the pressures to do well, it is not surprising that pitchers' rituals are often more complex than those of hitters.

A 17-game winner in the Texas Ranger organization, Mike Griffin begins his ritual preparation a full day before he pitches, by washing his hair. The next day, although he does not consider himself superstitious, he eats bacon for lunch. When Griffin dresses for the game he puts on his clothes in the same order, making certain he puts the slightly longer of his two outer, or "stirrup," socks on his right leg. "I just wouldn't feel right mentally if I did it the other way around," he explains. He always wears the same shirt under his uniform on the days he pitches. During the game he takes off his cap after each pitch, and between innings he sits in the same place on the dugout bench.

Tug McGraw, formerly a relief pitcher for the Phillies, slapped his thigh with his glove with each step he took leaving the mound at the end of an inning. This began as a means of saying hello to his wife in the stands, but it then became a ritual as McGraw slapped his thigh whether his wife was there or not. Many of the rituals pitchers engage in—tugging their caps between pitches, touching the rosin bag after each bad pitch, smooth the dirt on the mound before each new batter or inning—take place on the field. Most baseball fans observe this behavior regularly, never realizing that it may be as important to the pitcher as actually throwing the ball.

Uniform numbers have special significance for some pitchers. Many have a lucky number, which they request. Since the choice is usually limited, pitchers may try to get a number that at least contains their lucky number, such as 14, 24, 34, or 44 for the pitcher whose lucky number is 4. Oddly enough, there is no consensus about the effect of wearing number 13. Some pitchers will not wear it; others, such as the Mets' David Cone and Oakland's John "Blue Moon" Odum, prefer it. (During a pitching slump, however, Odum asked for a new number. Later he switched back to 13.)

The way in which number preferences emerge varies. Occasionally a pitcher requests the number of a former professional star, hoping that—in a form of imitative magic—it will bring him the same measure of success. Or he may request a favorite number that he has always associated with good luck. Vida Blue, former Athletic and Giant, changed his uniform number from 35 to 14, the number he wore as a high-school quarterback. When the new number did not produce the better pitching performance he was looking for, he switched back to his old number.

One of the sources of his good fortune, Blue believed, was the baseball hat he had worn since 1974. Several American League umpires refused to let him wear the faded and soiled cap. When Blue persisted,

he was threatened with a fine and suspension from a game. Finally he conceded, but not before he ceremoniously burned the hat on the field before a game.

On the days they are scheduled to appear, many pitchers avoid activities that they believe sap their strength and therefore detract from their effectiveness, or that they otherwise generally link with poor performance. Many pitchers avoid eating certain foods on their pitching days (actually, some food taboos make good physiological sense). Some pitchers do not shave on the day of a game. In fact, Oakland's Dave Stewart and Baltimore's Todd Worrell don't shave as long as they are winning. Early in the 1989 season, Stewart had six consecutive victories and a beard before he finally lost. Ex-St. Louis Cardinal Al Hrabosky took this taboo to extreme lengths; Samsonlike, he refused to cut his hair or beard during the entire season—hence part of the reason for his nickname, the "Mad Hungarian."

Many hitters go through a series of preparatory rituals before stepping into the batter's box. These include tugging on their caps, touching their uniform letters or medallions, crossing themselves, tapping or bouncing the bat on the plate, swinging the weighted warmup bat a prescribed number of times, and smoothing the dirt in the batter's box. There were more than a dozen individual elements in the batting ritual of Mike Hargrove, former Cleveland Indian first basemen, and after each pitch he would step out of the batter's box and repeat the sequence. His rituals were so time consuming that he was called "the human rain delay."

Clothing, both the choice of clothes and the order in which they are put on, is often ritualized. During a batting streak many players wear the same clothes and uniforms for each game and put them on in exactly the same order. Once I changed sweatshirts midway through the game for seven consecutive games to keep a hitting streak going. During a sixteen-game winning streak in 1954 the New York Giants wore the same clothes in each game and refused to let them be cleaned for fear that their good fortune might be washed away with the dirt. Taking this ritual to the extreme, Leo Durocher, managing the Brooklyn Dodgers to a pennant in 1941, spent three and a half weeks in the same black shoes, gray slacks, blue coat, and knitted blue tie.

The opposite may also occur. Several of the Oakland A's players bought new street clothing in an attempt to break a fourteen-game losing streak. Most players, however, single out one or two lucky articles or quirks of dress rather than ritualizing all items of clothing. After hitting two home runs in a game, infielder Jim Davenport of the San Francisco Giants discovered that he had missed a buttonhole while dressing for the game. For the remainder of his career he left the same button undone.

A popular ritual associated with hitting is tagging a base when leaving and returning to the dugout during each inning. Mickey Mantle was in the habit of tagging second base on the way to or from the outfield. During a successful month of the season one player stepped on third base on his way to the dugout after the third, sixth, and ninth innings of each game. Asked if he ever purposely failed to step on the bag he replied, "Never! I wouldn't dare. It would destroy my confidence to hit." A hitter who is playing poorly may try different combinations of tagging and not tagging particular bases in an attempt to find a successful combination.

Another component of a hitter's ritual may be tapping the plate with his bat. A teammate of mine described a variation of this in which he gambled for a certain hit by tapping the plate with his bat a fixed number of times: one tap for a single, two for a double, and so on. He even built in odds that prevented him from asking for a home run each time at bat. The odds of hitting a home run with four taps were 1 in 12.

When their players are not hitting, some managers will rattle the bat bin, the large wooden box containing the team's bats, as if the bats were asleep or in a stupor and could be aroused by a good shaking. Similarly, some hitters rub their hands or their own bats along the handles of the bats protruding from the bin, presumably in hopes of picking up some power or luck from bats that are getting hits for their owners.

There is a taboo against crossing bats, against permitting one bat to rest on top of another. Although this superstition appears to be dying out among professional ballplayers, it was religiously observed by some of my teammates. And in some cases it was elaborated even further. One former Detroit minor leaguer became quite annoyed when a teammate tossed a bat from the batting cage and it landed on top of his bat. Later he explained that the top bat might steal hits from the lower one. In his view, bats contained a finite number of hits, a sort of baseball "image of limited good." For Pirate shortstop Honus Wagner, a charter member of baseball's Hall of Fame, each bat contained only a certain number of hits, and never more than one hundred. Regardless of the quality of the bat, he would discard if after its one hundredth hit.

Hall of Famer Johnny Evers, of the Cub double-play trio Tinker to Evers to Chance, believed in saving his luck. If he was hitting well in practice, he would suddenly stop and retire to the bench to "save" his batting for the game. One player told me that many of his teammates on the Asheville Tourists in the Class A Western Carolinas League would not let pitchers touch or swing their bats, not even to loosen up. The traditionally poor-hitting pitchers were believed to pollute or weaken the bats.

Food often forms part of a hitter's ritual repertoire. Eating certain foods before a game is supposed to give the ball "eyes," that is, the ability to seek the gaps between fielders after being hit. In hopes of maintaining a batting streak, I once ate chicken every day at 4:00 P.M. until the streak ended. Yankee catcher Jim Leyritz eats turkey before every game. Hitters—like pitchers—also avoid certain foods that are believed to sap their strength during the game.

There are other examples of hitters' ritualized behavior. I once kept my eyes closed during the national anthem in an effort to prolong a batting streak. And a teammate of mine refused to read anything on the day of a game because he believed that reading weakened his eyesight when batting.

These are personal taboos. There are some taboos, however, that all players hold and that do not develop out of individual experiences or misfortunes. These taboos are learned, some as early as Little League. Mentioning a no-hitter while one is in progress is a widely known example. It is believed that if a pitcher hears the words "no-hitter," the spell will be broken and the no-hitter lost. This taboo is still observed by many sports broadcasters, who used various linguistic subterfuges to inform their listeners that the pitcher had not given up a hit, never mentioning "no-hitter."

But superstitions, like most everything else, change over time. Many of the rituals and beliefs of early baseball are no longer remembered. A century ago players spent time off the field and on looking for items that would bring them luck. For example, to find a hairpin on the street assured a batter of hitting safely in that day's game; today women don't wear hairpins—a good reason why the belief has died out. To catch sight of a white horse or a wagonload of barrels were also good omens. In 1904 the manger of the New York Giants, John McGraw, hired a driver and a team of white horses to drive past the Polo Grounds about the time his players were arriving at the ballpark. He knew that if his players saw white horses they'd have more confidence, and that could only help them play better. Belief in the power of white horses survived in a few backwaters until the 1960s. A gray-haired manager of a team I played for in Quebec would drive around the countryside before important games and during the playoffs looking for a white horse. When he was successful, he'd announce it to everyone in the clubhouse before the game.

Today most professional baseball coaches or managers will not step on the chalk foul lines when going onto the field to talk to their pitchers. Detroit's manager Sparky Anderson jumps over the line. Others follow a different ritual. They intentionally step on the lines when they are going to take a pitcher out of a game.

How do these rituals and taboos get established in the first place? B. F. Skinner's early research with pigeons provides a clue. Like human beings, pigeons quickly learn to associate their behavior with rewards or punishment. By rewarding the birds at the appropriate time, Skinner taught them such elaborate games as table tennis, miniature bowling, or to play simple tunes on a toy piano.

On one occasion he decided to see what would happen if pigeons were rewarded with food pellets every fifteen seconds, regardless of what they did. He found that the birds tended to associate the arrival of food with a particular action—tucking the head under a wing, hopping from side to side, or turning in a clockwise direction. About ten seconds after the arrival of the last pellet, a bird would begin doing whatever it had associated with getting the food and keep it up until the next pellet arrived.

In the same way, baseball players tend to believe there is a causal connection between two events that are linked only temporally. If a superstitious player touches his crucifix and then gets a hit, he may decide the gesture was responsible for his good fortune and follow the same ritual the next time he comes to the plate. If he should get another hit, the chances are good that he will begin touching the crucifix each

time he bats and that he will do so whether or not he hits safely each time.

The average batter hits safely approximately one quarter of the time. And, if the behavior of Skinner's pigeons—or of gamblers at a Las Vegas slot machine—is any guide, that is more often than necessary to keep him believing in a ritual. Skinner found that once a pigeon associated one of its actions with the arrival of food or water, sporadic rewards would keep the connection going. One bird, which apparently believed hopping from side to side brought pellets into its feeding cup, hopped ten thousand times without a pellet before it gave up.

Since the batter associates his hits at least in some degree with his ritual touching of a crucifix, each hit he gets reinforces the strength of the ritual. Even if he falls into a batting slump and the hits temporarily stop, he will persist in touching the crucifix in the hope that this will change his luck.

Skinner's and Malinowski's explanations are not contradictory. Skinner focuses on how the individual comes to develop and maintain a particular ritual, taboo, or fetish. Malinowski focuses on why human beings turn to magic in precarious or uncertain situations. In their attempts to gain greater control over their performance, baseball players respond to chance and uncertainty in the same way as do people in simple societies. It is wrong to assume that magical practices are a waste of time for either group. The magic in baseball obviously does not make a pitch travel faster or more accurately, or a batted ball seek the gaps between fielders. Nor does the Trobriand brand of magic make the surrounding seas calmer and more abundant with fish. But both kinds of magic give their practitioners a sense of control—and an important element in any endeavor is confidence.

13

Social and Cultural Change

There has been life on the earth for some $3\frac{1}{2}$ billion years. In this time span the human species is a relative latecomer. Recent findings have pushed the existence of humanlike animals back perhaps as much as 4 million years, but it was not until about 40,000 years ago that the first "modern" *Homo sapiens* appeared. It is not our purpose here to trace human evolution through the various species of the prehistoric past; such a study lies in the realm of physical anthropology, paleoarcheology, or human biology. But it is relevant to note here, in a chapter on social and cultural change, how recently modern *Homo sapiens* has come onto the scene and how quickly changes have resulted. Only within the last few thousand years or so has culture begun to expand beyond the limits of the most primitive stone age technology; agriculture, the basis for any kind of large permanent settlement, is less than 10,000 years old; urbanism, even in its earliest forms, is perhaps 6,000 years old; and as we all know, the industrial revolution has occurred only within the last 250 years. If we were to compress the entire span of human life on earth into a single day, agriculture would be invented around 11:56 p.m., people would begin to settle in towns and cities at 11:57, and the industrial revolution would begin shortly after 11:59:30. More change has occurred during the last 30 seconds of this "human day" than in all the time leading up to it. We might ask two very logical questions: What were people doing during all this time? And why has so much change occurred in such a short time?

Innovation and Diffusion

As we noted earlier, for most of their history, men and women lived by hunting and gathering food. Indeed, some hunting and gathering societies are still in existence, and much of what we know about human prehistory is based on the way modern tribes live as well as on the archeological record of the past. Many of these groups have adapted well to their environment and appear to have a great deal of free time for other activities besides obtaining food.

Even so, hunters and gatherers could not be expected to change very rapidly—certainly not at the pace that we have experienced in the past few thousand years. Technology tends to increase geometrically: The more there is, the faster it grows. Technological change is like compound interest, and hunters and gatherers don't have much in the bank. Although they find enough food for themselves, surviving is still a day-to-day task for everyone. The band cannot afford to have many members who do not work to support themselves. Furthermore, the development and exchange of new ideas is limited. A given area can support only a certain number of people, and this tends to create isolated pockets of hunters and gatherers who grow more unlike their neighbors over time. They become not only physically isolated but culturally separated as well. These two conditions—living from day to day and being isolated from others—prevented any major changes from occurring for hundreds of thousands of years. Moreover, since they had a fairly successful and secure life style, hunters and gatherers were under little pressure to seek radical changes.

Anthropologists tend to look at cultures and how they change in terms of two basic processes—the rise of new elements and their spread from one group to another. These two processes are called **innovation** and **diffusion**. Innovations or inventions do not come out of the blue; they are recombinations of existing elements to create something entirely different. We would not expect an Inuit hunter to invent a rifle, even though the need might be there, because the invention of the rifle depends on the existence of a level of technology not available to Inuit culture. However, today we might not be surprised to find an Inuit hunter *using* a rifle, since diffusion, or the borrowing of a cultural item, does not always require a sophisticated level of technological development. In looking at

A Laplander with a sewing machine. Diffusion accounts for a far greater proportion of a group's culture than invention.

the overall pattern of cultural change, anthropologists recognize that diffusion accounts for most new elements in a culture, and while innovation is very important, innovations tend to be relatively infrequent in non-Western societies.

Not all innovations result from purposeful attempts to create a new idea or object. In many cases accidents that occur in the course of normal daily activities can result in innovations—as was probably the case when someone accidentally dropped a piece of meat into a fire and "invented" cooking! We also recognize that many inventions are based on others and involve the combination of existing elements of a culture into something new. Thus we can see some inventions as "products of the time" that were likely to happen regardless of the chain of events that led a particular person to them. History is full of examples of inventions and discoveries being made at the same time in different parts of the world by people who were not in contact with one another. Although Charles Darwin is usually given credit for developing the theory of natural selection, Alfred Wallace arrived at the same conclusion independently and even presented a paper on the subject at a meeting attended by Darwin in 1858. We generally credit Alexander Graham Bell with the invention of the telephone in 1876. However, Bell's invention merely put together existing knowledge about electric current and the induction of sound, based on the telegraph, which had been in existence for some 30 years. It is not surprising that someone else might have some to the same conclusion at about the same time, and in fact this did happen. Elisha Gray arrived at a similar concept in the same year that Bell presented his invention. The list of such "coincidences" is quite long.

Once an innovation has occurred and has been put to use by a group of people, the next step in the process of culture change is its spread or diffusion to neighboring groups. Nearly all the elements of any culture are borrowed from others; they are not innovations that occurred within the group itself. How cultural items are borrowed, which items tend to spread most quickly, and which ones tend to meet with the greatest resistance are all part of the study of diffusion. In areas where neighboring groups have similar cultures, innovations may spread fairly easily as people move back and forth from one group to another, bringing new ideas with them. But when the cultures of two or more groups are very different, diffusion may not occur easily. Anthropologists have devoted much effort to the study of such situations as a result of the massive change brought about by the expansion of Western cultures in the conquest and colonization of the native populations of every continent in the world. Social and cultural change that occurs as a result of this kind of culture contact is known as acculturation.

Acculturation

Acculturation can be defined as change that occurs when groups of individuals with different cultures come into continuous first-hand contact. This is a rather broad definition that covers many different kinds of change and contact. Here we will examine acculturation studies in some detail in order to see how anthropologists have viewed the changes that arise out of contact between different groups.

One factor that can affect the exchange of

An Inuit mother feeding her infant with a bottle introduced through contact with Western culture.

elements of culture is the type of contact that occurs between two or more groups. For example, in some situations the contact is between two whole societies, or at least a cross section of each. Thus when two nonhostile Indian tribes moved into the same region we might expect a blending of culture as members of the two tribes interacted, perhaps intermarried, and shared their ways of life. On the other hand, many other situations involve only a part of one of the two societies involved. The contact between the Spanish conquerors and the Mexican Indians involved only a small portion of Spanish society, which surely was not representative of the entire culture. Similarly, contact with the peoples of the Pacific Islands during World War II was limited to a small part of American society—the military. Other examples might affect the cultural exchange differently, as in the case of contact between missionaries, traders, or miners and the people of the area in which they work.

Other acculturation studies focus on the process of change. What traits were borrowed by one culture, in what order, and with what resistance? Was a new innovation adopted exactly as it existed in the original culture, or was it changed to fit in better with the borrowers' culture? Was there an element of prestige involved in borrowing? These and other questions have been asked in an attempt to understand the process of cultural and social change, not only to interpret past events, but to predict future change as well.

Plains Indian culture: The decline of tradition One early study of acculturation was carried out by Margaret Mead, who described the changing culture of a Plains Indian people who had been in contact with white society. At the time of her study (in the early 1930s), the contact had been so recent and overwhelming that adjustment had not been possible; therefore her study concentrated on the problems of disorganization that had resulted from the contact.

The Indians' initial contact with white culture was through fur traders, who introduced guns and steel traps to Indian culture. The second phase of contact was marked by white settlement of the region, the establishment of an Indian agency and a Presbyterian mission, and the disappearance of the buffalo. Finally, in the third phase the Indians were pressured to abandon their traditional way of life (living in teepees, hunting, trapping, and fishing) and encouraged to adopt the way of life of the typical rural white American. Mead points out that even with all these changes the Indians might have been able to get by, but after about 25 years they had to face the problem of increased white settlement, which took away their land. The white settlers did not mingle with the Indians but maintained a separate culture. This kept the two groups from getting along with each other. While the Indians were encouraged to adopt the white people's ways, at the same time they were prevented by prejudice from taking part in activities with white people.

As Mead shows in her study, Indian religion broke down under the pressure of white contact. At first all the Indians converted to Presbyterianism as a result of the efforts of the white missionaries. But the new religion failed to give them the rewards it promised, and the Indians soon turned to peyote cults, using hallucinogenic drugs to satisfy their religious needs. Peyotism also provided an outlet for their traditional ritual ceremonies, which did not fit into the Presbyterian service. At the time that Mead wrote about this situation, the peyote religion was still the dominant form among the Indians, and very little of either the original religious beliefs or the recently adopted white people's religion remained. Thus she described a situation of cultural breakdown in which contact between two cultures leads not to the sharing of elements of the two cultures but to the disorganization and breakdown of a traditional way of life and, at the same time, a rejection of much of the new way that is offered.

As a postscript to the study, Mead points to a positive result of the contact between whites and Indians. Because the subjugation of Indian culture to that of the whites took place throughout the country, the various Indian tribes began to develop a feeling of group identity. Formerly they had considered the tribes to be culturally distinct, but now they faced a common enemy that drew them together as allies. Thus, as a result of acculturation with whites, Indians developed a class consciousness that has built up over the last century to its current high level. In the days before white contact such as consciousness would have been unthinkable, but when faced with a common threat, Indians of all tribes began to look at one another in a new light, ignoring their differences and stressing their similarities.

Caribbean culture: The blending of traditions   In a study of acculturation in the Caribbean, Melville Herskovits describes the process of **syncretism**, the reinterpretation of new cultural elements so as to fit them into the already existing traditions. Herskovits studied the introduction of Christian ideas into the religion of black people in the New World—specifically, the relationship between African gods and Catholic saints. He emphasizes that non-European people do not easily abandon their native religious beliefs and

Often elements of another culture are borrowed and then made to fit in with existing ways of doing things.

practices when confronted with Christianity. Rather, they usually react in one of two ways: Either they try to keep the old way and reject anything new; or they adopt the new elements in their outward form, but reinterpret them to fit into the old way, keeping the old values and meanings alive.

Herskovits cites examples from Cuba, Brazil, and Haiti to illustrate this process. He says that while black people in these countries say that they are Catholic, they still belong to cults that are under the direction of priests whose functions are basically African and whose training follows traditional patterns. He also points to specific links between African gods and Catholic saints, showing how the content of the old religion is carried over into the form of the new one.

Brought over to the New World as slaves, the Africans were baptized into the Catholic Church in these countries. The whites tried to erase their traditional cults, which they feared would serve as a focus for revolutionary activities. Although the cults were broken up to a certain extent, they managed to continue on the local level. However, since they were officially banned, they were forced to take on a new appearance to hide their real nature. Thus, in many of these cults, although Catholic practices were adopted to satisfy the whites, they were only a mask for the underlying traditional rituals.

Herskovits points to some examples of traditional African gods that have been reinterpreted in terms of Catholic saints. In Dahomey, Legba is a god who guards the crossroads and entrances to temples, residence compounds, and villages. He is also widely worshiped in Haiti, where he must open the path for the supernatural powers. Many Haitians believe Legba to be the same as St. Anthony. The reason for this identification is that St. Anthony is commonly shown as an old man, poorly dressed and using a cane to support himself as he walks. The use of a cane or wand is also attributed to Legba, who uses it to guard the path for the supernatural powers.

Damballa is a Dahomean rainbow serpent

Melville Jean Herskovits (1895–1963)

Melville Jean Herskovits is widely known as the first American anthropologist to specialize in African studies, particularly Afro-American cultures in the New World. At a time when American anthropology was concerned primarily with native American cultures, Herskovits conducted fieldwork in Africa. he then turned his attention to Afro-American cultures, particularly in the Caribbean, pointing out how African traditions were reworked into the way of life forced upon the people in the New World. Herskovits' study of Afro-American culture led him to an interest in culture change, and he was a leading figure in the development of a school of anthropology concerned with the process of acculturation, or culture change through contact.

god. He is connected with the serpent cult, which is said to be popular in Haiti. Yet in Haiti he is generally identified with St. Patrick, who is associated with snakes in the Catholic tradition (he is said to have driven the serpents out of Ireland). Following this logic even further, Moses is said to be the father of Damballa. This is because of the Bible's description of Moses throwing his staff on the ground in front of the pharaoh, whereupon it turned into a serpent.

Many other traditional gods have been worked into the Catholic belief system. Sometimes the Catholic saints are even equated with natural phenomena such as the sun, moon, and stars. For example, in some areas of the Caribbean St. John the Baptist is worshiped as the god who controls thunder and lightning. This is because he is often shown holding a lamb, and in Dahomean mythology the ram is the emblem of the god of thunder. In the same vein, saints are added to the Catholic hierarchy to cover certain areas of the African tradition that are absent from the Christian tradition. For example, many Caribbean black people worship such deities as *St. Soleil* (St. Sun), *Ste. la Lune* (St. Moon), *Sts. Étoiles* (Sts. Stars), and *Ste. la Terre* (St. Earth).

Herskovits' study of the contact between traditional African and European white cultures in the Caribbean shows how flexible people can be in adopting new ways. Such flexibility is not always possible, and instead, culture contact may lead to breaks in the continuity of traditional patterns, as is illustrated by the following example.

Australian aborigine culture: The reversal of tradition The Yir Yoront are a tribe located on the northern peninsula of Australia; they are described in a study by Lauriston Sharp. Before white contact their culture was of the Old Stone Age type. They supported themselves by hunting, fishing, and gathering fruits and vegetables. The most important tool in their culture was a polished stone ax with a short wooden handle, and this had meaning not only in their economy but in their social ranking system as well. The ax was a masterpiece produced only by men. It required specialized knowledge of the natural resources of the area, such as wood for the handle, bark for the binding, and the right kind of stone. While the ax could be used by anyone—man, woman, or child—it could be obtained only by trading. Thus complex trade networks arose among men (and only men) to acquire stones for the axes. Since only men owned the axes (even though women did most of the work with them) women constantly had to ask the men to borrow the axes; this reinforced male dominance in the group and clearly marked out the patterns of authority.

This traditional pattern of ownership and use of the stone ax and the social relationships it created were shattered when the Yir Yoront came into contact with white culture. Around the turn of the century the Australian government established three mission stations in the Yir Yoront territory, and through them many items of Western culture were dispensed. The missionaries encouraged members of the tribe to work for the mission, and they were paid in what were considered useful goods, including steel axes. However, the steel ax was introduced in large numbers to all who worked for the mission. The new ax was much more efficient than the old stone ax, and it soon replaced the stone ax as a status item in Yir Yoront culture.

It is easy to see how the introduction of the steel ax might affect the Yir Yoront. For one thing, axes were no longer the property only of men—women and children also got axes from the mission. The dependence on men that had been created by the stone ax was transferred to the mission through the steel ax. Men who had been the head of their families lost their power over women and children; this was especially true of men who were too proud and independent to work for the mission and so did not have a steel ax. In short, the introduction of the steel ax upset most of the traditional patterns associated with the stone ax. Men sometimes became so desirous of a steel ax that they would sell their wives or daughters into prostitution to acquire one from a Westerner or even from a member of their own tribe. The values associated with age, sex, and kinship ties were not reinforced by the use of the steel ax. Furthermore, along with the decline in ownership patterns surrounding the ax came an overall decline in patterns of ownership of many other things, with a resulting increase in stealing and crime in general. The old culture lost much of its meaning and began to die out—all because of an ax!.

The author of this study does not offer any value judgments about the changes that took place in Yir Yoront culture. He does not suggest that the male-centered society that existed prior to white contact was better (or worse) than a society in which women have some authority. He notes that while crime increased, the standard of living also rose. His main purpose is to show how complex the process of change can be, and that it can have unexpected effects on other areas of life. As such, he presents us with a valuable picture of acculturation.

Modernization

Modernization is a major theme in recent history. It embraces the social and cultural changes resulting from the agricultural revolution, the industrial revolution, and more recently the atomic revolution. It occurred first in Western societies, but it has spread throughout the world, both by design and by chance. Although many of the factors that led to modernization were not of Western origin, the various processes that produced the industrial societies of the twentieth century reached their peak in Europe and the United States; only recently have non-Western countries, such as Japan, been industrialized.

Anthropology has an important stake in the study of modernization. Since modernization is occurring in every country in one way or another, there is an urgent need for comparative studies to provide a cross-cultural perspective on the problems encountered in various parts of the world. Moreover, in most of the societies that have traditionally been studied by anthropologists (that is, tribal and peasant peoples), cultural patterns have been changed by contact with the West. Such changes affect technology, economic order, patterns of social relationships, ideologies—in short, every aspect of traditional life. However, we also recognize that whereas industrial technology grew up in Western countries, and thus was molded to the cultural patterns found in those countries, when it was transplanted to Third World countries it does not always fit into their cultures. As a result, anthropologists who have studied the traditional way of life of these peoples are interested in how it is being changed by contact with the West. Often they find that the changes that take place in non-Western countries do not follow the pattern of industrialization as it occurred in Europe and the United States; the new technology must be modified to fit existing values and traditions.

Modernization is a broad term that covers a number of separate processes. It is generally assumed that these processes occur together and that they are interrelated. By modernization we usually mean at least the following: economic growth, or industrialization; urbanization; and westernization. In this section we will look at each of these processes separately, comparing the changes that took place in the West with changes that are taking place in the developing nations of the Third World.

Industrialization   The growth of industry in any society cannot occur without related changes in agriculture. Because industry requires a large number of people to work in factories rather than on farms, there must be a transformation of agriculture so that fewer people can produce more food in order to supply the nonagricultural work force. The conditions of the industrial revolution were not really laid down until the seventeenth century, when the application of science to agricultural production began to take effect. (This period has been called the second agricultural revolution; the first was the domestication of plants, which took place in prehistoric times in the Near East.) But increasing production is not enough in itself, for there must be a way to make the surplus available to the work force. Thus along with the **industrialization** of a country must come

In this scene from Iran, note the combination of foreign and indigenous elements.

the commercialization of agriculture so that surplus products can be transported to markets.

The significance of this process to the anthropologist who studies rural people in non-Western countries is clear. Traditionally, such people were **subsistence agriculturalists**; that is, they produced food mainly for their own consumption, with only a little surplus to take care of a few basic needs. They were not integrated into a national or international market system, and many of them even got along without cash, by trading their surplus directly for other products that they needed. Industrialization also means a major change in the structure of the rural population because, at least in its early stages, it requires a larger work force than is available in the cities. Therefore mass migration from rural areas to towns and cities is characteristic of industrializing countries. But it is a selective migration of people in a narrow age group, usually about 15 to 35 years of age, which leaves the countryside with a rather uneven population made up largely of old people. This has an effect on rural life: Without new ideas and pressure for change from the young, traditions become solidified and rural communities become even more conservative.

Another important result of industrialization may be seen in the nature of the family. In a rural farm community the typical family is a large one made up of several generations, not just parents and their children. The farm is an ideal place for such a family unit. There is a variety of tasks for persons of both sexes and all ages, and in an operation designed to produce food for the group, all the members of the family can carry their weight. But when the family moves to the city and enters the industrial work force, this is no longer the case. Here the crucial factor affecting the family becomes *mobility*, both geographic (or physical) mobility and social mobility, the ability to rise in the system of social stratification. The urban industrial family moves often, and extra members merely hold it back. In addition, the work situation in the city does not permit extra members to contribute their share to the family economy, as they could on the farm, and they become a liability to those who must support them. As a result, the process of modernization has caused a shift from the extended family toward a nuclear family made up of parents and their unmarried children.

Other factors that accompany the increase in industry and the decline in subsistence farming include the growing independence of young people, the rising status of women, a trend toward individually arranged marriages as opposed to marriages arranged by parents, a decline in plural marriage, and a trend toward neolocal residence, with newlyweds setting up a new household separate from that of either spouse's parents. All of these cultural changes can be traced directly to the effects of industrialization on a rural, agrarian population. For example, as land becomes less important to the economy,

Industrialization has brought with it a new way of life to the Western world, but has also created many problems along the way.

young people who can offer their labor power on the open market gain a measure of security and become independent from their parents and families at a much earlier age. Women also enter the labor force, and with their new economic position they gain a higher status coupled with greater independence from their husbands or fathers. Further, in a rural farm community marriage was based mainly on economic factors such as how much land a potential spouse was likely to inherit, where it was located, and how it would fit in with the plans and assets of the other party. For members of the industrial labor force, however, these questions no longer have much meaning, and as a result marriage becomes a personal bond between the spouses rather than an economic arrangement between two families. In addition, the independence of the couple from their families leads them to separate themselves from them physically as well as emotionally, and this is reflected in residence patterns.

Urbanization   Urbanization means not only an increase in the size of cities but also an increase in the number of cities and in the percentage of the population living in urban locations. Urbanization is related to industrialization because industry is usually located in cities, and people who work in industry must live nearby. In addition to the demographic (population) factors involved in the growth of cities, we generally mean something more by the term **urbanization**: a change not only in the physical nature of the city but also in the psychological and cultural makeup of the people who live there. Of course, with the growth of cities there must be parallel growth in communication and transportation networks, market systems, technological advances, and division of labor.

Anthropologists who study urbanization are concerned but only with these broad-scale changes, but also with the effects of city life on rural people. For example, in rural areas an individual is generally thought of first in terms of his or her family and then the community. Rarely does a rural resident think in terms of national goals or identify with the nation as a whole. Yet when rural people move to the city they find that their local outlook is no longer useful and that they must think in terms of the country of which they are a part, rather than the village or even the city. This change from localism

This Kikuyu tribesman looks rather out of place in the modern city of Nairobi, Kenya. Urbanization does not always lead to immediate change for migrants to the city.

to nationalism is connected with a major shift in the values of the individual, and can be seen as one of the most sweeping effects of urbanization.

Another difference between life in a small village and in the city lies in the nature of personal interactions. In a rural community everyone knows everyone else personally. People know each other's life histories, interests, and peculiarities; it is hard to keep anything secret in a small village. On the other hand, the city is an anonymous place where a person can disappear. People are thrust into situations in which they must interact with others whom they have never met. Personal knowledge can no longer serve as the basis for interaction; instead, people develop ways of dealing with one another in a formal manner, according to prescribed rules of behavior. For the new city dweller this can be very hard to adjust to and a source of frustration. To some extent it can be avoided by creating stronger neighborhood ties. Thus we often find sections of large cities that are solidly ethnic, in which the language spoken is different from that spoken in the rest of the city and people still seem to have the kinds of personal relationships that we might expect to find in a village. Such ethnic neighborhoods are adaptations

Although the city is a place for rapid social change, some ethnic communities are able to retain parts of their traditional cultures.

to the city, attempts to maintain some of the old traditions and offer some comfort and security to newcomers who are turned off by the impersonal nature of the city.

Another feature of the impersonality of the city and people's reaction to it is the attempt to create smaller groups in which one can maintain strong personal ties. In a village this is not necessary because everyone is thrown together by the nature of village life, but in the city a person must actively go out and look for a small group. It is typical of city life that there are large numbers of what we call **voluntary associations**, or groups that a person must seek out and join. Such associations are commonly based on shared interests rather than factors, such as residence in the same neighborhood, over which most people have less control. A voluntary association might be formed by people with the same occupation or the same interest in leisure activities. The basis for such a group can be almost anything.

In moving from the country to the city, migrants experience a change from what anthropologists call the "folk" culture to the "urban" culture. They move from a small, relatively isolated, homogeneous village to a large, impersonal, heterogeneous community. The family becomes less important as they are integrated into the industrial economy, and they turn instead to secular institutions and groups of people who share the same special interests. Of course, this does not happen overnight. In many cases studied by anthropologists it has been found that even second-generation immigrants cling to many of the traditions of the rural areas from which their parents came. In the classic study Oscar Lewis followed Mexican migrants from a small village to Mexico City in an attempt to see how the pressures of city life affected their rural "folk" culture. He found that there was very little breakdown of traditional culture among first-generation migrants. Family ties remained strong, and the people formed what might be called an **urban village**—an attempt to create an artificial folk culture in the midst of the city.

Similar trends have been observed in other studies. Even today rural migrants to U.S. cities have been known to resist the pressures of urbanization and maintain many of their folk traditions. For example, in the past three decades there has been a massive migration of Appalachians to urban areas in the Midwest. This migration is a result of the decline in the two basic economic activities of the Appalachian region: subsistence agriculture and coal mining. Countless studies of Appalachian migrants to the city have found that they maintain very strong ties with their families "back home." The migrants tend to live in parts of the city known as "Little Appalachia," such as "Uptown" Chicago, where an estimated 50,000 Appalachian migrants reside. They work in the same factories, worship at the same churches, and, in general, resist the intrusion of urban culture into their lives. Many migrants still communicate and visit regularly with their families in Appalachia; on any Friday evening you can see an almost endless stream of cars heading south across the Ohio River at Cincinnati, Portsmouth, or any other city along the river.

What do these two contradictory trends— the simultaneous breakdown and maintenance of folk culture among urban migrants—tell us about the process of urbanization? For one thing, we can see how the traditional way of life that is functional in a small community can be a disadvantage to a person living in the city. There will be pressure for migrants to give up their old ways if they are to succeed in their new home. But at the same time we can learn a valuable lesson about the nature of culture. Culture is basically conservative. We learn patterns of behavior easily in childhood, but we give them up only with great difficulty as adults. This is why it takes at least one generation—and usually more—to go through a complete change from folk to urban culture. The migrants themselves tend to cling to their traditions and fight off newfangled, "citified" ideas. Their children grown up in a dual environment: Their parents teach them the old values, and their peers and other people with whom they come into contact teach them a new and different set of values. Sometimes these people make the transition smoothly in one generation, but depending on the strength of the urban culture in which they are raised and the conservatism of their own cultural heritage, the process can take much longer.

Westernization Of all the aspects of modernization, **westernization** is the hardest to define. This term is generally used to refer to the adoption of cultural patterns that are characteristic of Western society. Many of these changes have already been discussed— the trend toward a nuclear family type, the rising status of women, the growth of a market economy and a market mentality. But westernization can occur without movement to the city and without industrialization; as the term is used here, it refers to changes in values, attitudes, and beliefs, that is, in the psychological makeup of people in non-Western societies.

Throughout the developing world westernization is taking place in a number of ways simultaneously. Such things as the construction and staffing of schools are major factors in bringing about social change. Throughout the 1960s, 1970s, and into the decade of the 1980s, as Asian and African countries gained political independence, one of their top development strategies was to improve the educational systems left by their colonial masters. A literate population that can process various forms of the printed media is a vital component in producing social change. Since most print media are urban-based, one effect of spreading literacy can be the development of a sense of nationalism. Newspapers and magazines cover what is taking place in the national capital or in major cities. Intentional or not, this is a unifying process.

Radio, and increasingly television, play an enormous role in the westernization process. Thanks in large measure to inexpensive, battery-operated transistor radios, today there are relatively few places in the world where

In Mexico, as in other developing nations, a very important priority for the government is to improve the level of literacy of their population.

music, soap operas, and news are not heard. As a medium for diversion as well as for edification, the radio is highly effective in carrying out westernization. Like most of the print media, radio broadcasting has a strongly urban-based content. Consequently, even though they might be hundreds of miles from the nearest large city, residents of rural Nigeria and Colombia know substantially more about urban life than did previous generations.

Television is having much the same impact in many parts of the world today. One major difference is that while radio might have a local or regional thrust and focus, much of TV broadcasting consists of foreign programs dubbed into local languages. People all over the world follow *Miami Vice, Dynasty, Hotel,* and *Dallas* regularly. Reflect for a moment on what sort of image other peoples might have of the United States when their primary source of information about us is our popular television shows.

Through communication with the outside world, new products and materials are made available to people in isolated areas, and high prestige is attached to those items. At the same time, although people are unaware of

this, it is impossible to adopt a new material culture, including the products and higher standard of living of an industrialized and urbanized society, without some of the values associated with industrialization and urbanization rubbing off. For example, a man who used to work on his family farm cannot take a job in a factory without adopting some of the values that go with industrial labor. He will develop new attitudes toward time and efficiency, things that were not as important on the farm. He will begin to calculate the cash value of his labor; on the farm his labor had no cash value. Punctuality and precision are basically Western values that were not found in most agricultural societies prior to the spread of Western culture and the beginning of modernization. This is not so much because Westerners are different from people in the rest of the world as because the conditions of industrial labor impose certain requirements (we might call them constraints) that bring about these values. The same might be said for city life, with its anonymity and specialization: It is not that these cultural patterns are characteristic of people who live in Western countries; rather, the first urban industrial centers in which these values and patterns were functional were located in the West.

Another important factor in the spread of Western culture is known as *culture lag*, a term that refers to the fact that certain kinds of ideas and innovations are adopted more readily than others. This is true not only of cross-cultural change but also of change within a single society. For example, ever since the invention of the atomic bomb, commentators in the United States have suggested that although we have the capacity to kill the entire population of the world ten times over, we have not developed the technological and moral capacities to ensure that we will not do so by accident. The well-known novel *Fail Safe*, the more recent movie *War Games*, and many similar stories describe how a mechanical failure or the actions of a powerful but mentally unbalanced individual or an inquisitive computer jockey could launch the world into nuclear war. This is a clear example of culture lag in which values lag behind technology.

Andre Simić, an anthropologist who has

studied urbanization in Yugoslavia, writes of rural peasants who attempt to become westernized but are unable to do so because of technological barriers. He tells of a family that purchased a refrigerator because of its prestige value but was unable to use it because the village had no electricity. Other anthropologists have noted similar cases in which refrigerators were used as storage vaults, clothes closets, or even illegal stills—in each case because of the lack of electricity. And Simić tells of another family in the village he studied that had purchased a radio and placed it in the living room for visitors to admire, despite the fact that it would not operate without current.

We should recognize that westernization is not a necessary part of industrialization. There is no single model of an industrial society that must be followed by an industrializing country. Each culture has its own traditions and its own history and direction, and these differences will affect the form that modernization takes. For example, it is generally assumed that part of the process of

Watusi men enjoy ice cream for the first time. They prefer to keep the refrigerator door open since it is cooler.

westernization is a change from ascribed to achieved status—the introduction of the "merit system" and the elimination of nepotism in industrial settings. In our own society nepotism is unacceptable, for it is considered inefficient to promote someone on any basis other than merit. However, in Japanese society, in which industrialization has been highly successful, this is not the case. A Japanese factory is thought of as a family, and people are brought into it on that basis. The factory management is very paternalistic toward the workers—a far cry from our own system, in which benefits have often been won only after bitter battles between management and labor unions. The Japanese example proves that a country can successfully industrialize without transforming the native value system to conform to a Western model. While it is true that Western values usually make for more efficient production and thus are commonly adopted (sometimes unknowingly) by the people of industrializing nations, it is important to recognize the flexibility of culture and its ability to accept change without undergoing a total transformation.

Modernization: A case study The village of Kippel, where one of the authors worked, is nestled in a valley high in the Swiss Alps, surrounded by mountains on four sides. Until recently traffic into and out of the valley was almost nonexistent, and the way of life of its few hundred residents was much the same as it had been in the Middle Ages, when the valley was first settled. The villagers practiced a mixed economy of agriculture and livestock raising, growing enough grain and potatoes to provide for their needs and relying mainly on dairy cattle for the remainder of their diet. A marriage partner would be chosen from one of the four villages in the valley, for it was necessary to combine two people's inheritances to provide enough land to support a family; in addition, the limited contact of young people with the outside world almost forced them to look for a spouse at home. Village life was marked by cooperation in tasks that required more labor than one

household could supply, and the difficulty of farming steep slopes and transporting crops or building materials vertically meant that there were many such tasks. The Roman Catholic Church dominated every aspect of life, with many festivals and a great deal of ceremony surrounding daily activities.

After World War II the Swiss government undertook a program of industrialization in the mountainous regions of the country. Railroad lines were extended into more isolated areas; dams were constructed; and factories were built in mountain regions to promote industry there. A number of men from Kippel left during these years to take jobs in industry, first building railroad lines, dams, and factories, and later working in the factories. In 1961 a large aluminum factory was built less than an hour's drive away from

An elderly farmer in Kippel, a remote valley in Switzerland, using the traditional scythe to mow hay.

Kippel, and today more than 20 men from the village work in the factory. Most other men between the ages of 35 and 55 work as unskilled or semiskilled laborers at similar jobs, and commute to work daily, sometimes weekly, from their homes in Kippel.

The shift from agriculture to industry shortly after World War II led to many drastic changes in Kippel. All at once the younger generation became free to advance and get away from agriculture. Whereas formerly it was expected that when a boy finished primary school he would go to work on his father's farm, he was now expected to continue his schooling and learn a trade or, in rare cases, to obtain even more training and take a white-collar job. Agriculture became something of a hobby for the old men, who were the only full-time farmers left in the village. But the new working class did not give up farming altogether, for they felt insecure in their industrial jobs and were still attached to the land and to the values of subsistence agriculture. As a result, these men became what is known as **worker-peasants**, that is, people who go to work in factories but maintain a small agricultural operation on the side. In Kippel most of the work done on these farms is performed by women and young girls who are related to the male head of the household. The man helps out on weekends and during his vacation, but the main responsibility for farming has shifted to the women. Younger men who have completed school and have better-paying jobs than their parents have abandoned the idea of farming altogether and do not even maintain a small agricultural operation to qualify them as worker-peasants. Thus within a generation Kippel has changed from an agricultural village to a working-class suburb.

Other major economic changes have affected the village life style as well. More than a decade ago a group of investors purchased a large tract of land above the neighboring village and began to develop a ski resort. In all more than $1 million was paid to the owners of this land, many of them residents of Kippel. Within a few years the tourist industry in Kippel, and throughout the valley, mushroomed. Villagers now obtain low-interest government-subsidized loans to build new houses, and the typical house includes one flat for the owner's family and at least one or two flats to be rented to tourists. A man with such a house can earn as much from the rent he collects as he does from his unskilled job. Several new tourist-oriented projects have sprung up to the villages below the planned ski resort, including a new hotel in Kippel. And of course all of these projects create jobs for local residents, so that the village has again been transformed, this time from a working-class community into a tourist center whose main source of income is the provision of services.

These economic changes have spelled the end of many traditional aspects of village culture. The cooperation that used to be such an important part of village life is now almost nonexistent. Since there is no labor force engaged in agriculture, there is no interest in maintaining community projects, and when people need help they usually have to pay for it. There is a new emphasis on inheritance. In the past everyone tried to put together a complete agricultural unit, including land in various parts of the valley and at various altitudes, but today people compete for land near the village that can be used as housing sites. Formerly valuable agricultural land outside the village limits now has little value.

Marriage patterns have changed in recent years as a result of the economic transformation of the village. Improved transportation and more experience outside the village have led to more marriages with outsiders. People tend to marry younger than they did a generation ago, for they are able to gain financial security much earlier then they could when they were planning to become farmers and had to wait for their share of inheritance. There is a growing trend toward emigration, since young people find that they cannot apply the skills they have learned without going to the city. Finally, there has been a steady decline in the influence of the church on younger people because they have broadened their outlook on life as a result of their experiences away from the village.

What has happened in Kippel in the past 40 years is typical of the effects of modernization on small communities throughout the world. Industrialization draws these communities into the national culture, overcoming the differences that were such an important source of identity for the villagers. Some individuals are attracted to the cities by the promise of fame and fortune. Others, like the people of Kippel, remain in their village, only to find that it, too, is becoming urbanized, if not in size, then at least in culture. What we are seeing in Europe, and to a lesser extent in the Third World, is the spread of a mass culture, a unifying influence that affects rural people as well as city dwellers. As the world becomes smaller, media intrude into even the most isolated village; farmers are uprooted and drawn into factories, or forced to become rural business people; and the process of modernization continues to erase the traditional cultures that anthropologists have studied for so long.

Planned Change and Applied Anthropology

The study of cultural and social change often involves problems of planned change. In recent years many anthropologists have been engaged in programs aimed at promoting and carrying out change, that is, **applied anthropology**. In such a program the anthropologist must start with some basic assumptions about the people he or she is working with and the changes that have been proposed. First of all, we must assume that something that originates in one culture and fits the ideals and patterns of that culture may not be acceptable to people who have a different way of life. People tend to accept innovations from another culture in bits and pieces, reworking them to fit their own way of life and discarding aspects that they dislike.

The results might be that the most important aspect of the program is not accepted while trivial or unnecessary elements are adopted wholeheartedly. For example, one of the most prominent changes to take place early in the development of many Third World countries is the creation of a national airline. To Westerners these airlines are "irrational" and "unnecessary." For us, an airline is a means of transportation; in a country that does not need mass air transportation and does not have the wealth to support it, it seems foolhardy to operate an airline. The point is that the developing countries have borrowed a Western innovation that is an important symbol of their entry into the modern world. They are not really concerned about whether or not they need air transportation.

Armed with the assumption that innovations must fit a new context, the anthropologist must see that before a program is presented to the people toward whom it is aimed, it is reworked so that it is acceptable to them, but still is organized in a way that will achieve the goals of the plan. This raises some ethical questions. To whom does the agent of change owe allegiance? To the government that pays for the job? To his or her beliefs about what is best for the people? Or to the people's own values? Often the anthropologist is placed in the role of a counselor whose job is to convince people to accept something they might otherwise reject. The anthropologist must understand the people's way of life in order to get them to accept the change, even if this means engaging in a small-scale con game. Yet at the same time the anthropologist is hired because of his or her ability to operate between two cultures, an ability that includes not only awareness of how people live in a small community halfway around the world, but also familiarity with the technology of the West. By virtue of greater education and knowledge, the anthropologist has a responsibility to help those who are less educated and less knowledgeable.

Certainly an ethical question is raised by vesting this kind of power in anthropologists, but if we accept the assumption that there are some basic values that we must adhere to in carrying out such programs, then their benefits will outweigh the drawbacks of intruding on other people and unduly influencing their way of life. These values include a preference for health over sickness, the belief that a full stomach is better than an empty one, and the assumption that every person has a right to an education as a step toward gaining control over hs or her future.

A second assumption of applied anthropology is that all change operates within a cultural context. Earlier we defined culture as an integrated system, so that a change in one aspect would have an effect on others. Consider, for example, what the invention of the automobile has meant to American culture. It has not only led to easier transportation, it has become the focal point of the U.S. economy. People have moved from cities to suburbs, changing the whole pattern of residence from what it was a century ago. With more than 45,000 people dying in traffic accidents on our highways each year, most of them still of childbearing age, the population structure of our country has changed. In addition, farming has become more commercial because crops can be grown and transported to markets more quickly. Recreation patterns have responded to the new mode of transportation. And of course the automobile has taken a heavy toll on our environment, polluting the air in our cities and depleting the resources of our land.

It is amusing to ask: What if Henry Ford had known what was going to come of his great invention? Would he still have carried it through? The automobile is a fait accompli and the changes it has wrought are irreversible. But this kind of question is not idle in the context of developing societies. In fact, such questions are precisely the ones anthropologists must ask in evaluating a proposed program of planned change. We know that there is no such thing as a "simple" change—any change will produce other changes, and many of those secondary changes, or ripple effects, will be unexpected. The goal is to anticipate as many of them as possible, and

to evaluate the overall results of the program, not just its immediate goals. Perhaps after all the relevant factors have been weighed, adjustments can be made so as to avoid unwanted results, but the primary duty of the anthropologist is to consider the project in terms of its overall effect on other people—and to reject a program, no matter how noble its goals might be, if the means for achieving those goals cannot be justified. This duty is especially important because the anthropologist almost always works with other specialists who are not trained to consider the native culture and plan around it. Someone who is trained in the methods of administration can easily lose sight of the effects of a program while trying to make it more efficient. It is the anthropologist's job to inform those who carry out such a program of the problems that might arise and to point out ways to avoid those problems while still achieving the program's goals.

Many programs of planned change are merely programs of westernization—the introduction of Western technology, along with training in the use of that technology. However, through their experience with another way of life, anthropologists learn that it is not always desirable, let alone possible, to change the way of life of other people in order to raise their standard of living. If we adhere to the value of cultural relativism, by which we grant every culture its own integrity, we are bound to look for ways of helping others without remaking them into people just like us. Whether the planned change is to introduce tractors into rural farming areas, set up health clinics in areas with high rates of disease, or operate birth control programs in overpopulated countries, we must recognize the right of each culture to keep its own traditions. We must find ways to introduce these changes without transforming the society.

Some programs have taken this approach with great success. The Peace Corps, for example, has adopted a policy of working with the people of Third World countries to solve the problems that they themselves consider serious. Peace Corps volunteers follow closely the basic requirements laid out by Malinowski for anthropological fieldwork, which were discussed in Chapter 4. As part of their training they learn the language of the people with whom they are to work; they live among those people, preferably in the same village or community; they observe their customs and try to fit in with their way of life as much as possible. In short, they do not force their ways on others so much as try to determine what the people want for themselves. While we do not mean to imply that the Peace Corps has no problems, clearly these methods (which have been adopted by other agencies with similar goals) and preferable to operating in complete ignorance of the local culture.

Barriers to change   Books on applied anthropology contain story after story about how a planned program of change failed and

For three decades Peace Corps members have applied anthropological insights in their work. Here a Peace Corps volunteer is working with agricultural students.

how, during an analysis of the failure, it was discovered that a minor adjustment in the program would have led to improved results, if not total success. George Foster, in *Traditional Societies and Technological Change*, discusses applied anthropology programs in terms of two factors: barriers to change that exist within the traditional cultures and must be overcome if the program is to succeed; and stimulants to change that can be injected into the program, taking into account the nature of the culture and the planned change. Many of the examples that follow are cited in Foster's book, an excellent introduction to the study of applied anthropology.

In describing the situation in which many applied anthropologists find themselves, Foster cites an ancient oriental fable:

Once upon a time a monkey and a fish were caught up in a great flood. The monkey, agile and experienced, had the good fortune to scramble up a tree to safety. As he looked down into the raging waters, he saw a fish struggling against the swift current. Filled with a humanitarian desire to help his less fortunate fellow, he reached down and scooped the fish from the water. To the monkey's surprise, the fish was not very grateful for this aid.

Like the monkey in the fable, the person who is not aware of cultural differences might feel hurt and surprised. It may seem to us that we are rescuing people from the problems that plague them, while to them it appears that we are forcing upon them unwanted changes that threaten to destroy their traditions and the way of life that has been a part of their culture for generations. Is it any wonder that they are not grateful?

Cultural values can act as strong barriers to change, and the anthropologist must find a way to present the change so that it is not seen as conflicting with those values. For example, in the United States we tend to value change—any change—for its own sake. We are deluged with advertisements for "new, improved" detergents, foods, and other products. Our cars look different every year, as do our clothing styles. One major

U.S. company has had as its slogan "Progress is our most important product." Indeed, it seems that we are more willing to accept change than anyone else in the world. And that is exactly the point. In most societies, especially in nonindustrial countries, people tend to rely just as heavily on tradition as we do on change. They feel a strong attachment to the ways of their ancestors, and any attempt to replace their traditions with new ideas will be rejected out of hand. To get a program accepted, the anthropologist must find some way of convincing the people that it will fit in with their tradition. Christian missionaries found this out when they learned to work their teachings gradually into an existing system of beliefs, rather than abruptly replacing an entire religious tradition with a new one. The same principle can be applied by anthropologists to other kinds of change.

Other cultural values, such as pride and dignity, can enter into the success of a program of planned change. For example, most Americans would offer little resistance to adult education. Many U.S. corporations encourage their employees to seek further training, and some even require it. We admire people who return to school after a long absence, and at many universities and colleges there are programs that seek to attract senior citizens by offering them student status without the customary tuition fees. Yet not all cultures have our regard for adult education. In some societies school is for children, and the idea that adults should return to school would meet with disapproval. If adult education is to be successful in such a setting, it must be presented as something other than a return to school—perhaps by offering instruction informally, outside of the school building and in a manner as different from the traditional schoolroom pattern as possible.

Questions of pride and dignity can be recognized in advance and dealt with, provided there is someone in the program who has a thorough knowledge of the local culture. For example, a program to sell improved seed to farmers in a village in India failed because, while the poorer villagers participated, the wealthier and more influential villagers would have nothing to do with it. The reason, it turned out, was that the best farmers were able to raise enough seed by themselves to feed their families and provide for next year's crop. To buy or borrow seed was a sign that one could not raise a large enough crop, and for the most successful farmers this would mean a loss of face.[1] If someone in the program had realized this in advance, an alternative could have been worked out. Perhaps some of the new, improved seed could have been traded for some of the old seed from the farmers' last crop. But the assumption that everyone would recognize the value of the new seed ignored the cultural barriers to change in this village.

Besides the problems of introducing changes that conflict with basic cultural values, norms, tastes, and the like, there are potential barriers on a "social" level, that is, in the area of group relations within a community. For example, in many small, tightly knit communities tasks are carried out in groups, so that people interact closely and form strong bonds associated with their work. In a village that has no running water and no bakery, women gather to do their washing at the central fountain or stream, and bake their bread in the communal oven. Facilities like the fountain and the oven thus are important not only for their obvious functions, but also because they allow the women to gather together, talk and gossip, and pass the time while doing their work. It might seem to an outsider that piping running water into the home or supplying ovens for each household would improve the standard of living, but for these women it would not improve the *quality* of living. Indeed, it would have the opposite effect, for it would break up an important peer group from which they receive much satisfaction.

[1] Morris E. Opler and R. D. Singh, "Economic, Political, and Social Change in Villages of North Central India," *Human Organization*, 11, no. 2 (1952):5–12.

Women in India attend a family planning course given by a government worker. In many cases it is necessary to do more than just explain how birth control works. Cultural considerations must be taken into account as well.

Authority is another aspect of the social structure of a community than can serve as a barrier to change. An innovation, if it is to be accepted, must be introduced to the members of the community who are in positions of authority, and their leadership must be seen as an important factor in its acceptance. In a village in Peru several wells were dug to supply water to the villagers. However, the villagers did not take advantage of the wells because they were drilled on land that was owned by people who were not leaders in the community, and people who did hold positions of authority were not consulted. As a result, they used their influence to reject the plan.[2]

A third kind of barrier to change is what Foster calls a psychological barrier. Such barriers often take the form of a failure to communicate. In trying to communicate the nature of the planned change and the benefits to be derived from it, the anthropologist must realize that the message the people receive is not always the same as the message intended. Or, other elements of the program might convey an unplanned message without the project directors realizing it. For example,

it has been said that Mexican Indians are reluctant to call the priest to administer the sacraments and last rites of the church when a relative is seriously ill, despite the fact that they are devout Catholics.[3] However, from their point of view their reluctance makes perfect sense. Because they hesitate to send for a priest until the person is obviously dying, almost every time the priest comes, the patient dies shortly thereafter. Thus the message conveyed by the Catholic Church, which is that all members should have the benefit of the sacraments when they are gravely ill, is not the message understood by the Indians.

A similar problem concerns the role of the hospital as it is seen by the residents of a rural community. When people are relatively isolated and hospitals are far away and expensive, they are taken to a hospital only for the most serious illnesses. As a result, a smaller percentage of those who enter a hospital survive, for they do not make the more casual use of the facilities that most city dwellers do. It is easy to see how this could lead to the belief that a hospital is a place where someone goes to die, and that con-

[2] Allan R. Holmberg, "The Wells That Failed," in Edward H. Spicer (ed.), *Human Problems in Technological Change* (New York: Russell Sage Foundation), 1952.

[3] Georgetta Soustelle, cited in George M. Foster, *Traditional Societies and Technological Change* (New York: Harper & Row, 1973), p. 130.

finement (like the last rites of the church) should be avoided. If a rural health care program is to succeed in the face of such psychological barriers, it must be preceded by an educational program to relieve the people of such fears. It may be necessary to take some patients to a hospital when there is nothing seriously wrong with them in order to show their fellow villagers that people can survive the experience of hospitalization. Such a practice would normally meet with resistance from doctors and program directors who lack the insight of the anthropologist, but in the long run it would be much easier and more efficient to take this approach than to simply expect the people to adapt to the program.

Another such failure to communicate can be seen in the way people perceive various roles. People in one culture might see a specialist as having a different role than that specialist is supposed to have. For example, in some cultures a folk curer is expected not only to cure a patient but also to diagnose the illness by discovering the symptoms without the aid of the patient. What happens when people used to this idea enter a modern Western clinic and the first thing the doctor asks them is to describe their symptoms? If they believe the "doctor" is supposed to find out through magical means what is wrong with them, they are not likely to respect a modern physician who can't get past the first step in the diagnosis. To them it is obvious that such a doctor is incompetent.[4]

Stimulants to change Our discussion so far might make it appear that any attempt to introduce change will be rejected. In part, rejection can be avoided by a thorough study of the culture with an eye toward uncovering potential barriers and taking them into account in the planning stage. Yet even the most observant anthropologist will come up against unexpected barriers, for there will always be unforeseen effects—new problems that arise after an innovation has been intro-

[4] Foster, *Traditional Societies*, pp. 138–139.

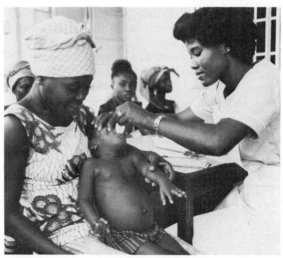

A nurse giving medication in a West African clinic often faces difficulties in getting people to participate in public health programs.

duced. To counter the effects of such barriers, the anthropologist can recommend a number of elements that will stimulate acceptance of the change, regardless of the problems that might be encountered.

We have already mentioned a few such stimulants. In some societies, especially those in which industrialization has already begun and therefore Western culture has become a model, many innovations are accepted simply because they are identified with the West, which is synonymous with progress, wealth, and power. Even though people do not perceive a need for latrines or vaccinations or other Western innovations, they can sometimes be persuaded to accept them simply for their prestige value. While the reasons for the success of the program might not seem valid to the directors, the results are every bit as real.

Economic gain and competition can also serve as stimulant to change. If it can be shown that an innovation will mean more money or a higher standard of living, it is more likely to be accepted. Likewise, encouraging competition between individuals, between factions in a community, or even between communities in a region can often lead people to accept innovations that they might otherwise reject. The competitive instinct can be used to overcome the strong tendency of people throughout the world to cling to their time-tested traditions.

Friendship or a close relationship between a member of the program staff and the people for whom it is designed can serve as a stimulant to change. It is not enough to send in trained people to administer a project, for if they are not trusted, their suggestions will not be heeded. On the other hand, if a project worker has a close tie with a community member, he or she can get that person to try the innovation. This is an important aspect of training programs for such groups as the Peace Corps, in which the personal relationship between the volunteer and the people with whom he or she is working is a major factor in the success or failure of the program.

Finally, it is important to point out that any innovation will have a better chance of success if it fits in with existing cultural patterns. It is important to maintain traditional values and to adjust the roles of those engaged in the program so that they fit in with local conditions. For example, many rural health programs aim not only at curing sick people but also at teaching them the value of preventive medicine. In such a situation a doctor may take the role of instructor rather than that of curer. The anthropologist should examine the roles of teacher, curer, and doctor in each community in order to find out which role has the best chance of stimulating the desired change. If there are no schools, or adult education is unpopular, then perhaps the role of curer would be the best one in which to present the doctor. If the villagers' experience with doctors has been negative, then perhaps the doctor should be presented as a teacher. If there is fear or mistrust of government, the program should not be linked to any government agency. If clear patterns of authority already exist in the village, they should be used to

stimulate acceptance of the change. In sum, it must be recognized that any innovation that is introduced into a new cultural setting will have to exist in a new context, and no matter how well it might have fit into the culture in which it originated, it must be reworked to fit into another one. Showing how well it fits in can act as a stimulant for its acceptance by overcoming people's tendency to stick with what is familiar and accept what is new only after a very cautious trial.

Unexpected effects: The pitfalls of planned change Throughout this discussion of applied anthropology and the problems faced by programs of planned change, we have stressed the fact that by introducing an innovation into another culture we unleash a series of changes, not all of which can be predicted. Knowing that such actions will have unexpected effects, the anthropologist takes on the additional task of evaluating the program as it progresses and determining whether its success will not be at too high a price. If the anthropologist is lucky, he or she may even anticipate some secondary effects, and an experienced anthropologist will apply the results of other, similar programs to predict secondary changes and call them to the attention of those who are running the program.

Anthropologists and others engaged in public health programs have long been aware of the hazards of programs that involve changes in diet. For example, in an area where people live almost entirely on a diet of raw fish, many people suffer tapeworms. At first sight it might seem logical to introduce a program (including education and the necessary materials) that encourages people to cook their fish, thereby killing the tapeworms before they are consumed. But what are the secondary effects of cooking fish? We have also learned that where people eat mainly fish and have few other sources of vitamins, their vitamin intake will be reduced by such a program, because cooking lowers the food value of the fish. We might simply be trading the problem of tapeworms for the problem of vitamin deficiency.

In India public health officials found that in many villages where cooking was done inside the hut, with no chimney and poor ventilation, there was a high rate of respiratory and eye ailments. They set out to solve this problem, assuming that it would be a simple matter to introduce chimneys and windows and a new kind of stove that would eliminate smoke inside the house. But they did not take into account the secondary effects of such a change. Many of the huts had thatched roofs that were infested with wood-boring ants. The high smoke level kept the ants under control. When a new, low-cost, smokeless stove was introduced, the ants began to multiply and ate up the roofs more rapidly. This in itself might not seem serious, except that for Indian peasants the cost of a new roof is a large portion of their income—income that they would otherwise spend to maintain their already meager standard of living. By causing them to replace their roofs more often, the innovation had the unexpected effect of lowering their standard of living. In effect, the people traded respiratory and eye diseases for a poorer diet and fewer clothes, which also affected their health. The lesson we should learn from such experiences is not to abandon all hope of helping people, but rather to try to anticipate the effects of any program of planned change, and to compare similar programs in other parts of the world in order to avoid making the same mistakes over and over again.

Applied Anthropology and the Future

Most applied anthropology has dealt with planned change in Third World countries, and perhaps this is as it should be. Attempts to spread the wealth and knowledge of the Western world and put them to use to raise the standard of living in less wealthy countries and to help less fortunate people have been all too few. It is indeed a tragedy when the attempts fail for lack of knowledge of foreign cultures, knowledge that anthropologists may be better equipped to provide than anyone else. If anthropology is to be criticized, it is not for the role it has played in planned change—the benefits have far outweighed any abuses that may have occurred—but rather for its failure to take a stronger stand and to force itself on programs that were doomed to failure because they did not make use of basic anthropological insights. This problem is still with us today. Anthropology is still a misunderstood and little-known field, making its use by government and private agencies far less frequent and efficient than it should be.

The challenge for applied anthropology lies not only in the Third World but also in our own society. It is time to abolish the distinction between anthropologists who study foreign cultures and social scientists who study their own society. We are all students of human behavior, and if our science is to have any validity, it must be applicable to our own society as well as to others. If we have learned from our study of others, we ought to be able to apply that knowledge to ourselves. The authors look forward to a day when anthropology is more important in dealing with the cultural differences behind many of the severe problems in our society, including race relations, sexism, drug addiction, alcoholism, and crime. It is not necessary for every government employee to be a trained anthropologist or for every poverty program to be run by someone with a Ph.D. But it is important that the message of anthropology—and it is an important message—be made available to as many people as possible and as clearly as possible. This is the subject of the final chapter of this book.

Summary

For millions of years human beings survived by hunting and gathering their food, using a relatively simple technology. Although there was cultural change during this period, it occurred at a slow rate compared to more recent times.

However, as population density increased and people came into contact with one another on a more regular basis, the rate of change increased. One kind of change that occurs when groups of people came into contact is called *acculturation*.

More recently, the major theme in cultural change has been *modernization*, which can be seen as three processes of change that tend to occur together: urbanization, industrialization, and westernization. However, as the case study of Kippel, a small village in the Swiss Alps, shows these three processes need not occur together; industrialization and westernization can take place without movement to the city because of the impact of modern media in transmitting urban mass culture to the rural countryside.

Another major source of cultural and social change has come from programs of planned change, often associated with the field of applied anthropology. Anthropologists contributed to the programs of planned change following World War II, and they continue to make important contributions to the planning and, hopefully, the ultimate success of programs of change in the developing countries of the world today.

In any attempt to introduce new cultural elements to people there will be barriers to change. Traditional values of modesty, conservatism, pride, and even taste can spell the doom of a program of planned change if they are not taken into account. Authority patterns must be considered, and factions or group dynamics cannot be overlooked in the administration of such a program. Psychological factors such as people's perception of the changes and of their traditional way of life may also serve as barriers to change.

To overcome the barriers to change, the applied anthropologist can use stimulants to achieve the aims of the program. Occasionally the changes can be made to appear prestigious in order to get people to adopt them. Economic gain can also be a strong motivation for change, as can close personal friendship or rapport between the change agent and the people of the community.

In every case of change there will be secondary consequences, many of them unanticipated. It is the role of the applied anthropologist to try to predict these secondary changes, and to plan for them in advance. The elimination of one problem may create another problem even more serious than the first, thus threatening the success of the entire program.

The ability of anthropology to aid in the solution to the world's pressing problems will be the key to the success of the discipline in the future. Our understanding of other cultures has enabled us to make valuable contributions toward improving the living conditions of countless people throughout the world. At the same time, we are recognizing the growing need to contribute our knowledge and understanding toward the solution of problems on the home front as well.

Glossary

acculturation A process of culture change that occurs when groups of individuals having different cultures come into continuous first-hand contact.

applied anthropology The use of the knowledge gained in studying other cultures toward the solutions of practical problems.

culture lag The differential rate of diffusion or adoption of various innovations.

diffusion The spread of an innovation from its point of origin throughout an area and ultimately, through contact with other cultures, to neighboring regions.

industrialization The growth of industry, usually accompanied by a change in agriculture, the family, and many other elements of the social structure.

innovation The creation of new elements in a culture, usually as the result of recombinations of existing elements into something qualitatively different.

modernization A broad term covering at least the following separate processes: economic growth, or industrialization; urbanization; and westernization. It is usually assumed that these processes occur together, and that they are interrelated, although this is not always the case.

syncretism The process of reinterpreting new cultural elements to fit them in with the already existing traditions in a culture.

urban village An ethnically homogeneous community within a city that retains much of the culture of its inhabitants, in contrast to its urban surroundings.

urbanization The growth in the size of cities, the number of cities, and the proportion of the population living in urban locations. Urbanization has frequently been associated with a heterogeneous, impersonal, and individualistic life style.

voluntary associations Groups in which membership is based on any common interest, such as similar occupation or leisure activities.

westernization The adoption of cultural patterns characteristic of Western society. Changes in non-Western societies include the predominance of the nuclear family, the rising status of women, and the growth of a market economy, as well as changes in values, attitudes, and beliefs.

worker-peasants People who have gone to work in factories, but have kept a small agricultural operation on the side.

Questions for Discussion

1. When we speak of the "melting pot" in American culture, we generally think of the assimilation of immigrants into a traditional American way of life. But at the same time, these groups have had a part in changing American culture in the process of acculturation. Discuss some of the everyday aspects of your life that are foreign in origin and have resulted from contact with immigrants in recent American history.

2. Can there be modernization without adopting certain Western values and patterns of behavior? Can you conceive of a factory where workers showed up whenever they felt like it, or a market that opened and closed whenever the traders

decided they wanted to work? What is it about our way of life that requires punctuality and efficiency?

3. In recent years the rate of technological change has increased so rapidly that we are now faced with numerous social problems. Can the rate of change continue to increase, and if it does, what will be the consequences? Do you see any efforts in our society to slow down change?

4. American society is currently undergoing some drastic changes and is facing some rather awesome problems, such as our pollution of the environment, depletion of resources, and current economic troubles. From what you have learned about the field of anthropology, how might you apply some of its techniques to help solve these problems?

Suggestions for Additional Reading

MICHAEL V. ANGROSINO (Ed.), *Do Applied Anthropologists Apply Anthropology?* (Athens, Georgia: Southern Anthropological Society, Proceedings no. 10, 1976). A collection of essays on current problems and accomplishments of applied anthropology.

JOHN H. BODLEY, *Victims of Progress*, 3rd ed. (Menlo Park, Cal.: Benjamin/Cummings, 1990). A moving book that deals with the difficulties many indigenous peoples have in the face of social change.

JOHN H. BODLEY (Ed.), *Tribal People and Development Issues* (Mountain View, Cal.: Mayfield Publishing, 1988). A collection of articles dating from the mid-nineteenth century to the mid-1980s on the impact of development on tribal people.

JULIAN BURGER, *Report from the Frontier* (London: Zed Books Ltd., 1987). A book describing the state of the world's indigenous peoples whose cultural survival is threatened by national development schemes.

ROBERT CHAMBERS, *Rural Development: Putting the Last First* (Essex, UK: Longman Scientific & Technical, 1983). The definitive argument for making rural development more genuine by taking local people's values, knowledge and behavior into account in development planning.

SHELTON H. DAVIS, *Victims of the Miracle: Development and the Indians of Brazil* (Cambridge, England: Cambridge University Press, 1977). An examination of the history of the development of the Amazon basin and the effects of various activities on the indigenous population of Brazil.

GEORGE M. FOSTER, *Applied Anthropology* (Boston: Little, Brown, 1969). A discussion of the field of applied anthropology, its methods and goals.

GEORGE M. FOSTER, *Traditional Societies and Technological Change*, 2nd ed. (New York: Harper & Row, 1973). A summary of the barriers to planned change and stimulants that can be used by the applied anthropologist to overcome some of these barriers.

JOHN FRIEDL, *Kippel: A Changing Village in the Alps* (New York: Holt, Rinehart and Winston, 1974). A case study of modernization and its effects on a small village in the Swiss Alps.

SHU-MIN HUANG, *The Spiral Road: Change in a Chinese Village Through the Eyes of a Communist Party Leader* (Boulder: Westview Press, 1989). The biography of 40 years of change as told by Ye Wende.

BENJAMIN D. PAUL (Ed.), *Health, Culture and Community: Case Studies of Public Reactions to Health Programs* (New York: Russell Sage Foundation, 1955). A collection of essays dealing with a specific type of applied anthropological program, analyzing some of the general problems encountered in health programs.

PERTTI J. PELTO, *The Snowmobile Revolution: Technology and Social Change in the Arctic* (Menlo Park, Cal.: Cummings, 1973). A case study of social and cultural change following the introduction of snowmobiles to the Skolt Lapps of northeastern Finland.

ANDREI SIMIĆ, *The Peasant Urbanites: A Study of Rural-Urban Mobility in Serbia* (New York: Seminar Press, 1973). An interesting account of the changes brought about by industrialization and urbanization in a formerly peasant population.

EDWARD H. SPICER (Ed.), *Human Problems in Technological Change: A Casebook* (New York: Russell Sage Foundation, 1952). Although much of the material is now almost 40 years old, this is still an excellent collection of essays for students interested in social change.

JACK O. WADDELL and O. MICHAEL WATSON (Eds.), *The American Indian in Urban Society* (Boston: Little, Brown, 1971). A collection of articles dealing with the problems of cultural breakdown and adjustment among Indians in modern American urban society.

MICHAEL B. WHITEFORD, *The Forgotten Ones: Colombian Countrymen in an Urban Setting* (Gainesville, Fla.: University Presses of Florida, 1976). A case study focusing on the process of migration and adjustment of rural families to a provincial capital in southern Colombia.

Bali's New Gods

COLIN TURNBULL

In the following reading Colin Turnbull discusses the impact of tourism on the island of Bali. While he points out that this activity is very important in attracting needed foreign revenue, he notes it is not accomplished without other types of costs to the Balinese culture and environment.

To the Balinese their home is known as Pulau Dewata, or "Island of the Gods." But sometimes it seems that in the last few years the gods of Bali have descended in the form of tourists. With swimsuits and cameras as their sacred symbols, they appear to hold the power of both desecration and consecration.

The Balinese have traditionally considered their island to be safe as well as sacred, but tourism has changed that too; from tourism and tourists there is little safety. The government of Indonesia has done its best to contain the damage, both social and environmental, by confining tourists to the southern point of the island. But Bali is not much more than a hundred miles long and since it is both encircled and traversed by motor roads, only the western jungles are effectively free from the pollution that tourism brings. Even there, however, the people are not untouched. On this small and densely populated island (approaching three million people for its two thousand square miles), every village, if not every family, has somehow been affected by the massive influx of tourists, an influx so sudden and rapid, the islanders have had little time to adapt.

It would be easy enough to paint a totally negative picture of the impact of tourism on Bali. The once beautiful sandy beach at Kuta, for instance, is now littered with bodies in various stages of undress, interspersed with pimps, hawkers, and masseurs who move from body to body, plying their services. When I was there last year the beach was patrolled by two well-dressed prostitutes riding on scooters for ready pickup and delivery. Even the water was not entirely safe; to reach it one ran the risk of being run down

Colin Turnbull, "Bali's New Gods," *Natural History*, 91 (1) 1982: 26–32. Reprinted by permission of the author and the author's agents, Scott Meredith Literary Agency, Inc., 845 Third Avenue, New York, N.Y. 10022.

by tourist youths racing and trick riding on motorcycles. And once in the water there was the danger of being hit by speedboats, towing large rubber dinghies loaded with shrieking tourists who seemed to have come thousands of miles to do what they could have done at home.

Yet the local fishermen, whose beach it used to be, continued to go about their business as though none of these intrusions were going on. And sunset was still a beautiful time of day. Kuta Beach is renowned for its sunsets, but apart from some scattered photographers, few tourists are to be found there in the twilight; after all it is cocktail time, and sunsets look just as good from a comfortable lounge, with drink in hand.

Bali's modernization, urban development, and extraordinary economic growth, with all the corresponding benefits of medical, social, and educational services that had previously not existed, also have their negative aspects. It could be argued that prior to the descent of the tourist gods, for whose benefit the island seems largely to be administered, some of these services were not needed; they are needed now to combat problems brought by tourism itself. The economic benefits touch only a few, and the cost to all is high in terms of damage to the social fabric. How high might be measured by the increase in the rate of teen-age suicide.

Nevertheless, tourism is of major, often paramount, economic and even political importance in many remote parts of the world, and one of the major issues that has to be faced is how to weigh the complex advantages against the equally complex disadvantages. Here my focus is on one small segment of the overall problem of the social change induced by tourism: the interaction between the tourist and what is sacred to the people of the place he is visiting. In a vast subcontinent such as India even the most profane tourists are likely to have little effect on what is sacred to the Indian; on a small island like Bali, it is another matter. The Balinese people's way of life is intimately bound up with their religious belief and practice, and there are some 30,000 temples on the island, so the possibility and danger of desecration are very real. But in looking at the desecration and how it takes place, most often unconsciously at the hands of tourists, we find there is also a kind of consecration taking place.

In line with my ongoing analogy between tourism and pilgrimage, of all tourist meccas surely Bali is one that is truly sacred. The quest of most tourists going there involves an ideal of perfection of beauty and goodness—which, incidentally, are qualities by which the Balinese religion defines the sacred. Since for the Balinese the land itself is sacred, the very environmental and ecological changes wrought in the name of tourism or by tourists are a form of desecration. And since reciprocity in human relationships is also sacred in their essential egalitarian traditional way of life, the abuse of money is also a form of desecration. With money they have learned to "purchase" human services for individual gain, without involving any further reciprocal personal obligation. Money all too easily and subtly short-circuits mutual concern and consideration. This effect of tourism is perhaps most insidious and most pervasive in a cultural setting such as Bali. What is a small amount of money for the tourist may be a small fortune to the Balinese. Individual wealth in such measure, together with other material appurtenances of Western civilization brought by tourism, readily lures young men and women, even boys and girls, away from their homes and villages. Too late, they discover they have also been lured away from the security their traditions offered and from the ideals their lives were built around.

At the individual level, desecration by tourists may be conscious or unconscious. On Bali it is most often the latter; vandalism, such as the scarification of sacred monuments by graffiti and pilferage from sacred sites, is not yet as common as elsewhere. But it is curious that the most conscious, blatant, and offensive insults are given at the most sacred places and on the most sacred occasions. Sometimes it is the tourist industry itself, through the initiative of local entrepreneurs, that overtly desecrates what is holiest, but individual tourists do their share of conscious profanation. For instance, even at Pura Besakih (the Mother Temple) on Mount Agung, probably the holiest shrine in Bali, I saw some tourists openly ignore polite requests not to enter certain areas. They swaggered wherever they wished, openly ridiculing the

sense of propriety so sacred to the Balinese, making loud and coarse jokes concerning customs of modesty in dress and nonadmission of women during their menstrual period. And down the coast at Goa Lawah, the sacred home of the mythical serpent Basuki is noted by most tourists merely for the quantity of bats that infest the cave. The associated temple, a holy place reserved largely for death ceremonies, is ignored or paid scant courtesy at best. Crowds of tourists press through worshipers to see and photograph the bats or push among mourners to take snapshots of a funerary ritual. I saw three particularly unkempt and scantily dressed youths force their way up the steps, ignoring requests to put on the required ritual waist sash readily available to all foreign visitors and ridiculing the offered wraparound apron that would have concealed the immodesty of their very short shorts. They burst among the mourners with whoops and jeers, and one tried to throw stones into the cave to dislodge the bats. Eventually a little old Balinese priest came up to them and politely asked them to leave. There was something about that tiny man that stopped them in their tracks. They looked at each other in surprise, then with a few more self-conscious gymnastics and coarse comments they bounded down the long flight of steps, laughing as they knocked people aside.

I caught up with them on the nearby beach of volcanic lava. All their bounce and bravado had gone; they were arguing about just why they had listened to that silly little old man. After all, they had come all that way to see the bats and they had as much right to be there as anyone else. But none of them suggested turning around and going back. They had been touched by something—and stopped. The Balinese might say that the youths had been stopped by the gods. It was certainly no threat of physical coercion that had prevented them from "having their fun"; and plainly they had no respect for the "silly little old man" or the religion he professed. But evidently he somehow commanded an air of authority that was just as effective as that of any armed policeman or bouncer. I will not insist that the authority was sacred in the sense that any supernatural force was at work, but whatever the source, it was powerful enough to prevent an act of desecration. It touched the desecraters, too, and for a moment compelled them to acknowledge the existence of something sacred to others.

The abusive and offensive behavior of these three young men also affected the rest of us. It annoyed the photographers and those trying to film the mourning ceremony, particularly when one of the three bearded, bandannaed heads popped into a viewfinder. It caused a few to stop taking photographs. What it did to the Balinese I cannot say; apart from the priest who intervened they seemed to pay no attention. Perhaps it merely heightened their awareness of the sanctity of the place and the worship they were about; perhaps that is what it did for all of us.

For those who are uncomfortable with the word *sacred*, some Balinese whom I talked with about this and similar incidents use the word *respect*. The young manager of a beach resort was very clear and emphatic. He did not object to the behavior itself; Basuki, after all, was perfectly capable of looking after himself and could have struck the youths dead. It was rather the lack of human consideration that offended him. More than this overt act of desecration or, only slightly less overt, the insulting condescension of tourists in his hotel, on the beach, or on the streets, he found their manner of dress objectionable. This for him was true desecration. To attack the gods directly is merely foolhardy and ignorant. But to attack the sanctity of "proper human relationships" is an insult and a threat that is as real as it is mortal. Much of Balinese social structure is built around the concept of propriety, and despite the outward appearances of freedom and relaxation, there is an underlying code, which is specific and rigorous, concerning mutual relationships. That code clearly defines the acceptable limits of behavior, and dress is an important element. Other than when bathing, men in shorts are indecent, and without shirts they offer open insult; the same is true for women. On the beach, the pimps, hawkers, masseurs, and even the two motorized prostitutes were all impeccably dressed, the women with blouses buttoned up to the neck and the men in long trousers and open-neck shirts fastened as high as they would go. Even the totally naked fishermen somehow gave the appearance of being fully clad, in respectability at least, as they entered or emerged from the water casually concealing their genitals with the left hand, their neat piles of clothes close to the water's edge.

The hotel manager came from the north coast of Bali and talked longingly and lovingly of "the other side of the island," of its beauty and safety. By "safety" he was not referring to physical safety. His home was only a few hours' drive away, but he had never been back and said he could not return there. "Like the rest of us who have left our homes, I am not clean. Look at how I dress." He was considerably better dressed than I was, but in Western style. Yet he was in no way bitter or hostile to tourism. He was grateful for the new horizons it had opened up to him and to the island, and while aware of the damage being done to the traditional way of life, he pointed out that he and others were now more aware that they had something to lose. When I asked him what he had gained, other than this knowledge, his Western clothes and dark glasses, his home without a family, and his scooter (all things that he listed), he gave an odd answer. He said, "Now I know there is even more for me to respect."

At the beginning I referred to tourists as the new gods of Bali, with swimsuits and cameras as their sacred symbols, holding the power of desecration and consecration. This was not entirely flippant. One brochure in front of me describes Bali, not as "Island of the Gods," but as a "Photographer's Paradise." And under "Emergencies" it lists four: police, hospital, ambulance, and finally, camera troubles. Since so many of us take cameras with us when we travel abroad we should be aware of the possible sacral power of this device and the way that we handle it.

One could do an amusing study of the ritual behavior of photographers, but that is not what I have in mind. I have in mind what is very clearly in the minds of Muslims when they prohibit photography of the human form, and what the Jewish scriptures had in mind when they forbade graven images. It is the ancient idea of "quintessence," that fifth and *essential* ingredient that was thought to be latent in all being—the stuff of the stars, some thought, the stuff of sanctity and divinity. No representation of man (or God) that does not show that inner reality can do justice to man or God. Since the quintessence is invisible, any pictorial or graven image is wanting, and failing to do justice to a divinity is a desecration.

I think most of us—even the most profane, the most irreligious—have something that to us is sacred. I doubt if many could put their finger on what the invisible quintessence of that sacredness is, any more than the ancients could when they coined the word. But we are aware of its presence. It is what sometimes motivates us to take photographs, and it is very definitely what sometimes motivates us *not* to take photographs. Probably most of us have had moments when, camera in hand, we have seen something deeply moving, so beautiful that it seemed made for photography, yet somehow we came away with the shutter still cocked, the camera unused. The Balinese would call that an act of "respect." We might say it was because the light was not right, but even that excuse is to say that our mechanical apparatus was, at that moment, incapable of making a perfect image of what we "saw."

Or we might recognize that what we saw with our eyes was not really what we wished to capture, that any photographic rendition without the smell, the touch, the feeling, without that indefinable quintessence, would be a failure. Like most other tourists at Kuta Beach I watched sunsets. I watched *every* sunset, and I watched from the beach, bare feet in the sand. And like others I took photographs. They are probably like those everyone else took, and while they are spectacular, they do not have that essential that made some moments standing on the beach in the warm air, with the smell and sound of the surf, sacred. All the photographs do is to help recall the sunsets that were sacred because they occurred when I deliberately went out to the beach *without* my camera, to be a part of the sunset instead of a detached, objective observer.

So it was at the temples of Bali (and of course elsewhere). The act of photography seems on the one hand to diminish what is being photographed by making it commonplace or to insult it by the futility of trying to capture its invisible essence; on the other hand the photographer is demeaned if he or she doesn't realize that there *is* an invisible essence. I observed Balinese noting with obvious approval or disapproval the manner and mood of the photographer. There were times when a cluck of disapproval was heard as a tourist took a quick snapshot of something particularly sacred, hurrying on with hardly a pause or second glance. Then there were times when the photographer's intense concentration, and rigid requirements for perfect conditions, conveyed a sense of respect and brought a quiet sigh of approval; for respect, whatever its origin, can only serve to heighten rather than diminish what is sacred. The drawback is that the act of taking a photograph too often puts a distance between the photographer and the object being photographed. For the tourist in par-

ticular there is often neither the time nor the opportunity to empathize and identify in a way that makes for outstanding photography, which is a true art. The snapshot is literally a "taking" and may serve to remove the tourist even further from the very thing he most wants to approach and share.

The cost of using the lure of photography to attract tourists to Bali can be high. The narrow streets of Kuta are lined with indigenous tourists agencies, car hire firms, and bus operators. Outside their one-room offices are blackboards and posters advertising their "specials." The sacred gets top priority and commands the highest price, but how long can the sacred remain intact when subject to such commercialization? Even death is not immune. The most lurid and colorful posters call tourists to come and enjoy cremations—one advertised a mass cremation. For many Balinese the cost of living has grown so enormously that they can no longer afford to finance a cremation for a single family member, so the dead are pooled, so to speak, and the conflagration is made even more dramatic by the glare of floodlights, the explosion of flashbulbs, and the presence of the new gods.

There was even an "underground" tourist traffic in death, surreptitious visits to a lakeside beach where the bodies of the dead are laid out in the open. I wonder how many have the stomach to show such photographs to their friends, and what they say about the custom. I found I did not have the stomach to go and find out. I confined most of my photography thereafter to the profane; mainly to photographs of other tourists at work with their cameras.

14

Anthropology and the Modern World

One of the most important justifications for any scientific study is the extent to which the results can be applied to real-life problems. Indeed, this is what separates science from art. We study music, literature, and philosophy to expand our knowledge and gain a broader perspective on life. But when we seek to apply our knowledge to the problems that plague us, we turn from the humanities to the sciences.

Anthropology, like any other field of study, is a product of its time. It responds to the issues of the day, and those who engage in anthropological research and writing reflect what is of interest to those who fund their research and read their publications. So we should not be surprised to learn that anthropology has changed over the years, just as American society has changed economically, politically, and socially. In this final chapter we will present our own views on how anthropology has changed, and how it is trying to meet the new challenges of the 1990s and beyond.

For many years most individuals who wanted to be anthropologists stayed in school until they acquired a Ph.D. degree and then took jobs in an academic setting. The typical anthropologist's job combined teaching and research at a college or university. With relatively few exceptions this was what anthropologists did until approximately twenty years ago, when a combination of factors changed this pattern. In part as a result of a constriction of the job market in academic settings, and in large measure in response to a widespread feeling that anthropological theories and methods had extensive usefulness in the "real world," beginning in the early 1970s anthropologists began looking at employment opportunities outside of the academic environment. In fact, today approximately half of the new Ph.D.s and the vast majority of holders of Master's degrees take nonacademic jobs.

Occasionally we hear students say, "Anthropology is an interesting subject, but what relevance does it have to what I plan to do after I graduate?" Perhaps for some incorrect reasons, students have assumed that studying anthropology is fun but of little practical value. In reality, anthropologists work in an impressive range of jobs. Today an ever increasing number of anthropologists are employed in various aspects of the business world. Some use their social scientific skills to study potential consumer acceptance of new products, while others are involved in personnel issues, where they can utilize their competencies in studying human behavior and interactions. Other anthropologists work in international business, often with management in an effort to present important dimensions of the cross-cultural perspective or indoctrination in values and attitudes. Some study social organizations or ethics because business leaders frequently want not only ethnographic information, but also orientation to cross-cultural sensitivity. What makes up appropriate or inappropriate behavior? These are questions and issues that anthropologists can effectively address. As Brian Burkhalter so cogently notes: "Conducting international business in general and international marketing in particular demands sensitivity to cultural differences in behavior and expectations, and the scope for practical advice from applied anthropologists is tremendous. Vast differences in cultural norms determine what is considered proper and tasteful advertising, what are appropriate colors for packaging, what are the most appealing sizes of units offered for sale, and what are the most effective means of promoting a product."[1]

Noncommercial international groups interested in social change also employ anthropologists. Organizations like CARE, the World Health Organization, and the Peace Corps, as well as agencies like the United States Agency for International Development (USAID) look to anthropologists to assist

[1] "If Only They Would Listen: The Anthropology of Business and the Business of Anthropology," *Practicing Anthropology*, 7, no. 4 (1986): 19.

them in understanding their client population and in introducing new ideas and concepts in ways that are culturally appropriate.

The United States government hires anthropologists in a variety of positions. For example, for the past three decades anthropologists have been working with the Census Bureau in understanding why some groups systematically are undercounted. The Bureau is interested in the use of common anthropological techniques to help gain greater participation in the census. In certain areas anthropologists have been consulted on the design of questionnaires and the procedures for administering them. In the Pacific Islands suggestions were made for changes in enumerator's manuals in order to deal with such things as how to interpret hereditary titles or how to compute annual fuel costs if interviewees purchased kerosene by the can. Anthropologists, working as consultants, helped select and frame questions that would be valuable to understanding what is taking place in U.S. Pacific territories.

Recreational development is another growing area of interest. In many areas anthropologists work with other members of interdisciplinary teams to develop management plans involving human and ecological considerations for developments of parks and other recreational areas. Tourism is an important generator of income in many areas of the world. Among other concerns, anthropologists often address such issues as the impact of recreation development on local people.

Environmental and ecological concerns draw upon anthropological talents and expertise also. Along these lines, anthropologists have been involved in everything from being part of a multidisciplinary research team looking at the problem of chemical contamination of groundwater in assessing the potential social impact and community reaction to the construction of a Superconducting Super Collider in the state of Michigan, to the cultural impact on local residents of the planned construction of a nuclear power station in the state of Washington, to the effects of deforestation and outside encroachment in the Amazon basin on the indigenous population of the area.

An increasing number of anthropologists find work in the corporate environment, and the following illustration certainly is not as unusual today as it might have been only a decade ago. Several years ago Eleanor Wynn was a graduate student in linguistic anthropology at the University of California at Berkely. She was studying social interactions and status differences using data gathered on office complexes when she had an opportunity to get a summer job at the Xerox Palo Alto Research Center (PARC) studying dissemination of information in offices. The "summer" job lasted a total of four years, and Wynn wound up doing her fieldwork and completing her dissertation while on the job. She now works as a researcher in the marketing department of Bell-Northern Research in Mountain View, California. Wynn is a market researcher whose fieldwork involves looking at state governments and Fortune 500 companies. Her specific research varies but is always "applied" in nature—she needs to solve particular problems or address specific questions that enable management to make choices regarding how they wish to spend their development money.

Many others find satisfying work in a wide variety of jobs in which they constantly use anthropological concepts. One dandy example is James Lett, who has a Ph.D. in anthropology from the University of Florida and works as a broadcast journalist with the CBS television affiliate in Ft. Pierce, Florida. He notes that his job is somewhat out of the ordinary for an anthropologists, but says, "As far as I'm concerned, however, I'm doing what I was trained to do: observe, record, describe, and explain human behavior—I'm just doing it in what is, for anthropologists, a nontraditional medium."[2]

---

[2] James Lett, "An Anthropologist on the Anchor Desk," *Practicing Anthropology*, 9, no. 1 (1987): 1.

Anthropology Comes Home

There is a longstanding tradition in cultural anthropology that a student who wants a Ph.D. should do field research in a foreign culture, in which he or she will be required to speak a foreign language. And the unwritten rule is that the more that culture differs from our own, the better. This is not to say that anthropologists who have not had field experience in a foreign country are not "real" anthropologists; rather, it is to say that the ideal training includes a heavy dose of culture shock that can come only from total immersion in a different way of life.

Many graduate anthropology departments still maintain this ideal. Yet a growing number of students do not do fieldwork overseas—often not through any fault of their own, but because of the changing nature of anthropology itself. We are "coming home," so to speak, and turning our attention toward the problems of our own society. Unlike the nineteenth-century anthropologists whose fascination with the bizarre practices of so-called savages led them to study non-Western societies, today we are less concerned with gathering knowledge for its own sake and more concerned with the potential applica-

tions of that knowledge to the solution of social problems.

There are a number of reasons for this dual trend toward home-based studies and an emphasis on application, and not all of them are found in our own society. To be sure, the shift from the study of the exotic for its own sake to the study of more familiar Western cultures is to some extent an outgrowth of the demand for greater relevance in education that arose in the late 1960s and continues today. Not too many years ago few students would have asked why a course was offered as part of a college curriculum. But today there is a growing emphasis on justifying the content of the entire curriculum, including anthropology, and often that is translated into answers to the question: How can I apply what I will learn in this course to the "real world," that is, to the social reality of my own society? Since most anthropologists are associated with universities, the field reflects the concerns of students—which, in turn, reflect the concerns of their parents and of the society at large—with the relationship between what is taught in the classroom and what is applied in nonacademic settings.

At the same time, many anthropologists have turned toward the study of their own "backyard" because of changes that have af-

The study of urban gangs has become popular in recent years among urban anthropologists.

fected their ability or desire to do research in foreign settings. For one thing, in recent years, unfortunately, anthropology has not had a good reputation in a number of countries, and this has made it difficult for research plans to be approved and carried out. Anthropologists (or people posing as anthropologists) have engaged in studies that have angered foreign governments.

Quite frankly, in some instances governments have been less than enthusiastic about having anthropologists witness the sufferings they are imposing on segments of their rural population. The Brazilian government has conducted a running and heated dialogue with local and international anthropologists on its treatment of Amazonian tribal peoples. By presenting the injustices perpetrated on the populations they study to the outside world, anthropologists have engendered the wrath of governments in several parts of the globe.

The changing international political scene also heightened the problems faced by anthropologists. U.S. influence had already begun to slip by the mid-1960s, but the Vietnam War hastened the process. By the end of the war the United States was no longer seen as a kindly big brother but as an imperialist exploiter of the Third World. Most of us are familiar with the effects this has had on our life style as well as on U.S. relations with other countries throughout the world. But few people outside of the field realize the tremendous impact that this period of change has had on anthropology. Several countries that formerly welcomed anthropologists with open arms are now off limits for anthropological study. India, long a favorite place for anthropological fieldwork, closed its doors for a while to those who wished to engage in participant observation within its borders. Several countries in Latin America stipulate that for each anthropologist who comes to study there, arrangements must be made to train a student from that country in the United States. In addition, the country's students must be hired as assistants. While these rules may appear sound, they have the effect of eliminating almost all research by American anthropologists because they impose budgetary requirements that are far beyond the means of any individual and are likely to turn off most, if not all, sources of funding.

Other political factors have reduced the

As the American image declined in many countries, societies formerly open to anthropologists no longer accepted them.

number of opportunities for anthropologists to study in various countries. Even in our own society anthropologists are running into greater difficulties in studying certain groups. On many Native American reservations tribal councils are placing restrictions on anthropological studies and requiring anthropologists to gain permission to work with the group. Again, the overall effect has been to limit opportunities for more traditional studies and to encourage work in some familiar areas of American culture.

Along with these political problems has come a noticeable shift in the funding of anthropological research. In the past much of the support for anthropological research came from private sources, if not from the anthropologist's own pocket. But as the U.S. dollar has declined in value and economic woes have tightened the budgets of funding agencies, less money has been available for foreign research. The exchange rate, which used to allow an anthropologist to conduct a summer's field project on a shoestring, now requires sums of money that are beyond the means of almost any academic employee. The bottom line is that funding for cultural anthropology, from whatever source, is drying up at the same time that more applicants are competing for support. And as the competition increases, a key factor for the granting agency is the expected return per dollar in terms of useful, applicable knowledge. It would seem that the descriptive anthropological study of a generation ago is doomed to extinction.

One result of the shifting pattern of funding for anthropologists has been a tendency for prospective researchers to seek support from agencies that have traditionally been more closely aligned with other disciplines. A growing number of anthropologists apply for research money to sources such as the National Institutes of Health, the National Institute of Education, and other agencies of the federal government. But in so doing they are forced to change their tactics in order to compete with applicants from other fields. Some of these agencies are unwilling to support foreign fieldwork unless the knowledge obtained can be applied to the solution of the problems of American society. Money for travel outside the United States is difficult to obtain, as is support for an extended stay in a foreign country. Again, it would seem that anthropology has "come home" largely in response to factors that have arisen not within the field itself but as part of the large-scale changes taking place in American economics and politics.

Another factor that cannot be overlooked in analyzing the reasons for the changing focus of anthropology is the evolution of the middle-class life style in the United States in recent years. Traditionally, most anthropologists have been associated with universities, and therefore have tended to follow the same general patterns as the middle-income population throughout the country. This means, among other things, that there are probably more families with both spouses working at full-time jobs. The reason this pattern might have a greater effect on anthropology than on some other disciplines is that anthropologists often take a year off to do fieldwork. This is more difficult if it means taking one's children out of school for a year and also asking one's spouse to take a leave of absence from a permanent job—something that is not always possible, let alone desirable. We know several anthropologists who, after doing research in a foreign country, developed an interest in some aspect of American society once they had married and started a family. It is much less disruptive to families to spend a couple of summer months in the hills of Appalachia, on a reservation in Arizona, or in a lobster fishing village in New England than it is to take off for Mexico or Africa or Asia.

Finally, there is a growing commitment among anthropologists of all ages to help solve the problems of their own society. From the turmoil of the 1960s many of us gained greater awareness of the need to take a more problem-oriented approach. This is not intended as a criticism of those anthropologists who have maintained their interest in other countries, nor is it a put-down of those who do not engage in applied anthropology. But there can be little doubt that the field as a whole is moving toward greater emphasis on the application of anthropological concepts and research findings, and we suspect that this change reflects what has been going on outside academic circles for some time.

What Anthropologists Study at Home

In discussing recent changes in the field of anthropology, we don't mean to suggest that before the 1960s it was taboo for anthropologists to write about American culture. Indeed, there are a number of excellent and well-known examples of anthropological research in American settings—not just studies of such ethnic groups as Native Americans, chicanos, or oriental Americans, but studies of other, less easily identified groups as well. In 1945 Carl Withers, who used the pseudonym James West, wrote about a middle American town that he called Plainville. Also in the 1940s W. Lloyd Warner returned to the United States after doing research among the Australian Aborigines and became involved in the question of social class in American society. In 1954 Earl Koos wrote about health beliefs and practices in a typical American town that he called Regionville. These are but three examples of early studies of American culture; there are hundreds more.

As more anthropologists have turned toward research in the United States, a number of trends have appeared. Perhaps partly because most anthropologists are employed at universities, which tend to be located in cities, and partly because most Americans live in or around cities, it is not surprising to find a number of studies dealing with urban topics. Several anthropological publications are concerned with questions related to ethnic groups in American society. African-American culture, which in the 1950s was seen as the province of urban sociology, now is equally popular as an object of study by

anthropologists. Mexican Americans and other Spanish-speaking groups in the United States have also become popular subjects for anthropological study, as have a large number of other ethnic minorities, including Asian communities.

In addition to the emphasis on urban studies, there have been several other trends in anthropological research. A number of researchers have begun to focus on some of the major institutions in American society—a far cry from the more traditional tendency to study small groups in isolated settings, ignoring their ties to the wider society. Studies have been done on subjects ranging from major segments of federal, state, and local governments, to other pillars of American society, such as the schools and hospitals, to such common features of our daily lives as McDonald's. Likewise, anthropologists have looked into various aspects of life in American society, including the world of sports, religious life, and even the programs we watch on television. It is hard to imagine most anthropologists of a generation ago accepting these studies as "legitimate," but today many of us not only openly admit to such interests but even encourage our students to do research in their own backyards as part of their training.

New Subfields of Cultural Anthropology

Another result of the return of anthropology to American soil has been the tendency of many professionals to branch out into other fields and combine them with their anthropological background and training. Many of these areas might not have fit in which fieldwork in a foreign culture, at least not as they were formally taught in university classrooms in the United States, but once anthropologists began to apply them to their own culture the fit became more obvious. For example, anthropologists who studied law, dispute resolution, and social control in non-Western societies rarely had any formal training in law school because detailed study of the United States legal code would have been of little use in understanding the legal processes of those societies. We don't mean that they did not study anything about law; rather, that most of the courses that are part of a law student's training were not applicable to the anthropologist's anticipated fieldwork. But this is not the case for the anthropologist who is investigating a problem to which U.S. laws do apply. As a result, a growing number of students are supplementing their graduate training in anthropology with formal training in law, and recently several programs have been established that award a joint degree in law and anthropology.

The same is true in other fields. Most anthropologists who studied illness and healing in non-Western societies had little, if any, formal medical training, but as anthropology became more interested in health problems and the health care system in the United States, the value of such training increased. Anthropologists who studied education in other societies, especially those lacking formal schools, probably had little training in education; today there are many anthropologists with combined degrees in anthropology and education who are applying their training to the study of the U.S. educational system from an anthropological perspective. The point is that as anthropology has come home, the requirements for fieldwork have changed and ties with other fields have become stronger. Students are branching out, either during their graduate training or after they complete their degrees. In the course of their careers many anthropologists find that they need to learn more about another field in order to become better anthropologists, both at home and abroad.

Urban anthropology The trend toward combining anthropology with other disciplines has led to the rise of several new subfields. Many university departments now offer a course in urban anthropology, recognizing the growing interest in urban-based research among professionals and students alike. This does not mean that until recently anthropologists did research only in rural areas—we could cite numerous examples of urban anthropology going back to the beginning of this century. However, they were not labeled "urban anthropology" until recently, a fact that reflects their relatively recent acceptance as a "legitimate" subject of study.

In the past 15 years or so, urban anthropologists have focused on several new topics. One of the most obvious, and certainly among the most strongly debated, is poverty. In 1959 Oscar Lewis introduced the concept of a "culture of poverty." Even though Lewis never directly identified this culture of poverty with the city, it became linked with urban anthropology, largely because most studies of low-income populations were done in cities. Urban anthropology in the United States has also focused on the problems of segregation and race relations, crime, and urban policy and planning, to mention but a few. Several books describe the culture of street

Every year rural-to-urban migration results in thousands of people living in squatter settlements on the edge of town. Cities have real difficulties providing these people with the basic necessities of water, sewage disposal, public safety, schools, and medical facilities.

gangs, low-income ethnic neighborhoods, or skid row alcoholics—major social problems that are usually linked with cities. Not surprisingly, much less attention has been devoted to the suburbs, and there is little anthropological writing about this side of American life, even though such problems as alcoholism and family breakdown are found there as well as in the inner-city ghettos.

Medical anthropology Medical anthropology is another new subfield, despite the fact that several anthropologists engaged in research on the health and healing practices of non-Western societies more than 50 years ago. This area of study has become a separate subfield because of the growing interest of anthropologists in bringing together the biological and cultural components of anthropology and the many different subfields of medicine. Although much of the research by medical anthropologists still focuses on the more traditional areas of folk medicine and unorthodox medical care systems and practices, there is a growing trend toward looking at the formal health care system from an anthropological perspective. Some recent examples include the ethnography of a hospital ward, a comparative analysis of childbearing practices among ethnic minorities in the United States, and the problems of communication between physicians and clients who do not come from the same cultural backgrounds—to mention but a few. As in the case of urban anthropology, many of the issues currently being addressed throughout American society are gaining importance among anthropological researchers; they include aging, population and birth control, and nutrition.

Nursing and anthropology is a rapidly growing and very natural area of interest. With the huge number of ethnic groups in this country, nurses often have to care for patients from cultures about which they know very little. Often the communication barriers extend beyond language. Right off the bat, as health care practitioners, nurses need to recognize, understand, and reduce their own notions of ethnocentrism. Anthropological concepts can help in that area. Frequently nurses and clients have radically different notions about illness and about practices and expectations in care. Cultural context is becoming an increasingly vital part of the nursing education curriculum. Some programs offer courses in cross-cultural healing practices involving acupuncture, ethnic healing, spiritual healers, touch therapy, and spiritual healing. Not only do nurses obtain some appreciation of these different approaches—which allows them to more effectively communicate with their clients—but also they gain a broader perspective and better understanding of Western cosmopolitan medicine. Anthropology's holistic perspective can be shared by nursing, making anthropological concepts and knowledge beneficial to an important segment of health professionals.

Applied medical anthropologists are involved in health care research and service both in the United States and in many foreign countries. In the U.S. they may work for community health agencies, for universities, and for health planning councils. Often they are called on to assess community health needs and then translate them into health program objectives. Anthropologists frequently direct research programs designed to evaluate obstacles to prenatal health care, investigate causes of infant mortality, gather data on the epidemiology of violent death, study the role of placebos in medical care, or analyze patient-physician communication, to name but a few types of work being done.

Applied medical anthropologists are also very active in the field of international health, working with the U.S. Agency for International Development (USAID), the World Health Organization (WHO), the Pan American Health Organization (PAHO), as well as with many nongovernmental programs. Frequently the objective is to bring their anthropological training and expertise in these programs in order to provide guidance on how to increase survival rates for the especially vulnerable, high-risk populations of women and children in the developing world. Much

One of the authors, participating in a program in nutritional anthropology, weighs a child in a Honduran peasant community.

of the international work focuses on programs as for increasing immunization rates, evaluating growth-monitoring efforts, or promoting oral rehydration techniques. Based on their cultural knowledge and understanding of the recipient population, anthropologists have been able to more effectively promote breastfeeding of infants and to improve prenatal care for women. Thus, applied medical anthropologists are actively translating anthropological knowledge into understanding and aiding the contemporary world.

Educational anthropology   While anthropologists have long been interested in the transmission of culture from one generation to the next, the development of a field called *educational anthropology* is fairly recent. In many studies in non-Western societies in which formal educational institutions were not as clearly defined as our school systems, this area fit into the larger category of "socialization." But as anthropologists have turned toward their own society, a more narrowly defined subfield has emerged to reflect the distinction we make between the overall socialization process and the formal but limited educational process. Recent anthropological studies have focused on many

current issues in the area of education, multicultural education, bilingualism and its role in education, learning outside the formal educational system, and the role of formal education in the transmission of culture.

The cultural landscape of the United States is rapidly changing. For example, while children from a non-European background currently make up 42 percent of California's school age population, by the end of the decade that figure will exceed 50 percent. Even the most casual observer can't help but be impressed by the increase in ethnic diversity that is taking place all over the country. One of the important challenges facing educators is the need to develop skills to teach a multicultural settings, and equally important the need to teach students how to function effectively in an increasingly multicultural environment.

Ecological anthropology   Another relatively new subfield in anthropology, and one that parallels a major area of concern throughout American society, is ecological anthropology. Anthropologists who conduct field research have always pointed out the importance of the environment, not only in the subsistence practices of the people they study, but in many other aspects of their life as well. A standard chapter of any ethnography is devoted to how people make a living from the land, and it always includes a discussion of what today would be termed the ecology of the area—the relationship among all the elements of the environment, including human beings. Thus "ecological anthropology" was around long before the ecology movement. However, many of the problems with which anthropologists are concerned today have grown out of the concerns of the wider society, such as pollution, overpopulation, the interaction of human populations with their environment, and the impact of human culture on the environment. There is still a great deal of interest in the ecology of non-Western societies, and many anthropologists have found that in complex Western societies using advanced technologies to exploit the environment, it is very difficult to sort out the many variables in the impact of humans on their surroundings. They turn to areas in which the technology is not as advanced and in

which the environment has not been disturbed as much as it has in the West, seeking to develop ecological models that they can then apply to all societies. But in doing so they allow us to see how energy utilization, pollution, population density, and a host of other variables can affect behavior in our society. In this sense ecological anthropology is as much a product of the times as the other "new" subfields of the discipline.

Applied Anthropology, Then and Now

In its early days anthropology was much more descriptive than analytical. It was the study of "strange" and "bizarre" cultures in "uncivilized" areas of the world. Its main goal was to describe the native practices. Sometimes different societies were compared, but rarely was there any analysis of the practices themselves or of the ways in which they fit into the rest of the culture. It was not until the late nineteenth century that the potential of anthropology as an applied science was considered and government officials began to ask how anthropological data could be used. Anthropology became a tool of European colonial governments, which recognized that by gaining greater understanding of the native peoples and their cultures, they could create a more efficient colonial policy. Colonial administrators and officials in Africa, Asia, and the Pacific applied anthropological insights to local policies (although they rarely thought of themselves as anthropologists), working within the structure of native culture to achieve their governments' aims.

If the people had a strong hereditary chiefdom, the colonial government would try to set up an administrative system that maintained the continuity of the position of chief, incorporating the chief into the new administrative structure. When a large migrant labor force was required to support the economic enterprises of the colonial government (e.g., the diamond and copper mines of South

Concern for the past damage to the environment has led to increased interest in ecological anthropology.

Africa or the plantations of Latin America), migration was encouraged and even forced, depending on the traditions of the native people. For example, in a region where it was customary for men to migrate for trade while herding their animals, or for any of a number of other reasons, the colonial officials merely redirected the migration routes so that they would lead to the mines or plantations. On the other hand, if the population consisted mainly of sedentary agriculturalists, another means would have to be found to get people to move, such as placing a tax on the land that would force them to work for cash wages. Adopting policies that fit in with the local culture amounts to applied anthropology, that is, applying the knowledge gained in studying another culture to the solution of a problem.

In the United States the early efforts of applied anthropology were tied in with the so-called "Indian problem." There were various views on how to deal with the Indians. Some thought they should be helped to become assimilated into white society. Others wanted to force them to maintain their own culture and prevent them from coming into contact with white society. Given the violence that characterized the westward movement, and the frequent and often fanatical hatred of the Indians by some whites, there was not much support for simply leaving the Indians alone to do as they wished. Nor was it widely believed that they should be forced to maintain their own culture and identity, for such independence was feared by many whites. The dominant opinion, and the ultimate policy of the U.S. government, was to try to assimilate the Indians into white society. This was a difficult policy to carry out, however, for it had to be combined with a policy of racial segregation. The task for the government officials, therefore, was to find a way to make the Indians conform to white standards while keeping them from intruding on white society. Although this has not been the case for some time, prior to 1934 anthropologists employed by the Bureau of Indian Affairs and other government agencies were assigned to study Indian culture and discover

Assimilation is not always the answer. Native Americans, seen here in Harrisburg, Pennsylvania, are protesting remarks made by the local mayor regarding their use of city property.

how it could be altered so as to speed the process of assimilation.

Concern with the "Indian problem" continued into the twentieth century, when it was overtaken by the "immigrant problem." In the early decades of the century large numbers of Europeans, Latin Americans, and Asians poured into the United States, settling mainly in the major cities on the East and West Coasts and around the Great Lakes. While immigration was nothing new, the problems that arose in the cities, and espe-

cially in ethnic communities within the cities, were alarming. One need only recall the conflict that took place among ethnic groups in Chicago during the Prohibition era to understand the dramatic effect of immigration on American culture. Once again, as specialists in foreign cultures, anthropologists were occasionally called upon to contribute their insight and knowledge to the solution of the "immigrant problem." In fact, however, anthropological knowledge was put to very little concrete use, either in the nine-

Immigrants streamed into New York and other American cities in the early twentieth century, raising new questions for a generation of anthropologists. In recent years other waves of immigrants have arrived in this country, posing other interesting queries for contemporary social scientists.

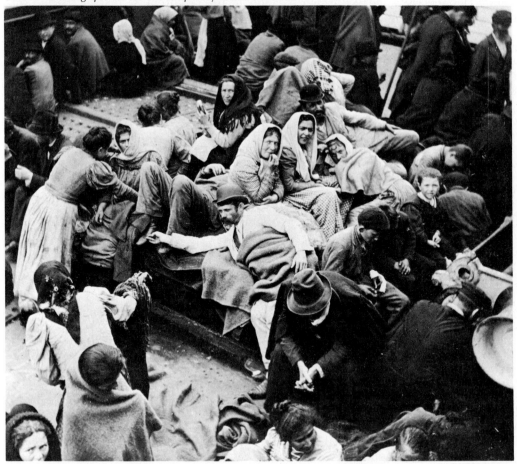

teenth century with the Indians or in the twentieth century with the urban ethnic communities. This was not really the fault of anthropology as a discipline. Public officials distrusted social science and social scientists, ignored their suggestions, and acted to uphold the vested interests of those who had voted them into power. Clearly, anthropologists had much to contribute to the solution of those social problems, just as they do today. The failure of public officials to recognize this fact is a serious problem for the future of anthropology, which we will discuss shortly.

During World War II anthropologists contributed their knowledge of foreign cultures to the war effort. They studied both allies and enemies in detail in the hope of learning more about them and thus about how to deal with them. Where fieldwork was impossible, available literary sources were examined. Immigrants were interviewed, radio broadcasts and newspapers were analyzed; even novels were studied in an attempt to determine what policies would be most effective in dealing with the countries in question. Some benefits were derived from this effort. For example, studies of Japanese culture influenced American policymakers in 1945 to take into account the role of the emperor and the strong feelings of loyalty and respect for his authority among Japanese soldiers. The decision to allow the emperor to retain his position (though stripped of his power), and to have him give the order of surrender directly to his soldiers, probably saved countless lives. Had the U.S. Army tried to force a surrender without the order from the emperor, no doubt many Japanese soldiers would have fought to their death, ignoring any command of a foreign leader whose authority they did not recognize.

After World War II the focus of applied anthropology changed once again. Two very important tasks were undertaken by the United States and the Western world in general: the reconstruction of those countries that had suffered enormous losses in the war, and an attempt to raise the standard of living in the so-called developing countries of the Third World, where the level of poverty and suffering seemed to grow even faster than the rapidly expanding population. In both cases, but especially the latter, anthropologists had valuable information to contribute, and in the years just after the war a number of trained anthropologists occupied government positions in this area. The primary concern of the programs undertaken during this era was to plan and carry out the social and cultural changes required to build or rebuild the economies and societies of the Third World and the wartorn countries. Special emphasis was placed on improvements in agriculture, health, and medical services, education, and social welfare programs. It should not be forgotten that the period following the war was one of political tension and conflict between the capitalist countries of the West and the socialist countries of the East, and Western development programs, especially in the heavily populated Third World, were carried out in competition with similar attempts financed by the Soviet Union. Even today the United States foreign aid program is spurred at least as much by political purposes as by humanitarian goals, which means that anthropologists' contributions are usually tempered by political considerations.

Despite some early successes in the development program of the postwar era, applied anthropology never reached its full potential in this area. There are several reasons for this, most of them having to do with the nature of foreign aid programs rather than with the ability of anthropology and anthropologists to make a meaningful contribution. Plans to develop another country's resources and introduce new programs from the West usually become quickly embroiled in local and national politics, so that compromises must be reached. Appointment to leadership positions in such programs is usually political as well, meaning that vested interests must be served at the same time that goals are being set and implemented. What this means in practical terms is that anthropologists usually take a back seat either to program administrators in the U.S. government agencies that propose and carry out the programs, or else to local political figures whose goals may differ from those of the program. An objective analysis of the program and its needs may bear little resemblance to the final results, leading to frustration for the anthropologist and doubts on the part of the administrators as to his or her usefulness. While most anthropologists could probably point to at least a few cases in which applied anthropology made a valuable contribution, we doubt that the majority of the American people can think of a single example of successful applied anthropology. It is this failure to identify anthropology as an applied science that has limited its success. As a discipline, anthropology is still thought of as the study of bones and ancient cities and exotic tribes in the jungles of Africa or Brazil or New Guinea. Tell someone that you are an anthropologist who studies African-Americans or inner-city schools or hospital wards and the most likely response will be one of disbelief.

But applied anthropology is changing, and will continue to change, as anthropology acquires a new image in this country and elsewhere in the world. For one thing, universities are producing anthropologists in large numbers—not just Ph.D.s, but students with a B.A. or an M.A. who majored in anthropology. Clearly, there are not enough teaching positions for all these anthropologists, as there were a decade and a half ago. As a result, a growing number of professional anthropologists are obtaining jobs in a variety of nonacademic settings—some in government, others in business—where they can bring a new perspective to their duties. As more people in our society come face to face with anthropologists doing other things besides studying bizarre cultures or digging up old bones, they will help to spread a new image of the field, giving it greater legitimacy in the eyes of society and drawing more attention to it as an applied social science.

In addition, academic departments throughout the country are dealing with the changing employment scene by shifting the emphasis of their training programs toward nonacademic careers. An example of this trend is the journal *Practicing Anthropology*, which is published by the Society for Applied Anthropology. The journal, unlike all others before it, is aimed not at anthropologists in academic professions but at the growing number of people trained in anthropology who are working (or looking for jobs) in the so-called real world. A quick glance through any issue will tell you that anthropology has many applications that have not been tapped before. Biographical sketches confirm the fact that a growing number of people are applying their anthropological training to a wide variety of situations that just a few years go no one would have thought of associating with anthropology. Anthropologists are working as legislative assistants in Congress, highway engineers, nurses, city planners, senior citizen program and day care center administrators, and more.

At one time, when students asked for advice about a career in anthropology, we would advise them first to obtain a marketable skill and then to get as much training in anthropology as they wanted or needed. We hesitated to advise them, no matter how dedicated they might be, to go into anthropology with the idea that they would find a job in this field when they finished their studies. And we felt guilty when we saw a student put in four years of undergraduate work and at least five more years of graduate study, and then be unable to find a job teaching anthropology and not want a job doing anything else.

But today we are beginning to see a bright future for anthropologists, largely because of their increasing exposure to the general public and the changing image of the field itself. Anthropology is an important part of any liberal arts education, and the perspective one gains from studying different cultures and life styles can be invaluable in rounding out one's views on one's own culture. No longer are students of anthropology limited to preparing for academic occupations, and no longer must an anthropology major look toward the Ph.D. as the only way to become employable. The future requires imagination and creativity, but it is a challenging one that offers many rewards and satisfactions. We hope that, after having read this book and taken your first step into the field of anthropology, you will agree.

Summary

In the last two decades anthropologists have begun to pay more attention to applying their knowledge to the solution of problems in Western societies, in addition to continuing their interest in non-Western peoples. This tendency reflects many changes that have affected anthropology: the closing of several countries to anthropological fieldwork; the dollar's fall with respect to other currencies, which has made fieldwork prohibitively expensive for many American anthropologists; the growing number of anthropologists competing for limited research funding; the public's increasing demand for relevance in education and application in research; the assimilation of many tribal peoples into the industrializing nations of the Third World; and a growing commitment among some anthropologists to applying their knowledge to problems in their own "backyard."

At the same time, we have seen the emergence of a number of new subfields of cultural anthropology that are applicable to the major social concerns of Western cultures, including medical anthropology, urban anthropology, ecological anthropology, and educational anthropology. As trained anthropologists move out of the university setting and into business and government, applied anthropology is taking on a new focus, different from the focus of a generation ago on ethnic minorities in the United States or developing countries around the world.

Questions for Discussion

1. What are some of the "new" directions being taken by anthropologists today? How does this contrast with the type of work anthropologists used to do?

2. What are some of the advantages, as well as some of the disadvantages, of having more anthropologists study U.S. culture?

3. It has often been said that anthropology, by nature, has always drawn heavily from other fields, such as sociology, history, zoology, and economics. Looking at some of the new and very exciting subfields emerging in cultural anthropology, why is this even truer today?

4. Some observers note that ethnocentrism often emerges in planned social-change projects. In what ways can anthropologists work to prevent that from occurring?

5. In what specific ways can anthropological perspectives be useful in helping to improve the human condition on a global scale? Are there any messages to be derived from studying anthropology for an academic term that will influence the way you look at things from now on?

Suggestions for Additional Reading

Applied Anthropology

Human Organization (Washington, D.C.: Society for Applied Anthropology, 1941–). The journal of the Society for Applied Anthropology, containing the latest research and commentary on the field, as well as providing an excellent historical perspective on applied anthropology since 1941.

Practicing Anthropology (Washington, D.C.: Society for Applied Anthropology, 1978–). Aimed primarily at the growing number of anthropologists in nonacademic work settings, this journal contains a wide variety of information about the potential for applied anthropology beyond the walls of the university.

ERVE CHAMBERS, *Applied Anthropology: A Practical Guide* (Englewood Cliffs, N.J.: Prentice-Hall, 1985). This book is designed to introduce readers to applied anthropology and how it is carried out.

JOHN VAN WILLIGEN, *Applied Anthropology: An Introduction* (South Hadley, Mass.: Bergin & Garvey Publishers, 1986). This is a comprehensive overview of applied anthropology, its development within the discipline, and how it is carried out. Questions of ethics are discussed and there is a large section on policy research.

Urban Anthropology

City and Society (Washington 1988–). A new journal focusing on the anthropology of cities.

Urban Anthropology (New York: Plenum, 1972–). A journal devoted to anthropological studies in cities.

JOHN FRIEDL and NOEL J. CHRISMAN (Eds.), *City Ways: A Reader in Urban Anthropology* (New York: Harper & Row, 1975). A collection of articles outlining the field of urban anthropology and focusing on several problem areas in the study of urban cultures.

GEORGE GMELCH and WALTER ZENNER (Eds.), *Urban Life: Readings in Urban Anthropology*, 2nd ed. (Prospect Heights, Ill.: Waveland Press, 1968). A cross-cultural reader on the anthropological study of cities.

SALLY ENGLE MERRY, *Urban Danger: Life in a Neighborhood of Strangers* (Philadelphia: Temple University Press, 1981). An excellent ethnography of a neighborhood in a major American city, concentrating on how the residents conceptualize and manage danger.

Medical Anthropology

Medical Anthropology Quarterly (Washington, D.C.: Society for Medical Anthropology, 1987–). A journal containing articles, book reviews, and a variety of current information about the latest developments in the field of medical anthropology.

CAROL A. BRYANT, ANITA COURTNEY, BARBARA A. MARKESBERY, and KATHLEEN M. DEWALT, *The Cultural Feast: An Introduction to Food and Society* (St. Paul: West Publishing Co., 1985). The authors pull together work from several disciplines in outlining the relationship between people and the food they eat. The book deals with global food issues and offers suggestions on how the nutritional and social sciences can assist in dealing with world food problems.

PAUL FIELDHOUSE, *Food & Nutrition: Customs & Culture* (London: Croom Helm, 1986). An enlightening book for anyone interested in food and people, it promotes the message that eating is not merely a biological activity, but a behavior which has profound social and cultural influence.

GEORGE M. FOSTER and BARBARA GALLATIN ANDERSON, *Medical Anthropology* (New York: John Wiley, 1978). A survey of the major areas of interest in medical anthropology, summarizing research in both Western and non-Western cultures.

RONALD C. SIMMONS and CHARLES C. HUGHES (Eds.), *The Culture-Bound Syndromes* (Dordrecht, Holland: D. Reidel Publishing, 1985). This book examines the role of culture-specific beliefs and practices affecting variation in the character of illness and its treatment in different societies.

Ecological Anthropology

DONALD L. HARDESTY, *Ecological Anthropology* (New York: John Wiley, 1977). A presentation of the field of ecological anthropology, combining theoretical perspectives with a broad consideration of several problem areas.

EMILIO F. MORAN, *Human Adaptability: An Introduction to Ecological Anthropology* (North Scituate, Mass.: Duxbury Press, 1979). A thorough and interesting introduction to the subject.

Anthropology and Your Future

American Anthropological Association, Newsletter (Washington, D.C.: 1960–   ). The major source of communication among anthropologists in the United States, including news of the profession, job listings, and a wide variety of information of importance to anthropologists.

Special Publication of the American Anthropological Association, No. 14, *Getting a Job Outside the Academy* (Washington, D.C.: American Anthropological Association, 1982). This book discusses job opportunities outside of academic settings and addresses a variety of subjects, ranging from how to prepare a résumé to tips on how to do well on interviews. A major portion of the book deals with how anthropological skills can be effectively used in the nonacademic work world.

H. RUSSELL BERNARD and WILLIS E. SIBLEY, *Anthropology and Jobs: A Guide for Undergraduates* (Washington, D.C.: American Anthropological Association, 1975). A survey of career opportunities outside college teaching open to those with degrees in anthropology.

CHARLES FRANTZ, *The Student Anthropology's Handbook* (Cambridge, Mass.: Schenkman, 1972). A guide to what you can expect in a career in academic anthropology.

MORTON H. FRIED, *The Study of Anthropology* (New York: T. Y. Crowell, 1972). A practical guide to some of the most common questions concerning the study of anthropology.

Educational Anthropology

JUDITH FRIEDMAN HANSEN, *Sociocultural Perspectives on Human Learning: An Introduction to Educational Anthropology* (Englewood Cliffs, N.J.: Prentice-Hall, 1979). A survey of the anthropological approach to the study of education from a cross-cultural perspective.

GEORGE SPINDLER (Ed.), *Doing the Ethnography of Schooling* (New York: Holt, Rinehart and Winston, 1982). Clarification and exemplification of what anthropologists can do to solve educational problems.

Rituals at McDonald's

CONRAD P. KOTTAK

*The success of this fast-food chain may be based, not so much on the taste of a
Big Mac, as on the security offered in ordering one.*

The world is blessed each day, on the average, with the opening of a new McDonald's restaurant. They now number more than 4,000 and dot not only the United States but also such countries as Mexico, Japan, Australia, England, France, Germany, and Sweden. The expansion of this international web of franchises and company-owned outlets has been fast and efficient: a little more than twenty years ago McDonald's was limited to a single restaurant in San Bernardino, California. Now, the number of McDonald's outlets has far outstripped the total number of fast-food chains operative in the United States thirty years ago.

McDonald's sales reached $1.3 billion in 1972, propelling it past Kentucky Fried Chicken as the world's largest fast-food chain. It has kept this position ever since. Annual sales now exceed $3 billion. McDonald's is the nation's leading buyer of processed potatoes and fish. Three hundred thousand cattle die each year as McDonald's customers down another three billion burgers. A 1974 advertising budget of $60 million easily made the chain one of the country's top advertisers. Ronald McDonald, our best-known purveyor of hamburgers, French fries, and milkshakes, rivals Santa Claus and Mickey Mouse as our children's most familiar fantasy character.

How does an anthropologist, accustomed to explaining the life styles of diverse cultures, interpret these peculiar developments and attractions that influence the daily life of so many Americans? Have factors other than low cost, taste, fast service, and cleanliness—all of which are approximated by other chains—contributed to McDonald's success? Could it be that in consuming McDonald's products and propaganda, Americans are not just eating and watching television but are experiencing something

comparable in some respects to a religious ritual? A brief consideration of the nature of ritual may answer the latter question.

Several key features distinguish ritual from other behavior, according to anthropologist Roy Rappaport. Foremost, are formal ritual events—stylized, repetitive, and stereotyped. They occur in special places, at regular times, and include liturgical orders—set sequences of words and actions laid down by someone other than the current performer.

Rituals also convey information about participants and their cultural traditions. Performed year after year, generation after generation, they translate enduring messages, values, and sentiments into observable actions. Although some participants may be more strongly committed than others to the beliefs on which rituals are based, all people who take part in joint public acts signal their acceptance of an order that transcends their status as individuals.

In the view of some anthropologists, including Rappaport himself, such secular institutions as McDonald's are not comparable to rituals. They argue that rituals involve special emotions, nonutilitarian intentions, and supernatural entities that are not characteristic of Americans' participation in McDonald's. But other anthropologists define ritual more broadly. Writing about football in contemporary America, William Arens (*see* "The Great American Football Ritual," *Natural History*, October 1975) points out that behavior can simultaneously have sacred as well as secular aspects. Thus, on one level, football can be interpreted simply as a sport, while on another, it can be viewed as a public ritual.

While McDonald's is definitely a mundane, secular institution—just a place to eat—it also assumes some of the attributes of a sacred place. And in the context of comparative religion, why should this be surprising? The French sociologist Emile Durkheim long ago pointed out that some societies worship the ridiculous as well as the sublime. The distinction between the two does not depend on the intrinsic qualities of the sacred symbol. Durkheim found that Australian aborigines often worshiped such humble and nonimposing creatures as ducks, frogs, rabbits, and grubs—animals whose inherent qualities hardly could have been the origin of the religious sentiment they inspired. If frogs and grubs can be elevated to a sacred level, why not McDonald's?

I frequently eat lunch—and, occasionally, breakfast and dinner—at McDonald's. More than a year ago, I began to notice (and have subsequently observed more carefully) certain ritual behavior at these fast-food restaurants. Although for natives, McDonald's seems to be just a place to eat, careful observation of what goes on in any outlet in this country reveals an astonishing degree of formality and behavioral uniformity on the part of both staff and customers. Particularly impressive is the relative invariance in act and utterance that has developed in the absence of a distinct theological doctrine. Rather, the ritual aspect of McDonald's rests on twentieth-century technology—particularly automobiles, television, work locales, and the one-hour lunch.

The changes in technology and work organization that have contributed to the chain's growth in the United States are now taking place in other countries. Only in a country such as France, which has an established and culturally enshrined cuisine that hamburger and fish fillets cannot hope to displace, is McDonald's expansion likely to be retarded. Why has McDonald's been so much more successful than other businesses, than the United States Army, and even than many religious institutions in producing behavioral invariance?

Remarkably, even Americans traveling abroad in countries noted for their distinctive food usually visit the local McDonald's outlet. This odd behavior is probably caused by the same factors that urge us to make yet another trip to a McDonald's here. Wherever a McDonald's may be located, it is a home away from home. At any outlet, Americans know how to behave, what to expect, what they will eat, and what they will pay. If one has been unfortunate enough to have partaken of the often indigestible pap dished out by any turnpike restaurant monopoly, the sight of a pair of McDonald's golden arches may justify a detour off the highway, even if the penalty is an extra toll.

In Paris, where the French have not been especially renowned for making tourists feel at home, McDonald's offers sanctuary. It is, after all, an American institution, where only Americans, who are programmed by years of prior experience to salivate at the sight of the glorious hamburger, can feel completely at home. Americans in Paris can temporarily reverse roles with their hosts; if they cannot act like the French, neither can the French be expected to act in a culturally appropriate manner at McDonald's. Away from home, McDonald's, like a familiar church, offers not just hamburgers but comfort, security, and reassurance.

An American's devotion to McDonald's rests in part on uniformities associated with almost all McDonald's: setting, architecture, food, ambience, acts, and utterances. The golden arches, for example, serve as a familiar and almost universal landmark, absent only in those areas where zoning laws prohibit garish signs. At a McDonald's near the University of Michigan campus in Ann Arbor, a small, decorous sign—golden arches encircled in wrought iron—identifies the establishment. Despite the absence of the towering arches, this McDonald's, where I have conducted much of my fieldwork, does not suffer as a ritual setting. The restaurant, a contemporary brick structure that has been nominated for a prize in architectural design, is best known for its stained-glass windows, which incorporate golden arches as their focal point. On bright days, sunlight floods in on waiting customers through a skylight that recalls the clerestory of a Gothic cathedral. In the case of this McDonald's, the effect is to equate traditional religious symbols and golden arches. And in the view of the natives I have interviewed, the message is clear.

When Americans go to a McDonald's restaurant, they perform an ordinary, secular, biological act—they eat, usually lunch. Yet, immediately upon entering, we can tell from our surroundings that we are in a sequestered place, somehow apart from the messiness of the world outside. Except for such anomalies as the Ann Arbor campus outlet, the town house McDonald's in New York City, and the special theme McDonald's of such cities as San Francisco, Saint Paul, and Dallas, the restaurants rely on their arches, dull brown brick, plate-glass sides, and mansard roofs to create a setting as familiar as home. In some of the larger outlets, murals depicting "McDonaldland" fantasy characters, sports, outdoor activities, and landscapes surround plastic seats and tables. In this familiar setting, we do not have to consider the experience. We know what we will see, say, eat, and pay.

Behind the counter, McDonald's employees are differentiated into such categories as male staff, female staff, and managers. While costumes vary slightly from outlet to outlet and region to region, such apparel as McDonald's hats, ties, and shirts, along with dark pants and shining black shoes, are standard.

The food is also standard, again with only minor regional variations. (Some restaurants are selected to test such new menu items as "McChicken" or different milkshake flavors.) Most menus, however, from the rolling hills of Georgia to the snowy plains of Minnesota, offer the same items. The prices are also the same and the menu is usually located in the same place in every restaurant.

Utterances across each spotless counter are standardized. Not only are customers limited in what they can choose but also in what they can say. Each item on the menu has its appropriate McDonald's designation: "quarter pounder with cheese" or "filet-O-fish" or "large fries." The customer who asks, "What's a Big Mac?" is as out of place as a southern Baptist at a Roman Catholic Mass.

At the McDonald's that I frequent, the phrases uttered by the salespeople are just as standard as those of the customers. If I ask for a quarter pounder, the ritual response is "Will that be with cheese, sir?" If I do not order French fries, the agent automatically incants, "Will there be any fries today, sir?" And when I pick up my order, the agent conventionally says, "Have a nice day, sir." followed by, "Come in again."

Nonverbal behavior of McDonald's agents is also programmed. Prior to opening the spigot of the drink machine, they fill paper cups with ice exactly to the bottom of the golden arches that decorate them. As customers request food, agents look back to see if the desired item is available. If not, they reply, "That'll be a few minutes, sir (or ma'am)," after which the order of the next customer is taken.

McDonald's lore of appropriate verbal and nonverbal behavior is even taught at a "seminary," Hamburger University, located in Elk Grove Village, Illinois, near Chicago's O'Hare airport. Managers who attend choose either a two-week basic "operator's course" or an eleven-day "advanced operator's course." With a 360-page *Operations Manual* as their bible, students learn about food, equipment, and management techniques—delving into such esoteric subjects as buns, shortening, and carbonization. Filled with the spirit of McDonald's, graduates take home such degrees as bachelor or master of hamburgerology to display in their outlets. Their job is to spread the word—the secret success formula they have learned—among assistant managers and crew in their restaurants.

The total McDonald's ambience invites comparison with sacred places. The chain stresses clean living and reaffirms those traditional American values that transcend McDonald's itself. Max Boas and Steve Chain, biographers of McDonald's board chairman,

Ray Kroc, report that after the hundredth McDonald's opened in 1959, Kroc leased a plane to survey likely sites for the chain's expansion. McDonald's would invade the suburbs by locating its outlets near traffic intersections, shopping centers, and churches. Steeples figured prominently in Kroc's plan. He believed that suburban church-goers would be preprogrammed consumers of the McDonald's formula—quality, service, and cleanliness.

McDonald's restaurants, nestled beneath their transcendent arches and the American flag, would enclose immaculate restrooms and floors, counters and stainless steel kitchens. Agents would sparkle radiating health and warmth. Although to a lesser extent than a decade ago, management scrutinizes employees' hair length, height, nails, teeth and complexions. Long hair, bad breath, stained teeth, and pimples are anathema. Food containers also defy pollution: they are used only once. (In New York City, the fast-food chain Chock Full O'Nuts foreshadowed this theme long ago and took it one step further by assuring customers that their food was never touched by human hands.)

Like participation in rituals, there are times when eating at McDonald's is not appropriate. A meal at McDonald's is usually confined to ordinary, everyday life. Although the restaurants are open virtually every day of the year, most Americans do not go there on Thanksgiving, Easter, Passover, or other religious and quasireligious days. Our culture reserves holidays for family and friends. Although Americans neglect McDonald's on holidays, the chain reminds us through television that it still endures, that it will welcome us back once our holiday is over.

The television presence of McDonald's is particularly obvious on holidays, whether it be through the McDonald's All-American Marching Band (two clean-cut high school students from each state) in a nationally televised Thanksgiving Day parade or through sponsorship of sports and family entertainment programs.

Although such chains as Burger King, Burger Chef, and Arby's compete with McDonald's for the fast-food business, none rivals McDonald's success. The explanation reflects not just quality, service, cleanliness, and value but, more importantly, McDonald's advertising, which skillfully appeals to different audiences. Saturday morning television, for example, includes a steady dose of cartoons and other children's shows sponsored by McDonald's. The commercials feature several McDonaldland fantasy characters, headed by the clown Ronald McDonald, and often stress the enduring aspects of McDonald's. In one, Ronald has a time machine that enables him to introduce hamburgers to the remote past and the distant future. Anyone who noticed the shot of the McDonald's restaurant in the Woody Allen film *Sleeper*, which takes place 200 years hence, will be aware that the message of McDonald's as eternal has gotten across. Other children's commercials gently portray the conflict between good (Ronald) and evil (Hamburglar). McDonaldland's bloblike Grimace is hooked on milkshakes, and Hamburglar's addiction to simple burgers regularly culminates in his confinement to a "patty wagon," as Ronald and Big Mac restore and preserve the social order.

Pictures of McDonaldland appear on cookie boxes and, from time to time, on durable plastic cups that are given away with the purchase of a large soft drink. According to Boas and Chain, a McDonaldland amusement park, comparable in scale to Disneyland, is planned for Las Vegas. Even more obvious are children's chances to meet Ronald McDonald and other McDonaldland characters in the flesh. Actors portraying Ronald scatter their visits, usually on Saturdays, among McDonald's outlets throughout the country. A Ronald can even be rented for a birthday party or for Halloween trick or treating.

McDonald's adult advertising has a different, but equally effective, theme. In 1976, a fresh-faced, sincere young woman invited the viewer to try breakfast—a new meal at McDonald's—in a familiar setting. In still other commercials, healthy, clean-living Americans gambol on ski slopes or in mountain pastures. The single theme running throughout all the adult commercials is personalism. McDonald's, the commercials tell us, is not just a fast-food restaurant. It is a warm, friendly place where you will be graciously welcomed. Here, you will feel at home with your family, and your children will not get into trouble. The word *you* is emphasized—"You deserve a break today"; "You, you're the one"; "We do it all for you." McDonald's commercials say that you are not simply a face in a crowd. At McDonald's, you can find respite from a hectic and impersonal society—the break you deserve.

Early in 1977, after a brief flirtation with commercials that harped on the financial and gustatory benefits of eating at McDonald's, the chain introduced one of its most curious incentives—the "Big Mac attack." Like other extraordinary and irresistible food cravings, which people in many cultures attribute to demons or other spirits, a Big Mac attack could strike anyone at any time. In one commercial, passengers on a jet forced the pilot to land at the nearest McDonald's. In others, a Big Mac attack had the power to give life to an inanimate object, such as a suit of armor, or restore a mummy to life.

McDonald's advertising typically de-emphasizes the fact that the chain is, after all, a profit-making organization. By stressing its program of community projects, some commercials present McDonald's as a charitable organization. During the Bicentennial year, commercials reported that McDonald's was giving 1,776 trees to every state in the union. Brochures at outlets echo the television message that, through McDonald's, one can sponsor a carnival to aid victims of muscular dystrophy. In 1976 and 1977 McDonald's managers in Ann Arbor persuaded police officers armed with metal detectors to station themselves at restaurants during Halloween to check candy and fruit for hidden pins and razor blades. Free coffee was offered to parents. In 1976, McDonald's sponsored a radio series documenting the contributions Blacks have made to American history.

McDonald's also sponsored such family television entertainment as the film *The Sound of Music*, complete with a prefatory, sermonlike address by Ray Kroc. Commercials during the film showed Ronald McDonald picking up after litterbugs and continued with the theme, "We do it all for you." Other commercials told us that McDonald's supports and works to maintain the values of American family life—and went so far as to suggest a means of strengthening what most Americans conceive to be the weakest link in the nuclear family, that of father–child. "Take a father to lunch," kids were told.

Participation in McDonald's rituals involves temporary subordination of individual differences in a social and cultural collectivity. By eating at McDonald's, not only do we communicate that we are hungry, enjoy hamburgers, and have inexpensive tastes but also that we are willing to adhere to a value system and a series of behaviors dictated by an exterior entity. In a land of tremendous ethnic, social, economic, and religious diversity, we proclaim that we share something with millions of other Americans.

Sociologists, cultural anthropologists, and others have shown that social ties based on kinship, marriage, and community are growing weaker in the contemporary United States. Fewer and fewer people participate in traditional organized religions. By joining sects, cults, and therapy sessions, Americans seek many of the securities that formal religion gave to our ancestors. The increasing cultural, rather than just economic, significance of McDonald's, football, and similar institutions is intimately linked to these changes.

As industrial society shunts people around, church allegiance declines as a unifying moral force. Other institutions are also taking over the functions of formal religions. At the same time, traditionally organized religions—Protestantism, Catholicism, and Judaism—are reorganizing themselves along business lines. With such changes, the gap between the symbolic meaning of traditional religions and the realities of modern life widens. Because of this, some sociologists have argued that the study of modern religion must merge with the study of mass culture and mass communication.

In this context, McDonald's has become one of many new and powerful elements of American culture that provide common expectations, experience, and behavior—overriding region, class, formal religious affiliations, political sentiments, gender, age, ethnic group, sexual preference, and urban, suburban, or rural residence. By incorporating—wittingly or unwittingly—many of the ritual and symbolic aspects of religion, McDonald's has carved its own important niche in a changing society in which automobiles are ubiquitous and where television sets outnumber toilets.

Photo Credits

Chapter 11: Rene Burri/Magnum Photos. 297 Standard Oil Company of New Jersey. 298 Eugene Gordon. 299 Michael Whiteford. 300 Library of Congress. 303 S. M. Wakefield.

Chapter 12: 314 Hubertus Kanus/Photo Researchers. 316 American Museum of Natural History Neg. #328285. 318 George Holton/Photo Researchers. 319 George Holton/Photo Researchers. 322 Michael Whiteford. 323 Tomas Friedmann/Photo Researchers. 324 Charles Gatewood. 325 UPI. 326 S. M. Wakefield. 328 Ewing Galloway. 330 Odette Mennesson-Rigaud/Photo Researchers. 332 James Frazer/The Bettmann Archive. 336 Pennsylvania Dutch Visitors Bureau. 339 Marc P. Anderson.

Chapter 13: Hubertus Kanus/Photo Researchers. 354 Burt Glinn/Magnum Photos. 356 American Museum of Natural History. 357 Courtesy Northwestern University Archives. 359 Muldoon, Jr./United Nations. 360 United Nations. 361 Marc and Evelyn Bernheim/Woodfin Camp. 362 Laima Druskis. 364 John Gutmann/Pix, Inc. 365 Williams/Frederic Lewis. 366 John Friedl. 370 Watson/Peace Corps. 372 United Nations/ILO. 373 B. Wolff/United Nations.

Chapter 14: 383 Bernard Pierre Wolff/Photo Researchers. 386 Charles Gatewood. 387 Jaques Pavlovsky/Sygma. 390 Bernard Pierre Wolff/UNICEF. 392 Michael Whiteford. 393 I. B. Shavitz. 394 AP/Wide World Photos. 395 Library of Congress.

Index